WITNESSES OF WAR
Children's Lives under the Nazis

WITNESSES OF WAR

Children's Lives under the Nazis

NICHOLAS STARGARDT

JONATHAN CAPE
LONDON

Published by Jonathan Cape 2005

2 4 6 8 10 9 7 5 3 1

Copyright © Nicholas Stargardt 2005

Nicholas Stargardt has asserted his right under the Copyright, Designs
and Patents Act 1988 to be identified as the author of this work

First published in Great Britain in 2005 by
Jonathan Cape
Random House, 20 Vauxhall Bridge Road,
London SW1V 2SA

Random House Australia (Pty) Limited
20 Alfred Street, Milsons Point, Sydney,
New South Wales 2061, Australia

Random House New Zealand Limited
18 Poland Road, Glenfield,
Auckland 10, New Zealand

Random House South Africa (Pty) Limited
Endulini, 5a Jubilee Road, Parktown 2193, South Africa

The Random House Group Limited Reg. No. 954009
www.randomhouse.co.uk

A CIP catalogue record for this book
is available from the British Library

ISBN 0-224-06479-7

Papers used by The Random House Group Limited are natural,
recyclable products made from wood grown in sustainable forests;
the manufacturing processes conform to the environmental
regulations of the country of origin

Typeset by Palimpsest Book Production Limited,
Polmont, Stirlingshire

Printed and bound in Great Britain by
Clays Ltd, St Ives plc

CONTENTS

PART FOUR: Afterwards

LIST OF ILLUSTRATIONS

LIST OF MAPS
(drawn by Paul Simmons)

ACKNOWLEDGEMENTS

In the spring of 1994, I visited the Jewish Museum in Prague to study their collection of pictures by children from the Nazi ghetto of Theresienstadt. I had seen some of the pictures the previous year in a small exhibition in Prague about the murder of Czech Jews, and I knew others from the Museum's publications. But I had no idea how many and how varied they were. Some were painted on recycled packing paper; others on old Czech forms which dated from the town's pre-war past as a military garrison. The paints were not as bright as in the reproductions I had seen and it was evident that it would be all too easy to mistake the particular colours available to children in a Jewish ghetto for those they had chosen to express particular emotions. I found myself increasingly fascinated by line drawings of scenes from the children's daily lives, most of which had not been exhibited anywhere. To make any sense out of them I needed to know a great deal more about the conditions in which the children had lived, and here two scholars who were also survivors, Anita Franková in Prague and Erik Polák in Terezín, proved invaluable guides to the ghetto's archival records.

This first exploration of what it means to write history from a child's point of view convinced me that it was worth doing and I wondered what kind of sources existed about other groups of children living through the same period in Nazi Germany. A year's leave in Germany in 1997–8 gave me the opportunity to find out. Some leads did not work out well: reading the files of the traffic police for the 1930s and 1940s, in order to see how children had been playing when they became involved in street accidents, turned out to be a very time-consuming way of verifying something which many memoirists recall well. Other chance encounters led to extraordinary finds, like the case files of children taken into 'care' homes, or the very large private collection built up by the novelist Walter Kempowski. Everywhere I was met with generous help, and curiousity that someone who was obviously neither German nor of the generation of war children should want to know such things. Many of my older German colleagues spontaneously volunteered their own childhood memories, which stayed with me and helped me to think about the sources I was reading. It is not possible to read children's letters to their parents from reformatories or wartime evacuation without wondering about what it means to maintain family relationships during long periods of separation. And here I owe my greatest debt to my son, Anand, who inspired me across great distances from the beginning.

Having deliberately chosen to work on a historical problem for which there were no models, I knew that this would all take time, and I am grateful to a number of institutions for making that possible. The Central European University hosted my stay in Prague and the Australian National University a visit to Canberra. The Alexander von Humboldt Foundation funded a year at the Max Planck Institute for History and the University in Göttingen. Terms of sabbatical leave from Royal Holloway, University of London, and Magdalen College and the Faculty of Modern History, Oxford, as well as one funded by the Arts and Humanities Research Board, gave me clear time to begin drafting the book. A year-long British Academy research fellowship saw the completion of a bulky first draft. I would also like to thank the editors of *Past & Present* for permission to use material which they first published in an article of mine on children's art from the Holocaust.

As in all long projects, this one has been reshaped many times and under the stimulus of many people. Discussions with students, colleagues and friends in Britain, Australia, Germany, Israel, Switzerland and Austria have broadened my understanding of the Nazi period and the history of childhood, and they have taught me much about which questions can be answered historically and which ones must remain open. In particular, I would like to thank the following people, who I hope will recognise something of themselves in this book: Lynn Abrams, Charlotte Appel, Stefan Berger, Richard Bosworth, Ruth Bottigheimer, Laurence Brockliss, Catherine Clarke, Martin Conway, Ning de Conning-Smith, Niall Ferguson, Anthony Fletcher, Mary Fulbrook, Saul Friedländer, Robert Gildea, Helen Graham, Abigail Green, Ewen

Green, Valentin Groebner, Atina Grossmann, Rebekka Habermas, Christa Hämmerle, Anthony Harris, Liz Harvey, Paula Hill, Gerhard Hirschfeld, Yigal Hoffner, Georg and Wilma Iggers, Ian Kershaw, Hartmut and Silke Lehmann, Peter Longerich, Helga and Alf Lüdtke, Petra Lutz, Guy Marchal, Hans Medick, Hans Mommsen, John Nightingale, Jeremy Noakes, Bill Nowak, Richard Overy, Johannes Paulmann, Daniel Pick, Alexander von Plato, Hartmut Pogge von Strandmann, Mike Roper, Ulinka Rublack, David Sabean, Karen Schönwälder, Reinhard Sieder, Gareth Stedman Jones, Willibald Steinmetz, Cornelie Usborne, Nik Wachsmann, Tom Weber and Paul Weindling. Jane Caplan, Richard Evans, Jan Lambertz and Adam Tooze all generously commented on draft chapters and Jan also shared material which she had found in her own research in the UN archives. Had he lived, my father might have found it strange to see parts of the world in which he had grown up through my eyes. But having spent their own lives studying other cultures, my mother and he gave me the strongest reasons for believing that such intellectual curiosity is life-affirming.

I have depended much on the help of a number of archivists and librarians, especially Anita Franková and Michaela Hájková in Prague, Anna-Maria Klauk and Christoph Schönberger in London, Günter Müller in Vienna, Christina Vanja in Kassel and Peter Widmann in Berlin. And I owe a very special debt to Walter and Hildegard Kempowski, who opened their home and their invaluable private archive to me, where I was also assisted by Dierk Hempel. I learned a great deal from my former doctoral student Shirli Gilbert's work on music in the ghettos and camps. She also tracked down and translated the Yiddish songs which I have used and checked the whole manuscript. In the last stages, I have benefited from Zofia Stemplowska's help with Polish materials and she compiled the glossary of place names. Julia von dem Knesebeck and Anna Menge located the last few German secondary works, and Anna assembled the bibliography from my notes. Anna, Zofia and Abigael Candelas all helped me with the final checking of the manuscript.

Clare Alexander, my literary agent, took the book on with an intuitive understanding of what I was trying to do and with all the wisdom that comes of a lifetime spent working with manuscripts and their authors. And Sally Riley has made the adventure of finding publishers willing to translate into other languages fun. I have been equally fortunate in my editors. At Jonathan Cape, Will Sulkin and Jörg Hensgen share a love of books with a passion for arguments and ideas which has made for a wonderful collaboration, right down to the last entry in the index. Rosalind Porter has been unflaggingly efficient at dealing with queries and Ilsa Yardley copy-edited with great care, while Tom Drake-Lee has been a delightful guide through the other side of the publishing house.

When I wrote my first book, I was too shy to show it to anyone. With this one I have had the luck to have friends willing to read the whole thing: Rosamund Bartlett, Dick Bessel, Etienne François, Ruth Harris, Heinz Lubasz, Iain Pears, Lyndal Roper, Mark Roseman, Richard Sheppard and Bernd Weisbrod each brought their very different and formidable skills to bear, and each found mistakes that the others had missed. They all also prodded me in the same direction, telling me, whenever the wider context of the Second World War or Nazism threatened to divert the narrative, to put the children first. Without their criticism, I know that this book would be a much worse one. And without their friendship and encouragement, I might not have managed to rewrite it one more time.

To Ruth, Iain and Lyndal I owe much more: over the last decade, they have read and heard more about this period of history than they ever bargained for, and have helped me to work out what I was trying to say. When I began, I wondered whether the experience of children counted as 'real' history. My partner, Lyndal Roper, gave me the best advice: work on what you really care about. In the intervening years, I have learned more from her than I can possibly thank her for. It is to Lyndal and to my sons, Anand and Sam, who have constantly reminded me just how freshly children look at the world, that I dedicate this book.

Nicholas Stargardt
February 2005

THE RIGHT TO A NAME

POSSESSING one's own name is one of the most elementary forms of personal identity. For prisoners in Auschwitz, the number tattooed on their forearms replaced their names, and a great deal of Holocaust remembrance is concerned with naming the victims of Nazi genocide: only then can they be properly recalled as people. Sometimes their names went through a number of different versions as they changed language and jurisdiction. Where possible I have reverted to the names people used at the time: so, for example, Mary Berg – as she became known when she published her diary in New York in 1945 – is referred to here as Miriam Wattenberg, as she was in the Warsaw ghetto.

I should have liked to have given all the children in this book their names. But that was not to be. Under German Federal law governing data and personal records, the identities of individuals are protected during their lifetimes and those of their immediate family. This ban on revealing the real names of persons creates immediate problems for any historian who sets out to treat all equally. It is not only former members of the Hitler Youth who may not be named. The ban applies also to naming child psychiatric patients who were killed in the asylums of the Third Reich: they have become the anonymised victims of the Holocaust. In a book with such a large cast of children, many of whom share the same first names, it would have been confusing to refer to them by their first names only. So I have had to create pseudonyms for those, mainly German and Austrian, children whose identities are protected by law. In these cases, I have retained the original given name and chosen a family name which starts with the same initial and comes from the same part of Germany. The reader can easily establish where this has been done by consulting the endnotes: Dierk Sievert, for example, becomes Dierk S. in the notes, the initial indicating that the name in the text is a pseudonym. In a very few cases, I was not able to establish what the family name was, usually because of the way the person has been anonymised in another publication, and so have simply used the first name on its own.

Names of places turn out to be just as complex as names of persons. Often, towns had several different names for centuries, which altered with the language spoken by their multicultural population or the political juris-diction under which they fell. The solution of realist cinema where everyone uses her or his own language and name for a place seemed certain to confuse the reader, although the alternative – to have Germans speaking of Poznań and Poles of Posen – also grates on the ear. On the whole, I have followed the rule of accepting the name used by the political author-ities at the time: so, Theresienstadt reverts to its Czech name of Terezín in 1945. Poland presents a particularly difficult case, because of its history of partitions by the great powers and its shifting borders during the period 1939–45. I have used Polish names for places until the start of the German occupation and again after liberation. For the period of German occupa-tion, I have generally used the Polish names for towns within the rump territory in Central Poland which was designated as the General Government, whilst employing the German names for places which were formally annexed to the Greater German Reich. I have made two excep-tions to this rule, however, for Łódź and Gdynia, where I have kept the Polish names throughout, because the Nazi names Litzmannstadt and Gotenhafen had no prior history: much of Gdynia was built in the 1920s to give Poland a port on the Baltic, and, until 1939, the German minority had always referred to Łódź as Lodsch. I have called the Lithuanian city of Vilnius, or Wilno as it was named under Polish rule in the 1920s and 1930s, throughout by its Yiddish name: for it is Jewish Vilna which features most often. For the sake of simplicity, I have also not tried to Russianise the names of towns in Eastern Poland during the period of Soviet occu-pation in 1939–41. Hopefully, most confusions will be clarified by consulting the maps and the glossary of place names, and I can only apol-ogise for any lingering errors. Names are not neutral and, in writing this book, I have discovered that the right to name people and places remains a very present part of the legacy of the Second World War.

DRAMATIS PERSONAE

Yehuda Bacon	Czech–Jewish boy in Theresienstadt and Auschwitz
Martin Bergau	German teenager from Palmnicken in East Prussia
Lothar Carsten	Hitler Youth in Wuppertal
Janina Dawidowicz	Jewish girl in the Warsaw ghetto
Thomas Gève	Jewish boy from Berlin, deported to Auschwitz
Liselotte Günzel	German schoolgirl from socialist family in Berlin
Janina	Polish girl from village of Borowa-Góra
Wanda Przybylska	Polish girl in Warsaw
Klaus Seidel	Hitler Youth and anti-aircraft auxiliary in Hamburg
Dawid Sierakowiak	Jewish boy in Łódź
Dierk Sievert	6th former in Osnabrück at start of war
Fritz Theilen	Teenage 'Edelweiss Pirate' in Cologne
Uwe Timm	Young child in Hamburg and Coburg
Miriam Wattenberg	Jewish girl in the Warsaw ghetto

INTRODUCTION

LOOKING back at her childhood, Katrin Thiele could not reconcile her happy memories with what she had learned about Nazi Germany: 'Could all the Nazis I had known –' she wondered, 'just about everyone I loved – really have been the loathsome brutes subsequently portrayed?' Katrin, like many other children of her generation, simply could not equate the overwhelming evidence of mass murder with all the Nazi ideals she 'had been taught to revere, notions like self-sacrifice and dedication to duty'.[1]

In Katrin's case, the end of the war abruptly ruptured a stable and comfortable family world. Her father, who for twelve years had served as a Nazi functionary and then an officer in the *Wehrmacht*, was pursued by both American military and German civilian police. Arrested and interned for reasons she could not fathom, he disappeared from Katrin's life for the next three years. In the meantime, Katrin's mother – having been born in London before the First World War – was 're-patriated' with her two children to a country they had grown up thinking was their national enemy. Katrin left Germany as a ten-year-old in 1946, to live in Britain. Overnight, she went from being Katrin Thiele to Kay Norris. With the change of name went a wholesale change of language, national identity, permissible topics of conversation and social reference, as Kay learned how to be an English schoolgirl. The memories, mostly from the war, which broke out when Katrin was only three, had to be locked away in her mind until a time came when she could explore them more safely.

Despite her parents' subsequent divorce, Katrin had two opportunities to visit her father and try to make sense of this sudden destruction of her family. In 1949, now aged thirteen, she and her older brother, Udo, spent a weekend with him and his new wife during the Christmas holidays. In many ways a happy reunion, it also shocked her deeply. Both her command of German and her emotional relationship with her father had stopped at the point she had left, three years before. She could not express the new ideas and concepts she had acquired in England and he seemed only too glad to accept her as the little girl he had last seen. He also looked quite different from both her memories and her imaginings. Gone was the sharp-featured, brisk man in uniform, preaching fanatical dedication to the cause. But he was not the broken, despairing prisoner she had imagined during his two years of internment. Instead, she saw a balding man, more careworn and overweight than before, but who did not seem to need her help. He had remade his life, finding a good job and a charming home in the Harz, where he had settled down with a beautiful woman – an old family friend – who had long adored him.

Katrin found she could not fathom her father's beliefs. What had happened to those inner convictions he had carefully instilled in his children? Even when Katrin went to visit him in 1956, during the first summer of her studies at Oxford, she found that she slid back once more into the emotional collusion of 'papa and his little girl'. Of his former Nazi self she could find no more than a deep nostalgia for the Third Reich, especially for his time as a soldier; and he refused to accept the scale of the genocide committed against the Jews. By now settled in Canada, he appeared to have simply signed up to a fresh set of goals, becoming a new, hard-working and ambitious member of the community of German immigrants. She felt misunderstood. He did not seem to realise that his daughter had remained true to the virtues he had inculcated in her. Where she still recognised the Nazi collective virtues of *Pflicht*, *Treue*, *Wille* and serving the *Volk* – duty, loyalty, will and serving the nation – in the everyday English good conduct of 'dutifulness', 'integrity', 'determination' and 'making the world a better place', he mocked her dreamy idealism. In their two English-speaking countries on either side of the Atlantic Ocean, the generation which had made Nazi Germany and the generation which had been made by it were as far apart as a loving father and daughter could be.[2]

In some respects, Katrin's experience was less different from that of her contemporaries who had remained in Germany than she thought. Many German war children also found it difficult to talk to their parents, especially in establishing emotional contact with fathers who had spent the years from 1939 to 1948 at war or in prisoner-of-war camps. There were many topics which German families avoided in the 1950s. It was the generation of children who had been most deeply marked by the Third Reich. The men and women who had carried the swastika across Europe could often look back on childhood memories untouched by Nazi emblems and slogans. Like Katrin's father, many found it easier to shed those values and goals afterwards that did not make for success in the post-war world. Their children had known no other world in their most formative years and had often imbibed Nazi values and sayings alongside exhortations to wash carefully, look after their clothes and be polite. Small wonder that members of this generation should feel that any serious post-war confrontation with the world their parents had helped make menaced their very identity as responsible individuals. For many it was easier to go on being dutiful and serving others within the new institutions of East and West Germany.[3]

In fact, Katrin did not go back and investigate her family history until the early 1990s. In this, too, she was not peculiar among her generation. Both children of Nazi fellow travellers and Jewish children who had survived the ghettos and camps of the 'final solution' often did not write their memoirs until after they had retired and began to wonder how best to tell their grandchildren about the events they had often tried to keep from their children.

In 1988, West Germans marked the fiftieth anniversary of the Nazi pogrom against German Jews on the night of 9 November 1938, a night of mob violence and murder, burning of synagogues, and looting of flats and shops, which had left nearly a hundred dead and had seen 25,000 Jewish men sent to the concentration camps. For 1988, in a halting and ham-fisted fashion, the West German government sponsored a full national commemoration of the anniversary, prompting many localities to follow suit. In the course of this anniversary, the well-known south German journalist Lore Walb found herself plagued more often than ever by dreams about the Jews. In one recurring dream, she became a young student in Heidelberg during the war once more, when a Jewish classmate from her school years suddenly turned up on her doorstep, begging to be taken in, just for a day or two. Each time

Lore Walb awoke from the dream she had not made a decision. The daughter of convinced Nazis, she had emerged from the war unscathed herself and had soon begun a career in radio in southern Germany.

By 27 November 1988, less than three weeks after the main commemorations of *Kristallnacht*, she was noting a different dream in her diary. A young woman once more, she found herself in the street walking alongside an older Jewish man clad in a long coat, broadbrimmed hat, his narrow, decent face sporting a goatee. Laying her hand on his bony shoulder, she leaned her head on it and said, almost weeping with relief and joy, 'I am so glad that you are back.' Like so many wish dreams, Lore Walb's posed the problem, not the resolution. The Jews had not come back and she could not ask their forgiveness. Nor had she yet made her own self-reckoning or forgiven herself. Instead of closing this chapter of her life, the sixty-nine-year-old retiree embarked on what she called, in a suggestive and laden phrase, 'the stations on the way towards the work of memory'.[4]

The result of Lore Walb's journey was a kind of public confession through the medium of private self-analysis, in which the older woman reread and commented upon her own youthful diaries. There was the family photo album with that proud moment in 1932 when the thirteen-year-old had stood before the Führer in the local sports stadium while a crowd of 25,000 looked on. Then, in November 1933, for the tenth anniversary of Hitler's Beer Hall putsch, came another public moment when she recited a poem, with the top education officials of the province in the audience. When the war broke out she started her studies at university. Like almost everyone else, Lore Walb celebrated the fall of France in June 1940, sharing, too, in the general mood of hatred against Britain for needlessly prolonging the war. 'The Führer should not be too humane this time,' she wrote on 17 June, 'and should give the English a hefty warning for once – for they alone are guilty of all the unhappiness and misery into which so many nations have been plunged.'

On rereading her own entries, Lore Walb realised that she had possessed no inner barrier to absorbing and making such key phrases of Nazi propaganda her own. After the attack on the Soviet Union, she somehow skated over even the death of the boys in her circle of friends, dwelling on the military and political importance of the cause for which they had died. 'Bolshevism' and 'Russian sub-humans', 'Japan's fabulous successes' against the United States' Pacific fleet, her own ideas of how to win her mother round to letting her study for a doctorate and her sympathy for the German soldiers freezing on the eastern front; the clichés chased each other across the page. At every turn, she took from the media the key phrases she needed to make sense of events, dressing up Goebbels's slogans and epigrams as her own private reflections. Half a century later, steeped in the starkly contrary values and verities of another era, this confontation with her own outwardly uneventful Nazi past came as a profound moral shock.[5]

Lore Walb's diary provided ample testimony to that attitude of inner moral engagement which Katrin Thiele found so much harder to shed after the war than her name, nationality and language. Even at the very end of the war, when Walb heard that her town had been surrendered to the French in order to avoid further bloodshed, she wrote about her disappointment, rather than her relief. In her heart, she still clung to the romanticism of loyalty and national sacrifice, whatever her head might dictate. As, finally, the local authorities hung out white flags, she felt 'most deeply shamed and humiliated'; writing on 26 April 1945, she grieved for the 'millions of soldiers who have fought for years and are still fighting at the front for no purpose'. Nothing made sense at that moment.[6]

When Lore Walb tried to take stock of what she had learned in the decades since the war but which was not in her diary – such as the hundreds of thousands of concentration camp inmates sent on increasingly pointless 'death marches' by their captors in the final months – she tried to imagine the individual plight of those who were lucky enough to survive. And yet, the faces her memory summoned up when she thought of the war were of the young German men who had died: Rolf, Günther, the brothers Gerhard and Heinz, her one-time boyfriend Walter who died in the final week of the war, fighting in Vienna. And, like so many women born between 1909 and 1929, Lore Walb had another reason to remember them. There was no one left to marry.[7]

In March 1988, Martin Bergau joined other middle-aged war children at a quiet weekend reunion in Cologne. It was the annual gathering of families from Palmnicken, a formerly East Prussian town on the Samland Peninsula. Most had fled to the West ahead of the Red Army in 1945, others afterwards, and among them Bergau met a woman who reminded him of events he had witnessed as a fifteen-year-old

Hitler Youth in those fateful days of early 1945. The woman's mother, Bertha Pulver, had hidden a young Jewish woman, the survivor of a massacre of – mostly Jewish – concentration camp prisoners which the SS had carried out with the help of the local militia forces of the *Volkssturm* down at the edge of the frozen Baltic. Afterwards, the SS and local militia had hunted down the Jewish women who had escaped from the seashore. Armed as members of the *Volkssturm*, Bergau and some of his teenage Hitler Youth friends had been called by the SS to help guard a line of Jewish women at an abandoned mine, while the women were led in pairs round the corner of the building. Bergau could hear the shots of the two SS men who were killing them. Eventually, the line became so short that the fifteen-year-old Bergau accompanied them round the corner too. As he looked on at the executions, he saw one of his Hitler Youth comrades walking among the prostrate bodies firing a revolver at any who still moved. A few women who had escaped from the massacre on the ice evaded capture and survived. One of them was the young woman Bertha Pulver had hidden.[8]

Prompted by his chance encounter with Bertha Pulver's daughter, Martin Bergau set to work writing his own memoir of the war years and his three years as a prisoner of war in the Soviet Union. In contrast to the reflex response, still widespread in Germany, of having heard nothing and seen nothing of actual camps or killing, Bergau painstakingly set about including this particular massacre of camp prisoners in his account. He wrote off to the Yad Vashem archives in Jerusalem to ask for survivors' testimony, which he added in a special appendix to his memoir. The book did not become a best-seller.

Martin Bergau was the only one of these three German memoirists who had been directly caught up as a teenager in the murderous end to the war. His achievement was to chronicle his own sense of inner engagement with Germany's cause, rather than to probe it deeply. Lore Walb's sense of guilt came from a recognition that she, a talented teenager and young woman, had freely dedicated herself to Nazi precepts and Nazi goals, remaining true to them until the end. As she grew older Katrin's sense of guilt was nourished not from anything she had done as a young child during the war, but from her apprehensions about what her father might have done to be arrested. When historians began interviewing the children of the Third Reich in the 1980s, they, too, were principally concerned with exploring the feelings of guilt which Katrin Thiele, Lore Walb and Martin Bergau were trying to address. But they were more interested in the children's responses to what their fathers did during the war than in the children's own experiences.[9]

In all wars, children are victims. The Second World War differed only in the unprecedented extent to which this was true. One of the most famous photographs of the Holocaust is the picture of the child holding his hands up as he is driven at gunpoint to the *Umschlagplatz* in the Warsaw ghetto. He was just one of the 1.1 million children who perished in the 'final solution'. Children were shot by soldiers and militiamen in their thousands in occupied Poland and the Soviet Union. Starvation and disease killed the elderly and the very young throughout occupied Europe, but especially in the East. Children were incinerated with their mothers in the firestorms of Hamburg, Dresden, Elberfeld, Darmstadt and a host of other German cities, or froze to death in the mass flight of German civilians along the snowbound roads from Silesia and East Prussia in 1945.

Some of this suffering of children has become familiar in the telling, while other areas remain relatively unknown. But the 1990s marked a watershed. Many people write down their memories only after they have retired and their own children have grown up. This was as true for Austrian children who remained with their mothers throughout the war as for Jewish children who lost their whole families in the Holocaust, and for the generation of younger war children the time to tell their stories came during the last ten years.

Three books were published in 2002 which brought the dimensions of German suffering back into the mainstream of German public discussion. Antony Beevor's *Berlin: The Downfall* prompted much talk about the rapes perpetrated by Red Army soldiers at the end of the war. Günter Grass's novel *Crabwise* was seized upon for his treatment of mass flight, while Jörg Friedrich's *Der Brand* (*The Fire*) focused on the bombing of the cities. None of them was the first to treat his subject, but each captured the German public imagination in a way their predecessors had not. Friedrich was alone in talking about German suffering in the war in terms which set it on par with the Holocaust, casting Winston Churchill as a 'war criminal', referring to asphixiating air-raid cellars as 'gas chambers' and calling the RAF's Bomber Command '*Einsatzgruppen*' as if they were SS killers. After so much public discussion of German responsibility for the murder of the Jews, most commentators found these terms unacceptable and strongly rejected any attempt to equate German and Jewish suffering. But other elements of Friedrich's vocabulary, especially his more general emphasis on innocence, victimhood and trauma, have gained widespread acceptance. And this has set the tone for the handful of works which have now appeared based on interviews with war children. For the first time, interviewers have wanted them to tell their stories, rather than hear their responses to the deeds of their fathers, most of whom are now dead. Amid talk of 'breaking the silence', the new emphasis has been on the worst moments of their wars, on bombing, flight and hunger. Giving voice to the suffering of innocent German children can make their memories sound like those of Holocaust survivors, opening the prospect of 'empowering' the victims by according them high moral standing and political recognition.[10]

In many ways this evocation of the suffering of innocent children is not as novel as it appears. In West Germany, mass flight from the eastern provinces and mass rape by the Red Army had received enormous coverage in the 1950s. Although the mass bombing by the country's new British and American allies quickly became a non-topic in West Germany, it did become a feature of Cold War commemoration in East Germany. The child's perspective also appealed to West German writers like Heinrich Böll in the early 1950s as they looked for symbols of hope in the post-war world. But as the literary critic and survivor of the Warsaw ghetto Marcel Reich-Ranicki remarked in an acid review of Böll's early work, the limited horizon of the child could also provide an excuse for avoiding all the broader issues of the Nazi war of annihilation waged in the East.[11]

As new national identities were being encouraged in the 1950s, in Poland, in Israel and in West Germany, innocent suffering often provided the raw material for morally uplifting parables of renewal. In Poland, this way of viewing the country's huge losses during the war and the German occupation connected back to an older tradition of seeing the nation, its martyrdom and its resurrection in terms of Christ's Passion. But this was also a tradition under attack by the Stalinist ruling party, which preferred to focus more on the heroism of its own resistance, while simultaneously attacking the record of the much larger nationalist forces, the Home Army. In West Germany, the tales of ethnic Germans expelled from Eastern Europe and of prisoners of war starving in Soviet camps were sometimes couched as a kind of

Protestant expiation. Through their suffering many Germans of the 1950s felt that they had paid their – generally unspecified – moral debts. In the new state of Israel, the fact of genocide underwrote the state's very foundation. But in a country which saw its armed forces as vital to its existence, many Israelis were also afraid that European Jews had passively acquiesced in their own slaughter: for the first decade and more, commemoration dwelt exclusively on heroic resistance like the Warsaw ghetto uprising. In Poland and Germany, children's essays were collected and their drawings exhibited soon after the end of the war. In Israel it would take longer to commemorate them: the very scale of their tragedy may have made it too painful to contemplate.[12]

Confronted with such suffering, it is natural to turn to a notion like trauma to understand its impact. Certainly, many children as well as adults must have been traumatised by their experiences. But trauma is also very difficult to apply to the past. Like its cultural neighbour, victimhood, trauma is often treated as a psychological – and moral – absolute. They foreclose the past, telling us what we will find before we have looked. Trauma is also a concept which was designed for understanding individuals, not whole societies. As oral historians working on other subjects have listened to stories and conducted interviews, the most self-reflective have noticed the similarities between their work and that of psychoanalysts and psychotherapists; but this has tended to make them more, not less, cautious about how final and definitive their interviewees' accounts are. Such caution would be advisable here.[13]

Instead, since the 1960s there has been a strong tendency in the Federal Republic to treat public debate itself as a kind of social therapy, as if by *talking* out the Nazi past, the Holocaust, collaboration in the former East Germany with the *Stasi*, or – most recently – German suffering in the war will itself cleanse and cure society of their effects. As Lore Walb and Martin Bergau addressed the questions of responsibility for Nazism and the Holocaust, they asked themselves very difficult questions which involved a precarious balancing act between their deep childhood memories and the moral positions of adulthood. By contrast, little self-interrogation is demanded of witnesses once their childhood suffering is endowed with the unquestionable status of 'survivor testimony'. And this easily shades into redemptive views of suffering like those which were current in the 1950s, founded on a belief that suffering ennobles people by helping them to reform themselves, a doubtful claim about a conflict as destructive as the Second World War.[14]

So much emphasis on innocent suffering can also make children appear strangely passive within the accounts of harm done to them, the objects rather than the subjects of history. But most children were still able to engage with their environment and lived the war in a network of social relationships: if we want to find children's own wishes and responses to events it is here that we should look. From a historical perspective, it is better to restrict the use of 'trauma' to extreme cases which cannot be explained in any other way: like the small German girl who could only think of rescuing her shoes from the rubble of her house, or the five-year-old Polish girl who had to be taught to speak again after her liberation from a concentration camp.[15]

Children established their own chronologies of the war through key events; the moment when *their* war became real. When exactly their secure world collapsed became a defining moment, dividing the war from a previous 'golden age'. For Jewish children in Germany, Austria and the Czech lands, that moment almost certainly came before the war, often with their emigration, especially if that involved family separations. For Poles, this often happened in 1939–40, with the mass shootings, deportations and – for Polish Jews – ghettoisation. For German children in the cities of the Rhineland and Ruhr, it came with the onset of heavy bombing in 1942. For children in the eastern German provinces, that moment was usually the mass flights of 1945. For many other German and Austrian children, their intact and safe world did not end until occupation and the collapse of the Third Reich: for them, the events shaping their inner sense of time were more likely to be the capitulation of 8 May 1945 and the hunger years which followed than the Nazi period itself.

As children's memories of Nazi Germany divided between those who remembered it as a time of normality and those who recalled it with fear and horror, the exact events they recollected mattered. For dates and events marked that emotional boundary. Often, too, crossing the boundary spelled the moment when children had to take over responsibilities from their parents, looking after their siblings and parents or becoming beggars and smugglers to feed their families. At some point – as their parents broke down in the starving Jewish ghettos, or as they fled before the Red Army in the snows of 1945, or while they hid in their cellars during bombing raids – many children shouldered premature responsibilities.

Such dutifulness tied them to their families, especially their mothers, long after they would normally have gone their own way.[16]

Most children did not experience these things in isolation and, especially for younger children, their memories of these decisive moments would be shaped by the stories they were told about them afterwards. For many Jewish children this was not so. Few of the Jewish children who survived the war still had close family members, and most would emigrate from Continental Europe, setting them on journeys to self-knowledge that they would have to chart through unfamiliar languages and traditions. But for most European children and their families, post-war reconstruction was a national and family affair, and their memories and much of their capacity for empathy would be channelled exclusively by their own wartime national and ethnic communities: there would be no European consensus about the meanings of 1939, 1940, 1941 or 1945, or about what counted as victory, defeat or liberation. The full impact of the Third Reich can be measured by the ways in which habits of thought remained intact long after its outward symbols and structures had been dismantled.

The Nazis' aims were above all racist and nationalist, but they projected these goals into the future through the enormous importance they ascribed to childhood. Children provided a crucial measure of Nazi success in realising their utopian visions. They saw the pure-bred, well-educated and upright German child as the racial future of the nation, and they were only too aware that this was the first generation they could nurture and shape from infancy. During the war, this involved a whole raft of measures, from signing up ten-year-olds to the junior branches of the Hitler Youth and League of German Girls, the *Jungvolk* and *Jungmädel*, and sending them out to gather medicinal herbs, to providing evacuee placements in hostels for children and giving them special food supplements. More generally, the regime tried to shield the home front and make it as 'normal' as possible.

Nurturing German youth also meant protecting it from harmful influences. German drop-outs and juvenile delinquents had to be taken out of society until they had been re-educated into lives of duty and diligence. Disabled children had to be excluded and, in the summer of 1939, Hitler launched a policy which directed medical personnel to kill them in the country's asylums. As the German racial future became the sole measure of value and utility, the Nazis abandoned all other ethical criteria in their dealings with children.

The campaigns in the East, first in Poland in 1939 and then, from 1941, in the Soviet Union, opened the way to colonial settlement for Germans which was meant to be as permanent as white settlement in America, Australasia or southern Africa. Teenagers might prefer to read exotic novels about colonial Africa, but young men and women from the League of German Girls, the Hitler Youth, the Students' League and the Labour Service helped the police and SS in expelling Polish peasant farmers and settling ethnic Germans on their land. Schoolchildren evacuated to the newly annexed territories of western Poland, Bohemia and Moravia conducted their own marches through Polish and Czech towns, symbolically demonstrating German presence on all their national days. And woe betide the locals who failed to uncover their heads before the flags of the *Jungvolk* or Hitler Youth as they marched by, singing 'Deutschland, Deutschland über alles'.

For Polish and Polish-Jewish children, colonisation ripped apart the whole structure of legal norms and replaced it with arbitrary rule by decree. They saw their elders humiliated and were often forced to work clearing the snow in winter or mending the roads in summer. Instead of schooling they became acquainted with a racial system of rationing and segregation. On both sides of the deepening divide between Gentiles and Jews, children smuggled food and traded on the black market, and the networks that Jewish child smugglers built in Warsaw and other cities served as one of the few ways for them to escape into hiding. By the time that Martin Bergau witnessed the massacre of Jewish women in Palmnicken in January 1945, even German children in rural backwaters of East Prussia were becoming acquainted with the extremes of Nazi racial violence.

In the end, the regime would devour some of the very children it had sought to protect from racial pollution and air raids. In the last phase of the war the Nazi regime would call upon German teenagers to sacrifice themselves on the 'altar of the fatherland', sending teenage girls to flak batteries and boys out to fight Soviet tanks. With this suicidal climax of the Nazi cult of Gothic romanticism, the regime called up the last reserves of youthful idealism it had cultivated and sent the young to their deaths. In their wilful destruction lay some of the seeds of the post-war myth that the German nation had fallen victim to the Nazis. But, as Lore Walb's diary testified, the appeal of heroic and doomed gestures extended well beyond the Führer bunker in Berlin. With the sinews of state power snapping, this was a destruction which could not have occurred without the tacit consent and co-operation of many people, including, as often as not, the boys' own families.

How did this transformation occur? How did sufficient numbers of Germans come to believe the national struggle was worth the lives of their teenage children? One answer might be that they did not; that the Nazi regime held on to the bitter end through terror alone. There is some truth in this: of the 16,000 judicial executions carried out in Nazi Germany, over 14,000 took place after 1941. But the principal targets were Poles and Czechs, rather than Germans. And the Germans who were executed were more likely to be petty criminals caught looting after air raids than political opponents or defeatists. From the start of the war, German military discipline had been far more draconian than either the Western powers' or its own practice in the First World War: some 33,000 German soldiers were executed during the war; most of them as deserters, and probably half of them in the final twelve to eighteen months. Both against German soldiers and civilians, terror was greatest in the final months of war, as the regime and its armed forces battled for German territory, region by region. But terror alone did not keep Germans fighting: even in this end phase, both adult and teenage soldiers often fought on in small detachments, without anyone except their own officers and peers to prevent them from slipping away. Over one million German troops died in the last four months of the war. The Third Reich did not collapse until it was militarily defeated.[17]

This climax could not have been predicted from Germans' responses to the first years of the war. The easy victories of 1939 and 1940 over Poland, Denmark, Norway, the Netherlands, France, Belgium and Luxembourg provided grounds for jubilation, but also relief that the war had been shorter and cost far fewer casualties than people had feared. The Allied bombing and the war on the eastern front changed all that, confronting German society by the end of 1942 with a painful, frightening test of endurance. In the north and west, mass air raids affected all in the towns and cities under the flight paths. The wailing of the air-raid sirens sent families stumbling into claustrophobic and cramped cellars, often several times a night. There they waited to hear if this time the planes would strike. As German cities burned and turned to rubble, and the number of military and civilian dead rose, it did seem to many adults and teenagers as if this was a war of annihilation being waged against the German people by implacable enemies. The apocalyptic 'all or nothing' tone which Hitler's speeches had always had now suited the circumstances of 'total war' as never before. While teenagers and young adults like Lore Walb pledged their faith and commitment in their civilian diaries, many older people felt that they were helplessly tied to their nation's fate. But many, who might have walked by with disapproval during the anti-Jewish pogrom of November 1938, were now ready to follow the German media and blame the bombing on the influence of the Jews in Washington and London. And they knew that 'total war' would demand sacrifices. As early as February 1943, parents were accepting that their fifteen-year-old sons could man anti-aircraft batteries along the North Sea coast or in cities like Essen, Berlin and Hamburg. Many were dying in action before the German home front became subject to Nazi terror.

The Nazi 'national community' was riven with real and rhetorical contradictions. The regime's demands for blood and military sacrifice were absolute, and yet it was extraordinarily timid when it came to civilian morale. Desperate to avoid the collapse of the home front that had occurred in 1918, Hitler's regime struggled to maintain a kind of pseudo-normality, keeping civilian rations the highest in wartime Europe. Increasingly, forced labourers and prisoners from the East would endure the 'ruthless sacrifices' on the home front which German civilians were spared. Many of the German men in photographs taken in the bombed cities show them standing by in uniform, guarding the camp prisoners and forced labourers who had to clear up after the air raids. The longer the war lasted and the worse it went, the more foreign workers were executed in public, first by the security forces and, in the final weeks of the war, by lynch mobs. Nazi racism needed the fear of defeat and 'terror bombing' to persuade others to share in its Manichean visions of killing or being killed. Through everyday exposure to Nazi racial violence in a society fighting for its survival, those parts of the German home front which had been least Nazi in the 1930s – the industrial cities of the north, the Ruhr and Saxony – gradually absorbed these values which had lain at the core of Hitler's concept of racial conquest from the outset.[18]

When the war came home to children, they registered it as a set of physical events without precedent, spectacular and terrifying by turns. With a different sense of danger and threat from adults, young children often marvelled at the sights of fires burning across the cities in which they lived; even teenage boys competed to collect shell splinters the next morning on their way to school. Children were also sharply divided by their age and capacity to make sense of what they had seen. While younger children seem often to have been left with vivid but fragmentary images, older children strove to form abstract ideas about what was happening to them: from the radio, the Hitler Youth, their parents and their teachers they drew the moral of their national predicament, often redoubling their efforts to help fight fires or set up soup kitchens for bombed-out refugees. It is often said that the Nazis stopped adolescents from developing a sense of responsibility by presenting them with a ready-made set of authoritarian precepts. It could also be said that the Nazis inculcated an excessive sense of moral commitment, a personal responsibility to contribute to the war effort, which finally culminated in teenagers' willingness to sacrifice their own and others' lives in the final months of the war.[19]

I first heard of the Nazis as a child, my brother with childish prescience calling them 'the nasties'. My father had been born into a socialist and assimilated Jewish family in Berlin. The city from which he finally emigrated in 1939 remained his great love. We often asked him about his childhood in the late twenties and early thirties. His own political memories began with sitting inside his grandfather's bookcase and quietly listening in as the adults in the room – including leading Social Democrats – discussed how to react to von Papen's coup in Prussia in 1932 and how to defend the Republic. When Hitler took power, my father was on the cusp of adolescence and was severely reprimanded for unthinkingly whistling the 'Marseillaise' as he climbed up the stairs to visit a cousin who had joined a left-wing resistance group. Like many refugees and exiles, he preserved much of his moral and intellectual universe intact. For the rest of his life, he continued to identify with left-wing causes and with the 'other Germany' which had not voted for the Nazis in 1933, and which social historians have done so much since the 1970s to rediscover.[20]

My brother and I were fond of joking that, but for Hitler, we would not have been born; for otherwise our parents would never have met in 1950s Australia. We knew too that the odds had also been against our father surviving Hitler. But it was not until I read a statistical analysis of German military losses that I realised what surviving Hitler meant for *non*-Jewish men of his generation. Of his cohort of men born in 1920, 40 per cent died in the war, half of them in 1944 and

1945. The worst year to be born in twentieth-century Germany was 1920. This book begins after my father had already left Germany and after the closest and non-Jewish friend he had left behind – the one with whom he had marked all the grammatical mistakes in an early edition of Hitler's *Mein Kampf* in red ink – was serving in the German Army. He was killed by a landmine in early 1945. But it is not primarily their generation that fills the pages of this book.

I am concerned with something my father's stories awakened in me: a search for historical empathy and understanding. The more I found myself out of sympathy with some of my subjects, the more taxing that search became. It also felt more worthwhile. It is easy to identify with noble victims, but hard to think oneself into the mind of a child plying his trade on the black market or of a girl imagining herself ready to sacrifice her own and her brother's life on the 'altar of the fatherland'. It is difficult to imagine what a fifteen-year-old boy thought as he guarded women waiting to be shot.

As I wondered how to recapture what it felt like to be a child under German rule in the Second World War, I felt a need to weigh what adults remembered of their childhoods against contemporary sources. How else could we know what had been retained and what forgotten? How could we know what meanings and values children had given to events at the time, or what the adult world around them had encouraged them to think? Over the last decade, I have tried to track down children's school work, juvenile diaries, letters from evacuation camps, letters to fathers at the front, letters from reformatories and psychiatric asylums, children's artwork in the Jewish ghetto of Theresienstadt and German villages in the Black Forest, as well as adult accounts of children's games. Such sources are always fragmentary. They vividly illuminate some aspects of children's activities while leaving others in the shade. They are particularly precious because they embed experiences and emotions in the form they were expressed at the time – not just as they were remembered later.

Novelists can 'know' things about their subjects which historians cannot. Where novelists can be certain of the emotional logic at work within their characters, the historian needs to remember the openness of real protagonists' lives. Novelists, after all, do not need to test their intuitions against a barrage of incomplete sources. These constraints give historical understanding a different quality, and I have found myself constantly reminded that witnesses are not there simply to illustrate historians' favourite arguments, but to make us question again what we think we know. These things matter, because otherwise we cannot give an appropriate shape to the shards of societies broken apart by their experiences of the war and Holocaust.

Much of that destruction was fully intended: the Nazis were enacting a utopian vision of German colonisation in which children would be saved and damned according to their racial value. But to reconstruct what happened to children, let alone what they experienced, is a complex and delicate task. It also involves breaking a scholarly taboo. For good reasons of empathy and moral justice, Holocaust historians have generally focused exclusively on either the victims or the perpetrators. But, as historians of Nazism have come to realise, the Holocaust permeated German society even when it remained almost entirely invisible to people like Lore Walb at the time. We cannot grasp the extent of the transformations wrought by the war upon the colonisers and the colonised unless we bring their lives and viewpoints within the same frame. Because the Third Reich shaped their lives so profoundly, children are particularly appropriate subjects for such a history. Their capacity for treating the exceptional as normal reveals how deeply Nazism reached into society, dividing them between those who were destined to rule and those who were to serve; ultimately between those who were to live and those who were to die. Children's experiences deserve to be understood across the racial and national divides, not because of their similarities but because their extreme contrasts help us to see the Nazi social order as a whole. Children were neither just the mute and traumatised witnesses to this war, nor merely its innocent victims. They also lived in the war, played and fell in love during the war; the war invaded their imaginations and the war raged inside them.

PART ONE

THE HOME FRONT

I

GERMANS AT WAR

JANINA came out of the privy at the bottom of her grandparents' garden on the morning of 1 September 1939 to see two planes circling overhead. The sound of their machine guns opening up brought her parents, grandparents and brothers running out of the house to join her. Then they all rushed back inside again to listen to the radio. They just caught the announcement of the German attack on Poland, which had begun at daybreak, then the voice faded away as the batteries died. 'Grandpa turned the switch off and looked at our anguished faces,' ten-year-old Janina noted in her diary at the end of that long day. 'He knelt in front of the picture of Jesus Christ and started to pray aloud.' They joined him in the Lord's Prayer. Janina had been expecting to return with her parents from the little village of Borowa-Góra, where they had spent the summer holidays with her grandparents, to Warsaw for the start of school on 4 September, and had been happily anticipating the set of new school books they had promised to buy her. The ten-year-old knew that something momentous had just occurred, but had no images yet of war. Even those adults who had lived through the First World War in Poland could have no conception of what the second would be like.[1]

That September the start of the new autumn term was seriously disrupted across Europe. In Germany, schools remained closed at the end of the summer holidays and children hung around the gates to catch a glimpse of reservists as they poured in to register at these temporary mobilisation centres. In the rural calm of the Eifel, west of the Rhine, two little girls enjoyed the envy of all their friends for being allowed to stand in the village square with a bag of apples and throw them to the passing troops. Unfortunately, for many older children, like sixteen-year-old Gretel Bechtold, the excitement soon died down: the French fired no shots at the West Wall and soon she had to go back to school.[2]

As street lights were turned off and windows blacked out, Germany's towns and cities were plunged into a night-time darkness they had not experienced at night since the pre-industrial era. In Essen, little girls started pretending to be the nightwatchman who patrolled the streets reminding people to conceal their lights by calling out 'Blackout! Blackout!' All too soon classes began again. Dangling gas masks and satchels over their shoulders on the way to school, many children found they had to write assignments when they got there about blacking out and other measures of civil defence against air attack. What with trams and trucks colliding in the unlit streets and pedestrians missing their footing as they stepped off the kerb, the most significant change to strike one Hamburg boy, after four months at war, was the increase in traffic accidents.[3]

In September 1939, there were no scenes in Germany reminiscent of the jubilation of August 1914, however short-lived and partial that mood of public ecstasy may in fact have been. Even strongly Nazi families were unsure how to view the outbreak of war. As fourteen-year-old Liese listened to the radio broadcast of the Führer's Reichstag speech in Thuringia in central Germany, she squealed with pleasure. But after only two weeks of war, she was asking her father what he thought the chances were of bringing things to a speedy conclusion:

If we get into a real war with England, don't you think it will last at least two years? For once he starts a war the Englishman throws everything into it and mobilises his whole empire, for the Englishman has never lost a war yet.[4]

Her father, a reserve officer who strongly supported the regime, agreed. As might be expected from someone with experience of the terrible blood-letting of the First World War, he told her that France remained the key. Meanwhile, Liese's mother purchased a good-quality radio, a Telefunken-Super, and they set up a map of Poland next to it so that – just like in schools across the Reich – they could mark the advance of the German troops on it with little swastika flags after each news broadcast.[5]

When the German attack began at dawn on 1 September, the *Wehrmacht* found the Polish Army still in the midst of mobilisation. With the advantage of surprise, the *Luftwaffe* destroyed many of the 400 largely obsolete planes of the Polish Air Force on the ground, gaining immediate air supremacy. Thereafter, its 2,000 aircraft practised their new tactics of war, giving battlefield support to the German Army, while its sixty well-armed divisions swept over the borders from East Prussia in the north, Slovakia and the recently occupied Czech lands in the south, and along a broad front in the west stretching from Silesia to Pomerania. Defending such borders was impossible, and the Polish High Command abandoned its attempt to do so on 6 September. Even the attempt by the Poles to defend the major industrial and urban centres involved spreading their forty ill-equipped divisions and 150 tanks too thinly; the *Wehrmacht* could pick out its battleground and concentrate its 2,600 tanks there.[6]

As Germans flocked to the cinemas, far more eager to see the newsreels of the war – the *Wochenschau* – than the feature films which followed, their senses were bombarded with a new and sensually stimulating kind of photography. Aerial photography had been tried out since the First World War, but now the spectators could feel themselves being swept downwards in a furious nosedive, at a speed of over 150 metres per second. For once, police reports showed satisfied audiences, as they viewed the Polish campaign through the eyes of the German dive-bomber pilots. Small children in Essen queued up to jump off the chicken coop, screeching 'Stuka!' as they mimicked their screaming wail. By late September 1939, the well-informed American journalist, William Shirer, could find no one in Berlin, 'even among those who don't like the regime, who sees anything wrong in the German destruction of Poland'.[7]

Marion Lubien from Essen was one of many German teenagers who kept war diaries. On 3 September, she noted the capture of Tschenstochau (Częstochowa), on 6 September, 'the industrial area of Upper Silesia virtually unharmed in German hands', and on the 9 September her bulletin read, 'Lodz occupied. The Führer in Lodz.' But this fourteen-year-old girl kept to the clipped and stilted language of the *Wehrmacht* bulletins to the home front. Like most of the rest of the country, she may have been glued to the radio, fascinated by the first newsreel images, and temporarily intoxicated with a sense of victorious power – but the war itself remained distant and unemotional.

Not until the first bombs fell near her house in October 1940 would her chronicle of the war leap into the first person.[8]

On 5 October Warsaw surrendered, bringing hostilities to a close. But by mid-October, Poland had already become a non-subject in Germany and an undercover reporter for the German Social Democrats could find 'hardly a single person who still spoke of the "victory"'. Some hoped that now that the dispute over Poland had been settled with the country's dismemberment, peaceful relations with the Western powers could be restored. And Hitler played to such sentiments when he addressed the German Reichstag on 6 October. Insisting once again that he had no territorial claims against Britain and France, the Führer suggested that, with Poland's demise, the *casus belli* had also disappeared. This was a line the German public was more likely to appreciate than the French or British. When Daladier and Chamberlain rejected Hitler's olive branch, many German citizens joined Liese and her father in concluding that it was primarily British intransigence that was preventing a settlement. By mid-October, children were singing ditties about Chamberlain in the street and mimicking his famous habit of carrying an umbrella.[9]

However much the regime might insist that the British and French declaration of war on 3 September, rather than Germany's attack on Poland, had started a conflict which the German government was only too anxious to end, nothing could conceal the fact that the war was not yet popular at home. Even some of his military commanders had openly warned Hitler that Germany could not expect to defeat France and Britain. Hitler's foreign policy triumphs had done much to realign public opinion during the three years before the war, but they had not removed the fear of war itself. When German troops had marched across the Rhine in 1936, working-class districts, renowned for their earlier anti-Nazi sentiments, had hung out swastika flags for the first time. Few objected to rolling back the conditions the Allies had imposed on Germany and Austria after their defeat in 1918. Hitler's success in reversing Bismarck's 'Little German' unification of 1871 by drawing Austria back into a 'Greater German Reich' was an achievement German and Austrian Social Democrats could also endorse. After all, they had themselves attempted it at the end of the First World War, only to be thwarted by the Allies. Whether they believed in the pan-German creed of bringing all Germans 'home' into the Reich, or in restoring Prussia's and Austria's eighteenth- and nineteenth-century territories at the expense of the East European successor states, or simply subscribed to Nazi demands for colonial 'living space', by 1938 and 1939 few Germans objected in principle to Hitler's demands against Czechoslovakia or Poland. Success had nurtured both ambition and a growing complacency among the population at large.[10]

But the Czech crisis had lasted long enough – from May to October 1938 – to reveal just how much the German people feared a new conflict on the scale of the First World War. At the height of the crisis, the regime staged a grand military parade in Berlin on 27 September 1938 to impress the world with Germany's might, but there were no crowds, with passers-by literally ducking into doorways to avoid the spectacle. When the Munich Agreement was signed three days later, Hitler might storm in private that he had been 'cheated' of his war, but almost everyone else was deeply relieved. Goebbels had to give explicit instructions to the German press to remind the population of the 'world historic' achievement of Munich, to counter the universal rejoicing that war had been averted.

What Germans had feared in September 1938 came to pass in September 1939. As Hitler set out to address the Reichstag on 1 September, formations of storm troopers lined both sides of his route from the Reich Chancellery to the Kroll Opera House, but the crowds stayed away. In other big cities it was the same: the streets remained empty and deserted, as the period of painless and peaceful Führer miracles abruptly ended. At work, at school and at home, Germans gathered around the radio instead.[11]

Images of the blood-letting and chronic shortages of the First World War haunted national consciousness, and people of all walks of life, one Social Democrat noted wryly in his secret report on public opinion, 'speak far more about provisioning than about politics. Each person is entirely taken up with how to get his ration. How can I get something extra?' After only a few weeks of rationing, the Sunday trains were full of people leaving the towns to go 'hamstering' for foodstuffs in the countryside. Teenagers did not even bother to change out of their Hitler Youth uniforms before going. Ditties started to circulate in Cologne about the utter failure of the local *Gauleiter*, Josef Grohé, to set a good example for modest living, while neighbours began to fear that someone in their block of flats would denounce them to the police for having succeeded in laying by soap, clothes or – best of all – shoes. People who had lost their savings twice before feared wartime inflation and rushed to turn their cash into anything that could be traded later on. All unrationed luxury items, such as furs, swiftly sold out. By October 1939, the conviction was already growing that the country would not be able to hold out as long as in the last war 'because there's already nothing left to eat'. Only the soldiers, everyone agreed, had enough.[12]

Grumbling and anxiety do not make a revolution, but the Gestapo was taking no chances and had swiftly arrested all the former Reichstag deputies from the Left. Yet socialists, who had hoped for the last six years that war would bring down the Nazi dictatorship, had to admit in late October 1939 that it would take a great deal more than a few shortages: 'Only if famine takes hold and has worn their nerves down, and, above all, if the Western powers succeed in gaining successes in the West and in occupying large portions of German territory, may the time for a revolution begin to ripen.' Not until early 1945 would such conditions prevail, and by then much had happened to make a German revolution an improbable outcome of this war. In this respect at least, Hitler would have his wish: there would be 'no second 1918'.[13]

For now, the government did all it could to reassure the population that the war had made little change to life. While snaking lines of London children, cardboard labels slung round their necks as they clutched their small suitcases and gas masks, provided the media with its first vivid images of the British war, in Germany there was no mass evacuation of children from the cities. Hermann Göring was so confident in the power of the *Luftwaffe* he had built up, he joked that if a single German city was bombed, then people could call him 'Meier'. Still hopeful of negotiating a peace settlement with Britain, Hitler explicitly reserved to himself any decision to commence what he called the 'terror bombing' of its civilian population.[14]

Fearing the *Luftwaffe*'s air supremacy, the British government was not prepared to launch air strikes on German civilian or industrial targets for fear of sparking German retaliation. So, despite all the evidence of German bombing raids on Polish cities, during the first winter of the war, the RAF largely confined itself to dropping millions of leaflets on Germany explaining the causes of the war in the hope of winning over German hearts and minds. As Carola Reissner picked them up in Essen, her bewilderment turned to outrage. 'They are apparently trying to inflame the population,' she wrote to her relatives, adding meaningfully, 'these are obviously Jewish ploys.' The thought came naturally, for she had heard for years how the Jews had manipulated and tricked their way to power and influence in Germany. In a barrage of publications, including the lavish photo collection of *Die verlorene Insel* (*The Doomed Island*), German propaganda extended these images to Britain, revealing the Jewish huckster, the freshly minted aristocrat of city finance, as the true enemy who was busily winding up the creaking clockwork mechanism of the English class system and exploiting Germany's 'blood brothers' across the North Sea.[15]

On 9 November 1939, news spread across Germany that an attempt had been made on the Führer's life the previous evening. At 9.20 p.m. a bomb had exploded in the Munich beer cellar where the 'old fighters' of the Nazi movement were gathered for their annual celebration of the 1923 putsch attempt. Hitler had left to catch the train back to Berlin a mere ten minutes before, but the bomb killed eight people and injured sixty-four others. Many employers called special workplace meetings and schools held special assemblies where the children gave thanks for the Führer's providential escape by singing the Lutheran hymn which had been composed to celebrate the end of the Thirty Years War, 'Nun danket alle Gott . . .' ('Now thank we all our God . . .').[16]

Surprised, shocked and angry, even religious and working-class circles where many had cause to resent the Nazis, rallied behind the regime. People spoke bitterly about those they presumed to be responsible for the attack, 'the English and the Jews', and expected retaliation against both. Only the year before, at the same Beer Hall reunion of old Nazis, Goebbels had launched a nationwide pogrom against the Jews, blaming them all for the assassination of a German consular official in Paris at the hands of a Polish Jew. In the *Kristallnacht* pogrom, ninety-one Jews had been killed outright and 25,000 men bundled off to concentration camps where hundreds more had been murdered. Now, when the Führer's own death had been plotted, nothing happened. Two British agents were arrested on the Dutch border and the media contented itself with pointing the finger of blame at the British. There was no fresh pogrom against the Jews in November 1939. But where the public in cities with large Jewish communities like Frankfurt or Berlin had been shocked by the wanton violence and destruction of a year before, now the Jews were not a physical target. Instead, they were quietly ostracised within their neighbourhoods, as Germans turned into a nation at war to which Jews could not belong.[17]

By 1939, 82 per cent of Jewish children under sixteen had emigrated from Germany. Even conservative and nationalistic German Jews realised, after the pogrom of November 1938 and the expropriation of Jewish business which followed, that an independent Jewish existence in Germany was not possible. Where the Nuremberg race laws had reassured some religious Jews that their separate cultural identity would be respected, that illusion had been destroyed. Through the rescue efforts of the *Kindertransport*, 10,000 Jewish minors were brought from Germany, Austria and Czechoslovakia to Britain.[18]

At 4 p.m. on 2 September 1939, Klaus Langer left Essen with a large suitcase and backpack. A telegram had arrived that morning from the Aid to Jewish Youth, telling him to be in Berlin, ready to embark for Denmark the next day. His parents – who now abandoned their plans to emigrate together – had to bid a hasty farewell to their only son. As fifteen-year-old Klaus noted in his diary, the parting was 'short and difficult'. He had no idea when he would see his parents again and reflected sombrely that 'To be in a war in Germany as a Jew means to be ready for the worst'. The short ferry crossing of the Baltic from Warnemünde to Gedser the next day was beautiful. It was also, Klaus learned later, the last boatload to leave carrying Germans, because Britain and France declared war a few hours later. Safely in Denmark, Klaus took up his pen again on 8 September and his thoughts turned to the parents and grandmother he had had to leave behind in Essen 'and then', he found, 'only sad thoughts come to mind'.[19]

Jewish emigration peaked in 1939, as 78,000 Jews left Germany under the impact of the 1938 pogrom and a renewed fear of war. But not all could surmount the enormous bureaucratic and financial obstacles to leaving or securing entry visas for other countries. At the outbreak of war, 185,000 registered Jews remained in the Reich, perhaps 40 per cent of the Jewish population of 1933. From this ageing and increasingly destitute community, concentrated mainly in the cities, especially Berlin and Frankfurt, another 21,000 managed to leave before emigration was banned in October 1941. But by then, 30,000 of those who had fled had been overrun by the German armies of conquest; on the eve of the 'final solution', 25,000 Jewish children and young people under the age of twenty-five were still trapped within the 'old Reich' of Germany's 1937 borders.[20]

When rationing was introduced on 28 August 1939, it drew attention to the Jews. Speckled with 'J's for '*Jude*', their ration cards reminded neighbours, shoppers and sales assistants alike to enforce the host of new regulations stipulating where Jews could shop and which foodstuffs they were prohibited from purchasing. Different local authorities set their own restrictions to prevent Jews from inconveniencing German shoppers. In Breslau, the Jews could shop only between 11 a.m. and 1 p.m. In Berlin, where the hours were set between 4 and 5 p.m., one small girl found her path blocked by one of her neighbours as she tried to leave their block of flats with a shopping bag. Pointing to the large clock diagonally across the street in front of the chemist's, which showed the time as just before four o'clock, the woman stood her ground and told her off roundly, 'You're not allowed to go shopping yet, I won't let you out of here.'[21]

As shops put up notices warning that 'Foodstuffs in short supply are not sold to Jews', more and more regulations engulfed their daily lives. Between the 9 November 1938 pogrom and the outbreak of war, 229 anti-Jewish decrees had been issued. Between the outbreak of the war and the autumn of 1941, agencies worked out a particular anti-Jewish variant to every new measure governing the German home front and published another 525 decrees constraining the daily lives of Jews. They were prevented from buying underwear, shoes and clothing, even for their growing teenage children. Household pets, radios and record players all had to be surrendered. Thomas Gève's grandfather found it hard to cope without his crystal set and earphones. Blinded in the First World War, the former army doctor could no longer follow events. This most patriotically Prussian and assimilated of German Jews, who liked singing the quitessential soldier's song, 'Ich hatt' einen Kameraden', for his ten-year-old grandson when he was in a good mood, became cut off in his increasingly silent world, a blind old man unable to grasp how his fatherland had changed.[22]

Young Thomas still found life exciting. In his own block, the local boys would not play with a Jewish boy like him. But by going to neighbourhoods where he was not known, he was able to enjoy the anonymity of the streets and join other Berlin children in their games. His half-Jewish friends helped him find playmates too. For most Berlin boys, the war had not yet made much impact on the normal routine of their games. As Christmas approached, children pressed their noses against the shop windows, or best of all went to big department stores. On his excursions to the largest shop in Berlin, the KaDeWe, Thomas Gève was amazed by reconstructions of scenes from films in its shop windows. But most children went there because its collection in Berlin continued to outdo all others with its life-size figures from the fairy tales and its huge armies of toy soldiers. Otto Prescher and his companions in the working-class neighbourhood of Kreuzberg took over the pavements as soon as they were free of snow and ice to play with their tops, whipping them to jump from one large paving slab to another. In summer they continued to run barefoot behind the water carts spraying the streets, dodging the jets of water which they really hoped would hit them. When the brewers' drays were not drinking out of the troughs set into the kerb, the children sailed boats made out of discarded newspaper there.[23]

In a mania which gripped boys far more than girls, every school playground saw a frantic trade in cigarette cards, with pairs of boys leaning their heads over their packs of cards to the accompaniment of their satisfied drone of 'Goddit, goddit, goddit', until they found new cards they could barter and exchange. Even a sixth-former like Dierk Sievert filled three albums with Reemtsma cigarette cards of Renaissance and baroque art, not to mention the exciting ones about 'Germany awakes' and 'Adolf Hitler'. In this respect, too, Thomas Gève was no different from other boys, except that, for a few months until the outbreak of the war, he had access to English cigarette cards as well. Expecting his family to join him in Britain, Thomas's father had gone ahead in the summer of 1939 to make arrangements and maintained contact with his son in the meantime by sending back cigarette cards with their extracts of encyclopaedic knowledge. The idea that the world could be divided into such capsules of information would profoundly influence Thomas. At the end of the war, when he started to pick up the threads of his life again in Buchenwald, he would turn to this idea once again as he looked for a way to share his knowledge with his father once more. But there were no cigarette cards to describe the world from which he was emerging: he would have to make his own.[24]

Although Thomas had to take care to disguise his Jewishness in finding German playmates in 1939, few German children had any direct contact with Jews any longer. The 1935 Nuremberg race laws had excluded Jews from 'German' schools, but even before that many Jewish pupils had left to escape discrimination and bullying. Anti-Semitism had also swiftly curbed the trend to marry outside the Jewish community, which had become so strong in the Weimar years, and the young especially began to look far more towards the youth groups and friendships that the Jewish community provided. With the exodus of most of the young in the wave of Jewish emigration which followed the 1938 pogrom, German children had even less contact with Jewish children of their own age: in the big cities they saw mainly elderly and increasingly impoverished Jewish men and women. In Nuremberg, Hugo Riedl wrote a prize essay for Christmas 1938 on the Jews: referring approvingly to both his local *Gauleiter*, Julius Streicher, and his rabidly anti-Semitic paper, *Der Stürmer*, the eleven-year-old boy duly recycled the clichés he had learned. Beginning with the Jew's 'cunning', 'deceit' and 'murderousness', Hugo went on to declare that, while 'Germany wants permanent peace', 'everywhere the Jew is war mongering'; and 'after a Jew shot the embassy secretary in Paris, National comrades' anger was boundless. They stormed the Jewish businesses. Now the Jew will have to pack his bundle and move abroad.' Hugo's drawing of the Jew in morning dress, mopping his bald pate with a handkerchief as he clutched his bag could have come straight out of the pages of *Der Stürmer*.[25]

Not all children were as admiring of this variety of Nazi anti-Semitism, but there was also little resistance to it. From school, the Hitler Youth, the radio and often from their families too, the young picked up negative associations about the Jews. When the Weissmuller family moved to Munich in January 1939, they found they had Jewish neighbours. Each afternoon when ten-year-old Rudolf returned from school in his *Jungvolk* uniform, kindly old Frau Wolfsheimer would greet him in the stairwell, and he would reply with '*Grüss Gott, Frau Wolfsheimer*', in winter doffing the cap he wore. She would reach out to stroke his hair, and he would flinch inwardly, as if her touch were contagious. To Rudolf's great envy, his older brother Helmuth had joined the junior branch of the Hitler Youth for ten- to fourteen year-olds, the *Jungvolk*, in 1933, and Rudolf, then only four, had spent the next six years coveting the uniform, tassles and, above all, dagger. Now he had earned them, and along the way both boys learned that they were not to play Felix Mendelssohn in music classes at school 'because a Jew cannot think like a German'. However much he liked Frau Wolfsheimer, Rudolf felt a physical barrier separated them.[26]

The war injected the normal activities of the Hitler Youth with a still greater sense of purpose, as children were sent around their towns to collect goods for industrial recycling or to distribute to the needy via the Nazis' 'Winter Relief' programme. They went out into the woodland and gathered prodigious quantities of herbs, especially camomile and nettles which, they were told, would be made into ointments. As schools and the Hitler Youth cooperated in making these efforts a regular part of the week, taking up Saturday mornings and afternoons after classes, the children could feel they were doing their bit for the war effort. Hans Jürgen Harnack and his Hamburg classmates went out collecting bones from neighbours, which were sent off to a factory in Lüneburg to be turned into bone-meal. This was all necessary, he solemnly explained in a school essay, because after the 'world war Germany lost its colonies because England occupied them. So we have to wrest the raw materials for ourselves.' In the first year of the war, the pupils at another Hamburg school collected 2,054 kilograms of bones, while pupils who absconded could expect a beating from their teachers. By April 1940, the authorities were even worrying that people were donating valuable artworks to the collecting drives for scrap metal in their desire to 'offer a sacrifice to the Führer'.[27]

In the meantime, Thomas Gève and his street companions started collecting other things. They began to pester passers-by for their lapel pins. Each collecting drive for a good cause gave out miniature carved wooden dolls, aeroplanes, guns, or shells to pin on their coats and show that the wearer had already contributed. As the boys stopped people in the street to ask if they could have these badges and pins, many adults assumed that their requests were simply part of another recycling drive.[28]

Membership in the Hitler Youth had been made compulsory for all fourteen- to eighteen-year-olds in March 1939, and the Nazis' last major competitors, the Catholic youth organisations, were destroyed. In April 1940, for the first time all ten-year-old boys and girls had to join the *Jungvolk* or *Jungmädelbund*, the junior branches of the Hitler Youth and League of German Girls, swearing oaths of loyalty to the Führer as part of their induction:

> You, Führer, are our commander!
> We stand in your name.
> The Reich is the object of our struggle,
> It is the beginning and the Amen.[29]

Although many parents, especially those with strong Catholic, Social Democratic or Communist leanings, may have been less than enthusiastic about their children's enrolment, the sense of belonging and putting on the uniform exercised a powerful pull. One Berlin girl bitterly rued her parents' refusal to buy her an outfit when her whole class at school was admitted to the *Jungmädelbund*. It was bad enough that her thin and dark hair would never match the thick blonde plaits of the happy, confident and successful girls in her class.[30]

The Catholic Church and anti-Nazi parents might fear the Hitler Youth for its ideological indoctrination of the young, and both parents and teachers might resent its challenge to their authority, but precisely these things often appealed to the young themselves. With their dichotomy between good and evil, their appeal to feeling and their demand for moral commitment, Nazi values could have been designed for adolescents, and it was among this group of the German population that their purchase would last longest during the Second World War. Summer camping trips and cycling tours could often be tremendous fun, especially in those local groups which remained closest to the old ideal of 'Youth leads youth'. The feeling of not just having to obey adults at home and at school could endow the ordinary elements of afternoon drill and evening meetings with a close-knit sense of belonging and being grown-up.[31]

The League of German Girls started sewing slippers for the military hospitals out of woollen blankets or plaiting them out of straw. They went to the railway stations to hand out coffee, soup and packets of sandwiches to the soldiers on the troop trains. They came to help out in the Kindergartens run by the Nazi Welfare Organisation and tried to make good the chronic shortage of teachers by acting as teaching assistants. In Thuringia, Liese now threw herself into her work as a League of German Girls leader, proudly reporting the rounds of collecting 'used paper, scrap metal, used fabric and rose hip and medicinal herbs' she had organised to her father at the front. As she catalogued all the reports she had written in addition to her school work, she teasingly addressed him with the double greeting of 'My dear daddy (Most respected Captain Sir)' and signing herself off as 'Special Reporter Liese'. Liese might mention her mother's whirl of coffee parties and weddings without commenting directly on their frivolity, but she had already shown her father how much closer she stood to his serious world. With a single word she was able to equate her work in the League of German Girls with the adult male world of his military service: that word was '*Dienst*' (service). For his part, he recommended that she learn shorthand typing so that she could be of even more use to her country – and make him proud.[32]

But many mothers had a great deal more to do than drink coffee and eat cake. Although women were not conscripted into the war economy, the shortage of labour still had an immediate effect. Married women returned to the classrooms to replace men of military age, working-class women took up jobs in armaments factories and labour suddenly became scarce in traditional – and badly paid – sectors of female employment, such as agriculture and domestic service. For middle-class women, a distinct 'servant problem' developed, even though Hitler refused steadfastly until 1943 to countenance conscripting housemaids into the arms factories. However much the government tried to avoid overtaxing the patience of the home front and producing a collapse of civilian morale on a par with that of the First World War, the war made itself felt at first in small dislocations of routine and a series of minor adjustments. Mothers had to ask their older children to watch over the younger ones more often, as they queued for items in short supply, went to local government offices, or took over the running of the family business.[33]

School hours became erratic. Even after schools ceased to operate as military registration centres, classes often had to be doubled up because rooms were requisitioned for first-aid stations, by officials issuing ration cards, and as collecting points for salvaged paper. Lack of classrooms or limited space in the air-raid shelters forced many schools to cut the hours of tuition, especially for the younger age groups, and to teach the pupils using a morning and afternoon shift system. Each time the hours changed, mothers had to rearrange their routines to cope with childcare and, throughout the war, managers of armaments factories complained about the absenteeism and poor time-keeping of German women workers. No sooner had mothers adjusted to a new school calendar than the schools closed again. The winter of 1939–40 also saw chronic shortages of coal, which closed virtually all Berlin schools between 28 January and 28 March 1940. Children might celebrate these 'coal holidays', but their mothers were less pleased.[34]

Some children turned to hobbies to fill their spare time. Boys were often able to devote drawing and handicraft lessons to building scale models of gliders and aeroplanes – one area, as a teacher from the Berlin working-class district of Spandau proudly recalled, where ordinary Volksschule boys could beat the pampered grammar school pupils.

From building models, boys might graduate to the air-training corps of the Hitler Youth where they would employ the same principles to construct real gliders.[35]

Others found their place in the Hitler Youth through the arts rather than the standard routine of shooting and square-bashing. The intensely musical Ermbrecht from Königsberg in East Prussia was taken into their radio choir, while fourteen-year-old Herbert K.'s gift for playing the accordion was spotted on a summer camp for boys from Berlin and he was asked to join the Reich Youth Leadership radio band. In order to make the live evening broadcasts, the fourteen-year-old was issued with a special pass so that he could travel home at midnight without falling foul of the new curfew restrictions on juveniles. Herbert's mother became so worried that he was really absconding to meet a girlfriend in secret that one evening she followed him to the studio and back. She need not have worried. For him, the new opportunities and freedom of his single-sex organisation were quite intoxicating enough.[36] For women who were effectively single mothers, the childcare offered by these activities during wartime was often welcome. Many must have worried about losing influence over their children, but the Hitler Youth also had to respect the integrity of the German family, including parents' right to refuse to let their children attend evening meetings. The Hitler Youth for its part often reminded children to be polite and respectful in public places, especially to mothers, and there seems to be very little evidence for the later myth that children were made to spy on their parents. In fact, very few denunciations to the police originated within families at all. The young may have made eager local sleuths, but they proved less likely than adults to shop their neighbours.[37]

Despite all the talk of belt-tightening and duty, the war also provided the opportunity to be more, not less, self-indulgent. Dierk Sievert welcomed the opportunities to escape from the monotony of his final years of school and training ten- to fourteen-year-old boys in the *Jungvolk*. By the start of April 1940 he was spending far more evenings going out to the theatre and cinema than at the Hitler Youth. In the space of a single week, he managed to see *Peer Gynt* at the opera, a romantic film, *Dein Leben gehört mir* (*Your Life Belongs to Me*), at the cinema and Goethe's *Iphigenie* at the municipal theatre. Part of the allure of military life itself was the escape from parental strictures. Dierk's elder brother Günther brought back new and easy ways on his spells of leave from the front and introduced Dierk to serious binge-drinking and cards. He even let his kid brother break the curfew restrictions on minors and join his friends and girlfriend when they went out on the town. By 21 December 1940, Dierk was ruefully confessing to his diary that Günther was well on the way to turning 'everyone in the family into a drinker'.[38]

But dropping out of the Hitler Youth altogether came back to haunt working-class boys when they left school. Thirteen-year-old Fritz Theilen wanted to work for Ford in Cologne, only to find that the Hitler Youth exercised a closed shop over the apprentices, and the local leader would not relent even when his father returned from leave and intervened in person, threatening the young youth movement functionary with his service revolver. An appeal to one of his old colleagues, a master craftsman in the workshop, proved more successful and Fritz soon found himself not only back in the Hitler Youth but, alongside the other Ford apprentices, in the elite motorised section.[39]

At most, absent fathers could influence their children's behaviour through their letters. The father of nine-year-old Richard appealed to his sense of manliness. As he urged the boy to prepare himself for his future as a soldier by learning to darn his socks, he assured him that he was himself 'doing it here as well and it's good if you can do it too'. Fathers wrote, asking their children about their progress at school. Children, wondering what to tell their fathers about, were often keen to discover a ready-made topic of interest. Failure to keep up playing the piano was reported with misgiving; good marks in maths, English and Latin with pride. Some children reported how their mothers celebrated their successes with special outings. Some fathers remembered to send back money as a reward. Richard's father even got him to post him his homework so that he could read it. Since the boy preferred drawing pictures, his father took it upon himself to 'improve' the pictures in order to teach his son how to get the proportions right.[40]

But fathers also had to write explaining why they could not come home for birthdays, Christmas or Whitsun, without being able to say what they were actually doing. Oblique references to preparing for 'great events' hardly satisfied children's curiosity, who found it hard to imagine where their fathers were or what they were doing. Ten-year-old Detlef was so excited about the start of the war that he begged his father to draw a picture of his bunker so that he could imagine it for himself and sent his father his own version with the caption, 'Does the bunker look like this?'[41]

Another father advised his daughter to look at photos in magazines, since he could not take a photograph of the interior of his blockhouse. In the period of 'phoney war', letters from the western front resembled travelogues. Rosemarie's father wrote from his inactive artillery position along the Rhine border with France about the snow-capped peaks of the Black Forest. As temperatures plummeted to −25 Celsius, rare birds began falling off the branches and he and his comrade Sepp started feeding them on the windowsill of the blockhouse. The setting had become so homely, he reflected, that a casual passer-by would hardly believe that he could prepare his well-concealed guns to fire within three minutes. Fortunately, so far the 'decent' Frenchmen had not opened fire, even when their snipers could easily have picked out his officer's cap at 200 metres. Perhaps they too liked watching him feed the deer by hand.[42]

Throughout the Second World War children played war games. From her boarding school in Krumbach, twelve-year-old Rosemarie wrote back to her father in his artillery battery, revelling in her deeds in battle during that first winter of the war. On one occasion the girls trounced the boys who had tried to imprison them in a wall of tables and chairs while they were all left unsupervised in the school gym. In his town in Westphalia, ten-year-old Detlef was able to convey some of the excitement of his battles to his enlisted father, as the boy described how his side had retaken their position under 'murderous fire'. His side had used sticks as hand grenades, but the enemy had thrown stones. Then Detlef had led the charge with his 'sabre' raised, putting the enemy temporarily to flight. 'None of us cried and we won,' he wrote triumphantly to his father.[43]

Just as younger children had envied their elder brothers' Hitler Youth uniforms before the war, with their tassles and braid, so now they lusted after military trophies and the trappings of the enemy. Eight-year-old Christoph Meyer wrote to his older brother Werner begging him to send home a French kepi and epaulettes so that he could kit himself out properly as the 'General'. 'Please, get hold of them for me as quickly as possible,' he urged, 'I'm already waiting for them.' Two years later, Christoph was still writing to his brother about the charges he was leading the boys from Eisersdorf 'in the war against Rengersdorf'.[44]

Desperate as Christoph was to bring his war games up to date, he was continuing a fine old tradition of the boys of one village taking on those of another. In the cities, working-class boys joined gangs who battled for neighbourhood territory, across tramlines and canals. Similar battles had been waged in town and country for hundreds of years. Everywhere in these unsupervised games, the lead was taken by the older boys. Only the roles for which the children competed altered over time. In 1810, Cologne children had wanted to be the 'king' or the 'robber captain'. By the inter-war period, German and Austrian children were playing *Räuber und Gendarme*, cops and robbers.[45] Adding the accoutrements of the war, like Christoph's kepi, may have brought him glory by association without changing his appreciation of the game he and his friends were playing. The role-play and the games had not changed fundamentally from the days when boys played at being 'king' and 'robber captain'. At the war's end, role-play would change character in Germany; and in occupied Poland such games were already being dramatically transformed.[46]

For the time being, most German children experienced this war through coloured maps at school and stilted military bulletins on the radio, by hearing grown-ups' talk and composing letters to absent fathers and brothers requesting special items like real pens to replace the glass nibs which squelched ink all over the page. Within two months of his father's call-up, Detlef had attached himself to a soldier in the Medical Corps who was good with horses, and sometimes gave Detlef sweets or let him try his army rations of bread and sausage. Some small children made the soldiers laugh as they marched past by calling out, 'Papa, papa!'[47]

Soon, asking for news of the war simply became a good ploy for distracting a difficult teacher from giving out homework or spelling tests. This was how Martha Jahn and her classmates dealt with their severe English teacher with a wooden foot in Hindenburg in Upper Silesia. Often the war news was not very interesting, and the absent fathers were becoming more distant and remote. Teachers set aside time during German lessons for children to write to their fathers and brothers at the front but, perhaps just as often, it was a chore and they frequently could not think of much to say. Some teachers even dictated letters for the children to take down. Invisibly, the children were gradually losing contact with their fathers.[48]

Secondary schools also encouraged teenage girls to form new attachments, when they arranged for them to start writing to servicemen. Reviving a practice pioneered in Germany and Austria during the First

World War, girls knitted socks and gloves for the men at the front as patriotic 'gifts of love'. Some of these penfriendships blossomed into vivid correspondences, fostering romantic ties between men in the services and girls on the home front. Periods of military inaction during wartime allowed soldiers to impress civilians with the glamour of their martial calling, and the physical presence of troops in German towns turned individual adoration into a mass – if often sexually innocent – phenomenon. In her East Prussian village near Rastenburg, Dorothea Dangel spent so much time standing on the street with her girlfriend waving and throwing flowers to the passing soldiers that she got into trouble with her father.[49]

Up near the Dutch border, the townsfolk of Viersen could not remember anything like it. Unit after unit was quartered on the town in the winter and spring of 1939–40, bringing a buzz to the bars, theatre and cafés, and turning the girls' heads. First came the infantry, and Lieutenant Lemke was given the guest room in Herta Slenders's large family house. His batman Robby immediately hit it off with their parlourmaid, Martha. After the infantry came two pioneers; then the Lewinski Tank Regiment and they stayed for six months. Whereas the captain quartered in their guest room liked to spend his time quietly reading and writing in the living room, the batmen would hang around the kitchen. Sometimes the other officer in the house, a senior lieutenant whom they all learned to call 'the boss' because he commanded a company, would join them in teasing the maids and charming the children in the kitchen. By the time the 'boss's' younger brother, Max, arrived as well, he immediately became part of the family, the children quickly learning to call him simply 'Mäxchen', his nickname at home. Herta's four-year-old sister Ulla soon had the run of all the men, snuggling up on their laps as officers and men slipped into the roles of older brothers and uncles. Fresh from the Polish campaign, the men were well rested and in high spirits, and, to the older children's delight, the two brothers often had to climb in over the balcony rail and tiptoe upstairs in their socks when they came back too late. One night Herta's mother found the men playing with the electric train set, which they had discovered on the floor of the attic. Herta and her brothers soon learned snatches of the soldiers' songs by heart. The only thing that grieved Herta was that even after she had had her hair bobbed, no one thought she was grown-up. She could only watch and dream of being older than her thirteen years, while the men played, for one last time, at being teenage boys.[50]

On 10 May 1940, the tank regiment moved up to the border, following the German attack on the Netherlands at dawn. Before leaving they took a final group photo in the garden with Ulla on Mäxchen's lap and sent it home to his mother at the family estate in the eastern provinces. For the next few days, soldiers poured through Viersen en route to the Netherlands and the whole town turned out to offer them food and drink. Often the men were too tired to talk and had no time to stop, so that the children had to run alongside them to retrieve the cups they had used. Herta Slenders soon heard that their first lodger, Lieutenant Lemke, had led the infantry assault across the Dutch border. By 16 May, the children were sitting at the top of the cutting, waving to the men who were standing in the open doorways of the long troop trains taking them to the front. Often the trains had to halt and wait for a second locomotive to pull the long lines of cattle trucks, their roofs camouflaged with evergreen, up the small incline.

Then the children would run down the embankment to bring the men something to drink. On 17 May, a telegram arrived telling them that Mäxchen had been wounded in the back and was being treated in a military hospital in Aachen. Unable to visit him while all the trains were restricted to military use, his mother had to rely on the news Herta's mother relayed of his wound and recovery, deepening the bond between the two families. On 24 May came the news that Max was over the worst. On the 28th, Herta noted the capitulation of Belgium in her diary, and on 4 June she celebrated the fall of Dunkirk, with the hope that the regiment would come through Viersen on its return. On 14 June, a mere five weeks after crossing the Dutch border, Herta heard that the *Wehrmacht* had entered Paris and began to count the days until the tank regiment's return. Finally, after a trickle of individual visitors and several false alarms, the regiment paid a visit at the start of December, holding a victory concert in the town hall, replete with marches from Beethoven, Verdi, Wagner and the Condor Legion. The commander of the first company, Senior Lieutenant Fritz Fechner, gave an interval talk on the regiment's 'experiences in France', but for Herta the high point of the evening was being allowed to accompany Max and miss school the next morning.[51]

Throughout the 1920s, German schoolchildren had been taught to see France as 'the hereditary enemy'. Now, like a mythological monster, it lay vanquished. The *Wochenschau* brought the images of the perfectly dressed ranks of German soldiers marching out into the sunlight from under the shadow of the Arc de Triomphe to every cinema audience in the country – and attendance had doubled over the last two years. Forgetting that Britain was not yet defeated, forgetting their normal gripes about shortages and the arrogant venality of Nazi officials high and low, people focused their euphoric exultation on the figure of Hitler himself, recognising, as the *Regierungspräsident* of Swabia reported, 'wholly, joyfully, and thankfully the superhuman greatness of the Führer and his work'. Those who had still had their doubts after the *Anschluss* with Austria, or the dismemberment of Czechoslovakia, could now perceive the national messiah. Hitler had preached to the German people endlessly, telling them how the capitulation of 1918 had left them encircled by a steel ring of enemies. Even after conquering Poland, few Germans had felt like celebrating. But now a clamour for new photos of the Führer accompanied lively discussion of his expression, his look, whether he was serious or laughing. People scanned the *Wochenschau* for his image and came away disappointed when they only saw other leaders.[52]

Hitler had achieved something that had seemed impossible a mere nine months earlier: he had delivered the German people from another world war on the scale of the first. Blitzkrieg had made war short, sparing the civilian population the terrible privations it had suffered from 1914 to 1919. Above all, German casualties had remained low. The *Wehrmacht* reported 26,500 dead from the French campaign, compared with the 2 million dead of 1914–18. The *Wehrmacht* would have to revise its death toll upwards, but even so, if the war had ended that summer, as everyone now expected, the country would have lost 60,000 men in the conquest of Czechoslovakia, Poland, Denmark, Norway, the Netherlands, Belgium, Luxembourg and France. When Hitler ordered bells to be rung for a week and flags to be flown for ten days, most people enthusiastically complied.[53]

Gretel Bechtold's mother was among the few who did not join in the rejoicing. For her, the triumph was overshadowed by the death of Walter, her son in the artillery, near Langemarck. Neither his proximity to the legendary battlefield of November 1914, nor the assurance that her son 'had given his life for the greatness and preservation of the *Volk*, Führer and War', comforted her. Frau Bechtold never hung out the flag again. In fact, the number of casualties was relatively high for so short a campaign, and Frau Bechtold began obsessively cutting out the death notices from the local newspaper. Walter was the fourth man from their locality to fall. Gretel, his younger sister, had last written to him on 16 May, breathlessly telling him about their new dove, and how their father's clutter in the cellar had prevented them gaining entry during their first, brief, air raid by the RAF. Now she found she had lost her family confidant.[54]

When Rosemarie watched the depiction of war in the film of *The German March into Holland and Belgium* that June in Krumbach, she was shocked by the destruction, even though the film-makers had taken great care to exclude images of human suffering. The highly sanitised footage seemed 'very true' to her. In place of the ripening corn and the haymaking that was already under way in southern Germany, she could not bear to imagine what it would be like 'if the shell craters and shot-up villages, above all the completely devastated land were Germany'. Hoping that the war would soon be over, she contented herself with imagining a future for herself in the colonies. Although many German children shared her interest in the colonies, few seem to have shared her worries that summer. For many children and adults, the roar of the *Luftwaffe*'s engines, the singing and comradeship inside the cockpits, intoxicated them with the breathtaking technological power in the skies; the bombs fell in slow motion to an orchestral accompaniment before pulverising the Polish roads on impact. The film confirmed once again that Poland had started the war at the behest of England and France. Meanwhile, the first newsreel pictures of black French prisoners of war sparked spontaneous outrage among cinema audiences and calls to shoot them immediately.[55]

Across the land children and adults alike listened eargerly to the veterans' tales of war. In Bochum that summer, Karl-Heinz Bödecker met a friend of his father's in the street and brought him home. The thirteen-year-old boy was amazed and delighted by the way 'the Prussians' had transformed this careless man into a dashing and bemedalled soldier. He also impressed Karl-Heinz by having remained as courteous and considerate as ever, refusing to put his mother to the bother of running a bath or making up a bed for the night, though he did doze off as he listened to their record collection that afternoon. When Karl-Heinz's father came home, he poured out liqueurs and everyone fell silent as the man began to talk. He spoke of his own transient fear of being hit during an attack and made light of his wound. Reading this rather typical schoolboy effort to retell the war, Karl-Heinz's German teacher awarded it a 'Good'.[56]

By now the Armaments Inspectorates were reporting that even workers in protected occupations were impatient to join up. In Osnabrück, Dierk Sievert went to volunteer for the Motorised Infantry, only to find that, at seventeen, he was too young and, in any case, still had to discharge his compulsory labour service. Bored by their study for the *Abitur* and duties in the Hitler Youth, he and his friends took to lobbying the Reich Labour Service offices to find out when they could expect a posting. The army, with its powerful motorbikes, automatic weapons, leather coats, field glasses and, above all, its victorious tanks, had eclipsed all else. As these older teenagers jibbed at having to do Latin homework and lead group discussions of ten- to fourteen-year-olds in the *Jungvolk*, they felt that everything they had done had prepared them for this moment. Now they seemed to be in danger of missing out on the war altogether. But power and military technology exercised its pull even on those who did not think that Germany's war was a moral one. In Berlin, Thomas Gève donned a Hitler Youth uniform as a disguise, so that he could slip into the exhibitions of captured French war material barred to Jews.[57]

That summer of 1940, the school holidays were extended so that children could go out to the countryside and help bring in the harvest. For many children these summer camps with a sense of purpose may well have been summed up by the song,

> *Aus grauer Städter Mauern*
> *ziehn wir durch Wald und Feld . . .*

> Out of grey city walls
> we cross wood and field.
> Whoever stays can grow bitter
> We are travelling into the world.[58]

In any case, the Hitler Youth kept a list of the small minority who had stayed behind and passed the names on to their schools at the start of the autumn term, so that they could take appropriate disciplinary action. But it was not only German women and teenagers who were being 'volunteered' to help bring in the harvest. That summer and autumn 1.2 million French and British prisoners of war were brought to Germany. Most stayed in the prisoner-of-war camps no longer than it took to allocate them to farms and construction sites.

The operation ran smoothly: the Army High Command, Ministry of Labour, German Labour Front, police and local Party and government functionaries had learned how to coordinate their efforts after deploying some 300,000 Polish prisoners of war during the previous autumn and winter. By July 1940, another 311,000 Polish civilian workers had followed.[59]

The Labour Offices put together a wish list of unattractive jobs suitable for the racially inferior Poles, descending from timber, mining and building work to brick-making, stone-quarrying and peat-digging, all forms of the punitive 'hard labour' that the SS was used to inflicting on prisoners in its concentration camps. Officials from the Party and police busied themselves with limiting social relationships between Poles and Germans to those befitting 'master' and 'helot' races. Hitherto, Nazi policy had aimed at forging an ethnically homogeneous German nation state, but now the country found itself awash with ideas and policies that had previously been principally enforced in colonies overseas. Between the spring and autumn of 1940, German bureaucrats threw together a system of economic and social apartheid; it quickly expanded to include civilian workers from Western Europe, in a complex mesh of police regulations, racial rankings, petty privileges and harsh penalties. The Nazis had promised to make Germany into a racially pure 'national community', a true *Volksgemeinschaft* of solid citizens, pulling together for the common good. Instead, more foreign languages were to be heard on the streets than ever before.[60]

Defeated and beset with unemployment, many of the Poles had accepted German assurances about pay and conditions, and flocked to join the trains leaving for the Reich in January and February 1940. By April, enough news had filtered back from Germany to make recruitment dwindle and the German authorities would depend ever more on compulsion. All fifteen-year-olds were bound to report to the local Polish administation for work. In September 1941, the age at which teenagers had to register for work in the new – and formerly Polish – province of the Wartheland was reduced to fourteen. But German practice was already running ahead of their own regulations. In Posen, twelve-year-old Helene B. was taken directly from her class at school and shut in a dark goods wagon. The train stopped at small villages on the way to Berlin so that the farmers could buy girls straight off the train to work on their properties; she remembered them paying over money per head.[61]

Katya F. and her cousin were picked up on the street in March 1940 and sent straight to Germany. Katya was thirteen. She was treated quite well on the farm to which she was taken in the district of Halle, but the work was long and hard. In addition to milking the cows, feeding the pigs, ducks, chickens and geese, and mucking out the yard, Katya was put to work in the house, where she cleaned all the rooms once a week. But what drew her into the heart of the family was childcare. She helped Gerhard, who had just started going to school, with his homework and so learned German herself as well as establishing an enduring relationship with the boy. Four-year-old Erika and five-month-old Brigitte became particularly attached to Katya; for she washed, fed and bathed them.[62]

During the month Katya arrived, the government issued a series of new decrees. Polish labourers now had to wear a yellow 'P' against a violet background, were barred from public transport and German places of entertainment, put under an after-dark curfew and the clergy were instructed not to allow Poles to attend German church services. Employers were strongly discouraged from all fraternisation with Poles, especially permitting them to eat at the same table. And they were to stop them from writing home, lest their letters harm labour recruitment. In the countryside, farming communities could often decide for themselves how far they would observe this regime. Katya's German family not only allowed her to eat with them and accompany the farmer's wife to the local Catholic church; they also let her write home to her family. She stayed with them until the end of the war.

Much of the new labour was to guarantee adequate food supplies to the German population, a goal also met by levying delivery quotas across occupied Europe. Compared with the last frantic eighteen-month phase of the pre-war arms race, let alone the first nine months of the war during which fats, proteins and a range of other essentials had been in terribly short supply, Continental victory now brought an immediate improvement in food distribution for citizens of the Reich. Fresh fruit and vegetables continued to be scarce, but for now Germans were to be the best-fed civilians in the war. Such good fortune was bought increasingly at a direct cost to the occupied territories: even the French and the Belgians would see their rations fall, though not to the levels that were being inflicted on the Poles.[63]

In Logelbach, little Tomi Ungerer's abiding memory of the friendly German soldiers who marched into Alsace was the speed with which they bought up all goods from the shops, even before they expelled the Jews. On 21 July 1940, Dierk Sievert caught the 7.28 a.m. train from Osnabrück to visit his brother Günther at his *Flak* battery in Friedrichsfeld on the Lower Rhine. He brought home all kinds of goodies that Günther had bought in Holland, including Sekt, wine, soap and cocoa. Two months later Günther sent a parcel home from Greven with lard, butter and a chicken. As a member of a motorised unit, he was particularly well placed to transport goods back from the occupied territories and managed to purchase a hefty but much sought-after Phillips radio for himself. France in particular was viewed as a veritable cornucopia where everything of quality from stockings to fine wines was to be had. When Maranja Mellin's father returned from Paris in April 1942, their table was soon groaning under the weight of luxuries, from almonds and pears to cinnamon, pâté and carrots wrapped in ham; and that was not counting the notepaper, sewing material, stockings, gloves, belts, detergent, shoes, soap and sheets that he had also brought home. As she marvelled at it all, Maranja reflected in her diary that 'this has become the norm in Germany now. Wherever the men are, there they buy. Whether in Holland, Belgium, France, Greece, the Balkans, Norway, etc.'[64]

As fathers, brothers and uncles sent home rationed items in short supply, like meat and fruit or clothing, shoes and good-quality soap, a small black market began to develop too. Cigarettes became one of the standards of simple exchanges, a kind of barter currency, which the Security Police noticed when they found that many more women were drawing their full cigarette rations than actually smoked. As the war went on, the black market would become more elaborate, fuelled at one end by the goods flowing into German households from abroad and at the other by the hunger of millions of foreign workers. Entirely open to their mercy, many forced labourers on the farms tried to endear themselves to their employers by mending the children's playthings or carving them wooden toys.[65]

All kinds of foreigners and Germans were being drawn towards each other by the black market and work, religious observance and family meals, sexual attraction, childcare and the cinema, however much police regulations, watchful neighbours and public hangings of Polish men strove to keep masters and helots apart. In the Palatinate, boys in Hitler Youth uniform were seen taking Polish girls to the cinema. Everywhere, German children threw stones or snowballs at Polish men. But in the summer of 1940, all this exposure to foreigners with their odd languages and customs promised to be temporary. It was good to be German and it only remained for the British to recognise that they had lost the war.[66]

The Royal Navy had sunk half of Germany's surface warships during the fighting for Norway in the spring of 1940, and by 1 July it had only one heavy and two light cruisers and four destroyers ready for action. On 3 July, British ships attacked and sank the French fleet at Mers-el-Kebir to prevent it from falling into German hands. The only way the German Army that was being marshalled at the Channel ports could effect a crossing was for the *Luftwaffe* to win control of the skies and bomb the Royal Navy from the air. So, from 13 August, German squadrons based in Norway, France and the Netherlands began to pound Britain's airfields and radar control centres.[67]

As losses on both sides mounted, and the RAF's defensive capabilities were stretched to the limit, an accident occurred. On 24 August 1940, a hundred planes bombed the East End of London, bringing the war to British cities for the first time. They had acted without – and indeed against – orders from Hitler, for the Führer had explicitly reserved this decision for himself, realising that it would entail an escalation of the war, probably best timed to coincide with the land invasion, as the bombing of Warsaw and Rotterdam had done. Although it was much easier for the *Luftwaffe* to reach England from their new Continental bases than it was for the RAF to strike at Germany, Churchill ordered an immediate response. On the night of 25–26 August, twenty-two Hampden and Wellington bombers struck at Berlin, causing slight damage. But the psychological and strategic consequences were enormous. On 4 September 1940 Hitler vowed to a packed Berlin *Sportpalast*, 'We'll wipe out their cities! We'll put an end to the work of these night pirates.' By the time this first and heaviest German blitz tailed off at the end of May 1941, Britain could count 43,000 civilian dead, but it had won back control of its skies.[68]

Although Hermann Göring remained very popular, he also began to be mocked for having promised that no bombs would fall on Germany and that people could call him 'Meier' if they did: the name began to catch on. As the German authorities began constructing a system of deep bunkers in the capital of the Reich, the new and rare bomb-sites themselves became a tourist attraction. Thomas Gève found them as least as fascinating as the exhibitions of captured war material. Putting on his Hitler Youth uniform once more to conceal his Jewish identity, he compiled lists of bombed buildings in the capital, drawn like a twelve-year-old voyeur by the revelation that 'all their intimate interiors could be seen'.[69]

German children's images of their enemy were as disparate as their elders'. Full of enthusiasm for the cause, ten-year-old Detlef had sent his father pictures of an airman and a bomb in his letter of 30 September 1939, 'with which the English are getting something on their Jewish noses', adding excitedly, 'And have you yet seen the Blacks too?' But the same schoolteachers who impressed the power of the world Jewish conspiracy upon their pupils' minds also taught them English throughout the war and fostered an enormous respect for English culture, sporting ideals and literature. Children referred to the 'English', never to the British, perhaps because the Celtic fringe would have made them seem less Germanic; and if they were confused about their 'English blood brothers', that is not altogether surprising. Much of the regime's image of a German Continental empire drew its inspiration from the 'English world empire'. Not only had Weimar Germany seen an extraordinary flowering of Anglophilia, but the Nazi regime had craved social acceptance in Britain as well as a tangible alliance. Waiting for the attack on France to begin, Rosemarie's father turned his thoughts to her future and advised her to learn English. 'Even if the English are our enemies,' he opined, 'it is nevertheless necessary and useful to learn their language, because as far as I know more than 300 million people speak English (just think of America and of the possibility that we get colonies in Africa whose inhabitants can only speak English).' He need not have worried. Her marks in English continued to be excellent. As the Battle of Britain raged, children were offered a new board game, 'Stukas attack', and encouraged to sing 'Bombs, bombs on Engeland'. Shakespeare remained the most performed dramatist in Nazi Germany.[70]

More bizarrely, in February 1940 a swing festival in Hamburg attracted more than 500 young people. The music was English and American, and only swing dancing and jitterbugging were allowed. In a calculated assault on Nazi sensibilities, teenage boys with the money to spare dressed in English sports jackets with a shirt stud in the buttonhole and donned Anthony Eden hats, turning Chamberlain's much-ridiculed umbrella into a fashion accessory. The girls wore their hair long, lacquered their nails, pencilled their eyebrows and, to complete their attack on the Nazi ideal of the unadorned, flat-heeled German woman, laid on the lipstick. They even tried to converse only in English, though this proved too difficult and some tables lapsed into French. As if this were not bad enough, 'The dancers,' a Hitler Youth observer fumed, 'were an appalling sight.' He watched two boys dancing with one girl and other dancers jumping, rubbing the backs of their heads together, then bending double as their long hair flopped over their faces. When the band struck up a rumba, the dancers apparently went into a 'wild ecstasy', singing along in broken English. And as the band played faster and faster, everyone got up and joined in. On stage several boys were dancing together, all with cigarettes hanging out of each side of their mouths.[71]

To the consternation of the leadership of both the Hitler Youth and the SS, private swing clubs sprang up in other cities which, like Hamburg, had traditionally looked towards Britain or France, cities like Kiel, Hanover, Stuttgart, Saarbrücken and Karlsruhe, as well-heeled teenagers were gripped by jazz and the cool English look. There were even some in Berlin, Dresden, Halle and Frankfurt. Despite their outrage, the authorities did not always close down such events, though they often did spark off violent confrontations with the Hitler Youth and police, as parties of German-speaking youths dressed as Nazis would doubtless have done in England at this time, and a number of the swing enthusiasts were sent to new youth concentration camps.[72]

At particular moments, such as the attempt on Hitler's life in November 1939 or the continuation of the war in the summer of 1940, anti-English sentiments became extremely shrill. But these were exceptions. When relations turned sour after Munich and British propaganda returned to its militaristic images of the Germans, propaganda in Germany tore into the brutal callousness of the English class system, particularly the evils it had inflicted on the Boers, the Irish and the English working class. While the BBC enlisted George Orwell for their wartime broadcasts, German propaganda reprinted his polemical investigations into poverty and fêted the Jarrow marchers. But Anglophobia did not run as deep as the current of admiration for English culture or, at the very least, respect for England's imperial power. Few people might have direct experience of Britain, but they did have well-honed stereotypes.[73]

The idea of a Jewish 'plutocracy' at work in London allowed the Nazi regime to maintain a clear distinction between fighting England

and hating the English. Rather than trying to reverse the Anglophilia, Nazi propaganda fed off it. Germans could feel that they were fighting to liberate the English from their 'plutocratic' and 'Jewish' masters. By September 1939, some imprint of these motifs, which would be endlessly repeated over the following years, had already lodged in the mind of a ten-year-old like Detlef, given his wish that German bombs should fall 'on their Jewish noses'.

Because England was an adversary worthy of respect, the terrible fear of bombing had haunted popular expectations of war in Germany as much as it had in Britain. Even though nothing much had been constructed in the way of bunkers and air-raid shelters before the outbreak of war, most German blocks of flats and houses had cellars. As the first bombs fell on Gelsenkirchen and the Ruhr in May 1940, people cleared their cellars and began to equip them with benches, chairs and bunk beds. During the second half of 1940, the burghers of Münster had to spend more hours in their cellars during air-raid warnings than they would again until November 1944. But for the whole of 1940 the city listed just six fatalities. Hamburg reported nineteen fatalities, and Wilhelmshaven four. Even in the middle of the industrial belt of the Ruhr, Carola Reissner could report in November 1940 that the bombing had not caused enough damage to put a single plant in Essen out of commission. All the same, that summer and autumn the capital of the Krupp armament empire was equipped with serious anti-aircraft artillery and a bunker-building programme began which would make it one of the best-defended cities in Germany. Still, the building of private shelters continued apace.[74]

Public anxiety registered itself in the very high response to the first official efforts at evacuating children to the countryside. Whereas mass evacuation from the cities had begun in Britain straight after the outbreak of war, in Germany nothing was done until the air war escalated in the autumn of 1940. On 27 September 1940, Hitler's Party secretary, Martin Bormann, sent out a secret circular to higher Party and state functionaries, ordering an 'extended sending of children to the countryside'. Even among the upper reaches of the regime, there was to be no talk of 'evacuation', lest mass panic ensue. The regime, which so fervently believed in the myth that civilians had stabbed the army in the back in 1918, felt it had to dissemble to the population whose moral resilience it did not trust. While Churchill was promising the British people 'blood, toil, sweat and tears', the German people were being encouraged to think of easy victories over coffee and cake.

Hitler also refused to follow the British example and make the evacu-ation of children compulsory for fear of sending out negative signals to the population at large. In Germany, evacuation was not even carried out by the state, although the government did pick up the bill. Instead, a quango was set up, pooling the efforts of the National Socialist People's Welfare Organisation, the Hitler Youth and the National Socialist Teachers' Association. The name itself, 'Sending children to the countryside', *Kinderlandverschickung* – or the *KLV* as it became universally known – had its origins in the summer camps for workers' children from the big cities which had been pioneered by Church and Social Democratic welfare organisations before and after the First World War – and which the Nazis had taken over and continued throughout the 1930s. Now, children were to be sent away from the 'areas threatened by air attack' for six-month spells in the countryside. Retaining the earlier name may have been comforting, especially since some children did continue, as late as the summer and autumn of 1944, to be sent from the Ruhr simply to 'recuperate' in the Bavarian Alps.[75]

Ironically, for a regime so bent on reassuring its citizens, the success of the scheme depended on parents' fear for their children's lives. Fear of bombing in this first phase of the war can be measured from the eagerness with which families sent their children away from home, overcoming their anxieties about separation, about their children running wild on farms and about teenage sex. In the first two months, during which only Berlin and Hamburg were involved, 189,543 chil-dren were evacuated. As the scheme was extended to the vulnerable cities of north-western Germany, numbers continued to rise, reaching some 320,000 by 20 February 1941, 412,908 by the end of March and 619,000 by late June. Parents were desperate to save their chil-dren from the danger of a direct hit. And early rumours in none too distant Dresden described Berlin as a devasted city, the children infected by English biological warfare.[76]

Hitler had entrusted Baldur von Schirach with the task of drawing up the guidelines and organising the *KLV*. As the former head of the Hitler Youth, Schirach seized upon the wartime evacuation as the opportunity for which he had longed during the 1930s, to elbow aside the schools and the Ministry of Education and implement his own educational programme. From his point of view, the showcase was to be the single-sex homes, or 'camps', established for ten- to fourteen-year-olds.

Redeploying youth hostels, buildings the People's Welfare and Hitler Youth already owned, and requisitioning hotels, convents, monasteries and children's homes, Schirach's men rapidly assembled a stock of 3,855 buildings with places for 200,000–260,000 children. This collective model had no parallel in the British evacuation programme and Schirach conceived his project as a permanent youth education scheme which would last into the post-war era. Having freed itself from the constraints of teachers, parents and the Churches, the Hitler Youth would immeasurably strengthen its hold over the young.[77]

Whatever the grand ambitions of the organisers, they were shrewd and experienced enough to know that the popular support crucial to the success of their voluntary scheme depended on 'good and plentiful provisions'; in addition to the normal child rations and supplements, they allocated 2 Reichsmark to cover the basic daily costs for each child. The National Socialist People's Welfare organised special trains, paid for the children's health care, and even arranged for families who would do their laundry while they were in the homes. Despite finding 140,000 uniforms for boys and 130,000 for girls, as well as 85,000 blankets and 139,000 straw mattresses, much of the organisation, especially at the outset, was improvised, with children sleeping on loose straw while bunks were being built in their dormitories. As children grew out of the two pairs of shoes they had been told to bring with them, they had to run barefoot or fit their feet into one of the 110,000 pairs of wooden shoes which the organisation provided in its first two years.[78]

Ilse Pfahl and seventeen other girls from her class left Essen on 27 April 1941, bound for the Moravian city of Kremsier, where they were met by a delegation of the local *Jungvolk* and *Jungmädel*. They marched together through the streets of the Czech town to a large, modern, five-storey building, a convent whose nuns stayed on to cook for the German girls. Here, things seem to have been more comfortable than in the 'old Reich'. Although, like all 'camp' novices, Ilse and her roommates were made to straighten their beds, clean their dorm, fold up the clothes in their lockers, turn out properly dressed for the morning flag-raising ceremony, reach their classes on time and quieten down after lights out, under the new Hitler Youth rules no teacher could beat them.[79]

Ilse's punishments ranged from not being served pudding the next day, or having to write rhyming couplets about good conduct and discipline, to having her post withheld for three days. And punishments were meted out collectively to foster group cohesion and discipline: on one occasion, the girls were led out to march up and down the high road for 5 miles in complete silence. None of this prevented Ilse and her friends from Essen having fun. Kremsier was a garrison town and they met German soldiers within days of their arrival when they went to see *Der Sieg im Westen* (*The Victory in the West*) at the cinema. Every Sunday afternoon, Ilse and her friends would walk in the castle park and, after coyly refusing to talk to the soldiers, look forward to their attentions all week. By late May they were turning up at the park in their gymslips to sunbathe and play football with the evacuee boys. By early June they were going there in their swimsuits to sing and play games. 'The soldiers,' Ilse crowed that night, 'were our most attentive spectators.' In mid-July they went out to pick wild flowers for the soldiers and chatted up a senior lieutenant in the park, who later lent them his field glasses during a military exercise and even arranged for them to ride across the grounds on an officer's horse 'under the eyes of the whole company'.[80]

As for the local Czech population, after an initial gesture at communication – Ilse bought a dictionary to make shopping easier – she and her brigade of the *BDM*, the League of German Girls, settled into a routine of going on 'propaganda marches' through the town whenever the opportunity arose. They marched to the station to meet their teachers and *BDM* leaders, and they marched to see them off. They marched on Palm Sunday to contest the public space with the Church procession. And they marched through the town again a week later as a spontaneous gesture when they heard that war had broken out with Russia. For the sports festival on 29 June, they marched behind a military band and Ilse noted happily that the 'Czechs are bursting with rage'. As they drank coffee in the French park at the end to another perfect day, Ilse reckoned that she had been photographed forty times. The castle park was the one place in Kremsier where everyone – except the Jews – could meet. But the soldiers saw to it that no Czech man dared approach the *BDM* girls.[81]

Finally, in mid-November, it was Ilse's turn to go home. Their hair freshly washed, the girls bought presents for their families, said goodbye to the castle park and entered the convent dining hall to find white tablecloths and pine twigs on the tables for their farewell evening. By the autumn of 1941, the numbers of older children going to the *KLV* homes was entering a steep decline. It may have been that the tales of those returning from their first six-month placements confirmed the worst suspicions of parents about institutions run on Hitler Youth lines. But there was also less reason to send them: the fear of bombing had faded.[82]

In fact, at least two-thirds of the child evacuees did not end up in such homes at all, but went to relatives or were placed in private families. The six- to ten-year-olds travelled in supervised groups, the babies and younger children with their mothers. As specially chartered trains took mothers and small children, and large numbers of older children, on their migration from the cities of the north-west to the countryside of the south and east, southern Germany quickly became a more popular destination than the east. Bavaria, Baden and the Czech lands had a traditional tourist trade with a whole infrastructure for looking after strangers, whereas Pomerania and East Prussia did not. Conditions there jarred abruptly with the urban expectations of both organisers and children. In the clash between town and country, between West and East, children who jeered at the 'cultural trash of the East' won few friends, while in Pomeranian towns like Friedeburg in der Neumark it became axiomatic to blame all acts of theft and vandalism on the Bochum boys. Coming from a centre for heavy industry in the Ruhr, thirteen-year-old Siegfried Nicolay and his Düsseldorf classmates took immediate offence when the farmers derided their softness.[83]

Even in the more popular south, the welcome was not always warm. In February 1941, Rudolf Lenz arrived in Meggesheim with a group of boys from Herdecke and Wetter in the Ruhr. The ten-year-old was lined up with the others in front of the village school, where their prospective foster-mothers inspected them. After the 'slave market' was over and they had settled into the daily routine on the small holdings, Rudolf learned that the local farmers had been persuaded to offer hospitality on the promise that strong and healthy boys were coming who could help fill the shortfall of labour on their farms. Luckily, Rudolf liked helping out with the hay, wheat and potato harvests more than he liked going to school. Having been brought up as a Protestant in a confessionally mixed and fairly secular area, the deep and undiluted Catholicism of Meggesheim came as a shock. His foster-mother's daily attendance at early mass was one thing. But sacred spaces outside of church were new. He was truly astonished by the sight of her kneeling down to pray wherever she happened to be, on the street or in the fields, as soon as the church bell tolled at midday and again in the evening. Still, he adjusted: within months, Rudolf's Bavarian dialect was so thick that his parents had trouble understanding him.[84]

Germans' fear of bombing slowly but decisively waned. Their worries about how seriously the English would pursue this war had clearly been misplaced. Before 1940 was out, Carola Reissner had stopped getting out of bed when the sirens started to screech in Essen. In Osnabrück, as Dierk Sievert sat up on New Year's Eve and watched the candles burn low on the Christmas tree, he looked back fondly on the victories in Norway and France. Although his own efforts to volunteer for the army had not yet come to fruition, they looked set to succeed in the coming year. 'But I don't want to forget one thing,' the seventeen-year-old jotted in his diary, trying to fend off the mood of warmth and mild inebriation, 'the air-raid warnings. When I think how terrified we were of air raids before the war, and how they have been! You could almost call them harmless.' All in all, Dierk reflected, as he bade 1940 farewell, 'war is not so bad if it goes on like this'. For the new year, he wished for 'victory and peace' and 'for myself, that I can contribute to it'.[85]

II

DISCIPLINED YOUTH

Determined as the Nazi regime was to rally the nation for war, it had not counted on the kind of popular euphoria which greeted the victories of 1940. Hitler was far from alone in believing that Germany's defeat in the First World War had come from the collapse of the home front. Anxious to avoid any repetition, Hitler often restrained those who wanted to push through emergency wartime measures, whether they aimed at making the evacuation of children from the cities compulsory or conscripting women into the armaments factories. Apart from his desire to be acclaimed by the German people as their national messiah, Hitler was also swayed by a sense of vulnerability. He feared that the German people did not have the heart for painful sacrifices and would abandon their historic mission – and him – if these became too great.

Such cautious calculation about how to shape social consent had already influenced the regime's recourse to violence and terror: by the end of 1934, fewer than 4,000 prisoners remained in the concentration camps through which over 100,000 had passed in the first fifteen months of Nazi rule. As trade unionists and Social Democrats were released back into their communities, the media worked to change the image of the remaining camps. From a key instrument of political terror, which had been vital to securing the dictatorship, by 1936 the camps were being depicted as a 'tough but fair' way of 're-educating' a small but incorrigible minority of hardened criminals, paedophiles and Communists. The sanitised photos of prisoners at Dachau being marched off to work were calculated to evoke approval among those who read the illustrated Nazi press. When the Greater German Reich went to war, the country had 108,000 prisoners in state institutions, and another 21,000 in concentration camps. By the end of the war, the prison population would double and the number of concentration camp inmates rise to 714,211. But, in keeping with the regime's racial priorities and efforts to police foreign workers, the overwhelming majority of these camp prisoners were not German. It was a mark of the strength of the Nazi regime that it was petty criminals, rather than political opponents of the regime, who predominated amongst the German prisoners. As they strove to prevent anything that might weaken the German war effort, the police became more concerned with crime and social order than with political revolution.

German children and teenagers found themselves caught up in the battle to secure social order, as a series of measures was introduced to prevent the outbreak of youth crime of the kind that had plagued the country during and after the First World War. In addition to the system of youth courts and youth prisons, the adult courts were given discretion to try 'serious young criminal offenders' over sixteen. In practice, wartime pressures on places kept the numbers in youth prisons low. Rather, it was the number of children and teenagers committed to foster care and reformatories by the Youth Welfare Boards which kept rising: by 1941, they had reached 100,000, probably their full capacity. Unlike the adult petty criminals filling the prisons, most of these children and young teenagers had committed no crime: they were generally sent away for preventive purposes, or simply because they were seen as a danger to the community.

In setting the standard of child behaviour so high, the Nazis were drawing on a stock of professional ideas which were common across Europe, North America and Australia about the inherent dangers of social degeneration should vulnerable youngsters be left to grow up in corrupting conditions. It was better to remove them before they became incorrigible criminals, and while there was still a chance of rescuing them from depravity: with the accent on prevention, the authorities were not just trying to combat youth crime. They were also trying to 'save' the young from their families and themselves. Still more important was weeding out 'wayward' children before they corrupted their peers. The war only strengthened such convictions further: if a collapse of the home front was to be avoided, then it was not just food shortages, but also theft, black-marketeering and youth crime which had to be prevented at all costs. With their belief in protecting children as the racial future of the German nation, the authorities were also committing themselves to cutting those who might jeopardise that future out of the 'national community': to be permitted to return, such children would first have to prove that they had been 're-educated'.[1]

High-flown ideas about perfecting the nation and race had a way of translating into mundane, hard-nosed and socially conservative actions. In March 1940, a police decree for the 'protection' of young people forbade them from attending dances, cabarets and amusement parks after 9 p.m., as well as 'loitering' after dark, smoking or drinking. Such measures were not enforced equally on all. As Dierk Sievert well knew, he had been constantly breaking this curfew by going out drinking with his friends and his brother Günther in Osnabrück. It was lucky for Dierk that, in his middle-class home, he had grown up expecting to do his Latin and Greek homework for his *Abitur*. Instead of acquiring a reputation as a wayward, teenage drinker, he had become a trusted local Hitler Youth leader. Not every German teenager felt as comfortable within the 'national community' as this. Entrusted with enforcing the new decrees and maintaining good order, youth welfare officials continued what they were doing already. They kept watch for the first signs of moral decay, hoping to nip crime and disorder in the bud. Truancy from school and hanging around street corners were most likely to attract their attention. Girls who roamed the streets were considered potentially promiscuous, and as such on the way to contracting and spreading venereal disease. So, for example, the Youth Court at Hanau sent Emmi Krause to a reformatory in May 1939, because it found that, far from missing school through illness, 'She loiters around outside with soldiers and other young men till late into the night and visits dance halls with them.'[2] Girls like Emmi presented, according to the youth courts and welfare boards, 'a social threat and a danger [by example] to their school fellows'. Boys who dropped out of school were clearly on their way to becoming thieves and 'habitual criminals'. Like the motif of the promiscuous adolescent girl, so the image of the thieving teenage boy, joyriding on stolen bicycles, remained remarkably resilient throughout these years.[3]

Even in Nazi Germany, there were not enough places or enough funding to remove all these potential threats to society, and everywhere the constraints on numbers produced a degree of arbitrariness: when the police found teenage runaways at the railway stations at night, instead of starting an investigation, they often simply re-united them with their families, having first checked that the parents would pay the costs of the long-distance telephone call. If sheer luck – as well as social class – affected which tearaway children were sent to reformatories and which were not, once that decision had been made, their correctional education followed a strict and predictable path.[4]

Breitenau was one of the toughest reformatories in northern Hesse. A former Benedictine monastery set in rolling countryside near a bend in the River Fulda, Breitenau had been opened as an adult workhouse in 1874 and, from 1903, it also served as a reformatory of last resort. Its tall baroque buildings, steeply pitched roofs and large gate, closing off an inner courtyard, were naturally imposing and forbidding. Upon arrival, children and teenagers went through a similar routine to adult prisoners and workhouse inmates. They were stripped of their clothes and possessions, and clad in simple browny-grey sackcloth. The guards wore cast-off blue Prussian officers' uniforms, the original buttons and insignia replaced by those of the Kassel Communal Administration. They carried short daggers and, when taking inmates to work outside, carbines with fixed bayonets. Under the Nazis, they were issued with revolvers for the first time, given shooting practice and, in 1937, the restriction on firing at unarmed escapees was lifted.[5]

Ever since Breitenau's foundation in Bismarck's time, its guards and their charges had come from the same humble social backgrounds. The working day was at least eleven to twelve hours for all of them; under the Second Empire it had been still longer, fourteen to fifteen hours. Inmates included beggars, the homeless, vagrants, the unemployed and criminals who were given a spell in a workhouse at the end of their prison term to help 'educate' them to a life of morality, discipline and hard work. The reformatory 'pupils' were housed in the women's wing of the workhouse. The poorly-paid and badly-trained staff were themselves punished for lateness at work by fines; the inmates by prolongations of their stay, unofficial beatings or an officially regulated spell in the punishment cells. This was an institution moulded in the image of the Prussian Army and staffed by graduates of its barracks, whose scant privileges led them to insist rigorously upon all the minor differences in status between themselves and those they were entrusted to 'educate'.

'*Labore et fame*' – 'work and hunger' – had been inscribed over the entrance to the workhouse in Vienna in the eighteenth century and both had been key elements in the management of the Breitenau workhouse, from its foundation in 1874 onwards. Local administrators did not need to be ardent Nazis or well-read racial hygienists in order to use hunger and work to break the wills of their charges. As it happened, both the directors of Breitenau during the Third Reich were old Nazis who had joined the Party before the rise to power. Like other youth welfare officials, Heinrich Klimmer, who ran the workhouse from 1933 until he was sent to take over a similar institution in occupied Poland in 1940, and his successor, Georg Sauerbier, rose through the middle ranks of local government bureaucracy. Deprived of generous funding virtually since their foundation, workhouses, reformatories and psychiatric asylums only provided scope for unspectacular administrative and medical careers in Germany. Like their non-card-carrying contemporaries on the Youth Boards and their predecessors at Breitenau, Sauerbier and Klimmer came from the provincial bureaucracy. They might lack any specialist training, but they were committed to a kind of conservative, provincial vision of Nazism, serving their Führer and *Volk* by upholding the authoritarian mission of the state and a patriarchal moral order.[6]

On 23 August 1940, soon after taking over at Breitenau, Sauerbier wrote to the Professor of Psychiatry and Director of the Marburg Psychiatric Asylum, asking him to recommend any medical preparation which could be mixed in the reformatory girls' food to curb their 'sexual drive'. In his chilling reply, the head of the Marburg asylum explained that in his treatment of such 'psychopathic' girls he had found medical preparations to be quite useless. Instead, he went on,

One only gets through to these girls by disciplining them: if those sorts of things happen here, then we lay them in bed and put them on water soup and the most restricted diet until they are small and ugly. Then things tend to go all right for a longish period till the next outburst of this type occurs. In my experience, you get nowhere by dosing them. I would also recommend that in such cases you proceed against these girls with all severity and set about them without any consideration. That still has the quickest success.

With best wishes and Heil Hitler![7]

While trivial infractions of discipline met with unsanctioned but routine beatings, serious breaches were almost always punished by *Arrest* – solitary confinement on reduced rations. In theory only those adults sent by the courts for 'correction', such as beggars and vagrants, could be confined for up to four weeks without bedding and put on a bread-and-water diet for two out of every three days. For juveniles the harshest form of *Arrest* was set at fourteen days, on three-quarter rations. But by the war years, juveniles were being given up to four weeks' *Arrest* in Breitenau, the full adult maximum and twice what the institution's own regulations sanctioned.[8]

Sentences of *Arrest* often had to be interrupted and resumed again later. When Liselotte Wildt was returned to Breitenau in December 1943, she was sentenced to three weeks *Arrest* for her attempted flight. Having served two weeks immediately, she was not deemed 'capable' of serving the third until May 1944. Others were not so fortunate. Waltraud Pfeil died within a month of being sent back to Breitenau after attempting to run away to Kassel in the summer of 1942. Ruth Felsmann died four days after serving a fortnight's 'night *Arrest*' in October 1942. In August 1944, the local hospital in Melsungen found that Lieselotte Schmitz's weight had dropped from 62 to 38 kilos. She had contracted tuberculosis in Breitenau and died soon after.[9]

Behind these deaths lay a history of mundane, public sector thrift, which had been pursued with peculiarly Nazi ruthlessness. During the financial crisis of the Great Depression, spending on child welfare was slashed from 45.2 million marks in 1928–9 to 14.4 million marks in 1932–3, and many welfare institutions had had to let their inmates go. When the reformatories filled once more in the 1930s, all administrators understood that costs had to be held down. In 1937, a record forty-four youngsters were sent to Breitenau; the next year, it held 124, of whom 101 were girls. But to balance the books, the daily cost of feeding an inmate in Breitenau was systematically reduced, falling from 48 pfennig in 1934 to 35 pfennig in 1939. Special rations for the sick were also abolished. By contrast, 2 marks was allocated as the basic daily rate for child evacuees to the countryside. These sums translated into a very meagre diet of 'two slices of bread in the morning and broth at midday and in the evening (anything in it was a rarity)' as one former Breitenau girl, Dora Z., recollected. Small wonder that Karl Bach's mother should have alleged that her fifteen-year-old son ran away from Breitenau because he was being starved. This was in October 1939, before rations were cut further and working hours extended, first to eleven and then to twelve hours a day, as part of wartime austerity measures. Food rationing turned solitary confinement in cold cells from a psychological struggle between prisoner and guards into a test of physical survival.[10]

Families with the temerity to object directly to the Breitenau authorities could expect to be threatened with prosecution for daring to write
in 'such a shameless manner'. Routinely censoring the mail, the governor
would write back to the parents warning them 'to adopt a different
tone', if they wished 'to maintain a correspondence' with their sons or
daughters.[11] It did not help when a mother took her daughter's part by
expressing her continued belief in her innocence and urged her in the
language of Christian martyrdom to bear her ordeal patiently – thus
implicitly casting the reformatory in the role of Christ's persecutors:

I sit alone at home and think of you, my innocent child, and cry myself dry
over your suffering but bear it with simple patience. They will all receive their
punishment . . . For they know not what they do and you must think likewise.[12]

But the power was all on this governor's side and the girl never read
her mother's words. By the time she was released from Breitenau six
months later, her mother had been brought to heel: she sent the governor
a letter of thanks with two cigars. For its part, the management had
already been told what to think of these families. In the girls' files, their
psychiatric assessments routinely described such a mother as 'biologi-
cally inferior' or the father as 'an inferior, easily excitable man'.[13]
    Such encounters with the families merely confirmed the local Youth
Boards and reformatory governors in their belief that only institutional
care offered an opportunity to re-educate the parents as well as the
children. If necessary they were prepared to use the courts to remove
parents' rights of legal guardianship altogether. Families' only hope of
success was to persuade other state or Party authorities to raise serious
questions about their children's illnesses or deaths, but here too the
Breitenau custodians generally blocked further investigation, claiming
that the girls had not eaten their rations, had given away their food,
or were simply addicted to smoking.[14]
    Breitenau had another means of proving its financial viability to the
Reich: hiring out labour. As rearmament began to mop up the army
of the unemployed, in 1935 Breitenau – like other penal institutions –
started once more to hire out cheap labour to German farmers and
firms. By 1940, acute labour shortages permitted the authorities to bid
up the rates they received per inmate from 1 to 4 marks a day. The
inmates of the workhouse and reformatory themselves received a tiny

proportion: of the 138,707 marks Breitenau earned in 1941, it paid them a mere 6,645 marks. Yet, in the spring of 1942, Anni Nagel wrote to her sister describing her wish to work outside the 'workhouse' on the land:

Dear Lina I am so unhappy that I of all of you am the only one who has to sit in houses like this. If only I had someone dear to me who would help me so that I too could go and work outside.[15]

Although the working day outside Breitenau was effectively lengthened beyond the normal twelve hours through the added travelling time, many preferred it because of the opportunities to glean provisions from the farms or to acquire small amounts of extra food from civilian workers in the factories.[16]

Most routes back into the 'national community' were slow and hard. Obedience, work and humility were what counted. Reformatory inmates did not know how long they had to serve or when they could hope to be released. The 're-educative' powers of the authorities allowed them to keep the juveniles inside until they came of age. Even at nineteen, a further application could be lodged – as it was in the case of Lieselotte Scherer – to keep the teenager inside until she turned twenty-one. Not knowing how long their sentences would last added to the sense of having fallen out of the known world when these teenagers and children passed through the portals of Breitenau and gave up their clothes and possessions. Anneliese Grimm wrote home warning that she would go mad if she were not released soon. In a mood of painful nostalgia and remorse as Christmas approached in 1943, fourteen-year-old Rudolf Schramm accepted that he was not worth his parents spending 30 marks on the long train journey to visit him.[17] These rare visits – reformatory 'pupils' were entitled to no more than a single fifteen-minute visit every six weeks – were hard to manage for many families during the war, with fathers absent and mothers burdened by work and other children. Rudolf feared that even his own parents had rejected him:

Dear parents please don't think badly of me for writing so badly but it's so cold here that i already have really cold fingers. i'm still just in the house of misfortune you believe me dear parents i'm definitely not like you perhaps think.[18]

By the time he finished his laborious letter on 3 December, Rudolf Schramm had come to accept that he would remain in Breitenau for Christmas, his semi-literate missive conveying both his misery and intense desire to be remembered by his family:

> . . . now i too won't be at home for the christmas festival please don't forget me at christmas and send me something. See for once if you can't get together a half a *Stollen* [German Christmas cake] & some ginger bread & if possible a couple of advent biscuits & a couple of sweets . . . [19]

These were dreams of hunger and loneliness. On 25 May 1942, a week before she died, Anni Nagel wrote to her sister, begging her to send some food:

> Lina send me something to eat too. The main things – bread, sugar, jam, brawn, butter, cake semolina, almond oil, honey, lemmens, sausage, cheese.[20]

Anni's fantasy took flight to jam, sausage and a craving for 'lemmens', while her body was losing vital vitamins and fats. But the food she begged her sister to send also represented an emotional life-line, a tangible demonstration of nurture and love at a moment when she despaired of both. In December 1943, Ruth Buchholz sent her mother a wish list, for an Advent calendar, Advent biscuits, apples, custard, sugar, soup cubes, gravy cubes, vinegar, salt, pepper, onions, tea, coffee, oat flakes, semolina, honey, butter, fat, sausage, bread, rolls and tooth-paste. As she realised that she had let her dreams run away with her pen, she hastily added, 'I do hope that this time at least I have my wishes granted as I've written them down. But I know that you don't have much and have to save.' Even so, in a final pre-Christmas wish letter, she could not resist her hunger again: 'And above all else I still want to eat.' This time, it was bilberries, green Hessian dumplings with gravy and meat that she imagined receiving.[21]

Even though the reformatory celebrated Christmas after a fashion, with a tree and a special distribution of letters and packets which made it through the censorship, the festival's association with hearth and home made it a particularly miserable time to be locked away. Longing to go home combined with envy of the gifts and letters that others received to form an explosive mixture of emotions. Dora Z. remembered that the atmosphere in the women's wing – where the juveniles were housed – was particularly bad on Christmas Eve, the high point of celebrations across Germany, a time when most families would gather around a small tree with some sort of lights in their main – or only – room, placing their gifts at its foot and singing carols. Women wept with homesickness and, as quarrels erupted, fighting broke out among the teenagers. Male guards were sent into the women's wing to restore order, which they proceeded to do in typically brutal fashion, administering beatings to all the women present.[22]

Many children could not cope with such pressures. The simplest response to so fearful and oppressive a regime was flight; but escape almost always ended in failure. When Herbert Pflaum ran away from Breitenau as the morning's work brigades were leaving through the front gate, it took him three days and four stolen bicycles to reach his mother's flat in Schmölln. About ten minutes after he arrived, a policeman came to arrest him. Home was the first place that the authorities looked. When fourteen-year-old Rudolf Schramm ran away from the reformatory in Hohenleuben in May 1942, the police eventually found him hiding in his mother's wardrobe. Two months later he fled to her again, sustaining serious enough injuries on his rearrest, carried out by two women welfare officers, to require hospitalisation.[23]

In Germany as elsewhere in Europe, identity cards and address registers helped the police to track runaways. It was assumed that all kinds of officials, whether employed in forestry, the railways, postal services or municipalities, would cooperate with the police. For those on the run, whether they were Jews in hiding faced with the full apparatus of the Gestapo and SS, or mere reformatory runaways, it was often these simple but most pervasive controls that proved the hardest to evade. Escapees faced the choice between keeping on the move and heading for home. Some had no choice but to travel, because they found themselves homeless. Even though she had been released from Breitenau, this was what happened to Waltraud Pfeil, simply because her foster-parents were in the midst of a messy separation and would not house her. After journeying for four months through Munich, Innsbruck and even to the town of Berchtesgaden at the foot of the Führer's mountain retreat, she was finally arrested on the street in Nuremberg and promptly sent back to Breitenau. In each place, Waltraud depended on strangers, in a vulnerable existence governed by unregistered work, chance, charity and – above all – fleeting sexual relationships, before she had to move on again.[24]

It is hardly surprising, then, that so many preferred to rely on their families, even if family life was far from ideal. Sometimes the authorities did not even bother sending welfare workers round at all. A letter sufficed. The day after Waltraud Brand fled from the reformatory in Bad Köstritz, its governor wrote to her parents warning them that 'Should Waltraud be staying with you or you know of her whereabouts you are bound to inform the relevant Youth Board and ourselves, otherwise you are committing a punishable offence'. In the event, Waltraud Brand was taken into police custody at Erfurt station, having tried to pretend on the train that she had lost her ticket. But clearly, such letters had an effect. For when Waltraud escaped again – on the day of her return to Bad Köstritz, this time through a toilet window clad only in her underwear – she was bought back by her father. As her file notes report, she described 'her flight in her petticoat, in a monotone, as if none of it mattered to her . . . her journey by express train, the way the people stared and how she was beaten by her father when she got home'. Such beatings almost invariably attracted favourable comment from authorities obsessed by the dangers of lax discipline at home.[25]

There were, of course, families who fought tooth and nail to prevent their children from being taken back into custody. When the secretary of the Youth Board, the social worker and a senior police sergeant went to take Maria Gerber back into care on 22 July 1939, she 'hid herself in the kitchen behind her small but stocky and strongly-built mother'. Maria's thirteen-year-old brother Walter, her boyfriend, and finally her twenty-seven-year-old brother Heinrich all came to her defence, forcing the officials to beat a retreat and wait for reinforcements from the police snatch squad. Indeed, her mother, a Frankfurt market trader, had actually engineered an escape attempt by car from the Homberg reformatory a month earlier and had succeeded in evading a police road block set up to catch them on the new motorway.[26]

Maria's parents had originally consented to her being taken into care in May 1938, just before her sixteenth birthday, probably at the time when her pregnancy began to show. After giving birth in January 1939, the teenage mother was allowed to nurse her newborn for the first ten weeks before being separated from her baby and sent to the home at Homberg. By mid-July, Alfred Brum had agreed to acknowledge paternity, to pay child support and even, apparently, to marry Maria. But as a minor in care, she now needed the permission of the Legal Guardianship Court to marry. Instead of reuniting Maria, Alfred and their child, the Hereditary Health Court was due to consider an application, brought presumably by the Youth Board, to have Maria sterilised. The hearing date had been set for 18 July, while she was still hiding out in Frankfurt. Once Maria was arrested on 22 July, she was sent first to the Monika Home, where it was established that this time she was not, in fact, pregnant. She was then taken to the psychiatric asylum at Hadamar, where a doctor undertook the full assessment required by the Hereditary Health Court before it could rule on the sterilisation application. Crucial to the outcome of Maria's case was the 'Intelligence Test', which encompassed much rote learning as well as mental arithmetic and ability to use language correctly. It also involved questions on general historical and political knowledge – 'Who was Bismarck? In earlier times he was just like our Führer' – and then there were the answers to moral questions such as:

Why may one not spread false rumours? Because they will always be distorted further.
May one act as a spy? No.
Why not? Because that is treason to the fatherland.[27]

Maria's general demeanour – 'willing, friendly and concentrated' – as well as her aptitude for mental arithmetic, impressed the doctor; moreover, there was no history of illness in the family; nor had any member of her family previously been taken into the welfare institutions. Instead of finding any signs of hereditary 'feeble-mindedness', which would have justified having Maria sterilised, the psychiatrist concluded that Maria had suffered 'harm in puberty' and was merely 'psychopathic'.[28]

Maria was relatively lucky. Other children were sent from reformatories to psychiatric asylums for nothing more than bed-wetting. And the files of the asylum at Kloster Haina reveal how key were the impressions of the medical referee and how easily Maria's sterilisation case could have gone the other way. Often, doctors blatantly broke the conventions of diagnosis, confused different maladies and attributed moral or hereditary qualities to accidents suffered by distant relatives in order to find genetic grounds for sterilisation. Even children who passed the intelligence tests might still be condemned because of their 'asocial behaviour'. Instead of being sterilised, in late August 1939 Maria was sent to Breitenau as 'ineducable', where she remained for the next nine months. Her stay included four weeks of *Arrest* as winter set in for trying – yet again – to run away. Eventually, the care order was lifted in June 1941 after she had turned nineteen. She was finally free to lead her own life, though it is doubtful if she ever found her first child.[29]

Arrest and return to Breitenau were inevitably followed by serious punishment, and the spells of solitary confinement and bread-and-water diet were duly noted on an inmate's file. For those strong enough to survive such a regime and brave or foolish enough to try to escape again, the vicious cycle of arrest, escape, rearrest and punishment could continue for years. Merely talking during working hours was treated as rebellion and insubordination. Heir to the nineteenth-century custodial tradition with its notions of breaking and remaking the individual mind in the spirit of moral obedience, institutions like Breitenau aspired to a degree of control over their young inmates which they could never truly attain.

A handful of love letters survive in the records of the institution: these were, of course, those that were discovered. Like the children's censored correspondence with their parents, such letters open a window on their emotional ties. Falling in love provided a form of inner escape into emotions which Breitenau's regime of work and short rations was meant to dampen if not destroy. Instead, the institution's terrifying and gloomy character lent a peculiarly intense quality to the infatuations which blossomed within its walls. The very act of writing defied Breitenau's self-image as a 'total' institution. Scrawled in blunt pencil over newspaper cuttings, letters had to be passed surreptitiously to the loved one under many eyes or tossed over the wall which separated girls and boys.

In August 1942, sixteen-year-old Elisabeth Bachmeier was sent to the cells for 'fourteen days' strict *Arrest*'. She had been found 'writing secret letters to the reformatory pupil M. and throwing the letters out of the window'. The letter she was caught trying to smuggle also made a pledge of love to a boy in the reformatory. She promised to give him her food as a token, saving up all her food and throwing it over the wall which separated them. 'You know,' she continued, 'for you I'll do anything.' Taking Goethe as her model, she pledged, 'Beloved, to you I shall remain true till death.' Elisabeth knew the value of her love token. She had already been punished a month earlier with two spells of *Arrest* for trying to send letters out of the reformatory. Just as these young adolescents measured the strength of parental loyalty through the food which could be sent from home, so they offered their own pledges of love in food also.[30]

Another sixteen-year-old, Hannelore Büchner, kept a little cache of letters in two cotton envelopes she had sewn by hand, which – judging by their absence from her disciplinary record – do not seem to have been found till after her release: probably she left them behind, rather than risk having them found on her body during the final strip search which accompanied her release from Breitenau.[31] Hannelore wrote to Heinz, calling him 'My *Sonniboy*', after Al Johnson's *The Jazz Singer*, and she sent him a picture of her mother, adding that she hoped it would bring him joy.[32] Hannelore wrote still more passionately to Lotti, a girl in her own wing of the building:

I waited the whole time till Käthi was gone. My little sun! Hopefully one day my wish to take you will come true. If only you knew how my heart bleeds when you are together with another woman. Or don't you believe me, my *darling???* You can have anything you want from me, for I give you every-thing. It should be not just here but also <u>outside</u>.[33]

She turned to English to address her loves as 'My *Sonniboy*' and 'My *darling*', saturating her letters to both of them with endearments, prom-ises, sexual longing, and her fear of being abandoned. With Lotti, Lore could express her '<u>deepest faithfulness</u> and <u>everlasting love</u>', and ask if she could 'hear my secret calling'; to Heinz, she confessed, 'I just can't tell you how madly in love with you I am.' She had heard that he was going to be released; and to Lotti she insisted that their love was not to be just here, 'but also <u>outside</u>' and asked her to write what she thought about that. We do not know how Lotti responded. Heinz reacted with male pride and, as he warned her off seeing another boy, borrowed turns of phrase from officialdom, speaking of the 'facts of the matter' and threatening that she 'would fare badly' if she did not heed his advice. Determined to force her to leave 'Lu' – presumably another boy – alone, Heinz knew enough to doubt her 'mad love' for him. He does not seem to have known about Lotti or anything else that was happening over the wall in the girls' wing. He warned her, 'You must be faithful to me. Woe unto him if you try to have an affair with another. You will fare badly.'[34] As if these doubts within the walls of Breitenau were not bad enough, for each of them the real test was whether or not the relationship would survive their release. Would the stigma of the reformatory lead the other to deny former friends and lovers?

Hannelore's expressions of teenage love might sound clichéd and her behaviour manipulative, but she had good reasons to look for a companion who would remain true to her. She was alone, an only child who had been sexually abused by her grandfather and had lost contact with her father after her parents' divorce. She knew too that in a reformatory like Breitenau girls could literally die for love. Discovery would lead to at least a fortnight in the unheated cells on starvation rations, enough to kill a girl in Breitenau during the war years.

Hannelore Büchner was by no means the only victim of sexual abuse who found herself in a reformatory. This was what had set Anni Nagel on her downward social descent too. Her file had begun in September 1932, just before her eighth birthday. The Youth Board in the small Thuringian town of Apolda – the home of the Dobermann – had started to investigate a number of boys in her neighbourhood for having 'played' with Anni. Each in turn strenuously denied the charge. 'I didn't do anything disgusting,' declared one boy who went on to accuse several other boys and one girl of having had sexual relations with each other or with Anni. And he was quite clear where it had all been taking place. 'They do it there, near the promenade. On the Kirschberg too. Everyone knows that Anni Nagel starts it all by herself.' Although he was three years Anni's senior, the youth welfare officials did not question his account of Anni's sexual leadership. Another boy was even older and he too denied the charges of sexual abuse when brought in for questioning. On 13 February 1933, a fortnight after Hitler became Chancellor, Anni herself was called before the Youth Board. Asked 'which adult man had played with her', Anni named her aunt's husband, Erich H. Challenged repeatedly as to whether she was telling the truth, Anni insisted that 'with Uncle Erich it is true, it is true. Otherwise no one apart from Fredi F. did it with me. Only I don't know exactly if my Uncle Erich is older than eighteen or younger. The rest is all true.'[35]

In fact 'Uncle Erich' was thirty-two. Unlike the boys in the neighbourhood, he did not even try to deny the charges of sexual abuse the police now brought against him. But like the boys before him, Uncle Erich insisted that Anni had seduced him in a tale of musical beds in his small, working-class flat. Despite obvious inconsistencies in his story, despite his admission to having infected her with gonorrhoea, and despite his own record of extramarital sex which included having an illegitimate daughter by a previous relationship, the Youth Welfare Court believed Erich; and it labelled Anni 'an utter liar'. In October

1934 the investigation finally came to an end and the Youth Welfare
Court made its ruling. Anni was placed in a reformatory for 'provi-
sional education by the welfare services'. Although the criminal courts
sent Uncle Erich to prison, this did not stop the Youth Welfare Court
from citing Anni's mendacity and incitement of 'her uncle to sexual
intercourse' as the most telling evidence against her.[36]

Anni Nagel's case was only too typical: she had to be taken out of
school and off the streets. As the Youth Court explained in its routine
phrases, Anni had to be placed in a home

so that through strict discipline her development is properly channelled. The
child is now already a real danger not only for adults but also quite particularly for her schoolmates.[37]

The local state might lack the resources to punish all the potential
cases of ill-disciplined behaviour, but it could try to deter others. And
in the cases they did pursue the authorities provided an intrusive and
humiliating object lesson in conservative moral values, which was meant
to educate the whole community.

Little of Anni's hopes and expectations emerges from the official
record. The ordeal of testifying about her sexual abuse to the disbe-
lieving, middle-aged men on the Youth Boards hardly encouraged Anni
to give voice to her inner life. Ironically perhaps, it was thanks to the
reformers of the Weimar Republic that Anni found the courage to make
her first statements about sexual abuse at all. The Weimar Republic
had seen a number of imaginative and humane experiments in youth
welfare, ranging from employing counsellors and therapists to work
with families to offering advice to young people within the reformatories. There had even been a woman social worker in Breitenau in
the 1920s, although the institution's traditional workhouse atmosphere
had discouraged anyone from staying in the post for long. By 1933,
over 90 per cent of qualified social workers in Germany were women.
At each of the crucial points of the investigation Anni was interviewed,
not by a man but by a woman, the local authority social worker to
whom she confided how her Uncle Erich had abused her. From this
point of initial trust, Anni then maintained her story – even when it
meant retracting statements she had made earlier to male investigators. The majority of the officials and employees of the Youth Boards
were men. They also lacked any social welfare or pedagogical training,

having come up through normal careers in the religious charities or local government administration. Anni could not know that the female social worker in whom she confided was not very powerful in the overall scheme of things. Nor did Anni know that she would not try to protect her. It had been the social worker who first endorsed the boys' allegations that Anni was a liar which were to prove so damning to her, and which the Youth Boards invariably flung in her face each time she appeared before them from then on.[38]

Anni's was an extreme case within a system where officials started from the assumption that girls were more likely to have instigated sex than been its victims. The Youth Board's first duty was to protect not the child, but society. And a girl whose morals had been corrupted was not so much a victim of child abuse as a threat to the order and morality of those around her. Anni's first spell in a reformatory was followed by probation on a farm. When she visited home in October 1939, Anni was subjected to further sexual abuse, this time by her stepfather. Again, she testified about her abuse to a woman social worker, and again she was accused of lying. Anni was now aged fifteen and pregnant. Her illegitimate son was consigned at birth to a children's home in Apolda and Anni herself sent to Breitenau, an institution its governor advertised for its 'closed, hard discipline'.[39] In February 1942, the governor advised the Youth Board in Apolda against placing Anni Nagel in outside employment too soon:

Normally with such girls at least a one-year stint is necessary so that she has a certain fear of being sent here, for only this [fear] can still make her into a useful member of the national community.[40]

In Anni's case we shall never know whether she could have been 're-educated' in this way. She died on 1 June 1942 of tuberculosis – contracted no doubt in the damp, unheated punishment cells of Breitenau – having spent ten of her seventeen years in 'care'.

Dreadful as Anni's life was, her tale was not unique to Nazi Germany. Religious conservatives and liberal reformers, jurists and psychologists were all disinclined to accept the testimony of children in sex abuse cases. The same categories of 'wayward' behaviour were being used across North America, Western Europe and Australia from the late nineteenth century till well into the 1950s, building a broad consensus that 'difficult' children needed to be placed in institutions to save them and society at large from a vicious circle of moral depravity. The same paternalistic traditions of children's homes and child welfare administered by private, often Christian, charities in conjunction with the local authorities could be found, for example, in the Dr Barnardo's homes in Britain.[41]

As in so many other areas of government, the Nazis had worked with rather than against many of the instincts of the professionals. When the Nazis came to power in 1933, they found that the public and private welfare lobby had already shifted under the impact of the Great Depression towards cheaper and harsher remedies. Ignoring the wide and conflicting range of ideas among the experts, the Nazis drew upon those proposals from both the conservative, Christian charities and the secular, progressive ones which justified punitive measures. Leading Weimar progressives like Ruth van der Leyen and Werner Villinger had helped move opinion along in the 1920s by arguing that particularly difficult children should be regarded as 'abnormal' and 'psychopathic'. The Nazis combined these eugenicist ideas about the social dangers of 'ineducable' children with conservative, Catholic calls for a law allowing for indefinite institutionalisation, or *Bewahrung*. In a health and welfare system saturated with eugenicist and parsimonious attitudes, reformers were rewarded for becoming increasingly ruthless in their search for ways of singling out those who might benefit society, separating the 'educable' from the 'ineducable', like so much wheat and chaff.[42]

Nazi policy began with the most radical measures in force elsewhere, such as the forced sterilisation being practised in some US states and Scandinavia. The fact that Anni Nagel, like Waltraud Pfeil, Ruth Felsmann and Lieselotte Schmitz, died as a result of her treatment in Breitenau testified to an erosion of institutional checks on disciplinary measures typical of the Nazi state. These deaths in custody also pointed to something else: however much the Nazis might worry about the effect of food shortages on German civilian morale, the war ended any effective restriction on starving those youngsters who had been taken out of the 'national community' and placed in closed institutions.[43]

On 22 December 1939, Heinrich Himmler's deputy, Reinhard Heydrich, convened a meeting at the new Reich Security Main Office to canvass the idea of empowering the criminal police to send young offenders to new 'youth protection camps'. On 1 February 1940, Himmler obtained ministerial consent and, in August, a workhouse in the old welfare system at Moringen near Hanover, was converted into a concentration camp for boys over sixteen. Two years later a camp for girls was opened at Uckermark, ominously near the women's concentration camp of Ravensbrück. These new camps created a direct passage from the traditional welfare system of children's homes to the specifically Nazi concentration camp system.[44]

Moringen and Uckermark became a laboratory for Professor Robert Ritter's Institute of Criminal Racial Biology that was attached to the Reich Security Main Office in Berlin. The 'pupils' were categorised and sent to different blocks according to their status: in Uckermark, the girls were divided into three blocks, those 'under evaluation', the 'educable' and, for the majority, the 'hopeless cases'; in Moringen, the boys were divided into six categories. The directors of the institutions reached back to the traditional arguments about the homogeneity of sexual promiscuity among girls, compared with the diversity of thieving and violent behaviour among boys to explain these differences in treatment. By March 1945, 1,386 boys between thirteen and twenty-one had been sent to Moringen and, by the end of 1944, at least 1,000 girls and young women to Uckermark. A few would be released; most merely moved on to other enclosed institutions, such as psychiatric asylums or adult concentration camps, where many perished. Moringen and Uckermark remained an experiment. As one of the harshest reformatories under the old welfare system, Breitenau was selected to provide some of the first intake. While only these two youth concentration camps were ever opened, and they never took in large numbers, nonetheless they demonstrated the *Reichsführer SS*'s intention to retain the concentration camp system beyond the war to 're-educate' young 'layabouts'. But with competing pressures on their time and resources as well as a hierarchy of racial priorities, it was not German juveniles who most pre-occupied Himmler's men.[45]

Ritter and his researchers were finding other children to study as well, the children of 'gypsies' who had been placed in a Swabian Catholic children's home, when their parents had been sent to the concentration camps of Ravensbrück and Buchenwald in 1942. For over a year, one of Ritter's keen young graduate students, Eva Justin, came and studied the children at the St Josefspflege. Some of the older children remembered her as the woman who had come and observed them before their parents were sent to concentration camps, from which they first received intermittent postcards and later urns with their parents' ashes. At the St Josefspflege, Justin measured the heads, registered the eye colour and photographed the Sinti children. She awarded them prizes for playing football and *Völkerball*, and, in contrast to the nuns' efforts to teach them to be orderly and clean German children, Justin encouraged the children to climb trees and run wild in the woodland as if they were primitives. Indeed, this was what Eva Justin thought she had established through her study of 148 'gypsy' children in care: their morals were 'even worse' than those who had remained with their parents and nomadic tribes. She concluded that assimilation made no difference and that the only solution was to sterilise all of them, including most of those who were 'half-gypsy'. By this time other solutions were afoot and Justin's work on the St Josefspflege children in fact postponed the date of their eventual deportation from the 'old' Reich: they stayed until 1944, by which time the strawberry-blonde racial hygienist had completed her doctoral thesis and the children were no longer needed. On 9 May, thirty-nine of them were packed off in a bus for a special 'outing': the Stuttgart police sent them to a place called Auschwitz, from which only four would return.[46]

Back in Breitenau, other developments in Himmler's domain had a more direct impact on the German reformatory pupils' lives. Soon after Georg Sauerbier became governor in 1940, he drew Breitenau into the new system of 'labour education camps', whose purpose was to issue short, sharp shocks to foreign forced workers. Some 8,400 would pass through its portals during the next four years, quickly becoming the largest group there. They also stayed there the shortest time, usually no more than a few weeks, compared with the months and years spent by the German reformatory 'pupils' and adults in the workhouse. Most foreign workers were then sent back to their German employers, although as many as a fifth found themselves bound instead for concentration camps, like Buchenwald and Ravensbrück.[47]

Breitenau was soon crammed to the rafters. Over a 1,000 people jostled for space, filling the attics above the old basilica of the former monastery as well as the stables and outhouses, and even the tiny cells for solitary confinement had to take up to six occupants at a time. This new regime meant that the SS guards responsible for 'educating' the foreign slave workers occasionally intervened in the German workhouse and reformatory as well. The ordinary Breitenau guards also learned a further degree of brutality from the weekly interrogations carried out in the yard by the Gestapo, in much the same way that German prison staff during the war years copied the violence of the concentration camps. As the German demand for forced labour rose, so the age of those sent to Breitenau kept dropping: in 1943 and 1944, thousands of Soviet children were being deported to Germany, where they were placed under the same draconian labour regulations as adults. Once German and Russian teenagers were sent from Breitenau to clear bomb damage in Kassel in the winter of 1943, one former inmate from the Netherlands remembered what happened when a sixteen-year-old Russian boy salvaged some curtain material from the rubble to make wrappings for his frozen feet. Roused by the former householder's shouts of thief, a guard promptly arrested the boy. The next day the other prisoners were made to stand in a circle, while he dug his own grave and was forced to kneel beside it waiting for the fatal shot. Three times the guard aimed his revolver at him, before finally relenting and holstering his weapon.[48]

The most draconian measures were aimed at preventing new temptations to 'defile the race'. From the outset, Polish men were threatened with execution if they had sex with German women. Sensitivity to public opinion in the neutral countries and the West seems to have held the German authorities back until after the victory over France. But from the summer of 1940, hundreds of Poles were hanged in Germany, many of them in public, including at least three Polish prisoners from Breitenau. After such scenes, the Polish civilian workers who had been forced to witness them would return to their barracks, cowed and silent, while the local Germans, who had chosen to attend, stood around discussing whether or not the executions should have taken place in public and whether the woman had been punished sufficiently, especially if she was thought to have 'seduced' the man. Often local rituals of humiliation were inflicted on women, as they were marched through the streets with shaven heads and placards hung round their necks to proclaim their racial crime. Usually, a spell in a custody followed; many were sent to the women's wing in Breitenau.[49]

Consistently patriarchal in its attitudes, the Nazi regime prescribed much more lenient sentences for sex between Polish women and German men. Unable to control the thousands of outlying farms on which Germans and Poles lived side by side, the police relied on nosy neighbours to bring cases to their attention. In much the same way, the Gestapo had relied on denouncers to catch Jews perpetrating 'racial defilement' after the promulgation of the Nuremberg race laws in 1935, prohibiting sexual relations between 'Germans' and 'Jews'. Even though cases concerning foreigners – especially those involving sex between Polish men and German women – now took up most of the Gestapo's time, the overall numbers involved remained very low: in 1942, the police made just 1,200 arrests out of a total foreign workforce of 3 million; here too, the main point was to exercise control through spectacular acts of deterrence rather than to attain complete surveillance and control over all foreign workers.[50]

In Breitenau these different classes of prisoners met, as German workhouse inmates and reform school 'pupils' were thrown together with their racial and national 'enemies'. For the Polish and, later on, Soviet forced workers it was a harsh and brief encounter with a particular kind of concentration camp. Even if they were returned to their original firms and escaped being sent to the camps for good, they would return to a world of hunger, barracks, forced labour and regular abuse by German foremen. For them, the whole country was hostile territory, alien and potentially lethal. The boys and girls of the Breitenau reformatory might be subject to social prejudice themselves, but in general they felt no sense of solidarity with the foreigners alongside whom they had to work. Lieselotte Scherer could not stomach being treated on one of her farm placements like the Polish woman she worked with and expressed her outrage 'that a reformatory pupil in free employment can be regarded as a forced labourer'. However low Lieselotte had fallen, she still saw herself as one of the German 'masters'. As a reformatory for German boys and girls, Breitenau truly was the last station in the 'national community'. Beyond it – and already for the foreign workers within its monastery walls – there was no road back.[51]

For most boys and girls, release from a reformatory came in stages, via probationary placements, usually on outlying farms. Here, the teenagers had to work extremely hard and in any dispute the farmers and their wives were swift to remind them of their reformatory pasts. Almost any complaint was sufficient to produce official threats to send them back to the reformatory once more. Girls' love affairs with soldiers led to tests for venereal disease, boys failing to feed the cows on a Sunday afternoon elicited official warnings about sabotaging the war effort. Children feared that their own families would line up with the rest of society against them.[52] After six years in various types of institutional care and probationary farm service, eighteen-year-old Lieselotte Scherer tried to justify herself to a mother she hardly knew:

I was a child at the time I left you and now I'm already grown-up and you don't know what kind of person I am. . . . Forget everything I did to you. I want to make it all up to you. I hereby promise you that I'll change my ways out of love for you.[53]

Lieselotte's fear that her own mother shared the official view of her revealed the deep bedrock of common sense and common prejudice upon which welfare experts, doctors, religious charities and local administrators built their version of the Nazi state. They knew that most people would support them in their fight against juvenile disorder. In a period of full employment, the 'work-shy' and the 'asocial' had broken the social contract. Indeed, as late as the 1980s, surveys of public opinion found that the punitive measures taken against so-called 'asocial' elements were recollected as a popular and positive side of Nazism. After the war, the burghers of Guxhagen could think of no one better after whom to name the street which led from their little town to Breitenau than Heinrich Klimmer, the Nazi governor of the 1930s.[54]

The only shortcut out of Breitenau was offered by patriotism. Here the teenagers' private emotional worlds and the public values of their custodians at last intersected. For girls, patriotic fervour may have done no more than strengthen a determination to conform to society, to fit into the 'national community'. But it was boys' patriotism that impressed the reformatory governor, and the Ministry of Justice had already agreed that teenagers could do their probation at the front. They could volunteer for the services and, having won the governor's respect, see their 'welfare education' orders lifted. In 1941 and 1942, the German armed forces had enough recruits to turn down reformatory boys who volunteered for elite arms like the navy and air force. Generally, they had to wait patiently until they turned eighteen and could be drafted into the army: the best they could hope for were the *Panzer* divisions.[55]

As delinquent and wayward children teetered on the edge of the 'national community', they risked falling out of it altogether; and as Nazi policy became more brutal and punitive, the fall was more likely to prove fatal. It could mean starvation in the punishment cells, a youth concentration camp, a sterilisation order, or a psychiatric asylum. In taking such draconian measures, the state benefited from a widespread consensus around the treatment of juvenile delinquents. In many ways, the Nazi glorification of work established a very simple yardstick for membership of the German nation. In the pre-war years full employment had helped harden attitudes towards the 'work-shy' and 'asocials'. Work had itself been fêted as a positive virtue in pageants for the 'beauty of labour', while on the shop-floor the autonomy of the skilled worker had continued to be respected. In the concentration camps, the allocation of work spelled the difference between life and death. In prisons, work separated 'asocials' and 'community aliens' from inmates who might be rehabilitated.[56] And in reformatories, readiness to work diligently separated the 'educable' from the 'ineducable'. If the stories in their case files tell anything, it is that reformatory pupils had this one lesson drummed into them from all sides: to work diligently and without complaining, despite hunger, taunts and beatings. Whatever their secret longings and whatever other skills reformatory children learned from each other, they had to master the art of showing the 'right attitude' not only to their custodians and employers but in their letters home as well. Ironically, the letters which were censored because their tone appeared insufficiently contrite often revealed that the authorities possessed a deeper ally than control over external behaviour: children truly feared that their parents had condemned them too.

III

MEDICAL MURDER

In July 1939, Hitler asked one of the doctors in his retinue, Karl Brandt, to visit a couple who had petitioned him several months earlier to have their severely disabled baby killed. Brandt visited the family, a Lutheran farm labourer and his wife who lived in Pomssen in Saxony: on 25 July, the local church register recorded the death from 'heart weakness' of the five-month-old boy, Gerhard Herbert K. This was only the beginning of medical killing: within a month, the Reich Committee for the Registering of Serious Hereditary and Congenital Illnesses made it compulsory for doctors to report all newborn children suffering from idiocy, Down's syndrome, microcephaly, hydrocephaly, spastic paralysis or missing limbs. The registration forms were forwarded to three medical experts, one of whom, Professor Werner Catel from Leipzig, had already been called in to give an opinion on Gerhard Herbert K. The three referees decided the infants' fate without seeing them, simply annotating their registration forms with a '+' for death and a '−' for life. Killing had become a positive outcome.[1] As a result of this pilot study, about 5,000 children were killed and the number of asylums which set up their own so-called 'children's units', or 'Kinderfach-abteilungen', gradually rose until some thirty were involved in selecting and killing children.[2]

If German youth was to live up to Hitler's famous challenge of becoming 'as tough as leather, as hard as Krupp steel and as swift as greyhounds', weakness and idiocy had to be eradicated. If beauty was to flourish, there could be no place for the deformed in the German Reich. Although some saw the 'children's units' as a long-term measure, which would be needed long after the war to eliminate those whom sterilisation and abortions should have prevented being born, the first priority was to clear the asylums of patients who could not contribute to the war effort. Hitler entrusted Karl Brandt and Philipp Bouhler, the man who had plucked the K. family's request out of the 2,000 petitions that his office received daily, with establishing a second and larger-scale initiative. Brandt and Bouhler took up new premises in December 1940, and called their secret operation to weed out and murder adult asylum patients simply 'T-4', after its Berlin address at Tiergarten 4.[3]

During the first six months of the war, about 3,000 asylum patients were summarily shot and gassed as two special SS and police units swept across Pomerania and western Poland. Within the rest of the 'old', pre-war, Reich, medical murder proceeded along more bureaucratic but nonetheless rapid lines. As leading psychiatrists and paediatricians joined the group of referees assisting the 'T-4' executive, the number of individual case files they could process swiftly rose. In January 1940, a demonstration of gassing at the former hard-labour penitentiary at Brandenburg established a method for killing at least twenty patients at a time. Over the next eighteen months, patients from asylums across the Reich were channelled through holding sanatoria to be killed at Grafeneck on the Swabian Alp, at Hartheim near Linz, the Sonnenstein asylum near Dresden and at Bernburg. In January 1941, a year after the 'T-4' operation began, a sixth centre was opened at Hadamar to replace Grafeneck.[4]

Set on the hillside above the little town of Hadamar, the asylum overlooked the forgotten winding valley carved out by the River Lahn between Marburg and Frankfurt, an area of small tin mines, Catholic observance and rural poverty. The asylum at Hadamar had opened in 1906, at a time when the area was already economically depressed. Occupying the late-nineteenth-century buildings of a workhouse, the main asylum had been cleared of patients on the outbreak of the Second World War in order to serve as a military hospital. This made it easy to convert, given the active support of the provincial administration in Wiesbaden. Twenty-five of the original staff were kept on, while others were brought in from Grafeneck and from Berlin or hired locally. Patients alighted from the branch line at the station down the hill in the town or arrived in the grey buses of the Community Patients' Transport Service, which brought them straight to the asylum grounds. Shepherded in by a side entrance, patients were led into a bright room with large windows on the ground floor, where they undressed and had their identities checked off. After a cursory examination a doctor decided which, of the sixty-one possible causes of death on his list, would best fit the patient. They were photographed for the growing collection of faces of mental patients and led in small batches round the corner to the narrow flight of stairs down to a small white shower room, with a tiled floor and wooden benches running along its sides. Here they were gassed with carbon monoxide and their bodies burned in the two crematorium ovens on the other side of the basement. Between January and August 1941, 10,072 people were gassed there.[5]

Unfortunately for the authorities, the crematoria chimneys gave off thick plumes of smoke, which confirmed the loose talk of the labourers responsible for disposing of the bodies. Public disquiet at Grafeneck on the Swabian Alp, where 9,839 people were gassed, had led to the transfer of operations to Hadamar in the first place. The sheer numbers led doctors to be careless in forging death certificates. Some relatives were told that patients had died of appendicitis who had had the organ removed long before. Even sending paper urns of ashes to families had its pitfalls. When relatives found a woman's hairpins in the urn for a man or received an urn for a son they had removed from an asylum two weeks before, they began to ask questions. In the immediate vicinity of the asylums, the gassing was no secret at all. When Bishop Antonius Hilfrich of Limburg wrote to the Reich Minister of Justice – a fellow Catholic – to protest, he cited the play of local children, who used to greet the grey buses as they drove through Hadamar with the chant, 'Here come the murder boxes.'[6]

On 3 August 1941, the Catholic Bishop of Münster, Clemens August Count von Galen, used his pulpit in the Lamberti church to preach a public sermon against euthanasia. Disclosing all he knew of the killing of patients, Galen warned about what would happen to the old, the frail and wounded war veterans, 'if you establish and apply the principle that you can kill "unproductive" human beings'. Galen's sermon made a significant local impression. It was read out in diocesan churches in the Münsterland, and the RAF dropped copies of it in leaflet form more widely.[7]

In his tirades over dinner, Hitler privately vowed to have Galen's head, but he realised that it was unwise to enrage the Catholics of the Münsterland after a summer of confrontation with the Church over enforced monastery closures. Lesser figures were not so lucky. Paula F., who worked in the provisioning section of the Hadamar asylum, was questioned by the Gestapo and sent to Ravensbrück concentration camp for six months for possessing a copy of Bishop Galen's sermon. Here, as in other areas of political control in the Third Reich, use of terror and intimidation was both brutal and selective, aiming to break and then reintegrate, rather than annihilate, many dissidents. When Paula returned to Hadamar, she found that she had not only lost her job but that the townspeople shunned her.[8]

The 'T-4' operation was put on hold and then wound down. Its key personnel soon made themselves and their expertise available to a new and much larger gassing project being developed by the SS to dispose of Jews at Bełżec in Poland. By the time the 'T-4' operation came to an end that August, it had already exceeded its target of killing 70,000 patients. 'T-4' staff occupied themselves by calculating the value of the eggs, marmalade, cheese and potatoes they had saved the Reich, and by weeding out 20,000 concentration camp inmates. But this was the end of only one phase of medical killing.[9]

One of the Saxon medical directors of the 'T-4' programme, Paul Nitsche, had been experimenting with other methods of killing. In his asylum at Leipzig-Dösen, he tried dosing his patients with Luminal; at Grossschweidnitz a further 5,000 patients had been killed by a mixture of drugs and starvation while the main 'T-4' gassing action was under way. These experiments paved the way for a more decentralised and discreet form of killing. At Hadamar, the gas chamber ceased its operations and the crematorium was dismantled after the 'stop order' of August 1941. Almost a year later, in August 1942, a new team was assembled at Hadamar under the gentle-mannered, sixty-six-year-old Dr Adolf Wahlmann and his chief administrator Alfons Klein. On arrival, adult patients were immediately divided between those who could and those who could not work. Those who could not received stinging-nettle soup three times a week until they died of starvation. Over 90 per cent of those sent there between August 1942 and March 1945 died, accounting for at least 4,400 deaths; so that the locals would no longer be dismayed by its tell-tale plume of smoke from the crematorium, they were buried.

Medical killing was now concentrated in Pomerania, Hesse-Nassau, Saxony and Bavaria, with the Meseritz-Obrawalde asylum in Pomerania and Hadamar in Hesse-Nassau becoming the two most prominent centres in the Reich. Even though other provinces were now sending their patients to these asylums, starvation continued to run rampant through their asylums too. Nearly half of the patients who died in this phase of medical murder simply starved to death in asylums which did not specialise in killing. Altogether, it is estimated that 216,400 mental patients were killed in the Reich, with more – an estimated 87,400 – falling victim to these disguised forms of killing than were gassed in the 'T-4' operation of 1939–41.[10]

The murder of disabled children had continued without a halt. Unlike the gassing of adults, killing children had also been disguised from the start, with doctors and nursing staff using different cocktails of drugs: powdered Luminal was mixed into the evening meals, children were injected with morphium-scopolamin, or given tablets of Luminal and trional. With symptoms of acute pneumonia or bronchitis, death was often neither instantaneous nor painless, but might drag on for several days. Alfred Völkel, a half-Jewish boy who was sent to Hadamar in 1943, was given the task of sorting the children's clothes in one of the attics. On his way there, he had to walk through the closed ward, where he heard the 'death rattles' of the twenty to thirty hungry and exhausted children as they battled for breath against the onslaught of the drugs. It has not been established yet how many of the victims of medical killing as a whole were children, but they certainly ran into the tens of thousands.[11]

At all times, those involved in the medical killings were resolved to maintain secrecy and to keep the families of their victims away. Much of the success of these efforts depended on manipulating normal bureaucratic procedures, by delaying informing families about each of the stages by which patients were transferred via a network of inter-mediary asylums to a killing institution like Hadamar until it was too late. Some asylums, like the Kalmenhof in Idstein, routinely used the excuse of military priorities on the railways to forbid visits. But a lot of the information which built up to the protests of 1941 came from leaks within the state bureaucracy, as well as local knowledge. With the resumption of killing in 1942, a greater emphasis was placed on secrecy within the bureaucracy, with the provincial authorities from which patients were sent no longer being informed of the name of the asylum to which they had been transferred. The savings on the asylum budgets had to be hidden too, with millions of marks secreted in 'building funds' and surpluses being ploughed back into other forms of civic expenditure, from memorials, to the Nassau provincial library and the Rhine-Main provincial orchestra.[12]

Killing with drugs was meant to reassure those few relatives, who succeeded in beating the administrative paperchase and arrived at the asylum before the children were buried, that their children had apparently died of natural causes. Their bodies were buried with at least the semblance of a service, although the local pastor in Idstein wondered why the child's coffin on the cart which passed his house on its procession to the graveyard always looked the same. In fact, it was. The mildly disabled teenager who did odd jobs in the town's Kalmenhof asylum had been set to fashion a trapdoor in the bottom panel, so that the body could be released in the grave and the coffin subsequently removed and reused.[13]

Insofar as it became public knowledge, the 'euthanasia action' divided public opinion deeply and led to some of the most outspoken protests of the war. It threatened to pit the Nazi regime and prominent health professionals against the majority of German society, as notions of 'social usefulness' competed with the idea of the sanctity of life. The medical referees used patients' ability to work as the deciding factor in reaching their '+' and '−' verdicts. This was in keeping with bureaucratic criteria elsewhere. Willingness to work was used in reformatories, prisons and concentration camps too as a way of separating the 're-educable' members of the 'national community' from 'asocials' and 'community aliens', and there had been no public outcry over these institutions. But using their incapacity to work as a criterion for putting psychiatric patients to death was quite a different matter and from the first the medical killing was conducted on the assumption that the German public would not approve of such measures. Although the 'euthanasia action', as they liked to call it, could call on the co-operation of a very wide range of professionals, including experts from both the Protestant and the Catholic Churches, it also produced the sharpest and most widespread criticism the regime had to endure during the whole war.

During the 1930s, expenditure on food and other outgoings was cut in asylums at least as vigorously as it was in workhouses and reformatories, and created an administrative culture steeped in balance sheets. Forcibly sterilising patients might protect German society from 'degenerating' into a 'nation of idiots', but it would not reduce the numbers of patients or free up hospital beds for the military. In the

First World War, as German psychiatrists had watched as many as 71,000 of their patients die of starvation and related illnesses, they had already learned to think in terms of a duty of care to the national cause and the state rather than to the individual patient. Karl Binding and Alfred Hoche attempted to redefine the concept of 'mercy killing' radically in their 1920 pamphlet, *Permission for the Destruction of Life Unworthy of Life*, by canvassing it as a legitimate means for society to dispose of 'useless ballast existences'. But mainstream medical opinion still baulked even at the notion of individual assisted suicide in the 1920s and was not ready for such an attack on individual rights, even if there was a broad consensus that many psychiatric patients were leading vegetative and worthless lives. Under the hammer blows of the Great Depression a growing number of health professionals were ready to speak about their duty in terms of a wartime national emergency, while more radical asylum directors, like Hermann Pfannmüller and Friedrich Mennecke, and some senior provincial officials, like Wilhelm Traupel, eagerly embraced the new idea of 'mercy killing' outright. Men like Pfannmüller might canvass his views when parties from the SS or the Hitler Youth visited his Bavarian asylum, but these discussions were not widely publicised.[14]

Goebbels realised that German society was not ready to endorse such extreme utilitarianism about the right to life. When it came to 'mercy killing', he promptly scrapped all the drafts for films along the lines of earlier Nazi pseudo-documentary propaganda about the waste of resources on 'idiots' or the benefits of forced sterilisation. Nazi educationalists might propose setting arithmetic problems for schoolchildren which contrasted the tax revenues spent on marriage loans and asylum patients. But most people continued to see disability as a misfortune. As adverse public reactions to compulsory sterilisation had shown, however shameful people felt disability to be, there was still a very widespread fear that this was something that could happen to anyone. It was no accident that when Galen chose to preach against the secret killing of asylum patients, he laid great emphasis on exactly this point. No one was safe from 'mercy killing', which targeted those who could not work. No soldier badly injured in battle, no worker who had given his health to the war effort, no old person who needed care would be safe. A complex but still largely comprehensive system of public health had been one of the signal achievements of German public policy, and one in which the Social Democratic labour movement had played a very active part alongside the Church charities. What might make sense to some bureaucrats and health professionals obsessed with rationing and steeped in a culture of racial fitness implicitly broke a well-established social contract about the right to care as well as deeply held ethical norms about the sanctity of life.[15]

Goebbels's response was to prepare public opinion gently, by having a film made about the assisted suicide of a woman who was dying slowly and painfully from multiple sclerosis. With a powerful musical score by Norbert Schultze and an all-star cast, Wolfgang Liebeneier's *I Accuse* was the big-budget release of the summer of 1941. By January 1945, 15.3 million people had gone to see it. Although the jurors in the film rehearsed the arguments about utility and rationing resources in time of war, it was the emotional drama which held centre-stage. As audiences discussed the psychologically engrossing dilemma of the woman's right to choose her own death and the doctor's to help her, many reflected on the advisability or otherwise of a law permitting euthanasia. But they did not generally connect this issue with the very different kind of medical killing already under way. Bishop Konrad of Passau sent out a pastoral letter spelling out the link, and in the Münsterland, where Galen's sermon had gained widespread coverage, people also made the connection with what they knew about the medical killing; and there the film flopped.[16]

Despite the public protests of 1940 and 1941, knowledge about the medical killings remained very patchy. Most parents of disabled children did not live close enough to the asylums to hear what was going on there and many were relatively isolated in their own localities, probably not even knowing other families with disabled children. When Frau Wally Linden signed the receipt on 12 March 1943, acknowledging the return of her dead son Dietrich's things, she gave no indication that she doubted he had died a natural death. Beyond the immediate neighbourhood of the asylum, knowledge remained uneven. Unsuspecting parents would have been guided by their prior experience of dealing with asylum staff. Although one of the tasks of the administrative staff at Hadamar was to fob off relatives' enquiries, very few parents asked any difficult questions.[17]

Why did so few parents challenge the faked death certificates they were given? Were they afraid of asking questions? Or were parents – as so many 'euthanasia' doctors claimed at their post-war trials – relieved to have a disabled child taken off their hands and wanted to be spared the truth? There is some evidence that both factors played a part in some families' reactions to the telegram, but to understand what such families experienced it is not enough to start with post-war statements, or even with the moment when they learned of the deaths of their children. These came at the end of a long tale, involving years spent in care in previous institutions, during which both the children and their families had learned what institutional care entailed.

One such institution was the Protestant Inner Mission's asylum at Scheuern-bei-Nassau. Karl Todt, the director of Scheuern, had fallen into line quickly. Pressure had come on him from three different directions. The president of the Inner Mission's Central Committee, Pastor Constantin Frick, was an ardent advocate of 'euthanasia', and proved ready to force recalcitrant directors to fall into line. Todt himself was informed at a briefing conference of regional asylum directors involved in the programme in Berlin on 20 March 1941 that Hitler had issued an order authorising the killing. But by this time, he and his staff were deeply involved in the 'euthanasia action', sending children in their care to be killed elsewhere, first at the Eichberg sanatorium, later at Hadamar. Of the 370 children taken into care at Scheuern, 228 were sent on to be killed at Hadamar, 89 in the period from January to August 1941, and 139 from August 1942 till March 1945. Scheuern also served as one of the network of transit asylums which held child patients on their way to Hadamar from asylums in the Rhineland and Hamburg.[18]

The key role in bringing Scheuern into line was played by the provincial administration in Wiesbaden. The provincial bureaucrat with responsibility for the asylums, Friedrich Bernotat, was an ardent supporter of medical killing, and was prepared to flatter, threaten and cajole his colleagues into falling into line. Bernotat did not simply try to have those who stood in his way removed. A former Uhlan from East Prussia, who had joined the provincial bureaucracy after the First World War, Bernotat enjoyed using his own Nazi Party and SS contacts to have his competitors and enemies called up to the *Wehrmacht*, in one case making sure that an old rival – and fellow 'euthanasia' enthusiast – Friedrich Mennecke, was sent to the eastern front. Bernotat could always threaten not to send any state-funded patients, leaving a private, religious foundation like Scheuern facing financial ruin; as early as 1937, Todt had agreed to place the asylum under Bernotat's control.[19]

The medical killing allowed a man like Bernotat to combine

professional advancement with ideological zeal. Whereas most public health officials seem to have participated without asking awkward questions, but without any special enthusiasm either, bureaucrats like Bernotat helped to connect Berlin with the provinces, and the state administration with the local *Gauleiter*. When he took over the provincial youth welfare and reformatory desk in 1943, he immediately began to look for ways to forge links between the asylums and the reformatories and children's homes under his care. His first opportunity came in May, when he was able to help officials in the Interior Ministry in Berlin rid themselves of forty-two half-Jewish '*Mischling*' children, by transferring them from children's homes to Hadamar. Alfred Völkel was one of the five who were fortunate enough to be released, thanks to outside interventions. He remembered how once or twice a week, a few of the children would be called to the 'office' and failed to return. When he was put to work sorting their clothing, he realised what had happened to them. Although few 'Aryan' reformatory pupils were sent to their deaths at Hadamar, Bernotat was beginning, in 1943 and 1944, to create a system which would integrate the reformatories into the machinery of medical murder. Those who showed no sign of 'improvement' could now be sent to 'labour education camps' for the young, Himmler's youth concentration camps at Moringen and Uckermark, or murdered in the Hadamar asylum. In this guise, as well as a means of eradicating newborn children with disabilities, 'euthanasia' looked set to become a permanent part of the Nazi system of 'social welfare'.[20]

By the time they were told that their children had died, parents had often come to trust the psychiatric doctors and nurses. Certainly, they frequently had greater grounds for trust than when they had handed their children over to the institutions. During the intervening period, which often lasted years, families' dealings with asylum staff developed through occasional visits and more frequent letters, creating their own complex dynamics of anxiety, hope, anger and trust. Much of the deception perpetrated on families depended on exploiting their hard-won trust. All tales of severely disabled children involve stories of family tragedy, sometimes tragedies which pre-dated the birth of a damaged or severely impaired child. While some single mothers gave up their children at birth, most parents tried to raise their children themselves even after they realised there was something wrong. When children became increasingly violent, breaking objects and lashing out at people, parents found that they could no longer balance the demands of the disabled child against those of their healthy children.[21]

The war also took its toll on families, burdening most mothers with the practicalities of single parenthood. Those who had to work outside the home, as happened in so many poor urban households, faced yet further strains. For some, putting a child into an asylum was a tactical concession made in the full expectation of collecting him or her at the war's end, in just the same way as poor people had made temporary use of orphanages since the eighteenth century. Willi Lorenz was a year and a half old when he came to the asylum at Scheuern in December 1937: his mother had drowned while washing clothes in the River Lahn at the beginning of the year and his father, living in poverty, had clearly tried and failed to bring up his son on his own. In February 1941, however, the father – having remarried in the meantime – attempted to regain custody over Willi. The asylum authorities at Scheuern, already heavily involved in the child 'euthanasia' programme, turned down the request of the local welfare office, claiming that 'the child is to a high degree feeble-minded (idiot) and is a fundamental case needing pure nursing care'. It then concluded, 'As a result he is utterly unsuited to being cared for in the family, including his father's house-hold. Institutional nursing care is probably unavoidably necessary on a permanent basis.' Two years later, Willi Lorenz was deported to Hadamar and killed there. Like so many other asylum patients' fami-lies, Willi's was poor. Their mothers were more likely to have suffered accidents while working during pregnancy or to have received less good medical care at all stages from conception to early infancy. In general, with less time, money and access to information than their middle-class contemporaries, working-class families had fewer choices. And, just as children of the lower classes were over-represented in the refor-matories, so they were more likely to have come to the attention of a doctor on the lookout for any evidence of 'feeble-mindedness' or 'idiocy'.[22]

Parents tried to maintain contact as best they could. One mother, herself a medical doctor, wrote to her nine-year-old son, probably in the summer of 1944 in block capitals:

DEAR LITTLE PETER,
    WE ARE NOT IN HANOVER ANY MORE. BECAUSE THE AERO-

PLANES KEEP COMING, WE ARE AT GRANDPA'S IN SCHRIMM. I AM
SENDING YOU A NEW TOOTHBRUSH AND GINGERBREAD. – I
HAVEN'T HAD ANY NEWS FROM YOU FOR SUCH A LONG TIME. DO
WRITE TO ME FOR ONCE.
    WITH LOVE
    YOUR MUMMY[23]

Few children could write back and still fewer of their replies are
preserved. The more common form of communication was to send the
children parcels, usually containing sweets or other delicacies. For Alfred
Kempe's twelfth birthday, his parents sent a packet with cake. The son
of a steelworker, Alfred was virtually dumb, although he compensated
for this by communicating through mime and regularly greeted the
doctor on his morning round by acting out his examination of the ears
and heart, on one occasion re-enacting an epileptic attack he had
witnessed so well that the medical staff thought it would convince the
general public. By the age of ten, he had also developed an unusually
large appetite, and the nurses attempted to stop him gobbling his food
by dividing his rations. Typically, one of the nurses also gave him his
birthday cake bit by bit. But since Alfred could not read or write, it
was for the asylum staff to write to his parents to tell them how much
he had appreciated their efforts:

Your birthday parcel for Alfred arrived on the 17th, his birthday. Alfred was
delighted by it. He even said that it was from 'Papa and Mama'. Frau Schulz
gives him some of the cake every day, he also is very pleased with the mouth
organ and likes blowing on it.[24]

In their eagerness to hear about their children, many parents
addressed their letters directly to individual ward nurses, even though
the asylum directors discouraged the practice. Whereas parents often
piled 'Heil Hitler!', 'with German greetings' and 'yours sincerely' in a
nervous litany in their missives to the management, they were able to
write in a warm and direct fashion to the nursing sisters, who generally came from equally humble social backgrounds as themselves.

Visits, especially in the war years, were difficult to arrange. Requests
for free travel passes by parents were inevitably unsuccessful (and
involved a paperchase of petitions to various different offices), and the
authorities often used military transport needs as a way of discouraging parental visits. Even when they did see their children the results

might be very mixed. So when Alfred Kempe's mother came to take him home to celebrate the Christmas of 1940, according to the management, she was 'very excited and provocative and was not satisfied with anything'. She would have had good reason to be shocked by the sight of patients running around unheated wards in nothing but a soiled nightshirt. Helena Donnahue, whose family came from Holland, could not speak, dribbled constantly and did not recognise her mother when she visited her in Scheuern in mid-May 1942, six months after the six-year-old had arrived. Apparently, the mother 'was extremely edgy, said that she was outraged by the condition of her child, although', the nurse added sententiously, 'she has not changed in any respect since she was admitted to the asylum'. In fact, patients had been put on starvation rations since at least 1937, when their costs had been set at 46 pfennig a day: in the first year of the war, a third of the patients in the province's asylums had died.[25]

But there were other problems, too. Although Alfred's home visit seems to have gone well and the generally cheerful and gregarious boy even stayed an extra week, he had not recognised his mother when she came to collect him: as one of the nurses noted in his file, 'K. did not show any particular joy at his mother's visit, does not appear to know her properly any more.'[26]

Not all parents reacted in this way, nor did they all hold the asylum responsible for the condition of their child. Six-year-old Rosemarie Roth's parents also visited her in December 1940. While they, too, both made 'a very edgy impression' on the nursing sisters and the father was unhappy with the way Rosemarie was being cared for, he felt that too much, rather than too little, was being done for her. At home, Jakob Roth told the sisters, they would have simply given the child a 'wet rag on which she had chewed the whole day. That way', he explained, 'she had been considerably more settled.' Rosemarie's father directed his resentment not against the psychiatrists and nurses, but against his wife. While she was absent, he cursed her, saying 'that she was not the right wife, that if he had a different one, the child would have turned out differently'. The family had originally attributed Rosemarie's disability to her mother having continued to cycle during pregnancy as she kept their milk delivery business going and to a breech birth. As so often, the admitting doctor had disregarded this tale and diagnosed the girl's 'feeble-mindedness' as 'inborn'. Now, as the father cursed the mother in the bleak and chilly asylum ward that December,

Jakob Roth was directing the Nazi and medical obsession with 'racial hygiene' and 'heredity' inwards, to the bickerings and miseries of his marriage and family life. Yet both he and wife continued to write, he from the eastern front, she from home, letters in which they made their attachment to their only child and their thirst for news of her very evident. When Rosemarie died, her mother even managed to attend the burial at Hadamar.[27]

For asylum children, life was sharply divided between day and night. The rules of darkness and silence at night enforced a solitude on the children which dormitory life did nothing to mitigate. Many children cried during the night, some uncontrollably. Although psychiatric observers routinely commented early on that a particular child showed no signs of homesickness, the same observers often went on to note a decline in night-time crying and in some cases of bed-wetting over the ensuing months, perhaps as the children began to feel more secure. Poor diet would also have contributed to the general level of incontinence, while many children were given sedatives at night lest their crying set other children off.[28]

Some children clearly thought that they had been sent to the institution as a punishment. Karl Otto Freimut connected it with a football he had damaged in another asylum. While many disabled children could not control their bowels, others wet themselves out of anxiety. So, when Gertrud Dietmar was seven, her nurse noted that 'If she gets a smack she immediately wets herself every time. If she is told off, she doesn't wet herself.'[29] But despite the similarities between life in closed institutions with short rations and low levels of staffing, a child's life in an asylum was very different from that in a reformatory.

At Scheuern, the children were separated between those only lightly impaired, who were able to attend the *Hilfsschule* attached to the asylum, and those whose disability was too great. The presence of the school introduced a strong gender bias, with boys outnumbering girls in a ratio of five to two, at least among those who were transferred to Hadamar in the second phase of the 'euthanasia' programme. Mildly disabled girls, it was thought, could be better used helping out their mothers at home and so did not need the special school, a gendered division which may have saved their lives.[30]

Friedrich Brauer was almost eleven when he came to Scheuern in

late May 1941. A child with a spastic gait who had not learned to
walk or talk till after the age of three, Friedrich had never attended
school. Still, he was given a standard intelligence test on his arrival to
see whether he should. Friedrich knew where he was, where he had
come from, could tell the days of the week and could count to twenty.
Even though he could not remember more than half the months of the
year, or say in which one Christmas fell, he unhesitatingly answered
the key political questions he was asked:

(What is the name of our leader?) Adolf Hitler.
   (Who is Hermann Göring?) That's the fat one who looks like this (holds
both hands to his head and puffs his cheeks out).
   (With whom are we at war?) With the English.[31]

The tests were constructed to examine knowledge far more than intelligence, offering a kind of photographic negative of what the authorities expected children to have learned in German primary schools,
even when, like Friedrich, they had never seen the inside of one. That
impaired children could unhesitatingly name the Führer was quite
typical of such tests, even when they failed many of the other categories. Most also knew that the war was being fought with England
and later with Russia, even when they knew nothing more about where
these places were or who ruled them.[32]
   Most of the Scheuern children were far too disabled to sit any kind
of intelligence test. They had no sense of the larger events like the war
and Scheuern itself remained remote from the actual bombing. In such
cases, the doctors focused their attention on a number of key markers,
such as physical coordination, the acquisition of language, toilet
training, the ability to play with simple toys, attitudes towards other
children and their relationship with the asylum staff. To some extent
such monitoring had a simple, regulatory function. Aggressive and
disruptive children as well as children who could not be toilet trained
were considered very demanding, at a time when numbers of asylum
staff and funding had been reduced to a minimum. Margarethe Günther,
who was twelve and a half when she came to Scheuern in 1940, was
so disruptive – endangering both herself and the other children – that
the staff tied her onto a 'night chair' during the daytime. A year and a
half later her last observation in Scheuern noted that she still 'sits rocking
on her little chair, has to be tied to it because of the permament danger

of falling off'. During the daytime, there were children who could not or would not join in any activity. Edda Braun, whose entire thirty-two months of life had been spent in the Bethany Children's Home in Marburg, was not physically impaired but she rejected all overtures and simply stood in a corner and faced the wall when she came to Scheuern in September 1942. The nursing staff duly took little further interest in her.[33]

Case notes which end in murder make for painful reading. At some point in the files the doctors and nurses were condemning the children whom they were observing to death. Abrupt breaks in the medical record suggest when a child's fate was being decided. The last few lines in each murdered child's medical file always provide the pretext for death, purveying a mixture of fact and fiction, real dates of transfer to Hadamar and – in all probability – of death there alongside ficticious fatal illnesses. In some medical files it is apparent that a new and highly negative assessment of the patient had occurred prior to this, indicating that some sort of medical 'selection' had taken place. So in Waltraud Blum's notes her last entry in Scheuern reads:

1.11.42: Mentally as physically no noteworthy improvements, no prospect of further development. Straightforward case for nursing care.[34]

By contrast, the previous entries charted Waltraud's slow but steady learning curve, from an inability to recognise even her own name or to engage with objects (at the age of two), to learning to walk six months later, to learning how to play with wooden blocks and paper (at three), to joining in circle games with other children by early 1941. The last such optimistic entry in Scheuern, from 15 February 1942, had noted that she 'continues to be calm, friendly, well-behaved, has no particular bad habits, creates few difficulties on the ward'. The next entry for Waltraud's stay at Scheuern followed: 'She does not speak yet, at least not intelligible words, just babbles to herself. Otherwise, no further mental development recognisable.' This last sentence, in a different typeface, may well have been added later, possibly at the same time as the final entry, preparing Waltraud's departure for Hadamar on the transport of twenty-three children and three adults which took place on 19 February 1943. Phrases like 'straightforward case for nursing care' and 'no prospect of further development' operated as code for the death sentence of a medical selection.[35]

When, just four days before her departure, the staff had lauded Waltraud as a 'calm, friendly, well-behaved' child, they gave no indication of what was about to come. In all likelihood, the nurse who wrote up the file did not yet know. Nor was her positive engagement with the children on her ward unusual. Nurses might be poorly trained and paid, suffer from low morale and high numbers of patients, and owe their primary loyalty to their superiors rather than their charges. They might oversee the chronic underfeeding of all patients, and their colleagues in the Eichberg and Kalmenhof asylums might come under police investigation for skimming off rations and trading in patients' clothing and ration cards. Despite all this, nurses often chronicled the children's little developmental advances as a series of minor victories, almost as if these helped them to maintain some belief in their own vocation.[36]

Waltraud Blum could manage no more than to sit in her chair, suck on her hand, and turn a celluloid ring round in her fingers during her first three months at Scheuern. She was two and a half, could not walk, did not respond to her name, did not react to other objects such as a doll or a ball. Her only words were 'Mama' and 'Baba'. Six months later, by mid-March 1940, she was starting to learn to walk and pushing around a small chair to give herself support. By the second half of June, she was walking unsupported in the garden and playing with building blocks and paper. Karl-Heinz Koch, his nurse noted, 'builds with building blocks, says what he has built is supposed to be'. Paul Egger who came to Scheuern at the age of three, was described on his arrival as 'utterly helpless, now and then, without particular cause, a friendly smile'. Three months later he was still unable to move or speak and had trouble swallowing even pap. But by his eighth birthday, both his physical coordination and his ability to engage with people and objects had developed to the point where he was observed playing with a ball and a cuddly toy, putting them under his pillow or his bed-cover and getting them out again.[37]

The asylum routines encouraged group as well as individual play, principally circle games. How far children were able to involve themselves in such games was observed as part of the psychiatric assessment of their mental and physical condition. Group games, especially cooperative ones without complex rules, like the circle games, were also clearly used as a means of fostering some sense of reciprocity between children, who were otherwise prone to react violently. Violence was often triggered by the interruption of individual play and quarrels over toys.[38] Even in this period, the musical talents of many disabled children attracted notice. Although the children were almost always more interested in performing than in listening, and although their concentration spans remained short and their awareness of other children slight, their singing, humming or playing on the mouth organ fostered gentle emotional states. Many disabled children could only play on their own or with adults.[39]

Whereas the reformatory at Breitenau encouraged their young charges to develop a 'definite fear' of the staff and the institution, so that they would learn to 'become useful members of the national community', the disabled children at Scheuern came to think of the institution as home. Where reformatory children saw their families as a lifeline and developed intense relationships with each other, many of the disabled children began to forget their families and were incapable of playing with one another. Reformatory children reacted to the harsh discipline and starvation rations by trying to escape; disabled children by fastening on to their nurses.

By the time he was nearly nine, Karl-Heinz Koch had developed an elaborate fantasy game. Going into the doctor's room, he would lift the receiver on the desk and call out 'Hello', chat away to an imaginary caller, at times covering the mouthpiece with his hand as if what he was saying in the room ought not to be heard. Then he would continue the telephone conversation further, say 'yes' a few times, and mention a watering can, before finally saying 'Goodbye' and hanging up. When asked whom he had been talking to, he would reply, 'Yes, Karl-Heinz with Sister Emma,' the name of the nursing auxiliary on his ward. While Karl-Heinz took on the speaking role of the doctor, like Alfred Kempe in his mime game of the doctor doing his morning round, his silent conversation partner, 'Sister Emma', was at least as important. 'Emmi' and 'Ida' were in fact the first names he learned in Scheuern, the names not of nursing sisters, but of the two young women who did the cooking and cleaning in his ward. Within three months of his arrival, even though he knew Emma's actual name, he had begun to call her 'mama'.[40]

Down's syndrome children, of whom there were many, may have been particularly prone to forming such strong attachments to these junior nursing personnel. These were the women who were always at hand and took over the intimate maternal activities of feeding, cleaning, dressing the children and taking them for walks in the garden, or, indeed, in many cases had given them the hard-won confidence to walk unaided in the first place. Emma often appeared in case files as the woman whose name the children learned. For Willi Barth, within a month of arriving at Scheuern, then aged four, going to 'Emma' meant returning from the disconcerting surroundings of a medical examination to the familiar world of his ward. When Alfred Kempe suffered an attack at night after being at Hephata for six months, he pointed to his head to show the sister where the pains were as she hurried to his bedside. He called her 'mama'. In Scheuern, he transferred the attachment again:

17.5.40: On walks in the asylum grounds K. is interested in everything new to him, jumps excitedly to the attendant whenever he sees something, points at what he has seen with every sign of excitement, only calms down when he sees that the attendant is interested in it as well.[41]

A few months later Harald Baer, at nearly five years of age, was observed to be doing no more than following the play of the other children; but when it came to walking in the garden, it was noted, he 'likes going there' and 'runs around the garden, picks flowers, brings them to the nurse'.[42]

Such transfers of affection were not always straightforward. For some children Christmas had no meaning because they could not relate to presents or toys in general and even the tree elicited no response. For others, the receipt of parcels from home evoked strong but ambiguous responses. When, at Christmas 1940, Gertrud Dietmar

. . . got a parcel from her mother, she was pleased, but did not ask where the parcel was from. When the attendant said it was from 'Mama', D. said, 'Yes, Mama.'[43]

In her case, the separation from her mother had already taken place. Two and a half years earlier, her case notes record that Gertrud had been receiving neither letters nor presents, even for her birthday and Christmas. Perhaps her parents could not afford them; perhaps, too, her mother had withdrawn after Gertrud's lack of enthusiasm at her visit the previous Christmas. A similar pattern can be found in the case of Karl Otto Freimut, although his own attitude appears still more

ambivalent than Gertrud's. At the same Christmas of 1940, Karl Otto
– only three months younger than Gertrud Dietmar – also received a
packet from home.

(What was in it?) 'Apples, toy . . . and clothes.' (Did you say thank you?)
'Yes.'
   (How?) 'Pray.' (Prayed for whom?) 'For dear God.' (Did you write?) 'Yes.'
   (What?) . . . [sic] (Did you write yourself?) 'Sister Malchen.' (What did she
write?) 'That I'd had the cap on in the living room.'44

Karl Otto's near blindness would have prevented him from writing in
any case, but two years before, in August 1938, he had already
expressed his confusion about where his home was. His mother had
come to collect him for a home visit. He had, apparently, been 'pleased
when his mother came, was friendly and loving to her, greeted her
with a kiss'. Asked if he would come back, he had said, 'Yes, I'm
coming back.' When Karl Otto returned from the visit, he was clearly
unsettled and played at being collected by his mother: 'I'm going on
holiday . . . My mama is coming tomorrow . . .' he had said, but
now, after spending time with his mother at home, he had gained the
confidence to say, 'I'm not coming back at all.' After this he 'even
laughs loudly about such conversations with himself'. The confusion,
the laughter, the visit and the shift of the centre of gravity from the
asylum to the parental home and back again all suggest Karl Otto's
inner disquiet as well as his anxiety about what others might expect
of him.45
   As the children fastened onto the nurses and auxiliaries of the
asylum as substitute mothers, their real mothers learned to write to
ward sisters to obtain news of their children. A bond of trust had
been forged between parents and those on the lowest rung of the institutional hierarchy. Through such confidences, parents who had feared
the consequences when they had first handed their disabled child over
to the public health system had gradually learned to trust the asylum
authorities.
   When Frau Wally Linden signed the receipt in March 1943 for her
dead son Dietrich's things, she did not question the fake death certificate. Born in July 1938, Dietrich had been diagnosed as suffering from
'idiocy' and taken into Scheuern at the age of two. For the next two
and a half years, his mother had written regularly to the director, Karl

Todt, to ask for news. Answering promptly by return of post, the asylum had sent her reassuring answers, designed to win her trust. On 5 May 1941, the director had written,

Dear Mrs Linden,

Further to your enquiry, I am informing you that Dietrich is getting along very well. Physically, he is in general completely healthy and otherwise really cheerful among his friends, he is also making some small progress in walking, if he can hold on to tables and chairs he can get around really nicely. He likes the food. Sister Otti's children's ward, in which he has been up to now, was disbanded for organisational reasons and as a result Dietrich is with another nurse. But she, too, looks after him with much care and a love that is touching to see. In Dietrich's name, best wishes,

Heil Hitler!

The Director[46]

The letter is typical in a number of respects – the upbeat tone; the children are recognised as a little band of 'friends' who are almost always 'cheerful'; the telling little details which suggest her son's continued progress; above all, the comforting reference to the nursing sisters directly responsible for him; and the bureaucratic punctiliousness in dispatching a reply the day after an enquiry was received. But perhaps the most important element in the letter was conveyed by the final formal phrase, 'In Dietrich's name'. As the authorities had already disclosed in an earlier letter, Dietrich could hardly speak: 'Now and then he says Mama; otherwise, he does not speak at all. In his name, best wishes.'[47]

The clinic had to – or at least offered to – speak on his behalf. The absent parents needed desperately to hear news from children who mostly could not communicate directly with them and the authorities slipped comfortingly into the role of go-between. Mediated by the postal service and punctuated by the still rarer, carefully controlled visits to the child, this relationship of trust became the principal passage along which parental love could flow. Parents had to believe implicitly in the information they were given; not to do so meant believing that they had already lost all contact with their child. In lending credence to the authorities families were not simply being gullible; they had had to learn to overcome their suspicions.

Trust was clearly a factor in the minds of the architects of this programme of medical murders. In the internal circular memorandum of 1 July 1940 in which the Reich Minister of the Interior established the decentralised system for killing children in centres like the Eichberg asylum, he had addressed the problem of how to persuade parents to give up their disabled offspring. The solution proposed was for the doctors to talk the parents round by feeding their hope 'that through treatment of certain illnesses some possibility may exist, including cases which were hitherto considered hopeless, of achieving successful cures . . .'[48]

From the outset, the architects of medical murder had worked on the assumption that even parents who might endorse euthanasia would prefer not to carry the responsibility of knowledge. This assumption derived from a survey of parents' views carried out in the mid-1920s by Ewald Meltzer, the director of the Katharinenhof asylum in Saxony. Meltzer's findings, especially the idea that parents would prefer to be told that their children had died of an illness, had been flagged again by Theo Morrell, Hitler's physician, in his proposals on the conduct of euthanasia in the summer of 1939.[49]

Parents may have been more willing to trust a religious institution like Scheuern than a state asylum, but theirs was also a trust which had been fostered by prompt replies to their letters, visits and letters telling them how their Christmas parcels had been received. The very banality of their trust in institutions which cared for their children made it easier to string together the entire chain of medical deceptions which the killing involved. And the bureaucrats contributed too, all the way to returning garments which siblings might wear along with unused clothing coupons. Feelings of guilt, relief and helplessness may have played their part as well, but the parents were dispersed across a society in which their children's disability remained a taboo subject outside the family. In a society unused to the murder of its own citizens, even the murder of thousands of children could be largely concealed from them. Small wonder that so few parents thought to question the spurious causes of their child's death.

The fact that the children also needed to find parental figures within the home made it more natural for the asylum staff to assume the role of guardian, foster-parent and go-between, playing their part both in the children's development and in the parents' continuing contact, and perhaps even fooling themselves for a time that these particular children would not be sent to Hadamar. Medical files cannot reveal how great was the despair of children denied attention, warmth, proper clothing or adequate food. But they do show that even in these most discouraging, impoverished and debilitating of environments, children turned instinctively to those they hoped would give them love.

PART TWO

THE RACE WAR

IV

LEBENSRAUM

THE screeching wail and vertiginous dive of the Stukas, which so impressed German cinema audiences, spread terror among the refugees thronging the Polish roads in September 1939. In the cities, Poles learned to listen for the deeper drone of heavy bombers on their way towards Warsaw, Poznań and Cracow, the ancient pilgrimage town of Częstochowa and Łódź, the brash capital of textile production. From the start of the war, the Germans made little distinction between military and civilian targets as they taught the world the meaning of a new word: blitzkrieg. The German air raids on Łódź turned serious on 2 September. Tired but elated from digging defensive ditches in the heavy clay soil outside the city, fourteen-year-old Dawid Sierakowiak joined a group of other teenagers hanging about outside the municipal administration. As they took cover in the air-raid shelter, he kept everyone entertained by mimicking Hitler's speech to the Reichstag of the day before. But there were not enough shelters for most people. Peasants who had come to sell their produce in town helped little Wacław Major and his friend Pietrek hide under a pile of potatoes. As Wacław, a devout Catholic boy of eight, looked up to see where the bombs were coming from, he concluded that God was 'angry': for what he saw outlined against the sky was a series of black crosses.[1]

Dawid Sierakowiak came off duty at 1 a.m. on 6 September to find panic spreading through a city deserted by the police and all other authorities. As civilians took flight, Dawid found his family and neighbours gripped by 'the psychosis of a crowd going to be slaughtered. Father loses his head – he doesn't know what to do.' The Sierakowiaks went to a meeting of their Jewish neighbourhood. They decided to stay put and Dawid was left with nothing to do but watch the mass exodus. First to leave were the local conscripts and reservists, then 'women with bundles on their backs – clothes, bedding, food. Even little children go.' Dawid and his friends then wryly appointed themselves in place of all the commanders who had fled. By the evening Polish Army columns began to move through the city in good order, followed by some of Poland's precious tanks. The next day, Dawid and his friends went out onto the road leading south to Pabianice to watch, hoping against hope that such a good military array heralded a battle to halt the German advance, a repetition of those miraculous changes of fortune brought about – he optimistically recalled – by the French at the Marne in 1914 and the Poles on the Vistula in 1920. A politically precocious fourteen-year-old, Dawid Sierakowiak possessed a rare gift among diarists of registering the emotional timbre of each turn of events. Observing the transformation of his own fate would become a major preoccupation over the long three and a half years to come.[2]

Miriam Wattenberg and her family joined the crowds of people streaming out of the city. Like most people they made for Warsaw, learning only later that most of those who had followed the Polish armies on the other road, towards Brzeziny, had been strafed by the Stukas. Between the four of them, they had three bicycles and managed to buy a fourth from a passing peasant 'for the fantastic sum of 200 złotys'. Thirst nagged them terribly in the glorious late-summer heat but, hearing the local rumours in Sochaczew that German agents had poisoned the wells, they dared not drink from them. Miriam's father spotted a house along the way with smoke curling up from the chimney and went to beg for water. Finding the windows shattered by bullets, which had killed the owner in his bed, Miriam's father took a big kettle filled with water from the kitchen. They cycled on, the kettle dangling off the bike. As they passed their first column of German prisoners of war, the men smiled insolently back at them, their faces radiant with confidence.[3]

In Warsaw, the Wattenbergs quickly found themselves under siege. They made themselves at home in a flat at 31 Zielna Street whose owners had fled. But the maid had stayed behind and served them a dinner of herring, tomatoes, butter and white bread on a white table-cloth as in pre-war days. It was their first solid meal since leaving Łódź. All too soon they found themselves queuing for bread in the intervals between the German bombardment, scuttling back to the cellar until the house – dangerously located next to the telephone exchange – took a direct hit; they had to move again.⁴

Dawid Sierakowiak was sitting in the park drawing a sketch of a girlfriend when the news reached him that Łódź had surrendered without a fight. German patrols had been spotted on Piotrkowska Street. The Grand Hotel was already bedecked with flowers to receive the German General Staff. He watched as members of Łódź's 60,000 ethnic German minority rushed out to greet the first detachments: 'civilians – boys, girls – jump into the passing military cars with happy cries of *"Heil Hitler!"'*. Meanwhile, Dawid and the rest of the Christian and Jewish Polish population retreated indoors. As he looked around him at the end of his first day of occupation he saw and sensed that 'Faces and hearts are covered with gloom, cold severity, and hostility'. On Saturday, the main force arrived and on Sunday came the first acts of German occupation: 'they are seizing Jews to dig'.⁵

In Borowa-Góra, a mere 20 miles from Warsaw, Janina could hear the shelling of the capital. She had to swallow the news of one defeat after another before she had anything cheering to add to her diary. Finally, on 11 September, came news that a British force had landed on the Continent. The ten-year-old shouted, 'The British are coming!' and her pretty aunt Aniela started to do the cancan polka. Janina began to imagine herself with a big platter of doughnuts mingling in a crowd of English soldiers, wearing her yellow organza dress and a friendly smile. '"How do you do?" I would say' – Aunt Aniela had already started giving them English lessons – 'and they would all comment on my perfect English.' On 16 September came the long-awaited news right on cue: the Germans had been 'repulsed on the western front'. But the French and British commanders failed to make good their governments' promises to the Poles and the French invasion from the west stopped just across the Rhine at Kehl.⁶

Militarily, Poland was defeated before the Soviet Union invaded. When the Red Army crossed its eastern border on 17 September – in accordance with the secret treaty Hitler's Foreign Minister, Joachim von Ribbentrop, had concluded in Moscow less than four weeks previously – it effectively cut off any chance for the Polish Army to retreat towards the natural cover of forest and swamplands, and regroup in depth. Now, any units retreating eastwards risked falling into the hands of the Red Army and the stiff defence of Warsaw against the Germans no longer served any strategic purpose. As the Red Army moved westwards towards its agreed demarcation line with the Germans, it encountered little resistance, losing a mere 2,600 men compared with the 45,000 casualties incurred by the *Wehrmacht* or the 200,000 Polish dead and wounded. Although most Polish military planning until 1938 had been directed towards a renewal of its 1920 war with the Soviet Union, now the Soviet invasion came as a surprise. Many of the villagers thought the Red Army was on its way to fight the Germans. And many welcomed the Red Army with the traditional courtesies of bread and salt, with flowers, or with hastily erected 'triumphal arches'. Some heads of the regional administrations actually told the local population to be friendly towards the Red Army because it was Poland's ally.[7]

On 18 September Henryk N. looked out of the windows of his parents' boarding house in Zaleszczyki. The golden autumn weather had just broken and it began to rain steadily as two tanks clattered round the corner and occupied the bridge which marked the border between Poland and Romania. The locals struck up conversations with the soldiers, addressing the Red Army men in Ukrainian. The soldiers kept telling everyone how cheap matches were in the Soviet Union, but were clearly under instructions not to venture into other comparisons. As the day dragged on uneventfully and their supplies did not come, the Red Army men loosened up and fell on the food provided by the guest house. 'We learned,' Henryk remembered four years later, 'that they never saw milk or eggs in the army and they continually asked that we give them "honey" which is what they called jam.' Even in impoverished eastern Poland people swiftly realised that their new masters looked upon them as privileged and prosperous.[8]

By 20 September news had filtered back to ten-year-old Janina in Borowa-Góra that the Russians and Germans had met at Brest-Litovsk. 'We are overwhelmed with sorrow,' she confided in her diary, 'Warsaw is on its last legs.' That day, the men buried the village guns in her garden and Janina went out into the fields to see the Germans marching in, only to be shot at. While she was crawling homewards through the meadow grass, a wounded cow suddenly startled her and she broke into a run. Her mother was so relieved when the girl arrived home safely that she spanked her daughter and sent her straight to her room.[9]

Meanwhile, the shelling of Warsaw grew more intense and – with no hinterland left – the government abandoned the capital and went into exile. The mayor continued to organise Warsaw's defence, setting a heroic precedent which would help to establish the Polish underground army after the city was finally forced to capitulate a week later. Fourteen-year-old Miriam Wattenberg and her parents spent the last night of the siege in the overcrowded cellar of a bombed-out building. Miriam could smell the gangrene which had already erupted around the shell splinter embedded in the little boy who lay convulsed on the concrete floor next to her. As news of the surrender spread in the eerie stillness of 27 September, they clambered out of the cellar to find that volunteer rescue crews had already set to work searching the rubble for survivors and loading the dead onto carts. Wrapped in blankets, the Wattenbergs struggled past people busy carving meat off the carcasses of horses. Some of them were still twitching. They found their last flat virtually intact and the concierge invited the Wattenbergs to join him for dinner: together they ate one of the last swans from the Krasiński Park.[10]

As they invaded the young Polish republic from east and west, the Soviets and Germans fanned the flames of ethnic civil war, drawing on the resentments and hatreds of the inter-war years to destroy Polish statehood as comprehensively as possible. In many of the towns and villages of west Prussia, the Poles had only narrowly outnumbered the Germans in the plebiscites that decided the exact demarcation of the national borders after the First World War; and the electoral campaigns had been conducted amid rising violence from paramilitaries on both sides, which led to a long-term separation of all civic associations along rigid national lines. In the east, the Poles were a minority. In 1921, Poland had seized territory from Soviet Russia and Lithuania, and set about colonising its new eastern districts. Like the Prussians and Austrians before them, the Poles had adopted the well-tried practice of giving subsidies and land grants to encourage Polish military settlers. But even by 1939, ethnic Poles counted for no more than 5.2 million of the 13 million Polish citizens of the eastern provinces which the Red Army now occupied.

The Ukrainian majority in eastern Poland needed little encouragement to settle old scores. There had been countless incidents of arson, beatings and isolated killings between the Polish military colonists and Ukrainians. In 1930 and 1936, the Polish Army had stepped in and waged brutal pacification campaigns. Now, in advance of Soviet ground troops, the Red Air Force began dropping leaflets, like the ones thirteen-year-old Zdzisław Jagodziński picked up in Krzemieniec, 'calling on peasants to occupy the estates of landowners, to beat them up'. Henryk N. remembered how 'Ukrainian bands attacked the returning Polish soldiers and robbed them of their clothes and let them go home beaten and naked'. As larger detachments of the Polish Army tried to evade capture, they made for the Romanian or Hungarian borders to be interned on neutral territory. En route, they set fire to a swathe of villages in the overwhelmingly Ukrainian district of Polesie, killing their inhabitants 'in reprisal'. To many, the arrival of Soviet rule came as a restoration of order.[11]

The Soviet occupiers rapidly confirmed Poles' belief in their own cultural superiority. Everywhere Polish boys were struck by the smell of the tar of Russian soldiers' footwear, the blare of propaganda songs broadcast from speakers in the streets and the new filth and decay, which quickly covered all public spaces. 'Within a week,' wrote a boy from Włodzimierz Wołyński, 'our town was completely changed: dirty all around, no one caring to keep it clean, heaps of refuse thrown away by the army disintegrating in the streets. Footpaths, trees, lawns all destroyed by trucks and tractors.' With the rouble and złoty set at an exchange rate of one to one and – still more important – an absence of the ration controls that operated in the Soviet Union, the Red Army men had gone on a buying spree in eastern Poland. For the soldiers and the army of officials and policemen that followed them, largely rural, eastern Poland represented a new world of bourgeois luxury. As they fell upon the seemingly unlimited supplies of butter, sour cream, meat, sausage, eggs and cheese, and bought up clothes, shoes and watches indiscriminately, they quickly exhausted stocks. Official policy played its own part here, as virtually the entire Białystok textile industry was dismantled and shipped east. So too were the wooden floors, stoves, brass and iron handles, tiles and doors of government build-ings, hospitals and schools. Meanwhile, oil, grain and cattle were being shipped west under the Soviet trade agreement with Germany. Within months in towns swollen by the influx of refugees from western Poland, people could only buy the salt, kerosene, matches and tobacco stocked in the official shops, but were able to amuse themselves with stories about the ubiquitous wife of the NKVD official who wore a pink nightie to the theatre, thinking it was a ball gown. Townsfolk made their way out into the countryside to barter second-hand clothes with the peasants in exchange for food.[12]

In many of the western districts which the Nazis would re-annex to the Reich, a wave of violence engulfed the mixed communities of Poles, Germans and Jews. In the small west Prussian town of Konitz, ethnic German – and Protestant – militiamen immediately turned on their Polish Catholic and Jewish neighbours. On 26 September, they shot forty Poles and Jews. The next day they killed a Polish priest; the day after, 208 psychiatric patients at the Konitz hospital. In October and November, 200 patients in another psychiatric unit nearby were shot. By January, with the assistance of the *Wehrmacht* and the Gestapo, the local militias had killed 900 Poles and Jews from Konitz and its surrounding villages.

In 1900, Konitz had been an overwhelmingly German and Prussian town. That year, the German and Polish communities had united: they had conducted a pogrom against the town's thriving Jewish community, in the wake of a ritual murder accusation, a belief that Jews killed Christian children and used their blood for religious rites, which still ran very deep in parts of Poland. Yet in 1919 the Association of Jewish Communities in West Prussia had declared their unmistakable allegiance to 'Germandom', decrying 'Polish arbitrariness and intolerance'. Twenty years later it was their German neighbours who would massacre them.[13]

Across the formerly West Prussian region around Bromberg such massacres were repeated. In the absence of complete figures, some order of magnitude is suggested by the fact that 65,000 people were killed in these first months, counting only the larger massacres in which over 1,000 persons died. Local German militias carried out nearly half of them. In towns like Bromberg, which had seen retreating Polish Army units attack ethnic Germans in the opening days of the war, many of the killings reeked of savage fear, fanned by lurid and grossly exaggerated German propaganda tales. In Rippin, Polish prisoners were made to run the gauntlet on their way to the cells, nails were driven into their backs and eyes were gouged out with bayonets. As Polish men fled into the forests, some local German men hunted down Polish women and children instead. In Bromberg itself, Boy Scouts who had acted as runners and scouts for the Polish Army were lined up against a wall next to the Jesuit church in the town square and shot alongside the priest who tried to give them last rites.[14]

Instead of declining as 'German order' was established, terror increased. Mass executions were coordinated by the new central SS and police apparatus in Berlin, the Reich Security Main Office. From late October 1939 and into early 1940, these men organised the 'action against the intelligentsia' as they put Hitler's – and their own – vision for their Polish colony into practice. Under this single heading, teachers, priests, academics, former officers and officials, landowners, former politicians and journalists all became liable to summary execution or deportation to concentration camps where further mass executions were carried out. Pursuing their own ideological common sense, the militias and the *Einsatzgruppen* of the SS routinely included Jews as well as psychiatric patients in their 'actions' without seeking further clarification. One of the few Polish witnesses to mass shootings in the forest outside Trischen testified to post-war investigators that here too the victims included boys in school uniform. But for him, 'The worst sight was when a truck came containing twenty to thirty Polish girls aged sixteen to eighteen dressed in their Girl Guide uniforms. They had gone white, were thin and were collapsing most likely from hunger.' They too had to lie down in the trench and were shot in the back of the head. The shootings continued until all the defensive trenches dug five weeks earlier to halt the German invasion had been turned into mass graves.[15]

As these part-time militiamen learned how to divide their large numbers of victims into small, easily controlled groups, how to make them literally lie face down in their own graves, and how to aim below the skull at the back of the neck, so they developed the precise techniques that would be passed on later in the war by the SS *Einsatzgruppen* and its auxiliaries. In the Ukraine, Belorussia, the Baltic States and in Yugoslavia, just as here in Poland, the SS, their local auxiliaries, the German Army and German police continued the same methods of mass execution by small groups of killers firing individual shots at their victims. First perfected here in western Poland, these techniques would account for the deaths of 2.2 million Jews and millions of Soviet soldiers and civilians. As in the Soviet Union later, so now at the start of the war in Poland, the perpetrators could never decide how secret they really wanted their deeds to remain. In many towns and villages they had to contend with horrified and fascinated throngs of German soldiers. Some were willing to lend a hand, others protested their shock and disgust. Many simply took photographs. As news filtered back to Germany, Goebbels's propaganda had ensured that the killings were generally regarded as legitimate retaliation for the massacres of ethnic Germans by Poles.[16]

In the mid-1930s, the concentration camp empire of the SS had been small and its scope for anti-Semitic action limited, as the Nazi regime brought its domestic enemies to heel and courted foreign opinion. As soon as Hitler launched his war, he let the most radical exponents of racial conquest off the leash. Centred in the SS and Security Police establishment built up by Heinrich Himmler, they began a wave of civilian killing without precedent in their own bloodstained history. When General Blaskowitz protested directly to Hitler, the Führer sided with the SS. Once the 100,000-strong ethnic German militias were disbanded in November 1939, many an enthusiast joined the SS or police, while the heads of the SS's *Einsatzgruppen* took charge of the new offices of the Gestapo and Security Police in Poland. The Poles were national and now also racial enemies, and the limits placed on Nazi violence in Germany did not count here, as small children were butchered along with their mothers.[17]

Even Polish children who had seen little or nothing of the violence quickly learned new dimensions of terror. In September 1939, fear began with a word, repeated on the radio and on the lips of adults: war. Boys had played soldiers in Poland as much as anywhere else, imagining themselves in the role of the victors; and some had really fought or run messages in the campaign too. But for many children, war was an entirely new concept and experience. In Borowa-Góra, for the first two weeks of September, ten-year-old Janina's war took place on the radio, punctuated by her grandfather's prayers and her auntie's dancing and her own English lessons as she happily awaited the arrival of the French and British. For Wanda Przybylska 'the war' was bound up with roses. The nine-year-old could not grasp why this strange word made her mother weep, surrounded by the white roses whose scent hung heavily over her parents' garden. One evening her mother came into the bedroom Wanda shared with her sister, to tell them that all was lost. As Wanda summoned up this moment five years later, her predominant impression was of her own incomprehension at the time. In 1939, she could not understand the word or her mother's tears. Soon after, the Germans occupied their village of Piotrków Kujawski between Bromberg and Kutno, and arrested her father, the local schoolteacher.[18]

Janina began to discover fear the day the Germans took Borowa-Góra, but in the nightmare she committed to her diary she did not relive the bellowing of the wounded cow or even being fired at as she crawled home through the meadow grass. Instead, she dreamed about a dead German soldier. Just before Christmas she and the other village children came upon his body sticking out of the snow in the forest. A few days before, they had taken great pleasure in building a snowman to look like Hitler and then destroying him. Now, terrified of the reprisals that would follow should the Germans discover the soldier's body in the forest, the men of the village returned to bury him secretly at night. Impressed by her father's injunctions not to talk about it, Janina's fears were amplified by those of the adults around her. That night she started seeing the dead soldier in her dreams. 'I dreamed that I was trying to run through deep snow and I was falling over the dead soldier's boot. I dreamed the same dream three times last night,' the ten-year-old added to her diary on 22 December, 'and on each occasion I woke up covered in sweat.' When the snow melted and spring came, Janina still thought of the dead soldier each time she walked in the woods and looked down at the mossy carpet of pine needles wondering where he lay. Occupation, even more than the military campaign itself, began to teach children the meaning of fear. And they learned it first from the sudden impotence of the adults who had seemed so powerful to them.[19]

Soon the traditional war games of boys changed too. Where German children were merely adding French kepis and epaulettes to their traditional war games, in Poland the games were now shaped by their daily reality. Children began to distinguish between revolvers and machine guns. In Bromberg, four- and six-year-olds began re-enacting the executions on the town square, acclaiming most those who cried, 'Poland has not yet perished!' before they died. In Warsaw boys played at liberating prisoners, but they were also observed acting out Gestapo interrogations, slapping each other's faces in this 'wild' game. As reality invaded the make-believe, children were torn between models of heroic resistance and the power of their conquerors.[20]

Fear, envy and hatred seeped into the pores of society, and their progress was marked in central Poland not by large massacres but by small events. With the *Wehrmacht*'s arrival in Łódź, Jews became fair game. Dawid Sierakowiak watched from his window as Jewish women were beaten and humiliated in the street, and men summarily marched off to forced labour. On the Wattenbergs' return from Warsaw, a string of *Wehrmacht* officers offered to 'buy' paintings from Miriam's father, a well-known antique dealer, but their most frequent and shameless visitors were their German neighbours, a railwayman's family, who came to 'request' bedding and other household items.[21]

One Sunday morning in October, there was a knock on the Sierakowiaks' door and they opened it to find that a German Army officer and two policemen had come to search their apartment. Dawid's father was in the midst of his prayers and began to shake with fear because they had come upon him while he was wearing his shawl and phylacteries, or *tefillin*, on his arms and forehead. Instead of assaulting him, as the whole family expected, the officer merely looked at the beds, asked about bedbugs and enquired whether they had a radio. Clearly disappointed by their abode – he did not even 'find anything worth taking', Dawid noted wryly – the party left.[22]

The following Saturday, Dawid was quietly reading a book when his mother rushed in to say that German officers were again searching for radios held by Jews. Although their possession was not formally prohibited until mid-November, the searches offered an excuse for private looting. Again the visitors found nothing worth taking from the Sierakowiaks, and the family's circumstances were such that no German would have wanted to take over their flat. But they did take Dawid with them and put him to work carrying the goods which they then confiscated from the rich Jews on Reymont Square. Dawid could barely lift the basket full of things he had to lug from a doctor's house. On this visit, the police officer was accompanied by a boy of about Dawid's age. Three days later, on 31 October, the boy came back again, this time bringing an SS officer, a *Wehrmacht* officer and a military policeman. They ransacked the wardrobe and took Dawid's razor and two old blades, and then demanded money and new underwear. 'The Aryan lad,' Dawid noticed, 'who was giving the tour whispered to the disappointed officer that he should at least grab me for work, but the officer didn't respond.' His mother continued to tremble for a long time after they left. The boy had apparently taken to harassing Jews and was bringing new searchers every day.[23]

Dawid's mother made him eat something and quickly packed him off to school to be out of harm's way. But at school things were not going well either. The headmaster had already summarily expelled Dawid and nine other boys in his class for non-payment of fees, and had only taken him back when a woman friend of the family collected enough money to pay for his classes until the December holidays. The altercation with the headmaster had taken place in public and Dawid had left, seething and humiliated. 'I cursed him in my soul with all my strength, and vowed to settle accounts with him some day "in another social system",' Dawid had promised himself, deferring his vengeance until the Communist victory.[24]

On 8 November, Dawid had the strange experience of going to 'school in everyday clothes and without a school badge (the proud ornament of schoolboys)'. Łódź had just been added to the area of western Poland annexed to the Greater German Reich and new restrictions had been announced in the German newspaper the previous day. Jews were barred from the main thoroughfare, Piotrkowska Street, and all uniforms were banned, down to striped trousers and the shiny buttons on school blazers. On 10 November, the eve of the Polish national day, twenty-two members of the Jewish Community Council had been arrested and – though Dawid did not yet know this – executed. On 15 November one of the synagogues was burned down because the Jewish Community Council did not have the 25 million złotys demanded as protection money. But when Dawid learned that local Germans were being called up to the militia, his fears of what they might do if the occupation authority was slimmed down began to outrun his fear of the German soldiers and administrators from the Reich.[25]

On 18 November the Jews of Łódź were forced to wear a yellow band. Rather than run the gauntlet of the streets, Dawid stayed home. First reports were reassuring: 'The Poles cast down their eyes at the sight of the Jews with their armbands; friends assure us that "it won't be for long".' But by early December it was hardly worth going to school any more. Teachers were vanishing in the mass arrests and there were scarcely any more classes. By 11 December even this boy, almost every page of whose diary testifies to his thirst for books and knowledge, felt completely discouraged: 'I don't even want to attend these substitute readings and shortened classes any more.' That day a new fear swamped Dawid's family. His father hurried back with the news that at six o'clock that evening the deportation of the Jews from Łódź would begin. They followed their neighbours' example and began to pack. Only Dawid decried it as a wild rumour and went to sleep. But by the evening of 13 December the Jewish Council confirmed that the deportation of the entire population would begin within four days. Those, like Dawid's uncle, who could pay for space in cars and carts fled southwards into Bohemia and Moravia, or undertook the more hazardous journey eastwards into the Soviet zone. But without even a menorah to light their candles at Chanukah, the Sierakowiaks could not afford to leave. Instead, they lit their first candle in a hollow potato with a wick made of cotton wool.²⁶

As the life of the Łódź Jews disintegrated, the news Dawid heard got better and better. On 19 November people were claiming to have heard the BBC report seven-hour battles between the Russians and Germans near Lwów. The day before, 2,000 British planes were said to have bombed Berlin, turning it into a second Warsaw. By 1 December people were saying that Hamburg had been occupied by English airborne troops, that Berlin was in flames, that the Rhineland lay in ruins and that Danzig was on fire. This time Dawid knew better: 'Nice images,' he commented ruefully, 'but how can they help us?' But as food prices kept rising and coal became scarcer, the streets more hazardous and the news of deportations more threatening, the owners of secret radios spread new hope. No speech from Hitler had been heard since he addressed the Reichstag in early October: he must have died or have been removed from power.²⁷

As rumour and counter-rumour swept through the city, it was not only the Jews who were puzzled. The newly established SS Resettlement Office was also in a quandary. In November 1939, the Łódź district had been added to the other Polish districts incorporated in the new German *Reichsgau* Wartheland. In consequence, another 300,000 Jews were added to the Greater German Reich from an area that had been ruled by Russia throughout the nineteenth century. Between 1 and 17 December, the SS completed the deportation of all the Jews from the western – formerly Prussian – part of the Wartheland. Despite their best efforts, the winter coal shortages forced them to scale back the operation, and leave the Łódź Jews where they were. As a stopgap measure, on 19 January 1940, the SS Resettlement Office decided to create a temporary ghetto to house the Jews of Łódź. With its population of 160,000, Łódź was the first of the large Polish ghettos to be created and for the next two years remained the second-largest Jewish centre in Europe. By the time the new ghetto in the run-down northern district of the city was closed off on 30 April 1940, Dawid Sierakowiak and his parents had been forced into the overcrowded confines of what remained of Jewish Łódź. He would never leave it again.[28]

Łódź, or, as the Germans now named it, Litzmannstadt, found itself on the eastern fringes of an extremely rapid and violent process of German colonial settlement. Partitioned for the fourth time in its history between German and Russian states, Poland was immediately parcelled up by further divisions within the German zone. From being a means of moving mass armies, the cattle truck now became a method of 'transferring populations'. East of the River Bug, the Soviets instigated four great waves of forced deportation, which saw 880,000 people shipped off to labour camps, orphanages and collective farms in the Soviet Union. As the Soviet authorities rounded up refugees from the west and expropriated businessmen, Jews made up some 30 per cent of deportees. Children were also over-represented, comprising a quarter of those taken: those who ended up in Soviet orphanages risked punishment for speaking Polish or admitting to believing in God.[29]

While the deportees to the Soviet Union underwent the ordeal of being Sovietised, the Germans were busy expelling Poles and Jews in order to clear territory for German settlement. Reversing decades of German out-migration from the eastern provinces, the Nazis now concentrated on bringing in German settlers, especially from Soviet-held territory, to people its two new *Reichsgaue* of Danzig-West Prussia, which stretched from the Baltic coast south to Bromberg and Thorn, and the Wartheland, which included Posen, Łódź, Kalisch and Kattowitz. From their 700-year-old communities in the Baltic States, 60,000 ethnic Germans were uprooted and sent 'home into the Reich'. Tens of thousands more followed from the mainly Polish-speaking regions of Volhynia and Galicia. A year later, ethnic Germans from Bessarabia, Bukovina and Dobruja were brought 'home' too, many of them spending months festering in temporary German camps, while they waited for homes, farms and businesses to be cleared for them. Some solidly constructed accommodation was found for the settlers by the simple expedient of taking over existing buildings. Many priests and nuns were sent to concentration camps as the Germans made clear that the Concordat with the Catholic Church only operated in the old borders of the Reich, while SS units which specialised in murdering psychiatric patients cleared the asylums.[30]

Secret guidelines within the SS's Central Resettlement Office warned that, while German farmers needed to be near the Polish farms they

The partition of Poland in 1939

were about to take over so that feeding and milking the livestock should not be disrupted, they should be spared the sight of the evictions. 'This,' an official, who realised that the German farmers from Soviet-occupied Poland spoke Polish fluently, noted, 'is not insignificant for the psyche of the Volhynian and Galician Germans.'[31]

The expulsion of Poles and Jews from the annexed territories was not just the work of German men in the SS, police and army. They were assisted by many young recruits from the German women's organisations, student volunteers, organisers from the League of German Girls and girls doing their obligatory Reich Labour Service. The head of the women's Labour Service in Danzig-West Prussia even published an article, explaining how four leaders and fifty of her girls were always deployed alongside an equal number of SS men in the resettlement actions. Some of the young women would go to the railway stations to welcome the German settlers, others would assist the SS in evicting Poles, then superintend Polish women in the clean-up operation afterwards. In an article she wrote in 1942, a German student analysed her own reaction to watching the SS herd Polish villagers into a shed during one such clearance:

Sympathy with these creatures? – No, at most I felt quietly appalled that such people exist, people who are in their very being so infinitely alien and incomprehensible to us that there is no way to reach them. For the first time in our lives, people whose life or death is a matter of indifference.[32]

Melita Maschmann arrived in Posen on a wet November evening in 1939. Fresh from Berlin where she had grown up in a prosperous, conservative family, she was aching to throw herself into work for the League of German Girls, reclaiming the old Prussian and Austrian territories in the East and bringing German culture to the new ones. The town, dominated by its massive castle, was cold, dark and unwelcoming. Although Melita was promptly given the best room in her lodging house, she met no one except the nervous and obsequious Polish landlady. But as she heard all manner of scruffling sounds behind walls and doors, and the murmur of voices, she gradually realised that the other rooms in the house must be heaving with unseen people. Away from home for the first time, the twenty-one-year-old was frightened by the world she had come to reclaim.[33]

Melita's senses, she recalled, were assailed by the 'particular smell of saturated clothes, stale bread, unwashed children and cheap scent'. Children came out of stinking yards with rags wrapped round their feet. Many were begging. Their visibly starving faces and bodies haunted her dreams. Meeting no Poles from the intelligentsia or upper classes, Melita swiftly confirmed her own presupposition that the Poles – unable to produce a ruling class themselves – had always been destined to be ruled by others. If she knew of the mass shootings of the Polish intelligentsia then under way, she did not say so when she 'rendered her account' in the early 1960s. In the street to the castle she stopped and watched the children creeping up in the winter evenings to steal coal from the heaps stockpiled there. As they tried to fill little buckets and sacks with the precious fuel, the armed guards would try to chase them off, throwing coke after them or firing warning shots. Any child who was caught was beaten.

Shaken by what she had seen, Melita fell back on her local colleagues in the Hitler Youth and League of German Girls for moral support. She remembered too her nationalist father's explanations of the Polish demographic threat and the brightly coloured population map that he had shown her back in her own pre-Nazi childhood. With its low birth rate, Germany was represented by a patch of blue on which sat a frightened little girl. On the yellow patch, just next door to the right, a sturdy little boy was crawling on all fours aggressively in the direction of the German frontier. Her father had warned her that the Polish boy would one day 'overrun the little girl'. The picture map stuck in her memory, keeping alive 'the feeling that the Poles were a menace to the German nation'. Such images were not just the material of Nazi propaganda. They advertised a wider-ranging nationalist and conservative consensus in Germany after the country's defeat and loss of its overseas colonies in the First World War that its national destiny lay in colonising the eastern lands. As Melita strove to master her own emotions, she would make sure that neither the Poles nor the German girls whom she directed on their obligatory labour service ever glimpsed any sign of fright beneath her commanding exterior.[34]

Meanwhile, the children of the new settlers needed to be re-educated and re-Germanised too. The teachers and activists from the League of German Girls who had come from the 'old Reich' routinely put the filthy and torn clothes of the settler children, their lack of shoes in the winter snows, their head lice and their mendacity down to their 'Polish education'. One headmaster, used to the ramrod posture of Hitler Youths in the Reich, reported how these children would slouch in front of him, their caps pushed back, their hands thrust deep into their pockets, while they thought nothing of yelling, whistling and throwing around paper during class. In the villages themselves the local ethnic Germans often resented the land and financial assistance granted to the new settlers. They dubbed Lithuanian Germans 'Communists' and those from Bukovina 'Gypsies', while fights broke out between the local German children and those from Bessarabia.[35]

By the time the deportation trains arrived on the other side of the border posts between the new eastern marches of the German Reich and the rest of German-occupied Poland, their Polish and Jewish cargo had been crammed together for days in unheated freight wagons. For Zygmunt Gizella the strongest impression was one of shame. As men and women were forced to go to the toilet in full view of the other thirty-eight people in his cattle truck, it was as if all the powerful taboos of early childhood were being broken in front of him.[36]

Along the way, the deportees were lodged in old factory buildings without heating or sanitation. While those better able to work were shunted off to farms and factories in Germany, children were left lying without beds or bedding on damp concrete floors strewn with loose straw in winter, sometimes for months on end. In the 'resettlement camps' of Potulice, Posen, Thorn and Łódź only the lice and bacteria thrived. Children fell prey to measles, scarlet fever, typhus and pneumonia. As eyewitnesses reported to the Polish Government in Exile, the 'coughing and the heart-rending sobs of dying children were the usual music of those camps'.[37]

By December 1940, 305,000 Poles – of whom 110,000 were Jewish – had been dumped into this rump Polish territory, which the Germans designated the 'General Government'. Eventually, 619,000 Polish citizens were 'resettled' there in order to make way for Germans. The great majority – some 435,000 – came from the Wartheland, where the new *Gauleiter*, Arthur Greiser, enthusiastically shared Himmler's vision of radical colonial settlement.[38]

In the winter of 1939–40, these transports were particularly brutal, the deportees forced onto the trains without adequate food, water or clothing. A Pole who watched as the doors of one of these trains were finally opened saw how the people who crawled out of them fell on their knees and began to eat snow. Women climbed out, still clinging to the frozen bundles which had been their children, and were forced to leave them in one of the trucks. As the train doors were pulled open at Cracow, Dębice and Sandomierz, station staff discovered whole goods wagons packed with Jewish children and their mothers who had frozen to death. The ever-ambitious SS and police chief of the Lublin district, Odilo Globočnik, was already proposing in February 1940 that Jewish evacuees 'should be allowed to starve' and planning to slow down their journeys in order to encourage 'natural wastage' in the freezing winter. Meanwhile, General Blaskowitz wrote from Poland, warning Hitler that such scenes were intensifying Polish antipathy 'into immense hatred'.[39]

The enormous numbers of Poles forcibly 'resettled' were surpassed only by the numbers of Poles who were taken to perform forced labour in Germany. By the end of January 1941, 798,000 Poles had been sent to Germany, many of them from the annexed territories. While the very young and old, the physically and the racially 'unfit' all continued to be shipped east to the General Government, mass labour recruitment was going on there too for the farms and factories of the Reich. In the spring of 1943 Hans Frank, the Governor-General, celebrated the success of German impressment by presenting the one-millionth 'volunteer' with a gold watch before his train left Warsaw. Hitler's belief that the mass of Poles should be held in the General Government as in a native reservation or giant camp in order to provide unskilled labour for the German economy was literally being fulfilled.[40]

For the Poles, the lessons in subservience came thick and fast. Although the exact measures in force varied from *Gau* to *Gau* and between the annexed territories and the General Government, the general intent was similar. In many places Poles and Jews had to step off the pavement to make way for Germans. In some, like the Wartheland and eastern Pomerania, they were ordered, in October 1940, to bare their heads in the presence of any German in uniform. Some officials took to walking the streets equipped with riding crops and dog whips to enforce the new code. A string of German decrees proscribed Polish schools from teaching anything properly, including German grammar, lest 'Poles should succeed in passing themselves off as Germans'. Sport, geography, history and national literature, the core elements of education in Nazi Germany, were all banned in Polish schools. In the Wartheland even instruction in Polish was forbidden. With their zealousness for shooting and expelling Polish teachers and priests, the authorities in the Wartheland now turned over huge classes, which only met for one to two and a half hours a day, to the wives of German farmers and non-commissioned officers. To drill them, as the new regulations stipulated, in 'cleanliness and order, in respectful conduct and obedience to the Germans', Polish children were to be instructed in standing up, stepping aside, sitting straight in class, in silence, in quick and polite responses to questions, cleanliness of clothes and hair, of ears, throat and hands, and, above all, discipline.[41]

Many of the Polish teachers expelled to the General Government ended up in Warsaw and helped to establish the Polish underground state. Its greatest single efforts were devoted to reversing the effects of the German occupation on the young. It took pride in 'the strengthening of their patriotic feelings', above all through clandestine schooling. By 1942, 150,000 pupils were involved in taking banned supplementary classes in national history and geography. Under the camouflage of technical-training courses, grammar and secondary schools were able to operate: 65,000 pupils graduated from high schools and thousands from university during the occupation. Attending illegal classes was exciting. For the pupils, illegal education in their national history easily led on to participation in the 'Grey Ranks' of the Polish scouts. Boys embarked on secret military training, while girls like Janina learned nursing skills. In the meantime, they all engaged in a round of good works similar to their German counterparts in the Hitler Youth and League of German Girls, with the crucial difference that they risked punishment from the Germans for doing them: collecting clothes and food for the orphans of 1939, sewing clothes for babies born in the prisons, helping to find lodgings for those who had been forcibly 'resettled'.[42]

Measured across society as a whole, the secret Polish schools could not undo the damage of the German occupation. The numbers were too small: most children, even in 'Aryan' Warsaw, did not go to school at all. As the German officials in the new *Gaue* watched Polish children hanging around on the streets, they worried about how to keep them under control. One League of German Girls activist wrote back to her family in July 1942, describing the children 'as cheeky as anything and [they] stare at us as if we were wonders of the world'. One solution she mentioned was to set them to work. Indeed, from October

1941, children of twelve and upwards were made to register for work in the new *Gaue* and, in the spring of 1943, forced labour was extended, in places, to include children as young as ten. In some districts every child of school age – seven–fourteen in pre-war Poland – had to work six hours a day, cleaning streets and gardens. Children were sometimes taken in lorries straight from school to work in quarries or on roads, with scant regard to their strength, clothing or the weather.[43]

German children coming from the 'old Reich' were meant to assume their new places within the 'master race' by keeping their distance. Children of middle-class Jewish families like Sonia Games, who had grown up in an ethnically mixed community in Silesia and had been brought up to venerate German culture, continued for a short time to enjoy living near German families. Her companions included Anna Weiner, a German official's daughter. She even went back to Anna's house for lunch. But once Jews were forced to wear a yellow star on the front and back of their clothes, Sonia remembered, 'little Anna stopped knocking at my door'. And when Polish and German school-children had to share the same school building, as they did in Hohensalza as late as 1942, both the inside and outside space was divided off to 'protect' the German children from socially contaminating contact.[44]

Jost Hermand was among the first cohort of children evacuated from Berlin in the autumn of 1940. At ten, he was also one of the youngest boys in his school to be sent to a *KLV* camp run by the Hitler Youth in the Wartheland. Jost had only joined *Jungvolk*, the junior branch of the Hitler Youth, that Easter. His experience was overshadowed by the sense of being one of the smallest and most vulnerable boys in the camp. With his slight stutter and puny build, he was always the last to be picked for team sports and spent his time during matches of *Völkerball* – a kind of volleyball in which members of the opposite team were the target – dodging the ball as it was hurled across the yard at him by the larger boys. In his dormitory a firmly established pecking order assigned each boy his special position. The sport kings occupied the top bunks, the weaklings – like himself – the bottom ones, where they could ill-defend themselves against nightly assaults after lights out. 'Everybody,' Jost remembered bitterly, 'knew exactly whose shoes he had to shine and who in turn would shine his, whose home-work he had to do and who would do his for him, even which of the boys he had to satisfy manually at night and who had to satisfy him.' His aspirations were focused entirely on moving up within this closed hierarchical world. During thirty-six months spent in five camps, much of it with the same classmates, this is just what Jost did.[45]

Jost did notice at once that food was still unrationed and, unlike Berlin, there was no shortage of meat, eggs or fruit. He immediately used some of the money he had brought from home to send two pairs of socks he had filled with several pounds of sugar off to his mother back home. Other boys, including the young Ralf Dahrendorf, soon realised that they could shoplift with impunity. In this world Jost Hermand had so unhappily entered, he was largely oblivious to the presence of Poles.[46]

But there were certain set-piece activities which all German boys and girls participated in, such as marching through the countryside and the Polish towns and villages, symbolically conquering public space. Although Poles were considered unworthy of giving or receiving the Hitler salute and were barred from singing the national anthem, 'Deutschland, Deutschland über alles', they did have to doff their caps and hats if it was sung in their vicinity. For groups of Hitler Youths, this was too good an opportunity to miss: they used their marching songs and flags as a good pretext for falling on anyone who did not uncover in time.[47]

In May 1940, one of the many German tourists visiting Warsaw's new 'Jewish residential district' was surprised when people did not automatically uncover their heads as he passed. Not realising that the measure in force in the Wartheland had not been extended to the General Government, he began to lash out at them and a panic ensued. At this point the crowds of ghetto children who had stopped to watch did something rather unexpected. They gathered in great numbers in front of the German, with an artificial look of awe on their faces. Bowing deeply, they kept on taking off their hats. Many made sure they passed him several times, so that they could repeat their obeisances all over again. As their fright subsided, a crowd of adults gathered to watch, finally sending him off with a resounding cheer and a gale of mocking laughter. 'This,' the sharp-eyed ghetto chronicler Chaim Kaplan observed with bitter irony, 'is Jewish revenge!'[48]

Mockery was not the only weapon of the weak. Fantasy also proved a fertile outlet for hatreds that could find no direct expression. For most of the occupation, the Germans remained untouchable. The result was a remarkable growth of Polish expletives, ranging from the hated 'bloody hangman' to the short-lived 'master for the season'. The Resistance might parody the restrictive notices hung on so many parks, swimming pools, sports grounds, theatres and children's playgrounds by daubing on walls 'Only for Germans' under a gallows, but the laughter would be cut short by any real German passing by.[49] Dreams of a revenge replete with gouged-out eyes and severed hands found expression in a 'Prayer for the Germans', in which God was implored to bring every possible misfortune to the land of the enemy. With its elaborate dream-scape of revenge and atrocities to be visited on the Germans, the prayer also expressed the ordeal of daily impotence, down to its inversion of the 'Lord's Prayer' in its closing refrain:

> For their base murders, crimes and cruelties,
> pardon them not, never forgive them for their guilt.[50]

Only God could decide the Poles' fate and, for now at least, vengeance was not to be had outside poetry and prayer. Meanwhile, the Germans remained powerful and attractive. Gangs of local lads strutted the streets of Warsaw in officers' riding breeches and high, elegant boots. 'This appearance was intended to let everyone know,' Kazimierz Koźniewski commented wryly in his account of the *demi-monde* of the Resistance, 'that the young man was body and soul a partisan and a fighter, [and] that under his loose-fitting jacket he carried at least two sub-machine guns.' Their models may have been the former cavalry officers who had taken charge of forming Poland's underground armies, but they had replicated, too, the Germans' own taste for riding breeches and boots. By ostentatiously advertising their preparedness to resist Nazi rule, teenage boys also made themselves easy targets for the Gestapo. Given the price of ordinary leather shoes, let alone high riding boots, when many people were reduced to wearing wooden clogs, the German-controlled 'reptile press' was not alone in dubbing such youths the new '*jeunesse dorée*'. Some Warsaw workers were clearly inclined to agree. But despite these obvious disadvantages, the fashion continued throughout the occupation.[51]

For teenage boys especially, defeat and occupation often profoundly challenged the sense of manhood and national duty which had been drummed into them in every schoolroom, namely to defend their women and children. Male failure and national defeat were refracted back by the street scenes of Polish men returning from prisoner-of-war camps, clad in threadbare greatcoats and shapeless garb sewn from blankets. By contrast, the resolute walk of the well-groomed woman turned all heads. In the cities women's fashions were changing too. As women cut down men's jackets and coats for their own use, female colours and cuts became more masculine. Above all, Warsaw's women impressed German men with something no longer much seen in the Reich, their fur coats. German-approved publications began telling people how to make their own make-up, soap, shoe polish, ink, dye, detergent and disinfectant. To be dressed well was more than a matter of display. It was a route to success; attracting favours which could smooth a way through regulations or open up a cornucopia of restricted goods.[52]

Envy of the power, purpose and dress of the Germans was involuntary and inevitable. Teenage male envy and hatred of the Germans was also tinged with misogyny. Polish women and girls often became their targets, threatened with incarceration in brothels for having German lovers, or singled out for breaking the resistance's vain boycott on attending the downmarket love stories, adventure and war films authorised in the Polish cinemas.[53] With their policy of shaving the heads of German women who had sex with Polish or Jewish men, the Germans had already shown Europe's resistance movements how to direct their violence when 'liberation' came. And, across Europe, many of those most eager to do so were boys still in their teens at the end of the war.[54]

Mingling among the new clientele of Warsaw's cinemas and bars were a large number of teenagers and children, visibly displaying the new financial independence they had won trading on Warsaw's streets. As the Resistance bemoaned the 'fall in the moral level' of young people who had become used to lying, stealing, spending, drinking and sex, it was reporting on the social consequences of one of the triumphs of life under occupation, the black market.[55]

The Polish countryside in 1940 and 1941 was not starving and agricultural shipments to Germany were still relatively low, especially compared with what was to come. But the citizens of Warsaw and other Polish cities were already hungry and the Jewish ghettos were famished. The first six months of German occupation saw infant mortality double among the Polish population of Warsaw and rise threefold among the city's Jews. Where official rations – when they arrived – covered just under half the food Poles needed to survive, Jews had to bridge a 90 per cent gap between official rations and physical survival. With the inevitability of supply and demand, a black market sprang up around the contours of official restrictions. Black-market prices for food were predictably highest where rationing was most severe, the ghettos.[56]

The Warsaw branch lines were crowded with mothers and children going to barter for food in the countryside. Older children went out to deal on their own account. They sewed hooks under their coat collars to hang sausages and meat, and stitched bags for butter and eggs into the hems of their coats. The railway workers provided an early warning system against police raids, though occasionally the smugglers would be faced with an unexpected inspection and have to choose between trying to throw the goods away and attempting to buy the Germans off. To avoid the German controls at Warsaw Central Station, many people got off at earlier stops and used the city's trams or crossed the Vistula by boat.[57]

All this activity took up a great deal of time, as well as often offering a better income than the low official pay scales. Employers had little choice but to tolerate rates of absenteeism, which reached 30 per cent by 1943. The furniture, household utensils and, above all, second-hand clothes sold on the Warsaw cattle market commanded greater sums than the libraries of impoverished scholars. Despite numerous police raids on trains, railway stations and city markets, the German authorities had to admit that they could not control the black market, the governor of Warsaw even confessing that it was essential for 'the provisioning of the population'.[58]

In January 1941, Stanisław Srokowski was among the suburban train passengers on their way in to work in Warsaw who listened to a boy of eleven or so, singing about the enemy and his destruction of their city, and the wonderful future awaiting Poland. He sang confidently and well, and the passengers wept openly and paid him generously for reminding them of their dreams before they returned to the frustrations of daily life. Awakening such dreams was important for morale; it also brought him money to contribute to his family budget.[59]

In the Warsaw ghetto, children sang too. People became used to the sight of children playing instruments, or simply stretching out their hands with the plea, 'Jewish hearts, have pity!' By 4 January 1942, Chaim Kaplan had noticed how little people were prepared to give any longer, how even pious men hurried away from the almost naked and barefoot little children wailing pitifully in the gutters amid the refuse. 'Every morning,' he continued bleakly, 'you will see their little bodies frozen to death in the ghetto streets. It has become a customary sight. Self-preservation has hardened our hearts and made us indifferent to the suffering of others.' When Miriam Wattenberg's group of girls held an art exhibition, people flocked to divert themselves. But they turned away from the drawings of beggars – 'They are no revelation to anyone,' Miriam noted – preferring to '"feast" their eyes on the apples, carrots, and other foodstuffs so realistically painted'.[60]

In songs like 'Koyft geto-beygelekh' ('Buy ghetto bagels') musicians celebrated the child peddlars who milled around the brigades waiting to leave the ghetto for work in the morning, trying to sell them food and cigarettes. As a father sings about his daughter, his Yiddish mimics the rhythmic and musical cries of the street-hawker:

> My dear parents, my brother Zshamele,
> My child Nekhamele are not here,
> My only little girl, in a little dress
> Now sells bagels, stands right here.
> Buy ghetto bagels . . .[61]

The song conjured up the brittle jollity of the famished child-vendor urging her customers to celebrate the little pleasures of the present in order to clinch a sale, to 'Sing ghetto songs, play ghetto fiddles', just as long as they would follow the refrain and 'Buy ghetto bagels . . .' Hunger drove children themselves to fantasise about food. Girls in Łódź played their mothers queuing up for their vegetable rations, fighting in the queue before a pretend window and complaining about the rations they received. As one of their teachers watched, a girl with short blonde plaits and a long, skinny face threw herself into the role-play, screaming, 'What a disaster! What a calamity! They swindled me, those robbers! They gave me rotten potatoes, the whole lot. What will I feed my children?'[62]

When the ghetto could give alms no longer, Jewish children went under or over the wall to beg on the streets of the 'Aryan' city instead. There the reporters of the occupation press and the underground resistance found them in their thousands, shivering in the slush and frost of the winter pavements. As the problem worsened that winter, the SS ordered the Polish municipal welfare authorities to investigate child begging. A Polish round-up in January 1942 confirmed that just over half those picked up on the streets – forty-nine out of ninty-six – were Jewish. They were washed, fed and sent back to the ghetto. The Polish children were questioned and medically examined. All but one of the thirty-six families they came from had no adult male breadwinner. Unemployment, war deaths, deportation to Germany, disability and the concentration camps had taken their toll. Most of these children were still seriously underweight. They suffered from scabies, fungal growths on the skin and tooth decay, and they all showed signs of tuberculosis. None of them attended school. But their greatest anxiety when they were picked up was how their families would eat. They were their principal breadwinners and had volunteered to feed their even sicker and weaker brothers and sisters. The German authorities in Warsaw accepted the Polish report, and quietly dropped the issue of child begging.[63]

It was smugglers, too, who provided a key point of contact between the increasingly alien and mutually hostile worlds of Gentiles and Jews. Because of the severe penalties all participants risked, their activities depended on a certain level of trust, and a considerable number of the networks of Poles willing to hide Jews on the 'Aryan' side of Warsaw would emerge out of the contacts of child-smugglers. Food parcels were thrown over the walls, smuggled through the gates – often with the connivance of guards – dropped from trams and brought in under hay by the returning garbage collectors once they had dumped their refuse outside the ghetto in Wolska Street. The German-controlled *Nowy Kurier Warszawski* taunted Poles who helped Jews in this way with becoming '*Shabbesgoyim*', servants to the Jews. But it was also good business. Janina Pładek's father, as well as working for the local German administration, took produce from their farm in Judrowice into the Łódź ghetto. As she saw her father gripped by sweaty anxieties each time he ran the gauntlet of German controls, which could all too easily land him in a concentration camp, he pointed out to Janina that the Jews needed the food. The returns on selling food to the ghetto were also higher than anywhere else.[64]

The Warsaw ghetto's smuggling operations rested primarily on the efforts of children. Halina Grabowska, who lived on the 'Aryan' side, kept the letters which her friend Wanda Lubelska sent to her from the Warsaw ghetto. In her last one, Wanda described watching the children re-enter the ghetto via the warehouse where she worked. 'If you could see this whole scene,' she wrote to her Polish friend. 'Small children, in whose clothing sacks of potatoes and onions are sewn, run between the cars and around the legs of the policemen.' Wanda worried that the daily toll of children shot as they tried to climb in and out of the ghetto no longer upset her the way it had six months before. They attracted Miriam Wattenberg's attention too. Now aged seventeen, she noticed how it was the older children who kept watch, signalling to the younger ones when it was safe to slip back again. The small children running the gauntlet looked to her 'like little skeletons covered with a velvety yellow skin'.[65]

The German gate guards, many of them middle-aged family men from Police Battalion 304, played a crucial role in the traffic between 'Aryan' and Jewish Warsaw. On each gate, three policemen were always posted, one German, one Jew, one Pole. As they tried to establish whether the Germans would be hostile, Jewish policemen might move closer, to see if the German shrank away or was willing to strike up a conversation in the boredom and cold of a central-European winter. If they would talk, then, one former Jewish policeman opined, the best move was to make basic human contact by drawing the conversation back to their families at home. Then they were most likely to cooperate in the illicit trades of goods and people. But most, Miriam Wattenberg's observations confirmed, remained only too ready to fire on them, leaving it to their Jewish colleagues 'to pick up the bleeding victims, fallen like wounded birds, and throw them on passing rickshaws', as they called the handcarts in the ghetto.[66]

Henryka Łazowert, a Polish poet who only turned to Jewish themes after she was forced into the Warsaw ghetto, celebrated the child-smugglers' hazardous endeavours too:

> Through walls, through holes, through ruins,
> Through wire there is also a means,
> Hungry, thirsty and barefoot
> I slip my way through like a snake.

She made her audience see the child slipping 'through holes, through brick, through walls', driven by 'anguish and hardship' to bring her mother bread, and knowing that sooner or later 'My life will come to an end'.

I don't want to come back any more,
You remain alone now, Mama,
The street will soon devour
The cry of your beloved child.

One thing causes me worries,
Not poverty, anguish and hardship,
Only who, Mama, will tomorrow
Bring you that little piece of bread?[67]

The motives and dilemmas Henryka Lazowert dramatised were only too real. For many children, smuggling turned them into the bread-winners for their families. Jack Klajman took his eight-year-old brother with him, sometimes working with the organised gangs, sometimes on his own account. For him, it was a matter of pride to replace his father, who had run his own business until the war; for his father, it brought great anguish to concede his dependence on his young son. By September 1941 both the father and mother had died, and the ten-and-a-half-year-old became the major provider for his sister and two brothers.[68]

Just as the Germans attempted to strip the Jews of their possessions at every turn, so the black market automatically sucked the remaining tradeable assets out of the ghettos. Through their very efforts to combat immediate starvation, the Jews were forced to collude in their own gradual economic and physical destruction: most of the goods they sold off to bring in food could not be replaced. By October 1941, typhus was rampant in the Warsaw ghetto; by mid-May 1942, Chaim Kaplan estimated that 60 per cent of the ghetto was starving, with another 30 per cent in a state of deprivation. Equally unstoppable was the new social order born of extreme privation. Those who rose to the top of the ghetto class system included the major black-market oper-ators along with the administrators, policemen, medical personnel and those in charge of provisioning. As relatives used their family networks to gain access to privileged and protected jobs, the size of the ghetto administrations in Warsaw and Łódź increased. The privileges ranged from extra rations to the special restaurants of the Jewish Council in Warsaw and the exclusive villa accommodation of the Łódź elite outside the main ghetto at Marysin. Whereas many of the official ghetto elite came from the middle-class professions, the *nouveaux riches*, who operated the smuggling rings and mingled with the official elite in the ghetto cafés and concerts, had often risen up from more shady and obscure backgrounds.[69]

With a once prosperous father who now set out to rescue the family's dwindling fortunes by joining the Warsaw ghetto police, Janina Dawidowicz was kept away from the gangs of boys who fought ferocious mock battles on the stairs. Some of the women in her block organised a children's performance of *Snow White*. When Janina landed the title role, the ten-year-old's ecstasy reached its height: for her costume she was given a purple dress – a cut-down twenties evening gown – fitted with a green sash and covered in sequins. The performance itself was a great success too, drawing the plaudits of the adult audience as the children danced and sang in a loose reworking of Walt Disney's 1937 film.[70]

To get her away from the dangers of roaming the ghetto's streets and their flat's refuse-strewn courtyard, Janina's mother found the money to enrol her in a private playground. Here, for three afternoons a week, girls queued to play netball. Forbidden by her mother from bringing any books to read, Janina – now aged eleven – formed a gymnastics group and found a ballet dancer to teach them until they could do splits, handstands and back bends with complete ease. Exercise away from the 'foetid air' that enveloped the rest of the ghetto was regarded as crucial in the battle to prevent children from succumbing to depression, not to mention tuberculosis. Even in the late autumn of 1940, mothers would look for a patch of sunlight on the pavement to sun their babies in. As the next spring turned to early summer, adults with 2 złoty to spare could hire a deckchair from the new 'Fairy Tale' café as long as they donned swimming costumes in keeping with the 'beach' theme of this reclaimed bomb-site.[71]

Janina Dawidowicz owed her good fortune to more than her father's opportunism in joining the ghetto police. Soon after the Warsaw ghetto was closed in November 1940, they received a surprise visit from one of her father's former lovers, Lydia. Janina took one look across their small, dark room at this tall, beautiful woman with her long honey-coloured hair coiled round her head like a crown, with her radiant smile and large blue eyes, and ran to bury her face in Lydia's coat. After ostentatiously breaking the curfew regulations on her first visit, Lydia came again to take Janina to stay with her on the 'Aryan' side over Christmas. Once again, style was everything. As they walked hand in hand out of the ghetto gate, Lydia's fur coat was enough to make the police look the other way.[72]

Janina found herself thrust into a very adult world of sex, deceit and loyalty. Lydia and her father had been lovers, back in the days when he had been a well-heeled provincial gadfly. Lydia was now married to a German-born hairdresser, Eric, who sided with the Poles during the occupation and steadfastly refused the advantages he could have had as a German. Lydia's current lover was a German officer, tall, blond and handsome, with sea-green eyes, and they were already planning to leave Poland and settle together in Italy once Germany had won the war. However sorry she felt for Eric, with his melancholy eyes, short, tubby build and bad stammer, Janina was as attracted as others were to Lydia's passionate, restless energy. She also knew that the tensions between the couple were replicated by her own parents' quarrels in their dingy single room in the ghetto, whenever her mother accused her father of being unfaithful. As she was drawn into a complex web of adult confidences and secrets, Janina quickly learned how much more complicated love, beauty and jealousy were than in *Snow White*.

If only very few Jewish children remained as privileged as Miriam Wattenberg or Janina Dawidowicz, on the 'Aryan' side of Warsaw the possibilities open to parents to protect their children remained far greater. Wanda Przybylska had also wound up living in a single room with her family after her father's release from prison. Leaving their village of Piotrków Kujawski behind, the Przybylskas moved to Warsaw, finding accommodation along with other refugees in a former university hall of residence. Here the parents were able to safeguard their girls' education, eventually enrolling them in a secret lycée. Theirs was a liberal and in many ways tolerant nationalism.[73]

For Wanda, the months she spent during the school holidays just outside Warsaw in the countryside were vital. At Anin she joined her best friend Danuta and her sister in playing volleyball, climbing trees and watching the sunset. The girls told their dreams to each other and on their walks in the forest they spoke in whispers so as not to ruin the beauty of its silence. Wanda could have no inkling that she would be killed two years later in the Warsaw uprising. As the twelve-year-old experimented with composing her own paeans to nature, beauty and truth, she also proved a ready reader for her parents' collection of patriotic poets, finding her own sense of the romantic melancholy aroused by the rustling of the trees given a moral purpose in the writing

of Roman Kołoniecki and Adam Mickiewicz. Imagining soldiers sacri-
ficing themselves heroically for the motherland was one thing, but
learning to hate the Germans was another. Wanda was embarrassed,
confused and deeply upset when she saw the triumphant glee with
which the people of Warsaw looked upon the German wounded: she
was moved by their frailty. In Wanda's short life, she still had a long
way to go before she could overcome the sense of common humanity
her parents had inculcated in her and learn truly to hate.[74]

Neither Wanda nor her parents were typical. Many Poles had already
espoused less tolerant values before the war, with the government
imposing a secret quota on the number of Jewish students permitted
at the universities, while the nationalist Right around Roman Dmowski
pushed for completely excluding the Jews and Ukrainians. Most children, including Wanda, also had fewer ties to Jews than their parents'
generation, and much depended on how they were taught to regard
Jews. Growing up under the German occupation, children learned the
new moral codes faster than their elders. As Dawid Sierakowiak had
discovered to his cost in the first days of the occupation, Polish boys
of his own age were playing an active role among those earning a livelihood from tormenting Jews. Many street children had little else to do,
and the Resistance became increasingly worried about the rise in juvenile criminality. For some on the Jewish as well as the 'Aryan' side
of the city, it may have made little difference which activity their
network provided for them: smuggling, blackmailing or working for
the Germans. Others saw their struggle for survival in more idealistic
terms, joking that after the war they should erect a statue to the
'unknown smuggler'. For the child-smugglers themselves, risking their
lives in order to win bread for their families did not guarantee success.
Even if they were not caught, some could not save their families. When
their parents and siblings died, they sometimes moved in with other
children they had come to know through the smuggling trade. They
turned to each other for the support no one else could give them,
creating small gangs whose fragile resilience depended on the children's
toughness and mutual trust.[75]

As middle-class Poles sold off their pre-war wardrobes, the former
bourgeois order visibly disintegrated. Old moral codes were dissolving
too. The German occupation was intended to smash pre-existing social
relationships of trust and solidarity, atomising society into a cowed
mass of self-centred individualists whose only hope was to obey their

German masters. Its system of rationing, prohibitions, fines and punishments established an elaborate hierarchy stretching from the Germans from the 'old Reich', through the ethnic Germans, the 're-Germanised' Poles and, on almost the same level, the Czechs, down to the Ukrainians, the Poles and, beneath them all, the Jews. These many gradations of entitlement were intended to enforce racial and national inequality, and foment mutual envy and hatred.[76]

The Nazis did not succeed as completely as they hoped. The very operation of the black market militated against social atomisation, revealing the venality of administrators with the power to forbid everything and sell everything. Large-scale traffickers needed German passes for their delivery vehicles to keep the bakeries supplied with white flour and chits to draw the petrol to run them. The German military sold off supplies of food and clothing, sometimes even weapons, to Polish dealers in operations whose scale and complexity was occasionally revealed by odd consignments no one wanted to buy, like the time when Warsaw markets were inundated with tortoises, offloaded by accident en route from Greece or Bulgaria to Germany.[77]

The corruption of the local German military and civil authorities selectively tempered their ideological ruthlessness. According to a 1941 London publication, an Aryan certificate cost 500 złoty for a Pole and 1,200 złoty for a *Mischling*, or half-Jew. To buy someone out of the Gestapo cost anything from 10,000 złoty to $10,000. And in Cracow, a German official was found willing to supply Jews with foreign passports. In February 1940, Ludwik Landau had already noted this predisposition to accept bribes for a whole range of services among the very Gestapo agents entrusted with imposing German 'order' and 'correctness'. The Polish 'blue' police and Jewish ghetto police followed suit so successfully that when Salomon Hercberg, the head of the Łódź ghetto police, was finally arrested in March 1942, German police found a haul of furs, food and jewellery as well as 2,955 marks in his three apartments. Corruption was essential to life in a society bound up by impossible regulations, fostering secret channels of communication of benefit to those who had some kind of 'pull' themselves.[78]

If smashing society altogether remained a utopian dream, the German occupation certainly succeeded in fostering communal fears and resentments. Jews resented Poles, who took over their 'Aryanised' businesses, or used the shadow of the German presence to abuse, attack and rob them. For their part, some Poles claimed that it was Jews who had started the atrocities against ethnic Germans during the military campaign, continued to imagine that they possessed vast wealth in furs and gold and diamonds, and resented the fact that Jews were exempt from forced labour in Germany. Reflecting on these real and imaginary differences, one of the reporters to the Polish Government in Exile in London warned that 'Poles and Jews equally have the typical human inclination to see only advantages in the situation of the other side, and only disadvantages and difficulties in what they experience themselves'. But their positions were not equal. As early as the winter of 1940 Jan Karski – himself appalled by the conditions he witnessed in the Warsaw ghetto – nonetheless felt that he had to explain the real state of public opinion to the Polish Government in Exile. Karski warned that by giving the Poles privileges over the Jews, the Nazis were able to turn the Jewish question into 'something akin to a narrow bridge upon which the Germans and a large portion of Polish society are finding agreement'. The Polish Government, anxious to present a liberal and emancipatory image abroad, responded by editing out these sections of Karski's report from the version circulated to the Allies. Back in Poland, such reciprocal hostility fed off both communities' relative, but unequal, powerlessness.[79]

What could Jewish parents and teachers tell their children? It was difficult to know what ideals or what future could possibly appeal to them. Paulina Braun, a composer in the pre-war Polish theatre, wrote a number of songs in the ghetto especially for the singer Diana Blumenfeld. In one hit that she sang in the prime venue of the Femina Theatre, she put herself in the position of a mother trying to answer her child's questions about what it means to be a Jew:

> Tell me, dear Mother, if it is a sin
> That I am such a small Jewish child? . . .
>
> – A Jew, my dear child, that is suffering,
> A Jew, my dear child, is a burden,
> A Jew, my dear child, can not avoid
> Evil fate, when hate comes.
> A Jew, my dear child, means faith,
> A Jew never loses his courage.
>
> The Jew is holy, my child, believe me,
> The only one who knows the taste of tears,
> Persecutions, troubles, suffering without end.[80]

But this was a lament performed primarily for adults, expressing their anxieties about their 'hour of misfortune'. And even here Paulina Braun had acknowledged how much children had seen and how little could be concealed from them. All the rage that hunger and powerlessness could awake in a Jewish child was concentrated in the eight-year-old whom Emmanuel Ringelblum heard screaming, 'I want to steal, I want to rob, I want to eat, I want to be a German.'[81]

V

THE GREAT CRUSADE

'INCREDIBLE, wonderful news!' Dawid Sierakowiak rejoiced on Sunday, 22 June 1941. He had just learned of the attack Germany had launched on the Soviet Union the previous day. The entire Jewish ghetto in Łódź, Dawid wrote in great excitement, 'has been electrified by this message'. For the first time, it looked as if Hitler had opened a front on which he would rapidly be defeated. After the fall of France the previous summer, Nazi power had seemed unshakeable and all the optimistic rumours of the first months of German occupation had faded. Dawid had learned to take such a sober view of good ghetto news that he did not even dare to believe in the Soviet war until it was confirmed by the German-controlled press on Monday. Only then did he start to hope for his imminent liberation by the victorious Red Army.[1]

Dawid's hopes would eventually be fulfilled. The Red Army would triumph, but not before the *Wehrmacht* had destroyed most of the forces it possessed in 1941 and had overrun the western Soviet Union. Soviet troops would not reach the gates of Łódź till 18 January 1945. By then the ghetto would be completely destroyed, and of the 190,000 Jews confined there at one time or another, only a few hundred would emerge from their hiding places to greet their liberators. Dawid himself would not live to see that day.[2]

The speed and success of the German assault on the Soviet Union rapidly drove Dawid to despair. 'I have completely lost my head since yesterday,' he wrote on 1 July. 'Can there be no end to the constant German victories? The myth simply has to burst some day! It has to!'[3] After he heard on 19 July that the Germans had completed their conquest of Belorussia by capturing Smolensk and opening up the road

3. Building models in the Hitler Youth, 1942.

Bomben auf Coventry

HEFT 84   20 PF.
Kriegsbücherei der deutschen Jugend

4. 'Bombs on Coventry': cover of weekly publication for German youth.

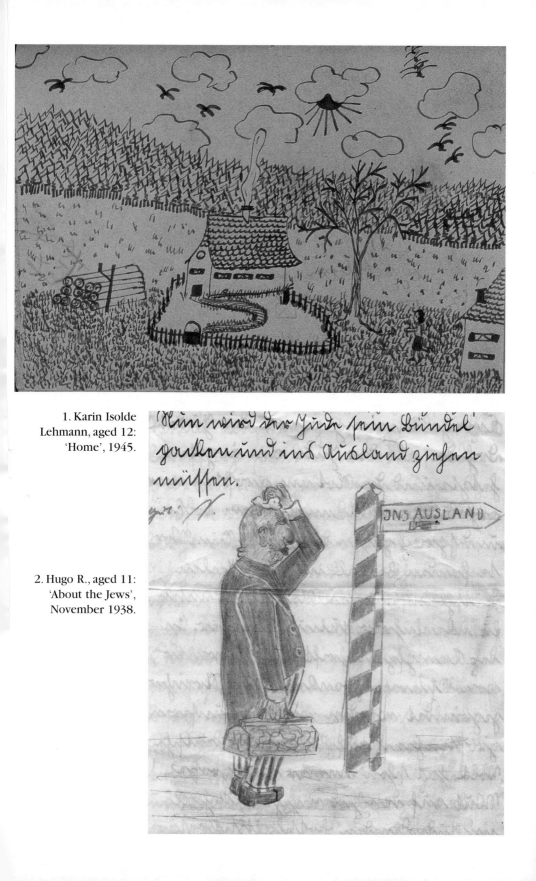

1. Karin Isolde Lehmann, aged 12: 'Home', 1945.

2. Hugo R., aged 11: 'About the Jews', November 1938.

prisoners digging another grave and was surprised to see the wounded man he brought tea to drink only that morning being led to it and made to lie down there before being shot by a non-commissioned officer. As the men began to argue about whether the shooting was justified, Robert heard that the wounded man had been a commissar. A devout and reflective man, Robert was finding that there were many things in this campaign about which he felt he could not write home to his wife. Instead, he confided them to the parallel entries in his diary, which he hoped to share one day with his wife and son, Rainer.[6]

The next day, Robert's machine-gun unit moved up towards the front line. As they drove past a village he saw male civilians digging a large hole, while women and children stood to the side. 'Some twenty in all,' he noted in his diary. 'Execution?' he asked himself as the truck sped on, soon reaching a stretch of road in which the ditches on both sides were full of war material, shot-up cars and dismembered horses. In the fields to the left and right there were more and more dead, including many civilians. By the evening, as they headed towards Minsk, they came upon the fresh graves of German soldiers on either side. They passed a mass grave on their right. Some said fifty Germans lay there, others that it was Russians.[7]

On 28 June, Robert's unit went into action for the first time. Trying to break through the fortified line between Stołpce and Koidanov, they took cover in the ditch by the side of the road where they came under heavy fire. Robert found that when he tried to speak to his comrades his mouth was full of earth from jumping into holes. Before them stood a field of tall golden corn which the scouting party had to secure. Behind them a petrol tanker burned out of control on the road. As they counted their dead and wounded afterwards, Robert was upset by seeing the chicks and young geese running around the wooden house nearby. When he ventured inside, he met the helpless gaze of the kids choking on their tethers. A small boy and girl came running over the field with their arms up, pale and with tears running down their cheeks, their looks asking whether they might enter the house. Robert was so thrown that he answered them in French, the language of his last campaign.[8]

On the same day, Robert confided in his diary that he had heard of a Führer order prohibiting the summary execution of prisoners. 'I am pleased. At last!' he commented. 'Many of those who had been shot I saw lying with their hands raised and without weapons and even to Moscow, Dawid had to find something else to occupy his mind. He turned his hand to translating Hebrew poetry into the ghetto's Yiddish idiom, choosing Saul Tschernichowsky's 1902 poem 'Baruch of Magenca'. In this harrowing account of a slaughter of Jews during the Middle Ages, Tschernichowsky had sought divine comfort in their martyrdom:

> Alas, my God, Thou hast delivered
> Thy sheep, like things abhorred,
> Into the hands of strangers, who abuse them.[4]

Many of the 3 million German soldiers massed for the attack in June 1941 felt a profound sense of participating in a historical undertaking. The Nazi-Soviet pact of 1939 had done little to eradicate the violent anti-Communism which united Nazis and mainstream Christian conservatives. Even some of the regime's most vocal conservative and religious critics now rallied to its side. Despite his own bitter feud with the Nazi regime over its closure of Catholic convents and monasteries in his diocese, and despite his mounting opposition to the murder of German psychiatric patients, Count August Clemens von Galen, the Bishop of Münster, joined some other Catholic bishops in offering prayers for this 'successful defence against the Bolshevik threat to our people'.[5]

Robert R., a Catholic schoolteacher from southern Germany serving on the eastern front, resolved that this time he would keep a diary charting the German crusade against Bolshevism, having failed to take notes on the French campaign. He crossed the River Bug, which had divided the German and Soviet zones in Poland, on the third day of the campaign, the thick dust blown up by his truck obscuring much of the countryside from view. On 25 June, he was woken by the sound of two shots as he tried to snatch a nap in the afternoon. Cross at the idea that someone was shooting at a dog, he got up to investigate and found a crowd of soldiers clustered around a grave that two Russian prisoners had been forced to dig before being shot in it. The men said that one of them had fired after surrendering and that the other had been found with dum-dum bullets. One of them still kept moving his arm for some time in a vain attempt to escape his grave after the earth had been shovelled over his body. Robert was in time to see four more

5. German children
entering an air raid
shelter early in the war.

6. Polish child's drawing of taking
refuge in the cellar.

7. Krzysztof Aleksander, aged 13, Częstochowa, Poland, 1946: 'Night Raid'.

8. Aleksandra Łabanowskia, aged 9, Inowrocław, Poland, 1946: 'Mummy's sad memories from Ravensbrück'.

9. S. Kwiatkowski, aged 13, Warsaw, Poland, 1946: 'Execution'.

10. German camp for Polish children in Łódź.

11. Jewish children playing at ghetto policemen, Łódź ghetto.

12. Jewish children playing on Krochmalna Street in the Warsaw ghetto.

13. Liliane Franklová, aged 11–12, Theresienstadt ghetto: 'Soup kitchen'.

14. Ilona Weissová, aged 11, Theresienstadt ghetto: 'Entrance to fantasy land'.

15. Maria Mühlsteinová, aged 11, Theresienstadt ghetto: 'Sold out!'.

16. Zuzana Winterová, Theresienstadt ghetto: 'Order of the day'.

17. German air raid shelter in the Ruhr.

18. Hitler Youths and League of German Girls helping feed the bombed out, Düsseldorf, 1942.

without belts. I saw at least a hundred lying like that.' In the first fortnight alone, Army Group Centre in which Robert R. was serving took over 300,000 prisoners in two huge battles of encirclement near Białystok and Minsk.[9]

Robert R. was wrong. There were orders from the Führer, but they said the opposite of what he imagined. More than once, Hitler had instructed his senior commanders that this war was to be one of conquest and annihilation, in which German soldiers must not look upon Red Army men as 'comrades' deserving dignity or respect. From the start of the campaign, unit commanders were under no compulsion to proceed against soldiers who committed offences against civilians or prisoners of war. The *Einsatzgruppen* were also ordered to shoot on sight all political commissars and Jews in Party and state offices, and it was left to their commanders to decide how broadly to interpret these orders. And when they came across Sinti and Roma, some *Einsatzgruppen* executed them without any orders at all.[10]

In September 1939, the German public and *Wehrmacht* had been deluged with propaganda about Polish massacres of ethnic Germans. So now the media concentrated on the need to avenge Soviet atrocities, such as the Lwów prison massacre carried out by the retreating NKVD. Many German soldiers wrote to their families, privately confirming the media's accounts. As one man put it, 'This time an end will certainly be put to this God-hating power', having seen 'evidence of Jewish, Bolshevik atrocities, the likes of which I have hardly believed possible . . . You can well imagine, that this cries for revenge, which we will certainly also take.' On the home front, the response was similar, with voices demanding what the Security Police happily called a 'radical treatment of the Jewish question at home in response to the horror stories about Jewish-Bolshevik atrocities on the eastern front'.[11]

Propagandists manipulated another powerful image, the gun woman, a Communist perversion of the natural order, the *Flintenweib*. There really were many Soviet female front-line troops, and German soldiers thronged to see and photograph them when they were brought in as prisoners in the summer of 1941. They often treated them as irregulars and shot many of them out of hand. As their propaganda contrasted the domestic ideal of the German wife and mother at home with the image of a cruel and untamed Russian woman of the steppes, the men of the *Wehrmacht* were seized by fascinated anxiety. When a middle-aged salesman from Bremen informed his wife that a *Flintenweib* had been handed over to his police battalion to be dealt with, he described her as 'a person of twenty, dark and forbidding, in uniform and high boots . . . Dreadful that women give way to such things.' He was fairly confident, he wrote home, that his comrades would shoot her. The second *Wochenschau* from the Soviet campaign set a captured *Flintenweib* before German cinema audiences, provoking a response not seen since the footage of black soldiers among the French captives of 1940. According to the reporters for the Security Police, the representative view was that such women 'should not be allowed to live'.[12]

On 27 October 1941, Robert R. was ordered for the first time to take part in a 'pacification action' himself. As his men drove civilians at gunpoint out onto the steppe before firing rockets into the thatch to set their villages ablaze, Robert found himself shaking with horror and praying constantly. He screamed orders to drive the women and children away, feeling 'like weeping'. Of all this, it was only his desire to weep which he could relate to Maria in his letter the next day, confining the details of the action to the pages of his diary. She can have had no inkling of the deeds underlying this sudden admission of weakness.[13]

Robert's sense of shame in the excesses of the German crusade grew, but still he held firm to his conviction that it was fundamentally justified. He had only to look at the Russian wounded, abandoned on the battlefield by their comrades, to reflect on how cheap life was in Russia. Indeed, he returned again and again to the thought that it was not only his patriotic duty to fight this war, but still more his paternal duty. If it would prevent his two-year-old son Rainer from having to come and fight a war here in the future, then he was ready to do it again and again. Robert, like every other German, had learned on 22 June that the *Wehrmacht* had attacked the Soviet Union in order to prevent an imminent assault by the Bolsheviks. Like most, he seems to have believed it. But his very need to repeat the point suggests how much emotional energy he had to expend in self-justification. Part of his problem, he wrote to Maria, was that he saw her and Rainer in the faces of all the Russian women and children. When his unit took the village of Pochep on 20 August, he had again been overwhelmed with feelings of shame, brought on by the old men, women and children who kissed his hands, embraced his boots and wept with gratitude when he told them that they would not be shot or burned out.[14]

This inner moral tension was compounded by Robert's growing

expectation of death, and his grief for his dead comrades. He had slept fitfully before going into the action at Pochep. He dreamed that he and Maria had gone to a memorial service in the cathedral in Eichstätt. He drew her attention to the many graves – 'Look, there are so many of them!' Then he knelt down before the altar for a long time, until someone snarled at him to move on. But in the altercation he lost sight of Maria and saw instead that a post office had been set up in the cathedral and people were working there at a frantic pace to process the soldiers' mail. As he looked for Maria in the packed congregation, people asked him whether it was true that he had died too. 'No,' he replied in his dream, 'but I'm alive!' While he went to kneel in the front pew – 'which I take to be reserved for me' – Robert found himself thinking, 'Oh, now I won't see Maria any more.' Full of forebodings of his own death, Robert's dream also conveyed something else, which became ever more prominent in his diary and letters to his wife: his sense of being cut adrift from his home and community by the ruthless brutality of this war. As he fought out his moral dilemma within himself, his sense of shame, gloom and inner tension grew and he concentrated his hopes on his wife and young son. Rainer, the son about whom Robert R. asked so often in his letters and whose toddler discoveries brought Robert so much joy, did not appear in his dreams. The boy had been born on the night German soldiers were mobilised in 1939, and when Robert appeared suddenly on his rare periods of leave, Rainer hid things in the large boots of the strange man in his mother's room.[15]

Mortally wounded near Kashira on 4 December, Robert was carried for 5 miles by his comrades until they found a suitable place to bury him. Whether with fitting respect or unintended irony, they chose the entrance to a school. The four plain exercise books that comprised his diary were brought home to Maria. But one of Robert's wishes did not come true: his diary did not become a family chronicle. Even half a century later, when Maria allowed two local historians to publish them, she still did not show them to Rainer.[16]

How much German soldiers wanted their families to know about the war they were waging in the east varied greatly. Robert R. was striking in his attempt to broker his civilian and military selves in a parallel sequence of letters home and a private confessional diary. Most men were not capable of maintaining such a sharp division between the front and home. As they acclimatised to the East, they often found they needed to explain themselves to their loved ones. One forty-year-old Bremen salesman serving with Police Battalion 105 wrote to his wife in a matter-of-fact tone about the actions of his unit in the 'complete extermination of the Jews' in his district, including 'men, women and children', but then – as if conceding the moral problem – he asked her 'to think no more about it'. He also invariably reminded her not to tell their daughter about such things. At the same time he wrote proudly about the home movie he was making for them about the deeds of his unit in Russia. Eventually, this selfish, callous yet physically squeamish clerk plucked up courage to watch while his comrades carried out one of their many executions. This, too, he wrote to his wife, he had filmed for their family record, though it would be best, he added with his characteristic hesitation, if they waited to see it till 'later'. Men like him drew a different moral and aesthetic line from Robert R. Instead of putting themselves under the moral stress of distinguishing between what they wrote home and wrote for themselves, as Robert had done, they left it up to their wives to censor their letters for the children. Such men drew no line between the front and the home front, leaving this task to their families back home: there the line ran between adults and children.[17]

From the start, Jewish men were shot, whether or not they had held any office or been Communist Party members, but until the end of August, some SS and police units included women and children while others left them out. At about 3.30 p.m. on 22 August 1941, a tractor pulled a cart up to a quiet spot near the woods outside the small Ukrainian town of Belaya Tserkov, 45 miles outside Kiev. A group of Ukrainian militiamen stood around waiting under the command of SS-Obersturmführer August Häfner. As he recalled, they were trembling. The tractor had brought some eighty or ninety children, aged from six or seven to only a few months old. There were no adults among them. The children, Häfner remembered, were lined up along the top of the grave that had been prepared and shot so that they fell into it. The Ukrainians did not – perhaps could not – aim for any particular part of the body and many of the children were hit four or five times before they died. 'The wailing was indescribable . . . I particularly remember,' Häfner testified, 'a small fair-haired girl who took me by the hand. She too was shot later.'[18]

Two days earlier, on 20 August, the children had been found lying

in two small rooms on the first floor of a house in a side street of
Belaya Tserkov. German soldiers quartered in the surrounding houses
had been disturbed by the whimpering and crying of the children, who
had arrived the day before. When the men entered the house they found
the children lying or sitting on the floor of the two rooms in their own
faeces. The soldiers, men of the 295th Infantry Division, were shocked
and turned to their Protestant and Catholic military chaplains for help.
They took the problem of the children up the hierarchy to the Protestant
Divisional Chaplain, Kornmann, and his Catholic counterpart, Dr
Reuss. Both men went to visit the house that afternoon. There were,
Reuss stated in the report he filed the same day,

flies on the legs and abdomens of most of the children, some of whom were
only half dressed. Some of the bigger children (two, three, four years old) were
scratching the mortar from the wall and eating it. Two men, who looked like
Jews, were trying to clean the rooms. The stench was terrible. The small children, especially those that were only a few months old, were crying and whimpering continuously.

There was 'not a single drop of drinking water', *Wehrmachtoberpfarrer*
Kornmann confirmed, 'and the children were suffering greatly due to
the heat'. 'The visiting soldiers,' Reuss reported to Lieutenant-Colonel
Helmut Groscurth, the General Staff officer for the Infantry Division
in Belaya Tserkov, 'were visibly shaken, as we were, by these un-
believable conditions and expressed their outrage over them.'

The children were Jewish children, whose parents had been shot by
SS *Einsatzkommando* 4a during the previous eleven days. Three truck-
loads of children had already been taken away to be executed the
previous evening. Helmuth Groscurth immediately went to visit the
house with Dr Reuss, the ordance officer and a translator, and found
things just as Reuss had described them. While he was there,
Oberscharführer Jäger of the Security Police arrived and confirmed
that 'the children's relatives had been shot and the children were also
to be eliminated'. Desperate to prevent this, Groscurth first proposed
going to see the local military commander, the *Feldkommandant*,
Lieutenant-Colonel Riedl. When Riedl supported the actions of the SS
Einsatzkommando, Groscurth decided to go over his head and filed a
report to the Commander-in-Chief of Army Group Centre, Field
Marshal von Reichenau, at 6th Army Headquarters. Meanwhile,

Groscurth used his own men to prevent the SS from moving a truck they had already loaded up with children, and dispersed the Ukrainian militiamen who were preventing food and water from being brought into the house for the children.

In making his case to Reichenau, Groscurth was not quite sure of his ground. While he could tell him that he had 'asked the *Feldkommandant* whether he thought that the *Obersturmführer* had also received orders from the highest authority to eliminate children as well as adults', he did not quite dare to make his defence of the children a clear-cut issue of humanity. Or rather, within the Nazi system, the definition of inhumanity no longer directly equated with killing. As Groscurth formulated it, there were other grounds for intervening. The first was that the planned execution of the children was already public knowledge. Indeed, he claimed, the troops stationed in the vicinity were outraged by their treatment and were 'waiting for their officers to intervene'. Alongside this pragmatic reason, humanity also featured, but in a minor key: 'Both infants and children should have been eliminated immediately,' he wrote in the conclusion to his report on 21 August, 'in order to have avoided this inhuman agony.' By this time, Reichenau had already confirmed his support for 'the necessity of eliminating the children' as Häfner and the Security Police were demanding. But, even when backed into a corner by the collective might of the SS and police authorities, the military administration and his own Commander-in-Chief, Groscurth could not resist pointing out the moral difference between executing *francs-tireurs* and women and children. Such measures, he insisted, 'in no way differ from atrocities carried out by the enemy about which the troops are continually being informed. It is unavoidable,' Groscurth continued, 'that these events will be reported back home where they will be compared to the Lemberg [Lwów] atrocities.'

Reichenau was predictably furious. Singling out Groscurth's accusation of moral equivalence with Bolshevik terror, the Field Marshal condemned it as 'incorrect, inappropriate and impertinent in the extreme'. Warning that the report had already passed through many hands, he concluded that 'it would have been far better if the report had not been written at all'. Five weeks later, on 28 September, *Einsatzgruppe C* telegraphed from his front, 'Measures taken to register all Jews, execution of at least 50,000 Jews planned. *Wehrmacht* welcomes the measures requests radical action.' Over the next two days, armed Ukrainian militiamen and members of *Sonderkommando* 4a drove 33,771 Kiev Jews down into the ravine of Babi Yar and shot them, one by one, in the back of the neck. On 10 October, Field Marshal von Reichenau issued a general order to all his troops to co-operate fully in exterminating the Jews. Within two days the commander of Army Group South, Field Marshal von Rundstedt, had sent Reichenau's order to all of his commanders. Once Hitler too had expressed his delight at Reichenau's 'excellent' formulation, the Army High Command instructed all subordinate commands to issue orders along the same lines. Helmut Groscurth went on serving in the 6th Army and died at Stalingrad. His rapidly stifled intervention was a far cry from the protests about the actions of the SS in Poland in 1939, which General Blaskowitz had carried all the way to Hitler. This was a different kind of war.[19]

On Sunday, 9 November 1941, Lev Abramovsky was woken by the sound of shooting in the streets of the small Belorussian town of Mir. At his mother's shouts, the family rushed into the street, joining their neighbours as people fled in panic. Lev was barefoot and only managed to put on some galoshes. His eldest sister Zlata and her husband were carrying their toddler boys, and his mother had his three-year-old twin sisters, Lea and Briandel. But he, his sister and three of his brothers were able to run. The whole family headed towards the Jewish cemetery. As they ran, many people were shot by local police. Near the cemetery Lev took refuge in a barn, climbing up into the hayloft from which he could look out at the raised landmarks of the Jewish and Tartar cemeteries, and Count Mirsky's abandoned castle.[20]

The same morning, Regina Bedynska, the daughter of the Polish schoolmaster, had seen German soldiers arrive by truck from Stołpce. Unlike the pogroms in the Białystok region or the Baltic States, the local population had not risen to massacre its Jews and the Germans had to instigate the murders themselves. But the actual killing was done by the local police force, a group of about thirty volunteers formed within the first two weeks of the German occupation from local Belorussian men with a few Poles and Tartars among them. Some had had relatives deported under Soviet rule; others were known as aggressive Jew haters. Regina saw them killing Jews at the slaughterhouse. Thirteen-year-old Jacob Lipszyc was herded with his family by the

German soldiers and the local police to the town square. As the police began to open fire, he heeded his mother's plea and ran for it. His mother, brother and sister were killed by two machine guns mounted at corners of the square. Small enough to slip under the stairs of the ruined pharmacy, Jacob watched as hundreds of people surged in the packed square. A covered truck backed in. As the tarpaulin was pulled back another policeman began firing the machine gun that had been hidden underneath into the panic-stricken crowd of Jews.[21]

From his hayloft, Lev Abramovsky saw how a large column of Jews, stretching all the way back to the Catholic church in the village, was escorted to the pit near the castle from which builders normally dug out their sand. He saw how his mother and father, his two brothers, Motia and Elia, his sister Zlata and her husband Yeisif Landa were shot in the Jewish cemetery. He also saw how his sister's small children were picked up by the legs and battered to death against the tombstones. Later that afternoon, Belorussian policemen and German gendarmes came into the barn, stabbing through the straw on the floor with their fixed bayonets, and Lev and his remaining brother, Bera, were discovered in their hayloft and added to the column of Jews still queuing for their deaths at the sandpit near the castle.

Too closely guarded to break out, they were herded and beaten as they shuffled along towards the execution site Lev had seen so clearly from his hayloft. Ahead of them came the rattle of four or five heavy machine guns; around them the sobs, pleas and prayers of those being driven to their deaths. Dusk was gathering as Lev approached the site. He saw how 'crazy Yeshil', one of the Jews who was being made to shovel dirt over each layer of bodies, turned and lunged with his spade at a policeman, only to be shot and fall into the mass grave before he could reach his killer. Lev and his brother were in the last group. As they stood next to each other looking over the edge of the pit waiting for the machine guns behind them to open fire, they saw blood spurting out of the heaving mass of the dead and dying. Lev's brother Bera was killed instantly. Lev fell with him, toppled by the weight of the people behind him. Five or six people fell on top of him and he passed out.

When Lev came to, he was surrounded by warm bodies and warm blood. Following the direction of a draught of cold air, he scrambled through the dark, tangled mass of the dead towards the top and climbed out of the pit. It was snowing lightly and the police had left. Only one man stood there praying, but at the sight of Lev he ran away. Dazed and weeping, and feeling suddenly chilled, Lev began to wash himself in the snow and to vomit up the blood he had swallowed in the pit. Then he realised that he had lost the galoshes he had been wearing and made wrappings for his feet from a jacket he found on the ground, before finally stumbling down the road out of town. He took refuge in the barn of a forester whom his father had known. The next day, they bathed him, gave him fresh clothes and sat him on top of the Russian stove. Lev could not stop crying convulsively until they gave him a herbal remedy. The forester even rubbed down Lev's frozen toes with badger's oil, but still he could not hold down any food. During the two days that followed, Lev stayed in the house while the forester found out what was going on in Mir. When he learned that those who had survived had returned to the ghetto and were being left in peace, and that his eldest brother Yankel – who had been away from the ghetto on the day of the massacre – was there too, Lev walked back to Mir and rejoined the survivors. Among them he found his two other sisters, El'ka and Lea.

Lev remained in the ghetto until August 1942. This time the Jews had advance warning of a pogrom and the small group of armed Jews in the ghetto chiselled a hole at night through the stone wall of the castle where they had been confined. Lev happened to be sleeping on the very staircase landing where they dug the hole and had no time to find his two sisters before making good his own escape. As the group with weapons tried to beat back those, like Lev, with none, this second group of some twenty unarmed Jews made their own way to the Tartar cemetery and into the forest. There Lev joined the partisans.

By November 1941, the German Army was reporting that the Belorussian countryside was teeming with Jews and regularly searched the former Soviet–Polish border region and along the Minsk–Brest railway. At the same time other Jews in ghettos like Baranoviči refused to believe the tales of mass murder brought by survivors from Gorodišče, Lachoviče and Ansoviči, and even when the Germans came to make selections, hoped they might be spared. In Slonim, a local Russian teacher observed how artisans and those with German language assumed that their skills were indispensable. In Baranoviči itself, 140 of the 157 arrested in a round-up in August 1941 had papers they expected the Security Police to respect. It did not. Lev Abramovsky was not alone in returning to a ghetto after a massacre. Even as late as the new year 1943, many of the ghetto dwellers of Iv'e believed German promises and returned voluntarily from the forests.[22]

The flat Belorussian countryside had inhospitable swamps, which defeated both the hunters and the hunted. But Jews were able to find sanctuary in the untamed forests of the region. Frida Nordau and her family dug two holes in the forest. They hid in one, leaving the other empty but with its camouflage of branches, so that raiding parties would think the occupants had moved on. The forests were full of runaways, especially Red Army men who had evaded or broken out of captivity. While the bands were still too weak and disorganised to worry the Germans, the small groups were a threat to each other as they competed for provisions and control of the forests. In eastern Poland and Belorussia, the German Security Police reported on numerous battles between Polish and Jewish groups, which usually ended with the complete destruction of the defeated party. As members of the Belorussian administration, police and other nationalist organisations set up by the Germans went over to the partisans in the later stages of the occupation, so, too, they strengthened the older anti-Semitic views of Jews as spies and poisoners of wells. Things became so bad that some leaders of Communist partisan brigades reported to their Soviet superiors that only recourse to the death penalty would enable them to contain the hatred for the Jews within their own units.[23]

What drove Jews back to the ghettos so often was hunger. Villagers sought to defend themselves from the ravages of the forest bands. As the German occupation became harsher and the bands larger, villages often found themselves caught up in the middle of the escalating cycle of reprisals and counter-reprisals that characterised the partisan war. Village elders usually had to play the leading role in selecting both forced labourers to work in Germany and those to be handed over to the Germans in reprisal for local acts of resistance. From mediators they were becoming enforcers.[24]

Even though some Jewish fighters were able to join these partisan groups – in March 1944 the 4th Belorussian Partisan Brigade had almost as many Jews as Russians among its 578 members – other ghetto escapees formed their own autonomous Jewish groups. By the turn of 1942–3, Jewish groups in the forests were strong enough to undertake joint actions with the Soviet partisans. But they often saw their purpose differently. A large group like the 1,200-strong Bielski partisans set up on their own, because they wanted to save lives as much as they wanted to fight the Germans. Like other bands, their fighters had great status, but they also took in – and fed – the old, the sick and the forest children. Tuvia, their leader, set a personal example by feeding children on the march with his own bread. In 1943, as German power began to wane, breakouts from the last of the ghettos reinforced the Bielski. When 150 people fled from the Novogrudok ghetto via a secret tunnel, some of the new arrivals brought their tools with them, and soon peasants who had been afraid of the bands were making their way to the forest to have metal and leather work done by the Jewish artisans who now existed nowhere else.[25]

Large groups of orphaned and abandoned children often followed the Polish, Ukrainian and Soviet partisan bands too. These '*besprizorniki*', or homeless children, the survivors of ghettos and villages that had been destroyed in anti-Jewish and anti-partisan actions, roamed the forests trying to live off nuts, mushrooms, berries and tree bark. But as many bands feared the loss of mobility which these hordes of homeless children entailed and drove them off, the children risked being shot not only by the Germans but also by Soviet or Polish partisans. Some tried to make themselves useful to the partisans, running messages and arms through the many German roadblocks, or spying out German positions and movements. Apart from the risk of German discovery, such children also risked the lives of the partisans who had trusted them – and who might avenge any suspected betrayal on their relatives. Like some of the groups of child-smugglers in the ghettos, these forest children often depended on one another for their survival: if their forest gangs became their new families, then they were as likely to have to act as the parent as the child.[26]

The Bielski children, wearing cut-down, cast-off adult clothing, mimicked adult behaviour, going off on their own to play at Germans and partisans, but also spending much time spying on the adults and watching the ebb and flow of sex under the trees. Among the Bielski, one small boy called Garfunk charmed everybody by springing to attention before Tuvia in the morning and announcing, 'Commander, allow me to report that in our *ziemlanka* whoring has been taking place.' Indeed, the one member of the Bielski who moved freely between all the partisan units in the Naliboki forest was Dr Hirsch. They all needed him to perform numerous abortions.[27]

*　　*　　*

While the Jewish survivors of Belorussia tried to salvage something of their lives in the forests, in the towns and villages all signs of their former presence were being rapidly eradicated. Like an army of locusts, the Germans stripped the land bare. Everywhere, they blamed the Communists and Jews for having robbed and exploited the populace before murdering and robbing it themselves. This was both official policy and unofficial business. The Higher SS and Police Leader for Central Russia, Erich von dem Bach-Zelewski, recovered 10,000 pairs of children's socks and 2,000 pairs of children's gloves, and had them sent via the *Reichsführer SS*'s personal staff to SS men's families as Christmas presents. As the *Feldpost* and men on home leave carried food parcels and Jewish loot back to Germany, the physical by-products of German destruction spread far and wide. It is doubtful how much children understood about the provenance of these goods, but they were often not entirely ignorant. In the Dornfeld kindergarten in Galicia, children learned to distinguish between the brass spoons 'from Jewish supplies' and the aluminium ones from their Lwów office, and their teacher reported that one three-year-old steadfastly refused to eat his soup until he was given a shiny aluminium 'Germany-spoon'. For this toddler, the difference between brass and aluminium had most likely been established by status and approval.[28]

Hitler had been 'prophesying' the 'destruction of the Jewish race in Europe' since 30 January 1939, and the Nazi Party ran off the Führer's prophecy as a poster for its 'Slogan of the Week' in September 1941. On 16 November 1941, Goebbels published an article in *Das Reich*, the upmarket weekly which he had modelled on the *Observer*, under the heading 'The Jews are guilty', warning that 'we are now experiencing the implementation of this prophecy'. 'In provoking this war, World Jewry,' Goebbels continued, 'has completely miscalculated the forces at its disposal and is now experiencing a gradual process of annihilation which it intended us to suffer and would inflict on us without any qualms if it had the power to do so.' Two days later, Alfred Rosenberg was even more explicit at a press conference. He lapsed from the official language of 'deporting the Jews' into speaking of the 'biological eradication of the entire Jewry of Europe'. It was as if the excitement of unleashing the long-awaited war against the Jews was too much for these men and, whatever their political circumspection about public announcements, they also had a great inner desire to lay claim to the momentous decisions they were helping to make.

But it would still have taken a keen-eyed reader to grasp from such utterances alone that the well-worn metaphors of the regime had changed their practical meaning.[29]

As the news percolated back to Germany of Jews, other civilians and prisoners of war shot in mass graves, there was already so much that people knew but did not want to know. The talk of soldiers on leave and the gossip of letters, some confessional, others matter-of-fact or even boastful, told wives and parents, mothers and even – inadvertently – children things they had not been told officially. In 1941, references to Jews being made to dig their own graves before being shot even found their way into a volume of soldiers' letters published by the Propaganda Ministry.[30]

The deportation of Jews from Germany had also begun shortly before Goebbels published his article, and adults who wanted to know had a pretty good idea of what happened to them. Michael Meister, a lawyer and run-of-the-mill Nazi Party member, carefully photographed the eviction of Munich's Jews, their construction work on their transit camp near the Milbertshofen Station and their further incarceration, in order to document the contribution made by the municipal economic office in which he worked to cleanse the city of Jews. In Minden near Bielefeld, by late November and early December 1941, people were talking about what was happening to the Jews from their town. They were able to stay on the passenger trains they had left on until Warsaw. 'From there on,' people reported back, they went 'in cattle cars . . . In Russia, the Jews were to be put to work in former Soviet factories, while older Jews, or those who were ill, were to be shot . . .' Over the next year and a half, the authorities noted but were unable to stop the flow of information back to Germany about the mass shootings. There had been too many separate actions, and too many spectators and witnesses. Whereas tens of thousands of German soldiers had seen the killing sites in Poland in the autumn of 1939, now hundreds of thousands, even millions, had seen the killings at first hand. The desire to take photographs and write home about them was just as strong.[31]

Whether teenage children had any idea of what was going on depended to a large extent on what their parents knew and told them. On 31 August 1943 the fifteen-year-old daughter of Berlin Social Democrats, Liselotte Günzel confided to the pages of her diary, 'Mummy told me recently most of the Jews have been killed in camps, but I can't believe it.' As if to check that reality had not escaped her sense of moral proportion, she reflected, 'It's good that they're gone from Germany, but actually to murder them!' Another girl from Berlin simply remembered this as the time her parents would fall silent in their conversation when she entered the room; her father was both a Nazi and a pastor. What caused her grief and confusion decades later was the thought of 'Uncle' Leonhardt, the elderly Jewish man who used to read her fairy stories in their block of flats. One day he was no longer there; he had left her his copy of Andersen's tales.[32]

Many husbands and fathers simply could not bring themselves to write about the war itself to their children, and returned to the techniques which had served absent fathers so well during the first winter of the phoney war. They tried to maintain a precarious sense of contact by writing about the war as a form of travel. Gisela's thirty-eight-year-old father was called away from his printing press in Leipzig in 1941 and sent to guard Soviet prisoners of war in Graudenz in West Prussia. But what he described to his twelve-year-old daughter in October 1942 was the tranquillity of sitting by the river watching the barge traffic and the anglers.[33]

Posted to the eastern front in time to experience the retreat from the Soviet Union in 1943, Ingeborg's father wrote home to the Rhineland about the heat of the early-morning sunshine, the lack of piped water in the huts, turning the squalor, which other letter writers roundly cursed as evidence of Communist and Jewish exploitation, into an exotic travelogue. Ingeborg could hardly have missed his physical joy in being alive as he described waiting for his 'Turkmen soldier' to bring him enough buckets of water to have a wash and shave in the summer warmth of an early morning. Like so much travel writing he moved easily from describing the Russian primitiveness of having to fetch unclean water from a distant well – 'Now you can imagine how much we long for a glass of water from the tap like you have in H. And how you ought to thank God that you have lovely clear water in the homeland' – to marvelling at the strange beauty the steppes held for European eyes, as the sun set over the wild flowers. He had picked some to press and send home, a solitary and peaceful activity, which – like the letter writing itself – took him away from the forced dependence and intimacy of his *Kameraden* by reminding him of the attachments to his family and home.[34]

Eleven-year-old Ingeborg wrote back to her father about looking after her siblings, especially her little sister, Lotte, who would snuggle up to her while she sat near the oven to pen her letters. Lotte's toddler games of the princess and the robbers, her 'Wu, wu, wu' at the dogs who surrounded them in the park, must have given her father a small piece of home. He treasured Inge's letters so much that he still had them on him when his unit faced capture in Romania. Before his war against the Russians ended, he buried them under a tree, and they mattered enough for him to return and dig them up again in the 1950s. From Leipzig in Saxony, Gisela wrote excitedly to her father in Graudenz about hunting for Easter eggs in her pyjamas. But as her silences lengthened, her father could not help upbraiding her for her 'laziness'. Searching for ways of maintaining contact, he eventually hit on making the twelve-year-old his secret agent, sending her out to buy her mother a present from him for their wedding anniversary.[35]

Up on the Dutch border, school was once more disrupted by the Russian campaign. So many teachers had been called up that eleven-year-old Trudi was generally home again by eleven o'clock. Otherwise, she assured her father, everything was normal. The only novelties at home were the collections for the soldiers, the new coloured maps of the front at school and the large numbers of Russian prisoners being put to work on the local estate. The children were curious and reported how 'stupid' they were said to look. But she knew that they were also dangerous. Writing as if they were wild animals in a zoo, Trudi reported to her father how one of them had 'broken out briefly and murdered a woman in the neighbourhood. He was caught,' she continued, 'and has been shot already for sure.' But, she assured him in September 1941, all was well and the family had enough to eat.[36]

In 1943, Hitler finally agreed to let the Labour Offices conscript German domestic servants to do war work. In many families with the right connections to the Party, the Labour Offices or in the occupied territories, they were almost immediately replaced by teenage girls from Poland, Russia and the Ukraine. Compared with most of the millions of foreign workers in Germany by the summer of 1943, the 500,000 forced nannies were situated at the relatively privileged end of this hierarchy. They also came into closer contact with German children than did the factory workers braving the taunts of the Hitler Youth on the streets. Children were often too young to realise the boundaries that were all too evident to their nannies and parents. A toddler at the war's end, Edith P. remembered Franziska, the young Slovenian woman her father had brought home from Ravensbrück concentration camp, as a warm, comforting presence. Franziska used to pick her up and caress her in the night when her own harsh and unpredictable mother dumped the wailing child in the bathroom.[37]

For German children, their tale of these relationships started with the nanny's arrival like a Mary Poppins of the steppes at the front door, with padded jacket, wooden clogs or boots and hair in bunches. She did not speak German, had never seen an indoor toilet or bath and the first act of the children's mother was usually to scrub the nanny clean and impose German hygiene upon her. For the teenage nannies, the lice and dirt were the end of a tale of hiding in forests after their villages had been burned, of being hunted down by army units with dogs and loaded onto cattle trucks for a long journey with little food or water. Andreas G. was seven years old when Nastasia took over as his nanny in 1943. She was probably no more than fourteen or fifteen, but to his eyes she already seemed very womanly and grown-up. She came from the Ukraine and he liked her. Unlike his previous German nannies, she stayed and even after her redeployment in an armaments factory the following year, she came back on Sundays to visit. She ate with the family in the dining room, rather than in the kitchen, in breach of all the guidelines regulating contact between Germans and *Untermenschen*. Nastasia became close to Andreas through physical intimacy, washing his hair in the bath and letting him splash around, even when he soaked both of them. And she taught him a secret language, Russian. She was fun, whereas his mother was a rather strict and distant officer's wife.[38]

One day Andreas shocked Nastasia by calling out 'Hands up!' in Russian when they were playing with his soldiers on the floor. It was not a phrase she had taught him. Even worse, she found the commissar's red star his father had sent him. Whatever these moments meant to Nastasia, for seven-year-old Andreas the red star was merely the latest accoutrement for his war, the 1943 version of the kepi Christoph had treasured in Eisersdorf in 1940. Andreas admitted later he had already formed an image of 'the Russians' as 'Bolshevik subhumans' from his family and school, but it had nothing to do with her. For him Nastasia remained a warm and playful companion. She may have taught him Russian, but she was not one of 'the Russians'. And he did not tell on her when they argued about who would win the war.[39]

'Fighting the Russians' may have helped young boys to assert their male identity in an increasingly female environment. Lutz Niethammer was so delighted when his father sent him a wooden locomotive from Belorussia that he chose it as one of the only toys he took with him when they were evacuated from Stuttgart to the Black Forest. With its bright colours and black German script spelling out 'MOGILEW' on the front, the locomotive symbolised Lutz's boyhood in his 'female nest'. This did not stop the four-year-old saying, 'He should go now,' when his father came home on leave: quite the reverse, Lutz was only too happy to play the 'man' of the house in his father's absence.[40]

When nineteen-year-old Karl-Heinz Timm heard that his little brother Uwe wanted 'to shoot all the Russians dead and then pile them up' with him, he wrote home to the three-year-old in Hamburg, promising he would play with him when he came home on leave. Three days later, the young trooper wrote to his parents in some surprise to describe the warm welcome his unit had just received from the Ukrainian girls in Konstantinovka. 'Obviously, these people down here have not yet had anything to do with the SS.' When Karl-Heinz saw the figure of a lone Russian sentry as a 'meal for my machine gun', he was playing at a very different war in his SS *Totenkopf* Division from the games of his three-year-old brother; but each continued to idealise the other in his own mind. Meanwhile, other boys were updating their war games. They were playing at shooting prisoners in the back of the neck. They were not pretending to be members of the *Einsatzgruppen* – a name few would have recognised – but of the fearsome Soviet secret police, the NKVD. The shot in the back of the neck had become the ultimate symbol of Bolshevik terror, and so an irresistible subject for imagining the cruelty of the enemy.[41]

As the war in Russia dragged on, so the list of those who had died a 'hero's death' on the eastern front grew ever longer. Statistics could be concealed, but the columns given over in the newpapers to death notices grew longer: Gretel Bechtold's mother had started to cut them out after her son was killed in 1940. The worst fears that had been expressed at the start of the Russian campaign were being realised: the war had now begun to be long and costly. Death was difficult enough for small children to grasp at close quarters, but at a distance the loss of someone whose absence had become a normal part of their lives impinged on them principally through the pain and grief of their elders. A month after Gertrud L. received the news of her husband's death they held his memorial service in the church where they had been married by the same priest eight years before. As the congregation in the packed church wept quietly through the sermon, Gertrud could only stare ahead, dry-eyed. *Pfarrer* Kurowski posed the question of her faith directly. 'You have to ask yourself,' he asked, 'is there a Lord God, who permits the loving husband of such a young woman to be taken and four children to lose their father?' Where another widow might have doubted, Gertrud was comforted, drawn by his answer back into a familiar pattern of belief and worship. 'God,' he assured them all, 'does not place greater burdens on us than we can carry.' It was 3 May and the church was decorated with laurels. As the congregation filed out of the door, they passed a single steel helmet and a pyramid of rifles, representing the fallen soldier and his absent comrades. They reminded the congregation of the dignity of the struggle in which he had died. They were meant to mourn but also take pride in his death.[42]

Such displays of grief provided an occasion for communal action, as neighbours, family and friends turned out for the services of remembrance. These funerals without a body to bury, in which they had to sit silent and still in stiff, uncomfortable clothes, must often have made children feel suffocated. When Gertrud L.'s little boy, Manfred, found the gloom of his father's wake more than he could bear, he began tugging at his aunt Selma's arm and telling her that they should all sing 'All my ducklings' and other children's songs. What comforted his mother appeared tedious and possibly frightening to him.[43]

Many of the services for 'Heroes Remembrance Day' in the early years of the war were so laden with emotion and pathos that children who had lost no relatives felt moved to tears by the rendition of 'Ich hatt' einen Kameraden' or the ritual lighting of candles for the dead. But, as German losses on the eastern front rose in 1942, the regime decided that people needed cheering up. In a shake-up of radio schedules, Goebbels ordered more airtime to be given over to light entertainment. Despite the complaints of the bereaved, he decided to ration the regime's invocation of pathos.[44]

In an effort to bridge the gulf between home and front, German radio stations transmitted family greetings to the men in programmes like *Blinkfeuer Heimat* or *Gruss aus der Heimat*, as well as that most popular of all wartime schedules, the Sunday musical requests dedicated to loved ones in the *Wunschkonzert*. To mark Mother's Day and Christmas, the radio tried out live link-ups between mothers and sons, and husbands and wives. For the 500th edition of the daily

Kameradschaftsdienst (*Comrades Service*), which went out between 5 and 6 a.m., the radio even hosted a wedding of a suitably fairy-tale number of twelve brides and grooms. Pledging their vows live on air, the wives' wedding dresses and bouquets of lilies were described to their new husbands on their distant postings.[45]

As they listened to the German airwaves, soldiers were both comforted by schmaltzy light programmes and occasionally wrote in to complain, especially when they were addressed as '*Kameraden*' by 'young ladies', as if the 'home front' had lost all sense of propriety and respect for the uniqueness of male honour. This was only the most audible echo across the imaginative and emotional gulf that had opened between men at the front and their families at home. It was now far wider than it had been in the first years of the war. There was so much the men had seen and done for which they had no acceptable words.[46]

In the eastern territories themselves, the immediate effect of giving away the Jews' clothing and furniture, tools and farm implements to the local population was to make them complicit in the killings. Even if their non-Jewish neighbours had disapproved of their persecution, in towns like Slonim they helped themselves to the empty apartments in the ghetto afterwards. The donations also eased the crisis of manufactured goods somewhat, especially clothing and footwear, which the German occupation had deliberately created. Even before the campaign began, German policy had been to condemn the Soviet cities. As soon as the first plans were drawn up for the invasion of the Soviet Union in December 1940, the Ministry of Agriculture had advocated leaving up to 30 million Soviet citizens to starve to death in order to feed the German armies without putting a strain upon the home front. Only the rich agricultural and mining areas which might benefit Germany were to be protected.[47]

By the time the German armies became snowed in to their first winter of the campaign, they were stripping the countryside far and wide in their search for livestock and grain, horses and sledges, winter clothing, snowshoes, skis, furs and boots. Even now, when the local population was starving, the middle-aged Bremen salesman with Police Battalion 105 derived his greatest pleasure from sending food home to his family. He was careful to split up the consignments into small parcels, in case they attracted too much attention, sending dozens of

1–2 kilo parcels at any time. No doubt, his feelings of being a father far away from home found solace in being able to maintain his position of breadwinner under such trying circumstances.[48]

As 'national comrades' back in Germany were exhorted to give up furs and skis as well, the very activism of the Hitler Youth and League of German Girls revealed the scale of the crisis to the population at large. Meanwhile, a compulsory requisition of furs took place over Christmas in the Warsaw ghetto: it netted 16,654 fur coats and fur-lined coats, 18,000 fur jackets, 8,300 muffs and 74,446 fur collars. The Polish underground cheered itself by putting up posters depicting a German soldier huddled in a woman's fox-fur collar while he warmed his hands in her muff.[49]

As German cinema audiences saw the long columns of Red Army prisoners on the newsreels in the first months of the campaign, they worried who would feed them, fearful that German rations might have to be cut. By early 1942, 2.5 million of the 3.3 million Soviet prisoners taken had died. Tens of thousands had been shot in notorious forts, like Fort X in Kaunas, but most had died of enforced starvation. German civilian rations were indeed reduced in the 'Old Reich' in April 1942 for a five-month period, immediately depressing morale. This was to aid the *Wehrmacht*, not its prisoners of war. As usual in the Third Reich, the greatest burden fell elsewhere.[50]

Although Polish agriculture had already suffered greatly from the loss of workers to Germany, from now on it would have to deliver large quotas to Germany as well, a trend replicated across occupied Eastern and Western Europe. As acute shortage precipitated black-market inflation and hunger, those who suffered most were those locked in prisons, welfare institutions, ghettos and prisoner-of-war camps, and so barred from direct access to the countryside and often to the black market itself. The largest numbers of deaths by starvation would come, not, as the German experts had envisaged, from the wholesale starvation of the urban populations in the East, but from these imprisoned populations. But everywhere infant mortality rose sharply, as crucial fats became scarcer; in Poland it contributed to the absolute decline in population which set in from 1942–3.[51]

In Łódź, the 'Elder of the Jews', Chaim Rumkowski, opened allotments for the children to dig in the fresher air of the privileged district of Marysin. Sometimes he ordered extra distributions of food to the schoolchildren. But Dawid Sierakowiak's diary entries dwelt increasingly on his 'never-ending hunger'. Despite his best efforts to supplement the household budget by teaching his private pupils Polish, French, German, mathematics and Hebrew on the way home from school or on the windowsill of their crowded room, prices kept going up. The inflation was augmented by the influx of well-heeled and -dressed Jews: the 20,000 new arrivals in Łódź in October and November 1941 had been deported from the Reich and, despite their 'wonderful luggage and cartloads of bread', quickly bought up local supplies as they adjusted to the reality of a Polish ghetto, further impoverishing themselves and most of the other inhabitants in the process.

Still, the string of German victories had created an eerie quiet: more workshops were opened to meet German demand and talk of the war died down. Even Dawid found his thoughts focused on his personal rite of passage, as he graduated from his Jewish *gymnasium* with top marks in everything except gymnastics. On the last day of school he felt filled with a nostalgic melancholy. For once, he relaxed his constant awareness of the war and fate of the community, and allowed himself to be 'moved by such a trifle . . . because it's about me, and a new epoch in my life begins'. He hoped to go on to the *lycée*, but, as the schools continued to house the Czech, Austrian and German Jews, and the competition for work increased, the best he could do was use his contacts to secure a job in a saddlery. Branding by 'race' affected everyone. While the *yekkes*, as the Jews from Germany were known, were providing ample new material for the ghetto satirists and troubadours, the 5,000 Sinti and Roma who came with them were quarantined off in a separate sub-camp under the ghetto administration's control. Within weeks they were succumbing to starvation and typhus, and the Sinti and Roma children were dying in great numbers.[52]

The Russian campaign revealed more than Hitler's military hubris. It also revealed the impossibility of implementing a grandiose policy of racial colonisation. The *Wehrmacht* might be unable to defeat the Red Army in a blitzkrieg campaign, but already it had taken far more *Lebensraum* than there were Germans to live in it. More Germans had to be found. As early as September 1941, Heinrich Himmler was sending out German racial biological commissions to scour the orphanages of Belorussia not only for concealed Jewish children, but also for children suitable for 'Germanisation'. The aim, the *Reichsführer SS* explained, was to 'distil' every 'drop of good blood' out of the racial 'mishmash' of the Eastern nations, taking children with or without their parents' consent. This marked a new departure. In the first period of German rule in Poland, from 1939 to 1941, the SS Resettlement Office had concentrated on the cattle truck to alter racial demography, moving Poles and Jews out, and bringing Germans in. There had been many wrangles between different German administrations about how stringently to apply the national classification system, and how many Poles became German had varied radically from *Gau* to *Gau*, but only after the attack on the Soviet Union did the SS begin an ambitious project of 'Germanising' individual children. At the same time as the SS was killing Jews for their racial impurity, it began to dilute its own criteria of 'Germandom'.[53]

Much of this 'Germanising' activity took place in the same territory that had been the focus of German settlement and to which so many German teenagers had been evacuated for their safety, the Wartheland. The Youth Welfare Boards there were ordered to cooperate with the experts of the SS Race and Resettlement Office and the SS's own homes run by its *Lebensborn* organisation. Several thousand children were brought to Łódź, Kalisch and Brockau. A mere 250 to 300 actually made it through these first selections, with their sixty-two racial tests and prolonged observations of character. In Pabianice, three men came to the orphanage in 1943 and lined all the children up against a wall. Ilona Helena Wilkanowicz was one of the seven they chose out of a group of about a hundred. But, like many children in homes, she was not an orphan. Her father had tried – and failed – to prevent her being taken away. In the first half of 1943 a further 4,454 children, aged two–fourteen, were sent to the homes for screening from the General Government, as SS and Ukrainian units once more worked in conjunction with teams of girls from the Labour Service and League of German Girls to clear Polish villages for German settlement, this time in the Zamość district.[54]

In the 'double-think' of SS racial experts, these were German children whose previous 'Polonisation' was now being reversed, whatever the status of their parents. 'Foreign orphans' now became 'foundlings' in the quasi-legal language of the bureaucrats of the Reich Interior Ministry. On 10 December 1942 it authorised the establishment of a secret registration office at the *Gau* Children's Home at Kalisch in the Wartheland, which issued the children with new, German, identity documents. Often similar-sounding German names were chosen to make them easier for the children to accept: Ilona Helena Wilkanowicz became Helen Winkenauer. With their official rebirth, the children's trail went as cold for any Polish relatives trying to track them down as for new German parents who wanted to trace the origins of their 'ethnic German orphan'.[55]

On 7 June 1942 Reinhard Heydrich, Reich Protector of Bohemia and Moravia, died from his wounds, one of the few assassination attempts launched by Allied intelligence on the Nazi leadership to succeed. Two nights later the villagers of Lidice were ordered out of their homes in reprisal: 196 women and 105 children were taken away by truck and kept in a school in nearby Kladno, while their village was razed to the ground and their menfolk shot. The women were then sent to Ravensbrück concentration camp and the children went to Łódź, for further racial screening. Himmler hoped that the 'humane and correct education' which 'children of good race' would receive in German homes would prevent them from trying to avenge their parents' deaths. As it was, they came to Collection Camp II in Strzelców Kaniowskich Street, one of four transit and deportation camps in the city. Housed in old factory buildings, the conditions were much the same as had faced the deportees from the Wartheland in 1940. There was still no real plumbing and the children, anxious and hungry, were barred from going to the toilet except in convoy, once in the morning and again in the evening. Only seven children passed the screening tests and only seventeen of the 105 orginally taken could be traced after the war. Most of the rest probably perished.[56]

The Czech children selected for Germanisation were taken first to a convent in Łódź where conditions were better and then, in August, to a Wartheland children's home in Puschkau, where their 'Germanisation' began in earnest. Four of the children came from the same family in Lidice. They were the three Hanf children, Anna, Marie and Vaclav, and their eight-year-old cousin Emilie, who had come to stay after her mother died. They soon learned through beatings and food deprivation not to speak Czech to one another and, completely immersed in a German environment, some of them began to forget their mother tongue by the end of the year. Emilie was adopted by a childless couple in Sassnitz, who took her sailing on their boat, let her play with their German shepherd dog Zenta and had the local prisoners of war make her a doll's house for Christmas. Her new father,

Otto Kuckuk, was mayor of the town and held officer's rank in the SS. Vaclav Hanf, on the other hand, was never adopted because he had resisted learning German. Instead, he was passed from one institution to another, where the staff found frequent reason to beat him. The two sisters also had completely different experiences from each other. While Anna Hanfová was taught to play the piano by her adoptive family, Marie was turned into a domestic servant by hers. Both families knew that the girls were Czech, but it was Marie who experienced this through daily jibes and beatings.[57]

For younger children, it was virtually impossible to resist 'Germanisation' in the homes in the Wartheland. At three and five, Daryjka and Alusia Witaszek were too young to keep the memory of their parents alive, though Alusia did retain fragments – her own red coat and the black boots the German wore – of the day on which the police came to arrest their mother. But by the time the two girls, separated from their two older sisters, had gone through the children's camps at Łódź and Kalisch they were longing for a kindly, motherly person to come and take them away. Alusia easily won over her prospective German mother, Frau Dahl, to the idea of adopting both of them, but the *Lebensborn* officials proved intransigent. They insisted on separating the two girls so that no trace of their Polish childhood should remain. Although they had succeeded in overlaying all of Alusia's associations with Polish language and culture, so that she would never be able to speak it again without a distinct German accent, they did not succeed in making the older girl forget her little sister. If anything, the loss of both parents, her two elder sisters and infant brother had concentrated her attachment to Daryjka in a stronger bond than ever. At her urging, Frau Dahl continued to try to trace Daryjka, only to be thwarted by the *Lebensborn* bureaucracy until the war's end.[58]

For older children it was easier to organise their associations into a memorable and communicable form. Many already had a vivid and profoundly hostile sense of who the Germans were. Moreover, as in children's homes to this day so also in wartime, it proved harder to place older boys than girls or younger children. Alexander Michelowski was one of those never claimed from the *Lebensborn* home at Oberweis Castle in Austria. Despite the Hitler Youth routines of marching, singing and drilling, twelve-year-old Alexander maintained a sense of the Polish identity. In this he was enormously helped by being in a group of other Polish boys, who kept their language alive on their secret food-hunting expeditions in the cellars and neighbouring orchards and their late-night feasts in the dormitories, though they knew they would be badly beaten if caught speaking it. On one such raid to gather fruit, they were discovered by a Polish woman who had been brought to the farm as a forced labourer. She agreed to send and receive mail on their behalf, reconnecting them to their homes. Although Alexander failed to make contact with any of his family, he had another, secret, link to his Polish roots, which he carried with him. As he had waited in the station at Posen for the train that would take his group to Kalisch, a middle-aged woman had whispered to him and given him a picture of the Black Madonna of Częstochowa. She was, she told him, the mother superior of a nearby convent but did not dare to wear her habit because she was on a wanted list. Alexander, who had served as an altar boy, remembered her parting blessing, 'May the Mother of God protect you.'[59]

As more and more institutions for children were designated as 'camps', or *Lager*, there were camps and camps. In the well-resourced *KLV* camps organised by the Hitler Youth, teachers and People's Welfare, German city children were learning a kind of self-reliant confidence in keeping with the Nazis' aims. For Ilse Pfahl and her seventeen classmates from Essen, the seven months of 1941 they spent in the *KLV* camp in Kremsier were one long summer holiday. They went swimming every day – save for three they devoted to a sightseeing trip to Prague – and they used every birthday as an excuse to borrow their camp leader's radio and dance. As the time to go home drew near, the teenagers penned teasing verses in each other's albums, pretending to a greater sexual knowledge than they had yet experienced:

Uns kann keiner, auch nicht einer,	None can touch us, not one
auf der grossen, weiten Welt	In the whole wide world.
Uns kann keiner, auch nicht einer,	None can touch us, not one,
oder erst wenn's uns gefällt	Or only if we want to.
	Gretel

Ein Seehund lag am Strande	On the beach a seal lay
setzte sich seine Schwanze im Sande	buried his tails in the sand
möge dein Herz, so rein	may your heart be as clean
wie des Hundes Schwanze sein	as the seal's tails became.[60]
	Helga

The girls also marched in their League of German Girls' uniforms through the streets whenever the occasion arose, to greet and see off their youth leaders, and to disrupt the Catholic Czechs' Palm Sunday procession, or to mark the outbreak of war with Russia. For the girls, if not the Czechs, these were fairly innocent activities, a festive celebration of their power in the Reich Protectorate of Bohemia and Moravia, but still a long way from their fathers' war in the East.[61]

Such carefree adolescence stood in stark contrast to the First World War, when German girls of this age had died of tuberculosis in their thousands.[62] By comparison, the Nazis had largely succeeded in their efforts to shore up the German home front and to protect German childhoods from the costs of their war. Although the regime could not protect children from the death of fathers, brothers and uncles, it could and did protect them from malnutrition and labour in armaments factories. In the first years of the war, the Nazi regime had drafted millions of forced labourers from the occupied territories to make up the shortfall of labour in the Reich. With the assault on the Soviet Union, the Nazis had taken this policy further, creating a Continental-wide system of rationing and agricultural delivery quotas, which imposed starvation and rising infant mortality on their subject populations, so that Germans would not suffer such things.

Mass shootings had taken place right across the eastern front and had drawn hundreds of thousands, perhaps even millions, of German witnesses. Yet, as relatives and friends chatted on trams and trains and in shopping queues about what they had heard, it was possible to have knowledge without incurring responsibility. Hitler might prophesy the destruction of the Jews with increasing frequency, but he did not make the policy of mass murder public or ask the German people to approve it. Some teenagers, like Liselotte Günzel, might learn this secret too; others only sense that something was being kept from them, when Jewish neighbours disappeared or their parents fell silent when they entered the room. Auctions and markets selling Jewish property brought furniture and clothing whose origins were readily known into German homes. But there was also no immediate reason for most young Germans to spend a great deal of effort trying to understand these things. From 1935, Jewish children had been barred from German schools. By the outbreak of the war, the de-assimilation of Germany's remaining Jews had been virtually completed. Especially among the young, the Jews had come to exist largely as abstract propaganda stereotypes, as 'treacherous exploiters' and 'warmongers', not as real classmates or neighbours.

The war had given all the abstract lessons in racial superiority a tangible aspect. The Nazis made no secret of their exploitation of Eastern Europe and had published accounts about the brutal expulsion of Polish villagers to demonstrate how the promise of *Lebensraum* was being fulfilled in the East. Young women volunteers and girls doing their obligatory Reich Labour Service had had to play their part in these 'resettlement actions', while the boys and girls of Hitler Youth age had done their bit in symbolically reclaiming the streets and squares of the Polish and Czech towns to which they were evacuated. In Germany, even reformatory pupils jibbed at being treated equally to Polish workers on their probationary placements. Racism often had a contradictory and gendered character: Hitler Youth boys were seen throwing snowballs and shouting abuse at Polish and Russian workers, but also taking Polish girls to the cinema. Stories of killing might still exercise all the fascination of censored and illicit news, but the violent assertion of German racial supremacy had become almost too commonplace to notice.

VI

DEPORTATION

ON 1 December 1941, *SS-Standartenführer* Karl Jäger, Commander of the Security Police's *Einsatzkommando* 3, filed his report on his unit's activities in Lithuania. By this time the Nazis' 'final solution of the Jewish question' was taking shape. Jäger reported a total number of 'Jews liquidated by pogroms and executions' of 137,346, setting out the dates and places of each of the 117 different actions his men had undertaken and, like a good bookkeeper, itemising the 'total carried forward' at the bottom of each page. He also made it clear that he had spared only those communities the German civil and military administration had insisted were making a vital contribution to the war effort. While the SS seemed to be setting the pace in the Baltic States and Soviet Union, back in the Reich, others were lobbying the Führer to permit them to take action too. Goebbels finally persuaded him to introduce the Jewish star within the Reich from 1 September 1941, a public branding which made Jews afraid to face anonymous passers-by. Pressure began to mount again among the *Gauleiter* to deport their Jews to the 'east': whereas objections by German officials in Poland to the overcrowding of the ghettos had curbed these efforts in 1940, no such arguments were of any avail now. The ghettos at Riga, Minsk and Łódź became their immediate destinations. Those sent on the first trains to Riga and Minsk were shot within days. On 23 October, Jewish emigration across all of German-occupied Europe was banned. All the key meetings and discussions about mass murder took place in secret and, judging from the appointments kept that autumn by one of its chief architects, Heinrich Himmler, most of the work of briefing other power-brokers, resolving conflicts of jurisdiction and formulating policy was done at unspectacular meetings of two or three people.[1]

After calling a meeting of the Reichstag on 11 December to declare war on the United States, Hitler followed it up with a lengthy statement to the *Reich-* and *Gauleiter* the next day on the general situation. According to Goebbels's diary notes of the speech, the Führer harked back to the prophecy he had made in his Reichstag speech of 30 January 1939: 'He prophesied to the Jews that if they once more caused a world war, they would experience their extermination. This was not rhetoric. The world war is there, the extermination of the Jews must be the necessary consequence.' And that was all. The words had taken on a fixed and formulaic shape, repeated in Hitler's public and private pronouncements. On 30 January 1941, Hitler had reminded the Reichstag of his 'prophecy' that world war would spell the 'destruction of the Jewish race in Europe', and he would continue to reiterate this grim warning in public and private until he wrote his political testament in his Berlin bunker.[2]

It was clear to the conference of *Gauleiter* in December that the metaphor of 'extermination' was now going to become reality. After Hans Frank had consulted the Reich Security Main Office about actual measures, he briefed his officials in Cracow about what to do with 'these 3.5 million Jews' in the General Government. 'We can't shoot them, we can't poison them,' he conceded, 'but we will have to destroy them somehow, above all in connection with the measures to be discussed in the Reich.' He had been told in Berlin, 'liquidate them yourselves!' Stationary gassing facilities were already being constructed in the General Government at Bełżec under the direction of the ruthlessly ambitious Viennese Nazi and police chief of the Lublin district, Odilo Globočnik. Making use of the currently unemployed expertise of the personnel who had run the 'T-4 action' to kill German psychiatric patients, the SS learned at Bełżec how to build and operate its first gas chambers that November. Compared with the death camps it constructed at Sobibór and Treblinka in the months that followed, Bełżec was relatively small. But compared with the small shower room at the Hadamar asylum, with its capacity for twenty to thirty psychiatric patients at a time, Bełżec was being designed on a much bigger scale, large enough to murder the hundreds of thousands of Lublin Jews at least. Nor were the SS the only bureaucrats thinking along these lines. Even before Bełżec was built, the official in Alfred Rosenberg's new Ministry of the East in charge of racial questions wrote to the Reich Commissioner for the Ostland, Hinrich Lohse, making the same connection: former 'euthanasia' personnel, he opined, could show them how to construct gassing installations to eliminate Jews who were 'unfit' to work.[3]

On 20 January 1942, Heydrich called a meeting of State Secretaries to impress upon them the overarching authority of the Reich Security Main Office in the 'final solution'. He made its European-wide scope explicit, down to a table estimating the numbers of Jews in each country under German control. They came to 'over 11 million'. Even the twice rewritten minutes of this conference on the Wannsee, which turned all the talk of killing and extermination into 'evacuation' and 'resettlement', still impressed on the State Secretaries that no Jew could expect to survive these measures and that for Jewish 'half-breeds' forced sterilisation would count as a privileged exemption.[4]

Once the deportation trains began to roll from Central and Western Europe directly to the death camps in the spring of 1942, the very scale of the operation would spread knowledge through many lesser agencies into the furthest reaches of the Nazi empire. Occupied Poland became the centre of this new industrial killing, partly because of the size of the Jewish ghettos of Łódź and Warsaw, partly because of the good railway connections to the west and partly, no doubt, because from the start of the war Poland had served as a murderous laboratory for racial demography.

To the Jewish communities of the great ghettos in Poland these months appeared fraught with danger but they had little or no inkling yet of what was being set in motion. Although even boys like Dawid Sierakowiak carefully collected all the news circulating in the Łódź ghetto, the only harbingers of doom were the new arrivals from the Polish countryside, who brought tales of the terrible violence with which Germans had swept them up into the great ghettos. And even as late as the end of August 1942 the adult chroniclers of the Łódź ghetto were troubled by their inability to 'discover any guidelines in all of this, which is precisely what grieves everyone most'.[5]

Thanks to Karl Jäger's *Einsatzkommando*, the Jews of Vilna already knew their likely fate. On 6 September 1941, the Jews of this 'Jerusalem of Lithuania' were forced into the ghetto, but thousands were slaughtered in the weeks immediately beforehand and afterwards.[6] In the improvised music halls of the ghetto, those slaving in the German workshops hoped they might yet 'work to live', as the ghetto leadership urged them to do, and listened to the popular Yiddish theatre song 'Papirosn' ('Cigarettes'). But the song now had a new text:

Es iz geven a zumertog,
Vi shtendik zunik-sheyn . . .

It was a summer's day,
Sunny and lovely as always,
And nature then
Had so much charm,
Birds sang,
Hopped around cheerfully,
We were ordered to go into the ghetto.

There were too many of us –
The master ordered
That Jews from the area be brought
And shot at Ponar.
Houses became empty,
But graves then filled up.
The enemy has achieved his great goal.

At Ponar one can now see on the roads
Things, rain-soaked hats,
These things belonged to the victims,
To the holy souls,
The earth has covered them for ever.

And now it's sunny and lovely once again,
Everything around smells wonderful,
And we are tortured
And all suffer silently.
Cut off from the world,
Blocked by high walls,
A ray of hope barely awakens.[7]

Alongside the horror of the round-ups in the streets and the shootings at the huge pits in the nearby forest at Ponar, Rikle Glezer evoked the sense of isolation and abandonment felt by the Jews who remained 'cut off from the world' in the ghetto. Hers was the lament of a whole community, forced in upon itself, and she was heard by those lucky enough to have been issued with the precious yellow work permits, which entitled them to remain in the 'greater' ghetto. Yitskhok Rudashevski was among those who returned to the 'lesser' ghetto after one of these first deportation 'actions'. As he walked the streets, Yitskhok also saw the debris and detritus left behind after the deportation, the broken phylacteries and religious books strewn in the synagogue courtyard. 'Ponar hovers among the old ghetto streets,' Yitskhok felt, as he looked at everything that had been destroyed and abandoned: his fourteenth birthday would come soon. He found his uncle, who had survived the liquidation by hiding in a little room concealed behind a cupboard for a week.[8]

Once children in the Vilna ghetto learned the meaning of the words 'action', 'death transport', 'Nazi', 'SS-man', 'bunker' and 'partisan', they began to transpose them into their games. They would play at 'actions', 'blowing up bunkers', 'slaughtering' and 'seizing the clothes of the dead'. The ghetto lent itself to that particular variation of hide-and-seek which Yitskhok's uncle and so many children had just been playing for real. The game began by closing off all the doors and exits of a deserted inner courtyard. The children were then divided between the Jews, who had to hide under chairs, tables, in barrels and garbage cans, and the Lithuanian policemen and the Germans who came to look for them. If a dressed-up 'policeman' happened to find 'Jewish' children, he handed them over to the 'Germans'. As one cohort of children succeeded another, the 'blockade' game continued until at least 1943: only the name of the 'Kommandant' changed to keep abreast of reality; but he was always played by the strongest boy or girl.[9]

This allocation of roles was no accident. Among the children's other games was one called 'Going through the gate', which was based on the fact that the adult workers came and went through a single wooden gate to work outside the ghetto. One of the most feared and hated figures in the Vilna ghetto was Meir Levas, the head of the Jewish gate guards, a man who, Yitskhok noted grimly in his diary, personally flogged the small, frail boy called Elke who lived next door for smuggling flour and potatoes into the ghetto. The most terrifying and powerful figure Jewish children knew was Franz Murer, the German official in charge of the food supply to the ghetto, a man the children designated as the head of the Gestapo. As they played being Jewish workers trying to smuggle food into the ghetto and Jewish guards searching them for it, 'Murer' would arrive. Immediately, the 'Jewish police' would intensify its brutality and the 'workers' try desperately to throw away the incriminating packages. As soon as 'Murer' found some, the 'workers' were put aside and later whipped by the police.

The two biggest boys always got to play Franz Murer and Meir Levas, leaving it to the smaller ones to take the role of the adult Jewish workers, who, in reality, would often have included their own older brothers, sisters, aunts, uncles and parents. Like the adults they were playing, they were powerless to protect themselves from the blows rained upon them, in this case by the bigger, stronger children.[10]

Power resided in the uniform, just like in the games of Germans fighting the French, which Christoph and Detlef were playing in Eisersdorf and Westphalia during the first years of the war, or of Germans against Russians which Uwe Timm was enjoying in Hamburg. But Detlef, Christoph and Uwe wanted to be just like their fathers and elder brothers in their far-off war. The Jewish children in Vilna did not vie to be their elders, but their enemies. German children might re-enact NKVD executions in their games, but the shot in the back of the neck was an imagined event, far removed from anything they had seen or experienced of the war. The Jewish ghetto children were re-enacting what they could not avoid witnessing on a daily basis. Some games, like 'Blockade', turned the terrifying reality of evading ghetto round-ups back into hide-and-seek, honing skills at remaining silent and unseen, which might save the children's lives. But, just like the Polish children's re-enactment of execution and interrogation scenes that they had seen or heard about, so these Jewish children's games had a profoundly ambivalent character. The main roles of Gestapo man and gate guard testify to the envy and longing with which children might regard the enemies they most hated; but, unlike the boy heard screaming that he wanted 'to be German' in the Warsaw ghetto, these children were also playing, turning what they most feared into the stuff of games.

In contrast to Vilna, the great Jewish communities of Łódź and Warsaw were not prepared for their own destruction. Between January and May 1942, 55,000 Jews were deported from Łódź to their deaths. They included 12,000 of the 60,000 recent German, Czech and Austrian arrivals. Their wealth had driven up food prices in the ghetto a few months before to the consternation of the Polish Jews, but they lacked the vital protection of relatives within the Jewish administration, which they needed to get them into reserved occupations and keep them off the deportation lists. In fact, some people volunteered for deportation from Łódź, thinking that any work camp would be preferable to starving where they were. Hunger helped to mask the true nature of the deportations.[11]

As the only major Jewish ghetto in the 'Greater German Reich', the Jews of Łódź – or Litzmannstadt as the Germans called it – were more effectively cut off from the outside than the Jews of Warsaw, Vilna or Białystok. It was much harder to bring in food from the increasingly 'Germanised' city on the other side of the barbed-wire fence. Winter meant starvation. During the month of February 1942, 1,875 died out of a ghetto population of 151,001. The following month 2,244 people died. In the fragment of her diary which survives for the three weeks from late February to mid-March, a girl in her early teens wrote almost entirely about food and the family conflicts it precipitated. As the youngest child, she kept house while her parents, brother and sister went out to work. Her father, she noted on 27 February, 'looks terrible. He's lost thirty kilograms.' Then his work as a painter and decorator took him to the kitchen of the ghetto division and he was able to bring her back some soup. 'I was in seventh heaven,' she celebrated. But her elder brother who did not get any 'was so upset that he cried like a baby'. As the housekeeper, she was the one to go and collect their food rations and cook the dinner. On 10 March, after standing for three hours in a queue she finally got three loaves of bread and 'just had to have a piece' when she reached home, promising herself to go without that evening instead. But that evening her father saw her sneaking a spoonful of the twenty decagrams of potato gnocchi she was weighing out. He 'started yelling at me and he was right'. She began to shout and curse back. Torn by remorse and unable to apologise, she confessed her guilt to her diary: 'All the fights are started by me. I must be manipulated by an evil force.' In fact, during these bitterly cold days of late winter, in which the daylight hours passed so excruciatingly, she longed for night to come. 'I love the night,' she wrote. 'O night! May you last for ever, through all the days of hunger.' The enforced hunger became a major element in the deception and disinformation of the Jews.[12]

Only on 1 September did it become plain that the deportees were not being sent to forced labour. That day all the hospitals were emptied. Survivors of other ghettos had told tales about how the Germans 'deal with' the sick and to Dawid Seriakowiak the panic and terror that now gripped the whole ghetto created 'scenes from Dante'. 'People knew,' he recorded that night, 'that they were going to their deaths! They even fought the Germans and had to be thrown onto the trucks by force.' When a team of Czech Jewish doctors entered his apartment block that day – 'old, mean, and sour deportees from Prague' – they carried out a very thorough examination of every tenant. They found nothing specifically wrong with his mother, but they did note that she was 'very weak'. These two words, he quickly realised, would be enough to secure her deportation. She was, he admitted, simply worn out and emaciated. Dawid's family had also been ripped apart by hunger. Watching while his father consumed their share of the rations, Dawid could see that hunger was inexorably driving his selfishness, but he knew that he and his mother were paying the price. As Dawid's rage and bitterness against his father grew beyond any bounds of adolescent conflict, he knew too that there was very little he could do.[13]

That day, Dawid could not concentrate on his work and could only think of his mother. It was 'as though I divide, I find myself in her mind and body'. He seemed almost numbed to the general calamity. 'Laments and shouts, cries and screams have become so commonplace that one pays almost no attention to them. What do I care,' he asked bitterly, 'about another mother's cry when my own mother has been taken from me!? I don't think there can be ample revenge for this.'[14]

On 4 September, Chaim Rumkowski, the capricious, authoritarian and ultimately impotent 'Elder of the Jews', made a final public plea for another 20,000 deportees, so that a part of the ghetto might live by proving itself useful to the German war effort. 'In my old age,' he cried from his microphone in front of the ghetto fire station, 'I must stretch out my hands and beg: Brothers and sisters, hand them over to me! Fathers and mothers, give me your children!' As his voice was drowned by the terrified and terrible wailing of the crowd packed into the square, no one could have illusions any longer. Someone shouted back, 'Mr Chairman, an only child should not be taken; children should be taken from families with several children!' But Rumkowski had only one reply: 'So which is better? What do you want: that eighty to ninety thousand Jews remain, or, God forbid, that the whole population be annihilated?'[15]

In Łódź, Ettie took her rag doll and held it close to her, speaking to it in a serious voice. 'Don't cry, my little doll,' the five-year-old said. 'When the Germans come to grab you, I won't leave you. I'll go with you, like Rosie's mother . . .' Wiping away her doll-child's tears with the hem of her apron, she continued, 'Come, I'll put you to bed.

I haven't any more bread for you. You've eaten today's ration, finished, I must leave the rest for tomorrow.'[16]

In Warsaw, too, the ghetto remained ignorant of its impending fate as winter turned to spring and spring to early summer in 1942. What they had heard since the previous summer and autumn were the terrible tales told by the survivors of the smaller Polish ghettos. Miriam Wattenberg was immediately struck by the refugees' appearance. Ragged and barefoot, 'with the tragic eyes of those who are starving', they stood out even in the ghetto. Most were women and children, and many had witnessed the rounding up, even shooting, of their menfolk. Most of the new arrivals, with few possessions and lacking any of the contacts vital to survival in the ghetto, fell upon its meagre welfare institutions. Swiftly sinking to the bottom of the ghetto's atavastic social hierarchy, the refugees evoked more pity than terror.

Miriam visited one of these refugee homes to see for herself. The separate rooms had been knocked together to make large halls along whose walls stood improvised cots made out of boards and covered in rags. She saw half-naked children lying listlessly on the floor. Without plumbing, they had nowhere to wash. She went over to 'an exquisite little girl of four or five' who sat crying in a corner and stroked her dishevelled blonde hair. When the child looked up at Miriam and said 'I'm hungry', Miriam found it impossible to look back into her blue eyes, and turned away, ashamed. She had already eaten her own bread ration and had nothing to give her.[17]

As the throngs of beggars increased in the streets, many had to sleep where they stood, unable to find space even in the refugee homes in this ghetto of 400,000 people. During the winter months, many had simply frozen to death in the night. Someone might lay a piece of newspaper over them as a gesture of respect, while others scavenged shoes or items of clothing. By May 1942, the famous paediatrician Dr Janusz Korczak was seeing famine deaths everywhere. He stopped in the street to watch three boys playing a game of horses and drivers next to the prostrate body of a dead or dying child. They ignored him until their reins got entangled in him. As Korczak jotted down in his diary, 'They try every which way to disentangle them, they grow impatient, stumble over the boy lying on the ground. Finally, one of them says: "Let's move on, he gets in the way." They move a few paces away and continue to struggle with the reins.'[18]

Janusz Korczak's very love of children would gradually destroy him,

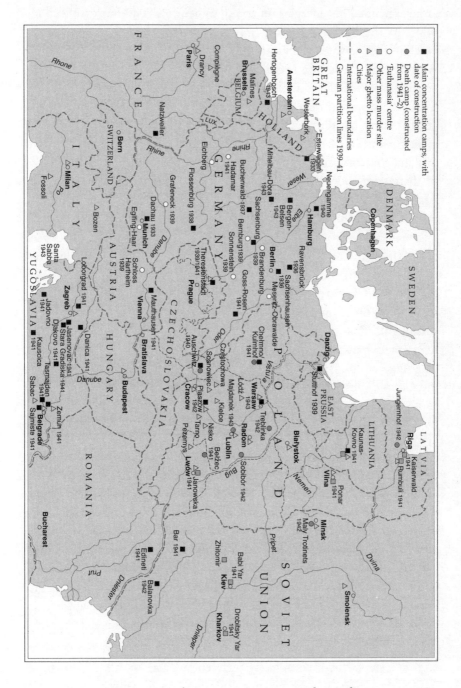

Major sites of Nazi persecution and murder

as he expended his energies on trying to help them in impossible conditions. In the Warsaw ghetto, only a very few children could participate in the private playgrounds and theatricals open to a Miriam Wattenberg or a Janina Dawidowicz. Many more were driven to street begging, smuggling or stealing. By the second year of the ghetto's existence, there were 4,000 children in different care homes. Korczak had dedicated his life to the care of abandoned children, having thrown up a successful medical career thirty years before to run a model orphanage. Korczak's orphanage at 92 Krochmalna Street, with its lack of distinction between Jews and non-Jews and its reform pedagogy, had become a cultural landmark to the liberal and secular-minded middle classes of Warsaw. When the Jews had been forced into the ghetto in November 1940, the orphanage had moved to Chłodna Street, in the small ghetto. The fact that Korczak went with it – and continued to refuse all offers to escape – became a matter of ghetto pride. It was the one child welfare institution to which the dwindling class of wealthy Jews went on giving generously. As he tried to bridge the widening social gulf that charted the ghetto's descent into absolute poverty, Korczak exhausted himself. He made the rounds of the ghetto elite, pleading for funds; he interceded with the ghetto administration and the German authorities; he even carried sacks of children's underwear to be secretly – and illegally – washed in a German laundry.[19]

When Korczak took over the public shelter for 1,000 children at 39 Dzielna Street, he inherited a child mortality rate of 60 per cent and a demoralised, hunger-stricken staff who stole the children's food. Korczak considered it 'a slaughterhouse and a morgue' and set about reforming and combating the existing staff. He failed on both counts. But, as they sought to protect themselves from Korczak's reforming ways, the Jewish staff in this home were not above denouncing Korczak to the Gestapo for not reporting a case of typhus, a charge which carried the death penalty. In this demoralising war of attrition, Korczak had to run around pulling high-level strings to have the matter dropped. He came away from his visits hungry because he could not bear to eat amid so much starvation and feeling 'all smeared, bloodstained, stinking'. The spartan but orderly Chłodna Street orphanage where Korczak slept was a completely different world: he could entrust the day-to-day management to his collaborator of thirty years, Stefa Wilczyńska.[20]

Meanwhile, footsore and exhausted from running all over the ghetto, the 'old doctor', as he was universally known, began to suffer from fatigue and dizzy spells. Unable to maintain his usual pace of work while subsisting on 800 calories a day, Korczak was troubled by his sudden bouts of forgetfulness and fading concentration. During the day he used little measures of vodka, or raw alcohol mixed in equal measure with water and sweetened, to give him 'inspiration' and quell the pains in his legs, the soreness of his eyes and the burning in his scrotum.[21]

The old doctor's strength ebbed and his interest in other people shrank. Only the children themselves exercised the same fascination over him as they had all his life. As a new day broke and Korczak still sat at his table writing by the carbide lamp, he tried to capture the utter disingenuousness of children waking up, struck by the gesture of a young hand stroking an ear, an arm holding a piece of clothing in the air as its owner stared motionlessly into space, the way a child wiped the corner of his mouth on the sleeve of his nightshirt.

The children in the orphanage were restless too, uninvolved in lessons or the Saturday ritual of reading aloud the newspaper they had helped write. Korczak encouraged them to keep diaries like him and read them aloud, even sharing a sanitised version of his own in return. Marceli vowed to give 15 grosze to the poor in thanks for finding the penknife he had lost. Szlama wrote about a widow who waited and wept for her smuggler son to return with something from across the wall, not knowing that a German policeman 'had shot him dead'. Szymonek wrote how his 'father fought every day to put bread on the table. Even though he was always busy, he loved me.' Mietek wanted a binding for the prayer book his dead brother had been sent from Palestine for his bar mitzvah. Leon haggled over the purchase of a French-polished box in which to keep his treasures. Jakob wrote a poem about Moses and, rounding out the children's shared wishes and anxious feelings of obligation, Abus worried that 'if I sit a bit longer on the toilet, right away they say that I am selfish. And I want to be liked by others.'[22]

On 7 June 1942, the head of the Jewish Council, Adam Czerniaków, realised a long-cherished ambition. He opened a children's playground on Grzybowska Street right opposite the ghetto administration.[23] The Jewish police band played introductory music while the 500 dignitaries gathered, striking up the 'Hatikvah' when Czerniaków arrived in a white tropical suit and a pith helmet. Urging everyone to ensure that the children survived these tragic times, he promised that this was just the beginning: he was going to open more playgrounds, as well as a training institute for teachers and a ballet school for young girls. The schoolchildren and their teachers marched past after he had spoken and then gave a display of singing, dancing and gymnastics. At the end the children were given little bags of sweets made in the ghetto from molasses. The ghetto's schools and day-care centres quickly arranged their timetables so that each class could visit the playground twice a week. The famous figure of the old doctor, Janusz Korczak, would bring up the rear as wards from his orphanage marched through the parks in good order.[24]

Czerniaków wanted to have regular weekly concerts at the playground. He issued instructions for children detained by the police to be brought there as well. When some of them crossed the road to see him in his office in the administration building, he was shocked by their appearance and their speech: 'They are living skeletons from the ranks of the street beggars . . . They talked like grown-ups – those eight-year-old citizens. I am ashamed to admit it, but I wept as I have not wept for a long time.' He gave a chocolate bar to each of them and made sure they all received soup as well. At the beginning of July, Adam Czerniaków was busy checking on the progress being made to open two further playgrounds and, on 5 July, he went ahead with an even bigger festive programme at the Grzybowska Street playground, in the teeth of religious opposition to all entertainments at this time of the year. The ghetto police band played and 600 children from the primary schools performed. A little girl made up as Charlie Chaplin came and sat with Czerniaków up on the stand. A week later, the two new playgrounds were opened, with even bigger crowds lining the streets, standing on the balconies and roofs, even perching on the chimneys. The performance of orchestral and choral music and ballet dancing was lavish and Czerniaków received an ovation from the children.[25]

For all his public reassurances and playground projects, Czerniaków had heard rumours of massacres since December 1941 and, during late April and May, the Germans ordered the ghetto to supply hundreds of deportees to construct a new 'labour camp' at Treblinka. On 8 July Czerniaków admitted that he was 'reminded of a film' when he looked at himself: 'a ship is sinking and the captain, to raise the spirits of the passengers, orders the orchestra to play a jazz piece'. At least to himself, in the privacy of his diary, the head of the ghetto administration was willing to acknowledge: 'I had made up my mind to emulate the captain.'[26]

Four days after opening the two new playgrounds, rumours of a mass deportation began circulating in the ghetto. The street beggars had been rounded up by the Jewish police and deported and, it was said, hospital patients and the prisoners in the Pawiak were being sent away too. On the same day, 16 July, Chaim Kaplan reported that Jews with foreign passports, who had once enjoyed special privileges, had suffered a sudden reversal of fortune and been marched off to the Pawiak prison. Miriam Wattenberg and her American mother were among them. It was said that Czerniaków was trying to buy the Gestapo off with a 10 million złoty bribe. He had in fact been told by the Gestapo that the rumours were unfounded and spent the day trying to reassure the population by driving through the ghetto streets and visiting the three playgrounds.[27]

On 22 July the mass deportations began. At 10 a.m. *SS-Sturmbannführer* Hermann Höfle and his deportation team entered Czerniaków's office and instructed him to have a contingent of 6,000 Jews ready for deportation by 4 p.m. This number was going to be the daily minimum until all Jews, with a few exceptions – who would include members of the Jewish police and administration and their families – had been deported to the East. As he listened, Czerniaków watched in consternation as the children were led away from the playground opposite the Jewish Community building. He pleaded for the children in the orphanages to be spared, but received no clear answer. On 23 July, the second day of the deportations, Höfle called Czerniaków back to his office at 7 p.m. and issued new directives to 'resettle' the 'unproductive' orphan children. As soon as Höfle was done, Czerniaków asked for a glass of water, closed the door of his office and wrote two farewell notes, one to his colleagues and the other to his wife Niusia: 'I am powerless. My heart trembles in sorrow and compassion. I can no longer bear this. My act will prove to everyone what is the right thing to do.' And he took the potassium cyanide capsule he had laid aside long before. Czerniaków's suicide was more than a private act of conscience. It also provided the Warsaw ghetto with a public warning.[28]

When the 'Great Action' began on 22 July, Chaim Kaplan immediately recalled the tales he had heard in the previous month from a German Jew, who had escaped from Sobibór, of a camp where people were killed by electrocution and lethal gas. The organiser of the ghetto's secret archives, Emmanuel Ringelblum, had heard similar stories in mid-June and not known how to interpret them. Feeling he did not have 'the strength to hold a pen', Kaplan could only chronicle his own dismay, 'I'm broken, shattered. My thoughts are jumbled. I don't know where to start or stop.'[29] On 3 August, the secret *Oneg Shabbat* archives were buried in milk churns and metal containers, so that at least a detailed record of Jewish life under German persecution would survive. The three young men who did the work added their last testaments to the archives. The words of eighteen-year-old Nahum Grzuwacz said it all:

Yesterday we sat up till late in the night, since we did not know whether we would survive till today. Now I am in the midst of writing, while in the streets the terrible shooting is going on . . . Of one thing I am proud: that in these grave and fateful days, I was one of those who buried the treasure . . . in order that you should know the tortures and murders of the Nazi tyranny.[30]

On the morning of 6 August, breakfast had just ended at the orphanage at Chłodna Street and the teachers and carers were clearing up when the long-dreaded call '*Alle Juden 'raus!*' rang through the building. Stefa Wilczyńska and Janusz Korczak instinctively moved together to calm the children and get them to gather together their things as they had been shown. One of the teachers went out into the courtyard and obtained a quarter of an hour from the Jewish police to allow the children to pack up and come out in good order. One hundred and ninety-two children and ten adults emerged and were counted off. As they lined up in fifty rows of four abreast, Korczak set off with the younger children in the lead so that they would not be outstripped by the older ones. Stefa Wilczyńska follwed with the nine- to twelve-year-olds. Among the older children came Abus, who had spent too much time on the toilet, and Mietek who always held on to his dead brother's prayer book.[31]

That day, all the children's homes in the ghetto were cleared by the Germans but, as ever, it was the news of Korczak's home that electrified the ghetto. With his disarming charm and self-deprecating irony, the old doctor had been adopted as the conscience of the ghetto. People had given gladly to provide the linen and food for his orphanage even as the halls for refugee children remained empty and bare. Now the crowds of people who had been forced to wait outside their houses during the 'action' watched while the children threaded their way along

the two-mile walk to the loading yard of the *Umschlagplatz*. The older
children took turns to carry their flag. On one side fluttered the blue
star of David against a white background, the Zionist flag but also the
colours of the armbands which the Germans had inflicted on the Jews
of Warsaw. On its other side the orphanage flag was green, after the
flag of King Matt, a mythical hero Korczak had invented twenty-two
years before. As long as they walked behind the green flag, the children held together as a group, following in the steps of the orphan
king Korczak had told them about so often.

After his return from the Polish-Soviet war of 1920, Janusz Korczak
had a written a story about a king who had let his land be ruled by
a parliament of children. When their enemies had finally overrun King
Matt's kingdom, he had been marched in golden chains down the streets
to his execution. It was, Korczak had written, 'a beautiful day. The
sun was shining. Everyone came to see their king one last time. Many
people had tears in their eyes. But Matt did not see the tears . . . He
was looking at the sky, the sun.' When King Matt finally reached his
place of execution, he refused a blindfold, to show that heroes die
'beautifully', only to feel cheated when he was exiled to a desert island
in a last-minute reprieve.[32]

As Korczak walked twenty-two years later, he did not look at the
sky and the sun. He had become a stooped figure by now, hollowed
out by hunger and anxiety beyond his sixty-four years, his nights filled
with dreams of food and pangs of guilt. As the procession came towards
the *Umschlagplatz* at the northern end of the main ghetto, Joanna
Swadosh, a nurse, looked up from her work and saw him carrying one
child, holding another by the hand, apparently talking to them quietly.
Occasionally, he turned to encourage the children behind. The children
were hot, footsore and thirsty, and – after so many months of scant
food – they tired quickly from the long walk through the little and
main ghettos. But even now the Jewish police were too in awe of
Korczak to shove or beat them as they normally did on such occasions. They simply formed a cordon on either side, separating the
column of children and their carers from the crowds on the pavements
who watched as they passed. Even after they left the ghetto gate and
crossed the road into the *Umschlagplatz* with its Lithuanian and SS
guards, and its thousands of distraught deportees waiting on the sun-
baked dirt with their bundles to board the trains to the 'East', Korczak's
children stood out. He refused to leave them alone for any length of

time lest they become overwhelmed with panic. Nahum Remba, a
Council official manning a first-aid station there that day, could only
watch as the Jewish police cleared a path for the children to board the
freight train. Following the same order as before, they walked in rows
of four. Once more, Korczak took the first group, Stefa Wilczyńska
the second. When a German asked Remba who that man was, he burst
into tears. The next day a red-haired boy delivered Korczak's diary to
a friend on the 'Aryan' side of the city who arranged for it to be hidden
in a Polish orphanage outside Warsaw.

When the deportations began, Mark Dawidowicz, Janina's father,
was in good spirits. As a ghetto policeman doing escort duty to the
'Other Side', he was able to smuggle in food every day. The danger
and his profitable new contacts to the ghetto underworld revived his
spirits, and he began to sing Russian Army songs from the First World
War. But the deportations continued, affecting his family too. In
September, as she was herded towards the *Umschlagplatz*, Janina
Dawidowicz lost her grandfather who had been holding her hand. She
and her parents managed to extricate themselves from the crowd and
return to their house; he did not. Janina wandered through the deserted
flats, playing with all the beads, paints and imitation precious stones
in a jeweller's, before moving on to salvage a beautician's make-up box
and some warm underwear from another flat. Yom Kippur, the Day
of Atonement, fell on 21 September and on that day, ghetto policemen
and their families lost their immunity and were liable to be deported
too. Once again, Janina's father succeeded in finding refuge that night
with someone who had remained exempt.[33]

In the previous three months 300,000 people had been deported.
Unprecedented in its speed, this 'great action' had left behind a mere
55,000–60,000 Jews. Men now outnumbered women two to one. Of
the 7,804 persons over the age of seventy, only forty-five remained and
of the 51,458 children under the age of ten, a meagre 498 hung on.
The shrunken ghetto was reorganised around a series of separate
'shops', or labour camps, managed by German entrepreneurs like
Walter C. Többens. On 17 December Miriam Wattenberg was still
being held with the other foreigners in the Pawiak prison, when she
learned about a camp at 'Treblinki', where naked people were being
killed by hot steam, gas and electrocution in the bathhouse, and where
the Germans were using a special mechanical digger to excavate mass
graves. That night no one in their cell could sleep.[34]

Gradually, the reports about Treblinka multiplied, and the Warsaw composer Shenker penned a lullaby to give voice to a father's lament for his murdered child:

Shlof, mayn kind, shlof,
Nit in betele dayn . . .

Sleep, my child, sleep,
Not in your little bed,
But in a little mound of ash,
My child, go to sleep.

You so loved
To sleep with your mother –
But do you lie today
Together with her?

The evil wind
Does not let you sleep;
It scatters you apart
So quickly.

In your young years
You had no calm –
And after your death –
Where are you? Where?

And the final refrain left no doubt for those who still hoped to hang on in the shell of Europe's largest Jewish community:

S'vet kumen, s'vet kumen,
S'vet kumen di sho . . .

It will come, it will come,
The hour will come,
It will come, it will come,
Also for me here.[35]

In Vilna, the ghetto had known about the mass shootings at Ponar from the outset. Deportation and murder had always been a part of the children's games and adults' efforts to 'work to live'. After the mass deportations from Łódź and Warsaw, the imminence of death filled the imaginations of those who had been spared. Buying one's way into the ghetto elite, purchasing exemption papers, carried no security any more. During the previous twenty months of ghetto 'normality' from November 1940 to July 1942, these things had served the smugglers and traders who ate the cakes in the cafés, and listened to the concerts and cabaret acts. They were among the few who could choose to live in a ghetto or try their luck by going into hiding 'on the other side'. While the ghetto had seen only 8,000 births, 100,000 people had died there, in 1941 reaching nine times the mortality rate for non-Jewish Poles in the rest of the General Government. But for Jews with resources and contacts the attrition rate within the ghetto had still remained low enough to offset the dangers of hiding on the other side.[36]

After the 'great deportation', the privileged began to invest in deeper and more elaborate hideouts, in *malines* which were connected to the town mains outside the ghetto walls and stocked – amid general star-vation – to survive for weeks before the hunted would run out of water or food. In Warsaw, the new SS official in charge inadvertently facili-tated this process by permitting the Jews to dig air-raid defences for themselves, an elaborate network of tunnels that proved invaluable during the uprising of the next spring.[37]

Some 6,000 Jews had fled the ghetto during the great deportation, while more than twice that number escaped to the 'Aryan' side after-wards. Until July 1942, leaving the Warsaw ghetto had been relatively easy: the child-smugglers and street beggars had done it every day. It was surviving on the other side that was difficult, although Warsaw, with its sizeable group of assimilated Jews who had never entered the ghetto and their Polish network of friends and helpers, remained a more attractive hiding place for Jews than other parts of Poland.[38]

The 'great deportation' changed all strategies for survival: whatever the risks of surviving on the other side, this now offered the only alter-native to staying in deep hideouts for weeks on end. The next German 'action' in the ghetto started on 18 January 1943. No longer exempted by her father's position in the ghetto police, Janina Dawidowicz and her mother Celia survived the two days of the action in a cramped cellar with strangers. The first shots had also been fired at the SS from Miła Street and sections of the Jewish underground were beginning to prepare in earnest for armed resistance. Before daybreak on the 20th Janina's father took her through the ghetto gate on a truck of workers he was escorting. They dropped Janina off at a street corner in the swirling snow, where a short, tubby man with a dog whispered to her to follow him. He was Lydia's husband Eric.[39]

After the great deportation had ended in September, it became relatively easy to leave the Warsaw ghetto once more. But hiding outside was extremely hazardous. To live openly required false papers and a great deal of confidence and knowledge. Poles especially were very good at spotting Yiddish inflections, Jewish looks and 'sad eyes'. The threat of blackmail or denunciation haunted all encounters. Children who were adopted into families as 'nieces' and 'nephews' from out of town had to learn and maintain their cover story at all times. They had to learn Catholic prayers, the catechism and the stories of the New Testament. They had to be ready to answer test questions like 'Are you going to school?' or 'What was your name before?'. But even if they passed all these tests, an inadvertent slip could be enough. A five-year-old boy had been playing the part of a Christian very well until the grandfather told a story at table about the horse-drawn trams on the streets of Warsaw in his youth. Forgetting that these pre-motor vehicles now only existed in the ghetto, the child chimed in that he too had seen a horse-drawn tram in Zamenhoff Street. His cover blown, he had to move, lest neighbours or professional blackmailers began to extort money.[40]

These dangers meant that families who went into hiding usually had to separate and to keep changing their abode. Like Janina Dawidowicz, Janina Lewinson escaped from the ghetto in January 1943. Many times Janina Lewinson and her mother and sister were forced to separate and they had to move hiding place frequently. They too were helped by someone with pre-war ties to the family, by Maria Bułat, the grandparents' former housekeeper and the mother's former nanny. In Janina Dawidowicz's case it was her father's one-time lover Lydia, who had fascinated her from the moment she swept into their dingy room in the ghetto with her perfume, glossy hair and sable coat, and who had brought the girl out to visit at Christmas and Easter time. These earlier visits to their family had forged such bonds of affection with Eric and his two boys that he was willing to run the risk of hiding her. The first thing they made her do was put on felt slippers to muffle her footsteps from the neighbours. She was told to keep away from the windows and hide in a broom cupboard when visitors came.[41]

Children had learned in the ghetto how to sit, cramped, immobile and silent for days, in *malines*. Now they transferred these skills to hiding in their protectors' broom cupboards. They had to learn not to betray themselves by reacting to what they overheard, however terrible. One boy, whose father had stayed behind in the Warsaw ghetto, only just had time to take cover behind the sofa when neighbours came to visit. The sound of explosions reminded the adults of the ghetto uprising then under way. When the visitors expressed their general satisfaction that the Germans were solving the Jewish question for the Poles, neither his protectors nor the boy himself dared to react to this turn in the conversation.[42]

Hiding often extended the claustrophobia of narrow and crowded living with other people into an unbroken rhythm of boredom. Hidden by former tenants, *pan* Wojtek and his wife, who lived in a fashionable street in the German part of Lwów, eight-year-old Nelly Landau divided much of her time between painting watercolours and reading the books a Communist friend brought for them. The paints helped her to escape through the walls of the apartment into the bright colours of the outdoors. Nelly read her way through Gorky, Dostoevsky and Alexandre Dumas, enjoying Jack London, Jules Verne and, that German children's favourite, Karl May, best of all. She was horrified by the plight of the slave girl, Alicia, in *Uncle Tom's Cabin* and painted pictures in which she escaped from her terrible master. But a lot of the time – especially when she felt lonely and sad – Nelly spent staring out of the window; her only contact with other children was to gaze at them in the street while she remained invisible behind the window.[43]

Nelly was not alone. Her mother was her constant companion and gave a sense of purpose to the cramped monotony of their days by dressing Nelly's hair each morning in ribbons as if they were going out. When she was not reading to her or retelling her the Greek myths, they played endless games of dominoes. As she waited for her father to come for her and watched the children and grown-ups passing by, Nelly painted pictures of children and adults at play. She painted her mother's knitting and their interminable games of dominoes. She did not paint the war, the police or scenes of danger and threat. Only once did she paint a solitary child, and this she called 'All alone'.

Nelly's father had chosen the Wojteks not just because they still had enough liking for and deference towards their former landlord to take the risk of hiding the mother and child. As the building's former owner, Landau also knew its secrets. Their flat – too small and dark to attract a German tenant – had a window that had been bricked up on the outside, but had remained accessible from the inside, creating a niche in which Nelly and her mother could hide behind a kilim during any search. Before he left, her father also showed them which floorboards to lift to retrieve the family jewellery.

Casual breaks in routine could shatter these long spells of boredom. When a neighbour knocked at the door of the Wojteks' flat one day, Nelly Landau's mother dropped a ball of red wool in her haste to get back to the concealed alcove in their room and unthinkingly tried to pull it under the door after her. Seeing the wool rolling over the floor, the neighbour immediately asked whom the Wojteks were hiding in there. Luckily, Nelly broke the thread on her side of the door in time for her host to convince the inquisitive visitor that the wool had rolled there by accident. Moments of near discovery like this left their indelible mark and Nelly duly reworked the incident into one of her pictures.[44]

Throughout the small towns and countryside, Jewish children had fled the liquidation of the ghettos, throwing themselves on the mercy of local farmers. Some were too frightened of being discovered and drove the children off. Some took the children in and claimed them as nieces or nephews, or exploited them as cheap farm labour. Others hid them despite the risk of denunciation by neighbours or even relatives, digging hiding places in the ground inside their barns. In such damp and confined spaces, as youngsters' eyes became unused to light, their muscles atrophied and they gradually succumbed to respiratory illnesses if they were lucky enough to survive undetected. Each time Dawid Wulf and his mother had to change their hiding place, she tried to prepare her seven-year-old son for the eventuality that they might be caught and shot by the Germans. After asking if it hurt very much, Dawid told her that he wanted them both to be shot with the same bullet. Local farmers and a group of Polish partisans joined in the hunt for these Jews on the run from the Cracow ghetto and the new bunkers became darker and more secret. When Dawid's mother suggested that he should draw their home and garden, with the sky and the sun above it, he confessed to her that he 'had forgotten what the sky and the sun looked like'. Instead, he built bunkers, tanks, cannon and ships out of the clay soil around him. Dawid also taught himself to read German and learned Heinrich Heine's poems by heart.[45]

But to remain on the outside entailed great risk. In the Zamość district in central Poland, the liquidation of the ghettos triggered what

Dr Zygmunt Klukowski, the director of the hospital in Szczebrzeszyn, described as a 'terrible demoralisation'. As he watched peasants bringing in Jews who had attempted to hide in the hamlets, he was horrified. 'A psychosis took hold of them,' he noted in his diary on 4 November 1942, 'and they emulate the Germans in that they don't see a human being in the Jews, only some pernicious animal, that has to be destroyed by all means, like dogs sick with rabies, or rats.' In Bełżec itself, even four-year-old Irena Schnitzer had heard that Jews were being killed in a bathtub filled with gas. When the SS began to clear the Polish villages from the district soon afterwards, the local peasants were terrified that they too would be sent to the gas chambers at the Bełżec camp but, at the time, many brought their farm carts to the squares, drinking and waiting to take over property left once the Jews had been loaded onto the trains.[46]

Children were no strangers to these scenes. On 1 August, Wanda Przybylska was on holiday at Anin once more, when she heard the sound of shooting in the distance. As the twelve-year-old went on with her diary, she noted that it came from the trains deporting the Jews, before turning back to two poems she was working on about autumn and nostalgia. It all seemed far away. But two weeks later Wanda and her family had to change trains at Falenica on their way back from swimming at Świder, a popular holiday spot for Varsovians. The next day, overwhelmed by what she had seen, she struggled for words to describe the 'crowds sitting without moving in the heat', 'all the corpses', 'the mothers hugging their babies'. As she sat on the veranda of the country house at Anin, she could not look at the stars. 'Everything is dead inside me,' the twelve-year-old wrote. With every round of machine-gun fire she could hear in the distance, she imagined a body falling. All the forests, the fields of wheat and the birds' song that had seemed to express her own inner vitality now felt totally lost to the barbarity and power of the enemy. For nights afterwards the girl lay awake weeping, unable to explain to herself why it was happening: 'Because they are of such and such a nationality? Because they are Jews? Because they don't resemble them?'[47]

With little else to entertain them, some children were eager to play an active part too. When a group of boys spotted ten-year-old Izak Klajman walking along the river bank outside Będzin, three of them grabbed him, pulled off his trousers to see if he was circumcised and began shouting 'Jew, Jew, Jew'. Then they twisted his arms behind his back and started deliberating whether to drown him or to hand him over to the German police. He was lucky. He managed to kick free and a woman who had known his father took him in. Once she had told the boys' parents and they had beaten them for what they had done, they left Izak alone. But in this maze of generous and mean, bold and frightened, sympathetic and anti-Semitic Polish neighbours, children had fewer ties to Jews than their parents' generation. They had grown up under the German occupation and it would seem that, in the countryside as well as the towns, they learned the new rules of hunting, tormenting and denouncing Jewish children faster.[48]

In the absence of any concerted policy from the Church or the Polish underground and in the face of the death penalty from the Germans, the profile of those willing to hide Jews was even more heterogeneous than those ready to denounce them. Janina Lewinson was aided at various times by a Polish aristocrat, Andrzej Szawernowski, and by Lily, a German prostitute whose brother worked on the railways as a policeman catching smugglers and Jews. She was helped by at least two ethnic Germans and a number of working-class Poles as well as members of the right-wing Polish resistance. Some ran the risk out of idealism, others for money, while some commercial relationships developed into friendships, with hosts going on protecting the family even when it had nothing left to give in return. But each time a hiding place was discovered by Polish blackmailers, new refuges had to be found, and Janina had to move thirteen times. As old networks unravelled and new ones needed to be thrown together, the Lewinsons depended utterly on the improvised efforts of a few self-sacrificing people. Some, like the courageous homosexual Stanisław Chmielewski – a man who had helped his Jewish lover to flee to the Soviet Union in 1939 before joining the Resistance – acted out of political conviction. Others, like the Lewinsons' former nanny, 'Auntie' Maria Bułat, or their former driver's ex-wife, Zena Ziegler, displayed a loyalty to their one-time employers far stronger than any of the Lewinsons' middle-class Gentile friends. It was above all these former servants who called upon their families and friends to hide the Lewinsons. When the family's funds were exhausted, 'Auntie' Maria even sold off a plot of land which Janina's grandparents had given her.[49]

The great deportation from the Warsaw ghetto finally gave Wanda Przybylska's parents the chance to leave their single room in the former student hall of residence in Tamka Street. The ghetto was reduced in size and they – along with other Polish families – were able to move into Pańska Street. No longer would Wanda have to play in the corridors or gather with her girlfriends on the windowsill on the first floor. On 24 February 1943 she learned that they had been allocated a four-room flat with its own kitchen. Even better, Wanda enthused in her diary that evening, 'To have a room just for me! What a marvel!' And so it proved. When they moved in a month later, it was at least as lovely as she had imagined. Her white and blue bureau was 'really pretty, just as I wanted it'. The room was simple, bright, warm and pleasing, with its few pictures and a crucifix on the walls, and flowers on a shelf. What Wanda did not write in her diary was that her parents were apparently sheltering two Jewish women in the flat as well. In fact, by the time of her thirteenth birthday, on 23 June, she would feel compelled to stop writing her diary altogether. Wanda did not do this willingly, but took her mother's warnings about exercising extreme caution amiss, as an unworthy injunction to be less than 'sincere'.[50]

In the autumn of 1943, six months after the destruction of the Warsaw ghetto, Józef Ziemian, a member of the Jewish socialist underground, spotted two Jewish teenagers as he entered the soup kitchen on the Nowy Świat. If Poles were attuned to picking up Jewish mannerisms and inflections of speech, Jews living under false identities like Ziemian had even sharper senses. The two boys recognised Ziemian as a Jew too and, overcoming their suspicions, struck up a conversation. They were 'Bull', whose dark-blond hair and blue eyes offered him some camouflage, and 'Conky' whose dark-blue eyes were, unfortunately in the circumstances, set off by the 'bad looks' of his long nose.[51]

On their second meeting the two boys took Ziemian to meet the others. There were over a dozen in their group, working the busy corners of Three Crosses Square, where the tram terminus stood. Here, in the heart of the German district of Warsaw, with a German gendarmerie post at nearby Wiejska Street and an SS barracks in the YMCA building on Konopnicka Street – with grocery shops, trams and restaurants reserved 'For Germans only' – this gang of Jewish kids plied their trade of selling cigarettes to passers-by. There was 'Toothy' Jankiel, a scrawny thirteen-year-old with buck teeth and bare feet, Zbyszek and Paweł who looked so 'Aryan' that even Ziemian doubted their Jewish origins. Outside the Institute for the Blind, Deaf and Dumb, he met Teresa. In a torn dress and dirty sweater, her fair hair falling down to her shoulders and a big scar above one eye, she shared her pitch with Yosef, whose limp had earned him the nickname of 'Hoppy'. Outside the YMCA building, Ziemian met 'Burek', 'the peasant', aged twelve, as well as a smaller boy whose frightened eyes belied their blue colour and the blondness of his hair. Ziemian had no difficulty in spotting 'little Stasiek' as a Jew. Then 'Boluś', at seven the youngest of the gang and everyone's favourite, arrived, dressed in a woman's ragged fur coat, tied around with a rope, his torn trousers fastened at the side with a safety pin. 'Boluś' – Bencjon Fiks – had already been spotted by the rival Polish boys who wanted to monopolise the trade on the square. He – and they – were at risk of being denounced as Jews.

The kids eyed Ziemian distrustfully, avoided his questions and moved on when he asked too many. He too was careful not to reveal that he worked for the underground Jewish National Committee. It was Bull, the leader of the gang and the first boy Ziemian had met, who grad-ually persuaded the others to accept him. He learned that they ate at several soup kitchens, frequenting the ones on Żurawia Street and Krucza Street, as well as Nowy Świat. Two women porters gave them lodging for a time. One had even slept in the alcove of a tomb in the Catholic cemetery on Okopowa Street until some observant neighbour had warned the police.[52]

Ziemian persuaded the Jewish National Committee to help the street children, but they did not want the clothes or money he offered them, preferring to trust in their own resourcefulness. Most had been smug-glers in the ghetto. Some, like Bull, had even escaped from deportation trains to Treblinka. One of the eldest, seventeen-year-old Mosze, or 'Stasiek', had managed to abscond from a pair of Polish blackmailers who had forced him to identify rich Jews for them so that they could live off the protection money. After playing cards with the Polish tram workers, Mosze-Stasiek would turn up on the square drunk, and encourage both the Jewish and the Polish boys to spend all their money on drink in a local restaurant. Ziemian quickly realised that, however much he wanted to drive Mosze-Stasiek out of the group, he was powerless to do so. The boy had won his place by defending the gang against attacks by the Polish boys. Now he helped to bridge both worlds. In any case, over the following year Ziemian watched their lives improve. They breakfasted each morning at the Różycki market, replaced their ghetto rags and had their pictures taken at the photographer's stand in the square.[53]

What the boys really needed from Ziemian were documents. By 1943, all adults needed both a German-style identity card, stating that they were employed and had a registered abode, and a certificate confirming that their employer held a work permit for them. Through its underground printing presses and its clerical network within the civil administration, the Polish underground was able to obtain thousands of these. As soon as Żegota, the Polish Committee for Aid to the Jews, was established in late 1942, it set up a special unit to produce large numbers of false identity documents, birth certificates, death records, marriage certificates, registration-card coupons and passes. Each time someone was tracked down and blackmailed, she or he would have to change address and, if living openly, identity as well.[54]

Some of the money that supported Jews in hiding came from America. The main socialist party, the Jewish *Bund*, received money from the Jewish Labor Party in New York, the Jewish National Committee from the World Jewish Congress, and Żegota from the American Joint Distribution Committee. As the sole united Polish-Jewish organisation, Żegota could draw on the resources of the Polish Government in Exile to handle communications with the outside world and to change dollars into Reichmarks. At the peak of what one historian has called 'the secret city', there were 25,000 Jews living illegally on the 'Aryan' side in Warsaw. Of these, Żegota supported some 4,000. The aid organisations simply did not have sufficient resources. But refugees, like the boys on Three Crosses Square, were also reluctant to entrust their lives to lists which might fall into the hands of the German or Polish police. Nonetheless, they were grateful to Ziemian for taking Boluś off the street. The youngest but also the most unmistakably Jewish child in the gang, he was beginning to draw attention to the whole group: a teacher from the Grochów district of Warsaw, Tadeusz Idzikowski, took him in.[55]

Blackmail was not restricted to strangers. Whenever *pan* Wojtek drank he would beat his wife Krysia. Eventually, devoted as the woman was to Nelly Landau and her mother, she turned the one weapon she had against him. She began threatening to denounce her husband for hiding Jews. In Lydia and Eric's flat, Janina Dawidowicz also found herself caught up in the quarrels and threats of a disintegrating marriage. Having been the one to offer Janina hospitality, Lydia quickly hit on the expedient of blackmailing her German-born husband for hiding a Jew. Eric soon found himself paying for a separate flat in town, which Lydia shared with her latest lover, her visits home alternating between terrible rows and tearful reconciliations during which the boys clung to their mother and Eric would temporarily lose his stammer. Gradually, Lydia took away the crockery, pictures, silverware, table linen and crystal glasses. Finally, the day came when Janina was alone in the flat and was too frightened of the things Lydia might scream on the stairs, if she did not let her in. She unlocked the door to find that Lydia had brought the removal men: by the time Eric and the boys returned, their home had been stripped bare.[56]

Even Eric now realised that Janina could no longer remain with him secretly. She would have to be hidden in a convent. He organised papers for her and taught her her new name, Danuta Teresa Markowska. According to her cover story, Danuta came from the port of Gdynia, a place which Janina had never visited. She also had to set about learning Catholic prayers and responses. This she did with great enthusiasm. For her, this was the fulfilment of a long-cherished wish to belong to the world of Christmas trees, a craving so strong that during her first visit to Eric and Lydia's in December 1940, she had tiptoed back into the living room after everyone else had gone to bed just to look at the decorations on the tree.[57]

The convent he chose outside Warsaw was set at the end of a long, curving avenue of lime trees with a vast vegetable garden nestling inside the curve. Janina and Eric arrived on a summer's day in 1943 amid the incessant buzzing of bees from the rows of conical hives. After the dappled shade cast by the avenue of limes with their big, dark-green leaves, the inside of the whitewashed house was dark and the corridor smelled of freshly scrubbed boards, stale food and too many bodies living closely together. Janina had to find her feet in this strange place, without ever letting her cover slip. Her first shock was the food. Even in the ghetto she had never faced anything so inedible, perhaps her most eloquent testimony to her father's efforts on her behalf. For the first months she starved.

Janina also had to find her place in the rigid hierarchy of power and privilege. To avoid the rare cold showers in a dank basement with frogs leaping about on the dark cement floor, she bribed the privileged senior girls to let her join them in bathing in the water left after the nuns had had their baths – and she discovered that some competed to bathe in the water left behind by the women on whom they had crushes. But it took till early December for her to be accepted by the senior girls. Volunteering for all the chores and acting as a substitute teacher for the junior classes did the trick. Finally, having shown a willingness to do all the hard work that Jews were believed to avoid, Janina was ready to call the bluff of those who muttered that she was one. In a game of 'What you look like', she herself declared that she looked Jewish, leaving it to fat Krysia, the senior girl, to step in and refute it. For Jewish boys, it was harder to carry off the subterfuge. In Zakrzówek outside Cracow, the brother superior of the home run by the Albertine Brothers told eight-year-old Zygmunt Weinreb 'to bathe in bathing trunks like the older boys'.[58]

While Janina cannily calculated her moves up to join the 'Old Guard's' table, she was racked by spiritual doubts. She wanted her conversion to Catholicism to be real and could not bring herself to take her first communion without being baptised. Finally, early in 1944, she found in Sister Zofia a nun to whom she could pour out her heart in private. A week before Easter, Zofia took her across Warsaw, so that she could be baptised away from the convent in a children's home. During the next week the fourteen-year-old joined the other girls in privately seeking forgiveness from all the nuns they might have offended in the previous year and, on Easter Sunday, Janina took her first communion alongside the eight- and nine-year-olds with a sense of having achieved a new, inner belonging. She would treasure the silver medallion Sister Zofia gave her.[59]

Just as the ghetto leadership had feared when the Church offered to take several hundred Jewish children into convents in the wake of the great deportation, it was winning their souls. But for so many Jewish orphans, it was the cult of the Virgin which was moving. It was not just that the worship of Mary occupied a central place in Polish Catholicism. Kneeling before the plaster statue with the sweet face, clad in a long white robe and a sky-blue girdle, her head crowned with tin stars, children could find something they missed bitterly: the presence of a mother.[60]

VII

THE FAMILY CAMP

IT was night when the door of Yehuda Bacon's truck was flung open. As he blinked in the glare of floodlights, he saw men in striped pyjamas, leaning on walking sticks. His first thought was that they had arrived at some kind of peculiar convalescent camp for invalids. Then, accompanied by strange shouts in a language he did not understand, Yehuda saw the sticks go into action, beating the men and women into two different lines on the ramp beside the tracks. Leaving their luggage behind, they had to clamber onto the backs of large lorries. As they drove off into the night, the floodlights illuminated the snow on the ground and reflected off the barrage balloons in the sky. The landscape was flat, picked out only by the winking of many lights. Unable to see the posts they were fixed to, let alone the barbed wire strung between them, Bacon could only guess at the size of the camp from the geometric patterns of light. It seemed vast, silent and empty. Eventually, the trucks turned off the road and the new arrivals were chased into an empty barracks block, its wooden bunks devoid even of straw matresses. Yehuda was too tired and disheartened to eat the food his father had carefully saved for him during their two-day journey.[1]

Yehuda Bacon arrived in Auschwitz-Birkenau on 17 December 1943. At fourteen, he already wanted to become a painter, a wish he would live to fulfil. He had spent the last year and a half in the ghetto Reinhard Heydrich had established at Theresienstadt to channel the Jews out of his 'Reich Protectorate of Bohemia and Moravia'. Moving among the many musicians and artists gathered in this small, eighteenth-century garrison town, the boy had been allowed to watch and study Leo Haas,

Otto Ungar and Bedřich Fritta while they painted. On 18 January 1945, Bacon would leave Birkenau, once again at night and in the snow, but this time on foot, with the columns of prisoners the SS wanted to evacuate ahead of the Soviet Army. By this time the young teenager had experienced an adolescence in the death camp in which his father and most of the other prisoners who had accompanied him from Theresienstadt had already died. During the final six months of Yehuda Bacon's incarceration in Birkenau, he and the handful of Czech boys who were spared were attached to the groups of men who worked in the gas chambers and punishment block, the *Sonderkommando* and *Strafkompanie*. Swayed by these powerful, terrifying but – to the boys – also generous men, Yehuda Bacon assimilated much of their secret knowledge and outlook into his sense of 'normality'.[2]

At each stage the future remained unknown. When Yehuda Bacon was in Theresienstadt, he knew nothing of Auschwitz-Birkenau, although he had seen cattle trucks packed with deportees leaving the ghetto when his own passenger train had arrived there. Yehuda was also unaware of the condition of the Polish ghettos or of their destruction. Nor had he heard of the mass shooting of the Jews in the Baltic States and Soviet territories. By contrast to the ghettos in all these places, Theresienstadt appeared 'privileged', although few of its inmates realised this at the time. When Bacon and his father arrived in Birkenau in December 1943, they were dumped in one of the most 'privileged' sections where the inmates did not have their hair shaved off on arrival or wear camp clothes. Their rations were better too. Above all, the men and women were only partially separated. Only in the neighbouring 'gypsy camp' in Birkenau did families actually live together. The transport of Czech Jews was housed in single-sex blocks but – to the great envy of prisoners in other sub-sections of the camp – they were not strictly segregated. From this strange semblance of 'normality', within sight of the crematoria chimneys, the Czech 'family camp' took its name. Above all, it had children, in a death camp where the overwhelming majority of children were sent straight to the gas chambers.

The 'privileges' granted to the Czech Jews in Theresienstadt and in the Birkenau 'family camp' derived from a series of improvised SS designs, going back to the autumn and winter of 1941. Reinhard Heydrich played a direct role in their fate from the outset. As head of the Reich Security Main Office, he would organise the deportation of the Jews across Europe, until he was assassinated in July 1942. As

'Reich Protector' of Bohemia and Moravia, Heydrich was at least as keen as other Nazi satraps to be the first to declare his fiefdom 'clear of Jews'. When the deportation of Jews began in September 1941, he originally planned to push them all out, sending them to the execution squads of the *Einsatzgruppen* and police battalions in the East or, at least, to join the influx of German Jews into the Łódź ghetto. By October, Heydrich had to concede that the military had priority on the railways and open a ghetto within his 'Reich Protectorate' instead. But Heydrich still meant Theresienstadt to be no more than a holding pen and transit point.[3]

When work began on refitting the barrack blocks of the former Czech garrison town in December 1941, the newly formed and predominantly Zionist and Communist Jewish Council assumed that, as in Vilna and the Polish ghettos, they would have to show their value to the German war economy if they were to survive. The average age of the Czech and Moravian Jews was forty-six and this plan seemed feasible to Jakub Edelstein, the first head of the Jewish Council. But within months, circumstances would prove him wrong. During the summer and autumn of 1942, 43,000 German and Austrian Jews were sent to Theresienstadt. Most were elderly. The average age of those transported from Berlin and Munich was sixty-nine, from Cologne, seventy, and from Vienna it was seventy-three. Theresienstadt was literally becoming an 'old people's home', and most of the inmates' work was devoted to meeting some of the ghetto's own needs.[4]

This influx of elderly German and Austrian Jews had its origins in an *ad hoc* alibi of the SS. By early November 1941, the first transports of German Jews to Minsk and Riga had led to over forty cases in which prominent Nazis had written to Heydrich to intervene. He quickly realised that Theresienstadt could be used to quieten fears among high-ranking Nazis, by convincing them that any German Jews under their protection were not being 'sent to the East', but would remain within the Reich. By the time of the Wannsee conference on 20 January 1942, this double role for Theresienstadt as a transit camp and a camouflage for the 'final solution' had become part of the general plan. As Heydrich explained, German and Austrian 'Jews over sixty-five years old' and 'severely wounded veterans and Jews with war decorations (Iron Cross First Class)' would be sent 'to an old-age ghetto'. With evident relief, he confirmed that 'with this expedient solution, in one fell swoop many interventions will be prevented'. But for many the 'privilege' of being sent to Theresienstadt brought only a brief reprieve: from January 1942 onwards, transports carried them on to the firing squads of the SS *Einsatzgruppen* around Riga and Minsk. By July 1942, trains were running from Theresienstadt directly to the gas chambers at Sobibór, Majdanek and Treblinka. As a transit ghetto, Theresienstadt offered precious little stability of any kind: by the end of the year, 96,000 Jews had come and over 43,000 had departed for that ominous but indistinct destination called 'the East'.[5]

Unexpectedly, on 16 February 1943 Himmler forbade Ernst Kaltenbrunner – Heydrich's successor as head of the Reich Security Main Office – to authorise any further deportation of elderly Austrian and German Jews from Theresienstadt. This in itself made any ruthless streamlining of the ghetto into workshops, along the lines of Łódź, impossible. In fact, no transports would leave the ghetto for the next seven months. Himmler explained that continued deportations would 'be at variance with the official statement that the Jews in the Theresienstadt ghetto for the old could live and die in peace'. What Himmler's real reasons were is not clear, although he may already have begun to think of Theresienstadt as more than just an alibi to comfort prominent Nazis disquieted by the 'evacuation' of 'their' Jews. On 18 December 1942, twelve Allied governments, including the Czechoslovak Government in Exile, issued a declaration condemning the extermination of the Jews. A month later, with the German 6th Army facing annihilation at Stalingrad, Himmler instigated the first of a number of contacts with the Allied secret services.[6]

By spring 1943 the SS was orchestrating a programme to 'beautify' the Theresienstadt ghetto, which would eventually result in a specially choreographed visit by delegates from the Swedish and Danish Red Cross as well as the International Red Cross on 23 June 1944. The International Red Cross team was also invited to visit a Jewish 'working camp'. This was the 'family camp' in Birkenau, and to this end it was built up with deportees from Theresienstadt in September and December 1943, and replenished in May 1944. From Himmler's point of view, opening Theresienstadt to outside inspection served to refute accusations of mass murder: great emphasis was laid on validating the claim that it was a 'final destination' and not the transit ghetto that it in fact was. Indeed, the very word 'ghetto' was removed and replaced by the designation 'Jewish area of settlement' – only to resurface unintentionally on the 'ghetto crowns' of its make-believe paper currency.

In addition, the apparently good condition of the Jews in Theresienstadt appeared to confirm Himmler's bona fides in beginning to pursue his own secret foreign policy: he would offer to exchange Jews for American dollars, German prisoners of war and American trucks, while he wondered how he could best broker a separate peace in the West, a strategy to which he only fully committed himself in the final weeks of the war.[7]

Like his own worst image of a Jewish huckster, Himmler was determined to have it both ways. As the German position on the eastern front worsened in 1943 and 1944, he sought to taint the *Reichleiter*, *Gauleiter* and the German generals with shared culpability for the murder of the Jews to prevent any other power bloc within the Nazi system from breaking away and making a separate peace. And he had Adolf Eichmann rush through the mass deportation of the Hungarian and Slovak Jews to the gas chambers of Auschwitz-Birkenau during the summer of 1944, partly in order to prevent the puppet regimes from splitting away, partly to make the genocide as complete as possible. At the same time, Himmler wanted to use the Theresienstadt ghetto and the 'family camp' in Birkenau to demonstrate that he himself would make a suitable negotiating partner, because he had Jews to sell. The key to Himmler's 'double-think' lay in the ideological character of his anti-Semitism and his actions are intelligible if he genuinely believed that the Jews were so powerful that they could deliver what he wanted – a separate peace with the West – which would allow Germany to turn all its resources back to the war against Bolshevism. To this end he would leave Hitler's birthday celebrations in Berlin on 20 April 1945, as the Red Army began its advance on the capital, to meet secretly with Norbert Mazur, as if this Swedish representative of the 'World Jewish Congress' really were an 'elder of Zion' capable of delivering a settlement with the United States.[8]

Jakub Edelstein and the Jewish Council, let alone the ordinary inhabitants of the Theresienstadt ghetto, knew nothing of these nascent priorities of the *Reichsführer SS*. What they did see were the new resources and the halt to deportations between February and September 1943. Even when the deportations were at their height in the summer of 1942, the Jewish Council tried to keep children off the transport lists and opened a series of children's homes. They were very different in kind from the ones that had depressed Miriam Wattenberg and driven Janusz Korczak to despair in Warsaw. There, Adam Czerniaków, the chairman of the Jewish Council, had been unable to realise his ambition of using the rationing system to protect the children.[9]

Without the SS's uncharacteristic decision to pump greater resources into Theresienstadt in early 1943, it is doubtful whether the Jewish administration's own cherished project of the children's homes could have been sustained for the twenty-six months in which they functioned fully. No other ghetto within the archipelago of West European transit camps and East European ghettos was able to establish anything like this system of separate homes for boys and girls, for Germans and Czechs, that were equipped with special ration supplements and later their own kitchens, and were capable of giving the children a measure of protection from their immediate surroundings. Some 12,000 children passed through Theresienstadt. At any one time, children under the age of fifteen numbered between 2,700 and 3,875. Approximately half of them lived in the voluntary children's homes, the remainder usually quartered with one or other parent in the adult, single-sex barracks.[10]

Against the odds, the children's homes worked. Child survivors have stressed the value of the daily routine, which contrasted sharply with the lack of structure for those children who remained in the adult barracks. In the children's homes there were cleaning rotas and order in the cramped dormitories. Daily communal breakfasts followed by a general assembly and roll-call, meetings on Friday evenings, special buns at the weekends – and continual well-organised evasion of the SS – all contributed to a sense of purpose. Under the bizarre and shifting orders regulating every aspect of the new society, children were generally forbidden by the Germans from attending classes, though these continued in secret regardless. In Yehuda Bacon's account of his time in the Czech boys' home, both the danger of discovery and his pride in evading it are apparent:

Two pupils kept watch, one by the house entrance, one by the doors. If an SS man crossed our way, they reported it. We already knew how to behave. You began immediately to talk about something or to read from a book. Our paper was quickly hidden . . .[11]

The homes were voluntary, but parents and other adult relatives in the ghetto usually had no means of caring for their children themselves. Discipline depended to a considerable extent on the children's own awareness that they formed an elite of sorts, that their conditions were better than those of the children in the adult barracks and that they were lucky to have gained places. Ruth Klüger recalled how she feared being excluded from the German girls' home for breaking the ban on drinking contaminated water. In the Czech boys' home, the core of the group was formed by boys from the Jewish orphanage in Prague, boys who already knew each other and institutional life. For some it was not so easy. Helga Pollak noted in her diary how bewildered, isolated and inconsolable her neighbour in the Czech girls' home was, a fourteen-year-old German girl, a fervent Catholic, deported under the regulations applied to so-called *Mischlinge*, or children of 'mixed' marriages. By contrast, both pre-adolescent boys and girls seem often to have 'paired' within their rooms, forming intense, same-sex friendships.[12]

The children also formed intense attachments to their adult room leaders. Whereas subject teachers moved from class to class, the leaders of each room were there all the time. Ella Pollak, who supervised the room of Czech girls, remained with them throughout their incarceration and further deportation. She became simply 'Tella' to them. Valtr Eisinger and his assistant Josef Stiassny moved their beds into the dormitory in the Czech boys' home and participated in the games and telling of bedtime stories. It was known that Stiassny had lost a brother in the Resistance, giving him a heroic aura. He became 'Pepek' to the Czech boys. The diminutive Eisinger won their respect by ridiculing the unsuspecting SS who came to inspect the room with that ultimate gesture of intellectual mockery, an overly elaborate show of respect. The boys dubbed him 'Tiny'. These allegiances were expressed through the use of the Hebrew title *madrich*, transforming the German title of *Betreuer*, carer, from teacher and guardian to youth leader and friend.[13]

The cultural atmosphere animating these educational experiments was of a peculiarly central-European kind: an eclectic mixture of progressive German reform pedagogy, Zionist and Communist ideals of the collective, tempered with some admixture of Freud. This was an intellectual atmosphere in which Eisinger had no hesitation in turning to the symbol of Goethe in order to explain to the children why they should not reject Germans and German culture as a whole or hold them collectively responsible for the persecution of the Jews. It was, he claimed, impossible to 'hate a nation that is one of the most cultured in the world and to whom, to a great extent, I owe my education'.

Instead, he encouraged the more intellectually precocious boys in his room to set up a 'Republic of *Shkid*' in imitation of a post-revolutionary orphanage in Petrograd, the Shkola Imeni Dostoevskovo. They, in turn, would demand lectures on Russian literature in the weekly journal *Vedem* (*We Lead*), which Petr Ginz, a half-Jewish boy from Prague, edited. The room was, Yehuda Bacon remembered with perhaps a tinge of nostalgia, 'democratically' run, with votes and vetoes. But there was discipline too: the bedding from badly made beds was thrown down into the courtyard and the boys could be punished with 'house arrest' on Saturday.[14]

The routine in the Czech girls' home was much the same. They too had order, a rota for chores, classes, a house song, better food than was to be had outside the homes and a uniform for special occasions. There was even a short-lived girls' journal, *Bonaco*, an acronym for the Czech *bordel na kolečkách*, a play on the words denoting both disorder and brothel. By intentionally turning to Russian and Hebrew for terms of address, such as *madrich*, in place of the more normal German or Czech, and by inventing acronyms, such as *Shkid* and *Bonaco*, which only those insiders could decipher, the children were drawn into an inner community with its own jokes and secret signs. They created their own codes which, for some, survived even their encounter with the camp slang of Birkenau.

A Viennese artist began to give the girls classes in drawing and painting. Friedl Dicker-Brandeis was a one-time member of the Weimar Bauhaus. Since the SS found nothing wrong with this, everything from old Czech Army forms to the packing paper from parcels could be officially recycled by the Youth Welfare Department as art materials. A shadow of Friedl Dicker-Brandeis's enthusiasm and creative intelligence survives in the notes she made for a guided talk she gave in July 1943. To celebrate the first anniversary of the children's homes, the art teacher mounted an exhibition of their pictures for their parents and other interested adults. She shared the passion of her own first painting teacher, Johannes Itten, for seeing art as a form of creative release – practising meditation and breathing exercises in conjunction – and built on his method of teaching pupils to break away from mechanical copying and to develop their own forms of self-expression. Friedl Dicker-Brandeis worried about how to encourage the children without telling them what to draw. Although she used books of reproductions of works by Giotto, Cranach, Vermeer and Van Gogh to show the girls how to analyse the rhythmic movement of brush strokes in their painting, she learned not to ask leading questions of the girls themselves, after one girl rushed off to improve her picture in order to please her. Perhaps to counter-act such tendencies, the girls were also given pencils to use in 'free' drawing time, giving rise to some of their most interesting pictures.[15]

Since nothing could protect children from exploring the ghetto beyond the homes, they brought back what they had seen into their free drawing time. Communal kitchens were the norm in Theresienstadt. Having witnessed these scenes as a seven- to ten-year-old, Inge Auerbacher remembered how long were the lines of people waiting to be served in the open courtyards. 'It was,' she wrote, 'especially hard in the winter, waiting in the bitter cold. Breakfast consisted of coffee, a muddy-looking liquid which always had a horrible taste. Lunch was a watery soup.' The food queue became a form of primary socialisation for new arrivals, as well as a source of endless complaints, charges and counter-charges of corrupt practice among adults. After the children had followed the bread cart through the ghetto streets and watched the struggle for existence into which the food queue drove most adults, including their own parents, they returned to the relative safety of their single-sex homes.[16]

Twelve-year-old Věra Würzelová's vision of a food queue lends a firmness and solidity to her figures, even though perspective is still lacking. Predictably, the figures in authority, the guard in attendance on the left and the cooks ladling out rations on the right, are considerably larger than the men and women, not to mention the child, waiting to receive them. In its top half, Liliane Franklová's drawing presents a similar scene: four adults wait patiently in line at a soup kitchen. A small child stands or waits on the wrong side. Below, a girl, or perhaps a woman, appears to be drowning in the sea and calling for help, while a boy and girl stand on the shore. In both the upper and lower halves of the drawing the girl seems to be immobilised in the wrong place.[17]

In Theresienstadt, like other ghettos that had a well-developed hierarchy, scarce resources were distributed unequally. Alongside official rationing, there existed a highly developed black market, as well as outright theft. At every echelon of the Economic Department people took their cut, from the members of the Council of Elders through the provisioning administration to the bakers, butchers, cooks and ghetto police. How the pot was stirred and what sorts of spoons were used to ladle out provisions became matters of fierce – and frequently recounted – struggles. Survivors remember that those who were well placed within this system used their own ration cards as currency, trading them for cigarettes, clothes, apartments, prostitution and luxury foodstuffs – sugar, apples, oranges, lemons – which had to be smuggled in or were released onto the black market from private food parcels. The only type of alcohol to be had was euphemistically called 'beer' – cold, black, ersatz coffee, slightly sweetened and left to ferment in bottles for a few days. Some of the paintings produced by the group of adult artists in Theresienstadt were commissioned by this new social elite of cooks and bakers.[18]

This is the world at which Liliane Franklová's child is gazing from the wrong side of the soup barrel. She may not have grasped the entire hierarchy of distribution in the ghetto through which power was brokered, but she and Věra Würzelová knew that those with authority were larger than those with none.

The Jewish administration cut rations for the elderly in order to boost those for children and adults in protected jobs. The effect on the mortality of the aged was immediate. In the second half of 1942, 14,627 elderly German and Austrian Jews died in Theresienstadt, equalling their numbers deported to Treblinka that autumn. Himmler may have prohibited their further deportation in February 1943, but that year, elderly German and Austrian Jews would account for 10,366 of the 12,701 people who died in the ghetto itself. May 1943 saw some improvement, as the SS permitted parcels from abroad in keeping with the general 'beautification of the ghetto', and tins of sardines started to arrive from Portugal for general distribution.[19]

With malnutrition came physical deterioration. Adult survivors testify how they became completely absorbed by food fantasies, conjuring up ever more elaborate recipes for Hungarian goulash well after interest in sex had disappeared. Hans Günther Adler, the most noted survivor-historian of Theresienstadt, intimated that although inmates of the ghetto never looked markedly more 'Jewish' than any other cross-section of European humanity, there was one respect in which they did come to resemble one another, as well as Nazi caricatures: they acquired the so-called 'Jewish look', the hooded gaze of the exhausted, the anxious and the prematurely aged. Flat-footedness became widespread; joints hardened and gestures became stiffer and more accentuated. Some writers describe feelings of perpetual irritability and a rapid decline of interest in and empathy with other people.[20]

The younger German and Czech Jews who ran the ghetto administration may have got along well enough, but many people simply turned in on themselves. The Theresienstadt diary of Martha Glass, deported from Hamburg at the age of sixty-four, refers constantly to 'the children'. By this she meant her own daughter and 'Aryan' son-in-law in Berlin, who kept her supplied with the regular food parcels on which her survival depended. In Theresienstadt she constructed a social world around the – mainly German – women in her room, and renewed old acquaintances from Hamburg and Berlin. Her only contacts with the rest of the ghetto were through the soup kitchens, the medical services and, above all, the free concerts of classical music. Of the children in the ghetto there is only one word in the whole diary, when she notes the tumult unleashed by the October 1944 transports: '22 October: . . . The ill, the blind, tuberculosis patients, the children from the orphanage, all are gone. There have never been such misery and cries of grief.'[21]

A wall of indifference grew up between the German-speaking elderly and the mainly Czech-speaking children in the homes. Yehuda Bacon accepted that, however much he continued to visit and encourage his own sick and dispirited father, in general he and his companions in the Czech Home for Boys shared in the general contempt among children for the old and the weak. Youth leaders like Stiassny might exhort him and his companions to maintain the scouting traditions of pre-ghetto society and help the elderly, bring them their rations from the soup kitchens, read to them and help lift their spirits, but the children reported how the barracks, the rooms and the very bodies of the aged 'stank'.[22]

Janusz Korczak had been shocked when he saw how indifferent street children had become to death in the Warsaw ghetto. They had ignored a corpse until it had become entangled in their game of horses and drivers and interrupted their play. It was as if such children had temporarily but also completely abandoned external reality and retreated into the world of their imaginations. The Theresienstadt children did not do this. They were hungry but, at least in the communal homes, they were not starving. For Věra Würzelová and Liliane Franklová food existed in a social setting. They dwelt on its distribution and its scarcity, but food still opened rather than closed their window onto the ghetto world. It was not – or not yet – an over-powering obsession, and they could still play with it in many ways. In Ilona Weissová's hands, food took on fantastical fairy-tale qualities as she drew all the food items she wished to consume.

In her drawing the eleven-year-old stands smiling pensively surrounded by the most extraordinary foods: a not very kosher pig and a hedgehog bearing fruit with forks stuck in them; a fish on a platter impaled on a fork; chickens walking up to her feet with forks sticking out of them; a winged figure delivering a basket of eggs from above; a bottle on a low trolley; jars of cocoa and coffee; and sardines, cheese, sweets, cake, milk and an apple. To make the subject quite clear, the sign behind the girl reads 'Fantasy land. Entry 1 crown'. With its pleasurable, rounded shapes and the girl, her hair tied in bunches, decked out in a party dress, Ilona Weissová had taken herself to *Schlaraffenland*, the legendary land where pigs fly into the mouths of sleeping peasants. In the early modern and nineteenth-century tales about the ease from work in *Schlaraffenland* the normal world was turned upside down; here ghetto life was being ruptured simply by importing foodstuffs from the old, pre-ghetto world.[23]

Ruth Klüger described in her memoirs how hours were devoted in the German girls' home – where she insisted that the food was worse than in the Czech homes – to fantasising about food while she and her friends whisked milk with a fork. The children's kitchens benefited from many of the parcels that could not be delivered because the addressee had died or been deported further. Crucial fats, vitamins and proteins came their way: meat, salami, cheese, eggs and butter, along-side fresh and dried vegetables, onions, marmalade, chocolate and fruit. Some of these luxury items appear on the labels adorning Ilona Weissová's baskets and jars, but for the most part the fantasy concerned what she did not have.[24]

In a remarkable drawing, Maria Mühlsteinová made the absence of food into the dominant feature. In this street scene in front of a grocery shop, two girls stand on either side of a kind-faced old woman. A street hawker in the upper left is selling newspapers to the occupants of a bus, an everyday enough event in the pre-ghetto world but quite out of place in Theresienstadt. The dog on wheels that is being led on a leash by the older girl might refer humorously to the time before the – pre-ghetto – ban on Jews keeping pets. Or it may be intended literally to represent a toy substitute, no doubt also lost with her deportation.

Both the flower the old lady has to offer the girls and her grocery shop belong to the pre-ghetto world. The very real emptiness of these imaginary shelves is reinforced by the sign above the shop, which reads *Vyprodáno!* (sold out). A ghetto policeman directs the traffic of a pre-ghetto town. Present and past become merged in these overlapping motifs, obliterating, as an image can do and words cannot, the moment of change itself. In place of the moment of transition Maria's drawing offered a composite of both worlds.[25]

As the children struggled with their experience of deportation, they seem to have been most concerned with understanding where they had come from and what they had lost. And so, in the free drawing time in their communal barracks, they depicted their former homes rather than the triple bunk beds they slept in now. They drew them in the same stylised way as they had done before their deportations, with pot plants flowering on the windowsills, curtains tied jauntily back and pendant lamps illuminating the table in the middle of the room.[26]

Edita Bikková, ten or eleven years old, exemplifies the optimistic order and satisfactory symmetry that also typifies non-Jewish German children's pictures of this period. All the figures in her living room are doing something. She is not present; only her brothers. The largest boy, in school uniform, is talking. The smallest is completing sums on a blackboard – and they all add up correctly. The curtains have a delicate floral pattern. Each child is identifiable by his clothes; the mother's costume, as befits the most important figure, is the most detailed. Even if Edita's parents and brothers were in Theresienstadt, she might only have seen them occasionally, sneaking out to the courtyards of their single-sex barrack blocks before returning to the dormitories for her evening meal. But their barracks' lives are not what she chose to commit to paper. Instead, the mother is kneading dough, perhaps to make *challah*.[27]

In format, Jiřina Steinerová's picture is similar. Three years older than Edita Bikková, Jiřina was struggling and not quite succeeding in mastering the three-dimensionality of objects. Perhaps as compensation the details of the two rugs and the tie-backs of the curtains are very closely observed. The picture presents the interior of a living room: a woman – the mother? – seated at a table covered by a fringed rug reads a book. A second woman waits behind her, maybe a servant or an older daughter. In the centre of the room a table stands on another rug and in the middle of the table we have what looks like a plate with eight biscuits. All this suggests order, cleanliness and comfort. But where is Jiřina herself? Is she present only in the portrait of the girl hanging on the wall? Below this portrait, the figure of a girl has been rubbed out and the lines of the wall drawn over her smudged shadow. The exacting details of this picture have a rather disturbing impact. There is the child's literal-mindedness – the painstaking representation of the fringes and geometric patterns of the two carpets, and the curtains with their tie-backs and pelmet board. Perhaps these were objects in her own past that she was fascinated by at a younger age and which she now recalled with longing in a place without carpets, let alone family life. Or she may have lavished so much effort on them to compensate for a lack of technical confidence and her inability to master perspective. There is also the cramped immobility of the figures, possibly, again, just a lack of artistic technique, were it not for the strange portrait of the girl on the wall, trapped in her frame as Jiřina herself was trapped in Theresienstadt, unable to re-enter the room that she is observing. Yet Jiřina Steinerová's home, like Edita Bikková's, remains intact, a world complete in itself. In both of these pictures the details are intricate and painstaking, and reinforce the sense of a discrete, pre-ghetto, time and space.[28]

In Zuzana Winterová's drawing, the orderly household takes the form of a triptych. The room below is neat and bright. A lamp hangs over the table. Flowerpots stand in the windows. The two chairs are confidently and squarely placed, and the boy sat like a cushion on top of one almost as an afterthought. Above, the mother cleans while the father reads his newspaper. Although both are facing the viewer, only the father is powerful enough to stare back, his eyes and eyebrows beetling over the paper. And here the old structure slips. The headline on his newspaper reads *Tagesbehfel*, a misspelling of 'Order of the Day'. Posted in the ghetto by the Council, in response to verbal instructions from the SS, the Order of the Day would have been read out to Zuzana in the morning assembly by the head of her home. In her picture she has effectively turned her father into the head of the home, or possibly vice versa, fatally undermining an otherwise consistent attempt to preserve the memory of a stable and secure family life.[29]

There is also some pattern to these slips and merging of different times. With the exception of Winterová's newspaper headline, the pictures of pre-ghetto home interiors tend to preserve their separate wholeness intact, even if the artist herself could not re-enter them.

There are no ghetto policemen. None of the people in them wears the Star of David so carefully observed in the other depictions of Jews. It is outside the parental home that time and circumstance proved malleable and unstable. The street was where children met the real face of the ghetto, where they found that the elderly 'stank'. If the present were a time and place before the world went wrong, the children's future Utopia is not the Zionism or Communism of their youth leaders, but the family living room of the past.

As news of a fresh transport departing from the ghetto spread, so the anxieties held so long at bay engulfed those whose names were on the list. Boys and girls, men and women ceased to be members of collective, single-sex barracks. They arrived and departed as families. Panic-stricken family groups had to sort out what to leave out of their 50 kilos of allotted baggage. Some parents tried to comfort their children by turning the transports into an elaborate game. The museum at Terezín contains a large doll dressed as a child, the Jewish star stitched onto its breast pocket, and carrying its own little suitcase. Like Yehuda Bacon, Eva Ginzová had arrived in Theresienstadt as a transport to Birkenau was pulling out. On 28 September 1944 it was her brother Petr's turn. Eva wormed her way through the crowd and crawled under the cordon to pass two slices of bread to Petr and their cousin Pavel before being driven back by a ghetto guard. There was so much shouting and crying around her that they could only communicate by their looks.[30]

Having been through this at least once before they came to the ghetto, people were better prepared to discard all but the most useful items for this next journey. There had been few deportations from Theresienstadt in 1943 and 1944. In September and October 1944 they resumed and the children's homes were liquidated during the mass deportations to the gas chambers of Auschwitz-Birkenau. The children and their teachers left behind 4,000 drawings and paintings. Very few of the children survived. But Willi Groag, the last head of the ghetto's youth welfare department, carried their drawings and paintings back to Prague in a suitcase when Theresienstadt was liberated in May 1945. That suitcase held an unparalleled record of children's art from the genocide, preserving, in their bright watercolours and faint pencil outlines, the frozen moments of children's imaginations.[31]

*　　*　　*

When Yehuda Bacon was deported to Birkenau in December 1943, he left many friends behind in the Czech boys' home. By the time the children's homes in Theresienstadt were liquidated in the autumn of 1944, the 'family camp' had already been wound down and most of its inmates killed or sent to other camps. Bacon had watched hundreds of thousands of Hungarian and Slovak women and children walking down the road from the railway siding or waiting patiently in columns on their way to the crematorium. He had had to help collect their belongings from the newly built ramp where the trains halted. He had heard about the enormous trenches behind the crematoria with their special drains and pots for human fat, in which thousands of corpses were burned when the crematoria could not cope with such enormous numbers. Bacon would have heard the Greek prisoners singing as they pounded the charred remains to dust in the open air, and he knew of strange acts of compassion, as when the SS sent a group of Slovak children back to the men's camp after they had already undressed in the changing rooms to the gas chambers.[32]

Yehuda Bacon had grown even closer to the dwindling group of Czech boys who had survived the destruction of the 'family camp', and he still treasured his time in the Czech boys' home in Theresienstadt. Whereas there he had dreamed of his old home in Mährisch Ostrau, this had become too remote, and in Birkenau he dreamed, instead, of the Czech Home for Boys in Theresienstadt. But by autumn 1944 he had also come to share so much in the lives of the men of the penal battalion that the outlook of the children freshly arrived from the homes in Theresienstadt might have seemed strange to him: he had little opportunity to find out. Like most of those on the September and October transports, Petr Ginz, who had single-handedly edited the boys' weekly newspaper *Vedem*, was sent straight to the gas chambers, as were Zuzana Winterová, Jiřina Steinerová, Edita Bikková, Maria Mühlsteinová, Ilona Weissová and Liliane Franklová. But Yehuda and his friends did pass food and valuable advice on how to survive through the electric fence to a group of children from Theresienstadt who were spared the gas chambers.[33]

The gradual transformation of those, like Yehuda Bacon, who were spared started on their admission to the Birkenau 'family camp'. The rituals of admission began with being marched to the showers to be deloused, tattooed and issued with camp rags, before being marched back and given their first food, camp 'coffee'. When Yehuda and the rest of his December 1943 transport were reunited with those who had established the 'family camp' in September, they learned the meaning of the hierarchy of ranks among the prisoners, the 'Kapos' and the 'Block Elders' with their armbands. For the first time since the Germans had marched into Czechoslovakia, Yehuda saw his father hit – not by an SS man but by a young Czech and fellow Jew – and he knew that he had to stand there and do nothing at all. Each morning Yehuda saw the corpses of those who had died in the night being stacked up in front of the block. He learned that if they were still there in the evening, inmates would swiftly try to exchange their own worse clothing and shoes for theirs. He saw how people attempted to report the dead as sick in order to go on collecting their rations. And as he looked across to the neighbouring enclosures in Birkenau, he caught sight of the beatings and of naked women running from barracks to barracks during selections in the women's camp.[34]

Within two or three weeks of Bacon's arrival, a 'children's block' was established in the family camp. Its instigator was Fredy Hirsch, a Kapo and a young, athletic and fair-haired German Jew, who had worked alongside Egon Redlich and Willi Groag in the youth welfare department in Theresienstadt. Modelling their efforts on the homes in Theresienstadt, Hirsch and the other youth workers set about securing basic material conditions for the children, inspecting their clothing each day for lice, and their hands, nails, ears and plates for cleanliness. Continuing the collective discipline they had learned in the children's homes in Theresienstadt, the whole class risked losing their special daily ration; the boys jokingly called it 'the prick parade'.[35]

With few pencils and little paper, most of their five hours of daily lessons were oral ones. They sang Czech folk songs and some Hebrew ones, as their teachers tried to impart their own Zionist vision. One ten-year-old, Otto Dov Kulka, who survived to testify at the trial of Auschwitz guards in 1964 and to become a historian of German Jewry under the Nazis, remembered how his teachers had told him about the struggle of the Maccabees and the Battle of Thermopylae. But he remembered the music even more than his history classes: the children's choir and playing the 'Ode to Joy' from Beethoven's Ninth Symphony on the mouth organ. The lesson that left the greatest impression on Bacon was the one where he had to imagine what it would be like if he were released from the earth's gravitational pull and could fly to the moon, the ultimate escape from Nazi imprisonment. But he also remembered performing a secret skit about a dream of going to heaven, only to find that the SS was there too. The boys' attitudes towards the SS were complicated by the fact that Yehuda and other child survivors remembered the 'fatherly' way in which a number of SS men, especially the doctors, behaved towards them, bringing them things they could use, including a football. For their part, SS men liked coming to hear the children recite German poems and brought their colleagues from other sections of the camp. They were so impressed with the paintings one of the teachers had made, based on Walt Disney's film of *Snow White*, that the next three months were dedicated to rehearsing a musical production in German. The stage and set were made out of tables, benches and sacks of straw. The dwarfs were meant to represent order and cleanliness, the wicked stepmother demoralisation.[36]

Fredy Hirsch made the greatest impact on Bacon and his friends. By making them exercise in the winter snow and wash their clothes as well as their bodies in the freezing water, he 'drilled' them and 'toughened them up', so that they would not be mistaken for the skeletal figures most camp inmates quickly became. As in Theresienstadt, the children's block soon had its own kitchen and ration supplements, once Hirsch had persuaded the SS to let them have the food parcels sent to non-Jewish prisoners who had died. In Birkenau, the gulf between young and old which had opened in Theresienstadt widened into a chasm. 'You oldie, what are you interfering for, it's no business of yours,' as Bacon characterised the children's style for addressing the aged, 'you've already got one foot in the crematorium!' The teachers themselves had none of the children's special entitlements to food, a deprivation that one of the young women, Hanna Hoffmann-Fischel, thought was hardest for the young male teachers to bear. She also remembered how attempts to inculcate Zionism often ended with the teachers standing by, swallowing hard as they watched the children eat.[37]

Left to their own devices, children played 'Camp Elder and Block Elder', 'Roll-call' and 'Hats off'. They played the sick who were beaten for fainting during roll-call, and they played the doctor who took their food away and refused to help those who had nothing to give him. As Hanna Hoffmann-Fischel watched the younger children playing these games, she realised the hopelessness of trying to protect their innocence.[38]

If the younger children wanted to play at wielding power, older children learned to use what power they possessed. They found that they could exchange their white bread ration for larger amounts of rye bread with adults whose stomachs rejected the heavy dark bread. Yehuda and his fellow stoker in the children's kitchen did a brisk trade toasting slices of white bread for the elderly, receiving half a slice for every five or six they did. Even Kapos and SS men came to warm themselves by the stove or give the boys gifts in return for their wood carvings. And older children learned to trade sex for food. Bacon remembered how a friend of his with a pretty sister became her pimp, charging a packet of cigarettes a time. Bacon believed that the boy did not understand what he was doing, beyond the pleasure of acquiring cigarettes and demonstrating his power. The practice spread even to the younger children. As one boy aged eight progressed from trading goods with a Kapo in another part of the camp to arranging for his mother to become the Kapo's girlfriend, so his food and dress attracted universal envy.[39]

Whereas adults generally tried to ignore their proximity to the gas chambers, the children played games with death, daring each other to run up to the electric fence and touch it with their fingertips, knowing the high-voltage current was usually – but not always – switched off during the daytime. As Bacon and his friends stirred the pot of soup on the stove, they could see the chimney of the crematorium and timed their cooking against its burning. While the adults clung to every shred of hope, he and his companions resorted to a dry, bitter sarcasm, vying to outdo each other with the sharpness of their 'gallows' humour': white smoke meant that 'this time it's fat people'.[40]

One day Hanna Hoffmann-Fischel came upon the younger children playing 'Gas chamber' outside their block. In their normal games of 'Roll-call', the bigger children would play at being Kapos and guards, beating the little children for 'fainting', much as the big boys in Vilna beat the smaller ones when they played at 'Going through the gate'. But now no one 'played' at dying. Instead of entering the hole in the ground they were calling a gas chamber, the children threw stones in, mimicking the cries of the people inside. It was one thing to envy the powerful guards, or get the smaller children to submit to being beaten in these other games. It was quite another to play at one's own death and, in the breakdown of the game, the children demonstrated the point where identifying with their enemies became too self-destructive to continue. It did not stop their curiosity. When Hanna Hoffmann-Fischel came over to them, they even asked her how to put up the chimney. Compared with the flights of wishful thinking that overtook so many adults, children's curiosity remained brutally centred on the present. But at the point where their role-play collapsed, they also defined the limits of imagining themselves in the death camp about which they had discovered so much.[41]

On 7 March 1944, the children's block had a party to bid farewell to the original September transport. The SS camp commander had just told them that they were being sent to a work camp at Heydebreck. Some people heard 'Heidelberg'. Others wondered where this 'Heidebrück' was and whether it was another concentration camp. The SS worked hard to create a false sense of security, taking down the professions of all men and women under the age of forty as if to facilitate their incorporation into a labour camp. But the *Sonderkommando* of prisoners who operated the gas chambers and crematorium had been sending warnings for weeks to the family camp of an imminent action, urging the Czech Jews to prepare to join in a general uprising. Fredy Hirsch and his assistant were too nervous to attend the children's party. But many adults clung to their hopes, their special rations and their post-dated postcards asking relatives to write to them at Heydebreck. Few of the older children seem to have had such illusions. Yehuda Bacon's friend and fellow oven-stoker, Cupik, said simply to Bacon as they looked at the chimney, 'Today I shall be a stoker in heaven too.'[42]

Early on 8 March the 3,732 survivors of the original September transport were taken to the nearby barbed-wire enclosure of the Quarantine Camp, where they were held in readiness till the evening. Otto Dov Kulka, who had sung in the choir for *Snow White*, was among the sick whom the SS kept back to maintain the illusion that theirs was a transport bound for the labour camps. Kulka watched through the windows of the sickbay, as hundreds of trucks drove up that evening to collect the rest of the transport. Under a hail of blows from the SS the men and women were separated and climbed aboard, still clutching the special food rations they had been given for their journey. The tailgates were closed and the tarpaulins lowered so that they could not see where they were going.[43]

The following morning those who had remained behind in the family camp learned what had happened during the night. Electricians and other prisoners whose skills entitled them to move between Birkenau's sub-camps brought word from the *Sonderkommando*, some of whose members felt ties of kinship to the family camp. Filip Müller, a Slovak Jew from Sered, had even left his post in the cremation room above the subterranean gas chamber and crept in among the women. He had been moved by the sound of their singing as they had waited for what seemed an eternity while all the trucks were unloaded and the doors closed. First they had sung the 'Internationale', then the Czechoslovak national anthem, 'Where is my home, my fatherland'. While the waiting continued they had struck up the 'Hatikvah' ('The Hope') and they sang the song of the partisans.[44]

As he tried to keep out of sight near a concrete pillar, Müller found himself confronted by a child looking for his mother in the crowded and dimly lit space. 'Do you know where my mummy and my daddy are hiding?' the little boy asked Müller timidly. The singing died away for a while. The room was still filling up when a group of Czech girls recognised Müller from the *Sonderkommando* uniform he was still wearing. Müller remembered them coming up to him and telling him not to stay. One of them, with long black hair and flashing eyes, urged him to tell those left behind in the family camp what happened so that they could fight against the SS. And she asked him to take her gold chain from her neck after she died and give it to her boyfriend Sasha at the bakery. 'Say,' she concluded, '"love from Jana." When it's all over, you'll find me here.' She pointed at the pillar where Müller was standing. As he was propelled out of the gas chamber, Müller was knocked down and beaten by one of the SS officers he worked under, before being sent back to man the ovens.[45]

After it was over and the fans had been run, Müller had to go back into the gas chamber and drag the corpses to the lift so that they could be burned in the crematorium above. As the doors were unbarred, the top layer of the corpses heaped against them tumbled out into the corridor. Filip Müller had witnessed this scene many times in the previous twenty-three months. Through the goggles of the gas mask he wore to protect his eyes and lungs from the pockets of concentrated gas among the heaps of bodies, he could see what had happened once the lights had been turned out and the gas released. People had rushed about as if in a 'subterranean labyrinth', knocking each other over, trampling on one another, as they struggled to suck the last of the oxygen at the top of the room. But below the gas vents in the roof, the floor was virtually empty. People had moved away from the smell of burning metaldehyde, fleeing the sickly-sweet taste as it scoured their throats and induced intense pressure within their heads. Their mouths covered in spittle, their legs in urine and excrement, the corpses were twisted around each other in uneven heaps. At the bottom lay those whose lungs had given way first, the children. The groups were virtually impossible to disentangle, Müller found, so tightly were they entwined. Some lay, he remembered twenty years later, 'in each other's arms, others holding each other's hands; groups of them were leaning against the walls, pressed against each other like columns of basalt'. He found Jana near the pillar she had pointed to and slipped her necklace into his pocket. The next day he made his way to the bread store and gave it to Sasha, a non-commissioned officer in the Red Army from Odessa, who had been among the first Soviet prisoners of war to arrive in Auschwitz back in 1941. From him, Filip Müller learned that Jana had been a children's nurse in Prague.[46]

The survivors in the family camp calculated that if the September transport had been given six months, then the December transports had only another three months to live. Prisoners who worked in the central records department confirmed these fears by sending word that their index cards carried the instruction 'six months' special treatment'. The atmosphere in the camp became strangely easygoing, with the survivors enjoying more plentiful rations, less work and better treatment from the new prisoner Kapos.[47]

When further transports arrived from Theresienstadt in mid-May, they refilled the family camp to bursting point. Another 7,500 – mainly German, Dutch and Austrian – Jews joined the Czechs and Moravians already there. At some point, postcards were issued on which inmates were allowed to write up to thirty words in German. Yehuda Bacon and his friends signed off the innocuous messages they felt confident would make it through the SS censors back to the boys' home in Theresienstadt with a special greeting in Hebrew: '*Moti*' or 'My death'. Anna Kovanicová wrote to her sister in Theresienstadt, so that reading down the last letters of each line spelled out 'GAS' and 'DEATH'. Although their messages arrived, they were not believed.[48]

Theirs were not the only messages to the outside world. Some members of the *Sonderkommando* hid written accounts in jars and empty beer bottles, which they buried that summer in the pits of ashes, hoping that their notes would be found after liberation in the place where they thought it was most likely that people would dig in search of the remains of those killed in Birkenau. Filip Müller knew that his fellow Slovak and friend, Walter Rosenberg, was planning to escape from Birkenau and briefed him in full about the gassing of the Theresienstadt prisoners. He also gave him a precious piece of material evidence about the poison gas to take with him: the label off a Zyklon B tin.[49]

A month later Walter Rosenberg escaped with another prisoner, Alfred Wetzler. With the help of Russian prisoners of war, who prepared and stocked a dugout under the horse stables in the third perimeter of the camp, the two men were able to hide until the SS gave up the search. After a harrowing eighteen-day journey, Rosenberg and Wetzler reached Žilina in Slovakia and the safety of friends, who gave Rosenberg a new Slovak identity as Rudolf Vrba. The two men compiled the first detailed report about the Birkenau death camp, including the gassing of the Czech Jewish men, women and children on 8 March. By the end of April, the Vrba and Wetzler report, as it became known, reached leading Jewish officials in Bratislava and Budapest. While the leaders of Hungary's Jews dithered, their Slovak colleagues set about smuggling it to the West, via the Vatican chargé d'affaires in Bratislava, Giuseppe Burzio, who took a full five months to deliver it to Rome. Other copies went by underground courier to Dr Jaromir Kopecky, the Swiss representative of the Czech Government in Exile. Within days of receiving it in late May, Kopecky passed it on to the Government in Exile in London, the World Jewish Congress and the International Red Cross in Geneva. On 14 June the Czech and Slovak Service of the BBC broadcast news of the gassings.[50]

The reaction to this news was disbelief, even among those who did not dismiss it out of hand. In Berlin, Ursula von Kardorff locked herself in a friend's toilet in December 1944 to read the Vrba and Wetzler report in the *Journal de Génève* in safety. Although she moved in Resistance circles, already knew in general about the mass murder of the Jews and had taken the risk of helping to hide Jews in Berlin, the stark detail of the Auschwitz death camp was too much for her. 'Is one to believe such a ghastly story?' the young woman asked herself in her diary. 'It simply cannot be true. Surely even the most brutal fanatics could not be so absolutely bestial.' But if it were true, she reflected, then the only thing to do was to pray for a speedy liberation from the Nazis. When another escapee from the family camp, Vítězslav Lederer, brought the news back to Dr Paul Eppstein, Edelstein's successor as head of the Jewish Council in Theresienstadt, the story was suppressed. Perhaps he was not believed. Perhaps the Council feared spreading panic through the ghetto. Even the 'family camp' in Birkenau had refused to believe the warnings of the *Sonderkommando* during the month before the March 'action'.[51]

Now, at least in the 'family camp', those illusions were gone. Bacon and the rest of the December transports began to count the days until 20 June 1944, when they reckoned their six months would be up. But still nothing happened. They could not know it, but three days later the long-awaited international inspection of Theresienstadt took place. The May transports reduced Theresienstadt's population to 27,000, completing the SS's 'beautification' of the ghetto. The new arrivals would make a healthier and less horrific impression in the family camp than the exhausted survivors of the September transports, should the International Red Cross delegate take up his German colleagues' invitation to go there.[52]

Dr Maurice Rossel, the representative of the International Red Cross, was accompanied by two Danish delegates on a carefully choreographed tour of Theresienstadt, which he described in a glowing report: 'Let us say that to our complete amazement we found in the ghetto a town which is living a nearly normal life . . . This Jewish town is remarkable . . .' He then went on to enumerate everything the SS had made sure he saw. Rossel even sent photos he had taken at Theresienstadt to Eberhard von Thadden at the German Foreign Ministry, including pictures of children playing in the park. Thadden thanked him and assured him that the photos would be 'used on occasions when foreigners turn to him again concerning alleged horrors in Theresienstadt'. Thadden also forwarded copies to the Swedish embassy, which had not bothered to send a Red Cross delegate of their own, and Rossel's testimony was presented to foreign correspondents in Berlin on 19 July 1944. Himmler had received a plausible denial of genocide.

What was remarkable was Maurice Rossel's willingness to disregard information which the Red Cross had received in the previous weeks, including the report by Vrba and Wetzler. Rossel had simply accepted SS assurances that Theresienstadt was definitely a 'camp of final destination' from which no one would normally be deported further. Nor did he bother to take up the invitation that Himmler had extended through the German Red Cross to visit the 'Birkenau near Neu Berun labour camp', to see if any of the claims about it were true.

The 'family camp' had served its purpose and in early July 1944 the

SS dissolved it. The SS procedures had changed considerably since March. The great victories which the Red Army had just scored in Belorussia hung in the air, and the evacuation of camp prisoners westwards was already beginning, in order to make good the shortages of manpower in the Reich. This time the talk of labour camps was no SS ruse: 3,500 able-bodied men and women were selected and sent away. A number of the SS guards at the selections were drunk and allowed some children they had turned down to rejoin the queue. Cowering as her skinny twelve-year-old's body was revealed in its nakedness, Ruth Klüger managed to slip through on her second attempt. But for many families the July selections spelled the moment of separation. At sixteen, Anna Kovanicová was picked to go for labour first time. But her mother was not, even though she also managed to rejoin the queue and present herself several times. Anna's father then decided not to report for the selection at all, preferring to stay behind with her mother. Yehuda Bacon's older sister and mother got through; he and his father were turned back, and so it went on, finally separating all those families whose lives had so far defied the normal logic of Birkenau. When it was time to leave, Anna's parents kept telling her to go but held on to her hands at the same time. Finally, she tore herself away. Turning to look back at them one last time, she took in the sight she would describe to her own children decades later. 'I can still see them,' she wrote. 'Thin, grey, cold, burned-out, forlorn.'[53]

Among the 6,500 people left behind in the family camp at Birkenau all order collapsed. No one bothered with roll-calls and people bathed in the water tanks outside the blocks without risking punishment. They knew that they were doomed. Then, a surprise selection was held by the head of the Birkenau camp, *SS-Obersturmführer* Johann Schwarzhuber, the officer who had so cynically given his word of honour to the September transport that they were going to Heydebreck. Now, the same man seemed intent on saving the boys and girls over fourteen. One of the SS doctors repeated the selection, weeding out all the girls and the younger children. But even on this occasion some of the most brutal SS men seemed to want to save some of the boys. When Otto Dov Kulka claimed he was twelve – which was still not old enough – SS man Fritz Buntrock looked down at his file card and back at him, before asking him why he was lying and waving him through to join Yehuda Bacon and the eighty or so other boys over fourteen.[54]

For fifteen-year-old Yehuda Bacon the parting from his father was excruciating. The relationship of care had gradually reversed itself between the son and the father. First in the Czech boys' home in Theresienstadt, then in the children's block in the family camp, Bacon had drawn strength from his special rations and a sense of pride from his peer group. He had already seen his father's vulnerability in the ghetto and, as he became weaker, Yehuda had continued to bring him food on his visits and to care for him. This had begun long before he saw his father beaten on the day they had arrived in Birkenau. But over the previous seven months, he had witnessed his father's accelerating decline and his sense of responsibility had increased. Yehuda knew that his father had accepted his fate: he even offered his son a gold tooth crown which had come loose. But still the boy found it impossible to leave the doomed remnants of the family camp behind, without looking into his father's eyes and promising him that they would meet again.[55]

On 6 July, Yehuda Bacon and the other boys were marched to the so-called 'gypsy camp', next to Crematorium 4. Like the Jews in the family camp, the Sinti and Roma enjoyed special 'privileges' and had been allowed to keep their own clothes and hair. They even lived in family groups. With a football pitch and playground for their children, they too had often been visited by off-duty SS men who enjoyed their music and dances. Some had also formed sexual relationships with the women there. Little suspecting what awaited them during the next month, the Sinti and Roma children taunted the group of Czech boys, pointing to the crematorium and calling it the 'marmelade factory', or the 'bread factory' for the Jews. By nightfall, the boys had been moved again, this time to join the Birkenau *Sonderkommando* and penal battalion.[56]

Within the week, a curfew order went out that always preceded an 'action' within Birkenau. Tense and subdued, the boys crowded at the tiny windows of their block, trying in vain to catch a glimpse of the people going into the crematorium. The next day the men of the *Sonderkommando* came, bringing photographs and small personal items to Bacon and his companions. They could doubt no longer that it was their relatives who had been murdered. 'We were very, very alarmed and upset,' Bacon recollected in his home in Israel in 1959, 'sad. But none of us cried.' The boys drew closer to one another and to their new protectors, the men of the *Sonderkommando*'s penal battalion, the *Strafkompanie*. For the first time, the boys began to pool their food, sharing it out equally and looking after those who fell sick.[57]

This dwindling group of Czech, Dutch and German boys became the young mascots of the Birkenau penal battalion and *Sonder-kommando* in whose block they were quartered. These men took them to the enormous warehouses known for their plenty as 'Canada', where the clothes and belongings of the murdered transports were sorted before being sent to Germany. Their new protectors saw to it that the boys were fitted individually for shoes, one of the greatest protections that could be afforded in the camp. Even the small group of Russian prisoners of war – so feared that even the SS and the ethnic German Block Elder treated them with circumspect politeness – took to the children, telling them their stories and joining in their games in the yard. On a Sunday evening the boys would accompany the Block Elder from one barracks to another, singing Czech and German songs for the prisoners.[58]

Bacon joined a group of twenty boys in the *Rollkommando*. Harnessed like horses, they pulled a wooden goods wagon from sub-camp to sub-camp within Birkenau. Bacon recalled this as relatively 'light' work, which also gave them privileged access throughout the camp, as they carted clothing, firewood and other goods from one enclosure to another, as well as collecting the belongings of incoming transports, which they proceeded to loot. One day the boys arrived at the crematorium when it was empty, and one of the men of the *Sonderkommando* showed Bacon around the installations. Back in Theresienstadt, the group of Czech boys who produced the weekly journal *Vedem* had started recording their 'rambles' through the ghetto by visiting the ghetto morgue and the newly built crematorium: they had explained its mechanical workings and capacity with a boyish enthusiasm for technological mastery as well as an adolescent fasci-nation with the fate of the dead. Now Bacon carefully observed 'all the technical details', noting how the shower heads in the gas chamber were not connected to anything and checking the dimensions of the vent for the Zyklon B cannisters. He and his friends listened eagerly and, remembering the men with walking sticks he had seen on the night of his own arrival in Auschwitz, Bacon looked in the room where the *Sonderkommando* waited with sticks to drive the unwilling from the changing room to the gas chamber.[59]

Among the men of the *Sonderkommando* and the *Strafkompanie*, the boys found individual protectors. Bacon's was Kalmin Fuhrman, a twenty-four-year-old Pole, whose duties included holding the arms or ears of those who were to be shot in the small execution room in the crematorium. Yehuda knew one of the men in the *Sonderkommando* from Theresienstadt; Fuhrman introduced him to the others. Some of these friendships between the boys and their protectors may have become sexual, but it was almost certainly the emotional intimacy with these powerful and terrifying men, who literally had the capacity to save them or kill them, which had the greatest impact. In Theresienstadt, Yehuda had only been admitted to the Czech boys' home thanks to the intervention of the Chairman of the Council, Jakub Edelstein, whose only son Arieh was one of Yehuda's close friends. Now it was Yehuda's new protector, Kalmin Fuhrman, who was able to tell him how his childhood playmate, Arieh Edelstein, had been shot alongside his parents.[60]

When Yehuda Bacon first told his story to an Israeli interviewer in 1959, he reached a point where his questioner did not wish to listen any further to this part of his tale and together they censored part of the transcript. 'Frequently,' Bacon related,

> the men in the *Sonderkommando* brought us children pieces of linen and told how whenever a transport came, they dealt with the most beautiful woman separately, namely they kept her back till last, brought her out last and led her into the gas chamber last. They then threw her last and with a certain piety into the oven on her own too, not with the others.[61]

Whether or not the men truly did so, the young teenage boys listened keenly to their stories in their shared barracks at night and went out during the day to sell bras and make-up to the women in the camp, crucial items which helped distinguish the healthy-looking 'prominents' from the rest during selections. It is not clear what Yehuda Bacon made of what he had heard, but judging from his one attempt to tell the story to someone else, he found it very difficult to communicate afterwards. Bacon was interviewed on several further occasions, but he did not try again to tell what this baffling and ambiguous tale of discovering the meaning of female beauty had for the men of the *Sonderkommando*. Perhaps he was put off by his first interviewer's reaction. He continued, however, to insist on how 'normal' the death camp had seemed to himself and his friends at the time, and how much it had been a part of his own adolescence. And in that admission lay

the terrible recognition that there was no pre-camp self he could rediscover after liberation. 'One should not forget,' he explained to a later
interviewer, 'that for teenagers it was *the* experience at a very impressionable age when you take in everything with an almost greedy
curiosity. We all treated the experiences as normality, almost as
romantic, virtually including the cruelties.' Yehuda Bacon grew up in
Birkenau, and this set him and the other boys apart from the powerful
and frightening men who protected them.[62]

To the outside world, Bacon and the other boys became closed and
'hard'. The genocide of the 400,000 Hungarian Jews that summer
brought a short age of plenty to the *Sonderkommando*. While the boys
openly traded food and clothes, the men secretly exchanged diamonds
and gold within the camp for weapons and ammunition for their
planned uprising against the SS. From the end of September until late
October, the final eleven transports from Theresienstadt arrived,
including most of the remaining children from the homes: of the 18,402
people on them, 1,474 would survive. During the abortive Slovak
uprising that summer the insurgents had immediately liberated the Jews
and the fear of the Czechs following suit may have finally prompted
Himmler to dispose of his Jewish bargaining counters. As fewer transports arrived, so the parasitic prosperity of the *Sonderkommando* ebbed
away. Even the boys knew that their own continued survival was inti-
mately linked to fresh transports entering the factory in which their
own families had died. By the time Himmler ordered the gas chambers to be dismantled in November and December, Birkenau was a
camp in terminal decline and the *Sonderkommando* was reduced to
melting down brass fittings to palm off as gold in their barter trade
with the SS. Shrouded in snow, both its prisoner functionaries and their
youthful camp followers once again felt the pangs of hunger.[63]

Still, Yehuda Bacon – like Filip Müller in the *Sonderkommando* –
did everything to stay in this little corner of Silesia they knew so well.
Between the summer of 1944 and January 1945, 63,000 of the 130,000
prisoners in Auschwitz and its subsidiary camps were shipped west.
Boy and man both calculated that here – even in the embers of a death
camp – their hard-won knowledge and connections would serve them
better than evacuation to unknown camps elsewhere. They both
succeeded in hanging on until, in mid-January 1945, they heard the
muffled boom of the Russian guns.[64]

PART THREE

THE WAR COMES HOME

VIII

BOMBING

ON 24 July 1943, sixteen-year-old Klaus Seidel was on duty at his anti-aircraft battery in Hamburg's Stadtpark. His had been one of the first to be re-equipped with the bigger 105mm guns in 1943. Just before 1 a.m. the battery went into action as the first of six waves of bombers swept over the city. The attack lasted fifty-eight minutes. Flying from north to south over the city, the 740 planes dropped 1,346 tonnes of high explosive and 938 tonnes of incendiaries, while the city's *Flak* batteries shot over 50,000 rounds into the night sky. Although Hamburg's fifty-four heavy and twenty-six light batteries, supported by twenty-four searchlight positions, amounted to one of Germany's strongest anti-aircraft defence systems, they only brought down two planes. That night the RAF had used 'Window' for the first time, letting fall a cascade of short aluminium strips, which jammed the German radar frequencies. Unable to lock onto bombers overhead, the *Flak* guns and the searchlights swung across the night sky at random.[1]

At 3 a.m. Klaus Seidel was called out again, this time to fight the fires at the Stadthalle. Dressed hastily in his pyjamas, tracksuit, steel helmet and boots, he and his comrades attempted to salvage goods and fight the fire with hoses. Luckily, another boy had sprayed him for a lark and this protected him from the sparks that came off falling timbers. As Klaus wrote to his mother later that day, he was so inexperienced he had wanted to go in sandals. After an hour and a half, they returned to the battery, where – still soaked – he ran messages until 6 a.m. That night, the police estimated, 10,289 people were killed. After three hours' sleep Klaus Seidel was back on duty again, preparing the anti-aircraft guns for the next attack.

It came at 16.30, from ninety American Flying Fortresses. At 0.35, six RAF Mosquitoes swooped over the city on photo-reconnaissance, to be followed at midday on 26 July by another fifty-four Flying Fortresses. The next day, 27 July, 722 bombers flew in, this time from the east, targeting neighbourhoods which had gone virtually unscathed till now: Hammerbrook, Rothenburgsort, Borgfelde, Hamm, Hohenfelde, Billwärder and St Georg. Tens of thousands of small fires united into a general conflagration, which remained easily visible to the next waves of attacking aircraft. As one RAF bomb aimer put it, the second and third raids were 'like shovelling more coal on the fire'. Freak weather conditions and the intense heat generated by the phosphorous bombs transformed the huge conflagration into a firestorm of unprecedented proportions. Objects and people vanished, trees up to a metre thick were flattened by the hurricane. Those who stayed in their cellars and air-raid shelters risked being incinerated inside them or asphixiated by carbon monoxide gases; those who fled risked being trapped and burned in the melting road surface or buried under the tumbling façades of apartment blocks. That night another 18,474 people were killed.

During the day, Klaus went in search of his grandparents. Unable to find them, he dug around in the ruins of their house to make sure they had not died there. He advised his mother strongly against returning from her summer holidays in Darmstadt. That day the *Gauleiter* of Hamburg, Karl Kaufmann, reversed his earlier orders not to leave, and issued instructions to enlist every available means – by rail, road and steamer – to evacuate the city.

Meanwhile, the bombed-out streamed into the Stadtpark, helping themselves to piles of bread, which large lorries dumped on the ground. Klaus Seidel was shocked by the way the refugees wasted the extra food delivered to them; he found tins of half-eaten meat slung into the bushes and heaps of plums left to rot on the ground. In their shock, the refugees had cast the whole code of rationing and frugality aside. The regime, anxious lest civilian morale collapse under the aerial assault, made a policy of issuing extra food and materials in areas affected by air raids. This had paradoxical results. After the firebombing of Wuppertal in May, the exhausted thirteen-year-old Hitler Youth, Lothar Carsten, numbed by fighting fires and helping the homeless, also remarked on how long it was since they had eaten so well. In Hamburg, Klaus watched bitterly as private cars, which had not run since the start of the war, were given petrol to evacuate refugees, while his *Flak* battery hardly had enough to keep its generator going. As he helped the refugees carry their odd assortment of salvaged belongings, he was surprised and embarrassed that they expected to have to pay him.[2]

On the night of 29–30 July the RAF returned in force yet again to Hamburg, killing a further 9,666 inhabitants. That night Klaus was able to write to his mother without candles, his paper illuminated by the glow of the 'fire-cloud'. On 31 July, Klaus finally had enough time off duty to check that his mother's flat was intact and to carry their own and their neighbours' valuables down to the cellar. It was as if his entire training in his Nazi home, at school, in the Hitler Youth and the *Flak* had prepared him for this moment. He professed not to understand why their own neighbours wanted to leave, arguing with cool logic that, since everything else around it had been destroyed, a fire break now surrounded their block of flats, making it safer than before.[3]

Klaus strove in his letters to maintain the kind of level tone befitting a young man of sixteen in uniform for the first time. He never mentioned a single corpse and never admitted to his own fear or that of his comrades – except obliquely when he said that he needed to smoke to get through an attack – but even this was an acceptable military practice. His account was drier and less emotional than the confidential report of the city's police president. When Seidel wanted his mother to know what they had gone through, he quoted the first lieutenant in his *Flak* battery who maintained that the bombing of Hamburg was worse than anything he had experienced during the Polish or French campaigns.[4]

What it cost these teenage boys to summon up such cool poise is impossible to calculate, but they did so in the self-image of having finally grown up and entered the world of men. For Klaus and the other boys in the sixth and seventh grades of the Lichtwarck High School who had joined the *Flakhelfer* in February 1943, the new air force and naval uniforms were not only the realisation of a dream long cherished through their years in the *Jungvolk* and Hitler Youth. The ordeal of serving under fire had made the uniforms sacred, setting them apart from the world of the Hitler Youth boys. Now they looked with contempt upon those they had left so recently. When Klaus heard that Hitler Youths had been awarded Iron Crosses for putting out incendiary bombs, he lost his self-possession for the first time in his correspondence to his mother. 'Anyone can put out incendiary bombs,' he raged, 'but when the direction finders call out "Plane dropping bombs", to go on working calmly demands quite other strengths.' Klaus Seidel could not know that many Hitler Youths would find themselves among the final defenders of the Reich, nor did he reflect on how many of his own survival skills had been honed in the youth movement. Without a second thought, Seidel had started bathing in the lake in the middle of the *Stadtpark* like a boy on summer camp, as gas, electricity, water and telephone lines were cut throughout the city. But Klaus Seidel was also still half a child. Before the raids began, he had been worrying that he could find no adult relative to sign his school report. Even during the first night and day of the bombing, his thoughts still turned to the model aeroplane he was building at school.[5]

Incendiary bombing changed the face of war. Pavel Vasilievich Pavlenko was one of the 450 prisoners from the Neuengamme concentration camp who were sent to clear the 2.5 square-mile 'dead zone' of Rothenburgsort, Hammerbrook and Hamm-Süd, where the streets were littered with the dead. For the seventeen-year-old from the Ukraine, the worst task of all was opening up the cellars. They might collapse at any moment and were sometimes still hot and glowing inside, with pockets of carbon monoxide. They were also, he recollected, 'full of desiccated people' still 'sitting there'. He helped collect the bones in a bathtub and carry them outside. Even though he thought of the Germans as his enemies, he still found it hard at first to look at their civilian dead. The Hamburg chief of police reported that many German soldiers on leave 'found only a few bones' in their search for their families. Reduced sometimes to less than half their size, the 'doll-like' corpses still remained recognisable, a phenomenon which the pathologist Siegfried Gräff attributed to the proportionate dehydration of all the internal organs when the body baked in such cellars after death.[6]

As whole districts turned to rubble and swirling dust, even seasoned locals became lost, disorientated and confused as they tried to search their own neighbourhoods. Those who had been bombed out often left notes pinned to buildings near their destroyed homes to let others know where to find them. It took Klaus Seidel a fortnight to discover that his grandparents had survived. Relatives searched for their dead through the streets and makeshift hospitals, trying to identify the remains by stray articles of clothing that had survived intact. Medical orderlies resorted to forceps to remove wedding rings after rigor mortis had set in. Then the relatives still had to report the death to the civic authorities. These fraught and exhausting preoccupations left many people too numb to think about the war for now.[7]

The bombing of Hamburg marked a turning point in the air war. Its scale was completely unprecedented, and it came at a time when both British and German governments thought that such attacks on German civilians might decide the fortunes of the war. Henceforth, RAF Bomber Command and Churchill would set Hamburg as a benchmark for what they were trying to achieve elsewhere. Both the local and national Nazi leaderships panicked. As order in the city disintegrated, the local *Gauleiter* even released political prisoners. Nationally, too, the Nazi leaders started imagining – just as their British attackers did – that civilian morale could not survive further assaults like these and, what with Mussolini's fall from power in Italy, they spent a summer full of grim forebodings about their own vulnerability. Hitler's perennial dread of the home front collapsing as it had in November 1918 seemed about to be realised. The government made special quotas of brandy and real coffee beans available to bombed areas. In an effort to re-equip those who had lost everything as quickly as possible, German agencies in the occupied territories began shipping the property they had looted from the Jews – and had planned to give to local German settlers – straight to the cities of north and western Germany. The government might understate the casualties, only for rumour to inflate them, and the city's evacuees spread tales of the complete collapse of political and social order in Hamburg to distant parts of Germany. To the consternation of both the Nazi regime and RAF Bomber Command, the Swedish press speculated that 100,000 people had died, a figure widely cited in post-war Germany. The reality was catastrophic enough. Between 35,000 and 41,000 people had been killed.[8]

The Hamburg raids were the culmination of an RAF campaign that had begun that spring and whose foundations Arthur Harris had been laying ever since he had taken over Bomber Command in February 1942. Starting on 5 March 1943 with raids on Essen, Bomber Command had launched a campaign of nightly raids by massed numbers of heavy bombers on the densely packed centres of working-class housing in the Ruhr. Justified by the argument that targeting the industrial workforce would disrupt war production, such attacks quickly became the main thrust of RAF bombing, partly because – for planes flying high to escape the *Flak* and equipped with inaccurate bombsights – the big cities were relatively easy to hit. The success of Operation *Gomorrah* over Hamburg led Churchill to agree to Harris's plans to inflict an even heavier series of raids on the German capital. 'We can wreck Berlin from end to end,' Harris promised at the beginning of November 1943, adding, 'It will cost us 400–500 aircraft. It will cost Germany the war.' Continuing until 24 March 1944, the cycle of attacks which the RAF mounted against Berlin proved to be the heaviest and most prolonged in the European war. But Germany did not capitulate by 1 April 1944, as Harris had rashly prophesied. Instead, by late March 1944, the RAF's losses to the German *Flak* and night-fighter squadrons of the *Luftwaffe* were becoming unsustainable. The whole strategy of 'area bombing' was put on hold. Harris would not have his way again until the new American long-range fighters had finished destroying the fighter squadrons of the *Luftwaffe*; and not until after the D-Day campaign in Normandy, during which Bomber Command performed highly effectively as German-style 'flying artillery' on the battlefields. By then it was also clear to all that Allied victory would be won on the ground rather than from the air.[9]

But for a long middle period of the war it was the threat from the air that preoccupied German civilians in the cities of the north-west. Constant repetition taught children to react to the sirens' screaming wail in their sleep. So one girl, who had been evacuated with her family from the bombing of Mainz, recollected how she cried aloud in her sleep at night at the sound of the sirens and begged her parents to take her to the bunker. A boy, born in 1940, traced his first memory back to the sound of the air-raid sirens as his parents roused him from his sleep. For these younger 'war children' it was quite common to associate the bombing either with their earliest or their strongest memories of the period. The conjunction of sudden awakening out of deep sleep and the sound of the sirens was particularly potent. Once RAF bombing became serious in 1942 and 1943, children practised going to bed dressed in tracksuits. In Bochum, Karl-Heinz Bödecker repeated each night as he got into bed, 'May the Tommies leave us in peace tonight.' Among Ute Rau's first stumbling words were 'Quick, quick, coats, cellar'. Some children carried little suitcases or rucksacks down into the air-raid shelters, presumably to give them a sense of focus and involvement in the proceedings. Many promptly fell asleep again on cots or bunk beds which had been rigged up in the cellars and bunkers. Others ran about and played games, sometimes cheering up the adults around them. One boy even remembered being visited by St Nicholas and given biscuits in the bunker.[10]

Sirens had such a powerful effect because of the sequence of events they inevitably heralded. At that time, 'I was four to five years old,' wrote one Essen boy, 'and still see the nights well during which we lay in the cellar and literally waited for the next raid. Amidst the howling and screeching of the sirens we then ran into a bunker, that was damp, humid and overcrowded with people. Here we felt almost nothing of the raid, but the fear stayed all the same.' Essen was relatively well equipped with concrete bunkers: given its prominence at the centre of the Krupp armaments empire, it had been singled out early as a city requiring air defences. Yet even in these massive shelters, where the sounds were muffled and the collapse, let alone the movement, of the buildings was cushioned, children registered the signs of bombardment. One girl remembered how severe quakes always put out the gas lamps in the bunker. But it was also the crush and clamour of frightened people that stuck in her mind.[11]

Sirens had similar effects on adults as on children. Even the report writers for the Security Police felt moved to note in May 1944, during a relative lull in the bombing campaign and nearly two months after the Allies' 'Battle of Berlin' had ended, that

the attitude of women raises the question of whether, under a longer contin-uation of present conditions, the discipline of the population, which has been maintained until now, can be sustained in terms of their nerves. Many national comrades . . . have had the wail of the air-raid sirens, the rumble of the engines of attacking aircraft, the shooting of the *Flak* and the explosion of the bombs continually in their ears and with the best will in the world can no longer free themselves from these impressions . . .[12]

Children often claim to have learned fear from the adults around them. As another boy at the Burg Gymnasium in Essen wrote,

I was born just at the outbreak of war so that I cannot remember the first [war] years. But from my fifth year on, much is ineradicably etched in my memory. I sat through long nights of bombing in the cellar or bunker between shaking adults.[13]

Or as a boy at the vocational school put it, 'Then it started in the bunker where people crouched in every corner and angle. With every bomb that fell the "Our Fathers" sounded louder.' Those – and in almost every German city they formed the great majority – who did not have access to a bunker, took refuge in their cellars, where every shudder and tremor could be felt. Children learned to listen for the different sounds, recognising the high-explosive bombs from their 'Crash bang!!!' and the 'muffled crack' of the incendiaries, whose 'clack, clack clack' reminded one child of 'when someone got a juicy slap'.[14]

As soon as Liselotte Günzel came upstairs from her Berlin cellar on 29 December 1943, she reached for her diary and began to write. 'It was another terrifying raid,' the fifteen-year-old wrote, as she tried to name her emotions and bring them back into some kind of intelligible order. 'We have one advantage over people from earlier generations,' she continued with teenage earnestness, 'we have become acquainted with mortal terror. Then everything falls away from a person; all the whitewash, everything apart from God that was most sacred in my life left me when death stretched out his finger towards me (I would never have believed it) . . . The sole comfort in my heart, the only comfort in mortal danger, remained: God's eternal love. It did not desert me.' Liselotte had taken comfort in prayer, repeating the words from her own confirmation nine months before:

My most beautiful ornament and jewel on earth art Thou, Lord Jesus Christ, I will that Thou mayest reign over me and that I may hold Thee at all times in my heart in love as in sorrow.

Thy love and devotion guide all things, no thing on earth standeth so fast, this I do freely confess, therefore shall neither death, nor fear, nor extremity separate me from Thy love.

Thy word is true and deceiveth not and keepeth its promises in death and also in life. Thou art now mine and I am Thine, I have surrendered myself unto Thee.[15]

When Liselotte had learned these words she could have had no inkling of how soon she would be put to the test, finding courage now in the literal truth of her pledge that 'therefore shall neither death, nor fear, nor extremity separate me from Thy love'. Almost as disconcerting as her terror in the cellar during the air raid was the eerie kind of normality that followed as the family climbed the stairs to their flat and resumed their customary activities. Liselotte found it hard to make sense of her rapidly changing emotions, finding her terror in the cellar suddenly strange as soon as she returned to the flat and picked up her diary once more.[16]

Living in Friedrichshagen on the eastern outskirts of Berlin, Liselotte Günzel's experience of air raids began on 22 November 1943, the night of the second major RAF assault on Berlin. Nothing fell on their quarter, but her father's office was completely destroyed and her mother fretted about their livelihood. Phone lines were cut, the overground *S-Bahn* and the trams were halted. The next night was just as bad: 'The whole inner city is said to be a heap of rubble. Friedrichstr[asse], [Unter den] Linden, Leipziger Strasse, Alex[ander Platz], everything destroyed, Auntie K. bombed out. My school burned out, can't go there any more.'[17]

In forty minutes the RAF had dropped 1,132 tonnes of high explosives alongside 1,331 tonnes of incendiary bombs. The destruction was so great that the fire brigade and the clean-up squads had enormous difficulty getting through to fight the fires. The fires raging around the Hausvogteiplatz looked set to unite into a general conflagration. Army units and the fire brigades had come from as far away as Stettin, Magdeburg and Leipzig, and the fires were finally extinguished shortly before the bombers returned the next night. By now the fire and air-defence personnel were worn out and a sharp, frosty wind threatened to turn the new conflagrations in the central administrative district into, in Goebbels's words, 'an inferno'. The greater spaciousness of Berlin's avenues and squares, as well as the smaller amounts of wood used in the buildings, prevented a firestorm from taking hold as it had done in the old city centres of Kassel and Hamburg. Nonetheless, between 22 and 26 November great damage was inflicted on the city and its inhabitants: 3,758 people killed, a further 574 listed as missing and nearly half a million made homeless. Compared even with the three air raids the city had endured in late August and September, this was a new level of experience. To cope with the enormous numbers bombed out who had nowhere to go, the municipal authorities erected temporary shelters in the city's outer suburbs and its green belt.[18]

Liselotte Günzel's district had remained on the fringes of the main events during these first air raids, so that their effect on her was incremental and psychological rather than sudden and physical. Nonetheless, the impact was overwhelming. At 3.45 a.m. on Christmas Eve she heard the air-raid sirens start to howl. She and her parents thought the raid would not be too bad because it was already nearly morning, much later than the normal air raids, but this time the bombs fell much closer to home. The Pathfinder squadron that marked the target area had had trouble with its navigational aids and the bombing was scattered over the city, reaching into eastern districts of Berlin like Friedrichshagen, which had been generally spared till now. During this seventh raid by the RAF, Liselotte and her parents had just stumbled down the stairs, dragging their suitcases beside them, and reached the cellar when with a terrifying bang the light went out. As she wrote later that day in her diary, 'We grabbed our cases and wanted to rush outside, thinking that the walls were going to fall in. Dust was swirling around, windows shattering.' Outside the clouds showed red against the glare of the fires burning in the city. 'Our men strove for order, forbade us from going out because the anti-aircraft guns were still firing and bombs were still falling. We sat for half an hour in the dark under appalling bursts of explosions and awaited our end.' For the first time, Liselotte also confessed to feeling truly frightened.[19]

Luckily the raid ended soon. Her father went upstairs and reported back to them that all the windows had been blown out and fires were burning in the neighbourhood. The family came upstairs, too, and matter-of-factly started to straighten things out. Every surface was covered in glass and dirt, their jars of preserves were smashed, strewing pickled cucumbers over the kitchen floor, and the clock had stopped at five minutes past four. The radio aerial was broken. Liselotte looked on as if in a dream. Then they began to clean up. They rolled up the carpets, took down their shredded blackout material and stitched it together again, carried the rubbish downstairs and flung it onto the street, in more peaceful times a prosecutable offence in Germany. Now, Liselotte noted with a hint of self-justification, everyone did it.

As she looked around her at all the houses with their windows gone, she was thrilled. In the darkness of the early morning all the windows in the neighbourhood were lit up for the first time in years. 'It was,' she noted, 'like an image of peacetime!! And today was Christmas Eve!! I was so delighted.' Soon nobody would be able to see out of the windows at all, as people hunted down sheets of cardboard to keep out the wind and cold: Liselotte went to the town hall and was given some there. The family went on with its Christmas preparations regardless.[20]

By the time she found herself reciting her confirmation prayers in the cellar on the night of 28–29 December, Liselotte had endured five weeks of continually disrupted sleep. The frequency of the air-raid alarms and severity of the bombing, the passivity of waiting in the cellar, were all taking their toll. In the few days since Christmas the bombing had infiltrated her sleep and her dreams. Even in the daytime she could not free herself of her fears. By the new year, Liselotte's efforts and constant moral demands on herself were narrowing in focus: she must not, she repeated to herself like a refrain, break down. 'As the bombs explode around you with unimaginable noise, death reaches for your heart with his icy hand,' she wrote on 3 January 1944. 'You have only one thought,' she went on. '"If only it would stop!" But it does not stop. You think, in a moment your nerves must crack, you'll have to cry out, but you're not allowed to, you have to keep your composure, you are not allowed to be weak, because that is what Frau L. told me . . .'[21]

Frau L. was Liselotte's German teacher at school and the focus of a full-scale teenage crush for about a year. Liselotte looked to Frau L., the nationalist wife of a Prussian officer, as the embodiment of her ideal of 'German womanhood' and found her own behaviour constantly wanting by comparison. Liselotte noted every one of her own failures with the same lofty intolerance that she judged the adult world around her. And, like Klaus Seidel in Hamburg, Liselotte Günzel was greatly preoccupied with projecting an attitude of composure. But whereas his battery could fire back, she was condemned to experience the air raids in claustrophobic passivity, knowing each time that if she survived, she would have to return to the dank cellar and endure it again and again.

Younger children experienced the bombing in markedly different ways from teenagers like Liselotte. In the mid-1950s, as the three- and four-year-olds of 1943 and 1944 tried to write about their war experiences, many had to confront early childhood memories which defied verbal expression. So, instead, they described the fear of those around them or repeated the tales their parents had told them about their childhoods, one boy even recounting his own loss of speech. In the mid-1950s there was much for which these children had no words. As eleven-year-old Marion stood in front of the ruins of their house, she could not grasp that it had been destroyed. The most dreadful experiences they did recount – one girl was dug out of the rubble of her house after five days – were often described in the most fleeting terms. A decade after the end of the war, very few of these younger children referred to seeing the dead.[22]

Some parents tried to show their children the devastation from a distance. Sigrid Marr remembered how her mother conducted her up to the third floor of their house where they

stared down at the sea of flames between the houses, looked at the glowing gables and window frames . . . 'This is one face of war,' my mother said to me. 'War has many faces, but all are terrible. It shows one of its faces here in the city after a bombing raid, the other out there at the front and in the field hospitals . . .' I nodded. Now I knew.[23]

In some respects the behaviour of children and their mothers was remarkably similar. Mothers counted the pieces of china that had miraculously survived the destruction of their homes. Their children grieved through the odd shoes and dolls they had retrieved. One girl, bombed out for the second time shortly after Christmas, sat quietly in the corner for the whole day. While her younger sister consoled herself with the doll their grandfather had rescued from the rubble, he retrieved her Christmas present and she immersed herself in the half-charred book about Queen Luise of Prussia whose heroic resistance to Napoleon had become a children's classic in the 1920s. Fifteen-year-old Liselotte could turn to the prayers she had learned for her confirmation and focus on preserving the appearance of outward calm she thought befitted her ideal of 'the German woman'. Older children and adults had words for expressing their disbelief and their pain, their grief and their rage. Younger children often did not.[24]

Three-year-old Uwe Timm could only summon up fragmentary images of the destruction of his Hamburg home in July 1943 – the two porcelain figures his elder sister carried outside; the line of burning torches down each side of the street; the small fires that seemed to hang in the air. Only much later did he learn that these were caused by burning curtains carried by the wind and that the torches had been trees. The missing hand of the porcelain shepherdess who survived continued to stand for all the family lost on 25 July 1943. Uwe's older brother, Karl-Heinz, by contrast reacted to the news of the bombing with outrage. When he read his father's letter, the young SS man wrote back from the Soviet Union immediately, 'That is not a war, but just a murder of women and children – and it is not humane.'[25]

Other children often watched these extraordinary but distant sights of destruction with awe and wonderment, thrilled by the vividness of the colours and wild beauty of the sights. Living in Hamburg before the July 1943 raids, Harald Holzhausen could see the oil tanks burning after a raid on the port of Harburg. For the thirteen-year-old boy, tired out from being woken twice by air-raid sirens in the same night, the colours were completely captivating and magical:

I gazed fascinated at the play of colours, into the yellow and red of the flames, which mingled and divided again against the background of the dark night sky. Neither before nor afterwards did I see such a clean, radiant yellow, such a blazing red, such a vibrant orange into which both colours merged. Today, fifty-five years later, I think this sight was the most significant experience of the whole war for me. I stood for minutes at a time on the street and looked at this symphony of colours, which only changed slowly. Later on I never saw such rich, radiant colours, not by any painter either. And had I become a painter . . . I would have spent a lifetime looking for these pure colours.[26]

Nor did the first appearance of Allied planes overhead necessarily evoke terror in children. One five-year-old girl, watching from her home outside Berlin as the planes flew in to bomb the city in 1943, remembered that 'the sight of the threatening and growling aeroplanes was such that I thought I was dreaming and in a magical world'. She wrote this in a school essay twelve years later, when she had very good reasons to replace her wonderment with fear. Another girl in her school imagined the planes as large animals flying over her home city of Essen, while in Breslau, Sabine Kaufmann found herself similarly captivated by the sight of American planes flying in formation, this time during daylight and very high, so high that in the early-morning light she thought they looked like 'silver birds beneath the blue sky'. 'It was a beautiful, majestic sight,' she wrote. 'My childish nature was so receptive to this spectacle that a feeling of happiness streamed through me. I had only one wish: to fly with them.'[27]

Again and again children compared such sights with being at the theatre, watching a show greater than any they had ever seen. Whereas children often found great beauty in these instruments of destruction, even in the fires themselves, only very rarely did adults comment on this aspect of the air war. An observer like Ursula von Kardorff confined her commentary on the 'wild beauty' of the bluey-black smoke swirling over the chalk-white pavements of Berlin after an air raid to the privacy of her diary; others might have found such comments tasteless. And yet, a shadow of the children's delight became embedded in adult slang. The different coloured marker flares that were used by the attackers to pinpoint the targets, or were launched by the defenders as decoys, descended slowly through the night sky on small parachutes. Their twinkling reds, greens, blues and yellows were called 'Christmas trees' in German, an illusion given completeness by the RAF's use of 'Window' to confuse the German radar systems. The cascade of small aluminium strips boys like Harald Holzhausen found on the ground after a raid looked for all the world like lametta, the silver tinsel families draped over the Christmas tree.[28]

After air raids adults turned to protecting their own homes and possessions, or to helping out their relatives and immediate neighbours, while Hitler Youths like Lothar Carsten assisted the emergency services. This thirteen-year-old went with the rest of his *Jungvolk* comrades to run messages and help the bombed-out carry their belongings after Wuppertal was struck on 29 May 1943. On their walk to school the day after a raid, younger children stopped to collect the strips of aluminium and fragments of anti-aircraft shells. These *Flak* splinters were particularly prized by boys, who traded them in their school playgrounds just as their older brothers had once swapped cigarette cards. But some other games no longer made any sense at all: the six-year-old girl who had loved playing 'Stuka' abandoned the game after Essen was bombed in March 1943. The make-believe had become all too real.[29]

Children gathered, too, in order to watch the teams who came to defuse unexploded bombs. Pavel Vasilievich Pavlenko was part of a team from Neuengamme concentration camp sent to defuse bombs in Wilhelmshafen. His whole squad had to dig in a circle round the unexploded bombs before one of them was chosen by lot to unscrew the fuse itself, the most dangerous part of the whole routine. Teams like his generally did the dirtiest and most dangerous jobs. But when children in Essen thought about the risks being run by the German experts and their neighbours, they ignored those facing the concentration camp prisoners in the team even when they remembered they had been present. For the most part, teenage diarists like Liselotte Günzel were too engrossed in exploring their own worlds to stop and notice the forced labourers who clearned up their streets at all.[30]

As a society of flat-dwellers, urban Germans concentrated their sense of community in their families and their immediate neighbours in the same building. They helped set up bunks in their cellars and put out fires together, forming spontaneous human chains to pass buckets of water from hand to hand. Neighbours relied on each other to guard their property and possessions against the wholesale theft of goods left on the streets. Children were told to keep an eye on the suitcases their parents had brought to the air-raid shelters with their papers and valuables. As their mutual obligations within this narrow community of neighbours deepened, so they turned inwards to their block of flats and their street. The 'national community' was shrinking towards the more visible dimensions of the neighbourhood and house. By the war's end, diarists would write about their 'cellar communities'. Already the criminal police was worrying whether the rise in theft and breakdown of solidarity spelled a decline in the national will for victory.[31]

Foreign workers were not always so invisible as when they worked in the bomb disposal units. When it came to looting, the police were on the lookout for them, even though they found that most of the people they arrested after the Hamburg raids were Germans, including SA men, Red Cross auxiliaries and solid citizens from the professional middle class. It was the foreign workers, especially the concentration camp prisoners on the bomb squads, who were punished most ruthlessly and for the most trivial offences such as scavenging a swede. Some were taken back to Neuengamme and hanged in front of the entire concentration camp for being caught with a piece of cheese or a matchbox they had hoped to trade.[32]

Klimenti Ivanovich Baidak was shocked to be met on the streets of Hamburg by schoolboys in Hitler Youth uniform, who accompanied their taunts of 'Russen kaputt' by pulling their ceremonial daggers out of their sheaths and drawing them across their throats. Even before the March raids on Essen, a French civilian worker wrote home from the Ruhr expressing his hope that 'it's over soon, because the people here have a mentality like a bunch of savages. Little five-year-old kids threaten us in the street. But you have to grit your teeth, because you can't say a thing, you just have to swallow it all.'[33]

The Hitler Youth did not have it all their own way. Informal working-class street gangs that had sprung up across German cities, especially in the Rhineland and the Ruhr, during the early war years had continued to grow. A new cohort of teenage workers and apprentices, like Fritz

Theilen, who were tired of being bossed around in the Hitler Youth and, accustomed now to earning their own money, wanted more freedom and less regimentation, wanted to hang out in the parks and play their guitars. Apart from impressing the local girls and breaking the night-time curfew, defending their territory against other gangs and, above all, the local Hitler Youth, these twelve- to seventeen-year-olds had progressed to setting out on their own hikes and cycling tours in libertarian imitation of the Hitler Youth. Often the young dissidents treasured the same things, making off with Hitler Youth badges and daggers of honour after evening brawls, while safeguarding their own sheath knives and home-made Edelweiss badges. In Hamburg, one such gang even took its name from the SS, calling itself the 'Death's Head'. Unable to tolerate and render such nonconformist youth harmless, patrols of Hitler Youths and SA men hunted them down, forcing several thousand to have their heads shaved, even sending some of them to reformatories, labour education camps and youth concentration camps. But a small hardcore of these gangs of 'Edelweiss Pirates' and 'Navajos' persisted, and the more the Hitler Youth and Storm Troopers harassed them, the more anti-Nazi their sentiments became. As Fritz Theilen and his friends in the Cologne district of Ehrenfeld turned their talents to political graffiti, they used air-raid alarms to daub 'Nazi heads will roll after the war!' under the Nazi slogan 'Wheels must roll for victory!'[34] But their songs celebrating the male camaraderie of fighting were tinged with an almost Nazi hue:

> For our fists, they are hard
> Yes – and our knives lie ready
> For the freedom of youth
> The Navajos fight.

And 'When the sirens sound in Hamburg', then, they sang – just like everyone else – 'The Navajos have to get on board'.[35]

Bombing must always have provoked feelings of individual helplessness. Nonetheless, this sense did not translate into a national feeling that Germany itself was helpless until very late in the war; not until the *Luftwaffe*, the *Flak* units and the *Wehrmacht* had been defeated. For civilians in the cities and small towns that fell prey to Allied bombing this moment did not arrive until the autumn of 1944 and the winter and spring of 1945. It was during this last phase of the war that the bombing became most severe and the loss of human life greatest, and the Nazi regime began, for the first time since 1934, openly to terrorise its own population. But, for the middle phase of the war, from the attack on the Soviet Union in June 1941 to the Normandy landings three years later, Germany did not appear helpless in the face of Allied bombing, even though it was precisely during this period that the Allies attached the greatest strategic importance to it. During this long and crucial middle period of the war, there were good reasons for German civilian morale to hold firm. Despite the bombing and the defeat at Stalingrad in January 1943, the *Wehrmacht* still controlled the European continent from the Channel and Atlantic ports to deep into the Soviet Union. The air war itself was not a simple battle between the RAF's Bomber Command and the civilian population either, and people had good reason to feel that Germany could fight back. At the end of March 1944, anti-aircraft artillery and the night-fighter squadrons of the *Luftwaffe* were still succeeding in decimating the bomber fleets.[36]

The loose talk about a change of regime or an end to the war, which had surfaced briefly during the summer of 1943 after Mussolini's fall from power, was swiftly silenced. Once the Special Courts started to hand out increasing numbers of death penalties for defeatist talk in the autumn of 1943, people retreated back into their shells again. Despite Hitler's opposition to diverting military resources away from offensive capability, they were quietly shifted back to defend the home front. Fighter squadrons were brought back from the eastern front, even though the Red Air Force had won control of the skies above the great tank battle at Kursk in July. The strains on German military capability caused by such multiple offensive and defensive commitments would be just as Hitler had feared. By the end of 1943, the *Flak* artillery had been built up to 55,000 guns, receiving three-quarters of the 88mm guns, which had already earned such a fearsome reputation as tank busters in North Africa and on the eastern front. Churchill might be exaggerating when he compared the air war with a second front, but the mass bombing of 1943 was starting to disrupt the flow of war material to the eastern front, even though the bombers were remarkably ineffective at hitting the arms factories themselves.[37]

Meanwhile, no one in the German government doubted the need

for immediate and massive measures for civil defence. A gigantic bunker-building programme got under way in the big cities. Huge underground shelters were constructed, like the one next to the Anhalter Station in Berlin, conveniently linked to the tunnels of the underground network. Bunkers were also contructed in Berlin, Bremen, Hamburg and other cities in the form of massive towers above ground, great windowless fortresses whose four-metre-thick walls of ferrous concrete also provided platforms for the anti-aircraft guns, radar equipment and searchlights mounted on their flat roofs. The three Berlin towers at the Zoo, Humboldthain and Friedrichshain could each accommodate 10,000 people and acted as strong defence points against attacks from the air and, in the final battle for the city, against ground forces. They also provided the population with a rallying point, a place of protection and a symbol of the national 'will to hold out'.[38]

All this required huge resources. The Berlin bunkers accounted for half the building programme of 1943, but even so could give shelter to only a fraction of the city's inhabitants. As elsewhere, most Berliners still had to seek shelter in the cellars of their blocks of flats. In small-town Germany the locals were less well drilled in civil defence and suffered proportionately much greater losses of life from single bombing raids than did known targets like Berlin and Essen, which had been bombed far more often. The schools did what they could, putting yet another cohort of children through civil defence drill, complete with gas masks, and acting as assembly points for those who were bombed out. In 1944, fourteen-year-olds like Mathilde Mollenbauer had to write out 'Into the air-raid shelter when there is danger of an air raid. Caution is not cowardice', a refrain she had to repeat until she had covered the whole page and learned it by heart.[39]

Within two weeks of the bombing of Hamburg, it was evident that the country was divided between those who had suffered from air-raid alarms and those who had not. The trains of refugees heading to safety were received with warmth and sympathy in north and central Germany. But as the trains headed south, the population was said to have responded 'coolly and to some extent even rejected' the evacuees. In southern Germany and Austria, the Security Police reported in mid-August, people simply had no idea 'of the catastrophe which the evacuees had undergone or of the accompanying physical and emotional suffering'. In East Prussia, locals referred to the mothers as 'Bombenweiber' and called the girls and boys 'Splitterkinder'. In

Bavaria they shouted '*Bombenkinder*' and the more traditional greeting of '*Saupreussen*' – 'Prussian sows' – at the girls as they marched in their uniforms through the countryside. Only in the 'extremely primitive conditions' enjoyed by ethnic German settlers in the Wartheland did the refugees encounter the warm and spontaneous welcome of those who had themselves been forced to move.[40]

For one Hamburg mother fleeing with her three children, arrival in the south was marked by the impossibility of obtaining clean nappies for her one-year-old baby. By the time she reached Linz in Austria, she and the children had nowhere to sleep but the floor of the railway station. As the children fell ill, she wrote to her husband begging him to send her the money for her fare home and assuring him that the basement of their home in Hamburg would be a 'thousand times better than here'. Above all, she asked him, 'Stop, wherever you can, the poor people from travelling to regions which lie in deepest peace . . . No one here in the *Ostmark* [Austria] understands. I wish that they would get bombed here too.'[41]

Further north things were quite different. Even in towns that had been spared, the sirens had sounded along the entire length of the flight paths taken by the fleets of bombers. Already in February 1943, eighteen-month-old Ursel had run to tell her granny she had 'Flyer-fear!' but, cocooned beyond Berlin, this was only the second time the toddler had heard the heavy growl of enemy aircraft engines overhead. From March till July, the RAF launched thirty-one major night raids on the much closer cities of the Ruhr, but kept changing the targets, partly to give the bombers – as yet with no long-range fighters of their own to protect them – better chances against the night fighter squadrons of the *Luftwaffe*. People got used to the routines of waking several times in the night, deciding whether or not to go down to the cellar and waiting for the all-clear. They often had more energy to discuss the bombing raids than the exhausted and dispirited refugees themselves. Dresdeners listened to the stories from Berlin with dread, imagining what it would be like to experience such raids themselves. Fear and rage were felt far beyond Berlin that winter and spring of 1943–4. Maria, the fourteen-year-old Polish domestic servant of a German family outside Danzig, was beaten by her mistress every time there was an air raid on the capital. The woman's husband, formerly a teacher in a German school in Poland, was employed on the military staff in Berlin and Maria was beaten often.[42]

If Germans did not yet feel defeated, the triumphalism of 1940 must have seemed a distant memory. Liselotte Günzel might have become ever more uncertain of her nerves by the end of 1943, but this did not make her a defeatist, even though her own father – an old Social Democrat – stomped about their flat muttering endlessly about revolution and did his best to convince her that Germany had lost the war. Instead, she looked eagerly for signs of German retaliation against England. This reaction had been well prepared throughout 1943. For the German defeat at Stalingrad in January had led Goebbels to give propaganda an increasingly shrill and pessimistic content. In the spring of 1943 he had launched propaganda campaigns about Soviet atrocities, Jewish war guilt and the promise to pay Britain back for the indiscriminate bombing of German cities. From the summer onwards, German propaganda began to invoke Germany's possession of a secret 'miracle weapon', which would help deliver 'final victory', but still nothing happened. By the summer both the Security Police reports on public opinion and Liselotte's diary were registering high levels of anxiety about how Germany was going to win the war and when the promised retaliation was actually going to come.[43]

Hitler had hardly spoken in public at all during the whole of 1943. In March, he had come back to Berlin from his East Prussian headquarters to mark Heroes' Remembrance Day, but had said nothing about the heroes who had just died on the Volga. Instead, he had rattled through his speech in such a rapid monotone that many people listening on the radio had wondered whether they were hearing a stand-in. After Hamburg, Hitler had refused Goebbels's urging to visit the bombed cities or to make a broadcast. Finally, after months of waiting, the Führer spoke to his people on 8 November 1943: it was one of the key dates in the Nazi calendar, the eve of the twentieth anniversary of his attempted putsch in Munich. By this time he was the only major figure whose reputation remained untarnished and could still command public credibility.[44]

The streets emptied to listen to the broadcast of his speech at 8.15 p.m. People were looking for reassurance and, most important, for confirmation that England really would be knocked out of the war by the new miracle weapons his Party propagandists had been promising all summer, or at least for some sign that real retaliation was on the way. They leaped on his rather vague threat of a strike against Britain with joy and relief: 'If the Führer says that, then I believe it. Tommy

will get his deserts . . .' or, as another stool-pigeon for the Security
Police noted down, 'A promise from the mouth of the Führer is worth
more than all the declarations in the press, radio and meetings of the
Party . . .'⁴⁵

In her parents' flat in Berlin, Liselotte confided to her diary, 'I am
just listening to the Hitler speech.' Despite her own unusually strong
misgivings about the Führer, she was buoyed up by his words: 'Hitler
has given me faith in victory again, he has spoken of a landing in
England and of retaliation for the terror bombing.' Then, in an echo
of Hitler's own obsessive reiteration that the capitalution of 1918 must
never be repeated, Liselotte took private refuge in apocalyptic public
sentiments: 'And even if all should go down, there will not be another
1918. Adolf Hitler, I believe in you and the German victory.' Catholic
clergy once more challenged the media monopoly of the regime by
using the pulpit to warn that vengeance was un-Christian. But in the
hard-hit Rhineland and Westphalia, their congregations often disregarded these moral lessons and, instead, fantasised about the scale
of the retaliation that would be launched against England. Pledging
these shared hopes in the form of solemn promises and vows may have
come naturally to adolescents like Liselotte, but teenagers were by no
means alone in subscribing to the power of 'strong hearts' and German
belief in victory.⁴⁶

Within seven weeks of Hitler's broadcast, whatever temporary hope
his words had given had evaporated under the tonnage of RAF bombing
and the news of a third freezing Christmas for the soldiers bivouacked
on the eastern front. A new rash of political jokes began to alarm the
Secret Police agents who wrote them down in late December 1943.
One ran thus:

Dr Goebbels has been bombed out in Berlin. He rescues two suitcases and
brings them onto the street and goes back into the house to recover other
things. When he comes out again, both suitcases have been stolen. Dr Goebbels
is very upset, weeps and rails: when asked what was so valuable in the suitcases, he replies: 'In the one was Retaliation and in the other Final Victory!'

Or more succinctly: 'On their last attack on Berlin, the English dropped
straw for the donkeys who still believe in Retaliation . . .'⁴⁷ In the
meantime people wished the bombers would strike some other city. In
the Ruhr, someone coined a popular ditty urging the RAF to fly on to

Berlin, because they were the ones who had all cheered Goebbels's great peroration in February 1943 in favour of 'total war':

> Lieber Tommy fliege weiter,   Dear Tommy, fly onwards,
> wir sind alle Bergarbeiter   We're all miners here.
> Fliege weiter nach Berlin,   Fly onwards to Berlin,
> die haben alle 'ja' geschrien For they all screamed 'yes' there.[48]

As people lay in bed at night and prayed that the bombs would fall on someone else's city they were hollowing out that feeling of national community which propaganda about vengeance and retaliation struggled to revive during the daytime.

But there was a darker side to German civilian morale. A string of letters to Goebbels survives from May and June 1944, advising the regime to use the Jews as human shields within German cities – even after they had in fact been deported – banning them from entering air-raid shelters and publishing the numbers of Jews killed afterwards, so that 'Even if this means has no effect on the terror from the air, at least this plague on humanity ought to be wiped out in part by the actions of their own people in the enemy countries'. Other proposals built on the German practice in occupied Europe of meting out collective reprisals: leaftets should be dropped informing 'the British and American government [sic] after every terror attack in which civilians are killed that ten times as many Jews and Jewesses and their children have been shot'. And a number of letter writers explicitly argued that such measures should have the effect on the British and Americans which the 'new weapons' and 'retaliation' had failed to deliver. Irma J., who called on Goebbels 'on behalf of all German women and mothers and the families of those living here in the Reich' to 'have twenty Jews hanged for every German killed in the place where our defenceless and priceless German people have been cowardly and bestially murdered by the terror flyers', also confessed to her own feelings of helplessness: 'because we have no other weapon available'. K. von N. took the same view, adding that this form of 'retaliation' against the Allies had the 'additional advantage of not putting our pilots at risk'. 'You should see,' he opined, 'how quickly the terror will cease!'[49]

The sense of helplessness and vulnerability which fuelled this murderous rage is perhaps most evident in another letter from Berlin, written by Georg R. on 1 June 1944. Headed 'I receive my letters *poste restante*, because in the meantime I have been burned out once and bombed out twice', Georg R. reminded the *Reichsminister* of his letter of a year earlier and entitled his proposal, 'No annihilation of the German people and German lands but complete annihilation of the Jews'. Instead of expelling all the Jews from Germany, he had a new idea: 'I propose that we should announce with an ad hoc plebiscite that, with immediate effect, we are not going to attack any towns or cities in England any more and hence the enemies may also no longer attack our cities and towns . . . Should our enemies nonetheless dare to attack even one of our towns or cities . . . then we shall have 10,000 or 20,000 or 30,000 Jews shot without mercy.'[50]

Goebbels's correspondents were sending back an amplified echo of the Nazi media. In April 1943 the Propaganda Minister had ordered anti-Semitic propaganda to be stepped up, until 70–80 per cent of radio broadcasts were devoted to the Jewish question, Jewish guilt in causing the war and the fate awaiting Germany should the Jews take revenge. The new 'Jewish school calendar' issued in April 1943 for the new school year was full of 'quotes' of planned Jewish revenge on Gentiles. At the centre of the campaign against British and American 'plutocracy' lay the secret manipulations of the Jew, the single and unitary image of all Nazi propaganda in the last two years of the war. Deep in the Austrian countryside, the slogan 'The Jew is guilty of the war' was drummed into small boys at school. Edgar Plöchl and his classmates had to chant it first thing in the morning. As soon as their strict teacher had checked that their necks, ears, fingernails and hankies were clean, and set aside those who were to be beaten, the boys solemnly repeated the words after him, 'The Jew is guilty of the war' – every day Edgar went to school filled with terror about the morning's punishments, then joined in the same chorus of boys chanting the magical words afterwards.[51]

If Goebbels's propaganda had only convinced Nazis, it might have had relatively little impact. But, as Victor Klemperer found out, Goebbels's orchestration of the Jew as the true protagonist in the war provided a focus for the fears and disorientation felt by people who were not Nazis and who would have been horrified at the idea of shooting Jewish hostages. The nice factory foreman, a fellow veteran of the First World War who had sympathised with Klemperer on 12 March 1944 for having lost his academic job just because he was

Jewish, turned a week later to the idea of Jewish 'billionaires' as he cast about helplessly to give Klemperer a reason for the latest, senseless American bombing of Hamburg. For people like him, the abstract idea of a 'Jewish plutocracy' offered an explanation which cut across their personal liking for individual Jews. This marked a new departure: even in the wake of the November 1938 program, enthusiasm for Nazi anti-Semitism had been generally restricted to groups and regions, like Hesse or Franconia, which had been anti-Semitic before 1933, and made least impact in cities like Berlin, Hamburg, Frankfurt or the Ruhr, where secular traditions and labour movement values ran deep. The war had altered this regional divide. To make sense of the ferocity of the 'terror bombing', the civilian population in the cities became more willing to believe in a conspiracy by an enemy who was filled with an implacable hatred of Germans and Germany.[52]

Belief in the 'Jewish' bombing went beyond hardline Nazis, and was strengthened by more than just anti-Semitic propaganda. It was conditioned by the widespread knowledge of the mass shooting of Jews in the East. The cultivated patrician, Lothar de la Camp, wrote from Hamburg to his siblings on 28 July 1943 in the midst of Operation *Gomorrah*: 'In private and even in bigger circles, simple people, the middle classes and the rest of the population make repeated remarks about the Allied attacks being the revenge for our treatment of the Jews.' In Munich, Essen, Hamburg and Kiel, voices were overheard that summer making the same point. Over 10 per cent of letters written to Goebbels in mid-August protested against the anti-Semitic campaign. Some pointed out that people had other worries; others that the Germans were now being punished for what they had done to the Jews. By 2 September 1943, the *Stuttgarter NS-Kurier* felt that it had to rebutt publicly the argument that world Jewry would not have fought Germany had Germany not solved the Jewish question so radically. Goebbels's anti-Semitic rhetoric was beginning to rebound on the regime. But he had nonetheless won a deeper victory. For neither Lothar de la Camp, nor the people he was citing, had any doubt that the Jews possessed the means to launch such devastating attacks on Germany. In spreading this sense of Jewish power, Goebbels's propaganda about the Jewish 'plutocracy' had done its work well, even if its present effect was to make Germans feel anything but confident.[53]

This pessimistic understanding of the national situation rose and fell in waves as the news from the different fronts altered during the long

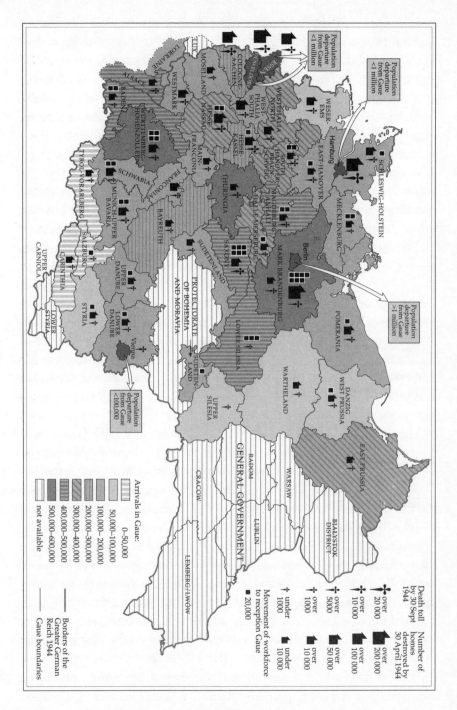

Impact of bombing on German cities (until 1944)

middle phase of the war. When the Americans reached Aachen in
September 1944 they found a population which expected to be collectively punished for what had been done to the Jews. But even critical
and unhappy citizens had internalised the deeper assumption that the
Jews had the unity and power to direct the Allied bombing campaign.
Goebbels was right to think that he could use fear and atrocity propaganda to prevent depressed civilian morale from collapsing into
outright defeatism.[54]

In the meantime, the regime was doing what it could to protect the
young from the bombing raids. After the heavy bombing of the spring
and summer of 1943, many schools were evacuated to the countryside
in their entirety. The model was the same as the earlier evacuations of
1940, 1941 and 1942; except now the scale of the operation was much
greater and the stint away was no longer limited to six months. In
Berlin, Goebbels used his position as *Gauleiter* and Defence
Commissioner to push through as complete a programme as possible.
Many other *Gaue* followed suit and this time, in contrast to the first
evacuations of September 1940, Catholic clergy came out in support of
the measures. By the end of 1943 a huge migration to the countryside
had taken place, from the north and the west of the Reich to the south
and east, which would be overshadowed only by the flight and migration from east to west at the war's end.[55]

The full-scale evacuation of whole schools to stately homes and
convents often depended on effective improvisation. When the
Pestalozzi Gymnasium for Girls in Berlin-Rummelsburg was evacuated
to Schloss Streben, a Polish count's residence in the Wartheland, the
girls had to sleep on straw on the floor and endure flea bites while
wooden bunk beds were built for them. But the rooms were large and
spacious, and the League of German Girls' camp leader would read
them ghost stories at bedtime by the flickering light of the kerosene
lamps. Breakfast always included soup. While the younger girls totted
up the bubbles on the surface as letters from home, the older ones
counted them as kisses. Nor did the kindly camp director, Herr Koethe,
who was always to be seen in his SS uniform, censor their letters home.

The Polish count moved into a flat off the main staircase, but the
girls never saw him and no one stopped them from sliding down the
banisters. For the most part, discipline was administered by the girls
themselves: twelve-year-old Renate Schwartz once had to lie on her
tummy on her bed without uttering a sound, while each of the other

nine girls in her room came up to her in turn and slapped her on the bottom for having run around lifting their skirts. Otherwise, Renate's memories were happy ones. She even landed the role of 'Thumbling', stumbling across the stage in their Sunday theatricals wearing Herr Koethe's oversized SS boots as she wielded a carving knife borrowed from the kitchen. As their theatrical ambitions grew, they put on a greatly extended version of the 'Giant with the three golden hairs' down in the village to the delight of the German families there.[56]

Small-town and rural Germany was less welcoming to the influx of refugee mothers and younger children into their homes and communities. Often they simply felt swamped. In September 1943, 1,241 evacuees from Bochum, Hagen, Berlin, Stettin and other cities were quartered onto the resident population of 8,000 in Rügenwalde on the Pomeranian coast. Overcrowding led to petty – but important and humiliating – daily conflicts, with hosts refusing to provide bedding or sufficient heating fuel, or even to let the refugees use their kitchens. In Rügenwalde the women and children had to bring their food from improvised communal kitchens and eat it in their bedrooms. As numbers of evacuees grew, so locals became ever more reluctant to take them in, and the village mayor and *Ortsgruppenführer* of the party – often, in fact, the same person – had to exert ever greater pressure to find them lodgings. When twelve-year-old Erwin Ebeling arrived in Lübow near Stargard in Pomerania, he was taken to a local inn, where the mixed transport of women, children and teenagers from Hagen were auctioned off to the local farmers. Most wanted to have a woman with only a single child, in order to derive most benefit on their farms. Erwin and ten other boys failed to find takers and had to sleep on bundles of straw in the swineherd's house until families could be found for them.[57]

In the Bayreuth district of Bavaria, two women and a child who had been compelled to share a tiny and inadequately furnished room found that no one was prepared to offer them a warm meal in the locality. They returned to Hamburg. In August 1943, no one in Naugard wanted to take in thirteen-year-old Gisela Vedder and her sister. Finally, the mayor gave them a bed in his kitchen, which he also used to conduct his business. While he sat there drinking with his visitors in the evening, the two girls hid under the covers. Unable to move or find anyone, including their teachers, who felt confident enough to intervene on their behalf, the two girls finally gave up. Dragging their wooden trunk along, they set off on a hot and dusty walk to the station. Again no one came out to help them and they had to lug it through the summer heat on their own.[58]

Everywhere the authorities had to contend with the difficulties of effecting a complete evacuation without compulsion. It was Hitler who had insisted on safeguarding parents' rights, the result of that residual caution about morale on the home front which prevented him from agreeing to the sort of full-scale emergency measures Goebbels had demanded in his 'total war' speech in February 1943. Despite a great deal of publicity, parents did not always give their consent. Local Party and Education Ministry officials often had to resort to secondary regulations to put pressure on parents to comply. When the schools were closed, recalcitrant parents were warned that they remained legally liable for sending their children to school. In cities like Berlin, some children travelled out to Oranienburg to attend the schools there, or used local contacts to board their children with foster-families in nearby towns like Nauen.[59]

As in the British tales of child evacuation, the more universal the evacuation measures became the more scope there was for the real abuse of children. Eight-year-old Peter Groote arrived in Massow in Pomerania in the summer of 1943, where he was looked after by two sisters, both Nazis and both spinsters. All went well, until the sisters decided to buy a dog, which they fed with a sizeable portion of Peter's rations. By the time his mother came to visit him in the winter, he was so thin that he had to be hospitalised. In other cases bed-wetting marked children's difficulties in adjusting. It was also treated as a physical or psychological weakness by the authorities. Just as it might lead to children being expelled from a reformatory and sent to a psychiatric asylum so, in a very few cases, bed-wetting led to the children being sent home to their families.[60]

Within two months, twenty-seven of the 306 pupils of one Hagen middle school had returned home. Their headmaster cited reasons from 'children's homesickness' and 'parents missing their children', to 'bad quarters', 'purportedly insufficient care of the children by their foster-parents' and 'entry of children no longer of school age to the workplace'. In an effort to stem the tide of returnees, the *Gauleiter* and Reich Defence Commissioner for South Westphalia, Albert Hoffmann, ordered that ration cards should be withheld from children who returned without very good reason, sparking a sit-in by women, and in some places their coal-miner husbands, until the authorities relented.[61]

But many children who stayed adjusted well to their new surroundings. Günter Kühnholz, one of three children, arrived in Rügenwalde to find that he had been taken in by a childless couple. The eleven-year-old sat on the doorstep the next morning and sobbed. But he stayed and quickly learned to call them 'uncle' and 'aunt' as he was meant to. He remained in Pomerania for the next three and a half years, enjoying a warmth and emotional intimacy he was unable to recapture with his own family later. Thirteen-year-old Friedrich Heiden joined the women and children in raking and tossing the meadow grass his foster-father and the farm servant had scythed down in Siebenbürgen; he learned how to load it onto a cart properly once it had all dried out. Unless it balanced, he noted, the cart would tip over. After bringing in over twenty-three loads of hay on his farm in Enzersdorf in the Bayerischer Wald, seven-year-old Karl Lukas was so proud of being able to help with the haymaking that he drew his mother a picture of it. While Nannerl, the daughter of the family, and the 'Pole' toss the hay onto it, the little figure 'Ich' holds the horse's harness. Friedrich was fascinated by the Romanians and gypsies whom he was working alongside for the first time, and amazed by how much food they could tuck away at his foster-father's expense. By June 1944, Karl was reminding his mother in secular and Protestant Hamburg to go to church. Farmers' wives had started by wanting to take in adult women at the 'slave markets' of evacuees, hoping that they would work harder, but it often proved easy to integrate children into the agricultural routine.[62]

Evacuee mothers frequently fitted in less well. Their urban ways and northern accents, dislike of the food and tales of the luxurious households they had lost all disturbed a sense of order and stability. Worst of all, many of the women would not work. Nor did they have to. Whereas a farmer's wife with four or five children had to make do with between 45 and 60 marks a month, the childless wife of a white-collar worker had about 150 to 180 marks to spend. If women from Essen, Düsseldorf and Hamburg evacuated to Württemberg looked down on the Swabian 'peasant women as simple and stupid because they work so hard', the farmers' wives resented the idle city women who 'seem to think that they should be waited on hand and foot, as in a hotel'. Swabians complained that they would not even help with domestic chores like washing and mending, let alone with the field-work, even when all hands were needed to bring in the harvest.[63]

As non-essential workers and especially women and children left the cities behind them, the war became physically distant. By the time Liselotte Günzel left Berlin for Droysen in Saxony, in February 1944, neither victorious retaliation against England nor the Jewish terror bombing were fashionable topics in the city any more. Those left behind settled for the propaganda slogan so carefully calibrated to describe what they could scarcely avoid doing anyway, 'holding out'. Or, better still, they tuned in to the radio with its new fare of romantic light-music requests, cleared away the furniture and began to dance. As she set out for her new boarding school, Liselotte Günzel reconciled herself to leaving her home and parents behind, by telling herself that 'beside the pain of farewell I feel the powerful pull to far-off places. The same feeling as drove the Nordic and Germanic conquerors to leave their homes thousands of years ago, rises powerfully in my breast today.'[64]

IX

FORCED OUT

In June 1944 the *Wehrmacht* was caught unawares. On the eastern front the Red Army launched Operation *Bagration*, its greatest single offensive of the war so far, as the third anniversary of the German invasion of the Soviet Union dawned. Enjoying tactical surprise, the Red Army fought a succession of huge encirclement battles at Vitebsk, Bobruisk, outside Brest and east of Vilna, close to some of its own most terrible defeats of 1941. By 4 July most of Belorussia was in their hands. The *Wehrmacht*'s losses in men and equipment were disastrous. Army Group Centre and Army Group North Ukraine were virtually destroyed, losing twenty-eight divisions and 350,000 men. The annihilation of Army Group South Ukraine followed, completing the liberation of the Soviet Union and pushing the Germans back to a line along the Vistula. In the west, the D-Day landings came on a sector of the coast German commanders had not expected to have to defend and on a day when the German air and sea reconnaissance had been called off because of the bad weather reported in the Channel. Once the Allies broke out of the ring around Normandy and the US 7th Army began to push up from the Mediterranean coast in mid-August, Hitler was forced to authorise a full-scale withdrawal from France. Paris was liberated on 15 August and, on 12 September, the first US troops crossed the German frontier south of Aachen.[1]

Until the end of May 1944, the Third Reich had controlled Europe from the Black Sea to the Channel ports. The output from the war industries was still increasing and civilian consumption at home had not had to be severely curtailed since the short-lived ration cuts of 1942. The mass bombing of the cities had abated, and – as ever a good index of their expectations – many parents wanted their children to come home again. An Allied landing had been widely anticipated in the west, but many expected it to fail as disastrously as the attempt at Dieppe had done in 1942.

Even with bitter fighting in Normandy, as the *Wehrmacht* tried to drive the Anglo-American invasion force back into the sea, it was still sustaining its greatest losses on the eastern front, where 1,233,000 German troops were killed in 1944 alone. They accounted for a staggering 45 per cent of German fatalities on the eastern front since June 1941. In the three months from July till the end of September, German losses peaked at a daily death toll of 5,750. But many relatives did not know that their menfolk had been killed and would continue to wait for news: for the *Wehrmacht*'s system for recording its own losses was also beginning to break down. By June 1944, it had under-reported its losses by 500,000; by the end of December another 500,000 men had died whose families did not know.[2]

The enormous defeats the *Wehrmacht* suffered that summer in both the east and the west precipitated the most profound crisis the country had faced so far. The losses of men and territory in France, the Ukraine and Belorussia made Stalingrad pale by comparison. Prescient generals had feared defeat once the blitzkrieg in the Soviet Union failed in the winter of 1941–2, and this led Army Group Centre to play a leading role in plotting Hitler's assassination, when they saw no other way of making peace in the west and concentrating their forces on the eastern front. But most of their fellow countrymen were not so well informed. By 1944, many Germans no longer expected an outright victory in this war, but defeat still seemed far off to most. Initial German reactions to the Allied landings had been optimistic, marked by a sense of relief that the decisive phase of the war had begun at last and that the air raids on Germany had ceased. Blanket coverage of the use of the first of the 'new weapons' against London and southern England had raised expectations that the long-awaited 'retaliation' had begun, which would knock England out of the war. But the propaganda had promised too much and, within three weeks, most people had become sceptical. In Danzig and Frankfurt already a few people were calling the 'V-1' flying bomb the '*Versager-1*', the 'No. 1 Dud'. German civilian morale oscillated in sympathy to German military fortunes: the stabilisation of the *Wehrmacht*'s lines in September and October was greeted with widespread feelings of relief, while the December offensive against the British

Soviet front line, mid-June 1944
Soviet front line, Dec 1944
Soviet front line Feb, 1945
Soviet front line, Apr 1945
Approximate areas of some principal Soviet operations
① Battle of the Dnepr, 25 Aug–23 Dec 1943
② Winter campaign, 1943–44
③ Belorussia, 23 June–29 Aug 1944
④ Lwów–Sandomierz, 13 July–29 Aug 1944
⑤ Jassy–Kishinev, 20–29 Aug 1944
⑥ Vistula–Oder, 12 Jan–3 Feb 1945
⑦ East Prussia, 7 Jan–25 Apr 1945
⑧ East Pomerania, 10 Feb–4 Apr 1945
⑨ Oder-Berlin, 16 Apr–8 May 1945
⑩ Prague, 6–11 May 1945
N
SWEDEN
FINLAND
Gulf of Finland
Baltic Sea
Leningrad
Tallinn
ESTONIA
Novgorod
Pskov
Riga
LATVIA
W Dvina
Siaulai
LITHUANIA
Königsberg
Danzig
Kaunas
Vilnius
Niemen
Vitebsk
W Dvina
Moscow
SOVIET UNION
Smolensk
Minsk
Mogilev
Oka
Briansk
Orel
Bobruisk
Schwerin
Berlin
Oder
Küstrin
E. PRUSSIA
Grodno
Poznań
Vistula
Warsaw
GERMANY
Elbe
Dresden
Neisse
Oder
Brest
Pinsk
POLAND
Breslau
Prague
Pilsen
UPPER SILESIA
Lublin
Kursk
Desna
Donets
Danube
Inn
Brno
Cracow
Vistula
Lwów
Kiev
Zhitomir
Innsbruck
Vienna
Bratislava
SLOVAKIA
AUSTRIA
Stanisławow
Kharkov
Vinnitsa
Dnepr
Dnestr
S Bug
Dnepropetrovsk
Zaporozhe
Budapest
HUNGARY
Cluj
Jassy
Kishinev
YUGOSLAVIA
Odessa
Belgrade
Galati
Kerch
Sarajevo
ROMANIA
Adriatic Sea
Bucharest
Constanza
Sevastopol
Yalta
Danube
BULGARIA
Black Sea
0 100 200 300 400 500 km

The Eastern Front (1944–5)

and Americans in the Ardennes brought surprise, hope and renewed speculation about the impact of 'new weapons'. Even at the year's end, many still thought in terms of a drawn-out stalemate, leading to a compromise peace, or, like the leaders of the regime, set their hopes on reaching separate terms with the Western powers.[3]

Having won air supremacy over the remnants of the *Luftwaffe*, the RAF and US Air Force resumed their bombing raids that autumn. Reaching deep into the south, their concentrated power was able to disrupt the railway network completely and hit those war industries that had been moved away from the Ruhr to central and southern Germany. By winter, finished weaponry was often no longer reaching the *Wehrmacht*. From a strategic point of view the bombing campaigns against the Ruhr, Hamburg and Berlin in the period from March 1943 to March 1944 had marked the most important single phase of the RAF's war against Germany. But the Allies now demonstrated what conquering the German skies meant. The British and American fleets of heavy bombers had continued to grow; so had the individual planes' payloads. Over half the total tonnage of bombs dropped on Germany rained down during this last phase of the war. And over half the German civilian deaths from the bombing came in the eight months from September 1944 to May 1945: 223,406 civilians of an estimated 420,000 for the whole war. In Heilbronn 5,092 were killed on the night of 5 December; on 16 December some 4,000 in Magdeburg. In Darmstadt, when 8,494 died in the firestorm unleashed on the night of 11 September 1944, their dead on this single night outstripped all the bombing casualties in Essen for the entire war.[4]

In the increasingly wrecked and depopulated shells of Germany's industrial cities, an atmosphere of lynch justice began to grow along-side the escalation in police brutality towards the 'eastern workers'. On 14 October 1944 the Duisburg *Volkssturm* – the local militia which had been formed less than three weeks before – seized a 'suspicious-looking' Russian working in a clean-up squad after an air raid on the city. They stood him against a wall in the street and shot him, merely because they had been told that some Russian prisoners of war had been eating jam – obviously stolen – in the basement of a demolished house nearby. Moral and physical panic began to grip the Nazi author-ities, as the Gestapo, police, SA and Hitler Youth struggled to main-tain control of cities whose population of foreign workers could no longer be rehoused when their barracks were bombed. The breakdown of the rail network meant that fewer supplies were getting through to the cities too: there was less work to be done in the plants and in places like Cologne shopkeepers were increasingly tempted to dispose of goods on the black market and blame their disappearance on break-ins by gangs of homeless foreign workers or German teenagers in the Edelweiss Pirates.

The very process of Nazi control, with its mixture of warnings to the families, sanctions at work and police controls over residence, could drive Edelweiss Pirates like Fritz Theilen, who persisted in growing their hair and strumming their guitars, into illegality. Once he and a few friends took to hiding from the SA and Hitler Youth in a shed on an allotment, they found themselves outside the system of rationing altogether. They decided to break into a storeroom to steal the special ration cards issued to travellers. A railway worker tried to stop them and one of Fritz's friends beat the man unconscious. By the evening in August 1944, when his friend Barthel Schlink pulled a pistol out of his pocket and fired at a patrol of SA men, Fritz Theilen knew that the Gestapo would hunt them down. Theilen was lucky enough to be arrested immediately and packed off to a military training camp. But that summer and autumn the remaining Pirates made contact with the new underworld of German black marketeers and foreign worker gangs; and in October, following a series of shoot-outs, the Cologne Gestapo seized some of the Ehrenfeld Edelweiss Pirates along with members of the Russian gangs. Public hangings in front of crowds of over a thousand spectators followed on 25 October and 10 November. Among those executed on 10 November were six German juveniles, including Theilen's friend, the sixteen-year-old Barthel Schlink, one of the supposed leaders of the Edelweiss Pirates in Cologne. The foreign worker gangs rather than the Pirates had been the major target of the Gestapo, but Schlink's body was left hanging all day as a warning.[5]

Dive-bombers and ground attack aircraft began to roam over the fields, country roads, villages and small towns without hindrance. In many rural areas such aircraft were often the first direct sign of the war. As these low-flying planes roared out of nowhere, some of them switched on sirens to reproduce the terrifying effect of the Stukas, making journeys trapped in slow-moving trains particularly terrifying.[6]

In Unterthurnbach in Austria, ten-year-old Helga set off with her two friends Edith and Anni to cycle home when the alarm sounded. As she heard a plane coming closer, Helga abandoned her bike and jumped into a ditch full of water by the side of the road. When the plane passed she clambered out and ran home across the fields. Edith did likewise. Later, when her grandfather went to fetch her bike, he found that Anni had been killed as she had tried to cycle on. 'Why,' Helga asked herself when she heard, 'why are they shooting at a ten-year-old girl?' The Bavarian and Austrian countryside no longer afforded a haven from the war. But even in the cities, veterans of many a bombing raid recalled how terrified they were of these airborne machine guns, raking the streets with virtually no warning, strafing, turning and strafing again.[7]

In spite of this onslaught, the basic structures of German society still remained largely intact. Having survived Stauffenberg's bomb on 20 July, Hitler's grip on power was, in any event, beyond political challenge. But as German society entered this new – and final – phase of the war in the autumn of 1944, the apocalyptic 'everything or nothing' alternatives of Nazi rhetoric began to look more real than ever. And still the regime's demands on the German people kept rising and its resort to violence against 'defeatists', looters and those who spread 'malicious slanders' became ever greater: court records show that Germans now made up the majority of those in the dock.[8]

While the *Wehrmacht* hastily re-equipped its pre-war fortified line of the West Wall and moved more divisions to the western front in preparation for its own counter-attack, 69,000 boys from occupied Europe – including 35,000 from the Soviet Union, 16,000 from Hungary and 18,000 from the Netherlands – were rounded up and sent to take over anti-aircraft duties or help the SS in the Reich. At home, the Party's *Gauleiter* were entrusted with raising a final levy of teenage boys and late-middle-aged men, to help make good the losses the *Wehrmacht* had sustained that summer. They were named the *Volkssturm* in order to evoke all the romanticism of the supposed national uprising of 1813 against Napoleon's occupation of Prussia, and were to be trained in infantry fighting and shooting anti-tank grenades.[9]

With the establishment of the *Volkssturm* the contradictions in Nazi views of children reached crisis point: what point was there in investing in child health, in protecting the children from premature and dangerous work through strict regulation, evacuating them from the cities, only to send them out against tanks on bicycles with a brace of anti-tank grenades strapped to the handlebars? The measures in child welfare had suited Nazi images of an Aryan Utopia of healthy, beautiful and happy families, but it was the competing image of the national future which was now preoccupying Goebbels and Hitler: sacrifice. It was morally preferable that the whole nation should be annihilated than that it should capitulate. Hitler's constant repetition of his political *idée fixe* that 'there must never be another November 1918' had come to the test. Many of the junior officers of that war now held high rank in the *Wehrmacht* and were not prepared to surrender either. Hitler had warned in his decree establishing the *Volkssturm* that the enemy's 'final goal is to exterminate the German people'. Once again, as in September 1939, Germany stood alone without allies. The struggle had become purer and simpler, and it would have to become still more ruthless.[10]

In keeping with the earnestness of the situation, media coverage of the Jewish threat and the red tide of Bolshevism became yet more shrill. In October 1944 Soviet troops crossed the pre-1939 German border for the first time, penetrating the East Prussian district of Gumbinnen and taking Goldap and Nemmersdorf. Scratch units of the local *Volkssturm* managed to hold the Russian thrust until mobile reserves could move up to give them support. When German troops retook Nemmersdorf they uncovered the first Soviet atrocities perpetrated in East Prussia and Goebbels's propaganda machine swung into action to publish stories that did justice to the photographs of the dismembered bodies of civilians and soldiers they had found. The journalists covering the story were so short on detail that the Propaganda Minister urged them to make it up in order to fill it with 'poetic truth'. In this case he was not far from the mark. For the first, but not the last, time East Prussia furnished evidence of Soviet barbarity.[11]

Although the men of the 11th Guards Army came overwhelmingly from Russia – and although it transpired later that some of the Soviet political officers had tried to shield civilians from their men – the atrocities themselves lent credence to those fears Goebbels had so ardently nurtured of the 'Asiatic hordes' whipped into a frenzy by 'Jewish commissars'. With blanket coverage of the massacres of prisoners at Lemberg (Lwów) and of Polish officers at Katyń and Vinnitsa, the German public had been prepared for three years for events like these. NKVD executions had even become the theme of children's games.[12] But the media campaign had its pitfalls. In early November the Security

Police in Stuttgart reported widespread outrage in all sections of the population over the publication of photos of the Nemmersdorf atrocities in
the local press. 'The leadership,' ran one view the police considered to
be typical,

> should realise that the sight of these victims will remind every thinking person
> of the atrocities we have committed in enemy territory, even in Germany itself.
> Have we not murdered thousands of Jews? Don't soldiers again and again
> report that Jews in Poland have had to dig their own graves? And how did
> we treat the Jews in the concentration camp in Alsace [Natzweiler]? Jews are
> human beings too. By doing all this we have shown the enemy what they can
> do to us if they win.[13]

Instead of blaming all of Germany's misfortunes on the Jews, many now
regretted their harsh treatment as the cause of present German woes.
On 12 September Stuttgart had been virtually destroyed in a firestorm
that killed 1,000 people. In their panic, the population had begun to
draw the opposite message from the one Goebbels intended: instead of
seeing the atrocities in East Prussia as grounds for resistance, in their
mood of defeat they saw them as a terrifying lesson in the revenge they
could expect to suffer themselves for the murder of 'thousands of Jews'.
Once again, severe bombing triggered German fears about Jewish
revenge, just as it had after the Hamburg firestorm. The strength of these
fluctuating responses was directly linked to how powerful people felt.
In their renewed mood of vulnerability, common sense dictated that, if
the Jews were as all-controlling as people had been told, it had been a
mistake to fight them. Now, the core nugget of Goebbels's propaganda
– that the Jews were directing the war against Germany – remained
deeply lodged in national consciousness. Even a trivial argument among
German passengers about an Italian worker's right to keep his seat on
a Berlin tram quickly elicited fearful and defeatist sentiments: 'There's
already enough guilt on our shoulders through our treatment of the Jews
and the Poles, which will be paid back to us.'[14]

　Whereas adult men, including many convinced Nazis, often sought
professional exemptions to evade active service in the *Volkssturm*, the
enthusiasm among teenage boys was such that many fourteen- and
fifteen-year-old boys joined up even though they were officially
supposed to be at least sixteen. They had gone the rounds of their
neighbourhoods, collecting for Winter Relief, recycling old paper, old

clothes and scrap metal. They had collected mountains of camomile and stinging nettles from the fields and woodlands, and turned out at the railway stations to help settle evacuees arriving from areas near the front or under threat of bombing. They had trained in the field exercises laid down in the infrantry training manual and had learned to shoot with small-calibre rifles while in the Hitler Youth. As air-force and naval auxiliaries, many had already manned searchlights and run messages while the bombs were falling around them. Some had even left their *KLV* evacuation homes to be given weapons instruction in premilitary training camps. To be issued finally with rifles, anti-tank grenades and revolvers from the depots of the reserve army came to many as an early reward, the logical culmination of their whole training. What if, as Dierk Sievert had worried four autumns earlier, the war ended before they could join up?[15]

In his *KLV* home in the little village of Prag in the Bayerischer Wald, Kurt Lutter was shocked to hear that the Hitler Youth was being made to dig trenches all over Hamburg. But in East Prussia, in Palmnicken on the Samland Peninsula, Martin Bergau and his friends each built up a motley collection of rifles, carbines and grenades, and went out on patrol, knowing they might run into Red Army units from the Memel. It was exciting to practise their field craft skills for real, slipping between the trees in the woodland and creeping across the heath, even when Martin and his friend Gerhard – after helping themselves to too much home-brew in a deserted house – ended up accidently opening fire on each other before stumbling home.[16]

The idea of 'commitment' and 'service' was often irresistible to children wanting to be taken seriously. Just as fourteen-year-old Liese had swung into action in September 1939 and proudly written to her father at the front about the deeds of her group of German Girls, so in September 1944 many answered the call. In Strasbourg, ten-year-old Monika Schypulla decided to begin her own 'war service'. As she wrote proudly to her father, she had to leave the house by 6.45 a.m. each day in order to take the number 16 tram to its terminus. She then had a forty-five-minute walk with the local Nazi Party leader so that she could carry messages for his office. 'But,' she continued, 'I am not allowed to open them! It is secret! There are things in them like how far the enemy is from us, etc.' Seven days a week till 3 p.m., Monika was doing her bit. '*Ja*, Daddy,' she wrote to him proudly, 'it is total war after all. Every single one of us counts!!' Helplessly cut off by the

Red Army on the Courland Peninsula, her father could only read her letters weeks later and listen keenly to the *Wehrmacht* reports for news of the western front. In the event, family crisis moved faster than the military retreat on the western front. Monika's mother died on 1 November and the ten-year-old girl, an only child, was packed off to stay with her godmother in Saxony, and instead of continuing with her 'war service' her father enjoined her to 'study hard' so that they might both prove themselves 'worthy of Mummy'.[17]

On 12 January 1945, the Soviets launched their long-awaited winter offensive. In the south, Marshal Konev's 1st Ukrainian Front opened a huge offensive across the Vistula, attacking through the dense forest, which the German General Staff had assumed would protect their elevated positions in Małopolska. On the night of 22–23 January, the first of his armies reached the River Oder and established a bridge-head at Brieg, crossing the last natural barrier to Berlin. As the Soviet armies swept through Warsaw, Łódź, Kalisch and Cracow, across the Wartheland, West Prussia and Silesia, the resilient structures of Nazi rule collapsed in panic and mass flight.[18]

Downstream from Brieg, the *Gauleiter* of Silesia, Karl Hanke, ordered the evacuation of women and children at the very last moment, on 20 January, and declared Breslau a fortress. Elsewhere, many Party leaders fled. Having hitherto forbidden evacuation, they often left it to local military commanders, farming communities, volunteers from the People's Welfare and aristocratic estate holders to organise mass 'treks' westwards as best they could. As the SS also marched their concentration camp prisoners west, their columns jostled for space on the roads and railway lines with the millions of civilian refugees, the prisoners of war, and units of the *Wehrmacht* and the *Volkssturm*. For the first time, the pretence that had been maintained for so long of physically separating German women and children from their racial enemies broke down completely. But on the whole, Germans would remember their flight as if only Germans were suffering on the snow- and ice-bound roads. This was more than a matter of later memory: for human empathy and solidarity had been thoroughly nationalised. In their plight, refugees could only look to their fellow countrymen for aid, and that, too, was far from secure, often forcing people to fall back on networks of education, friendship, family and village.[19]

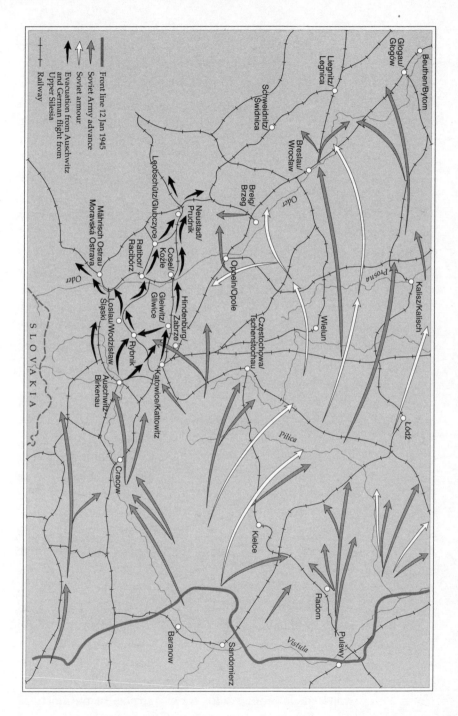

The Soviet advance on Silesia (January 1945)

As entire communities in the eastern provinces uprooted themselves and trekked westwards, the deep structures of traditional order often proved remarkably resilient. Whole East Prussian and Silesian villages set out together, following the carts of their aristocratic landlords. Wives of civil servants, like Lore Ehrich, would have to rely at key moments on the chivalry of men of their own social class, seeking out courteous SS and *Wehrmacht* officers, or on the good luck that friends would scan the lists of new arrivals on the lookout for them. As the general social solidarity the Nazis had tried to propagate frayed and proved unreliable, Germans returned to types of communal action they knew. But a sense of national identity did not disappear altogether: the abstract lines of national and racial division, which had been so violently enforced under Nazi rule, mattered more than ever. Just because nothing could be taken for granted, Germans used their shared fear of the Soviets, the Poles and the prisoners to elicit sympathy and help. Close to the affected provinces, farmers were often extremely open-handed at feeding and giving shelter to the treks of refugees; but the further the refugees fled from the eastern provinces the less generous and under-standing they found their fellow citizens to be.

In Upper Silesia, Konev's forces embarked on a huge encirclement of mines and factory towns from the east, north and south, leaving the *Wehrmacht* with a narrow escape route westwards, in the hope that the Germans would leave the invaluable industrial belt intact. Cracow fell on 19 January, the Germans for once simply pulling out, surrendering their defensive positions and the capital of their General Government without destroying it. After reaching the Oder at Brieg, D.N. Gusev's army turned to attack the German garrisons in Silesia from the west, cutting civilian escape along the main line through Breslau. Even after the fall of Cracow, the *Gauleiter* had permitted only women with small children to be evacuated. But now most of the 1.5 million Germans in Upper Silesia began to flee. The sheer speed of the Soviet advance often left villagers with less than twenty-four hours to get away. Still, almost the entire rural population – some 600,000 out of 700,000 people – escaped from the area between Oppeln and Glogau. Few of the urban refugees had access to the horses and carts country folk possessed and over 200,000 simply had to walk along the crowded roads, bound with snow and ice, in the hope of reaching the railway line through southern Silesia. As they thronged the small stations from Ratibor and Schweidnitz to Liegnitz, their numbers overwhelmed the volunteers from the National Socialist People's Welfare who had come to offer food, hot drinks and blankets. Many had to wait days before they could clamber aboard the trains. Others had to make their way to the safety of the German lines west of the Oder on foot.

But half a million German stayed behind in the industrial towns of Kattowitz, Beuthen, Gleiwitz and Hindenburg, which Gusev's forces were now encircling from the west. Many had been forced to continue working for the mines and industrial plants of the region until the end. It was also true that during the German occupation this was one Polish area where the great majority of the Polish population had been quietly classified as German, in order not to disrupt industrial production and where the apartheid system so brutally enforced just to the north in the Wartheland was at its mildest. Now most German workers may have assumed that the same pragmatic calculations would apply to them too.[20]

It was through these Upper Silesian towns that the SS marched its prisoners from the camps at Auschwitz – 14,000 men and women set out in ranks of five abreast to the railway at Gleiwitz. Another 25,000 were marched along the 41 miles of snowbound roads to Loslau. At least 450 prisoners were killed along the way. Such was the SS's fear of the Red Army that, for the first two days, they did not halt at night. Even when they did, there was no food or drink. Wooden clogs, broken shoes and foot rags afforded little protection against the snow, the threadbare 'zebra' jackets and trousers offered none against the cold. The SS set fire to the warehouses before they left Auschwitz, leaving a blaze which burned for five days, and only well-connected prisoners like Filip Müller and Yehuda Bacon had managed to 'organise' sufficient clothes, provisions and food to withstand the march. On the first day, the children who had come to Birkenau from the oldest and most famished of Polish ghettos, Łódź, began to collapse with exhaustion. Those who marched on had already passed the misshapen bundles of prisoners who had fallen out from the columns ahead of them. Their corpses lay in the bloodstained snow beside the road. Prisoners could see what awaited those they left behind even before they heard the shots or the thud of the rifle butts.[21]

Polish villagers who brought bread and milk for the prisoners were chased back by the SS, though many still turned out to watch. And it was here that most attempts at flight occurred as prisoners slipped out of the ranks and into the knots of people lining the streets. Elsewhere, especially when the columns marched through predominantly German villages or at night, the prisoners received no aid at all. Many Germans, who had hitherto accepted Nazi notions of camp prisoners as dangerous criminals, child abusers, foreign terrorists and Jews, were still shocked by what they now saw – 'Incredible!' and 'Can't grasp it!' were common reactions – but few of the survivors of these Silesian marches remember them as offering aid. No doubt many, as they turned away, were already more concerned with their own immediate future. To the German refugees the prisoners were simply another obstacle they had to contend with, alongside the overturned carts, dead horses, *Wehrmacht* units and columns of Soviet and British prisoners of war. All were clogging the roads, forcing the refugees onto field and forest paths, and reducing their chances of escaping westwards before the Red Army overran them.[22]

The longer the prisoners marched, the stronger their desire became to lie down, to eat snow and to sleep. Janina Komenda was only able to stop herself because of the bond she felt to her comrades and the knowledge that rest meant certain death. As the column passed the fields by the edge of the forest outside Ćwiklice, Janina was buffeted by the icy wind. Marching like an automaton, she endlessly repeated the same thought: 'On, on! Don't fall down!'[23]

At Loslau, Natan Żelechower and his column were brought into the engine sheds to wait, hobbling along on their numb legs. Met by a warm stench as they stumbled in from the cold, they were driven out again at dawn and herded by the hundred into open trucks that already had 20 centimetres of snow in them. As Jan Dziopek waited for hours, unable to move in his truck, he saw three young men being led into the field next to the station and shot. They had tried to hide under the straw in a barn where they were sniffed out by the dogs. Zofia Stępień-Bator and other women were finally allowed to drink the water the railway workers brought them – but there was too little to go round. Some of the railway workers gave out sips of coffee they had brewed until an SS man from the escort came over and forbade them to continue. A miner, Henryk Michalski, helped two women to escape as he came off shift – Monika Zatka-Dombke and Zofia Brodzikowska-Pohorecka. He took them in and they sipped their first drops of coffee as they warmed themselves against his stove. He too had been shocked into action by the shootings of prisoners – 'a disgrace', Monika heard him say.[24]

On the station the prisoners had huddled together to warm each other, but once the trucks jolted into motion they were pressed so close to one another that they could not move at all. They began to freeze. Only the disposal of each night's corpses provided relief for the living, giving them space to sit down, take off their shoes and work their frozen feet. No rations were handed out, but Filip Müller at least had enough saved from his time in the Birkenau *Sonderkommando* to have a little bread to spare when the train arrived in the Austrian camp at Mauthausen a few days later. Yehuda Bacon and the other children who had survived the march were put into two closed goods wagons, which gave them a little more protection from the cold. For the second time since he had left Theresienstadt, Yehuda looked out of a sealed train as it trundled through Mährisch Ostrau, the city of his birth and pre-war memories.[25]

At 4 a.m. on 20 January, Gero Hilbert was ordered to pack. The *KLV* camp in Burgstadt near Posen was going to be evacuated in four hours' time. He took his school books, his clothes and bedding, shoe polish and sewing kit, pictures of the town, and knife and fork. Six carts took their luggage to the station. After months of practice, it only took them three hours to march the 10 miles on foot. The eighty boys were allocated to three open coal trucks for the 130-mile journey to Züllichau. Their double blankets gave them scant protection against the wind, and the jam and butter they had brought with them froze during the night. Still, they had enough dry bread to eat the next day. After taking a roundabout route lasting thirty-six hours, the sixty wagons of their train trundled into Züllichau at 2 a.m. As they tried to keep warm on the station, they were surprised to see welfare workers turn out at 4 a.m. to bring them bread and warm coffee, and lead them to a barracks for the night. The next morning, while they devoured their first hot soup of the journey, they learned that ten young children had frozen to death elsewhere in the train that night. Later on their coal trucks were coupled to a train packed with refugees, which took them to Frankfurt on the Oder. Here, Gero's experiences were mixed. The local guards posted to watch their baggage stole 9 pounds of butter and their sweets, but the rest of their journey to Dresden and Zwickau in Saxony was uneventful and they were even able to sit in a proper compartment.[26]

Renate Schwartz and the other girls from Schloss Streben in the Wartheland shoved and squirmed their way onto the trains. The girls overnighted where they could at other *KLV* homes and were looked after by their teachers and the National Socialist People's Welfare. Even when Renate became separated from the others she found strangers willing to help her. People lifted her in and out of crowded trains through the window. As she shivered in the corridor in her thin coat, a stranger lent her his travelling blanket. Compared with Renate's previous journeys, the two days it took her to reach her home in Berlin – which included having to talk her way off the Schlesische Bahnhof in Berlin without a ticket – were terrible. But compared with most flights that January, the re-evacuation of the *KLV* children went like clockwork.[27]

Fleeing from Breslau with his mother, ten-year-old Jürgen Ingwert was exhausted by the time they reached Cottbus and lay down on the platform. A family of Volhynian Germans came across and gave him two handfuls of sugar lumps to see him through. At Leipzig, they were helped through the chaotic crush on the platforms by groups of Hitler Youths and Red Cross nurses. Glancing across the tracks as he got off his train to take shelter from an air raid under the great station hall at Leipzig, he saw an open goods train filled with motionless, snow-covered figures. They were wearing the striped clothing of camp inmates and, he surmised, had already frozen to death. In any case they were not brought down into the air-raid shelter. When someone suggested that they might be Jews, Jürgen remembered a woman replying coldly, 'They weren't Jews. They have all been shot in Poland already.' Jürgen went on wondering about them.[28]

Among the convoys of prisoners passing through Leipzig at this time was a fifteen-year-old German-Jewish boy from Auschwitz. Thomas Gève arrived in Leipzig, huddled with other Auschwitz prisoners in the open wagon they had ridden in from Loslau. As they had crossed Upper and Lower Silesia, he had been struck by the envious and resentful looks the crowds of German refugees waiting on the station platforms had cast at the prisoners. For the first time – and at such a desperate moment – concentration camp prisoners appeared privileged in their eyes: they already had places on a train. In Leipzig, the prisoners saw a hospital train on the next platform and called out in desperation, begging the Red Cross nurses to bring them some water for their own sick. The nurses pretended they were not there, but a little girl with pigtails had not yet learned to ignore these strange teenagers. Her neatly ironed black skirt whirling, she came running towards the train, pointing out the young faces she saw in the open wagon to her mother.

Gève and some of the other boys pulled themselves up to greet her.[29]

Meanwhile, on 27 January, the day Kurochkin's rifle divisions achieved their southerly objective of reaching Rybnik, they came upon Auschwitz. The 9,000 prisoners who stayed behind in its camps, deemed a grave security risk by Dr Haffner, the State Prosecutor, had in reality been too weak and sick to move. In the nine days since the massed ranks of the marchers had left the gates, 2,000 of those left behind had already died. In July 1944, when the Red Army had captured Lublin, they had been horrified by what they found at the camp at Majdanek. The Soviet advance had been so rapid that the SS had had very little time to destroy the camp. As the liberators viewed the commandant's house, the building materials depot, the barracks for SS guards and the barracks and workshops for prisoners, they also found the three gas chambers nearby, the crematorium and behind it the trenches for mass shootings, the piles of clothes and the heaps of shoes and the mounds of human hair. Although the SS had done their best to hide their traces at Auschwitz-Birkenau, blowing up the gas chambers and burning their central records, the Soviets knew what they had found. Medical personnel and journalists were rushed in to help the survivors and to publicise the horrors. Once again, as at Majdanek, the articles in the Soviet Army newspaper referred to the victims only as Soviet citizens; Jews and Poles were not mentioned. For the soldiers of the Red Army, Majdanek had already become an emblem of how the Germans had treated their comrades. Coming on top of the exhortations penned by Ilya Ehrenburg and other writers for Soviet soldiers to avenge themselves on the Germans for their crimes of occupation, the images of Majdanek and Auschwitz gave new grounds for wishing 'Death to the German occupiers!'. Two days after the liberation of Auschwitz, on 29 January, the Soviet armies completed their capture of the Silesian industrial region.[30]

On 13 January 1945, the day after Marshal Konev had launched his offensive in the south, Marshal Chernyakhovsky launched the 3rd Belorussian Front in a huge direct assault on East Prussia from the north-east. With their 1,670,000 men, 28,360 guns and heavy mortars, 3,000 tanks and self-propelled guns and 3,000 aircraft, the Soviets greatly outnumbered the much depleted forty-one German divisions, which faced them with 580,000 men, 700 tanks and self-propelled guns and 515 aircraft. But the Soviets had to contend with heavily fortified lines, which had been periodically updated and extended since before the First World War, and the Red Army was approaching these defences from their strongest side. Unlike Konev's eleven-day dash to the Oder, it would take the 3rd Belorussian Front until March to batter its way across East Prussia and eastern Pomerania, and reach the mouth of the Oder. Gdynia and Danzig held out till the end of March, and, to the east of the Vistula lagoon, the East Prussian capital Königsberg did not surrender till 9 April.[31]

East Prussia would see the most bitter fighting of the Soviet winter offensive. It would also witness terrible atrocities against German soldiers and civilians alike. To the 126,464 Soviet soldiers who died in the conquest of East Prussia were added another 458,314 wounded. By far the heaviest losses were experienced by the infantry, the backbone of almost all assaults, as Soviet commanders spent the lives of their men in order to hold their valuable tanks in reserve until they knew where they could be used to decisive advantage. A medical orderly with the 65th Army, Svetlana Alexeieva, looked into the faces of the infantrymen who came to her dressing station fresh from combat and was so dismayed that she looked away again. There was, she still remembered half a century later, 'nothing human there, they were somehow completely strange faces. I simply cannot describe it. You would think you were among the really mentally ill.'[32]

As he watched Gumbinnen burn on 24 January, Yuri Uspensky, a Russian officer with the 5th Artillery Corps, felt the rage of the just: 'It is vengeance for everything the Germans have done in our country. Now their cities are being destroyed and their population is experiencing what war means.' Three days later, on 27 January, crossing the Wehlau district en route to Königsberg, Uspensky was shocked by the sight of a woman who had been murdered with her two children. As he wrote in his diary that day, he reflected on the frequency with which he was seeing the bodies of murdered civilians on the roads. Uspensky involuntarily registered his disquiet by retreating into the passive voice while he searched for an abstract justification. 'One only has to think,' he reminded himself, 'of Majdanek and the theory of the Master race to understand why our soldiers are happily bringing East Prussia to such a pass. Sure, it is unbelievably cruel to kill children, but the German cold-bloodedness in Majdanek was a hundred times worse.'[33]

On the Hohendorf estate in the Königsberg district the order to evacuate came on the night of 20 January. The schoolteacher, who now insisted on being addressed as 'Captain', had told the children to take their school books with them; their parents told them to empty their school bags and take only clothes and bedding. Charlotte Kuhlmann and her siblings quietly packed some of their toys and she took her doll. Wearing their warmest clothes and their Sunday best, they released the cattle and set off. To the lowing of the cows, they fell in, while the nursemaid sang the songs she had learned during her training in Silesia. At the village inn, three of the children were put on one wagon, the two fourteen-year-old boys were given the handcart to pull, the nursemaid the pram to push and one of the girls the bike to ride. The rest of their large family were distributed over different carts. Like other villages in this most feudal of Prussian provinces, theirs was a collective endeavour in which the whole community moved together, often led out by the ageing landlord or, more often, his wife.[34]

When the Kuhlmanns reached the Vistula a week later, exhausted, wet and chilled, their trek was forced to take the carts over the frozen river: the *Wehrmacht* was reserving the bridge at the old Teutonic Knights' town of Marienwerder for military traffic. As Charlotte took her turn to guard their dwindling store of goods on the night of 28 January, she noticed a young woman from their village standing nearby, waiting for a cart. Carrying her newborn baby in a bundle in her arms, she stood there motionless, the frozen tears on her cheeks shining like pearls. Charlotte did not dare to approach, suddenly afraid that the baby had died.

Theirs was one of the few treks to make it out of East Prussia overland. For, on 20 January, the Soviets attacked up the middle of the province from the south, aiming straight for the Vistula lagoon, the *Frisches Haff*, in order to encircle all of East Prussia east of the Vistula, and so cut it off from Danzig and eastern Pomerania in the west. Driving north-west N. S. Oslikovsky's 3rd Guards Cavalry Corps burst into Allenstein on 21 January, taking most of the townsfolk as well as the *Wehrmacht* by surprise. The same happened in Osterode, trapping many of the 400,000 East Prussians who did not manage to flee. Once the Red Army had broken through the fortified line around Allenstein, they were able to advance by the shortest road to the coast. Heading through Preussisch Holland on 23 January, Captain Dyachenko drove his lead group of seven tanks straight through the evening traffic in Elbing, with his headlights on, passing trams and pedestrians, some of

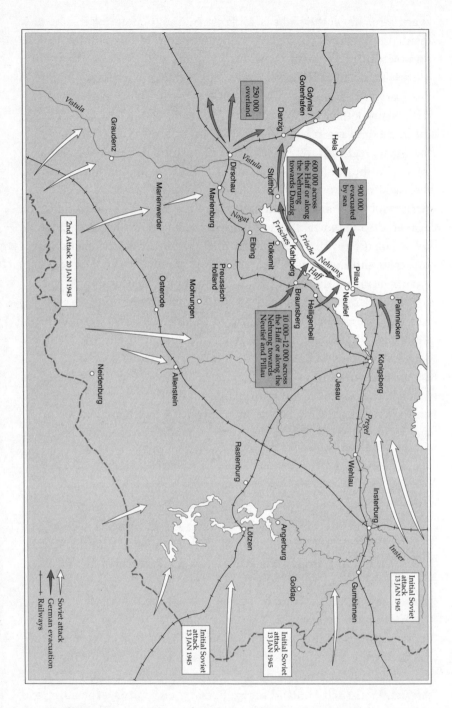

The Soviet conquest of East Prussia (January–April 1945)

whom took his vehicles for a German training unit. By the time the rest of the tank spearhead arrived, Elbing's defenders had recovered from their surprise and the tanks had to swing east of the town, linking up with Dyachenko the next morning at Tolkemit on the shore of the *Frisches Haff*.[35]

Hermann Fischer's trek from the Mohrungen district turned northeast in a bid to reach the Heilsberg triangle, but it was overrun by the Red Army on 24 January. Even after persuading the local Party leader to let them bury his Party badge in the rubbish, Fischer and his wife were held at gunpoint against a wall and saved thanks only to the intervention of Polish farm maids. That night a whole Soviet tank unit began the gang rape of one girl; it lasted for the following thirteen hours. For the next month, Fischer and two of his neighbours tried to keep their three daughters safe by hiding them in the forest. But on 25 February he was seen as he went to the wood and the next day, after a month of extreme cold and hunger, the two young women in their early twenties and the thirteen-year-old girl came out of their hiding places. Gerda, the thirteen-year-old, was lucky enough to be sent to work for the Russians, but the two older ones, Elise and Trude, disappeared without trace. As Hermann Fischer stayed behind on the farm where he had been overtaken and whose owner he had seen shot before his eyes, he watched an entire way of life being destroyed in front of him. He saw most of the other men, women and young girls being transported east to work in the Soviet Union, leaving the wreckage of multiple lootings lying in the abandoned dwellings or blowing about in the winter winds.[36]

Red Army soldiers did not just want to kill Germans. In spite of strict orders to the contrary, many of them wanted to wear the German military caps, jackets and boots they found in the houses they plundered. While the Germans could not discard such items fast enough, the junior officers and men of the Red Army began gleefully putting them on, even though in the misunderstandings that inevitably ensued Red Army men fired on each other. It was as if in their euphoria at conquering those who had once seemed so invincible, they needed to clad their own bodies with what had most terrified them. One dead Soviet soldier was found dressed in a complete Party uniform of the NSDAP.[37]

There were now only two ways out of East Prussia. Refugees from the northern districts headed towards Königsberg and the Samland

Peninsula, hoping to leave by sea from Pillau. Those from the south-east and central districts made for the *Frisches Haff*, attempting to cross the ice to Kahlberg, a small summer resort which lay on the long, thin sand spit – or *Nehrung* – separating the Vistula lagoon from the Baltic Sea. From Kahlberg, they took the road along the sand dunes of the *Nehrung* to the amber-rich silt lands at the mouth of the Vistula, passing Stutthof concentration camp as they headed towards the ports of Danzig and Gdynia and, beyond them, the safe haven of eastern Pomerania.

Harried by ground attack aircraft and hurried onwards by news of the Soviet advance, hundreds of thousands of refugees joined the remnants of twenty-three German divisions in an enclave along the southern edge of the Vistula lagoon around Heiligenbeil. The *Wehrmacht* held onto this pocket, measuring no more than 12 miles across at its greatest extent, from late January. Until the ice began to melt at the end of February, trek upon trek of refugees set out to cross it from the shore between Heiligenbeil and Braunsberg. Within range of the Soviet artillery, they set out at night, the farmers driving their carts in single file over routes marked by occasional torches, and with improvised bridges strung across the stretches where the ice had broken up. When Lore Ehrich crossed on 12 February with her two small children, she owed her ride to the SA men at Braunsberg who had forced the farmers at the point of a pistol to take refugees on foot. Within the first half-hour on the ice, the colt ambling along beside the cart broke both legs and had to be left behind. Later on, one of the two carthorses fell into a hole in the ice in the dark. Trembling with fear of losing his horse – and with it the ability to pull most of the goods he still possessed – the farmer carefully cut it free with an axe. The ice had been thawing and breaking and, as they waited, they found that the freezing surface water was gradually rising. In the light of widely spaced torches, the slow-moving treks looked like a long funeral procession. As the cold enveloped them, creeping into their limbs, Frau Ehrich kept her thoughts focused by looking at the broad back of the farmer in front of her.[38]

In the morning light the wreckage of the treks, the broken trucks and cars, and the people who had escaped from them and were trudging on across the ice on foot, became visible. Wounded soldiers lay on top of hay wagons, exposed to the wind and the snow. As night came Frau Ehrich's trek continued, the cracking of the breaking ice ominously loud in the silence of the *Haff*. Her children had become quiet, exhausted by the cold. When they reached Kahlberg, they did not want to get down off the cart. Her two boys both had the 'highway sickness', chronic diarrhoea. Tormented by thirst even more than by hunger, Frau Ehrich went on a hopeless tour of the port and the district Party leader's office where all she saw was rage and disappointment. The risk of typhoid meant that the water was undrinkable. She returned to the trek, which now inched its way along the narrow, boggy *Nehrung* road into whose holes carts ahead of them were continually falling or overturning. The whole line behind had to stop and wait for damaged wheels to be repaired and loads to be repacked. The soldiers whom they passed had no bread to give them. That first day they got no further than 3 miles. Their cart, with its rubber wheels, two horses and solid roof, was one of the strongest, but the farmer's fear of joining the growing number who had had to abandon their carts and property was betrayed by his hoarse shouts as he tried to guide his horses along. As they passed more wreckage, they saw that old people and mothers huddled with their young children lay beside the dead horses.

On their right was the military road and the tree break of evergreens, protecting them from the wind off the Baltic; to their left the glittering ice of the *Frisches Haff*, over which occasional artillery shells flew. At one of the many long halts on the road, thousands of Russian prisoners were driven past. Frau Ehrich saw many of them go up to the dead horses and cut off strips of flesh, which they ate raw. Whatever sympathy she felt for them was overwhelmed by the fear lest they overpower their guards and fall upon the trek. Nothing happened and soon they reached the end of the *Nehrung* road. Arriving at the huge assembly camp at Stutthof, she left the farmer and realised suddenly that she was on her own. No one was willing to help her queue for hours till soup and bread were distributed and she could not leave her children lying on the straw alone. While she tried to interest others in her plight, her luggage and her handbag, containing all her jewellery, savings books and money, were stolen. Eventually, thanks to the successive assistance of an SS officer, a policeman and a railway official, Frau Ehrich made it to Danzig. Here, too, connections helped and acquaintances who had read their names on the list of arrivals collected them from the refugee camp and looked after them until they were well enough to board a ship for Denmark three weeks later.

Dorothea Dangel's trek from her village near Rastenburg was led out onto the ice, as it had been all the way from home, by the elderly mistress of the estate. Dorothea, the woodcutter's daughter, was no longer the twelve-year-old who had got into trouble with her father in September 1939 for spending hours throwing flowers to the soldiers as they marched off to war. Nor was she the confident sixteen-year-old who had been chased home one night by an over-amorous German soldier; or the girl who had enjoyed carrying the heavy leather post bag down the avenue of village lime trees, but had found it hard to meet the expectant gaze of the wives and mothers to whom she had to deliver the telegraphic message 'Fallen'. She was cold and frightened, especially when her trek was forced back onto the ice from the *Nehrung* by military convoys that needed the road. They could only evade repeated strafing by Soviet planes at night, but it was then that the ice was at its most dangerous. As Dorothea walked along the trek in the dark to bring food back to her family one night, she was accosted by a woman carrying a baby who begged her for some: Dorothea refused. When she reached her family, her feeling of shame was made worse because they had been fed by an army field kitchen in her absence.[39]

Over 600,000 people fled over the *Haff* or along the *Nehrung* towards Danzig. Some 10,000–12,000 fled along the *Nehrung* in the other direction, away from Danzig, heading eastwards to Neutief and, abandoning their horses, carts and most of their belongings, embarked from Pillau on one of the ships which had begun to evacuate refugees from the Samland Peninsula on 25 January. This eastern end of the Danzig Bight was the last part of East Prussia to fall to the Soviets, holding out even after Königsberg surrendered in April. As Martin Bergau and the other Hitler Youth boys in the Palmnicken *Volkssturm* went out on night patrol, in their excitement often opening fire at the play of shadows on the snow, they, too, met some of the soldiers who were slipping away towards Pillau under cover of darkness. When Bergau challenged them to stay and defend their land together, the sixteen-year-old was given a lesson in survival: 'Do you think we want to get a frozen arse here?' he was told.[40]

On the night of 26–27 January, Martin Bergau heard shots outside his house in Palmnicken. He automatically did what he had been trained to do in his anti-aircraft unit and in the *Volkssturm*: he threw on his clothes, grabbed his gun and headed out of the house. He saw a woman who had tried to hide in the front garden run back out onto the road where she was gunned down. Shaking himself out of his 3 a.m. daze, Bergau saw the silhouettes of a long column of ragtag figures moving along the road, driven on by the shots. Pulling Martin back into the house, his father warned him off getting involved with a transport of prisoners. The next morning he found frozen shreds of bloodstained clothing on the garden gate. All along the route into the town local Germans had seen prisoners being clubbed to death with the butts of carbines or shot in the back of the head as they knelt in the snow by the roadside. They were some of the concentration camp prisoners who had been marched from the work camps at Heiligenbeil, Gerdauen, Seerappen, Schippenbeil and Jesau, all eastern *Aussenlager* of the Stutthof concentration camp.[41]

Around 90 per cent of these prisoners were Jewish women, many the survivors of the extermination of the Hungarian Jews and the Łódź ghetto. They had prepared themselves as well as they could, tying bowls and cups made of cans round their waists with telephone wire, but they still wore summer clothes and their feet were wrapped in rags or shod with wooden clogs, which got stuck in the deep January snow. Without a clear route or destination, provisioning or places to stay, the escort of SS men and Russian auxiliaries drove them on at the double, shooting those who could not run fast enough. When the Red Army excavated one mass grave in April in the Ellerhaus woods, a couple of miles from Germau, all the bodies they exhumed were louse-ridden and emaciated, some still carrying pieces of fish, potatoes and – like the Russian prisoners Frau Ehrich had seen on the *Nehrung* road – turnips in their pockets.

Only half of the 5,000 prisoners who had set off from Königsberg made it to the town of Palmnicken. There, they were penned in a disused factory and fed at the behest of the local *Volkssturm* commander. Four days later they were marched down to the seashore at night, driven out onto the ice and gunned down with automatic weapons. The perpetrators included not only SS and Gestapo men, anxious to be rid of their prisoners and save their own skins, but also members of the local *Volkssturm* and Hitler Youth. As he rode along the seashore that February, Martin Bergau saw bloated corpses which had come free of the ice being washed up on the beach. Revolted, he turned his horse away. He had already had to stand guard duty while some of the 200 women who had escaped the massacre were shot in their turn. Half a century later, the only ones of his Hitler Youth companions he could yet bring himself to name among the killers were two boys who later died in Palmnicken. Even so, Martin Bergau had observed exactly how the kneeling women were executed, and just how professionally the SS changed the magazines on their 7.65mm pistols.[42]

A few of the women who survived managed to find locals willing to hide them. Dora Hauptmann had escaped from the ice with a bullet wound to her hand and, knocking on a door, found a German family to hide her for a time. But as the nine German divisions in the Samland Peninsula continued to hold out, she had to move again. A crowd of children rapidly surrounded the dazed and exhausted woman on the Hexentanz Square, screaming 'We've got one, we've got one!' until a strong-minded local woman, Bertha Pulver, undertook to hand her over to the authorities. In fact, Pulver took Dora Hauptmann home, rang the doctor and got instructions on how to clean and tend her wounded hand. Despite at least two intimidating enquiries, Bertha Pulver continued to hide Dora Hauptmann until the Soviets finally took Palmnicken on 15 April.[43]

As the Red Army pushed forward into the Samland Peninsula in February, an NKVD unit reported finding the first mass graves. Other Red Army soldiers were more struck by the prosperity in Samland; one wrote home to his wife, 'The people live well here. Though the soil is sandy, they live better than us. When you enter a house, you don't know where to look first. You find so many beautiful things before you. Almost every householder has a piano. That's sort of something,' he added informatively, 'on which you play.' Meanwhile, Yuri Uspensky was increasingly repelled by the violence of his own side. By 2 February he could no longer justify it to himself by comparing it with the German occupation of Smolensk or the atrocities at Majdanek: 'I hate Hitler and Hitler-Germany with all my heart, but this hatred does not justify such conduct. We are avenging ourselves, but,' he added, finally giving vent to his disquiet, 'not like this.' On 7 February he was in the village of Kraussen and saw a soldier shoot a woman and her baby in front of their tanks because she refused him sex. In mid-February the nine divisions of the *Wehrmacht* that were bottled up on the Samland Peninsula counter-attacked, driving the Soviet forces back and reopening the passage linking Königsberg to Pillau and the Baltic. At Metgethen, they found further examples of Red Army atrocities. On 19 February, near Kragau, Yuri Uspensky was killed in the fighting.[44]

Luckily for Martin Bergau, he did not have to stay and defend the pathetic wooden barricades he had helped erect across the roads into Palmnicken. At the end of February, he and the other boys born in 1928 were ordered westwards, enduring a very rough crossing from Pillau to Danzig as the breakers rolled into the Bight from the open sea. One woman was so scared by her flight and crossing that she started to babble that she was the Empress of China. In the meantime, after travelling on from Danzig to Stettin by train, Martin Bergau found that no one was expecting his group. Without relatives in the West, he promptly talked his way onto an SS train and went straight back to Danzig, hoping to recross the bay to Pillau and fight in the victorious defence of his homeland. Doubtless he also hoped to reclaim the cache of small arms he had hidden under the floor of the garden shed, a romantic gesture which would nearly cost his father's life when a Red Army horse kicked through the rotten boards that spring.[45]

Just at this time, the strange quiet which had endured over the belt of land along the Baltic coast from Danzig to Stettin throughout February came to an end. While nearly a million refugees – of whom 800,000 came from East Prussia – were pouring in, the *Wehrmacht* had established a new defensive line 65 miles inland, which ran through Graudenz, Zempelburg, Märkisch Friedland, Stargard and Pyritz to the Oder, overhanging the Soviet armies to the south. Over half the refugees stayed on in this part of eastern Pomerania, as did the local population: whatever pressures were exerted upon them by the local civil and military authorities, they clearly also still believed that the line could be held.[46]

At the beginning of March, Zhukov's and Rokossovsky's forces attacked from the south, cutting eastern Pomerania in two and sweeping west to the Oder, before turning east once more towards Gdynia and Danzig. As German troops and refugees fled eastwards towards Danzig and westwards to Kolberg, the province was rapidly broken up into a series of encircled pockets along the Baltic coastline, which were reduced one by one. Once again, horse-drawn carts on overcrowded winter roads were rapidly overtaken by armoured columns. In the first weeks of March, huge numbers of East Prussian, West Prussian and Pomeranian treks heading for Danzig were overrun in the area around Stolp. This was no time for charity, even towards *KLV* children. As thirteen-year-old Herbert Hagener was pushed back off a boat in Rügenwalde harbour to make way for a local, he was told that since no one had asked the *KLV* children to come east, he could now find his own way home. Other boys from Hagen decided to go home, rather than stay and fight for a part of Germany that was not their home-land. By 10 March almost all of east Pomerania was occupied.[47]

Between the end of January and the end of April, some 900,000 people were evacuated by sea from the Danzig Bight and the east Pomeranian ports. Continuing to serve as a gateway to the Baltic to the very end of the war, the little fishing village of Hela on its narrow sand spit which separated the Bight from the Baltic was so isolated it was easy to defend, even if troops and refugees who crowded onto the sand bar had little protection from the air: the trenches which Martin Bergau helped dig in the sand promptly fell in again. But, still, 387,000 people managed to embark from here in April alone, after the port cities of Danzig and Gdynia had fallen. Martin Bergau was one of them, making his second escape from Danzig, this time in a U-boat and dressed in the blue and white uniform of a naval auxiliary.[48]

Most Germans were completely amazed and shocked by the Red Army's breakthrough from the Vistula to the Oder. Coming so soon after the upsurge of optimism engendered by their Christmas offensive in the Ardennes, few thought that, within weeks, they would be fighting to prevent the occupation of their own country. In the eastern provinces themselves, the great majority had waited until the last moment to flee because they had believed what they were told. Even in February, most of the population of eastern Pomerania – and half of them were refugees from East Prussia – had believed that the *Wehrmacht*'s new defensive lines were secure and stayed where they were.

When the news broke of the fall of East Prussia and eastern Pomerania, the disillusionment with everything the regime had claimed was all the more complete for being so delayed. In Hamburg, embit-tered refugees found audiences ready to repeat their tales; how all the Party bigwigs had forbidden the local population to leave before fleeing themselves. Officials in Party uniform were getting a hostile reception on public transport and people were tired of upbeat propaganda speeches. Even in the most loyal circles in Baden they were saying, 'They shouldn't always tell us that we will win the war, because we have to win the war. Rather, they should just show us how the others can still lose it.' Instead of criticising the Allied leaflet drops, it was their own media that people tore into, the 'whole talk in the press of heroic resistance, of the strength of German hearts, of an uprising of the whole people, of the whole high-flown rhetoric that was so empty of meaning'. Even belief in the Führer was beginning to crack, but this was as nothing compared with the disdain and contempt felt for the rest of his regime.[49]

People had known that victory was increasingly remote. Many undoubtedly did think that Germany would be defeated, others that the war would drag on in a stalemate. Many still hoped too that the Western Allies might make a separate peace with Germany, perhaps even joining the Reich in a renewed crusade against Bolshevism. But few had expected a German collapse on the eastern front, and its impact on public opinion was immediate. In those parts of the Reich facing the British and Americans along the Saar and the Rhine, defeatism began to gather momentum. A new hail and farewell had emerged in the cities to replace the increasingly rare Hitler salute: *'Bleib übrig'*, ('stay alive'), a sardonic fatalism sometimes abbreviated simply to *'BÜ'* on walls. But this was not the case everywhere else.[50]

On 3 February Berlin endured its heaviest raid of the war, the smoke and dust creating strange tricks of light in the darkened streets. Yet, even now, with another 3,000 killed from a single raid, there were still those willing to repeat the old slogan that had seen them through it all before: *'Durchhalten*, the most senseless of all words,' Ursula von Kardorff fumed at the end of that long day. 'Well, they will hold out until they are all dead, there is no other solution.' According to reports to the *Wehrmacht*, every conversation in the capital turned on the eastern front, the terror bombing, the lack of anti-aircraft defences and the promise of 'new' German weapons. People put together what they knew about the food situation, the coal shortage and the armaments industry, as they tried to make their own local assessments of the national position. They blamed the length of the war on those who had betrayed the Führer's trust and some even speculated that, but for them, it might already have been won. Above all, Berliners still wanted to hear 'positive facts. Every report', the *Wehrmacht* found, 'of a success, even only a small one, has a beneficial effect. Although many people still talk as if the war can no longer be won, people generally still hope for a change for the better.' As they teetered between hope and fear and as news spread that the diplomatic corps was leaving the capital, many women could not decide whether their small children should stay or go.[51]

During the summer and autumn of 1944, Goebbels had scripted the dying words of the German nation. Like Himmler, when he reviewed the *Volkssturm* for the first time on the 131st anniversary of the 'Battle of the Nations' at Leipzig, Goebbels returned to the war against Napoleon and the idea of a general, popular rising. But unlike Himmler, he chose a historic defeat to illustrate the value of sacrifice for the nation. Costing twice as much as the next big-budget colour movie and employing tens of thousands of soldiers, sailors and horses as extras, Veit Harlan's *Kolberg* bore unmistakable signs of Goebbels's part-authorship. The siege of Kolberg in 1807 had ended in French victory, but the unrelenting point of Harlan's film was that a new spirit of resistance had been born there. The locally born mayor of Kolberg, Nettelbeck, persuaded the Prussian commander, General von Gneisenau, that he 'would rather be buried in the ruins than surrender', and only rose from his knees once the legendary Prussian general had replied, 'That's what I wanted to hear from you, Nettelbeck. Now we can die together.' Again and again the film invoked the words of Theodor Körner, the patriotic poet of 1813, that Goebbels had himself used during the climax of his 'total war' speech in February 1943: 'Now, people, arise – and storm burst forth!' The marooned German garrison at La Rochelle was symbolically chosen for the premiere on 30 January 1945. Little did Goebbels know that by then a string of Prussian cities would be besieged. When Kolberg capitulated on 18 March – after a siege, which, unlike Königsberg, Posen or Breslau, had lasted less than a fortnight – Goebbels prevailed on the *Wehrmacht* to keep the news off its daily bulletin lest it spoil the propaganda effect of his film. Even though few Germans ever saw the film during the war, its central message of heroism and honour through self-sacrifice and death had been well prepared.[52]

German morale was increasingly divided not only by region, but also by age. Early in 1945, Ruth Reimann ran out of paper for her diary and felt that the art nouveau album which her aunt had given her was far too fine to spoil with her own 'profane' teenage preoccupations. Instead, she stuck a photo of the Führer, caught in a visionary moment in the mountains, into the front and inscribed opposite it the most beautiful words she knew, Hermann Claudius's 'Prayer':

> *Herrgott, steh dem Führer bei*
> *daß sein Werk das Deine sei . . .*

> Lord, stand by the Führer
> that his work be Yours
> that Your work be his
> Lord, stand by the Führer.
> Lord, stand by us all
> that his work be ours
> Our work be his –
> Lord, stand by us all.[53]

Nazi values, with their polarisation of good and evil and their exhortations to commitment, belief and self-sacrifice, had always held a particular fascination for adolescents. Back in January 1944, as she had steeled herself for further air raids, Liselotte Günzel had been forced by her Social Democratic father to consider the likelihood of defeat. For her the idealism of Gothic self-sacrifice had already offered an alternative:

'If victory is no longer to be had, then there is still honour,' shouted Teja to the Ostgoths, still fighting as they fell. Can one not shout to Germany's enemies: 'You can murder me, but you cannot kill me, for I am eternal!'[54]

In January 1944, no one was demanding that she put it to the test. Instead, she had been evacuated to Saxony. Through the system of evacuating whole schools, hers was also the age group that had been most protected from the war. Unlike children under ten, most of these children had not had to adapt to foster-families in villages, but had taken over castles and monasteries with their classmates, preserving and deepening that sense of peer-group belonging which the Hitler Youth had always encouraged. Although some remained stranded in the East, often their re-evacuation westwards had been assisted by volunteers from the Nazi organisations who could not do much for the general flood of refugees. Cocooned from the war in the solidarity of their *KLV* homes, many teenagers still continued to believe in the promise of 'final victory' and, even after the chaos they witnessed in January and February 1945, to see Germany as one nation, rather than the collection of villages and family networks upon which so many refugees had to fall back in their flights.

Many teenagers continued to respond in the ways that the regime encouraged. In *Kolberg* Goebbels and Veit Harlan projected the heroic qualities needed for national rebirth into the figure of Queen Luise of

Prussia. Although few teenagers saw the film, many girls brought up on her story of courage and sacrifice spontaneously turned to her example too. Ruth Reimann, as became a good member of the League of German Girls from the Elbe town of Burg, chose this as the time to inscribe the queen's words in her new album:

For me, Germany is the most sacred thing I know. Germany is my soul. It is what I am and what I must have to be happy . . . If Germany dies, then I die too.[55]

X

THE FINAL SACRIFICE

DURING the battles for the eastern provinces the Hitler Youth battalions had generally been held in reserve. This was about to change. With the Soviet armies poised on the River Oder opposite Küstrin, only 50 miles of motorway separated them from the capital. In April 1945 Hitler personally authorised sending 6,000 Hitler Youth boys from Berlin to reinforce the Seelow Heights, where they faced Zhukov's forces across the Oder. Hitler and his regime were revealing what prospect they were offering those they had so long extolled as their nation's future: death.

The Nazis had long celebrated the heroic death. Films for the young like Hans Steinhoff's 1933 production *Hitlerjunge Quex* had idealised the boy who died for the cause. In 1934 the regime had moved the main commemoration of the First World War dead from autumn to spring and christened it 'Heroes' Remembrance Day', in order to turn their 'blood sacrifice' into a fertility rite essential to national rebirth. The war had saturated society with the notion of heroic sacrifice. Millions of families had to phrase death notices for their fallen. Many chose the message encouraged by the regime: '*Für Führer, Volk und Vaterland*' ('For the Führer, Nation and Fatherland'). Others expressed a sense of greater distance from the regime or attachment to the Churches by placing God or the *Volk* before the Führer, or even omitting all reference to Hitler. But the German conservative and Christian traditions had also done much to school their adherents in bearing the burdens of sacrifice in both world wars. By the end of the 1920s there was no shortage of veterans' associations and groups wanting to cultivate 'Loyalty upon loyalty, faith upon faith, the spirit of sacrifice upon the spirit of sacrifice.' In March 1943, Marianne Peyinghaus went to comfort a couple who had recently lost their only son, a nineteen-year-old, a leader in the Hitler Youth who had looked set to take over his father's building firm one day. The mother simply said to Marianne quietly, 'The Fatherland can demand any sacrifice.' As they wept, Marianne could see that they were also trying to draw meaning from their anguish with these beliefs.[1]

When the Hitler Youth levy was raised for the *Volkssturm* in October 1944, parental consent was not sought: unlike evacuation to the countryside, this was no longer voluntary. By the end of 1944, parents were being threatened with legal sanctions if their sons did not enlist. Many families must have viewed the call-up of their teenage sons with horror, but few tried to stop them going. During the battle for Berlin, some of the young fighters would still go home for the night, returning to the battle each morning with a lunch packed by their mothers. Through Hitler Youth drills, field exercises, relief work in the bombed cities, and call-up to the *Flak*, families had been gradually accustomed to the idea of teenage service: over 100,000 had served already. In August 1944 the Reich Hitler Youth Leader, Arthur Axmann, had issued a call for boys born in 1928 to volunteer for the *Wehrmacht* and, as whole cohorts of Hitler Youths answered the summons, within six weeks 70 per cent of the age group had signed up – before they were compelled to do so. The 'final levy' of October 1944 brought the contradictions at the heart of Nazism to a crisis point.[2]

The Nazi regime had set itself up as the protector of German youth. It had justified its claims to purify the nation, to fight for 'living space' and to struggle against the forces of 'Judaeo-Bolshevism' so that Germany could be made safe for the next generation, the nation's racial future. This had been the reason for Hitler Youth summer camps and the evacuation of children from cities threatened by air raids; and this had justified channelling resources away from 'ineducable' delinquents, sterilising 'feeble-minded' girls and deporting the Jews. Now the very youth in whose name the Nazi regime pursued its utopian vision was to be sacrificed for its defence. To the next generation the destruction of the Hitler Youth in the last weeks of the war retained a profound significance, standing for the manipulation and betrayal of German society as a whole by the Nazis. But at the time, many young fighters saw things differently, regarding themselves as heirs to the proud tradition of the German student volunteers of 1914. And like that doomed generation, it was not only official propaganda that urged them to make their sacrifice: it was the role for which they had prepared themselves.[3]

In January 1945, Werner Kolb turned sixteen and the news of the Soviet breakthrough in Poland filled him with impatience to serve at the front, as he whiled away the hours in boredom at an insignificant airbase at Immenbek. For now he could only confess it to his diary, ruefully aware that 'Everyone has a secret longing, for a loving girl, for some other kind of secret. This is mine – to join the battle somewhere, on any front in this great war, for you, Führer, and for my homeland . . .' Ten days later he was rewarded: his company of Air Force Auxiliaries were relieved by girls doing their obligatory Reich Labour Service. As girls donned uniforms too, and took over support roles so that the boys could fill the ranks of the *Volkssturm*, they were sworn in also, pledging their personal loyalty to the Führer, in a nationalist dedication redolent of a religious vocation: 'I swear that I will be true and obedient to Adolf Hitler, the Führer and Commander-in-Chief of the *Wehrmacht* . . .' After the rallies were over, the reality was rather more makeshift and prosaic. In February 1945, two months before his sixteenth birthday, Hugo Stehkämpfer was called up to serve in the *Volkssturm* in the Rhineland. They were given old black SS uniforms, brown Organisation *Todt* coats, blue Air Force Auxiliary caps and – what was particularly galling for fifteen-year-olds who wanted to show what they could give for the fatherland – French steel helmets. Desperate not to be shot as partisans, these part-time soldiers preferred any uniform to wearing armbands over normal civilian clothes. Across the country, a frantic search for uniforms and equipment had been under way to make the *Volkssturm* look like soldiers. The stores of the *Wehrmacht*, police, railways, border guards, postal service, Storm Troopers, National Socialist goods drivers, the Reich Labour Service, the SS, the Hitler Youth and the German Labour Front, down to the zookeepers and tram conductors, were all turned over to provide uniforms for the *Volkssturm*.[4]

But there was precious little equipment or training to be had. The levy was simply too large. With the *Wehrmacht* itself short of 714,000 rifles in October 1944 and a monthly output of 186,000 standard pattern infantry carbines, there was never going to be enough to arm a full-scale national militia as well. By the end of January 1945, the *Volkssturm* had managed to accumulate a mere 40,500 rifles and 2,900 machine guns in its central armoury, a heterogeneous array of mainly foreign and out-of-date weapons for which there was often little if any compatible ammunition. There were also too few experienced instructors. Most of the middle-aged men could be given no more than ten to fourteen days' total training. The emphasis was on improvisation. Quadruple 20mm anti-aircraft guns were widely converted to infantry use; machine guns from planes were remounted on tripods and even flare pistols converted so that they could fire grenades.[5]

One press report about the heroic deeds of Hitler Youth in East Prussia concluded, 'Germany can be proud of this its most valuable miracle weapon.' But the boys of the *Volkssturm* had been largely protected till now. Although Hitler Youth units had played a crucial role in some of the battles in East Prussia, Silesia and Pomerania, it was no accident that Martin Bergau and his cohort of 1928 had been evacuated from the Samland Peninsula to the West. It was the elderly men whose lives had been squandered in the defence of East Prussia: at least 200,000 had been killed, with casualty rates in some areas running as high as 80 per cent. The Hitler Youth levies were seen as more valuable, and were meant to be held in reserve until they could be trained properly, replenishing the ranks of the SS and the *Wehrmacht*.[6] While Martin Bergau was being shipped from Danzig to the West, his contemporaries in the Ruhr were marching towards the gates of a camp run by the Reich Labour Service at Lavesum in Westphalia. Having graduated from Hitler Youth and military training camps, Heinz Müller and the other boys from Duisburg were intent on showing the raw farm boys in their group how cool they were. They dragged their feet and sang jazz numbers all the way:

> Black as coal to his soles is the nigger Jim
> His best white waistcoat wears the nigger Jim
> Like a tiger slips the nigger into the nearest bar
> He drank whisky, always more whisky, till he was totally tanked.[7]

As the boys reached the gate of the Labour Service camp, Heinz was doing a tenor solo. After greeting his new recruits with a heavy display of mock respect, the officer on duty bawled them out, ordering them to lie face down in the mud and do press-ups. To emphasise the word 'down' and make quite sure that all their civilian clothes got thoroughly filthy before they were kitted out in worn-out socks, underwear, boots and Labour Service uniforms, he pressed his boot on the boys' backs. It hardly mattered under whose auspices the training camps were run; the informal induction into military life remained the same. Those who answered the call for volunteers with clerical experience were sent to clean the toilets, while the 'Easter bunny' who turned out on parade without his carbine became the unit's scapegoat. Composing favourite recipes in their spare time, and competing for extra helpings of potato mash at meals, the boys from the Ruhr towns quickly learned to swap their tobacco rations for a share in the country lads' food parcels from home. Heinz Müller, the son of a Communist father who had been imprisoned in a concentration camp, was also eager for the chance at last to retaliate for all the bombing raids he had endured.

Heinz was soon happier than he could ever remember. He completed his basic training with machine guns, hand grenades and the *Panzerfaust*, and learned to cradle the 98K carbine firmly against the right shoulder to cushion the shock of its recoil. He also found time to fall in love. Issued with bikes and sent off to liaise each evening with the *Wehrmacht* unit in nearby Haltern, Heinz and his friend Gerd were excused normal duties, and Heinz soon worked out a system whereby Gerd covered for him while he dated a local farmer's daughter whom he had met during an air-raid alarm. When spring came, he was cycling the 8 miles to Haltern drunk on the prospect of seeing her, holding her hand and – after filling up on her mother's cooking – kissing her farewell under the fruit trees.

In Franconia, Rudi Brill and the other fifteen- and sixteen-year-old boys in his Hitler Youth group were marching over the hill between Fürth and Lautenbach to reach the fortifications they were building on the morning of 3 March, when two American fighter bombers suddenly swept out from behind a wood. Caught in the open with no cover, the thirty boys could only fling themselves to the ground. As the planes roared towards them, they could see the faces of the pilots and their eyes. Praying, Rudi thrust himself harder against the bare ground. The planes circled twice and then left them, without opening fire. After sprinting down the hill to the relative safety of their trenches, the boys hugged each other, intoxicated at having survived. They guessed that the pilots had mistaken them for forced labourers. Within a day or two, Rudi remembered, the boys' talk as they drifted off to sleep in the dormitories at night had returned to its normal groove, sex. They had mastered their fright. But unlike the heavy bombers which flew high or at night, these aircraft were not remote enemies: they had seen the pilots' eyes.[8]

As the Allies closed in, Hitler vacillated between over-optimistic plans and choreographing his own destruction, between gazing at the model for the rebuilding of Linz and calls for last-ditch resistance. Many of his strategic decisions revealed a self-destructive overconfidence during this final phase of the war: tank divisions were not sent to reinforce the eastern front in December; the western front was forced to defend German territory beyond the Rhine; and the 2 million German troops stationed elsewhere in Europe were not brought home to protect the Reich. Hoping to repulse or split the Allies, Hitler did not wish to give up control over Swedish iron ore, Baltic submarine bases, or the German 'fortresses' from Breslau to La Rochelle, imagining that these positions might be needed again. Ever the gambler, Hitler still thought there was something to play for and that a supreme sacrifice might yet turn the tide. For him the war was not yet lost. Without an armistice in the West or a concentration of all German armed forces, it was the *Volkssturm* that was going to have to provide much of that supreme sacrifice.[9]

But unlike Hitler's own past gambles, on this occasion he did not take the initiative. And for him, too, rational strategy now easily shaded into suicidal Gothic romanticism. When the Führer assembled his *Gauleiter* for the last time on 24 February, he mooted for the first time outside his inner circle his belief that if the German people failed the supreme test of war, then it would have shown itself to be too weak and would merit its destruction. This was hardly the stuff of propaganda and even Goebbels's close associates in the Propaganda Ministry were shocked when he began to speak about suicide as if he was helping them take roles in a historic film. Hitler and Goebbels would choose to kill themselves, but not until the only alternative was capture by the Red Army, and both went on hoping until the very end that a miracle would save them.[10]

Hitler was too exhausted to broadcast his customary speech to the German people after meeting the *Gauleiter* on 24 February. What proved to be his final public address was read out on the radio by his old Party comrade, Hermann Esser, instead, but the speech was redolent with the Führer's characteristic phrases: 'this Jewish-Bolshevik

annihilation of peoples and its West European and American pimps',
'freedom of the German nation', fighting till 'the historical turning
point', or at least long enough to mete out vengeance. 'The life left to
us can serve only one command,' the Führer demanded at the close,
'that is to make good what the international Jewish criminals and their
henchmen have done to our people.' After hearing Hitler's proclama-
tion the local Party boss in Lüneburg was driven to quip bitterly, 'The
Führer is prophesying again.' Even Goebbels's most loyal correspondents had given up calling for Jews to be shot in reprisal for Allied
bombing and – more aware of Germany's weakness than of its lack of
Jews – were pinning their hopes on leaflet drops to persuade British
and American troops not to allow themselves to serve as the pawns
of 'world Jewry'. As the director of the training school for engineers
in Kaiserslautern put it, 'Help us to found the United States of Europe
in which there are no more Jews' and, in a final, pseudo-Marxist
flourish, 'Europeans of all countries unite!' Or, as another enthusiast
wrote on the day the Red Army liberated Auschwitz: 'Goy awake!
Non-Jews of the whole world unite!' Even such true believers had to
hope that propaganda would serve where force was failing them.[11]

During the last week of March 1945 the Western Allies crossed the
middle and lower reaches of the Rhine, launching a huge encirclement
of the German armies in the Ruhr. On Easter Sunday, 1 April, American
tanks met at Lippstadt, closing the northern and southern pincers in
a ring which they could tighten around the Rhineland and Ruhr cities.
As they had marched up the picturesque, winding Taunus valley from
Frankfurt towards their rendezvous at Marburg, the American forces had
liberated a series of unimportant little towns. On 26 March they
had occupied Hadamar. When local residents told them about the murders
up the hill at the psychiatric asylum, they arrested the director, Dr
Wahlmann, and some of the nursing staff, doubled the rations of the
starving patients and let them come and go as they pleased. The new
director, Dr Wilhelm Altvater, arrived to take charge in early May and
found two large tubs in the dispensary, each containing about 5 kilos
of Veronal and Luminal. On 28 March the town of Idstein was occupied and the last witness to medical killings at the nearby Kalmenhof
asylum came out of hiding. Ludwig Heinrich Lohne, a mildly disabled
teenager, had been used to do odd jobs and had seen the nurses stir
the Luminal powder into the children's food. He had had to dig their
graves and drop their bodies out of the trapdoor in the bottom of the

little reusable coffin he had made. Lohne was used to being beaten and bullied in the asylum, and his front teeth had been knocked out, but in January he had seen how the epileptic patient and housekeeper, Margarethe Schmidt, had been injected and left to die in the locked air-raid shelter. So when the doctor sent for him, Lohne fled and hid in a barn until the Americans came. In other asylums, where most of the medical staff stayed on, many inmates continued to starve to death well beyond the final collapse of Nazi rule.[12]

In the early morning of 31 March 1945 the Americans reached Guxhagen near Kassel. They liberated all the inmates from the work-house and reformatory at Breitenau, among them German vagrants and juvenile delinquents as well as foreign forced workers – except for twenty-eight prisoners whom the Gestapo had hastily executed the previous day. Georg Sauerbier, the institution's Nazi director, remained at his post, venting his spleen by writing notes about 'enemy troops' on the case files of all those who had got away in this unheard-of fashion.[13]

While the Allies tightened their ring around the Ruhr, their guns on the left bank of the Rhine continued to shell the cities on the right bank and the bombers continued to pound them from above. The electricity had been cut in Duisburg since February. On 22 March the RAF hit Hildesheim, a small medieval town of half-timbered houses with a famous, 1,000-year-old monastery. The intense heat melted the great bronze doors to the cathedral dating from 1015, as the wooden houses turned into a funeral pyre for over 1,000 people. In Hella Klingbeil's working-class neighbourhood in Hanover, the women and girls busied themselves peeling potatoes so that the Hildesheimers should at least get their 'Bombensuppe'. Hitler Youth boys returned from helping clear up, telling tales of how 'some of the dead sat there as if they were alive and, if someone touched them, then collapsed in ashes'. Working alongside Germans to clear a bombed-out food warehouse, Italian military internees were encouraged by the German guard to help themselves to the largely spoiled produce. When the police discovered 'plundered' food on hundreds of Italian prisoners, the SS hanged 208 people – 120 of them Italians – in batches of five, while some of the shell-shocked townsfolk looked on, according to eyewitnesses, 'fairly impassively'. It was no longer just the security forces that terrorised foreign workers. At Oberhausen, a group of boys joined in the interrogation of an Eastern worker, beating the man until he was covered in blood and had confessed to stealing some potatoes. With a pistol borrowed from a *Wehrmacht* office, a telephone operator led his captive onto the Konkordia sports field, while the growing crowd beat him with clubs and wooden fencing. At the edge of a bomb crater, the telephone operator fired, hitting the man in the stomach. The crowd finished him off.[14]

As Nazi Germany broke up into different regions, the regime increasingly resorted to terror against the German population as well. After the firebombing of Dresden on 14 and 15 February, Hitler and Goebbels wanted British and American prisoners of war to be executed in retaliation. Only the united opposition of Jodl, Dönitz, Ribbentrop and Keitel succeeded in talking the Führer out of issuing the order. Instead, on 15 February, the Minister for Justice issued a decree establishing summary courts martial for civilians, aimed especially at the population in western Germany. Instead of fleeing before the Americans in the Saar and Mosel region, west of the Rhine, the local population had hung out white flags from houses. In one place German civilians stopped German troops from shooting; in another, the German soldiers trying to detonate charges under a bridge were attacked by farmers with pitchforks. A group of soldiers who broke through to the German lines after escaping the Americans were greeted with shouts of 'You're prolonging the war'. In late February, when the *Wehrmacht* retook Geislautern near Völklingen, the local SS commander found that the Americans had shared their rations, their chocolate and cigarettes with the population and treated their houses better than German troops had done. He warned that the good reputation of the Americans was preceding them throughout the territory. German propaganda tried to retaliate by warning the population that these had only been front-line troops and that the atrocities would start once the rear services and 'above all the Jews' took control.[15]

Under a presiding judge, three-man tribunals representing the Nazi Party, the SS and the *Wehrmacht* were empowered to dispense summary justice to defeatist civilians. Most of the 500 civilians sentenced to death by these courts martial were on the western front. On 9 March, even more summary 'mobile courts martial' were established for the military. It has been estimated that between 5,000 and 8,000 soldiers – perhaps a quarter of the total military executions during the war – were condemned by these 'mobile courts martial'. After the collapse of the Ruhr, much of their activity took place in south-west Germany, where units like Major Erwin Helm's or Lieutenant-General Max Simon's 13th SS Army Corps used terror to force soldiers and civilians to do what common sense told them was now pointless and go on fighting. Terror extended the war by a few weeks, but the main loss of life was still in combat with the enemy: 10,000 men were killed every day in the first four months of 1945; a total of 1.5 million from December 1944 to April 1945. This was double the rate of loss of even the catastrophic defeats in Belorussia and the Ukraine during the previous summer.[16]

Encircled in the Ruhr, the *Wehrmacht*'s morale on the western front quickly disintegrated. Faced by the armour and artillery of 2 million Allied troops, the 320,000 men under Field Marshal Walter Model's command could not break out. Exhausted and inwardly defeated, the *Wehrmacht* and civilian population surrendered most of the major cities of the Ruhr with scarcely a shot being fired. Everywhere Allied troops met small civilian units who had remained behind in the factories and mines, not to defend them but to ensure their safe delivery into American hands. German workers and managers united to prevent Hitler's much-trumpeted scorched-earth policy from being carried out. In Hanover, some of the Hitler Youths were fetched home by their mothers. But American commanders often cited the 'fanaticism' of the Hitler Youth as one of the stumbling blocks in their mopping-up operations, and at the important railway junction at Hamm the US 9th Army ran into a 'hornets' nest' of *Volkssturm* units. Outside the village of Oberdorf in the Aalen district, a young SS lieutenant directed his fourteen- to sixteen-year-olds to hold back the Sherman tanks from their trenches. In small engagements like these, the teenagers surprised their conquerors by their capacity to endure deadly fire. They seemed to exhibit the transitory adult emotions of battle in a heightened degree, and on capture astonished the Americans once more, transformed in their eyes into completely overwrought children, shaking, bleeding and weeping 'hysterically'.[17]

As the Americans entered Hanover, Hella Klingbeil ran out to look, even though her mother had warned her there might be black soldiers among them. Hella was overawed. Their uniforms looked new, their faces well fed and expressionless. They did not march, sing or shout 'hurrah' and they threw no flowers. Instead, they drove everywhere, ten to a truck and armed to the teeth. They were utterly unlike the hordes of German stragglers who had poured down the same roads a few hours previously. As he had watched the enormous tanks and motorised infantry race along the road between Kleinottweiler and Altstadt on 20 March, avoiding all the ditches that he and his comrades had been digging for the last six months, Rudi Brill had similar feelings to Hella: he was awed by such overwhelming force. In Essen the population even cheered as the tanks rolled in on 10 April. Many *Volkssturm* units quietly threw away their armbands and derisory equipment and went home.[18]

Under the guidance of their junior officers, some of the Hitler Youth battalions were not ready to give up yet. They made for the forests and hills, trying to head eastwards out of the reach of the Americans. Jürgen Heitmann's unit was out training when they saw the American tanks firing into their camp at Lieberstein, north of Fulda. The seventy boys ran across the fields with the weapons they had been carrying, reaching a Reich Labour Service camp at mid-afternoon on the next day. Here they were plied with food and sweets, before the locals made them move on by telling them the tanks had reached the village. As they escaped they could see the white flags of surrender already fluttering from the houses. At Lavesum, Heinz Müller's budding love affair was rudely broken off on 28 March, when he learned that the Americans had reached Haltern. As the 360 Ruhr boys marched out of camp filled with the thought that they would finally have their opportunity to retaliate for the bombing of their cities, they were told by fleeing soldiers to throw away their heavy anti-tank grenades, or *Panzerfäuste*. They would be useless against the nets which had been fitted to the tanks. But the fifteen- and sixteen-year-old boys ignored this sound advice and, still lugging their rifles and grenades, marched on for a further 30 miles that night.[19]

While Jürgen's company split into small units to make their way undetected through the Thuringian Forest, Heinz Müller's crossed the Teutoburger Forest together. But gradually the country boys from the Münsterland peeled off as they passed their family farms, leaving the cool, jazz-loving city boys to carry on. Goading them onwards with threats of the terrible cruelties that attended capture and the promise of the wonderful pea soup waiting for them on the other side of the bridge, their non-commissioned officers brought them over the River Weser. Too tired to worry about the pea soup or their hunger, they fell asleep on the meadow, surrounded by refugees and a motley array of stragglers from different army units who had been rounded up at gunpoint to hold the river. Only eighty boys – a quarter of those who had set out six days before – made it this far. On Wednesday, 4 April, as they climbed out of the ditches along the road to Stadthagen, after a plane had strafed their column, Heinz met a girl from Duisburg riding a bicycle. She told him that his mother had been evacuated to the next village, Nienstedt. Heinz got three hours' leave from his commander and borrowed a bike to ride there. Everyone came out to stare at his worn-out boots, torn clothes and dirty, pinched face. They competed to feed him and then, at 4.15 in the afternoon, his mother insisted that he go to bed for his last hour of leave. While Heinz slept, his mother burned his Labour Service uniform, scrounged civilian clothes from the neighbours and persuaded the old major in charge of local defence to sign his release papers. Heinz was so tired that he did not wake up till two and a half days later.

The same morning that Heinz went to Nienstedt, Jürgen's unit passed a forced march of concentration camp prisoners. From the bodies in the ditches, he could see the SS had been shooting stragglers and as they passed he saw another one being killed. Jürgen's group pressed on into Thuringia for another ten days, keeping halfway up the hills along the River Werra. They gathered food from *Wehrmacht* camps and passing units, and lodged in farms, on the floors of school build-ings and in the forest. Finally, they realised from the noise of American lorries roaring along the nearby motorway that they were already surrounded. They remained in the forest and a major wearing the Knight's Cross set about organising them to make a last stand, but Jürgen's own commander told them to bury their weapons and parts of their uniforms in the woodland. At 9 a.m. on 16 April he released them from their service oaths, leaving them to get home as best they could.

Meanwhile, between the eastern and western fronts, a strange semblance of normality continued. Eleven-year-old Anna-Matilda Mombauer was trying to please her crotchety middle-aged school-teacher with an essay about the onset of spring. The world could well have been at peace in her corner of Braunschweig for she had come across primulas and snowdrops in the shadow of the hill.

Out on the flat moorland of the Lüneburg Heath, Agnes Seidel cele-brated the first anniversary of the evacuation of her Hamburg class on 9 March. The children brought her flowers. Ten days later she was playing 'cat and mouse' with them in the big barn. Her son Klaus – who had won his spurs in the anti-aircraft battery of the Hamburg

Stadtpark in 1943 – was sending her rather depressing letters from Stettin about the mud and bad food in the trenches of his first tour of duty with the army. On the night of 26 March she even cried as she went to bed; but from nostalgic melancholy: the children had decorated her chair with flowers and played on the flute and mouth organ in honour of her forty-fourth birthday. Only in mid-April did she begin to register the acute danger of her situation. When the arms dump was blown up and the army stores at Melzingen thrown open, she was seized by a fit of weeping; as she sorted through the family photo albums she finally realised that all the certainties of her world were collapsing. On 16 April Agnes Seidel woke up from her afternoon nap to hear the sound of English trucks and tanks pouring through the village in an endless stream. Still, she was outraged when the polite English officers and an aggressive American 'half-nigger' came later that day to arrest the German officers on her farm. She ran after the car to bring some food to the two seventeen-year-old SS men inside and to clasp their hands one more time.[20]

Stalin wrote to Roosevelt expressing his amazement at the way the Germans were prepared to fight like madmen against the Russians to hold onto every minor Czech railway station while surrendering cities as important as Osnabrück, Mannheim and Kassel without any resistance. Now, as the US and British Armies drove virtually unopposed across the north German plain, it seemed possible that they might reach, not just the Elbe, but Berlin itself before the Russians.[21]

By mid-March, *Wehrmacht* surveillance teams in Berlin were reporting a widespread resurgence of the fear of Jewish revenge. Two workers in the Moltke Strasse in Spandau-West agreed on 19 March, that 'we are ourselves to blame for this war because we treated the Jews so badly', going on to draw the familiar conclusion: 'We needn't be surprised if they now do the same to us.' This foreboding arose as predictably as it had in September 1944 in Aachen and Stuttgart. While the mood in the capital teetered between hope, resignation and despair, the regime could draw some public support for its increasing use of terror at the front. On the *S-Bahn*, two workers talked approvingly of how three soldiers and the local leader of the Party had been hanged from telephone poles in Seelow on the Oder front, bearing placards proclaiming their desertion. Others called for the press to publish the numbers of deserters executed and worried about foreign workers who answered back. Meanwhile, the number of military executions being carried out at the Spandau fortress prompted the garrison commander to beg the Berlin commander to relieve his men of this duty. He refused.[22]

On 12 April Liselotte Günzel was listening to the radio in her parents' flat in Friedrichshagen when she heard the death sentence pronounced *in absentia* on the garrison commander of Königsberg for surrendering after a siege lasting months. She had just returned to Berlin after fourteen months at her boarding school in Saxony and the broadcast made her furious: 'His family is to be arrested. Is that not the rule of terror? Oh, how can German people and our *Wehrmacht* bear it. Because the brave officer did not want to sacrifice all his soldiers, they hang him and his whole family who are sitting at home ignorant of it all. To hang a German, a Prussian officer!' She was so angry, felt so betrayed by the regime to which she had pledged her loyalty so many times in the two and a half years since she had begun her diary, that for the first time she swore, cursing 'the whole Nazi brood, these war criminals and Jew-murderers, who now drag the honour of the German officer into the dirt'. Liselotte had been unable to believe the news that Jews were being murdered in the camps when her left-wing mother had told her about it back in August 1943, but she had not completely forgotten it either. The knowledge had lain dormant, ready – in her current mood of outrage and despair – to burst out again.[23]

Both Liselotte's brother and father had been called up to dig anti-tank traps. After inspecting the hurried barricades being thrown up in her neighbourhood in the eastern suburbs, Liselotte endorsed the joke going the rounds of Berlin. 'The Russian tanks will stand at the entry of Berlin for two hours splitting their sides with laughter, then drive over them in two minutes.' But still the work of digging two rings of fortifications around Berlin continued. The bridges were mined and the handful of out-of-date foreign artillery pieces available to the *Volkssturm* were added to the 128mm, 88mm and 20mm guns of Berlin's anti-aircraft defences. The three massive reinforced concrete bunker towers at Zoo, Humboldthain and Friedrichshain now assumed a central role. From their flat roofs the Berlin Anti-Aircraft Division had tried to defend the city from air raids. Now they would try to defend their immediate districts from ground attack.[24]

Liselotte found herself inwardly divided, just as she had been during the air raids of 1943–4. Like her defeatist Social Democrat father, she did not want Berlin to be defended. Yet even now in her new, resolutely anti-Nazi mood, she could not resist the emotional pull of the heroic death, of a final resistance whose futility and certain failure only increased its grandeur in her eyes. Confronting the prospect that her brother Bertel would soon be fighting with the *Volkssturm* in the battle for Berlin, she wrote, 'I'm terribly afraid for Bertel, because it would be so dreadful for Mummy. I myself,' she confessed chillingly, 'would be ready to sacrifice him, Frau L. sacrificed her life's joy after all.' Would Bertel's death make her equal with her teacher, who had already lost a husband? Was this to be her coming of age?[25]

Two days later, on 19 April, seventeen-year-old Liselotte stood and watched the boys of the *Volkssturm*, many of them younger than herself, cycling through Friedrichshagen to defend Münchehofe. Her feelings were still mixed. 'I am so proud of our boys, who are now throwing themselves against the tanks when the order comes,' she wrote the next day, adding, without any trace of personal responsibility, 'but they are being hounded to their deaths.' By now no one in her eastern neighbourhood of the city – designated as Sector B on the German military maps – was prepared to follow Goebbels's instruction and hang out flags for the Führer's birthday. Liselotte thought that most people had already burned theirs and thrown away their Party badges out of 'fear of the Russians'. That morning, Hitler had congratulated and decorated twenty boys of the Hitler Youth who had distinguished themselves in battle. In the last film footage of the Führer, he is to be seen patting one of them on the cheek in the Chancellery garden, before they were sent back to face the enemy.[26]

No one had any illusions any longer that the Soviet offensive would come soon. Along the road from Barth on the Baltic coast, Helga Maurer was taking her first ride in a motor vehicle. Looking down from the back of the open military truck, the toddler saw the spring fields slip away behind, while her mother held baby Edith on her lap. Their two brothers followed in the car behind them, carrying a packet of rusks. Helga's abiding memory was not of fear, but of excitement at their adventure and of sitting on one of the soldiers' laps: when their military convoy rounded a corner and her brothers and the all-important rusks disappeared from view, Helga had burst into tears and the soldier had picked her up.[27]

In Brigittenhof outside Berlin, the loyally patriotic middle-aged schoolmaster noted how his three-and-a-half-year-old daughter was running around the living room deciding which of her things they should take in the pram if they 'had to flee'. While the air-raid alarms wailed on 4 April, little Ursel ran to her mother and told her that the planes should stay away so that she could repack: 'Unpack now, for the dear God protects us, after all I pray every day,' the toddler continued, 'protect us from the wicked enemy.'[28]

Zhukov's artillery bombardment began at 5 a.m. on 16 April, but like so many of the refugees from the eastern provinces before them, Ursel's parents waited until they were told to pack. Karl Damm and his fellow Air Force Auxiliaries were lying in the shallow trenches they had dug two days earlier. Before being sent from Berlin the boys had been hastily issued with French rifles of a First World War pattern and each company had been given several of the single-shot rocket *Panzerfaust* grenades they were meant to use as a 'tank-hunting' unit, but there had been no time to instruct the cadets in how to fire them. Around noon, small, disorganised groups of retreating soldiers began to appear in their trench, dirty, terrified figures who belonged to the elite *Gross-Deutschland* Division. As Karl came off sentry duty at dawn, the boys could see fifty Soviet tanks moving along the road past their trenches. Yelling at them to move out, their sergeant led them over the first corpses they had seen, the dead bodies of their comrades in the communication trench. Their retreat was only halted by an officer brandishing a pistol, who ordered them to hold their positions while German tanks counter-attacked – successfully, for now. But Marshal Konev's 1st Ukrainian Front had burst through the German lines to the south, while further north the Hitler Youth battalions were still helping to hold Zhukov's tanks back on the three fortified lines of the Seelow heights. Completely vulnerable as they felt after their first experience of battle, the air-force cadets were still held together by their sense of discipline, teenage heroism and fear of falling into the hands of the Russians.[29]

Ursel and her parents did not leave Brigittenhof until it had been under artillery fire for twenty-four hours. At last, at 4 a.m. on 19 April, they set off, with Ursel's granny pushing her in the pram while her mother shoved the big handcart with the suitcases and bedding, and her father the little one with their provisions. Despite the crowds of soldiers and refugees on the bumpy roads, Ursel kept falling asleep, her head nodding forward, looking, her father thought with all the anguish of a respectable man made suddenly homeless, 'like a gypsy child's'. After a day and a night of wandering they had covered 20 miles, reaching

Buchwalde-Senftenberg. Even though bombs and shells were landing close by, they were too tired to continue. A soldier warned them not to stay longer than an hour, but it was there that their flight ended. The Russians arrested the father and held him for twenty-four hours. When he was released he could find no trace of his family: two months later, on 16 June, he would discover his mother's corpse near their last halt; but he still had no sign of where or if his wife and daughter had been killed.[30]

As 1.5 million Soviet troops converged on the German capital from the north, east and south, some 85,000 German troops were mustered to man defences which lacked all the qualities that had made the Red Army pay so dearly for its conquest of East Prussia. Nearly half of them came from units of the Berlin *Volkssturm*, many of whom had been forced to hand over their weaponry to arm scratch battalions of *Luftwaffe* and naval personnel. Ranged alongside them were 45,000 *Wehrmacht* and SS troops, drawn from the remnants of five different divisions. All told, they had mustered some sixty tanks. Concerned as ever to reassure the population of the capital, the *Völkischer Beobachter* merely carried a warning to keep off the streets the following day because of the danger of *Flak* splinters from a planned artillery exercise. As the first rocket flares illuminated the city that evening it looked to a boy in Prenzlauer Berg as if the Russians wanted to photograph Berlin. Meanwhile, the remnants of the *Gross-Deutschland* Division joined the *Volkssturm*, SS and Hitler Youth units in closing the barricades across the district's streets and bridges.[31]

On 21 April, the battle began, with the 3rd and 5th Shock Armies, the 2nd Guards Tank Army and the 47th Army of the 1st Belorussian Front fighting their way through the outer defence perimeter towards the northern and eastern districts of the city. Sixteen-year-old Rudolf Vilter was completely unprepared for the sight of a T-34 tank bearing down on him. His *Volkssturm* unit had received little training and none against moving targets. 'I thought it was coming directly at me,' he remembered years later, 'and I wanted to hide ten metres underground.' His sergeant, an old and experienced soldier, stood out in the open and shot at the tank with his *Panzerfaust*, showing the boys that the tanks were just as vulnerable as they were themselves. In Prenzlauer Berg, Erwin P. and his brother could not resist joining a friend of theirs who used a rope to climb into one of the trees on the Falk Platz to get a good view of the position. In the Gleim Strasse, a group of girls mistook the sound of the artillery barrage for bombing and went on playing in the street until a policeman told them to go inside because the Russians were coming.[32]

Across Berlin, families moved downstairs into their cellars, turning their lively neighbourhoods into cellar communities, with a speed and practice born of the months of bombing. But this time many families would not let their children leave the cellars again for the next twelve days. In Prenzlauer Berg, Renate and Helga's father fetched bottles from the cellar while their mother boiled water. Everyone put on a double layer of clothing, Renate – the youngest – adding her tracksuit and two overcoats on top. Carrying their gas masks and satchels with their daily provisions, the three sisters went down to the basement. Once the electricity and water mains were cut the next day, the population either had to depend on what they had already collected, or set out on hazardous forays to replenish their buckets from fire hydrants and street pumps.[33]

It was difficult to keep children occupied in cellars for so long. When she came to write about her experiences eight months later, one girl remembered spending the whole time painting pictures of fairy tales with her girlfriend. Some families like hers used lulls in the bombardment to queue for food at the shops or to fetch water; others to return to their flats. The small cellar in Hochmeister Strasse 29, where Helga and her two sisters were staying was so crammed with refugees that they had to sleep sitting up. To stop them suffocating in the bad air, their parents took them upstairs during night-time lulls in the fighting.[34]

Returning to her flat in Wilmersdorf, the novelist Hertha von Gebhardt even caught the broadcast of *The Magic Flute* on the radio: it was being performed at the *Schauspielhaus* on the Gendarmenmarkt that day. She went to the patisserie on the corner to take coffee with her grown-up daughter, while its owner, Herr Walter, strutted around in his SA uniform. While she felt confident that the older *Volkssturm* men would throw away their weapons before Wilmersdorf could be destroyed in the fighting, she watched the troops of fourteen- to sixteen-year-olds, lugging rifles almost as big as they were, and worried that they might not be so pragmatic.[35]

As Lothar Loewe ran messages under fire, he was flitting through an area of Berlin he knew like the back of his hand. His commander was a lieutenant with a medal and a wooden leg, who disappeared each night to visit his girlfriend. Lothar and the rest of his Hitler Youth unit returned at night to their parental homes, reassembling each morning to continue the war. Taking cover in a cellar, Lothar and an older soldier with campaign stripes fired at three tanks through the doorway. As the backblast of fiery gases from the *Panzerfaust* hit the wall behind him, the sixteen-year-old was jubilant: one of the tanks had been flung into the air by their grenades, and the Russians pulled back. But almost immediately Lothar was shocked to see a group of SS men drive all the men from a house which had hung out white bed sheets and shoot them in the middle of the street.[36]

As civilians ran out of water, these conflicts with SS troops became more frequent. On 25 April they shot 130 women and children in the Landsberger Allee for trying to return to the Soviet side of the city. Many had probably crossed the lines in search of water. In Prenzlauer Berg, a boy remembered going with his 'house community' to fetch water when the fighting had died down at 4 a.m. As they stepped around the dead horses, overturned cars, weapons and wounded soldiers littering the Ystader Strasse, a group of SS men jumped out of a house and wanted to shoot all the men for wearing white armbands. In the Schivelbeiner Strasse, young Hans Joachim S. blamed 'were-wolves' for picking out water carriers with white armbands from their snipers' eyries in the rooftops: he was probably referring to Hitler Youths. But still civilians needed water and still they donned white armbands, because they found the Soviet troops would let them pass. In fact, in an attempt to reverse the reputation they had earned in East Prussia and Silesia, the Red Army had started to send both civilians and even German prisoners of war back across the lines to persuade others that they would be treated well.[37]

In her cellar in Wilmersdorf, Hertha von Gebhardt realised finally that 'the Americans don't seem to be coming. Incomprehensible.' All the rumours of the last few days of a separate peace with the Western Allies or a new alliance with them against Bolshevism had evaporated. The only member of their 'cellar community' who was utterly amazed to learn that Germany was losing the war and that the Russians were already in Berlin was a late returner from a *KLV* camp, a twelve-year-old boy. Local children had already stopped yelling in fright at the ear-splitting detonations, and as curiosity got the better of their fear, were returning to play in the streets after the day's artillery bombardment had abated.[38]

At 2 a.m. on the 23rd, Ingeborg D. heard the sound of tank tracks and heavy engines grinding along the street above, but no one dared to go upstairs to see if they were German or Russian. Finally, at 5 a.m. they decided to go up and sleep in their own beds for a couple of hours. In the house entrance Ingeborg, aged ten or eleven, saw her first Russian soldier. As they continued up the stairs, they could see that the Krüger Strasse was full of tanks, field artillery and soldiers. Her first thought as she looked at the fresh-faced men without their steel helmets was how different they looked from the exhausted and dangerous-looking types she had seen among Russian prisoners of war. 'We soon saw,' she wrote in early 1946, 'how we had been lied to. They gave cigars to the men and sweets to the children. Towards midday on the 23rd the women of our house went out shopping. There was a pound of fat pork per person.' By 25 April, the future *Kommandant* of Berlin, Colonel-General Nikolai Berzarin, had set about bringing in provisions for the civilian population.[39]

Thursday, 26 April was a warm spring day and the *Wehrmacht*'s northern front line now ran from Prenzlauer Allee to the great *Flak* bunker in Friedrichshain. On the southern side, Hertha von Gebhardt had hardly slept that night and at 6 a.m., just before the 'Stalin organs' – or Katyusha rockets – opened up, she roused the rest of the house and made them move into the adjacent cellar as they always did in case of danger. Even here the blast of the Russian rockets nearly knocked them over. By midday Gebhardt and her companions were dividing up all the schnapps and tobacco of their absent neighbours. That afternoon they kept busy with a search-and-destroy mission for weapons, uniforms, insignia and military maps, anything which could provoke the Russians. As the bombardment became more intense and they suffered their own first casualties from their 'cellar community', Gebhardt began telling the children 'Little Red Riding Hood' and then 'Sleeping Beauty' in a voice loud enough to drown out the sounds of the rockets.[40]

As fourteen-year-old Wera K. ran from Alexanderplatz, criss-crossing the maze of narrow streets of Mitte back to their condemned cellar in the Landsberger Strasse, her usual five-minute walk from school seemed to take an age. Masonry was collapsing from above, horses and cattle had broken out of the livestock yard, their neighing and bellowing rising above the sounds of gunfire. 'And I have to admit,' Wera confided half a century later, 'that during this run I shat myself. Simply from panic-stricken fear.' Safely back in the cellar below their

bombed house, Wera, her mother and grandmother joined a few neighbours sitting in near darkness, around their buckets of water. Oblivious
to the passage of day and night, they gradually exhausted their supply
of candles, too apathetic to say much any more, though bitter quarrels could suddenly flare over sharing out the water supply. Towards
the end, people began to pray. Then, Wera remembered, a cow suddenly
appeared outside and they had milk.[41]

On 27 April the Hitler Youth fighters in Prenzlauer Berg were still
being extolled in the German press, boys for their tank-hunting, girls
for keeping the artillery positions supplied with shells despite heavy
fire. Meanwhile, the Soviet gunners established their positions on Little
Berlin's hill of Viktoria Park, from where they were able to fire down
onto the Anhalter Station, into whose cavernous concrete bunker tower
thousands of refugees had crammed as tightly as the sardines that had
been laid in to feed them. The gunners were amazed to see a column
of 400 Hitler Youths marching down the Kolonnen Strasse towards
them, holding their *Panzerfäuste* as if on parade. Those at the head
of the column died under the first artillery shells. The rest fled. They
could not yet know, but the last slim chance of reinforcements had
now gone. General Wenck's 12th Army had been stopped 10 miles
from Potsdam.[42]

By the end of 30 April the 10,000 German troops who had retreated
into the central government district were looking for a way out. While
sailors, Hitler Youth and SS units joined the battle for the control of
the Reichstag building, many did not know that the Führer had already
killed himself that afternoon. Goebbels initiated the first negotiations
with the victor of Stalingrad, Vasily Chuikov, to surrender Berlin; from
the Zoo bunker in the Tiergarten, the German *Flak* guns still held the
circle to the north; and to the west the Hitler Youth battalions occupied the Heerstrasse and the Pichelsdorfer Bridge over the Havel. Arthur
Axmann, the Reich Youth Leader, had spent most of his time with
them. Fleeing westwards, Captain Gerhard Boldt paused when he
reached the trenches in which the Hitler Youths lay singly and in pairs
on both sides of the Heerstrasse. As dawn had broken on 30 April,
revealing the silhouettes of the Russian tanks with their gun barrels
pointing at the bridge, Boldt had listened to their adult leader,
Obergebietsführer Schlünder, tell him how their original contingent had
been whittled down after five days of Russian shelling. With only their
rifles and anti-tank grenades to hold their trenches, a mere 500 of the

original 5,000 were still fit for combat; none had been relieved and all were exhausted. But bitter and disheartened as he sounded, Schlünder continued to follow his orders to hold the position. Even this experience of seeing their friends and comrades lying wounded or dead next to them had not undermined the resolve of these Hitler Youths to follow their orders. They would be among the last to surrender.[43]

At Spandau, just over a mile to the north, Hitler Youth units still held the Charlotte Bridge, while on the island where the Spree and Havel met German forces remained in control of the baroque citadel, though they knew they could not hold out for much longer. To the south, General Wenck's 12th Army had not been able to fight its way beyond Potsdam in its effort to assist the capital, but it was still just able to keep open an escape route for the remnants of the 9th Army to head towards the Elbe and the safety of the American lines. As Rudolf Vilter's unit joined the throng of women, children, wounded soldiers and prisoners of war, he spotted a major, along with two officers and a few military policemen, standing by the roadside, trying to catch German deserters. They had already seen the bodies hanging from the trees with signs reading, 'I was too cowardly to defend my fatherland.' As they pressed onwards, he saw an NCO in the *Waffen-SS* shoot a wounded Russian soldier in the stomach.[44]

In Prenzlauer Berg, the fighting did not end until the night of 2 May. At 2 a.m. the air-raid warden woke up the children in the cellar of Allensteiner Strasse 12, to tell them that 'the war is over'. As the menfolk returned to the house from the *Volkssturm*, they confirmed the news. When thirteen-year-old Hans Joachim went out into the street that night, he was thrilled. The German soldiers still had their weapons and were chatting and exchanging gifts of cigarettes and chocolate with the Red Army men. Eight-year-old Jutta P. ran out into Allensteiner Strasse to see the Russians, with their artillery pieces, cars and horses. But it was the soldiers' marching songs that really impressed her. This was only a local ceasefire, while the city's commander, General Weidling, negotiated the formal surrender of the Reich capital. At 6 a.m. he signed and, by mid-morning, Hans Joachim was bitterly disappointed to see the jovial comradely behaviour of the night before give way to the full humiliation of defeat, as German soldiers surrendered their weapons and were marched into Soviet captivity.[45]

In any case, not all the Germans had stopped fighting that night in Prenzlauer Berg. Caught in the battlefield of Schönhauser Allee from

23 April till 2 May, nine-year-old Christa B. was asleep in the cellar
when the SS set their large corner house ablaze on the last night of
the battle for Berlin. In their fear and confusion, the inhabitants abandoned their suitcases and broke through into the cellar of the next
house, where German soldiers with torn uniforms and blackened faces
brought them the news of the surrender. Coming up for air, they turned
to watch their house finish burning and collapsing in front of them,
an end to all the nights they had spent protecting it from incendiary
bombs.[46]

Berliners spent their first day of peace plundering the remaining
shops and military depots. The SS had set their own central stores in
the Schultheiss Brewery on fire during the fighting, but now it was
overrun with civilians eager to salvage what was left and put something by for the starvation conditions they expected defeat would bring.
Children who went to watch were shocked by the turmoil, the waste
and the sudden violence of adults who had enjoined them so often to
play in an orderly way and to recycle goods for the war effort. They
watched as the roofs were ripped off vehicles laden with provisions in
the brewery yard, until finally Russian soldiers began firing in the air
to restore order. Outside the Prenzlauer Berg water tower, twelve-year-
old Liselotte J. watched as those 'too cowardly' to go in themselves
fell 'like hyenas' on people carrying away their loot. When Walter B.
thought about the Soviet soldiers he saw taking photographs of the
fighting crowds, he was ashamed: 'Germany's conquerors did not get
a good impression.'[47]

On 1 May Lothar Loewe had been wounded, the physical shock of
the bullet instantly turning his bravura at his tank-hunting successes
to terror. That night, shortly before midnight – the agreed hour for the
surrender of the Zoo tower – he had joined an attempt to break out
of Berlin across the Charlotte Bridge over the Havel at Spandau. Against
the odds, they succeeded in storming across the bridge and breaking
through the thin Soviet line at its western end. Lothar was lured on
by the tale of hospital trains with white sheets waiting at Nauen to
take them straight to Hamburg, but when his unit reached the area,
they found a mass surrender under way: the town had fallen a week
before. Still unwilling to accept defeat, Lothar joined a group of a
dozen men in a further break-out effort, which finally came to an end
when their vehicle conked out and the six survivors had to jump down
and walk. Like the Hitler Youths who had been marching eastwards

through the Thuringian forests in a bid to escape American encirclement, the motives behind such doomed activity are not clear. Was
Lothar guided by instinctual fear or pride, or a refusal to accept defeat?
Or was he, like other *Wehrmacht* soldiers escaping from the Russians,
simply trying to surrender to the Americans?

Only when confronted with a line of Russian infantrymen advancing
on them in skirmishing formation did these diehards finally surrender.
They were then stood against a wall, the dead civilians already lying
on the ground confirming their worst expectations of the Russians:
they would be shot. But after a short discussion with one of the officers, suddenly the Red Army men came up to them and relieved them
of their rings and watches. Lothar also found they had pressed two
packets of German cigarettes into his hands. His image of the Russians
as 'sub-humans' finally and quite suddenly collapsed. When they were
handed over to a Ukrainian artillery unit in the next town, the unit's
woman doctor immediately tended the German prisoners. And they
were fed. But the gesture which shocked Lothar more than anything
else was when a Red Army man lent him his own mess kit. 'The idea,'
he mused decades later, 'that a German soldier would give a Russian
prisoner his own mess kit and spoon to eat from was simply unimaginable to me. And the fact that this Soviet gave me his, voluntarily,
happily, because he felt sorry for me, shook the foundations of my
image of them.' But before Lothar's revelation, in the final offensive
from the Oder to take Berlin, 361,367 Soviet and Polish soldiers and
458,000 members of the *Wehrmacht* had died. Of the Hitler Youth
levies, 27,000 had been killed in the last months of the war.[48]

On 5 May, the same day that Lothar Loewe was captured, American
troops finally reached a little Austrian camp riddled with typhus and
dysentery at Wels. There, Yehuda Bacon and Filip Müller were among
the prisoners who had survived the forced marches from Mauthausen
to wait among the lice, the starving and the dead for their liberation.[49]
Three days later the German *Wehrmacht* finally capitulated.

PART FOUR

AFTERWARDS

XI

THE DEFEATED

NINE-year-old Edgar Plöchl was out collecting firewood in a pram when he saw a Russian armoured column coming down the road towards his village in rural Upper Styria. Running home by back paths, the young Austrian boy was able to warn his family. Edgar's overwhelming memory of the war's end was not the arrival of the Russians itself, but the utter terror that preceded it. As he sat indoors waiting with his family, he experienced that mortal fear for the first time which Liselotte Günzel had felt during the bombing raids on Berlin in November 1943 and Miriam Wattenberg in Warsaw in September 1939. In sheltered parts of the Reich like Upper Styria, children's first and last experiences of the war often followed one another in rapid succession. To a young girl in Mecklenburg, in the days before the occupation it looked 'as if the grown-ups wanted to play hide-and-seek'. The watches and remaining jewellery disappeared into a glass preserving jar and were buried. Even her dolls were hidden under a woodpile, in case the teenage Polish girls working on the farm should find them: she may not have known how young they were, but she did know that they 'took childish pleasure in all toys'.[1]

Fear stripped adults of their normal authority and confidence, leaving them as physically helpless as the children. A girl whose trek from East Prussia was overrun by the Red Army, recalled as a teenager in the mid-1950s, how 'at the least suspicious noise we left our sleeping places and began to scream, to scream the way animals scream when they fear for their lives'. But, as soon as the soldiers entered, she continued,

. . . our cries ceased. Our hands clutched our mother even more tightly and silent, silent to the core of our innermost being we stared into the machine guns held before us. Some of the soldiers always fell upon our luggage. None of the adults dared to stop them. At the sight of the Russians all courage and all strength and all will-power went rigid with horror.[2]

From February 1945 onwards, Germany was swept by a wave of suicides. In April and May, 5,000 people killed themselves in Berlin alone. Fathers or mothers sometimes murdered their children, before killing themselves. Judging from the suicide notes the police found afterwards, most were terrified of the Russians or simply could not imagine any future after Germany's defeat.[3]

For many others the actual arrival of the Russians brought an enormous feeling of relief. As soldiers handed out sweets and chocolate, and reached out to caress the newborn, the Russians' love of children soon became legendary. In Vienna, the Russians scooped up six-year-old Karl Pfandl and sat him on their cavalry horses, while in Berlin children hung around the cavalry company quartered in Prenzlauer Berg. Karl Kahrs's small sister ran home screaming, chased by a Russian soldier who wanted to give her a sausage.[4]

On the first night of the Russian occupation of Friedrichshagen, Liselotte Günzel's mother was raped. In Wilmersdorf, too, the rapes started the night Red Army soldiers arrived. Hertha von Gebhardt tried to hide her daughter Renate behind her, hoping each time a Russian entered their cellar that he would take another woman. When a homicidal soldier entered who threatened alternately to shoot them all or blow them up with his hand grenade, she and the other women encouraged the Czech-speaking woman from the Sudetenland to go on talking to him until he stopped threatening them and took her off instead. In nearby Zehlendorf, a friend of Ursula von Kardorff's, who had hidden behind a heap of coal when the Russians came, suffered just such a fate: she was betrayed by a woman who wanted to protect her own daughter. The lively and pretty young woman told Kardorff on her first visit four months later how she had been gang-raped by twenty-three soldiers, one after the other, and had to be taken to the hospital to receive stitches afterwards. 'I never,' she concluded her tale, 'want to have anything to do with a man again.' She also did not want to stay in Germany. Mothers cut short the hair of their adolescent daughters and dressed them as boys. When a female doctor gave sanctuary to young women by putting up signs on the door in German and Russian warning of typhoid, the news spread like wildfire through the women gathered at the water pump in the street.[5]

Women were raped in cellars, on staircases, in their flats, on the street, while doing forced labour – clearing rubble, dismantling industrial plant, peeling potatoes for the Russians, as the ubiquitous shouts of '*Uhri, uhri*' – watches, watches – were mingled, especially after dark, with calls of '*Frau komm*'. Women were raped in front of neighbours, husbands, children and complete strangers, in a wave of sexual violence that began during the battle for the city and began to subside after German forces capitulated on 3 May. In the great capitals of Berlin, Vienna and Budapest, as many as 10–20 per cent of the women fell victim to rape. As the soldiers of the Red Army celebrated their survival and their victory, they were under strict orders to behave as 'liberators', not as 'avengers'. Shortly before the attack across the Oder, Soviet directives had changed dramatically: in place of the revenge propaganda, which the Red Army had circulated since 1942, came new injunctions to distinguish between 'Nazis' and ordinary Germans. Secure in the knowledge that his Anglo-American Allies would not prevent the Soviet occupation of eastern Germany, Stalin did his best to protect his new assets and, above all, to ensure that there were no East Prussian or Silesia-style massacres in Berlin. It was very late to implement such a dramatic change of ethos among battle-hardened armies which would go on sustaining enormous casualties. And when it came to rape, Soviet officers often found themselves choosing between doing nothing and resorting to summary executions to bring their men into line. Some officers even slept in the Berlin cellars themselves for the first few nights in order to offer civilians their protection; others laughed at the tales German women came to tell them.[6]

How did children see this explosion of sexual violence? In January 1946, children in the forty-seven schools in the Prenzlauer Berg district of Berlin were invited to write about the war. Many focused on the battle for the city. Even Liane H., the Communist girl who thanked 'Generalissimus Stalin for the liberation from Nazidom' and cursed the 'damned Nazi swines' and cowardly 'braggarts' of the Third Reich, admitted that 'the Russians violated our women and took a lot away from people'. One boy, who kept a diary, noted that five women were taken from his cellar in the Schivelbeiner Strasse and raped in the ground-floor flat on the first night of the occupation.

But his was a rare observation. Most of the boys and girls who mentioned rape insisted, like Liane H., that nothing happened to them personally, to their mothers, or even to the women in their building; unlike Liane, they did not express particularly pro-Soviet sympathies. When two of these girls were interviewed in the 1990s – nearly fifty years later and after the collapse of the East German state – they stuck by these tales. One of them, Christa J., gave a clue as to her silence when she conceded that in her class of fourteen- and fifteen-year-olds, 'Many of my classmates were raped. I cannot remember that anyone spoke about it.' Even so, she insisted, 'I too was hidden, somewhere in the cellar . . .'[7]

This pattern of simultaneously evoking mass rape and insisting on having evaded it went on haunting children's memories. The girl who had hidden her dolls under the woodpile in Mecklenburg remembered a decade later, in the mid-1950s, how her mother 'immediately put on an old dress and a headscarf over her hair, which she had powdered to look white'. About her own feelings towards the Russians she recalled: 'It all stirred up such a hatred of the Russian in me that, after relations had become more orderly, I screamed and kicked when a Russian wanted to sit me on his knee.' In the 1990s, when war children started writing their memoirs, their stories were much the same; only the details had become more elaborate. Hermine Dirrigl was fourteen when a very young Russian entered her flat in Vienna and immediately discovered her and her girlfriend cowering behind the curtain. While the girlfriend was able to run off, Hermine could not. Instead, her mother put her baby brother in her arms. 'The soldier gestured to make clear that I should pass the infant on,' Hermine recalled over fifty years later. 'My uncle tried to drag him out. The Russian threatened him with his gun. Finally he left.' Compared with adult accounts, there is something incomplete in Dirrigl's tale in the ease with which the Russian 'finally left'. Whether it is an adult interaction that she failed to comprehend at the time, a repressed memory, or something she shied away from including in a private memoir intended for her own children and grand-children to read is impossible to say. Even when she goes on to tell how the family then secured the protection of that ubiquitous guardian angel, a Russian officer, she glosses over whether this involved any sexual transaction on her mother's part.[8]

Where girls remained reticent about what exactly happened, a boy like Hermann Greiner was proud of the way he barred the entrance to his parents' flat in Vienna, preventing a Russian soldier from gaining access to a woman he had seen at one of the windows:

If I'd been bigger I would have attacked him and that's how I looked at him. Although nothing had been said the Russian must have realised this and quit the flat, slamming the door behind him.[9]

In protecting both his own mother and their neighbour, Greiner modelled his behaviour on what he thought his father would have done. And indeed, he recounts immediately afterwards how his father went out into the street to remonstrate – in Russian – with a soldier who was pursuing a young woman who lived opposite: 'in my eyes, all other male migrants and neighbours were wimps who hid themselves'. Hermann Greiner was eight at the time.[10]

Children's reticence stands in marked contrast to the frankness of adult women talking among themselves in Berlin at this time. As they had had to queue for water and rations during the battle for the city, even middle-aged women of the polite and educated classes had started to talk like soldiers. In the months immediately following defeat, they turned to comparing German and Russian soldiers' underwear, the way each side had spread venereal disease across the Continent during the war, and the different sexual preferences of Russians and Americans. They coined a new slang to contain the humiliation of finding officers to protect them, in phrases like 'sleeping for food', 'major's sugar' and 'violation shoes'. What is more doubtful is whether they ever spoke like this to their children, even their teenage daughters. Fourteen-year-old girls, who had had no sex education let alone sexual experience, did not have words for describing what had happened, and neither the schools nor their families seem to have helped girls or boys to talk about their experiences.[11]

As 'normality' was restored, rape gradually became a taboo subject. In the Soviet Occupation Zone, Walter Ulbricht told Communist Party members who petitioned him for an open discussion about Soviet rape in the Party that this would have to wait till a later date. By the time the Cold War set in, his new East German regime established a censorship on the topic, which persisted until its collapse in 1989. In the Federal Republic the Cold War had the opposite effect. The Mongol-eyed Soviet rapist appeared on the electoral posters of the Christian Social Union in Bavaria during the first Federal elections of

1949, before being adopted across Germany by the Christian
Democrats in the early 1950s and becoming a common motif in parts
of the Ruhr, whose cities had been razed to rubble by their new British
and American allies, but which no Soviet soldiers had ever reached.
As the anti-Semitic imagery of the bacillus of 'Jewish-Bolshevism' fell
completely out of favour in the Federal Republic, so Goebbels's final
image of 'European culture' pitted against an 'Asiatic' Russian
'barbarism' gained a new lease of life.[12]

None of this helped the victims of rape themselves. Routinely refused
government compensation during the 1950s for their injuries, women
were also increasingly discouraged from talking about their experiences. This growing social taboo reinforced the difficulty of finding
words to describe the pain and humiliation of an attack, which became
evident when oral historians began to ask questions about the subject
in the 1990s. Women who had been children at the time were reluctant to talk about what had happened to them, lapsing into third-
person accounts instead, and telling what happened to others but not
to themselves or their mothers. Part of the difficulty lay within the
family. Even in marriages where the couple had tried to maintain an
intensive and close correspondence throughout the war, women often
found that they could not tell their husbands that they had been raped
without triggering male shame and revulsion. It was not just that
German soldiers returning from prisoner-of-war camps had a double
morality for their own and their wives' sexual behaviour. They had
also been reared in notions of male honour, which saw rape as a violation of the homes it had been their duty to defend. It was both a
betrayal and a sign of their own impotence.[13]

If a pre-adolescent boy like Hermann Greiner was deeply troubled
by the failure of the male 'wimps' in Vienna to live up to the ideal of
male honour, for younger boys the collapse of fatherly authority came
as a revelation. The end of the war found Uwe Timm and his mother
in Coburg. After the firebombing of Hamburg, they were housed next
door to the widow of the district leader of the Nazi Party, who
continued to receive many Nazi functionaries. For five-year-old Uwe,
'From one day to the next all the big people, the adults, were small.'
The sounds of the Third Reich disappeared. The stentorian voices of
men he was used to hearing in the street and stairwell of the house
seemed to turn into apologetic whispers, just as the marching tramp
of German soldiers' hobnailed boots were replaced by the almost silent

rubber-soled walk of the American GIs. Even their petrol smelled different, sweeter, as if to go with the chewing gum and chocolate they threw to children like him. Just as Polish and Jewish children had often involuntarily envied the German soldiers, so German children could not help being attracted to all that their conquerors possessed.[14]

While adults remained fearful of approaching the Russians, they often sent out their children to deal with the conquerors. In Vienna Helga Grötzsch went to the Russians to beg for tobacco for her father to make roll-ups. On another occasion her mother instructed her children to cry loudly when they went to the Soviet *Kommandatura* to plead against being evicted from their lodgings: as she remembered wryly, 'Obviously, we bawled properly enough. We were allowed to stay.' More commonly, children were used as intermediaries. Helga Feyler remembered what happened when her grandmother sent her to the Russian camp near her village to beg for food; although her granny considered it too dangerous for adults, she was confident that the Russians would not harm children. The Russian camp was enclosed by a fence, from which ten-year-old Helga and her baby brother were shooed away by the first soldier to see them. Then a second soldier offered her white bread in return for her brother. When she shook her head, he showed her a photo of his own boy to win her confidence and pointed to himself, saying in broken German, 'I father . . . want.' She held out her bag to him and then lifted up the baby. The soldier, filled, she thought, with nostalgia for home, lifted the child high and swung him round in a circle before holding him close and stroking his hair. When the little boy began to cry, he passed him back over the fence. On top of the bag he had placed two loaves of white bread; underneath she found sugar and a piece of meat as well. Such incidents gave children a newfound sense of importance at a time when so many adults had lost stature in their eyes. Children were not simply observers of these scenes of conquest. They quickly became active participants.[15]

As adults burned their old uniforms, Party badges and many of their own books, including their children's, they ritually rid themselves of many things their children had been brought up to prize. When the British Army marched into Osnabrück, Dierk Sievert's family even purged his collection of cigarette cards from the album he had painstakingly assembled on the 'Robber State England'. Families threw away the braid and cloth from the Hitler Youth, the posters of *Wehrmacht* and SS uniforms, and dumped the youth movement's daggers along with other weapons in village ponds. Meanwhile, children going out to play in the fields and woodland secretly collected discarded weapons and played with them, sometimes with fatal consequences. In Vienna, which had fallen on 13 April, the population stitched new flags to hang out for May Day hastily sewing red cloth over the white circle in the middle of the old flags. As if to deride these efforts at solidarity with their 'liberators', the sunlight showed up the black swastikas underneath. For children and teenagers, the moment when they had to tear off their Hitler Youth badges and throw away their daggers was often particularly bitter and undermined all they had ever been taught about duty, obedience and honour. Some boys secretly noted where the weapons had been thrown, so that they could retrieve them later.[16]

Nor was the spectacle of returning German fathers reassuring. German psychiatrists and psychotherapists coined a new term to describe their condition, 'dystrophy'. As malnutrition brought on apathy, depression and a loss of all moral inhibitions alongside more measurable physical suffering such as liver damage, they painted a picture of defeated German manhood in colours the same commentators had reserved a few years earlier for the 'Slavic sub-humans'. Apparently, the 'endless space of the Russian landscape' and the 'completely different way of life' in the Soviet Union had changed German prisoners so that 'their nature and facial expressions have become Russian' and they 'had lost much of their actual humanity'. Psychologists, who had lauded the superiority of German manly virtues over Soviet barbarism such a short time before, now feared that the sex instinct might have died among the German prisoners held in the East. As the failure to rediscover intimacy filled the agony columns of German magazines, Beate Uhse found it a good moment to set up a rapidly growing business in contraceptive advice and marital aids.[17]

To many children and in all belligerent countries, the return of the father came as an unwelcome and unnecessary intrusion. In Prenzlauer Berg, Christa J. had developed an unusually close and intense relationship with her mother during the five years of her father's absence. In her own sixties, Christa looked back on this period as shaping a relationship remarkable for its comradeship and mutual respect. She was already eleven when her brother was born in 1942 and she felt that she and her mother were able to discuss their problems with each other during and after the war. This contrasted strongly with the feeling she had before her father was called up in 1941, of hearing her parents fall silent in their talk as soon as she walked into the room. Christa's father was a pastor and had a parish to return to when he was released from Soviet captivity in 1946. But he was no longer capable of throwing himself into his work. He lacked the 'inner drive' to do so. 'He was no longer ready,' she remembered, 'to talk much, and about himself and his experiences not at all.' He died early, living long enough to see his daughter start her medical studies and gradually lose her own religious faith.[18]

Many fathers could not easily resume their place in society. When Helga Maurer's father returned from British captivity in 1946, he found the family he had left in Barth in Mecklenburg had ended up in a village in Schleswig-Holstein. Quartered on the pastor's family, his four children and wife were living in a single, unheated room, an extension to the main building which had served for confirmation classes. After the excitement of Helga's flight on an army truck in April 1945, defeat had brought personal humiliation and hunger. She remembered how well fed the pastor's children were – the farmers regularly brought them produce – but when her two-year-old sister, Edith, begged for some bread and butter too, the pastor's wife had come that evening to demand bread coupons from their mother in return. The loss of status for a civil servant's family was dramatic and as a former *Luftwaffe* technician Helga's father experienced it intensely. Unemployed and looked down on in the village as an intellectual and a refugee, he did not know how to cope with his four children. They were all under eight and for the next four years, until he regained his civil service rank and was able to move the family to Braunschweig, he occasionally beat the children, especially the two older boys. Little Helga vividly remembered the time when they broke his ban on playing in the mud of the village pond one summer's afternoon. They were lined up outside the house in public view in order of age. First their mother scrubbed them down in the zinc tub and then their father beat them with a stick. What stuck in Helga's mind was the degradation of this public punishment and her younger sister Edith's fearful sobbing, as she saw her eldest brother Helmut being struck.[19]

It was not only frustration which turned fathers into disciplinarians.

Many knew no other life any more, and believed in the virtues of 'toughening up', or *abhärten*. One Berlin father, who had spent nine of the twelve years of his marriage away on military service and in captivity, found that his children scarcely recognised him. Shocked to find that his eldest boy, Hans, was behind in his reading, the father decided to remedy his son's backsliding by recourse to military discipline, making him do twenty-five knee bends. It was what he was used to. Indeed, in an army where officers had routinely addressed their men as '*Kinder*', the models of paternal authority were clear. For Rolf, the youngest, the return of the father was most unwelcome. He was used to climbing into his mother's bed in the morning and shouted at his father, 'Get away from here, can't you see it's occupied?!' While the two older children whispered about the father behind his back, it was little Rolf who gave voice to their feelings. During one mealtime argument, his mother recalled how the little boy stood up, his fists clenched and his face incandescent with rage. Coming round to where his father was sitting, he said to him, 'You, you, you're not the boss around here.'[20]

As the father discovered, his son was in many ways right. He did not understand the Berlin to which he had returned. He did not realise for the first week he was back that he needed to apply for a ration card. Far from the family begrudging him food, as he supposed, he found that he had been eating the children's rations. Nor did he grasp that Hans was behind with his reading because he had been helping his mother keep the household afloat. A former master craftsman, he did not understand how to live in an economy of makeshift or how to share cramped quarters with his in-laws. And he did not know how to talk to his children, or they to him. As fathers returned to families whom they hardly knew, to wives whom they had spent more years writing letters to than living with, to children who had been born while they were away, and to an extended family of parents and parents-in-law living together in the same cramped rooms, they found a Germany they did not understand. Many were unfit for work and there was, in any case, little work to be had in the first years of peace.[21]

The family had become the bedrock of society, as the Christian Democrats were fond of telling West Germans in the 1950s, but seen from the inside, as an economic and emotional unit, the family was more fragile than it had been even in the Great Depression. It only loomed so large in the late 1940s because so many of the more complex structures around it had collapsed. It was not just the German *Wehrmacht* and the Nazi regime that had been defeated and destroyed in 1945. With the collapse of the Nazi state, German welfare institutions had broken down also. Parents may have grumbled in the 1930s and even in the early war years about the intrusion of the Hitler Youth, but without it, without the women's organisations, without the Winter Aid, without the National Socialist People's Welfare and without an adequate health system, they were thrown back on their own resources. During the first decade after the war, American pollsters could not find anyone who did not remember the Nazi welfare services in entirely positive terms. For younger children, the *Jungvolk*'s recycling drives to collect scrap metal and paper, old clothes and vast amounts of medicinal herbs all belonged to an innocent, normal time. For post-war teenagers the orchestras and summer camps of the Hitler Youth quickly became a distant memory and the evacuation homes of the *KLV* a protected time of plenty, part of the 'intact world' which had now been destroyed.

Whatever the resentments Swabian farmers' wives had felt towards the working-class women who had been quartered on them during the war, however ready Pomeranians had been to blame all vandalism and theft on the boys evacuated from Bochum, they had been well paid for hosting these guests. Post-war refugees lacked the means to pay their way in the communities upon whom they were quartered. With the collapse of a complex national system of payments came a rapid rise in intolerance for outsiders. In Klein-Wesenberg in Schleswig-Holstein, Helga Maurer soon discovered that evacuee families like hers had lost more than their professional middle-class standing. They were seen as intruders, scroungers on the margins of society. When she and a girlfriend were spotted on the bank of the River Trave eating swedes, which they had plucked from a nearby field, their teacher made them confess to the theft in front of the whole class. They were then called to the front, so that all their classmates could point to them with outstretched arms, branding them as thieves. This public shaming confirmed what Helga thought everybody already knew about refugee children like her. And, as Helga's mother sent the children out to play in the cold and snow in the winter because she had no fuel to heat their single room, the children were literally made to feel it. Luckily, they found an old couple in the village who were happy for the four children to come and dry their wet clothes and shoes on their big, tiled stove. But such charity had become scarce.[22]

In the autumn of 1946 Victor Gollancz, the left-wing London publisher, went on a seven-week fact-finding visit to Germany. On his way from Düsseldorf to Aachen, he drove through Jülich, a little town of 11,000 inhabitants which had been 93 per cent destroyed in a single bombing raid on 16 November 1944. There were still, he was told by the *Stadtdirektor*, 7,000 or so people living in the flattened town, but walking through the rubble he could not fathom where. Then he saw a stove-pipe sticking out of the ground and after a little while found a sloping path down through the earth to the entrance. The cellar consisted of two tiny rooms housing seven people. There was a room for sleeping and a room for everything else. It had no toilet or running water, but inside he found two parents and their adult sons, and two younger children. Another child was out and the girl cradling her head on her arms did not raise it from the table even when the photographer's flashbulb popped.[23]

As he journeyed, Victor Gollancz looked at the broken shoes, the bodies swollen with water from hunger oedema and the skeletal bodies of adults and children when the water had drained away. He visited schools, with seventy to a classroom and no books. In hospitals without penicillin he stood by the bedsides and spoke to the dying. As a Jew and one of Fascism's earliest and most vehement critics, Gollancz now called for reconciliation and food aid for Germany, fearing that such conditions could only produce a new Nazism.[24]

By 1946, hunger was rife across the four Occupation Zones and infant mortality in the British Zone stood at 10.7 per cent, and in the British and American Zones, tuberculosis stood at three times its 1938 level. Basic rations were hopelessly inadequate. Ranging from 1,330 calories a day in the American Zone in mid-1946, through 1,083 in the Soviet, to 1,050 in the British, the basic ration reached its nadir with the 900 calories fixed by the French in their Zone of Occupation. In practice, as the *Manchester Guardian*'s correspondent discovered, the British daily norm was exhausted by two slices of bread with margarine, two small potatoes and a spoonful of broth with milk. Official rations were less than an adult could live on for any length of time. Even the millions of Care packets which began arriving from

North America in 1946, each with their individual donor and each containing 40,000 calories of dry or tinned goods, made little impact. Despite Berzarin's early efforts to ship produce in from the Soviet Union, Berliners soon dubbed the standard ration cards the 'Ascension pass'. The frequent late or non-delivery of key foodstuffs rich in fats, minerals and vitamins meant that, as in German-occupied Europe during the war, so in post-war Germany, the population subsisted on bread, potatoes and turnips. The spring of 1947 witnessed the physical and psychological low point of the occupation. The winter had been the harshest anyone could remember, the shaky rail network promptly collapsed again and shortages of fuel and food became chronic, leading to further ration cuts. As people struggled to survive on a 1,000 calories a day, German society disintegrated into its most basic nuclear structures.[25]

The rapid reopening of schools in the summer of 1945 brought little relief. Children collapsed from hunger in their classes. Over a quarter of all the Bremen pupils had no proper uniform and nearly a quarter could not come to school in winter because they lacked adequate shoes. Surveys in Darmstadt and Berlin drew a similar picture. Many schools also had to close again for lack of coal. Others, like Christa J.'s in Prenzlauer Berg, moved down into the air-raid shelter, to escape the gale blowing through the open windows. The day was cut, to allow the children to be taught in shifts, but already by the middle of November 1945 the toilets had frozen. One Berlin boy agreed with his teacher that he and the other ten-year-olds in his class were a 'living rubble heap'. They had no interest in learning or order or respect for the advice of their parents or teacher, until they had themselves become involved in helping to clear the school buildings and yard of actual rubble: with this, he wrote in his school essay – no doubt with his teacher's approval – their sense of purpose had returned.[26]

When children in Essen thought back about these years in the mid-1950s, many readily recalled the pain of going hungry. 'Yes, I remember, I cried from hunger,' Heinz Bader wrote in June 1956, while another boy in his Essen school thought that hunger left its physical traces behind in the body and memory. One teenage girl remembered the currency reform of 1948, because it was the time her father gathered the whole family to show them their first post-war orange; her younger brothers took it for a ball and would not eat it, because they were used only to 'water and milk soup', those thin soups dubbed by another child in the American Occupation Zone as 'Quaker fare', as if her hunger were a religious penance imposed by the victors. For another girl in her school, hunger robbed people of their humanity, turning them into animals: 'Hunger,' she continued, 'closes down feelings of joy and sorrow, it takes everything.'[27]

The crisis of provisioning stemmed directly from the failure of Germany's war of colonial conquest. Through its policy of compulsory delivery quotas from Eastern and Western Europe, the Nazi regime had protected the German population from food shortages, at the cost of enforced starvation in the Soviet Union and even inflicting 'turnip winters' during the later stages of the war in Belgium, the Netherlands and France. As Germany became more import-dependent, the malaise of its own agriculture grew despite the steady influx of forced labour. By the end of the war, Germany had been producing 50–60 per cent of its agricultural requirements. Once the Allies established the line of the Oder and Neisse rivers as the new eastern border with Poland, Germany lost – along with the industrial wealth of Silesia – 28 per cent of its agricultural land and about half its grain and livestock production.[28]

At the same time, population density rose steeply as much of the remaining German population was driven out of Eastern Europe. By 1947 the rump Germany of the four Occupation Zones had had to absorb 10,096,000 German refugees and expellees from Poland, Czechoslovakia, Hungary and Romania. In addition, as late as 1946, over 3 million wartime evacuees were still staying on in the country-side, rather than attempting to cross the often tightly policed zonal borders within Germany to return to the ruins of the cities they had left two or three years earlier. Nonetheless, by April 1947 some 900,000 people had crossed westwards from the Soviet Zone. A quarter of the entire housing stock in the four Occupation Zones had been destroyed. And many families were lucky to have one or two rooms in an apart-ment with shared facilities. In 1950, the Federal Republic still had a deficit of 4.72 million flats. Meanwhile, 626,000 households were living in Nissen huts, bunkers, caravans and cellars, and a further 762,000 families in camps and hostels. The wartime humiliations, which western evacuees remembered from landlords in eastern Germany who had not let them cook hot meals or provided coal to heat their rooms, were now visited on refugees from the East in even greater measure. Much as West Germans sympathised with their plight in general, they also told American pollsters that the country was too small to cope with such an influx, and this resentment was underlined by occasional riots.[29]

As hunger, exhaustion, cold and violence took their toll, many mothers found themselves shedding responsibility to their older children. For Gertrud Breitenbach the breaking point had come towards the end of her arduous trek from Czechoslovakia to Kneese in the Soviet Zone. She and the children had almost died: 'Just before getting there,' Gertrud wrote to her husband in his American prison camp, 'I just couldn't go on any more. I just couldn't any more . . .' On the way, their one-year-old daughter Britty became ill with enteritis for eight weeks, followed by whooping cough. As Frau Breitenbach faced physical and psychological exhaustion and near collapse, her nine-year-old daughter Ingrid took responsibility for the small baby. Her sense of needing to give succour to her run-down parents was reflected too in her determination only to report good news, which would cheer her father up: unlike her mother, she did not write to him about their trials but about her baby sister's 'red cheeks', her first words and her games of ring-a-ring-a-roses with her doll. For herself, Ingrid declared brightly as Christmas approached, 'I wish for nothing from the Christ Child but you, dearest Daddy.'[30]

In other families it was the economy of makeshift which forced over-burdened and effectively single mothers to cede responsibility, to send their older children out to trade on the black market, to leave their older daughter to care for the younger ones. Some mothers no longer trusted themselves to divide the meagre bread ration equitably and handed it on to one of the children. Others sent their children out to steal coal from the railway yards at night. Children's games quickly caught up with reality, with cops and robbers giving way to 'coal thief and engine driver'.[31] By 1946, the black market had become just as essential to post-war Germany as it had been in wartime Poland. Boys like eleven-year-old Peter Laudan graduated quickly from playing coal thief to doing 'shady barter' deals. 'If,' he recalled in respectable middle age,

. . . we hadn't seen all that as a game of growing up and growing up as a game, we would have been simply miserable – so it was often a pure joy to belt a grown-up over the head not with a bit of wood but with an extortionate price for a litre of fish oil, and we bragged a lot at school about our heroic deeds on the battlefield of the black market.[32]

In Berlin, centres of the black market sprang up on the Alexander-platz and the Tiergarten. In 1948 a pair of leather shoes cost 1,500 marks, 2 pounds of butter 560 marks, 2 pounds of sugar 170 marks, and 1 pound of coffee 500 marks, prices far beyond the reach of those on officially controlled wage rates. Just as in occupied Poland, factories began to pay workers partly in kind, to allow them to enter the barter trade themselves. As the cash economy fell apart, firms made wholesale barter arrangements with one another, further disrupting any chance of restoring an integrated market. Shops were stocked with lampshades, painted wooden plates, ashtrays, razor strops and buttons for which there were no buyers, while sewing needles, nails and screws counted among the luxury goods of the black market. Old social ties distintegrated, and families turned into joint units of production and exchange as well as consumption. One sixteen-year-old girl recalled how she and her mother had helped her skilled elder sister make dolls. Her father, a qualified saddler, supplied the stuffing by stripping down an abandoned car seat, while the women recycled old silk stockings for the arms and hands. In a good week they could make ten dolls, their efforts spurred on by her little nephew who, from the morning onwards, ran through the flat calling out, 'Mummy, cook lunch!' Their earnings went straight on foodstuffs.[33]

Going out to the countryside to barter directly with the farmers presented serious difficulties. The transport system remained chaotic and overcrowded, so that it was often easier to seek out branch lines and local trains, and this restricted the radius of the weekend foraging expeditions undertaken by women and children. Elsewhere children were sent out to smuggle across the German–Belgian border. At the crossing points near Aachen, a journalist from *Picture Post* guessed that the 1,500 children who had been arrested in the previous month represented 1 per cent of those crossing. They took household items across and brought back coffee and other luxury goods, including that currency of the black market, cigarettes, from 'prosperous' Belgium. If caught, many of the girls had learned already to offer themselves to the guards in the hope of keeping their haul intact.[34]

Across Europe, from Belgium to Poland, juvenile crime soared in the immediate post-war years, much as it had done after the First World War. In France, the Netherlands, Belgium, Denmark and Poland, it had taken off during the German occupation, as soon as rationing became short. By 1946 and 1947, it had spread in epidemic proportions to

Germany and Austria as well. It did not begin to recede there again until the late 1940s and remained high into the early 1950s. Psychologists, criminologists and social workers all began to discuss the moral crisis of the young. They found that across Europe children had apparently also lost any sense of respect for the law, for their elders or their communities.[35]

Trained to believe in nipping moral degeneracy in the bud, welfare authorities' inclination was to send the young to reform schools before the boys became incorrigible criminals and the girls prostitutes infected with venereal disease. In August 1946, thirteen-year-old Hella Wagner was sent to Breitenau – which had just reopened – for having had sex with numerous American soldiers whose drinking haunts she frequented. The stereotype of the delinquent girl had not altered since the 1920s. Only the prospective male partners changed: from 'young men' during the pre-war years to 'soldiers' during the war, to, in post-war Hesse, 'American soldiers'. In 1946 and 1947 more teenage girls were locked up in Breitenau than during the war itself. It was as if the local authorities were compensating for their political impotence, including their inability to prevent the 'fraternisation' of adult women with the enemy, by taking it out on teenage girls.[36]

As in so much of occupied Europe during the war, many of the children and teenagers plying the black market, smuggling goods over the border or stealing coal, saw themselves as breadwinners for their families. These were not signs of incipient 'degeneracy', but, in the conditions of chronic want and economic dislocation, signalled a contribution to the family as morally conscientious as staying at home to look after younger siblings. By allowing their children to take premature responsibility, their mothers not only loosened the bonds of parental authority; they also drew their children into their plight, their predicament, their hopes and their resentments. Instead of opening up an unbridgeable gulf between the generations, the dynamics of defeat and occupation helped to create a deep current of empathy between many mothers and their children that proved much more potent than their returning fathers' attempts to teach them obedience through beatings and military drill. They were needed, and nothing could be better guaranteed to ensure that they absorbed their mothers' views – and silences – about the lost war than such new responsibilities.

Communities became tighter-knit and smaller, deepening the gap between belonging and not belonging until it became an abyss. Adults and children had learned during the war to project their terror, rage and hatred at a string of 'enemies'. As the forced labourers were freed at the war's end, Germans, especially on isolated farms, were frightened by roving gangs of foreign workers at night, demanding food, clothes and money. Even in the Soviet Occupation Zone that moment of dependence – when German farmers had suddenly turned to their forced labourers to act as intermediaries with the invaders and vouchsafe their good treatment – had quickly passed. Instead, the German population began to turn to their conquerors to protect them from the foreign workers. In the West, an eleven-year-old girl on a farm near Donauwörth noted the comings and goings of the labourers who had slept in the barn and the roving bands in her diary during May 1945. The German police and local politicians lost no time in blaming the whole of the racketeering and violent crime that engulfed Germany in 1945–8 on the 'Displaced Persons', or DPs, as if they possessed the economic and institutional power to run the black market on their own. The fact that many black markets were located on the ground in front of 'Displaced Persons' camps, the boundary zone where Jews and Poles, Germans and Ukrainians mingled, seemed to support such claims, and the German authorities trotted out their arrest statistics to 'prove' the enormity of DP criminality. What they really showed was the attitude of the German police. The rates of criminal conviction did not substantiate such assertions, even in courts run by an unreformed West German judiciary not given to thinking kindly about impoverished and downtrodden foreigners.[37]

Faced with controlling the upsurge in lawlessness, the British and American military authorities began to come down hard on cases involving firearms, even if they had not been used, and started to impose the death penalty on DPs who only a few months earlier had attracted universal pity and sympathy in the Allied media. After listening to the pleas for clemency for a twenty-three-year-old Ukrainian armed robber in early 1948, the Chief Judge of the British Control Commission Supreme Court wrote, 'I saw D. in the Dock during the hearing of his appeal, and the impression that he made on me and on my colleagues on the Bench is that he is a rather low type of humanity unlikely to be of value to any respectable community at any time.' The terrible tales of youthful maltreatment former forced labourers told in their defence fell on increasingly deaf ears. The number of displaced persons continued to fall steadily, as East Europeans were sent home.

By early 1947 there were just under 1 million foreigners in Germany compared with the 8 million who had been liberated at the end of the war. Most of those who remained were in West Germany, with 575,000 in the US and 275,000 in the British Zones. As the Jews became a larger proportion of the remaining DPs, so the stigma of racketeering was applied to them too, giving a new shape to the still potent imagery of the Jew as a huckster and thief.[38]

In the Berlin district of Prenzlauer Berg, the schools reopened on 1 June 1945. After provisioning, school often counted among the first and most important steps towards creating a post-war and post-Nazi 'normality': children were to be returned to a sense of routine and given a sense of positive engagement. In Berlin, children were encouraged to monitor and describe the first year of rebuilding. On their way to school they could see the progress in re-laying the track and over-head cable of the tramlines, and monitor the mending of the sewers and gas and electricity mains that had to precede filling in shell craters. These things had a real meaning, not just to boys fascinated by civil engineering. In late August Christa J. was thrilled to find that the tap in their cellar was working; on 17 September, even though all the station clocks remained broken, she was impressed by the relative punctuality of the trains going out to Nauen; and on 15 January 1946 the whole household gathered in the kitchen to watch a pot of water boil when the gas was restored. It took two to three hours. Still, Christa urged patience, affirming, 'We are ready to go on building and helping our dear German fatherland where it has need.' For Liane and other children who heeded the Communist line, only 'Hitler and his consorts' were to blame for German atrocities in Russia. Most children did not mention them at all. For now, Berlin schoolchildren occasionally still wrote of the 'terror attacks' and 'terror bombing' of the British and Americans, though, within a year, these too would be hidden under the more neutral term, the 'effects of war'.[39]

Other children living in the Soviet sector of Berlin invoked the militant language of sacrifice which the Nazis had used in the war, to lend value and urgency to the peaceful efforts at reconstruction. As Christel B. reflected on the difficulties of pumping the flood waters out of the Berlin underground, she contrasted the 'bitter fighting' which had taken place there with the 'relentless work' which so many people were carrying out 'in so self-sacrificing a way' to restore the transport system. For some, this converted easily into the militantly pacifist values of the political Left. 'The burned-out ruins were still smoking,' Hans H. wrote in early 1946, 'and horny-handed workers set to. Over three hundred men do not ask for wages and bread. They know but one common goal: Rebuild! Nine months passed in the land and then came the long-awaited day, on which the call echoed through halls and workshops: "Fire under the kettle! Gas mains on!"' But even for Hans, all this work still had a nationalist objective, albeit a peaceful one. They were doing it so that 'Germany, which in its peaceful competition with the other people of the earth, meets a happy future!'. The confusion of the children was matched by their teachers: while younger 'new' teachers pushed the new Party line, their older colleagues often struggled between the new Communist language of 'the productive deployment of work' and older Nazi terminology of 'Ausmerzen' ('eradication'). Soon the Volk would be officially aligned with the 'anti-Fascism' of the new 'People's state', as it founded its 'People's Police' and, in the mid-1950s, its 'National People's Army'.[40]

In the Western Zones, talk of German sacrifice took on a quite different tone. Whereas the invocation of the 'Volk' would live on in the East, in West Germany appeal to the nation was often replaced by an appeal to local patriotism and regional belonging. By the early 1950s, thousands of teachers were sent to visit the United States so that they could contribute to the task of 're-education', a term which had previously only been applied to criminals and juvenile delinquents. Although people quickly learned that anti-Semitic views were not acceptable in public life, there was little pressure to revise opinions of 'asocials' or 'gypsies' and both groups were routinely denied compensation in the Federal Republic by the same judges who had ordered forced sterilisations under the Nazis.[41]

Angela Schwarz was the only Sinti child not to be sent from the Swabian, Catholic children's home, the St Josefspflege, to Auschwitz on 9 May 1944. Remembering that Angela had a German mother, one of the nuns, Sister Agneta, had held her back when the police came from Stuttgart to register the children, and sent her back to her dormitory when she tried to join the other children on the bus. The next day Sister Agneta had returned Angela to her German mother, Erna Schwarz, a person Angela had previously rejected, because she associated her with being forcibly taken away from her Sinti father and stepmother at the age of six. When the war ended Angela was eleven, but she clung to her Sinti roots, eventually learning the fate of her father and of the other St Josefspflege children. Angela took her father's name, Reinhardt: ahead of her lay a lifetime of scrimping at the margins of German society. The racial biological researchers, Robert Ritter and Eva Justin, who had studied Angela and the other St Josefspflege children, and built such close links with Himmler, went on to make respectable post-war careers in the public health department of the city of Frankfurt, Ritter as head of the *Nervenklinik*, Justin as a juvenile psychologist.[42]

The unprecedented geographic mobility of the German population meant that every classroom had pupils from other parts of the country, who spoke with unfamiliar dialects. Although there were few pupils who were not German, the West German educational authorities worried all the same about the impact of a new type of *Mischling* – the handful of children born of liaisons with black American GIs. Having failed to have the children 'repatriated', they now planned to train them for settlement in some tropical clime, supposing that their genetic inheritance combined 'German' and 'African' racial and national characteristics in a form which ruled out their making their future in Germany itself but made them ideal colonial emissaries. They stayed.[43]

The millions of ethnic Germans expelled from Czechoslovakia, Hungary, Romania and the German lands awarded to Poland brought with them terrible – and often true – tales of beatings, robbery and murder. As local militias in Poland and Czechoslovakia instituted pogroms against their German minorities, they often mimicked the rituals of German attacks on the Jews, down to the Czech practice of making them wear armbands marked with an 'N' for *Nemec*, German. In 1946 alone, according to Czech statistics, 5,558 Germans committed suicide. Sometimes a whole family would dress in their Sunday best before hanging themselves surrounded by flowers, crosses and family albums. Ethnic Germans who had so recently been terrified of the Red Army now turned to it to protect them from the vengeance of the Poles and Czechs. In Bad Polzin, eight-year-old Enno Strauss watched the columns of Russians, Poles and Jews loot the apartments of the Germans during April and May 1945. When the new Polish mayor told his aunt that eight members of his family had been shot by the

SS, she commented sarcastically, 'So say all Poles.' It was the same when the half-Jewish rector of her school carefully explained that the SS had killed twenty-three members of his family: she told herself that the Jews who had returned seemed to be doing rather well. Meanwhile, little Enno announced that he wanted a gun, so that he could go to Russia and break down the doors there. When his aunt asked him what he wanted to do there, he answered, 'Plunder and rape women.' On 13 June 1947, it was their turn to be driven across the Oder with a transport of 1,000 Germans.[44]

The liberated ghetto of Terezín – Theresienstadt – became an internment camp for Germans, who pleaded with the local Russian commandant not to withdraw, fearful that the Czechs would kill them all. The torments of forced singing and dancing, crawling and gymnastics, which had been the fate of the Jews, were now meted out by Czechs to German civilians awaiting cattle trains for Germany. On 30 May 1945, all 30,000 Germans living in Brno – or, as they would have called it, Brünn – were roused from their beds and driven out on foot. They were beaten as they walked to the camps on the Austrian border. Some 1,700 of them died on what Germans soon called the 'Brünn death march'.

The stories the expellees themselves told almost all began in late 1944 or early 1945. It was then that their world went wrong. To their minds, there was no prior story to be told. This was especially true for children. For her mother's birthday in 1949, twelve-year-old Monika gave her a thirty-one-page account of their flight from Silesia three years before, closing with a poem she had written in praise of the beauty of the lost Silesian meadows and woods. At fourteen, Hans-Jürgen Seifert mourned for the home he had left behind in the Lower Silesian town of Freystadt by drawing an exact architectural plan of its layout.[45]

Fewer than 1 per cent of the burghers of the Federal Republic seemed to think that the Germans had themselves to blame for the expulsions. The same people who might question the extent of Jewish suffering felt they needed to describe the expulsion of the Sudeten Germans as 'death marches'. For some, the stories of the expellees provided the only real atrocities of the war, to the exclusion of the Jews and all other nationalities. And these were conclusions which the official West German project to collect and edit their tales into a multi-volume record of German suffering invited readers and reviewers to draw. In these volumes, the harmony of a 'multinational community unlike any other in the world' was not broken by the German invasion of 1939, but by the Red Army in 1944 and 1945. This was a peaceful multi-ethnic world, in which German cultural and economic leadership was obvious, where Polish workers were grateful and loyal rather than in thrall and where there were no Jews. But the images made so public by the Allies at the end of the war of Jews in the death camps were being appropriated in German testimonies. In their tales from the internment and prisoner-of-war camps, it was German men and women who were sent to the left and to the right. It was German corpses which were piled in makeshift mortuaries and it was their gold teeth which were pulled out before the bodies were carted off to a mass grave in a Soviet camp. And the guards in this voluminous 'Documentation' wore Soviet, not SS, uniforms.[46]

When sociologists began to study children of refugees after the war, they found twelve-year-olds with the physique of seven-year-olds, suffering from malnutrition, bad teeth, rickets and tuberculosis. Their faces were white and puffy, and their skins covered in scratches and sores. Like starving children in the Warsaw ghetto, many had a lethargic, apathetic look and some had aged prematurely and resembled little old men. Parents and teachers confirmed that the children suffered from depressive moods and self-doubt, and were serious, mistrustful and reluctant to talk. Many suffered from headaches and asthma, had nightmares and regularly wet their beds. At the same time, their school work was often just as good as children who had not undergone their experiences, and even cases of psychological collapse often came with no forewarning. Margarete M. had fled west with her family from Silesia in 1945. To her mother, the girl appeared to be a 'very lively and jolly child', even though she had 'taken the loss of home and property very much to heart'. Margarete appeared to have adjusted well and attended school without any difficulties until 1951, six years after her flight. While she was preparing for exams, a single phrase tipped her over edge: it was a mundane reference at school to the 'amputated territories probably lost for ever'. The next day Margarete's mother saw that her daughter had suddenly become overwhelmed with fear that the Russians would get her, insisted on being told 'why she had had to leave the house and shop' and kept on talking about 'all events from 1945', until her mother sought psychiatric help.[47]

When she was brought to the asylum, Margarete only told her tale once to the doctor. The trek she had been on from Silesia had been overrun by the Russians, a neighbour had been bludgeoned to death with a rifle and her own father beaten. She told how the Russians had 'selected some girls from her trek, bound them upside down to trees and slit their stomachs open', and she told how she herself had had to run through the forest in a frenzy of fear while mines exploded around her. Having described all this, Margarete soon joined in conversations on her ward, played the piano and started to concentrate once more on preparing for her exams. Short of space and with a rapid turnover of patients, the doctor simply sent her home. Whether her attack was triggered by the stress of exams or whether it was the images her own memory supplied to go with the metaphor about the 'amputated territories' is difficult to say. But neither the onset of her crisis, nor its apparently speedy resolution was predictable. For their part, teachers, doctors and sociologists were torn between emphasising the suffering of innocent German children and claiming that they had succeeded in overcoming their experiences and integrating into West German society.[48]

In the war, 4,923,000 German soldiers died. Because of the way the last year of the war was fought, 63 per cent of all military deaths fell in 1944 and 1945. This was reflected too in the fact that the eastern provinces suffered the most, losing 20.2 per cent of their entire male population in military deaths alone, compared with the national average of 12.7 per cent. Most were men born between 1908 and 1925. At least a quarter and in most cases a third of the entire male cohort was killed in military service. In addition, at least 1 million German civilians were killed in the eastern territories and over 400,000 as a result of the bombing.[49]

It was a loss of life without precedent in modern German history. It was also a tragedy which families had to face, often without much information and with little help: many would have to wait years for the status of their men listed as 'missing' to be clarified. Although many of the war dead were too young to have had children of their own, 250,000 German children had lost both parents in the war and 1,250,000 had become fatherless. Many more lost brothers, uncles, aunts, sisters and grandparents. Like other divisions of labour within the family, the burdens of replacing their fathers were often distributed unequally between the orphaned children. Wolfgang Hempel learned in the autumn of 1945 that his father had been killed on capture in the final days of the war, while trying to lead a group of soldiers westwards from Berlin towards the American lines. The son was fourteen, the father forty-seven and, unlike many younger children, Wolfgang had clear memories of his father singing, telling stories but also listening to him. He crossed and recrossed the border of the Soviet Zone to visit his grave, bringing back his father's papers with him as well as a physical sense of the wood near Schopsdorf where he had died. As if to compensate for the demands she was placing on Wolfgang, his mother smothered his seven-year-old brother with so much protective care that he would eventually emigrate to the United States to live on his own. Meanwhile, Wolfgang slipped so effectively into the role of the dead father that in her last years his mother often mistook him for her husband.[50]

While families were waiting for news, they pinned pictures of captured or missing soldiers to the noticeboards of railway stations in the hope that a returning comrade might bring them news. When they had exhausted the avenues provided by the Protestant and Catholic welfare organisations and the Red Cross, people turned to the newspaper advertisements of dubious firms, including clairvoyants, who offered search services. As they strove to comfort and guide their flocks, the clergy published prayers for the missing in their parish newsletters and, by 1947, the Protestant Inner Mission dedicated a week of prayer in September to the prisoners and the missing. The services were to take Jeremiah, chapter 14 as their first reading. Its last verse runs:

'I will be found by you,' declares the Lord, 'and I will restore your fortunes and will gather you from all the nations and from all the places where I have driven you,' declares the Lord. 'And I will bring you back to the place from where I sent you into exile.'[51]

In April 1945, Martin Bergau had finally been taken prisoner in a farmer's barn in Mecklenburg. He endured forced marches and nights in the barracks of newly liberated concentration camps, experiencing the dizziness and acute thirst brought on by diarrhoea and seeing companions shot for lagging behind. Before they had finished crossing Mecklenburg and Pomerania, he and his fellow prisoners were fighting for scraps of potato peel. It would be three years before Bergau returned from captivity. Heinz Müller, who had been so proud of his jazz rendition of 'Black as coals to his soles is the nigger Jim', as his Hitler Youth unit had arrived at their training camp in Halvesum, was luckier. He simply resumed his clerical job in the Düsseldorf administration and pursued his career with the same dedication to service that he had once invested in the youth movement. Few of these boys returned to school. Werner Koll was captured but released within four months: as he readied himself to go home on 19 August 1945, he jotted in his diary, 'I left as an idealist, as the opposite I am going home.'[52]

Most prisoners of war returned by the end of 1948. Although the majority of the 17.3 million men in the *Wehrmacht* had served on the eastern front, most of the 11.1 million taken prisoner managed to surrender to the Western powers. Only 3,060,000 troops had become Soviet prisoners of war, but because the *Wehrmacht* had drastically under-reported its own losses in 1944 and then grossly underestimated them for 1945, many families continued to wait in vain for men to return who had been killed in the last year of the war. In 1947, when the Soviet Union announced that it had only 890,532 German prisoners of war, a Hessian statistician claimed that there must be another 700,000 prisoners in Soviet captivity, fuelling popular speculation about the fate of the 'missing million'. Further releases from the Soviet Union followed in 1953, but as the number of prisoners dropped, so the agitation in the newly founded Federal Republic for their return rose, until the last 10,000 were finally released in October 1955. Vigils, marches and moments of silence were held. In churches special prayers were said for both the prisoners of war and the missing. Some clergymen gave permission for gravestones to be laid over empty ground for men who had not returned, including men whose status was never clarified. The men who returned brought back terrible tales of hard labour felling trees in Siberia and of watching comrades die of cold and hunger. Even without the anti-Russian tinge of the late 1940s and early 1950s, the reality was grim enough: 363,000 prisoners died in Soviet captivity. At a rate of death of 11.8 per cent, this was far greater than that suffered by German prisoners anywhere else, including in the wretched French and Yugoslav camps.[53]

The numbers of German prisoners of war who died in Soviet camps stood at about a tenth of the number of Soviet prisoners who had died at German hands. But this was not a topic of general discussion in the early Federal Republic. Instead, the barbed-wire fences and watch-towers, the emaciated faces, hollow eyes and shaven heads, with which the associations of former political prisoners had adorned their posters publicising Nazi persecution in 1945 and 1946, now peered accusingly from the posters and booklets canvassing the suffering of German prisoners of war. Among the Churches, the plight of prisoners and refugees was viewed as a redemptive Passion which would lead German society back to Christian belief. While she awaited the return of her son in Hildesheim, Frau R. wrote to a Catholic priest on 2 September 1947 about her conversations with men who had already come home. She had become convinced that conditions of captivity in USSR were 'not comparable' to conditions in the 'German concentration camps', but were 'much worse'. Whereas 'innocent people who had only done their duty at the front' had to suffer for a long time, 'the people in the concentration camps were immediately anaesthetised in the gas chambers', even though, she added with a sudden burst of critical self-awareness, 'it was terrible and not nice to treat people like that'. Public intellectuals and parliamentarians debating restitution for the victims of war were content simply to establish the equivalence of German and Jewish persecution. Whether one read the stories of suffering of German expellees or of the prisoners of war in the 1950s, it was as if the genocide of the Jews had silently shaped their tales.[54]

These ways of expressing grief and mourning in public cultivated public solidarity for groups of Germans who could often expect to be met individually with hostility, condescension, suspicion or despair by their fellow countrymen and women. Stories of rape, expulsion from the East and imprisonment in Soviet camps may have testified, in West Germany at least, to the Russian threat, the unfairness of the Allied settlement and to German victimhood but, as refugee children learned, on the whole people did not want to engage with them personally. Rape victims continued to be regularly refused compensation and doctors and psychiatrists continued to worry that 'dystrophy' had turned former soldiers into 'asocial' and permanently dysfunctional beings. It was one thing to turn German suffering into a tale of German victimhood. It was another to accept moral responsibility.

On 17 May 1945, Liselotte Günzel spoke to one of the boys who had marched off with her brother Bertel to defend Berlin a month before. He described how the Hitler Youth of their district had been mown down in the Heerstrasse. Only now did she begin to wonder what Bertel had died for. For Hitler? For Germany? 'Poor misguided youth! Did your blood have to flow too?' Liselotte began to realise that she did not know him. He had always been so closed. Even as she now rejected the call to sacrifice that she herself had endorsed a month before, she could not entirely resist its allure. 'Should I curse your blind fanaticism or bow before your loyalty? Did you want to die rather than bear the yoke of the slave? . . . Could you be of no more use to Germany,' she asked in her diary, 'to our holy fatherland, through your life rather than through this senseless death?' Liselotte had been misinformed. Bertel returned from Soviet captivity that autumn, his health shattered.[55]

The one question Liselotte did not ask herself was whether she had played any part in his decision. Had her own continuous inner striving towards her ideal of 'the German woman' affected him? As the Friedrichshagen boys had cycled away with their anti-tank grenades strapped to their bicycles, she had confessed her own readiness to sacrifice Bertel on the 'altar of the fatherland', so that she might equal the sacrifice of the widowed teacher she so admired and loved. Now that none of this made sense, she did not turn back to read and comment on her own earlier entries. It was as if they had not been – but not quite. As she closed this, her last, entry in her diary her final words spoke not of her disappointment in the adult world around her, but of her disappointment in herself: '. . . It is all so terrible and the worst thing is that I am coming ever more to the realisation of how bad and petty I am.' Whether she felt like this because of the general humiliation of defeat is not clear, but even now, with her Gothic romanticism in tatters, Liselotte still forced herself to measure her behaviour against her ideal standard of 'the German woman'.[56]

When the Allied armies had swept over the German borders, many people had felt a kind of terrible and terrifying responsibility. In Berlin and elsewhere in March and April 1945, phrases like 'If they do to us what we have done in Russia, then God help us!' had served as a commonplace answer to those who questioned the point of further resistance. In the West, American intelligence officers thought that most people had expected to be punished by the British and Americans for what was 'done to the Jews'. When neither the much-anticipated Allied acts of arbitrary revenge nor collective punishment materialised, these feelings of guilt were quickly suppressed and with them the feeling that national survival hung in the balance.

Despite all the chewing gum their GIs had thrown to German chil-
dren, in August 1945, US intelligence in Germany reported that only
the Russians were hated more than the Americans. Whereas the
Germans who were questioned were willing to accept that Britain and
France had been forced into the war, they could not understand
American intervention. No German bombs had fallen on the United
States and no one knew of any German war aims involving America.
Interviewers found that the 'Jewish war' still provided the key explanation for American actions against Germany, and German defeat
seemed only to have strengthened and confirmed the 'power of world
Jewry'. Just as at times of plummeting public confidence in the war
effort – such as the summer of 1943 or the final months – when many
had blamed the bombing on the treatment of the Jews, so now the
same thought resurfaced in defeat: 64 per cent agreed that the persecution of the Jews had been decisive in making Germany lose the war.
But the Jews never served the same central function in most people's
thinking about the war as they did in Hitler's: unlike their Führer, most
Germans changed their attitude to the war radically as success turned
to failure. Each time the country had looked militarily vulnerable, the
fearful voices expressing regret about the Jews had multiplied. From
the vantage point of defeat, it was clear that it had been unwise to
antagonise the Jews in Washington by persecuting the Jews of Europe.
In fact, only 10 per cent of Germans polled now thought 'pre-emptive
war' had been a sound policy. Still, there were 37 per cent who considered that 'the extermination of the Jews and the Poles and other non-
Aryans' had been necessary for 'the security of the Germans', even
though almost nobody thought that the German people as a whole
was responsible for the suffering of the Jews. Whereas the taxes levied
to pay compensation to the German expellees were generally approved,
two-thirds of the population was opposed when the Federal Government agreed in 1952 to pay reparations to Israel.[57]

Before capitulation, all means were regarded as legitimate as long
as they prevented a German defeat, and Nazi leaders, *Wehrmacht*
generals, ordinary soldiers and Goebbels's wartime correspondents had
often called for an even more ruthless persecution of the Jews. With
capitulation, the question had changed from what Germany should
have done to win the war to what could have been done to make
defeat less disastrous. These calculations had influenced many of the
generals in Army Group Centre who had tried to assassinate Hitler in

1944: while some of the plotters had been moved by a deep, moral hostility to Nazism, many did not want to reverse the anti-Bolshevik policies they had helped to shape in the East; they only wanted to find a way of making peace in the West. And in this first post-war reckoning with Nazi crimes, the dilemma remained one of utility. It was in this pragmatic vein that many of the senior administrators and military men interrogated at Nuremberg by the Allies began to voice regrets about the persecution of the Jews too. It was obvious now that genocide had been a miscalculation, a strategic mistake, which had blocked a separate peace with the West. This was not yet a moral reckoning, more a switch from one set of calculations as Germany pursued total war to quite another now she had endured total defeat. And if such thinking revealed anything, it was how widely key tenets of Nazi policy had sunk into national consciousness during the war, cutting across differences in rank and power, gender, social class and age.[58]

By the time its political structures had collapsed on 8 May 1945, much of Nazism's racial and moral ordering had been imprinted deeply upon German society, down to the quite personal ways in which people who did not particularly favour the regime could hold racist and nationalist common-sense notions about crime, sexuality, war guilt, black marketeering, refugees, Russian 'hordes' and foreign 'Displaced Persons'. In over eleven polls conducted in the American Zone between November 1945 and December 1946, on average 47 per cent responded positively to the proposition that National Socialism had been 'a good idea carried out badly'. In August 1947, 55 per cent of those polled responded positively, a level of post-war disillusionment which continued to manifest itself until the end of the occupation. The level of support among the under thirties – those born after the First World War – was even higher, reaching 60–68 per cent, and this at a time when openly advocating National Socialism still potentially carried the death penalty. In a muted fashion, things had begun to change by the early 1950s. The very appropriation of motifs of Jewish suffering to describe the trials of German expellees and prisoners of war tacitly acknowledged what many Germans still sought to deny: the genocide. At the time, many people regarded Allied bombing and Russian atrocities as revenge. In many post-war accounts, German suffering began to take on connotations of the ritual cleansing of sins, a national expiation of guilt, even if that guilt was still only obliquely acknowledged.[59]

Unable to call their defeat a 'liberation', Germans referred to it as a natural disaster, 'a total collapse' like an earthquake, a '*Zusammen-bruch*'. Poland, the Soviet Union and Yugoslavia had sustained rela-tive losses in the war of a similar or even greater magnitude to Germany. Unlike them, the three post-war successor states to the Third Reich – Austria, East and West Germany – were not permitted to legitimate any cause for which their war dead had given their lives. There was no positive symbolism of liberty, resistance or national sacrifice that could be publicly associated with the German losses. While the new East German state tried to transform the anniversary of Germany's unconditional surrender on 8 May into a day of 'liberation', in the West people continued to refer to it commonly as a 'day of shame' and to revile the July plotters as traitors. But if they knew that those who had fought had done their duty, they could no longer say that they had died for their '*Volk*', let alone their Führer. When Emilie Most called friends and neighbours in Traben-Trarbach to mourn the death of her husband Rudolf in Russian captivity in 1949, she had no uplifting message for them: 'It is in God's hands that from the one we love most we must part.' But she wore mourning until her death in 1991.[60]

As post-war writers and public intellectuals started to write articles about the need to cleanse the German language of Nazism, they found it was easiest to shed Nazism's calls to total commitment and activism. Words like 'action', 'storm', 'movement', 'struggle', 'drummer', 'hard-ness', 'force', 'donation', 'courage to sacrifice' were all deeply tainted. In East Germany they lived on in the strange fusion of militaristic and anti-militarist appeals which had characterised the language of German Communism since the 1920s. But for West Germans more generally, disappointment in the 'miracle weapons' was replaced by astonishment at the 'economic miracle' and the 'fascination of the Führer' became the 'fascination with evil'. Talk of 'leading' the young switched to 'misleading' the young, as if the Nazis had manipulated the German people through language, rather than people having used that language to invigorate and pledge their own commitment in their private letters and diaries.[61]

It would take more than just reversing the values ascribed to a system of power to cleanse the language of Nazism. Words like '*Lager*' had covered everything from summer camps and evacuation homes to mili-tary barracks and death camps; '*Betreuung*' – caring – everything from kindergartens and reformatories, to the administration of concentration camps. Nazi German had made the banal portentous and trivialised the

horrific. Most of all, Nazi rhetoric had worked within existing traditions, fusing the clipped slang of military life and the poetics of German
romanticism to shape a language of heightened sensations and unmedi-
ated emotional experience, which encouraged the 'greatest loyalty' and
'fanatical will'. Even some of the first advocates of such a linguistic
cleansing happily retained more passive – but potentially even more
potent – Nazi terms, like *'durchhalten'* – holding out – for their own
use. As the language of active sacrifice fell away, in its place appeared
a passive, religiously tinged language of suffering; and in German this
shift in emphasis could occur without changing one central word:
'*Opfer*'. '*Opfer*' meant both active 'sacrifice' and passive 'victim'. Shorn
of the Nazis' and Communists' exhortations to active, militant, involvement, '*Opfer*' rapidly came to carry all the helpless feelings of passive
victimhood which clamoured for expression and public recognition.
For the children of the war this, too, was a burden.[62]

Children had known no other language. Racial categories and
demands to commit themselves, to maintain a brave face through the
bombing and to sacrifice themselves on the altar of the fatherland had
filled everyday speech. Often they had brought these notions to school
from their families; and children from anti-Nazi families had brought
them home from school or from the junior branches of the Hitler Youth
and League of German Girls. Only small children had been too young
to absorb the language of Nazism. Older children had to learn a
different way of formulating their ideas. As teenagers like Liselotte
Günzel stopped jotting down Goebbels's slogans in their diaries as if
they expressed their own private thoughts about the war, they began,
piecemeal, to forget their own language and points of reference at the
time.

In 1955 the pedagogue Wilhelm Roessler persuaded the education
ministries of the West German federal states to institute a mass collection of 75,000 school essays on themes such as 'My experiences at the
end of the war and immediately afterwards'. As they struggled to put
into autobiographical sequence their experience of bombing, evacuation, expulsions, deportations and post-war hunger, the young teenagers
of the mid-fifties frequently did what older children had done during
the war. They recycled a popular slogan of the day as their own moral
conclusion. In place of talk about 'holding out' or 'total war', the
teenagers of post-war East and West Germany often concluded their
personal accounts of the war with the popular slogan of the day: 'No

19. German children being evacuated to Marienbad, October 1941.

In den Jahren des Krieges wie des Friedens darfſt
du niemals mehr den ſtillen Dank und das verpflich-
tende Gedenken an jene vergeſſen, deren Opfer dir die
weihnachtliche Feier ermöglichten, deshalb brenne
am Feſt in jedem Hauſe ein Licht für alle die Getreue-
ſten, die an den weiten Fronten dieſes Krieges
Ewige Wache halten.

20. Medals ceremony for Hitler Youth
auxiliaries, 9 November 1943.

21. German advent calendar for home
and school, 1943.

22. German civilians
fleeing westwards, 1945.

23. Fritz Wandel, drawing of flight, from the exhibition 'Children See the War',
Berlin, October 1945.

24. *Volkssturm* defending Berlin, April 1945.

25. Children returning Nazi school books, 1945.

26. Karin Isolde Lehmann, aged 12: Christmas 1945 (note absence of father).

27. Boy looking for food in the rubbish, Hamburg, 1946.

28. Polish girl in Warsaw trying to draw her home after the war.

Pictures of his life in concentration camps by sixteen-year-old Kalman Landau, Switzerland, 1945.

29. 'Roll-call'

30. 'Organising'

31. 'Three prisoners sentenced to hang'

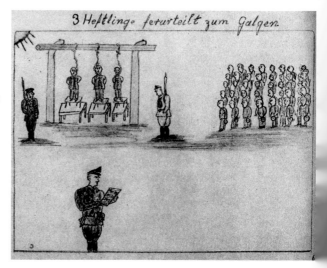

32. Death march

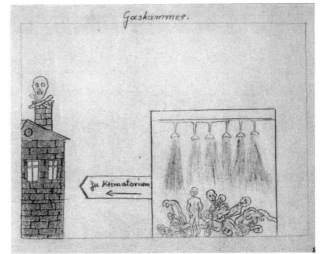

33. 'Gas chamber'

34. Liberation of Buchenwald

35. Thomas Gève, aged 16: 'The dead of the concentration camps admonish us', 1945.

36. Yehuda Bacon, aged 16: 'In memory of the Czech transport to the gas chambers', 1945.

war ever again!' As with the Nazi slogans during the war, this one was also heartfelt: neither East nor West Germany was able to make rearmament popular among the young.[63]

Yet it would have been difficult to discern attitudes from reading habits. Many children in West Germany went on reading the 'Red Indian' tales of Karl May and James Fennimore Cooper, while the popular novels of Willi Heinrich, Albrecht Goes and, especially, Hans Helmuth Kirst set the tone for writing about the war, with their focus on the suffering of generally decent and un-Nazi soldiers on the eastern front. Not until Bernhard Wicki's 1959 *Die Brücke* (*The Bridge*) would German audiences be confronted with a film with a clear anti-war message. While they watched seven boys fighting to the death to defend a strategically unimportant bridge which the *Wehrmacht* had abandoned, some audiences still responded enthusiastically to this image of heroic resistance to American artillery and tanks: one can only surmise what would have happened if the tanks had been portrayed as Russian.[64]

Uwe Timm had been too young to go to school under the Third Reich. But, with a father who had fought in both world wars and in the *Freikorps* in 1920, Uwe had learned while still a toddler how to snap his heels to attention to please him. He delighted his father after the war too when he refused the block of chocolate an American officer held out to him on a train. At every turn, Uwe knew he was being compared with his dead brother, his elder by sixteen years. Karl-Heinz had been the darling of the family. Tall, blond and blue-eyed, Uwe's brother was a courageous but also a sensitive boy who used to hide under a window seat in the house to read and draw on his own; and although he died in a field hospital when Uwe was only three, Karl-Heinz continued to overshadow his childhood. Karl-Heinz was always present in his parents' references and conversation, as they wished him alive again and mused about what would have happened if he had not volunteered for the SS, if he had been given more blood in the field hospital or if his shot-up legs had been operated on better; and, especially when old comrades came over for the evening, the father would relive the turning points of the war, discussing whether the battle of Kursk, in which Karl-Heinz had fought, could have been won. But Uwe could not ask what his brother had been doing in the SS or why he had volunteered; it was simply what 'brave boys' did. The family conversations always took the same course, so that Uwe began imagining and then dreaming of the brother he had hardly known. Eventually, he set out to discover who his brother really was by reading his letters and sparse diary of his months of service with the SS *Totenkopf* division, but Uwe waited until all those in his immediate family who tried to deflect his questions had died. The diary revealed little, breaking off six weeks before Karl-Heinz's own death with the comment, 'I think it's senseless to write about such cruel things as sometimes occur.'[65]

By the mid-1950s Uwe was only starting to formulate the questions he wanted to ask. But, like teenagers across Western Europe, he was beginning to challenge his father in other areas, rejecting his moral code of order, obedience, duty, upright bearing and insistence he be home by ten at night. Instead, the fourteen-year-old bought his first pair of jeans, and began listening to jazz and watching American films. Gradually the photos of Karl-Heinz in his Hitler Youth uniform and long boots, his face made more earnest by the straight parting in his hair, began to look as if they came from a different age.[66]

XII

THE LIBERATED

IN April 1947 the Berlin Philharmonic's legendary conductor, Wilhelm Furtwängler, was 'de-Nazified'. Yehudi Menuhin assisted in his international rehabilitation by performing the Brahms and Beethoven violin concertos with him at the Salzburg and Lucerne Music Festivals during the summer: EMI even recorded their Beethoven performance. In September, Menuhin continued the collaboration by visiting Berlin, where he gave two charity concerts with Furtwängler, in aid of sick German children. But when the virtuoso went on to perform for the Jewish Displaced Persons at the Mariendorf camp, he found that the Jewish residents boycotted him. Having read a letter of protest from Elijahu Jones, the editor of the Yiddish-language paper, *Undser Lebn*, Menuhin offered to come to a meeting with the DPs. He faced a hall packed with survivors of the camps to whom he pleaded for understanding and reconciliation. Jones, who had lost his whole family in the genocide, replied for them in Yiddish. In his letter to Menuhin he had already stated that their protest was as much against a concert given in aid of German children as against the so recently 'de-Nazified' German conductor. Now Jones warned that 'you and we find no common language'. Instead of trying to tell the musician what it felt like to lose his whole family, Jones asked him to imagine going for a walk together through the ruins of Berlin:

When you, the artist, see the ruins, you will say, 'What a pity that so much beauty has been destroyed.' When we, who have lost our families, see the same ruins, we shall say, 'What a pity that so much remained standing.'[1]

There was nothing more to be said. The silence that followed Jones's words was only broken when the audience rose to sing the 'Hatikvah', already the unofficial national anthem of the Jews in Palestine.

Despite everything, the Jewish population in Germany was growing in size: 50,000 Jews had stayed in Germany and Austria after their liberation, while their numbers were swelled by Jews fleeing from Poland's post-war pogroms. Of the 3.3 million Jews who had lived there before the war, 80,000 survived, emerging from the camps, from hiding and from partisan units in the forests. Another 13,000 returned with the Red Army while, of those deported to the Soviet Union in 1940–1, 175,000 opted to return to post-war Poland, hoping to find family members and to take up their lives once more. They returned to a country utterly devastated by war, its professional classes decimated and its makeshift state overstretched by the massive transfers of population and territory, as Poles were shifted from the Soviet Ukraine in the east to the newly annexed German provinces in the west. They also found Poland – especially but not only its rural provinces – rife with anti-Semitism. In town after town, taunts turned to stone-throwing and occasionally to murder. On 3 July 1946, a ritual murder accusation directed against the 200-strong Jewish community in Kielce sparked a pogrom in which forty-two Jews were killed. Within two days the Polish boy who had levelled the charge admitted that he had lied and the Polish courts sentenced nine of the ringleaders to death, but the pogrom had its effect: by the end of August over 90,000 Jews had fled Poland for Italy, Austria and Germany. Exceptionally, the US Military Government extended DP status to include these post-war refugees and to permit Jews, alone of all East Europeans, to return to Germany from countries to which they had been repatriated.[2]

Only in the American Zone were the liberated Jews treated as a separate group, and given their own camps. In the French, British and Soviet Zones, they were likely to be mixed up with former persecutors as the Germans' Eastern European collaborators fled westwards to the relative safety of DP camps. Most Jews in Germany duly moved to the American Zone where, by October 1946, they numbered 140,000, compared with just under 20,000 in the British and 1,200 in French Zones. Where there had been fewer than 2,000 'unaccompanied' Jewish children in the US Zone in July 1946, over the following few months 25,000 arrived, usually via Berlin. Many had organised themselves into autonomous youth groups with their own leaders, or *madrichim*, who advertised their plans to migrate to Palestine by calling their groups *kibbutzim*. By January 1947 most Jews had left Poland and the rush to enter the American Zone via Berlin came to an end. Those who remained in Poland were also less keen to leave: as the pogroms of the previous summer ceased, so news filtered back that the camps in Germany were overcrowded and food was scarce.[3]

The US Military Governor, General Lucius D. Clay, soon distinguished himself for his supportive and conciliatory tone towards the Jewish DPs. On 29 March 1946, eight US military policemen accompanied a raid by German police on a Jewish camp in the Reinsburg Strasse in Stuttgart looking for black-market goods. Although they found only a few eggs, 180 German police accompanied by dogs provoked a full-scale fight with the Jewish DPs. A concentration camp survivor who had only recently been reunited with his wife and two children was killed. The American Military Government immediately responded by barring German police from entering Jewish camps.[4]

Six of the eleven centres established for unaccompanied children in the American Zone were for Jewish children. By 1947, summer camps were being organised for all Jewish children aged over seven; 110 lucky ones were sent to Schloss Bruningslinden in the British sector of Berlin, where the chief American Jewish relief organisation, the Joint Distribution Committee, ensured that they received special food supplements and had the chance to exercise in the open air. At the end of their three weeks they gave a farewell concert at which they sang Hebrew songs about life in Palestine. Despite all these efforts, many remained small for their age and required extra supplies of fresh vegetables, fruit, butter, milk and meat. Meanwhile, the 'Joint' planned to send a psychiatrist around the youth camps to train staff to recognise the emotional problems of the children in their care.[5]

Next to the Bavarian town of Wolfratshausen lay the Jewish camp at Föhrenwald, lodged in a former IG Farben housing estate. When the 'Joint' sent her there in September 1945, Miriam Warburg established a school. Almost none of the adults with professional skills had survived the genocide and few – understandably – had any desire or ability to work. As Warburg listened to inmates tell her, 'Let the Germans work. We have worked enough,' or simply, 'I have died long ago. What does it matter what I do?' her enthusiasm wore thin. '*How* they speak, *how* they roll their eyes, *how* they wallow in their sufferings, *how* they repeat their stories,' the young Englishwoman fumed, unable to grasp what it meant to recover from such experiences. She found one man, tall, slim, pale and very timid, whom she persuaded to help her, even though he was afraid his nerves would not be up to it. After two days of teaching two to three lessons a day, he came back to see her, transformed by the experience. 'Yes,' he said, 'I can do it; please put me down for as many hours as you want. It was wonderful.'[6]

Miriam Warburg found the children exhilarating and exhausting by turns. Their thirst for knowledge seemed unquenchable, as she set out to teach them Hebrew, English and arithmetic without proper books or even enough chairs. But they could not concentrate long enough to do even elementary addition. The carers used group activities to build the children's confidence and give them a sense of identity. On Friday nights the children celebrated in their *kibbutz* style: there were piles of sandwiches on long tables covered with white sheets, candles fixed on some improvised candlesticks, walls decorated with bits of coloured paper and a huge Jewish flag. As Miriam Warburg watched and listened, a proper blessing was said and later the *madrich* read a play, and 'in between we sang and sang'.[7]

It was also very hard to win the children's trust. When the remaining Polish DPs in the camp were given shoes, the Jewish children immediately staged a strike and refused to believe that they would receive them the following week. When they heard of the plan to move children and adults from the nearby Feldafing camp to the one at Föhrenwald, they adopted old survival strategies and hid in the forest despite the torrential rain. In the former concentration camp at Landsberg a visitor watched the children discussing the fate of Moses in a Bible class. The teacher wanted to know whether his mother was right to hand him over to a stranger, even if she was an Egyptian princess. The children, most of them orphans themselves, had no doubt about it. At last, a boy stood up and pointed out that some of those in the class had been given to Poles by their mothers: 'That's how we survived.'[8]

No one knew how many abandoned and orphaned children there were in Europe at the end of the war. UNESCO put the figure at 13 million. There were the children of forced labourers and children brought for 'Germanisation', children from concentration camps and children whose parents had been sent to concentration camps. There were those who had survived the liquidation of the ghettos and those who had fled from villages where the whole population had been locked into barns or wooden churches before they were set alight. There were also German children who had been stranded with their schools in evacuation homes in Hungary, Romania, Czechoslovakia, Poland or other zones of Germany at the end of the war.[9]

Within Germany, child search operations fell under the aegis of the United Nations Relief and Rehabilitation Administration. UNRRA had missions in the different Occupation Zones, but lacked a common administration or set of policy guidelines, not to mention experienced personnel, to deal with the war refugees. By 1946 the scale of the relief operation had bankrupted the organisation and it was seriously alarmed by corruption and black marketeering within its own ranks. The French earned a reputation for refusing to allow outside agencies to search for missing children in their Occupation Zone and their sole child search officer had apparently been instructed to look only for children of French parentage. While the British had thirty-five child search officers in their Zone, few spoke the right languages. Only the Americans, with their forty-four officers, also used teams of East European volunteers. Some children had French fathers or Polish mothers but were being brought up by their German families, while others had handed their children over to the short rations and wretched conditions of orphanages and children's homes. No one knew how many children of mixed parentage there were, and both they and their mothers were often vilified and stigmatised.[10]

In France and Poland, the Channel Islands and Norway, the Netherlands, Denmark and Belgium, women who had 'slept with the enemy' had been hunted down by gangs of teenage boys and young men during the Liberation. While most of the policemen and government officials who had wielded power under the occupation were left alone, women were ritually marched through the streets with shaven heads. Sex and childbirth came high on the indices of post-war national virility and shame. In the summer of 1945, in both Norway and the Netherlands the new national governments at first proposed sending their 'German' children across the border, without consulting their mothers. In staking their claim that there were 200,000 Polish children in Germany, Polish searchers included all the children Polish women had borne to their wartime masters in Germany. And as if to counter the number of French children sired by German fathers during the occupation, the French government claimed that 200,000 children had been fathered by Frenchmen in Germany: in this early post-war statistical competition, remedying national humiliation trumped any thoughts about the possible compensation cases such claims might provoke.[11]

Relatives looking for missing children often lodged their first enquiries with the International Red Cross in Geneva. In January 1946, UNRRA opened a Tracing Bureau at Arolsen, near Frankfurt, where card indexes of unclaimed children in German and Austrian camps, hostels and orphanages could be compared with the often sketchy details supplied by relatives. Sometimes they had family photos as well, but these were often of little use in recognising children who had changed so much during the war years. By the summer of 1946, 65,000 enquiries had been lodged. Although 90 per cent of the cards for Jewish children were marked with a 'T' for *tot* (dead), the index occasionally produced extraordinary matches. One child was reunited with his parents on the strength of knowing only that he spoke French, that his father had a gold tooth and had called him 'Chou-chou'. The largest number of lost children came from Poland.[12]

In post-war Silesia, Roman Hrabar, an employee of the Polish Ministry for Social Welfare in Katowice, strove tenaciously to reunite Polish children who had been kidnapped from their families and 'Germanised'. These youngsters had been sent through the mill of German institutions, SS *Lebensborn* homes and camps until they came out the other end as 'ethnic German orphans' from the Wartheland, ready for adoption. In the autumn of 1946, the individual files of 5,000 children were discovered in the National Socialist People's Welfare Organisation's records in Łódź. Each card had a photograph of the child, the original Polish name and the – usually similar-sounding – new German one. Within a month, 443 children were traced. Using the index as a key to working out the ways other Polish children's identities had been disguised as part of their Germanisation, Hrabar devoted years to reuniting families.[13]

UNRRA child search officers in the British Zone were reluctant to do more than trawl through the German children's homes and welfare institutions. They were particularly keen to avoid delving into cases involving adoption or foster care, and generally argued against separating children a second time from successful families for fear of creating further emotional turmoil. As the SS racial experts had predicted, younger children had often integrated well and loved their new 'parents', who proved reluctant to believe that their 'ethnic German orphan' was really Polish or Czech. In some cases the children themselves were horrified to be told that they were not German. For years, letters and photos sent by Polish mothers might go unanswered by the German foster-family.[14]

Even when adoptive mothers responded well to learning from the Red Cross that their sons or daughters had been kidnapped in Poland, it could prove difficult for the child. Alusia Witaszek had been five in 1942, when her father was arrested and executed, and her mother sent to the women's concentration camp at Ravensbrück. In November 1947 she was ten and was settled with a German family, when her adoptive mother, Frau Dahl, reunited her with her real mother and siblings in Poznań. Alusia could not speak Polish and could only communicate with her eight-year-old sister Daryjka, who had also gone through the children's homes run by the SS *Lebensborn* organisation at Łódź and Kalisch. Taunted as Germans by their Polish peers in Poznań, and feeling like strangers in their own family, Alusia and Daryjka Witaszek ran away to the railway station hoping to return to Germany. They were caught and brought home again. Alusia never lost her tell-tale German accent.[15]

When the Germans destroyed Lidice on 9 June 1942 in retaliation for the assassination of Reinhard Heydrich, they sent the village's 105 children to Łódź for racial screening. Four of these Czech children came from the same family. They were the three Hanf children, Anna, Marie and Vaclav, and their eight-year-old cousin Emilie. Anna was the first to return. Her German parents, who had treated her well till now, simply gave her money for her fare and sent her on her way to Dresden. In the chaos of Dresden railway station, a Czech worker befriended her, put her up and made contact with the Czech authorities. Her father had been shot at Lidice in the massacre of 9 June and her mother had died in Ravensbrück. But an uncle came to collect her. Having kept in touch with her sister Marie and her cousin Emilie, Anna was able to guide the authorities to them. It proved much easier to bring Emilie away from the happy and privileged home of the Kuckuks than to separate Marie from her German family, who had treated her as an unpaid domestic servant. Marie had had her Czech inferiority beaten into her by her adoptive family, and it took her months to lose the habit of flinching during mealtimes. But by 1947 she found the courage to testify at the Nuremberg trial of the SS Race and Resettlement officials.[16]

The importance of having case workers in the field who spoke the right languages was underlined in finding the last of the Hanf children. Marie and Anna's younger brother Vaclav had been passed from one children's home to another where he refused to learn German and was frequently beaten by staff. A Czech team interviewing a Polish boy called Janek Wenzel suspected that he was not what he seemed. Their breakthrough came when they sang the Czech nursery rhyme 'I have horses, I have black horses'. The boy's face lit up and, laughing, he sang out the next line in Czech, 'The black horses are mine.' Only seven of the Lidice children had passed the racial screening tests and only seventeen of the 105 orginally taken could be traced after the war: most of the rest had been murdered or died in the camps. The stories of family reunions were the exception, not the rule. By September 1948 the International Tracing Service had succeeded in uniting a mere 844 of the 21,611 children on its books with their relatives.[17]

The British child search officers wanted primarily to repatriate children to Eastern Europe. This was general Allied policy and Soviet citizens were the first to be sent back, immediately undergoing screening for German collaborators by the NKVD in its 'filtration camps'. But the Western powers were also keen to send the DPs 'home' and rid themselves of an administrative headache. With the onset of the Cold War and the start of the post-war economic boom, Allied policy changed, and the British and the Americans began to see the remaining DPs as a labour resource rather than a problem. Where the British had previously tried to insulate Polish children from the anti-Communism of adult DPs who might talk them out of returning home, during the Cold War they became reluctant to assist Roman Hrabar in returning children to the other side of the iron curtain.[18]

Janina Pładek had ended her war in Westerstede, a pretty medieval town in the Ammerland between Bremen and the Dutch border. Having fled from Poland ahead of the Red Army, her parents had joined a local Baptist congregation and settled on a farm. But Janina did not find the congregation welcoming and was unable to make friends. Help came from the British: because Janina's father had worked for the Germans in the Wartheland and the family had been registered on the German National Lists, her younger brother had been called up to the *Wehrmacht*. But after his capture by the British, he had gone on to fight with the Polish Corps. Janina now took herself to the local DP camp and used this connection to receive preferential treatment in being selected to come to Britain.[19]

*   *   *

In February 1945, a month after Warsaw was liberated, Janina Dawidowicz emerged from hiding. She was reunited with Eric, the faithful German-born husband of her father's old flame, Lydia. In the chaotic conditions after the uprising and the destruction of the city, Lydia and her latest German lover had disappeared, and Eric had had to trawl through numerous homes until he found Janina's convent school. She was torn between Eric and his boys, whom she had come to love in the months of hiding in their flat, and her surviving family, two cousins whom she disliked. They were appalled by her Christian faith and hid the silver medallion Sister Zofia had given her, offending her still further with their obsessive talk about inheritance and reclaiming property. They finally let her live on her own once she turned fifteen, and in the summer of 1945 Janina returned to Kalisz, her home town, rented a room and settled down to await her father's return. Her cousins paid the rent and the fees when school started again in the autumn, while she hurried home each day from school to see if there was news: she knew that he had survived the final liqui-dation of the Warsaw ghetto and had last heard a year before – via Eric – that he had been in a camp near Lublin.[20]

One day, as so often before, Janina found herself in the cinema without having checked the programme. As the people around her wept, fainted and prayed aloud, she clenched her teeth and went cold inside. It was the Soviet film about the liberation of Majdanek, her father's camp. It took away, she wrote later, her 'last childish dream': 'There was no God.' In the summer of 1946 she met a fellow pris-oner of her father's in the town library, and he convinced her that her father had not survived. But still she could not grasp that he had died.[21]

Janina left Kalisz and its busy streets behind and sought sanctuary in the country cottage where she had spent the last summer before the war with her parents. Passing the days sunbathing in a swimsuit she had last worn as a ten-year-old, she relived the cinematic images of the death camp by night, until she was able to replace them with memo-ries of their life together in the ghetto: the 'old room, Mrs Kraut and her husband, Rachel, the Shereks, the Beatuses, the streets, the crowds, the gates of the *Umschlagplatz* which', Janina had to accept, 'I alone had not passed. Slowly, a word, a thought at a time, I began to name the unspeakable: my parents were dead.' Although she now felt ready to leave the summer cottage and Poland, it would take decades of wandering through France, Australia and Britain before she found a permanent home. Only then would she set about telling her story, in at least her fourth language, English.[22]

On 14 August 1945 a dozen Lancaster bombers took off from Prague's western airfield at Ruzyně, carrying 300 boys and girls to Britain. They were the first of 732 child survivors of the camps – all under sixteen – to be brought to Britain. They came as part of a special scheme negotiated with the Home Office by Leonard Montefiore and other veterans of the pre-war efforts to rescue Jewish children from the Nazis in 1938 and 1939, the so-called '*Kinder-transport*'. Only seventeen on this first post-war transport were under twelve. The six youngest, aged between three and four, were sent to Bulldog Banks, a cottage at West Hoathly in Sussex, which had been loaned to Anna Freud and Dorothy Burlingham's war nurseries.[23]

All six of these children came from the ghetto orphanage and had stayed in Theresienstadt even after the mass deportations to Auschwitz-Birkenau in the autumn of 1944. Having endured the last period of famine, typhus and disintegration in the ghetto, they had been so hungry in the ghetto orphanage that they still constantly cried and soiled themselves in their new home.

Alongside Gertrud and Sophie Dann, two sisters who had left Germany before the war, Maureen Livingstone, a Scottish nursery schoolteacher, cared for them. She was shocked when she first 'saw those six little children with shaved heads'. Anna Freud observed that they had turned in on their own bodies, engaging in prolonged mastur-bation and endless thumb-sucking; she put this down to their search for a gratification that was otherwise denied them. In Sussex the infants remained obsessed with food, but often would not eat it, refusing anything that was not made of wheat or maize. Even when they liked the food they would usually eat little. Instead, they concentrated on the things connected with food, checking and rechecking the way the table was set. Above all, they were possessive about their spoons. Gertrud and Sophie Dann could not understand the significance of the spoons until one of the workers from the Theresienstadt orphanage visited them in Sussex and explained that the spoons had been the only object the infants could call their own.[24]

Anna Freud reflected in the late 1950s on the apparent absence of powerful emotion. 'We do not know,' she confessed, which aspect or element of an experience will be selected for cathexis and emotional involvement . . . Where we expected to unearth buried memories of death, destruction, violence, hatred, etc., we usually found the traces of separations, motor restrictions, deprivations (of toys, pleasures) . . .[25]

Miriam Warburg noticed the same thing in October 1945, when women and girls in Föhrenwald told their stories in a 'strange, impersonal way'. 'It is, perhaps,' she reflected, 'a form of protection adopted, unconsciously, by all those who have suffered almost beyond human enduring.' When Anna Freud thought about how the children's sense of self had been affected, she returned to the familiar terrain of her long-running argument with Melanie Klein about the role of cognition and the Oedipal conflict in developing a sense of self, and concluded that it was the loss of parental figures, rather than children's experience of violence, which was central. When psychologists and directors of children's homes from across Europe met to discuss their experience of working with war orphans in 1948, there was no consensus on what harm the children had suffered. Some considered that the violence they had witnessed was crucial, while others thought this had made little impression compared with their loss of family, concluding – rather like Anna Freud – that their plight was similar to that of children who suffered such separations during peacetime. Some thought their memories needed to be repressed successfully for them to move on; others that they needed to express them through play therapy.[26]

In the early summer of 1945 the Swiss Red Cross invited 300 child survivors of the camps to recuperate in Switzerland for a few months. Many of the children came from Buchenwald. Among them were two Jewish boys of almost the same age: Kalman Landau was Polish, Thomas Gève, German. Both had survived the evacuation marches from Auschwitz and Gross Rosen, and both drew pictures to illustrate their experiences. Gève started drawing his in Buchenwald while he was regaining weight and too weak to go out of his barracks. One of the German Communist prisoners who had befriended him brought him a pad of blue Nazi forms. As his mania for drawing scenes from camp life became known, others crowded to see his work and bring him the stubs of coloured pencils.[27]

Thomas Gève wanted to create a visual encyclopaedia of the camps for his father. As he started to draw on the block of blue forms in Buchenwald, they reminded him of the cigarette cards he used to collect in pre-war Berlin. When his father emigrated to England in 1939, he had tried to stay in touch with his son by sending him English ones. To accumulate the encyclopaedic knowledge of a complete set required 200 cards. On his liberation in Buchenwald, Thomas set himself the task of producing that encyclopaedic knowledge about a world of which his father had no idea, and in which his mother had perished.[28]

Gève set out to explain how the camps functioned, by delineating how the barrack blocks were constructed and how the building *Kommando* on which he worked subdivided its tasks. He drew the armbands of all the different ranks of prisoner functionaries and the process by which new arrivals progressed through the different sections of the camp. As a boy in Berlin, he had admired the junctions of the Berlin *S-Bahn* and Nazi exhibitions of French war booty for their application of engineering and technology. As a future building engineer himself, his art dwelt upon the technical aspects of installations and the technical division of labour within the camps, often to the exclusion of the people. And true to the model of the cigarette card encyclopaedia, his cycle of drawings followed the logic of the world of the camps, rather than tracing his own personal history.[29]

In the Swiss children's home on the mountain above Zug, Gève's work was passed from hand to hand and used as a model to encourage the other children to express themselves through pictures. In a cycle of twelve pictures, Kalman Landau chronicled his passage through the camps, from arrival, through roll-call, forced labour, 'organising' food and the execution of prisoners who had attempted to escape. He drew the forced evacuation marches from Auschwitz on which prisoners were shot and clubbed to death in the snow; and he depicted the open goods wagons in which they had been taken to Gross Rosen and Mauthausen, where they had been crammed in their thousands in the quarantine barracks on arrival. Finally, his last two pictures told of the disarming and arrest of the Buchenwald SS guards by the prisoners, followed by the boys' arrival at the Swiss border in a railway train very similar to the one that had originally brought him to the camps. Even here at Rheinfelden there is barbed wire at the Swiss border post in his picture – as there probably was in reality.[30]

Like the child artists of the Theresienstadt ghetto, Landau made the figures in authority larger, giving the Kapos, SS guards and doctors recognisable features, whereas the prisoners – including himself – remained indistinguishable from one another, so many powerless, interchangeable units to be marched, stored and killed. The rifle butt used to club the stragglers on the forced march through the snow was enormous.

Only when the prisoners regained the autonomy to 'organise' – or loot – things in the camp do they become individual and distinct. But even when armed prisoners liberate the Buchenwald camp, the guards still remain bigger and more detailed than the prisoners. Like Thomas Gève's, Kalman Landau's drawings are notable for their spatial mapping. He strove not for due proportions, but for an architectural overview of the entire scene and the logical relationship of its parts, adding signs or captions in his broken German to make this logic unmistakable: '*Morgen Tempo*' (morning march), '*Zu[m] Krematorium*' (to the crematorium), '*Blok Äl[te]ster*' (block elder), '*Es stimmt*' (it tallies) and, more ominously in the late-night roll-call, '*Es stimmt nicht*' (it does not tally). Some of this concern with objects, architecture and technology is more generally characteristic of adolescent boys' pictures. In Theresienstadt the Czech boys who visited the ghetto crematorium drew and described its operation in their weekly newspaper, reporting knowledgeably about the technology, numbers of corpses burned and fuel consumption. In its flames were consumed mainly the bodies of the elderly and the sick, who died in the ghetto in their tens of thousands. The boys did not know at that time that death camps existed. Only when he joined the Birkenau penal battalion would Yehuda Bacon be allowed to look inside the crematorium there. Neither Kalman Landau nor Thomas Gève had seen the inside the gas chamber and worried that he had drawn the installation inaccurately. of a gas chamber. But each strove to depict them, as if their chronicle and mapping of the camps would otherwise remain incomplete.[31]

Looking at these pictures in 2003, Gève explained that he had not trusted himself to depict the prisoners inside the gas chamber and worried that he had drawn the installation inaccurately. But depicting the mechanics of control may have offered him the vehicle he needed for expressing his experience. Gève later became a building engineer.[32]

Some of Kalman Landau's images, like the skull above the gas chamber, bore the distinct imprint of Gève's drawings: he had placed the same skull at the centre of one his drawings, from which the names of the concentration camps fanned outwards. But whereas Gève's skull represented an enclosed system, Landau's drawings chronicled an unfolding tale. The very clarity of its chronology from the arrival at the camp at the beginning testified to his clear recognition of its end. It was a classic social narrative, whose closeness to events made it easy to chart and grasp, though it is harder to know what it meant to the artist himself. It was also a journey of survival told to an outside world, through the snows of the death march and the arrest of the SS by the prisoners to his arrival at the Rhine Falls near Schaffhausen, bringing Kalman Landau to the women looking over his shoulder in his home above Zug. Like Thomas Gève's drawings for his father, Kalman Landau's were already intended for an audience who had not been there.

Yehuda Bacon did draw the gas chambers he had seen, producing a technical drawing which was used in 1961 as evidence for the trial of Adolf Eichmann in Jerusalem, and four years later in Frankfurt during the trial of members of the Auschwitz SS. But Yehuda Bacon had already become absorbed by painting during his time in Theresienstadt, and he had gone on sketching in the Birkenau 'family camp' too. Among his first artworks after his liberation, Yehuda drew two portraits, one of Kalmin Fuhrman, his 'protector' in the Birkenau *Sonderkommando*, the other of his father. Fuhrman's was a conventional portrait, striking only for the tenderness invested in drawing someone so apparently hard and closed. Yehuda's depiction of his father was altogether different. His father's famished face with its dark, passionately brooding eyes is wreathed in the column of smoke ascending from the chimney of the crematorium below. In the bottom right-hand corner Yehuda noted the exact time of his murder, '10.VII.44, 22.00'. Like Kalman Landau and Thomas Gève, Bacon turned sixteen in 1945. He set out to continue what he had already begun in Theresienstadt and Birkenau, and trained to be an artist, with the conviction that 'through art – so I thought after the war, "I want to show people what a child's soul went through in the war." It was,' he added in 1964, 'the first reaction, but something of it remains.'[33]

Few of the Jewish children who survived the camps were reunited with close family members, and some of those who were could find themselves rebuffed and disappointed. It was not just that having cherished an idealised image of an absent mother or father through the ghettos and camps, children were unprepared to meet the real one. Many were also discouraged from telling their tales to their relatives. Having survived Auschwitz, Kitty Hart and her mother were immediately instructed by her uncle when he met them at Dover, 'On no account are you to talk about any of the things that have happened to you. Not in my house. I don't want my girls upset. And *I* don't want to know.' As the remnants of Polish Jewry were scattered across the world, all that would survive of their communities were the thousands of individual testimonies collected by the Central Jewish Historical Commission and the memorial books the diaspora communities helped jointly to construct.[34]

At the same time as a new, post-war diaspora was forming, the redefined states of Central and Eastern Europe sought to create more ethnically homogeneous nations within their new boundaries. The Soviet Union resettled 810,415 Poles, as they moved their border westwards to the line proposed by Lord Curzon in 1919, and now foisted by Stalin on Churchill and Roosevelt at Yalta. The cattle truck continued to service this demographic reordering, as it had done since 1939. Many of the Poles came from historical centres of settlement in eastern Galicia, from Lwów and Rivne. In parallel, 482,880 Ukrainians were moved eastwards into the newly enlarged Soviet Ukraine. Just as whole Polish villages had gone over to worship at Ukrainian Orthodox churches in the summer of 1943, in order to escape deportation by the SS from the Zamość region, so now 5,000 Uniate Lemkos in the sub-Carpathian region formally embraced the Catholic Church in the hope of demonstrating their loyalty to the Polish state. It did not help them, and between October 1944 and September 1946, 146,533 were forcibly resettled in the Soviet Union. Meanwhile, the Poles deported to Silesia from the western Ukraine hardly dared to discuss the harrowing details of their own recent explusion in public. Instead, as the last of the German population of Breslau was driven out, the new settlers were encouraged to believe that 'every stone of Wrocław speaks Polish'.[35]

Almost all Continental European countries, apart from Portugal, Spain, Switzerland and Sweden, had been defeated and occupied, sometimes more than once. In symbolic compensation, the 'Resistance' took on a significance often beyond all proportion to its wartime membership or role. In Denmark, Norway, the Netherlands, France, Italy, Belgium, Poland and Czechoslovakia, historians and the media, public memorials and education programmes celebrated unequivocal resistance, rather than the many little compromises and acts of collusion required by life under occupation. In these acts of public remembrance, children were left in an ambiguous position. On the one hand they represented innocence, with their persecution providing the most compelling evidence of national martyrdom; on the other hand, educators worried that children had been corrupted by their experiences, an anxiety which subtly undercut the taboo on speaking about the corrosive effects of occupation upon society as a whole.[36]

The Polish educational authorities celebrated children's sacrifice by publishing a collection of their memoirs, which emphasised their contribution to the Resistance and the persecution they had suffered through forced labour. The heroic example of boys who progressed through the Grey Ranks of the illegal boy scouts in German-occupied Warsaw, is still read by twelve-year-olds in Polish schools today. In 1946 the Warsaw illustrated magazine *Przekrój* promised a kilo of sweets to the winner of a competition for children's drawings. While some drew scenes of haymaking, ships on the sea and traffic in Cracow, many more reflected on the war. There were searchlights in the night sky, bombed houses in Warsaw, street round-ups of Poles and Jews, and executions. When children in the town of Oświecim (Auschwitz) drew the prisoners in the nearby concentration camp, their guards and Kapos were bigger and more detailed than the ordinary prisoners. In 1948 Professor Stephan Szuman of Cracow University collected a further 2,388 pictures by children, which illustrated similar scenes of war and persecution, with 45 per cent confirming that they had witnessed the scenes they were depicting. Adults worried about such pictures. When the first exhibition of children's drawings about the war was held in the Berlin suburb of Reinickendorf in October 1945, the *Berliner Zeitung* commented that 'from the child's perspective much is still distorted and the task of education has only just begun'.[37]

In Poland in 1945, the State Institute of Mental Hygiene studied the war's moral and psychological harm through a large-scale questionnaire. Many children claimed to have learned the patriotic virtues from their parents, teachers and the Resistance. But just as many children admitted that they had learned to lie, steal and deceive, hate, treat authority with contempt, feel indifferent to all ideals, and even to have lost faith in the sanctity of human life. Set against the evidence of teenage drinking, sex, absenteeism from work, theft and black marketeering which welfare workers, juvenile courts and psychologists were reporting across the Continent, such surveys confirmed their belief that the war had destroyed children's innocence. It had also taught these children how to survive.[38]

Across Europe, adults were offended by the energy and self-confidence
of children. During wartime and post-war occupations, and in the
Jewish ghettos, children had asserted themselves on the streets and
markets. They had had fewer norms to unlearn than adults and often
had more drive and energy to adapt. But their very success undermined
their trust in the adult world and increased their sense of having to
take responsibility for themselves. Some formed surrogate families with
other orphans; others, like the street beggars rounded up in Warsaw
in January 1942, saw themselves as their families' breadwinners.

*　　*　　*

The crisis unleashed by war and occupation was marked in many families by the time when parents ceded responsibility, especially to their
older children. In these instances the integrity of their family worlds
broke apart and children felt that they needed to patch them up again.
These specific moments shaped children's overall chronology of the
war, establishing when the 'safe' or 'intact' world of childhood was
destroyed. For Yehuda Bacon, bringing food to his father in
Theresienstadt had marked his assumption of premature responsibility.
For Ingrid Breitenbach it was taking care of her sister when her mother
collapsed during the expulsion from Czechoslovakia. For Wolfgang
Hempel it was setting out to find his father's grave and bring his papers
home in the winter of 1945–6. It was events like these that made the
preceding period seem like a 'golden age' of 'normality'. For many
Jewish children that 'golden age' had ended with German occupation
in 1939 or 1940; for German children it may have ended with the
bombing of 1943, the flights of 1944 and 1945, or the hunger and
expulsions that followed German defeat; and many other German and
Austrian children who lived in the countryside did not experience such
a break at all.

Hunger was the most common pain children experienced during
and after the war, and they soon learned that their parents could not
take it away. Like adults, children turned food fantasies into elaborate games, creating make-believe recipes or enacting the queues in
front of soup kitchens. They saw how hunger drove adults to fight,
steal and prostitute themselves; and they became participants in the
bitter accusations and counter-accusations of theft which tore families
apart, and which Dawid Sierakowiak and the anonymous girl in Łódź

chronicled with such grief, anger and shame in their diaries. Hunger drove children to beg and to risk their lives smuggling goods. It also taught them distrust of strangers: however unhappy their own families were, in most cases these remained the only social institution to which children could turn. The children's homes in Theresienstadt were the exception to this rule. In most other homes and orphanages children starved. In the extremities of the Warsaw ghetto, passers-by might throw a sheet of newspaper over the children who had died in the street, but hunger also drove other children to ignore the corpses altogether and to retreat into the make-believe world of games. Hunger invaded all social relationships, teaching children wariness and self-reliance, and it left its mark on their bodies and their minds.

Nina Weilová was ten when she was deported from Prague to Theresienstadt. In her memoir she chronicles her deportations, not through her own sufferings, but by the injuries inflicted on her doll. When she arrived at Theresienstadt, her doll was ripped open by the SS, and when she was sent to Auschwitz she lost her doll in the tumult on the infamous 'ramp'. It is as if she were withdrawing from the situation and seeing it through the eyes of a third person – except that this third person was a thing, her doll. When a German girl prepared to flee from Mecklenburg, she remembered hiding her doll along with the family valuables: perhaps the loss of the doll came to stand for the loss of her home. Small children use objects in place of words, expressing their own emotions through them. In Łódź, little Ettie comforted her doll about her hunger. In Essen, another girl was comforted by her doll when her house was destroyed. In some of these cases the child was alone and abandoned, in others she still had close family to care for her. But they all expressed their shock and fear, pain and loss through objects, finding something familiar which they had always loved; sometimes the doll stood for themselves, sometimes for their homes and on other occasions for their mothers.[39]

Loss of parents forced children to look elsewhere for love and for figures to protect them. In the asylum at Scheuern, some of the children called the nurses 'mama' and picked flowers for them when they were let into the garden. Loss stretched along a very broad spectrum from complete trauma to mildly disrupted family routines. At one extreme was the small Polish girl who had to learn to speak again when she was liberated from her concentration camp; at the other were German children, like little Detlef in Westphalia, who temporarily attached himself to a kindly soldier quartered in his town in 1939, because he missed his absent father. Even the teenage Czech boys in Birkenau seem to have looked upon their 'protectors' in the penal battalion in a paternal way, driven by fear and helplessness into a position of dependence which made them both younger and much older than their years.

There can be no comparison between the events of the Holocaust and the war which German families had lived through. There can be no cancellation of one horror by invoking another, although this was just what much of the public discussion in Germany in the early 1950s strove to effect. There were, indeed, similarities in the ways children responded to hunger, fear, humiliation and having to replace their parents. But to use a blanket term like 'collective trauma' for all the different kinds of loss and hurt children suffered, as some commentators are now doing, can only lead to confusion. Not all losses were traumatic: Detlef's feelings when his father was called up in 1939 could not have been of the same order as Wolfgang Hempel's when he learned of his father's death in the last days of the war. The two boys experienced very different kinds of loss, and it does not help our historical understanding to equate them. Behind such a search for emotional equivalence lurks the danger of making facile moral and political comparisons between all the groups of people who suffered in the war and the Holocaust. Indeed, this was what was at stake when the *Neue Wache* memorial in Unter den Linden was reconsecrated in reunited Berlin in 1993: the claim on its plaque to represent the 'Central Memorial of the Federal Republic of Germany to the Victims of War and Tyranny' immediately provoked a storm of debate about relativising the Holocaust.[40]

Trauma is a difficult category to apply historically. It is a concept designed to understand the hurt suffered by an individual, but it tends to be used to register the violence of an event. Even in individual cases, it is not possible to predict what will be 'traumatic', which injuries a person can deal with and which will lead to psychological breakdown. Working with a woman survivor of the Holocaust, the psychoanalyst Dinora Pines found that it took a long time: the woman needed first to tell her story, to be believed and evoke in someone else the anger that she could not express herself, before serious analysis could begin. Their experience is mirrored in the matter-of-fact and restrained tone of many Holocaust and war memoirs. To take a famous example,

Primo Levi cloaked his own emotions, leaving the reader of his Auschwitz memoir, *If This Is a Man*, to see and judge the world he calmly observed. His literary restraint propels his readers into a position not unlike Dinora Pines's with her patients, of engaging all the more intensely with the experience for being forced through the author's silences into imagining the emotional impact for themselves.[41]

Interpreting absence and silence as evidence of an underlying trauma is, however, always fraught with difficulty. Anita Franková was deported to Theresienstadt when she was twelve. She later became a historian in the Holocaust Section of the Jewish Museum in Prague but, despite these daily reminders, she could recall very little of her time in Theresienstadt. She ascribed this memory loss not to what had happened in Theresienstadt but to her later experiences in Auschwitz-Birkenau and Stutthof. In her case it was the traumatic period which she remembered and the more 'normal' one in Theresienstadt which she could not bring back. At the time, girls of Anita's age had observed much, drawing the queues of hungry people waiting at the soup kitchens and keeping diaries. They may have done this from a position of relative 'privilege', with special rations and kitchens in their collective homes, but they had also done it with great curiosity. The complexity of their circumstances and reactions to them underscores the importance of understanding children's experience in the terms in which they lived them at the time.[42]

In other cases children shocked adults, not by avoiding and suppressing the violence and death around them, but by speaking and joking about them. Whereas the adults in the 'family camp' in Birkenau tried to ignore the crematorium chimneys, Yehuda Bacon and his friends looked at the colour of the smoke and joked about whether the people were fat or thin that day. Whether these boys shared their Kapo Fredy Hirsch's belief that the 'family camp' would be spared that fate is impossible to say. They certainly did not deceive themselves about the reality of the crematorium, but they used their humour to protect themselves from it.

Danger often had to be immediate before children were touched by a fear of death. In Germany, for example, children frequently found distant fires from the burning cities were beautiful. One small girl gazed out at the firestorm in Dresden in February 1945, quite bewitched by 'that theatre', riveted by the 'blood-red' of the sky; from her vantage spot outside Dresden, 'the city itself looked like a drop of white-hot iron. And into this light fell "Chistmas trees" of all colours.' Soldiers in both world wars also remarked on the beauty of destruction, but they reserved this aesthetic appreciation for the destruction suffered by others, not by themselves. Children sometimes felt unthreatened by fires and bombing at close quarters, but were horrified when their own cellars shook and their own houses caught fire. From the first essays by older children in 1946, to the ones younger children wrote in the mid-1950s, they recorded how they stood and watched numbly as their homes burned down, taking with them the children's sense of insulation from the destruction they had been witnessing. In Birkenau, the normal ironic commentary Yehuda Bacon and the other boys kept up about the crematorium broke down when it was their parents who were going to the gas chambers. That night they had no words at all.[43]

Children's experience often comes in adult recollections, whether in the form of memoir or, for the recent past, the oral history interview, which inevitably blend the standpoints of child and adult. It is a rare memoirist, like the writer Uwe Timm, who tries to separate those fragmentary early childhood memories he had of the bombing of Hamburg, like the small fires hovering above the street, from his own later knowledge that these were burning scraps of curtains. And even for him it was virtually impossible to be sure which of his memories he had seen with his own eyes and which came from visualising the tales his mother told him so often that they took on a fixed photographic form in his mind.[44]

Among Lutz Niethammer's earliest memories were the red night sky. He thought he recalled that he had been sitting in his grandmother's house in the Black Forest, looking at the fires raging in Stuttgart. But this pioneer of German oral historians later realised that he could not have seen these fires 50 miles away from the burning city. His older brother remembered events Lutz could not recall, of being bombed out and rescued from their cellar in Stuttgart and then terrified when the bombers flew overhead during their train journey to the Black Forest. Niethammer came to the conclusion – at least for the time being – that he had turned his real fear of death in the cellar in Stuttgart into a comforting fairy tale of seeing fires from the security of his grandmother's kitchen. His desire to repress danger and restore his maternal protectors drove his memory to replace the collapsing cellar with the cosy hearth in the Black Forest.[45]

The problem that Lutz Niethammer touched on makes all memories difficult to equate with actual experiences. Five-year-old Karl Pfandl was more frightened by the tin crocodile – a Christmas present in 1944 – which chased him across the room shooting sparks out of its mouth, than by the flight from Budapest to Austria which he had just undergone. Perhaps, he had found the journey more exciting than frightening. Perhaps, like the Jewish DP children whom Miriam Warburg observed in Föhrenwald, he had minimised the threat to himself. Or maybe, like Lutz Niethammer, he had unconsciously substituted his more domestic anxiety over the new toy for the extraordinary threat of flight at some later point. Without earlier evidence than the memoirs and interviews composed in the last decade it is impossible to answer these questions.[46]

Historians who work on memories of Nazism and war have long warned about the difficulties of gaining access to the past. For example, many German and Austrian memoirs can be dated by the way in which they reflect the debate about public knowledge of the persecution of the Jews. The selection and publication of Holocaust memoirs has its own history too, not unconnected to the current norms of commemorating resistance and spiritual resistance. Many witnesses refuse to mimic the common prejudices of their own times, but they still have to engage with them, using time and distance to interrogate their own earlier selves. By 1998 Lothar Carsten had become deeply influenced by Buddhism and Hinduism, and had come to see the enthusiastic Hitler Youth who had kept a war diary in Wuppertal almost as a separate person. He could recall without self-exculpation the evening he had gone with his uncle, at eight proud to be with this big man in SS uniform, to watch the Jewish villas burning in 1938; and he could see himself once again as a fifteen-year-old Hitler Youth at the war's end, unwilling to rid himself of his insignia and dagger until a retreating veteran told him he had no choice. Lothar had kept the habit of writing a daily diary, but he was so aware of the changes in his own life that he did not need to justify or excuse his younger self.[47]

In a few cases the tensions between a person's childhood memory and adult moral position become evident in the telling. Like Lothar Carsten, Hans Medick lived in Wuppertal when it was bombed on 29 May 1943. But Lothar had been thirteen; Hans was only four. The next day he was taken by his father to see the bodies of the dead laid out on the town square awaiting identification. His description fifty-five years later, having grown into a left-wing, strongly Anglophile social historian, was still highly visual. What he remembered from childhood was no more than a single image, 'the green faces, their skin tightened into a permanent grin'. In the next breath he went on to say, 'But it was deserved,' because of the crimes of National Socialism and the bombing of Warsaw, Rotterdam and Coventry. Filling the gulf between the two thoughts, the memory and the moral conclusion, lay the passive construction 'it was deserved'. The 'it' could only apply to Nazi Germany in the abstract, never to the actual people he had seen in the square. Behind these two thoughts lay half a lifetime of strenuous moral engagement with the legacies of Nazism. The outcome had been to resist the allure of giving primacy to his own early and powerful memory, for which he may have had no words at the time; and the memory had remained an isolated fragment whose meaning stayed stubbornly unclear.[48]

In 1987, Wilhelm Körner noticed an advertisement in *Die Zeit* asking for diaries and letters from the war. It had been placed by the novelist Walter Kempowski and, after attending one of his public readings, Körner dug out his own war diary and sent it in. 'I very much wish,' he commented in his covering letter, 'that I had thought differently at the time, that I had seen through this disastrous regime and waged spiritual resistance against it.' But Wilhelm had come from a Protestant family of nationalist conservatives, his father rector of a school in Bremen and, from this background, Wilhelm found the beliefs with which he had filled the pages of his diary 'bog standard'. There was a gap at the end of the war: it had taken him a week before he could bear to pick up his pen again on 16 May, when he poured out his misery:

The 9th of May will definitely count among the blackest days of German history. Capitulation! We youths of today had struck the word from our vocabulary, and now we have had to experience how our German people after an almost six-year struggle has had to lay down its arms. And how bravely has our people borne all hardships and sacrifices.[49]

And on it went, for pages. These may have been the banalities of the age, the words he had heard from the radio and the Hitler Youth, school and his parents, the *Volkssturm* and his friends, and which formed his ideas and feelings in the immediate aftermath of defeat. But he had also believed in them and he would have died for them. Instead, the adult Wilhelm continued to follow in his father's footsteps, working like him in education in the Bremen area. After a thirty-two-year career in the upper schools of Bremerhaven, Wilhelm was shocked when the steady Gothic script of his rediscovered diary reminded him of that earlier self whose passionate convictions were so jarringly different from those he now held. For Wilhelm, as for so many of his generation, 'overcoming the past' had meant gradually losing contact with this earlier self. How could he have rekindled that sense of intense emotional communion of war without also feeling deep shame at the inner beliefs with which he had justified it at the time? These were long, not short, journeys and in many ways their moral purpose served to make West Germans' own personal past more distant and difficult to access.

During the war, adults and children in the German cities failed to notice the forced labourers who cleared their streets of rubble after the bombing, just as German refugees fleeing westwards in 1945 had ignored the death marches of the concentration camp prisoners in their midst. In this complete nationalisation of empathy lay the fatal work of Nazism, which had legitimated any act of barbarity towards *Untermenschen* as long as it helped the German cause. Despite all the evidence before them, many Germans did not reflect on what they were seeing.

Germans' wartime awareness of the murder of the Jews followed a similar pattern. In cities from Aachen to Stuttgart they spoke most about the genocide of the Jews after heavy air raids, or as they awaited the imminent arrival of the Western Allies. It was when they felt most terrified and impotent that people revealed what they already knew. For most of the time these things remained hidden. Seventeen-year-old Liselotte Günzel had known since the summer of 1943 that Jews were being murdered in camps, but it was twenty months before she returned to this knowledge in her diary: the information was there, ready to be used, when her own sense of national betrayal and impending defeat prompted her to summon it in April 1945 in a vitriolic diatribe against the Nazis. But her outburst was sparked, not by the murder of the Jews, but by the death sentence passed on a Prussian officer, the commander of the Königsberg garrison.

None of this meant that Germans were simply 'indifferent' to the fate of the Jews. The very knowledge of mass killings of Jews and Russians and Poles may itself have encouraged some people to think of them as a necessary part of a very difficult war on the eastern front.

Many more people seem to have worked hard to 'not know' what they knew, to keep the tales of mass shootings in the East separate from the media deluge about Jewish 'war guilt' with its repeated incantation of the Führer's 'prophecy' foretelling the annihilation of the Jews in retribution for 'causing' the world war. They had to make an effort not to think about the origins of the goods they bought at 'Jew markets' and 'Jew auctions', as the disappearance and murder of their former owners were buried within the 'total war' in which Germany was embroiled. Only spasms of fear brought what people knew to the surface again: the Hamburg firestorm triggered a chorus of complaints, all suggesting that German cities would not have been targeted if the 'Jewish question' had not been solved 'so radically'. Such anxious voices probably represented a much broader spectrum of opinion than the people who wrote to Goebbels urging the government to execute Jews in retaliation for the bombing. But the timing of these complaints about what Germany had done to the Jews suggests that they stemmed from vulnerability rather than humanitarianism: the bombing showed that 'Jewish plutocracy' was proving an enemy too powerful for Germany to vanquish.

As long as Germany looked as if it could survive – or even win – this total war, Nazi propaganda about the 'Jewish war' went unquestioned and unchallenged. Even old anti-Nazis found that 'Jewish plutocracy' helped to explain why the American and British 'terror bombing' was so pitiless. It was only after the war that it became common for Germans to compare their wartime tribulations with the murder of the Jews. During the war, whatever they knew and whatever their personal opinions about the 'solution to the Jewish question' remained part of the war's 'dark' side, overridden by their own hopes for its successful conclusion. But like all dark sides, the 'Jewish war' was never entirely absent or forgotten. The war itself created the key conditions for feeling that the future of the German nation itself hung in the balance; only at the very end did large numbers of people, especially in western Germany, begin to hope for their own defeat so that the war would finally come to an end.

The exclusively national focus encouraged in the post-war successor states also shielded children from some of their own vulnerabilities. Children sidestepped the issue of whether their own mothers had been raped, or what they had had to do to make ends meet during the occupation. As the German family was put back together again, these topics became taboo. Children avoided them when they wrote about mass rape in 1946 and 1955, and still avoided them when they wrote memoirs for their children and grandchildren in the 1990s. Taught not to ask their fathers about the war, many tried to preserve idealised images of their service records, despite the mounting evidence, including some-times from the men themselves, of their involvement in mass killing.[50]

As they grew up, children did not just repress the external events of the war. They also censored their own inner transformation. During occupation, children feared and hated their enemies, but also profoundly envied them. Polish boys had acted the 'Gestapo', and chil-dren in the Vilna ghetto and the Birkenau camps had played at being the SS searching for contraband, or carrying out round-ups and selec-tions. Defeat and occupation had altered German children's games too. Before they had even emerged from their Berlin cellars, children had started playing at being Russian soldiers. Waving make-believe pistols, they had relieved each other of imaginary watches, crying, '*Bangbang, pistolet, uri!*' As they assimilated the real and terrifying power of their enemies and masters into their games, children were also enacting their own impotence in all its starkly contrasting emotions, from shame and guilt, to rage and envy.[51]

In their fragmentary and elusive fashion, children's wartime games often expressed far more than the tales they told about themselves in the mid-1950s. There had been limits as to how far they would or could pursue such themes in their play. Once the Russians were in Germany, children stopped playing at NKVD executions; nor did they play at rape. In the Birkenau family camp, no child climbed down into the hole in the ground which they had made into a gas chamber. They could mimic the screams, but they could not be those people. Rather, they stood around the edge and threw in stones in their stead. The war was not just something that had happened to them. It had also been fought inside them, tearing apart their inner emotional world. When they recognised their enemies as the image of victorious strength and their parents as impotent failure, they had immersed themselves in self-destructive fantasies. As children tried to reconnect events into the continuous thread of their life stories, such games found no place in their autobiographies: whether they forgot them or hid them along-side other humiliations among their unspeakable memories we cannot know.

In 1955, Anne Frank's *Diary of a Young Girl* was published. In the

Federal Republic, as in the rest of the Western world, it became an instant best-seller. The following year the stage version was seen by thousands of young West Germans, causing an outpouring of emotions in special commemorative services and youth clubs founded in her name. Young people saw themselves in the talented and imaginative girl, forced into hiding with her family, sitting at the table with her notebook and watching the world outside from her upstairs window. And it was the house in Amsterdam where Anne had preserved her optimism intact – not Bergen-Belsen, the site of her physical and psychological destruction – which became a destination for pilgrims. Young Germans, like everyone else, were encouraged to see in Anne Frank the triumph of a universal 'humanity' and art, in its high romantic sense of spirituality, over Nazi brutality, and through her tale a mass audience in Germany began to engage at an individual emotional level with a fate which was not theirs.[52]

Anne Frank's diary drew so many readers because her voice never lost its integrity and no others competed for their empathy. Unlike the Jewish boys selling cigarettes in Warsaw on Three Crosses Square, who had managed their Polish competitors and German clients, unlike Janina Lewinson's family, who had to deal with networks of helpers and rings of blackmailers, Anne and her family stayed in their attic until the end. Most of the actors in her story remained off stage. In the 1950s, most storytellers were overwhelmed by the wealth of ambiguous perspectives and competing claims which memories of the war offered. They preferred to focus on the single, identifiable narrator and recover that integrity of the individual perspective which Anne Frank offered. Only at the end of the fifties would the modernist novel, with its multiple and contradictory points of view – and which had found such gifted exponents during the Weimar Republic – be given new life by authors such as Heinrich Böll, Uwe Johnson and Günter Grass. For millions of readers, Anne Frank's diary, with its individual voice, restored a sense of moral dignity and hope to the victims of Nazism.[53]

It was one thing for German teenagers to identify with Anne Frank as her diary moved them to tears, but it was quite another to bring her experience into any direct relationship with their own. Thinking about what Anne Frank endured meant *not* thinking about themselves. Insofar as a dialogue developed across national and communal divides in the first two decades after the war, it did so in spite, not because, of the pull of emotional experience. Feelings of victimhood and suffering might be universal across Europe in the 1950s, but in each nation people thought they had suffered in their own way. The common sense and common prejudices established under the Third Reich remained intact long after the outward symbols and structures had disappeared. For most of the generation of children who survived it, their own communities and the sufferings of those near them remained their primary concern. This was natural; it was also parochial, censoring out the experience of those who did not belong.

When the cohort of children born in the mid to late 1940s came of age, many followed the lead of the '1968 generation' and defined National Socialism by its crimes: increasingly, they regarded tales of German suffering as an embarrassing hangover of the 1950s, or dismissed them altogether as part of an attempt to ignore the scale of Nazi atrocities. The 'sixty-eighters' were mostly too young to remember the Nazi period and their revolt concentrated its attack against the residues of the Third Reich within their own families. Over the next decade, West Germans began to think less in terms of German suffering and much more in the terms of German guilt: they saw their Chancellor Willy Brandt kneeling at the site of the Warsaw ghetto, and in 1978 watched *The Holocaust*, an American mini-series, on their televisions. When the fiftieth anniversary of *Kristallnacht* fell a decade later many of those turning sixty were ready to reread their own teenage diaries; and some former Hitler Youths, like Rudolf Weissmuller, wrote to the town archives to discover the fate of their Jewish neighbours. He turned to autobiography to understand how he could have identified so closely with Nazism. Others, like Lore Walb or Wilhelm Körner, marvelled, not at what they had now come to believe, but at how they had ever believed the words they were rereading in their own diaries. But it would take an exceptional person to re-imagine both German and Jewish experiences at the same time. It would have been too disturbing to do so. For many people, the Nazi past had to be repressed to be 'overcome'.[54]

Witnesses are not, for the most part, historians. They see a part of what happened and they identify emotionally with only some of what they have seen. Even if they often take on the challenge of enlarging that picture in order to understand it better, the historical value of their testimony almost always resides in the specific things they witnessed. It is for the historian to fit the pieces of this huge and incomplete mosaic together, to restore the context of beliefs and everyday language, which the witnesses have often forgotten. Whereas much of the effort to remember has been focused on the possibility of future reconciliation in Germany, the task of the historian is to show the past as it was. Because children were so impressionable, they adapted especially fast to the shifting values of the world around them. To understand the fates of so many different children, Jewish, German, Czech, Sinti, Russian and Polish together, requires seeing their individual experiences within an overarching system of power. Their lives under the Third Reich were bound together by war and conquest, and their futures were traded through the balance sheets of food and starvation, settlement and expulsion, life and death. It was precisely what was irreconcilably different about their experiences that linked them together in a system of rule, in which officials badgered some parents to let their children be evacuated to the safety of the countryside and carefully logged the transports that took others to be killed. Whatever emotional similarities children exhibited across national boundaries in the ways they dealt with hunger or loss of home, the death of parents or physical terror, their experiences of the war would be for ever separated by the places they had occupied within the Nazi system of rule.

In 1945 Dr Walter Corti, the editor of the Zurich magazine *Du* which would publish Kalman Landau's drawings, launched an appeal on behalf of war orphans. Swiss children responded enthusiastically and raised £30,000 to build an international children's village. Teams of adult volunteers, including former combatants from opposite sides, flocked to the hillside next to the village of Trogen in the Canton of Appenzell, camping alongside the houses they were building. As each national house was completed, sixteen to eighteen orphan children were selected to come and live there under the supervision of a house mother and father. They were taught their national curriculum in their own language, but brought together with children from the other houses for joint activities aimed at building mutual respect and trust. By the end of 1948, nearly 200 houses had been built where only a single dwelling had stood two years earlier. The children had left camps and orphanages in France, Poland and Greece, Austria and Hungary, Germany, Italy and Finland behind, but brought their national languages and customs with them. The village was named in honour of the Swiss pioneer of child-centred learning during the European Enlightenment, Johann Heinrich Pestalozzi.[55]

The experiment was accompanied by enormous optimism about the prospects for international reconciliation and, in 1948, UNESCO sponsored leading figures in child rescue from across Europe to visit Trogen. Even though the iron curtain had already descended across Europe and the Cold War was undermining many of the humanist aspirations of the first post-war years, it was still hoped that the very shape of the children's daily lives would teach them the virtues of toleration, respect and an international understanding they could bring back to their countries of origin.

Dr Marie Meierhofer, the psychologist from Zurich who supervised the Children's Village, was often able to pluck only a single child from an orphanage where 300 or 400 boys and girls were looked after by no more than eight or nine nuns. In Switzerland, as everywhere else, such homes still usually ran on traditional authoritarian lines. Nurses ate meat, while the children made do with porridge. In the home at Zugerberg where Thomas Gève and Kalman Landau had come in 1945, another boy who had survived the camps tried to hang himself when he was punished by being shut in a dark cupboard. Many of the children arrived at Trogen with malformed vertebrae and symptoms of acute malnutrition. If Meierhofer could do nothing for those left behind, at least she knew that the handful of children she brought to Trogen would not be sent back after a few months to orphanages like those they had left. They were to stay and the emphasis was not on obedience but on gently winning the children's trust. There was a full-time psychologist and a room dedicated to play therapy. The 'village' still exists and, in 1956, was celebrated in an English children's story by Ian Serraillier. In *The Silver Sword* he recounted the adventures of four Polish children who, against the current of Allied repatriation efforts at the end of the war, struggled to reach Switzerland and find their parents.[56]

Even in his novel Serraillier did not pretend that recovery was easy for the children once they reached the International Children's Village. Before the Polish orphan, Jan, could leave his war behind him, he played at torture, firing squads and smuggling, and for a long time he stole, conducted night-time raids on the German house and threw rotten apples at the German children. These were the same games and the same difficulties that Dr Marie Meierhofer had observed. Meierhofer knew better than to try to stop such games: she thought it helped the children to re-enact what they had witnessed and was more concerned with children who lacked the ability to play at all.

When she went out to the different countries to select the children for the *Kinderdorf* at Trogen, she did not question them about their experiences, but waited for them to tell each other, to express them in role-play, or begin to draw. The children were all complete orphans, with no relatives to claim them. There were some who had fought in the Warsaw uprising and witnessed the mass executions that followed its defeat, and there was the little boy found in Hamburg who had seen his grandmother fall from the train during their flight from East Prussia. Meierhofer thought the difficulties faced by the young children who had been 'Germanised' were hardest of all, because they had twice had to change 'their language, social environment, culture, religion and, indeed, nationality'. She found that as a result 'their memory holds no past on which it might be possible to build'.[57]

Like war children elsewhere, they were emotionally volatile, impulsively warm and distrustful, attached to their dolls and, increasingly, to their house 'parents'. As they played, studied and helped with the daily routine in their homes, looking out over Lake Constance towards Germany, they were given the food, personal respect, security and tranquillity which would allow them to discover themselves. And as they grew up, Europeans were entering an unexpected era of relative prosperity and peace. Whatever hopes had been invested in these children, their greatest achievement was to have survived.

ENDNOTES

Archival abbreviations used in the notes

BA   Bundesarchiv, Berlin
DLA   Dokumentation lebensgeschichtlicher Aufzeichnungen,
          Institut für Wirtschafts- und Sozialgeschichte, University of
          Vienna
DöW   Dokumentation des österreichischen Widerstandes, Vienna
JMPTC   Archive of Jewish Museum, Prague, Terezín Collection
KA   Das Kempowski-Archiv, Haus Kreienhoop, Nartum,
          Germany
LWV   Landeswohlfahrtsverbandsarchiv-Hessen, Kassel
RA   Wilhelm Roessler-Archiv, Institut für Geschichte und
          Biographie der Fernuniversität Hagen, Lüdenscheid
YVA   Yad Vashem Archive, Jerusalem

Introduction

1. Katrin Fitzherbert, *True to Both Myselves: A Family Memoir of Germany and England in Two World Wars*, London, 1997.

2. Ibid., 257–65 and 285–7.

3. See Alexander von Plato, 'The Hitler Youth Generation and its Role in the Two Post-war German States' in Mark Roseman, *Generations in Conflict: Youth Revolt and Generation Formation in Germany, 1770–1968*, Cambridge, 1995, 210–26; Heinz Bude, *Deutsche Karrieren: Lebenskonstruktionen sozialer Aufsteiger aus der Flakhelfer-Generation*, Frankfurt, 1987.

4. Lore Walb, *Ich, die Alte – ich, die Junge: Konfrontation mit meinen Tagebüchern 1933–1945*, Berlin, 1997, 9.

5. Ibid., 14, 24, 36–8, 184–5, 225–32; 328–36.

6. Ibid., 333–4.

7. Ibid., 344–8.

8. Martin Bergau, *Der Junge von der Bernsteinküste: Erlebte Zeitgeschichte 1938–1948*, Heidelberg, 1994, 244–5; 249–75.

9. Gabriele Rosenthal (ed.), *Die Hitlerjugend-Generation: Biographische Thematisierung als Vergangenheitsbewältigung*, Essen, 1986; Dörte von Westernhagen, *Die Kinder der Täter: Das Dritte Reich und die Generation danach*, Munich, 1987; Peter Sichrovsky, *Schuldig geboren: Kinder aus Nazifamilien*, Cologne, 1987; and esp. Dan Bar-On, *Legacy of Silence: Encounters with Children of the Third Reich*, Cambridge, Mass., 1989.

10. Wolfgang and Ute Benz (eds), *Sozialisation und Traumatisierung: Kinder in der Zeit des Nationalsozialismus*, Frankfurt, 1998; on rape, Elke Sander and Barbara Johr (eds), *BeFreier und Befreite: Krieg, Vergewaltigungen, Kinder*, Munich, 1992; and Antony Beevor, *Berlin: The Downfall 1945*, London 2002; women's experience of the war, Margarete Dörr, *'Wer die Zeit nicht miterlebt hat . . .' Frauenerfahrungen im Zweiten Weltkrieg und in den Jahren danach*, 1–3, Frankfurt, 1998; bombing, Olaf Groehler, *Bombenkrieg gegen Deutschland*, Berlin, 1990; and Jörg Friedrich, *Der Brand: Deutschland im Bombenkrieg 1940–1945*, Munich, 2002; Günter Grass, *Im Krebsgang*, Göttingen, 2002; interviews with German children, Hilke Lorenz, *Kriegskinder: Das Schicksal einer Generation Kinder*, Munich, 2003; Sabine Bode, *Die vergessene Generation: Die Kriegskinder brechen ihr Schweigen*, Stuttgart, 2004; Hermann Schulz, Hartmut Radebold and Jürgen Reulecke, *Söhne ohne Väter: Erfahrungen der Kriegsgeneration*, Berlin, 2004; on Holocaust testimony, Tony Kushner, *The Holocaust and the Liberal Imagination: A Social and Cultural History*, Oxford, 1994; and Peter Novick, *The Holocaust and Collective Memory: The American Experience*, London 1999.

11. Robert Moeller, *War Stories: The Search for a Usable Past in the Federal Republic of Germany*, Berkeley, 2001, chapter 3; Lutz Niethammer, 'Privat – Wirtschaft. Erinnerungsfragmente einer anderen Umerziehung' in his (ed.), *'Hinterher merkt man, dass es richtig war, dass es schiefgegangen ist.' Nachkriegserfahrungen im Ruhrgebiet*, Bonn, 1983; 29–34; W. G. Sebald, *On the Natural History of Destruction*, London, 2003; in the GDR, the military published the autobiographical novels of Eberhard Panitz about the bombing of Dresden: see esp. his *Die Feuer sinken*, Berlin, 1960; Gilad Margalit, 'Der Luftangriff auf Dresden: Seine Bedeutung für die Erinnerungs-

politik der DDR und für die Herauskristallisierung einer historischen Kriegserinnerung im Westen' in Susanne Düwell and Matthias Schmidt (eds), *Narrative der Shoah: Repräsentationen der Vergangenheit in Historiographie, Kunst und Politik*, Paderborn, 2002, 189–208; Heinrich Böll, *Haus ohne Hüter*, Cologne, 1954, and the critique by Marcel Reich-Ranicki, *Deutsche Literatur in West und Ost: Prosa seit 1945*, Munich, 1963, 133; on this see also Donna Reed, *The Novel and the Nazi Past*, New York and Frankfurt, 1985, 55; Debbie Pinfold, *The Child's View of the Third Reich in German Literature: The Eye among the Blind*, Oxford, 2001, 27 and 149–50.

12. On Poland, see Edmund Dmitrów, *Niemcy i okupacja hitlerowska w oczach Polaków: poglady i opinie z lat 1945–1948*, Warsaw, 1987; Michael Steinlauf, *Bondage to the Dead: Poland and the Memory of the Holocaust*, Syracuse, NY, 1997; in general for the 'Resistance myth' in western Europe, see Pieter Lagrou, *The Legacy of Nazi Occupation in Western Europe: Patriotic Memory and National Recovery*, Cambridge, 1999, and his 'The Nationalization of Victimhood: Selective Violence and National Grief in Western Europe, 1940–1960' in Richard Bessel and Dirk Schumann (eds), *Life after Death: Approaches to a Cultural and Social History of Europe during the 1940s and 1950s*, Cambridge, 2003, 243–57; on Israel, Boaz Cohen, 'Holocaust Heroics: Ghetto Fighters and Partisans in Israeli Society and Historiography', *Journal of Political and Military Sociology*, 31/2, 2003, 197–213; on Germany, see Moeller, *War Stories*; Frank Biess, 'Survivors of Totalitarianism: Returning POWs and the Reconstruction of Masculine Citizenship in West Germany, 1945–1955' in Hanna Schissler (ed.), *The Miracle Years: A Cultural History of West Germany, 1949–1968*, Princeton, NJ, 2001, 57–82; and Habbo Knoch, *Die Tat als Bild: Fotografien des Holocaust in der deutschen Erinnerungskultur*, Hamburg 2001, 314–85.

13. On the widening invocation of 'trauma', see Andreas Huyssen, 'Trauma and Memory: A New Imaginary of Temporality' in Jill Bennett and Rosanne Kennedy (eds), *World Memory: Personal Trajectories in Global Time*, New York, 2003, 16–29; Peter Fritzsche, 'Volkstümliche Erinnerung und deutsche Identität nach dem Zweiten Weltkrieg' in Konrad Jarausch and Martin Sabrow (eds), *Verletztes Gedächtnis: Erinnerungskultur und Zeitgeschichte im Konflikt*, Frankfurt, 2002, 75–97; and Svenja Goltermann, 'The Imagination of Disaster: Death and Survival in Post-war Germany' in Paul Betts, Alon Confino and Dirk Schumann (eds), *Death in Modern Germany*, Cambridge and New York, 2005 (forthcoming); on problems of oral history, see Alessandro Portelli, 'The Death of Luigi Trastulli: Memory and the Event' in his *The Death of Luigi Trastulli and Other Stories*, Albany, 1991, 1–26; Luisa Passerini, 'Work Ideology and Consensus under Italian Fascism', *History Workshop Journal*, 8, 1979, 82–108; Gabriele Rosenthal, *Erlebte und erzählte Lebensgeschichte: Gestalt und Struktur biographischer Selbstbeschreibungen*, Frankfurt, 1995; Reinhard Sieder (ed.), *Brüchiges Leben: Biographien in sozialen Systemen*, Vienna, 1999; Karl Figlio, 'Oral History and the Unconscious', *History Workshop Journal*, 26, 1988, 120–32.

14. Alexander and Margarete Mitscherlich, *Die Unfähigkeit zu trauern: Grundlagen kollektiven Verhaltens*, Munich, 1967; *'Historikerstreit'*, Munich, 1987; Charles Maier, *The Unmasterable Past*, Cambridge, Mass., 1988; Richard Evans, *In Hitler's Shadow*, London, 1989; Jennifer Yoder, 'Truth about Reconciliation: An Appraisal of the Enquete Commission into the SED

Dictatorship in Germany', *German Politics*, 8/3, 1999, 59–80; Reinhard Alter and Peter Monteath (eds), *Rewriting the German Past: History and Identity in the New Germany*, Atlantic Highlands, NJ, 1997; Molly Andrews, 'Grand National Narratives and the Project of Truth Commissions: A Comparative Analysis', *Media, Culture and Society*, 25, 2003, 45–65; on the 1950s see n12 above.

15. RA, Luisenschule Essen, UI/5; Kyrił Sosnowski, *The Tragedy of Children under Nazi Rule*, Poznań, 1962, 167.

16. See esp. chapters 11 and 12 below.

17. On the centrality of racial, colonial war, see esp. Michael Burleigh, *The Third Reich: A New History*, London, 2000, and Ian Kershaw, *Hitler*, 2, 1936–1945: *Nemesis*, London, 2000; on civilian executions, see Nikolaus Wachsmann, *Hitler's Prisons: Legal Terror in Nazi Germany*, London, 2004, 314–18 and 402–3; for military executions, see Manfred Messerschmidt and Fritz Wüllner, *Die Wehrmachtjustiz im Dienste des Nationalsozialismus – Zerstörung einer Legende*, Baden-Baden, 1987, 63–89; and Steven Welch, '"Harsh but Just"? German Military Justice in the Second World War: A Comparative Study of the Court-martialling of German and US Deserters', *German History*, 17/3, 1999, 369–99; German military deaths, Rüdiger Overmans, *Deutsche militärische Verluste im Zweiten Weltkrieg*, Munich, 1999, 238–46 and 316–18; for a recent overview, see Richard Bessel, *Nazism and War*, London, 2004, 136–50; and see chapters 9 and 10 below.

18. See esp. chapters 8 and 10 below.

19. On arrested adolescent development, see Rosenthal, *Die Hitlerjugend-Generation*, 88–93.

20. See esp. Detlev Peukert, *Inside Nazi Germany: Conformity, Opposition and Racism in Everyday Life*, London, 1987; Tim Mason, *Nazism, Fascism and the Working Class*, Jane Caplan (ed.), Cambridge, 1995; Richard Evans, *The Coming of the Third Reich*, London, 2003.

Chapter 1

1. Janine Phillips, *My Secret Diary*, London, 1982, 46–8: 29 Aug. and 1 Sept. 1939.

2. RA, Goetheschule Essen, anon., UI/[1] (= unsorted in the archive, author's numbering); Gretel Bechtold, *Ein deutsches Kindertagebuch in Bildern, 1933–1945*, Freiburg, 1997, 98–9 and 102–3.

3. RA, Luisenschule Essen, anon. 19 years, UI/[5], 16 Jan. 1956: 'Verdunkelung, Verdunkelung!'; KA 3883/2, Hansjürgen H., b. 1929, 'Die Verdunkelung', school essays, Klasse 4: 15 Jan. 1940.

4. Herta Lange and Benedikt Burkard (eds), '*Abends wenn wir essen fehlt uns immer einer*': *Kinder schreiben an die Väter 1939–1945*, Hamburg, 2000, 21–3; Liese to father, 13 Sept. 1939.

5. Ibid., 18–27; Arbeitsgruppe Pädagogisches Museum (ed.), *Heil Hitler, Herr Lehrer: Volksschule 1933–1945: Das Beispiel Berlin*, Hamburg, 1983, 185–6.

6. Gerhard Weinberg, *A World at Arms: A Global History of World War II*, Cambridge, 1994, 48–53; Nicholas Bethell, *The War Hitler Won: The Fall of Poland, September 1939*, New York, 1972, 27–36.

7. Herbert Karowski, 'Film im Flug', *Filmwelt*, 24 Nov. 1940, cited in Erica Carter, *Dietrich's Ghosts: The Sublime and the Beautiful in Third Reich Film*, London, 2004, 207; Heinz Boberach (ed.), *Meldungen aus dem Reich: Die*

geheimen Lageberichte des Sicherheitsdienstes des SS 1938–1945, 3, Berlin, 1984, 829: 1 Mar. 1940; Kate Lacey, *Feminine Frequencies: Gender, German Radio, and the Public Sphere, 1923–1945*, Ann Arbor, Mich., 1996, 127–36; David Welch, *Propaganda and the German Cinema*, Oxford, 1985, 195–203; children's game, see RA, Luisenschule Essen, anon. 19 years, UI/[5], 16 Jan. 1956, 2–3; William Shirer, *Berlin Diary, 1934–1941*, London, 1970, 173: 20 Sept. 1939.

8. Dorethee Wierling, '"Leise versinkt unser Kinderland" – Marion Lubien schreibt sich durch den Krieg' in Ulrich Borsdorf and Mathilde Jamin (eds), *Überleben im Krieg: Kriegserfahrungen in einer Industrieregion 1939–1945*, Hamburg, 1989, 70.

9. *Deutschland-Berichte der Sozialdemokratischen Partei Deutschlands (Sopade) 1934–1940, 1939*, Frankfurt, 1980, 980; Adolf Hitler, *Reden und Proklamationen, 1932–1945*, 2, Max Domarus (ed.), Neustadt an der Aisch, 1963, 1377–93; Shirer, *Berlin Diary*, 182–4; Liese's father in Lange and Burkard, *'Abends wenn wir essen fehlt uns immer einer'*, 25–6; on songs, Marlis Steinert, *Hitlers Krieg und die Deutschen: Stimmung und Haltung der deutschen Bevölkerung im Zweiten Weltkrieg*, Düsseldorf, 1970, 109; Sudeten German children were playing at being Chamberlain in Sept. 1938: KA 2077, Erica Maria C., 'Keine Zeit zum Träumen: Erinnerungen 1935–1948', 7; on the fashion among Anglophile teenagers in Hamburg, see Peukert, *Inside Nazi Germany* 168; Arno Klönne, *Jugend im Dritten Reich: Die Hitler-Jugend und ihre Gegner: Dokumente und Analysen*, Cologne, 2003, 255–6.

10. Briefing session, see Wilfried Baumgart, 'Zur Ansprache Hitlers vor den Führern der Wehrmacht am 22. August 1939: Eine quellenkritische Untersuchung', *Vierteljahrshefte für Zeitgeschichte*, 16, 1968, 143–9; on popular opinion, see Steinert, *Hitlers Krieg und die Deutschen*, 76–87; Ian Kershaw, *The 'Hitler Myth': Image and Reality in the Third Reich*, Oxford, 1989, 121–47; *Deutschland-Berichte, 1938*, 256–70; on the Austrian '*Grossdeutsch*' dimension in Weimar, see Robert Gerwarth, 'Bismarck in Weimar: Germany's First Democracy and the Civil War of Memories (1918–1933)', D. Phil. thesis, Oxford, 2003.

11. Hitler, *Reden und Proklamationen*, 2, 1310–18; Steinert, *Hitlers Krieg und die Deutschen*, 91–3; Kershaw, *The 'Hitler Myth'*, 132–43; Kershaw, *Hitler*, 2, 87–125 and 220–3; Boberach, *Meldungen aus dem Reich*, 2, 72–3; *Deutschland-Berichte, 1938*, 684–9, 913–47, and *1939*, 975–89; on public reactions to the outbreak of the First World War, see Jeffrey Verhey, *The Spirit of 1914: Militarism, Myth, and Mobilization in Germany*, Cambridge, 2000; Christian Geinitz, *Kriegsfurcht und Kampfbereitschaft: Das Augusterlebnis in Freiburg: Eine Studie zum Kriegsbeginn 1914*, Essen, 1998; Nicholas Stargardt, *The German Idea of Militarism: Radical and Socialist Critics 1866–1914*, Cambridge, 1994, 141–9.

12. *Deutschland-Berichte, 1939*, 979–83; Steinert, *Hitlers Krieg und die Deutschen*, 110–21.

13. On repressive measures, see Klaus Drobisch and Günther Wieland, *System der NS-Konzentrationslager 1933–1939*, Berlin, 1993, 337–40; Wachsmann, *Hitler's Prisons*, 192–8; quoted in *Deutschland-Berichte, 1939*, 983.

14. On child evacuation, see Gerhard Kock, *'Der Führer sorgt für unsere Kinder . . .' Die Kinderlandverschickung im Zweiten Weltkrieg*, Paderborn, 1997, 69–81 and 343; in Britain, Angus Calder, *The People's War*, London, 1969,

21–40; Richard Titmuss, *Problems of Social Policy*, London, 1950, 101–11; for interviews with children, Penny Starns and Martin Parsons, 'Against their Will: The Use and Abuse of British Children during the Second World War' in James Marten (ed.), *Children and War: A Historical Anthology*, New York, 2002, 266–78; Martin Parsons, *'I'll Take that One': Dispelling the Myths of Civilian Evacuation, 1939–45*, Peterborough, 1998; on Hitler's order about bombing Britain, Kershaw, *Hitler*, 2, 309; Göring as 'Meier', see Steinert, *Hitlers Krieg und die Deutschen*, 367; and Göring's role in German air strategy, see Richard Overy, *Goering: The 'Iron Man'*, London, 1984, 172–204.

15. Martin Middlebrook and Chris Everitt (eds), *The Bomber Command War Diaries: An Operational Reference Book, 1939–1945*, London, 1990, esp. 19–21; Weinberg, *A World at Arms*, 68–9; Richard Overy, *Why the Allies Won*, London, 1995, 107–8; Reissner in Norbert Krüger, 'Die Bombenangriffe auf das Ruhrgebiet' in Borsdorf and Jamin, *Überleben im Krieg*, 92; Gerwin Strobl, *The Germanic Isle: Nazi Perceptions of Britain*, Cambridge, 2000, 141–50.

16. Lothar Gruchmann (ed.), *Autobiographie eines Attentäters: Johann Georg Elser: Aussage zum Sprengstoffanschlag im Bürgerbräukeller München am 8. November 1939*, Stuttgart, 1970; Boberach, *Meldungen aus dem Reich*, 3, 449: 13 Nov. 1939; *Deutschland-Berichte, 1939*, 1024–6; for the reactions of the Churches and Communists, see Steinert, *Hitlers Krieg und die Deutschen*, 111–14.

17. On 9 Nov. 1938, see Heinz Lauber, *Judenpogrom 'Reichskristallnacht': November 1938 in Grossdeutschland*, Gerlingen, 1981, 123–4; Saul Friedländer, *Nazi Germany and the Jews*, 1, *The Years of Persecution, 1933–39*, London, 1997, 275–6; for two outstanding local studies, see Dieter Obst, *'Reichskristallnacht': Ursachen und Verlauf des antisemitischen Pogroms vom November 1938*, Frankfurt, 1991; Michael Wildt, 'Gewalt gegen Juden in Deutschland 1933 bis 1939', *Werkstattgeschichte*, 18, 1997, 59–80.

18. Marion Kaplan, *Between Dignity and Despair: Jewish Life in Nazi Germany*, Oxford, 1998, 138–44; Paula Hill, 'Anglo-Jewry and the Refugee Children', Ph.D. thesis, University of London, 2001, esp. ch. 3; more generally, see Marion Berghahn, *German-Jewish Refugees in England: The Ambiguities of Assimilation*, London, 1984; Rebekka Göpfert, *Der jüdische Kindertransport von Deutschland nach England, 1938/39: Geschichte und Erinnerung*, Frankfurt, 1999; Wolfgang Benz, Claudio Curio and Andrea Hummel (eds), *Die Kindertransporte 1938/39: Rettung und Integration*, Frankfurt, 2003; Oliver Dötzer, *Aus Menschen werden Briefe: Die Korrespondenz einer jüdischen Familie zwischen Verfolgung und Emigration 1933–1947*, Cologne, 2002.

19. Klaus Langer in Alexandra Zapruder (ed.), *Salvaged Pages: Young Writers' Diaries of the Holocaust*, New Haven and London, 2002, 33–4: 8 Sept. 1939.

20. One of the best accounts of the stripping of Jews' financial assets through the Reich Flight Tax and punitive rates of currency exchange is in Mark Roseman, *The Past in Hiding*, London, 2000, 56–7 and 169–70; Herbert Strauss, 'Jewish Emigration from Germany, Part I', *Leo Baeck Institute Year Book*, London, 1980, 317–8 and 326–7; Kaplan, *Between Dignity and Despair*, 118 and 132.

21. Kaplan, *Between Dignity and Despair*, 150–5; small girl and neighbour, Hazel Rosenstrauch (ed.), *Aus Narchbarn wurden Juden: Ausgrenzung und Selbstbehauptung 1933–1942*, Berlin, 1988, 118.

22. Kaplan, *Between Dignity and Despair*, 150–5; Thomas Gève, *Youth in Chains*, Jerusalem, 1981, 21.

23. Gève, *Youth in Chains*, 18; KA 3666/3, Gisela G., 'Die Dinge des Herzens: Behütete Kindheit in gefahrvoller Zeit', MS, 1981, 10; KA 3024, Otto P., b. 1926, 'Himmel und Hölle: Eine Kreuzberger Kindheit', MS, 59–60: Otto P. does not date many episodes in his memoirs and these may be immediately pre-war, though no doubt other boys went on playing the same games.

24. KA 3024, Otto P., 'Himmel und Hölle, MS, 59; KA 3931/2, Dierk S., 'Auszüge aus dem Tagebuch': 3 Dec. 1940; Thomas Gève, interview with author and lecture, Southampton, Jan. 2003.

25. Kaplan, *Between Dignity and Despair*, 74–116; Benjamin Ortmeyer, *Schulzeit unterm Hitlerbild: Analysen, Berichte, Dokumente*, Fischer, 1996, and his (ed.), *Berichte gegen Vergessen und Verdrängen von 100 überlebenden jüdischen Schülerinnen und Schülern über die NS-Zeit in Frankfurt am Main*, Alfter, 1994; Museen der Stadt Nürnberg, Hugo R., class 5, 'Von den Juden', Nov. 1938. Marked as 'gut' by the teacher.

26. Stadtarchiv Munich, Familiennachlässe, Rudolf W., 'Erinnerung an Kindheit und Jugend', 71–84 and 146–7.

27. Jeremy Noakes (ed.), *Nazism, 1919–1945*, 4, *The German Home Front in World War II*, Exeter, 1998, 397–9; KA 3883/2, Hansjürgen H., b. 1929, school essays, Klasse 4: 19 Mar. 1940, 'Die Knochensammlung'; Hans-Peter de Lorent, 'Hamburger Schulen im Krieg' in Reiner Lehberger and Hans-Peter de Lorent (eds), *'Die Fahne hoch': Schulpolitik und Schulalltag in Hamburg unterm Hakenkreuz*, Hamburg, 1986, 364 and 366; Boberach, *Meldungen aus dem Reich*, 4, 959: 6 Apr. 1940.

28. Gève, *Youth in Chains*, 15.

29. Oaths varied between the *Jungvolk* and the Hitler Youth and changed with time: see Jeremy Noakes and Geoffrey Pridham (eds), *Nazism, 1919–1945*, 2, *State, Economy and Society, 1933–39*, Exeter, 1984, 422, and Noakes, *Nazism*, 4, 404–5; on the Hitler Youth, see Klönne, *Jugend im Dritten Reich*; Karl Heinz Jahnke and Michael Buddrus, *Deutsche Jugend 1933–1945: Eine Dokumentation*, Hamburg, 1989; Barbara Schellenberger, *Katholische Jugend und Drittes Reich*, Mainz, 1975; for Weimar background, see Diethart Kerbs and Jürgen Reulecke (eds), *Handbuch der deutschen Reformbewegungen, 1880–1933*, Wuppertal, 1998; Jürgen Reulecke, 'The Battle for the Young: Mobilising Young People in Wilhelmine Germany' in Roseman, *Generations in Conflict*, 92–104; on the Catholic Rhineland and the Saarland, see Horst-Pierre Bothien, *Die Jory-Gruppe: Eine historisch-soziologische Lokalstudie über nonkonforme Jugendliche im 'Dritten Reich'*, Münster, 1994; Bernhard Haupert, *Franz-Josef Schäfer: Jugend zwischen Kreuz und Hakenkreuz: Biographische Rekonstruktion als Alltagsgeschichte des Faschismus*, Frankfurt, 1991.

30. Lucia K., in Arbeitsgruppe Pädagogisches Museum, *Heil Hitler, Herr Lehrer*, 174–7; on Hitler Youth laws, see Noakes and Pridham, *Nazism*, 2, 420, and Noakes, *Nazism*, 4, 404.

31. On these issues, see esp. Rosenthal, *Die Hitlerjugend-Generation*, 80–6; Klönne, *Jugend im Dritten Reich*; Hermann Giesecke, *Vom Wandervogel bis*

zur Hitlerjugend: Jugendarbeit zwischen Politik und Pädagogik, Munich, 1981; for a more negative view, see Peukert, Inside Nazi Germany, 145–54; on parents refusing to let their daughters participate in recreational activities in case they became promiscuous, see Steinert, Hitlers Krieg und die Deutschen, 118.

32. Hertha Linde (ed.), So waren wir: Bildband zur Geschichte des BDM, Munich, 1997, 207, 215–20; Lange and Burkard, 'Abends wenn wir essen fehlt uns immer einer', 18–19: Liese, 5 Sept. 1939; 21–7; Liese, 13 and 30 Sept. 1939, and father, 5 Oct. 1939.

33. Dörte Winkler, 'Frauenarbeit versus Frauenideologie: Probleme der weiblichen Erwerbstätigkeit in Deutschland 1930–1945', Archiv für Sozialgeschichte, 17, 1977, 99–126; Ian Kershaw, Popular Opinion and Political Dissent in the Third Reich: Bavaria, 1933–1945, Oxford, 1983, 297–302; Noakes, Nazism, 4, 313–25 and 335–8; Norbert Westenrieder, Deutsche Frauen und Mädchen! Vom Alltagsleben 1933–1945, Düsseldorf, 1984; Stefan Bajohr, Die Hälfte der Fabrik: Geschichte der Frauenarbeit in Deutschland 1914 bis 1945, Marburg, 1979; Carola Sachse, Siemens, der Nationalsozialismus und die moderne Familie: Eine Untersuchung zur sozialen Rationalisierung in Deutschland im 20. Jahrhundert, Hamburg, 1990; Dörr, 'Wer die Zeit nicht miterlebt hat . . .' 2, Kriegsalltag, 9–37 and 81–99.

34. Arbeitsgruppe Pädagogisches Museum, Heil Hitler, Herr Lehrer, 192–5; de Lorent, 'Hamburger Schulen im Krieg' in Lehberger and de Lorent, 'Die Fahne hoch', 364–5; on female absenteeism, Ulrich Herbert, Hitler's Foreign Workers: Enforced Foreign Labour in Germany under the Third Reich, Cambridge, 1997, 249 and 307; Lange and Burkard, 'Abends wenn wir essen fehlt uns immer einer', 47: Rosemarie, 20 Feb. 40; KA 4718, Martha A., 'Ein Kornfeld in der Stadt', MS, 11; KA 2693/8, Dorothea D., MS, 4–5; KA 3931/2, Dirk S., 'Auszüge', 11 Jan. 1940.

35. Arbeitsgruppe Pädagogisches Museum, Heil Hitler, Herr Lehrer, 186 and 190–1.

36. Ibid. 177–8; similarly, KA 1759, Ermbrecht F., MS, 6; a 9 p.m. curfew was introduced in March 1940: Edward Dickinson, The Politics of German Child Welfare from the Empire to the Federal Republic, Cambridge, Mass., 1996, 238.

37. For an anecdotal exposition of the 'myth' of children denouncing their parents, see Richard Grunberger, A Social History of the Third Reich, New York, 1974, 151–2; for a detailed analysis of the social relationships of denouncers to those they denounced based on local records, see Eric Johnson, The Nazi Terror: Gestapo, Jews and Ordinary Germans, London, 2000, 362–74.

38. KA 3931/2, Dierk S., 'Auszüge', 4–10 Oct. and 21 Dec. 1940.

39. Fritz Theilen, Edelweisspiraten, Cologne, 2003, 15–18 and 26–31; similar system in the Saarland, Haupert, Franz-Josef Schäfer: Jugend zwischen Kreuz und Hakenkreuz, 166–89.

40. Lange and Burkard, 'Abends wenn wir essen fehlt uns immer einer', 238: 16 Dec. 1943; 41, 49 and 53: Rosemarie, 24 Jan., 3 Apr. and 15 May 1940; 155–6: Trude, 3 July 1944; 170–1: Marion, 1 and 7 Apr. 1943; 233, 240 and 243–4: Richard, 17 July 1943, and father, 1 and 26 Nov. 1943.

41. Ibid., 52: father to Rosemarie, 10 May 1940; 96: Detlef, 29 Sept. 1939; includes his own drawing of a bunker.

42. Ibid., 39–40: father to Rosemarie, 21 Jan. 1940.

43. Ibid., 45–6: Rosemarie, 15 Feb. 1940; 97–8, Detlef, 17 Oct. 1939.

44. KA 3936, MS letters from Christoph M. and sister, Regina, b. 1932 and 1933 to Werner, their elder brother by 13 years: second, undated letter and 20 Mar. 1942.

45. See the classic study by Iona and Peter Opie, *Children's Games in Street and Playground: Chasing, Catching, Seeking*, Oxford, 1969; DLA, Erwin M., b. 16 Apr. 1928, 'Verlorene Jugend', MS, 1994, 7–8; KA 3024, Otto P., 'Himmel und Hölle: Eine Kreuzberger Kindheit', 56; Jürgen Schlumbohm, *Kinderstuben: Wie Kinder zu Bauern, Bürgern, Aristokraten wurden, 1700–1850*, Munich, 1983; Eve Rosenhaft, *Beating the Fascists? The German Communists and Political Violence, 1929–1933*, Cambridge, 1983; Helmut Lessing and Manfred Liebel, *Wilde Cliquen: Szenen einer anderen Arbeiterjugendbewegung*, Bensheim, 1981; Reinhard Sieder and Hans Safrian, 'Gassenkinder – Strassenkämpfer: Zur politischen Sozialisation einer Arbeitergeneration in Wien 1900 bis 1938' in Lutz Niethammer (ed.), *'Wir kriegen jetzt andere Zeiten': Auf der Suche nach der Erfahrung des Volkes in nachfaschistischen Ländern*, Berlin, 1985, 117–51.

46. Peukert, *Inside Nazi Germany*, 154–60, for a more idealistic interpretation; Theilen, *Edelweisspiraten*, 32; Klönne, *Jugend im Dritten Reich*, 255. See chapters 5, 7 and 13 below for the development of these games.

47. Lange and Burkard, '*Abends wenn wir essen fehlt uns immer einer*', 99: Detlef, 12 Nov. 1939, and 191: Edith, 15 Apr. 1943.

48. KA 4718, Martha A.; 'Ein Kornfeld in der Stadt', MS, 10–11; Lange and Burkard, '*Abends wenn wir essen fehlt uns immer einer*', 258: Ulla; also, Radebold, *Abwesende Väter und Kriegskindheit*; and Schulz, Radebold and Reulecke, *Söhne ohne Väter*.

49. On Austria in the First World War, see Christa Hämmerle, '"Zur Liebesarbeit sind wir hier, Soldatenstrümpfe stricken wir" . . . : Zu Formen weiblicher Kriegsfürsorge im ersten Weltkrieg', Ph.D., University of Vienna, 1996, and her, '"Habt Dank, Ihr Wiener Mägdelein . . ." Soldaten und weibliche Liebesgaben im Ersten Weltkrieg', *L' Homme*, 8/1, 1997, 132–54; 'Liebes unbekanntes Fräulein Giesela!' in Ingrid Hammer and Susanne zur Niedern (eds), *Sehr selten habe ich geweint: Briefe und Tagebücher aus dem Zweiten Weltkrieg von Menschen aus Berlin*, Zurich, 1992, 203–22; KA 2693/8, Dorothea D., MS, 4–5.

50. KA 2694/9, Herta L., b. 1926, 'Einquartierung, 1939/40', MS, 1–4; and KA 2694/7, for her 'Erste Jahre und Überblick'.

51. KA 2694/9, Herta L., 'Einquartierung, 1939/40', 5–13; she also kept a copy of the book Fechner published about the period the regiment was in Viersen and on campaign, in order to recall particular moments such as his touching evocation of leave-taking on 10 May: Fritz Fechner, *Panzer am Feind: Kampferlebnisse eines Regiments im Westen*, Gütersloh, 1941.

52. Cinema attendance, see Welch, *Propaganda and the German Cinema*, 196; *Regierungspräsident* of Swabia, 9 July 1940 report and reports on the *Wochenschau*, cited also in Kershaw, *The 'Hitler Myth'*, 155 and 158–9; Boberach, *Meldungen aus dem Reich*, 3, 829–30, and 4, 978–9, 1179–80 and 1221–3: 1 Mar., 10 Apr., 27 May and 6 June 1940, cited also in Carter, *Dietrich's Ghosts*, 207.

53. Germany's official tally of military deaths in the First World War amounted to 1,885,245, with an additional 170,000 soldiers missing, presumed dead:

Statistisches Jahrbuch für das Deutsche Reich, 44, 1924–5, Berlin, 1925, 25: I am grateful to Richard Bessel for this reference. In 1944 the *Wehrmacht* calculated that 15,500 of its soldiers were killed in the Polish campaign and increased its estimate of those killed in France from 26,500 to 46,000: Rüdiger Overmans, *Deutsche militärische Verluste im zweiten Weltkrieg*, 304.

54. Bechtold, *Ein deutsches Kindertagebuch*, 108–13.

55. Lange and Burkard, '*Abends wenn wir essen fehlt uns immer einer*', 56: Rosemarie, 3 June 1940; the colonial novel by Hans Grimm, *Volk ohne Raum*, Munich, 1926, remained very popular throughout the 1930s; Welch, *Propaganda and the German Cinema*, 205–14; French prisoners in Boberach, *Meldungen aus dem Reich*, 4, 1222: 6 June 1940. In fact, the 90,000 French black prisoners of war were kept in France: Hans Pfahlmann, *Fremdarbeiter und Kriegsgefangene in der deutschen Kriegswirtschaft 1939–1945*, Darmstadt, 1968, 89.

56. KA 3187 b, Karl-Heinz B., b. 1927, 'Ein Urlauber': Klasse 4b Deutsch Heft, Bismarck-Schule, Bochum, 3 Feb. 1942 essay.

57. Kershaw, *The 'Hitler Myth'*, 156; KA 3931/2, Dierk S., 'Auszüge', 5–6 and 12–15: 1 July, 25–26 Sept., 29 Nov. and 21 Dec. 1940; Gève, *Youth in Chains*, 17–18.

58. Song, text by Hans Riedel, music by Robert Götz in Linde, *So waren wir*, 22; lengthening the summer holidays in 1940 for harvest work, Hans-Peter de Lorent, 'Hamburger Schulen im Krieg' in Lehberger and de Lorent, '*Die Fahne hoch*', 365.

59. Schools in Münster were requested to punish 12 per cent of pupils for not reporting for harvest work, Heinz-Ulrich Eggert (ed.), *Der Krieg frisst eine Schule: Die Geschichte der Oberschule für Jungen am Wasserturm in Münster, 1938–1945*, Münster, 1990, 60. Forced foreign labour, see Herbert, *Hitler's Foreign Workers*, 61–79, 95–7; Götz Aly, '*Final Solution*': *Nazi Population Policy and the Murder of the European Jews*, London, 1999, 43.

60. Herbert, *Hitler's Foreign Workers*, 95–124; Diemut Majer, '*Non-Germans*' *under the Third Reich: The Nazi Judicial and Administrative System in Germany and Occupied Eastern Europe, with Special Regard to Occupied Poland, 1939–1945*, Baltimore and London, 2003.

61. Herbert, *Hitler's Foreign Workers*, 61–87; Czesław Madajczyk, *Die Okkupationspolitik Nazideutschlands in Polen 1939–1945*, Cologne, 1988, 275; Helene B. in Annekatrein Mendel, *Zwangsarbeit im Kinderzimmer: 'Ostarbeiterinnen' in deutschen Familien von 1939 bis 1945: Gespräche mit Polinnen und Deutschen*, Frankfurt, 1994, 11.

62. Katya F. in ibid., 78–9.

63. Noakes, *Nazism*, 4, 510–22; Tim Mason, *Arbeiterklasse und Volksgemeinschaft*, Opladen, 1975, 1077–95 for general war economy measures; Lothar Burchardt, 'The Impact of the War Economy on the Civilian Population of Germany during the First and Second World Wars' in Wilhelm Deist (ed.), *The German Military in the Age of Total War*, Leamington Spa, 1985, 53; Rainer Gries, *Die Rationen-Gesellschaft: Versorgungskampf und Vergleichsmentalität: Leipzig, München und Köln nach dem Kriege*, Münster, 1991, 25–8; M. C. Kaser and E. A. Radice (eds), *The Economic History of Eastern Europe, 1919–1975*, 2, *Interwar Policy, the War and Reconstruction*, Oxford, 1986, 391–7.

64. Tomi Ungerer, *Die Gedanken sind frei: Meine Kindheit im Elsass*, Zurich, 1999, 38; KA 3931/2, Dierk S., 'Auszüge', 5–6: 21 July and 28 Sept. 1940; Mellin in Maja Bauer et al., *Alltag im 2. Weltkrieg*, Berlin, 1980, 14.

65. Dörr, 'Wer die Zeit nicht miterlebt hat . . .', 2, 15–20; Herbert, *Hitler's Foreign Workers*, 321–8; Wachsmann, *Hitler's Prisons*, 221–2.

66. On relations with foreigners and executions for 'race defilement', see Herbert, *Hitler's Foreign Workers*, 124–32; Robert Gellately, *Backing Hitler: Consent and Coercion in Nazi Germany*, Oxford, 2001, 166–75, and his *The Gestapo and German Society: Enforcing Racial Policy, 1933–1945*, Oxford, 1990, 159–214; for such offences Jews were executed behind the closed doors of prisons in the 'Old Reich': Alexandra Przyrembel, 'Rassenschande': Reinheits-mythos und Vernichtungslegitimation im Nationalsozialismus, Göttingen, 2003, 413–25.

67. Weinberg, *A World at Arms*, 118 and 145–9.

68. Hitler, *Reden und Proklamationen*, 2, 1560 and 1580: 19 July and 4 Sept. 1940; Kershaw, *Hitler*, 2, 303–10; Olaf Groehler, *Bombenkrieg gegen Deutschland*, Berlin, 1990, 172–5; Joseph Goebbels, *Die Tagebücher*, Elke Fröhlich (ed.), Munich, 1993–6, 4, 308, 311, 315, 324, 336 and 338: 5, 7, 9, 15, 24 and 25 Sept. 1940; British casualties, Alfred Price, *Luftwaffe Data Book*, London, 1997; bomber losses on the night of 7–8 Nov. 1941 would force Churchill to call off the Berlin raids.

69. On Göring, Steinert, *Hitlers Krieg und die Deutschen*, 172 and 366–7; bunker building, see Groehler, *Bombenkrieg gegen Deutschland*, 238–53; Gève, *Youth in Chains*, 17.

70. Lange and Burkard, 'Abends wenn wir essen fehlt uns immer einer', 97, 35 and 41: Detlef to father, 30 Sept. 1939, Rosemarie's father, 11 Jan. 1940 and Rosemarie, 24 Jan. 1940; Strobl, *The Germanic Isle*; German Propaganda Archive, Calvin College, Grand Rapids, Michigan, for board game, 'Stukas greifen an'; *Bomben auf Engeland*, Berlin, 1940.

71. Klönne, *Jugend im Dritten Reich*, 255–6.

72. Detlev Peukert, 'Arbeitslager und Jugend-KZ: Die Behandlung "Gemein-schaftsfremder" im Dritten Reich' in Peukert and Reulecke, *Die Reihen fast geschlossen*, 413–34.

73. Noakes, *Nazism*, 4, 526–31; Kershaw, *The 'Hitler Myth'*, 156; Boberach, *Meldungen aus dem Reich*, 5, 1645–8: 7 Oct. 1940; Strobl, *The Germanic Isle*, 132–60.

74. Eggert, *Der Krieg frisst eine Schule*, 92–3; Reissner, in Krüger, 'Die Bombenangriffe auf das Ruhrgebiet,' 92–3; Middlebrook and Everitt, *The Bomber Command War Diaries*, 31–8 and 56–130.

75. Kock, 'Der Führer sorgt für unsere Kinder . . .', 71–81; Gerhard Sollbach, *Heimat Ade! Kinderlandverschickung in Hagen 1941–1945*, Hagen, 1998, 14.

76. Parental attitudes and rumours, Boberach, *Meldungen aus dem Reich*, 5, 1648: 7 Oct. 1940; numbers of child evacuees, Kock, 'Der Führer sorgt für unsere Kinder . . .', 136–8; a total of 222 people were killed in raids on Berlin in 1940: Olaf Groehler, 'Bomber über Berlin', *Deutscher Fliegerkalender*, 1970, 113.

77. Kock, 'Der Führer sorgt für unsere Kinder . . .', 120–2.

78. Ibid., 125.

79. KA 2073, Ilse-W. P., 'KLV-Tagebuch', MS: 7 May, 3 and 13 June, 29 July, 18 and 25 Aug. and 19 Oct. 1941.

80. Ibid., 1, 11, 25 and 28 May, 2 June, 20 July and 8 Aug. 1941.
81. Ibid., 3, 4 and 5 May, 16, 22, and 29 June, 6 July, 14 Aug. and 18 Nov. 1941.
82. Ibid., 31 Aug., 18 Sept., 10, 25, 28 and 31 Oct., 14, 17 and 18 Nov. 1941; falling numbers, Kock, 'Der Führer sorgt für unsere Kinder . . .', 137.
83. Kock, 'Der Führer sorgt für unsere Kinder . . .', 137; Sollbach, Heimat Ade!, 14.
84. Rudolf Lenz in Sollbach, Heimat Ade!, 136–7.
85. KA 3931/2, Dierk S., 'Auszüge', 15: 26 Dec. 1940 and midnight on New Year's Eve.

Chapter 2

1. On Hitler, see his speech to the German press of 10 Nov. 1938: Wilhelm Treue, 'Rede vor der deutschen Presse', Vierteljahrshefte für Zeitgeschichte, 6, 1958, 175–91, and Kershaw, The 'Hitler Myth', 123–4; in general, see Gellately, Backing Hitler, 51–69 and plates 11–12; Wachsmann, Hitler's Prisons, 192–9 and 393; Lothar Gruchmann, Justiz im Dritten Reich: Anpassung und Unterwerfung in der Ära Gürtner, Munich, 1990, 910–11; Christine Dörner, Erziehung durch Strafe: Die Geschichte des Jugendstrafvollzugs von 1871–1945, Weinheim, 1991, 199–215 and 257–64; Patrick Wagner, Volksgemeinschaft ohne Verbrecher: Konzeption und Praxis der Kriminalpolizei in der Zeit der Weimarer Republik und des Nationalsozialismus, Hamburg, 1996, 311; Dickinson, The Politics of German Child Welfare, 213–4; Eckhard Hansen, Wohlfahrtspolitik im NS-Staat: Motivationen, Konflikte und Machtstrukturen im 'Sozialismus der Tat' des Dritten Reiches, Augsburg, 1991, 245; on the comparison with other countries, see n41 below.
2. LWV 2/8487, Emmi K., Beschluss, Jugendamtsgericht Hanau, 30 May 1939. For the development of Nazi measures, see Hansen, Wohlfahrtspolititk im NS-Staat, 281–2; Dörner, Erziehung durch Strafe, 157–71; Carola Kuhlmann, Erbkrank oder Erziehbar? Jugendhilfe als Vorsorge und Aussonderung in der Fürsorgeerziehung in Westfalen von 1933–1945, Weinheim, 1989, 201–2; Christa Hasenclever, Jugendhilfe und Jugendgesetzgebung seit 1900, Göttingen, 1978, 148–53; Dickinson, The Politics of German Child Welfare, 238–9.
3. Dickinson, The Politics of German Child Welfare, 238.
4. See Stadtarchiv Göttingen, Polizeidirektion VIII, Fach 59.2.185–59.3.31. for the period 23 July 1934–27 June 1944.
5. Wolfgang Ayass, Das Arbeitshaus Breitenau: Bettler, Landstreicher, Prostituierte, Zuhälter und Fürsorgeempfänger in der Korrektions- und Landarmenanstalt Breitenau (1874–1949), Kassel, 1992, 162–9.
6. Ayass, Das Arbeitshaus Breitenau, esp. 204–17.
7. Cited in LWV Bücherei 1988/323, Ulla Fricke and Petra Zimmermann, 'Weibliche Fürsorgeerziehung während des Faschismus – am Beispiel Breitenau', MS, 76–77.
8. Ayass, Das Arbeitshaus Breitenau, 253–4; Dietfrid Krause-Vilmar, Das Konzentrationslager Breitenau: Ein staatliches Schutzhaftlager 1933/34, Marburg, 1997, 213.
9. LWV 2/9565, Liselotte W., Hausstrafen, 3; LWV 2/9009, Waltraud P., b. 30 Nov. 1925, fled on 11 Aug. 1942, and returned on 17 Aug. 1942, admitted to the Stadtkrankenhaus Kassel with suspected meningitis on 7 Sept. and died

on 12 Sept. 1942, 57–8; LWV 2/8029, Ruth F., b. 14 Mar. 1925, d. 23 Oct. 1942; LWV 2/9163, Maria S., b. 24 Mar. 1926, d. 7 Nov. 1943, 30 and 32; Liselotte S. in LWV Bücherei 1988/323, Fricke and Zimmermann, 'Weibliche Fürsorgeerziehung', 86–7.

10. Ayass, *Das Arbeitshaus Breitenau*, 306–7 and 84–5; Kock, *'Der Führer sorgt für unsere Kinder...'*, 125; LWV 2/7780, Karl B., 14.

11. Cited in LWV Bücherei 1988/323, Fricke and Zimmermann, 'Weibliche Fürsorgeerziehung', 89; LWV 2/7823, Ruth B., Direktion Breitenau to Frau Ida B., 30 Apr. 1943, 16.

12. LWV 2/7823, Ruth B., letter from Frau Ida B., 13 June 1943, 22.

13. LWV 2/7823, Ruth B., letter from Frau Ida B. to the Breitenau Direktion, 14 Dec. 1943, and Thüringer Landesheilanstalt Stadtroda, Fachärztliches Gutachten, 2 Feb. 1943, 3 and 50; LWV 2/ 9163, Maria S., b. 24 Mar. 1926, d. 7 Nov. 1943, Thüringer Landeskrankenhaus Stadtroda, Fachärztliches Gutachten, Stadtroda, 24 June 1943, 9.

14. LWV 2/9116, Ursula R., 11, 20, 25, 85–90: Direktion Breitenau to father, 19 Feb. 1942 and 21 Oct. 1942. They had lost their rights of guardianship two years previously: Amtsgericht Gotha, 14 Sept. 1940; LWV 2/9571, Jula W.; 2/7780, Karl B., NSDAP interceded on his behalf.

15. LWV 2/8868, Anni N. letter to sister, n.d., 51.

16. Ayass, *Das Arbeitshaus Breitenau*, 307–9 and 335–6.

17. Extensions, Ayass, *Das Arbeitshaus Breitenau*, 308; LWV 2/8199, Anneliese G., 25–8: letter to parents and grandmother, 3 Nov. 1940; LWV 2/9404, Rudolf S., 17: letter to parents, 3 Dec. [1943].

18. LWV 2/9404, Rudolf S., 17: letter to parents, 3 Dec. [1943].

19. Ibid.

20. LWV 2/8868, Anni N., letter to sister, 25 May 1942, 51.

21. LWV 2/7823, Ruth B., 58, letter to mother, 28 Nov. 1943; and fragmentary letter to mother, n.d., 39.

22. For the distribution of letters, see LWV 2/9189, Lieselotte S., 16–19: letter to mother, 14 Jan. 1940; Dora Z., cited in LWV Bücherei 1988/323, Fricke and Zimmermann, 'Weibliche Fürsorgeerziehung', 80.

23. LWV 2/8978, Herbert P., 49 and 51–2; LWV, 2/9404, Rudolf S., 7.

24. See LWV 2/9009, Waltraud P., 49 and 51: Protokoll, 11 Apr. 1942.

25. LWV 2/7776, Waltraud B., 1, 8–9: Jugendamt, 15 Dec. 1944; Protokoll, 21 Dec. 1944; Personalbogen Breitenau, 30 Dec. 1944, 1. Very occasionally, the authorities worried about excessive – or even counter-productive – violence in the home, as in the case of Marie-Luise J. who was beaten by her mother and brother: LWV 2/8450, Marie-Luise J., 14–17: Abschrift 11 Mar. 1942, and letter of 27 Nov. 1943. Adam G. also ran home, only to be returned by his mother: LWV 2/8164, Adam G., 5: *Hausstrafen*, 22 July 1942.

26. LWV 2/8192, Maria G., 5–6: Jugendamt Frankfurt, 24 July 1939; Jugendamt Wiesbaden, 3 Aug. 1939.

27. LWV, 2/8192, Maria G., 1–4: Intelligenzprüfungsbogen zum Gutachten, Hadamar, 4 Aug. 1939.

28. LWV, 2/8192, Maria G., 7; on sterilisation on hereditary-psychiatric grounds, Bock, *Zwangssterilisation im Nationalsozialismus*, 326–39; on restriction of marriage loans on racial-hygienic grounds, see Lisa Pine, *Nazi Family Policy, 1933–1945*, Oxford, 1997, 104–16.

29. LWV 2/9245, Ursula S., who was sterilised before being sent to Breitenau;

for children sent to Haina, see LWV 1939/013, Heinrich G.; LWV 1939/037, Walter B.; also Klaus Scherer, *'Asozial' im Dritten Reich: Die vergessenen Verfolgten*, Münster, 1990, 66; 'Asoziales Verhalten': there were thirty-one juvenile cases in Breitenau during 1934–39, Ayass, *Das Arbeitshaus Breitenau*, 275–82; LWV 2/8192, Maria G., 14.

30. LWV 2/7811, Elisabeth B., 5 and *Hausstrafen* (the reference is to Goethe's 'Der König in Thule'). See also ten-year-old Margot S.: LWV 2/2018, Margot S., 54: letter undated but probably autumn or winter 1944–45.

31. LWV 2/7873, Hannelore B., 2 and 5: Jugendgericht Saarbrücken, 23 Jan. 1937; *Hausstrafen*, 21 Jan. 1941.

32. Ibid.

33. Ibid.

34. Ibid.

35. LWV 2/8868, Anni N., 8–9.

36. Ibid., 12, Thüringer Jugendgericht, Apolda, 3 Oct. 1934.

37. Ibid., 13, Thüringer Jugendgericht, Apolda, 3 Oct. 1934.

38. Including kindergarten teachers, there were 19,299 women compared with 1,830 men in paid employment as social workers in Germany in 1933: Dickinson, *The Politics of German Child Welfare*, 145, 172 and 204. In general, see Detlev Peukert, *Grenzen der Sozialdisziplinierung: Aufstieg und Krise der deutschen Jugendfürsorge von 1878 bis 1932*, Cologne, 1986, 258; Elizabeth Harvey, *Youth and the Welfare State in Weimar Germany*, Oxford, 1993; Hasenclever, *Jugendhilfe und Jugendgesetzgebung*, 124; Christoph Sachsse and Florian Tennstedt, *Der Wohlfahrtsstaat im Nationalsozialismus*, Stuttgart, 1992, 84–96, 152–6 and 162–6; Ayass, 'Die Landesarbeitsanstalt und das Landesfürsorgeheim Breitenau' in Gunnar Richter (ed.), *Breitenau: Zur Geschichte eines nationalsozialistischen Konzentrations- und Arbeitserziehungslagers*, Kassel, 1993, 44.

39. LWV, 2/8868, Anni N., 13–14, 21, 23 and 30: Protokoll Anni N., Apolda Kriminalpolizei, 30 July 1940; Protokoll Anni N., Breitenau, 15 Dec. 1941; Landesinspektor, Schlussbericht, Breitenau, 15 Dec. 1941; Direktor Breitenau to Jugendamt Apolda, 24 Feb. 1942.

40. LWV, 2/8868, Anni N., 30: Direktor Breitenau to Jugendamt Apolda, 24 Feb. 1942.

41. For a comparative context, see Linda Mahood, *Policing Gender, Class and Family: Britain, 1850–1940*, London, 1995; Lynn Abrams, *The Orphan Country*, Edinburgh, 1998; Sarah Fishman, *The Battle for Children: World War II Youth Crime, and Juvenile Justice in Twentieth-Century France*, Cambridge, Mass., 2002; Robert Mennel, *Thorns and Thistles: Juvenile Delinquents in the United States, 1825–1940*, Hanover, New Hamps., 1973; Adolfo Ceretti, *Come pensa il Tribunale per i minorenni: una ricerca sul giudicato penale a Milano dal 1934 al 1990*, Milan, 1996; Wachsmann, *Hitler's Prisons*, 364–9. On the Barnardo's homes and migration to Australia and Canada, see Barry Coldrey, *Child Migration under the Auspices of Dr Barnardo's Homes, the Fairbridge Society and the Lady Northcote Trust*, Thornbury, 1999; Patrick Dunae, 'Gender, Generations and Social Class: The Fairbridge Society and British Child Migration to Canada, 1930–1960' in Jon Lawrence and Pat Starkey (eds), *Child Welfare and Social Action: International Perspectives*, Liverpool, 2001, pp. 82–100; on racist policies in Australia and the United States, see Victoria Haskins and Margaret Jacobs,

'Stolen Generations and Vanishing Indians: The Removal of Indigenous Children as a Weapon of War in the United States and Australia, 1870–1940' in James Alan Marten (ed.), *Children and War: A Historical Anthology*, New York and London, 2002, 227–41; Anna Haebich, 'Between Knowing and Not Knowing: Public Knowledge of the Stolen Generations', *Aboriginal History*, 25, 2001, 70–90.

42. Dickinson, *The Politics of German Child Welfare*, 197; Peukert, *Grenzen der Sozialdisziplinierung*, 248–52; Weindling, *Health, Race, and German Politics*, 381–3, 444 and 578; Cornelie Usbourne, *The Politics of the Body in Weimar Germany*, New York, 1992, 134–9.

43. See Gisela Bock, *Zwangssterilisation im Nationalsozialismus: Studien zur Rassenpolitik und Frauenpolitik*, Opladen, 1986; Paul Weindling, *Health, Race, and German Politics between National Unification and Nazism, 1870–1945*, Cambridge, 1989; Usbourne, *The Politics of the Body in Weimar Germany*; Stefan Kühl, *The Nazi Connection: Eugenics, American Racism and German National Socialism*, New York, 1994.

44. Workplace infractions, LWV 2/8356, Sonja H., b. 4 June 1928; and LWV 2/8194, Anna G., b. 5 Jan. 1927. On Nazi policy and youth concentration camps, see Wagner, *Volksgemeinschaft ohne Verbrecher*, 376–84; Martin Guse, Andreas Kohrs and Friedhelm Vahsen, 'Das Jugendschutzlager Moringen – Ein Jugendkonzentrationslager' in Hans-Uwe Ott and Heinz Sünker (eds), *Soziale Arbeit und Faschismus*, Frankfurt, 1989, 228–49; Martin Guse, *'Wir hatten noch gar nicht angefangen zu leben': Eine Ausstellung zu den Jugend-Konzentrationslagern Moringen und Uckermark* (3rd edn), Moringen, 1997; Michael Hepp, 'Vorhof zur Hölle: Mädchen im "Jugendschutzlager" Uckermark' in Angelika Ebbinghaus (ed.), *Opfer und Täterinnen: Frauenbiographien des Nationalsozialismus*, Nördlingen, 1987; Ayass, *Das Arbeitshaus Breitenau*, 305.

45. Detlev Peukert, 'Arbeitslager und Jugend-KZ: Die Behandlung "Gemeinschaftsfremder" im Dritten Reich' in Peukert and Reulecke (eds), *Die Reihen fast geschlossen*, 413–34; Wagner, *Volksgemeinschaft ohne Verbrecher*, 376–7.

46. Johannes Meister, 'Die "Zigeunerkinder" von der St. Josefspflege in Mulfingen', *1999: Zeitschrift für Sozialgeschichte des 20. und 21. Jahrhunderts*, 2, 1987, 14–51; Michail Krausnick, *Auf Wiedersehen im Himmel: Die Geschichte der Angela Reinhardt*, Munich, 2001; Michael Zimmermann, *Rassenutopie und Genozid: Die nationalsozialistische 'Lösung der Zigeunerfrage'*, Hamburg, 1996, 150; Donald Kenrick and Gratton Puxon, *The Destiny of Europe's Gypsies*, London, 1972, 68–9; Eva Justin, *Lebensschicksale artfremd erzogener Zigeunerkinder und ihrer Nachkommen*, Berlin, 1944.

47. Richter, *Breitenau*, 96–215; Krause-Vilmar, *Das Konzentrationslager Breitenau*, 209–15; Ayass, *Das Arbeitshaus Breitenau*, 303; in general, Gabriele Lotfi, *KZ der Gestapo: Arbeitserziehungslager im Dritten Reich*, Stuttgart, 2000.

48. Overcrowding, Ayass, *Das Arbeitshaus Breitenau*, 303–4; violence, Krause-Vilmar, *Das Konzentrationslager Breitenau*, 213–4; in prisons, Wachsmann, *Hitler's Prisons*, 274–83; Russian boy, Richter, *Breitenau*, 124–5.

49. Herbert, *Hitler's Foreign Workers*, 69–79 and 131–33; Gellately, *Backing Hitler*, 179–82; Przyrembel, *'Rassenschande'*; Richter, *Breitenau*, 178–202.

50. Herbert, *Hitler's Foreign Workers*, 125.

51. Reactions to foreigners, LWV 2/7811, Elisabeth B.; LWV 2/9189, Lieselotte S., 69: Protokoll, Breitenau, 9 Nov. 1942.
52. LWV 2/9189, Lieselotte S., 41: Abschrift Jugendamt Kassel, 16 Mar. 1940, 41; LWV 2/8043, Fritz F., 40: letter from the Breitenau Direktion, 12 Feb. 1942; LWV 2/9009, Waltraud P., 51–2: Protokoll Breitenau, 11 Apr. 1942; and LWV 2/7881, Else B., 29, 33 and 38: farmer A.A. from Kaltenbach to Breitenau, 12 Nov. 1941 and 16 Dec. 1941, and medical report, 22 Jan. 1942.
53. LWV 2/9189, Lieselotte S., 16–19: letter to mother, 14 Jan. 1940.
54. Detlev Peukert, *Volksgenossen und Gemeinschaftsfremde: Anpassung, Ausmerze und Aufbegehren unter dem Nationalsozialismus*, Cologne, 1982; Gellately, *Backing Hitler*, 11.
55. LWV 2/7734, Anna Elisabeth B., 52: letter to parents, 21 Oct. 1940; LWV 2/7865, Werner G., 14, 21 and 36; LWV 2/8164, Adam G., 13, 17, 18, 23, 29, 30 and 40. As soon as Adam G. reached his tank training school in Erfurt, he sent an enthusiastic postcard back to Breitenau. In April 1941, the Justice Ministry established a system of probation for young offenders in the military, which was further expanded in 1944: Dörner, *Erziehung durch Strafe*, 275–80.
56. Peter Reichel, *Der schöne Schein des Dritten Reiches: Faszination und Gewalt des Faschismus*, Munich, 1992; Alf Lüdtke, *Eigen-Sinn: Fabrikalltag, Arbeitererfahrungen und Politik vom Kaiserreich bis in den Faschismus*, Hamburg, 1993, 221–350; Wachsmann, *Hitler's Prisons*, 258–68 and 299–314; Karin Orth, *Das System der nationalsozialistischen Konzentrationslager: Eine politische Organisationsgeschichte*, Hamburg, 1999, 106–12 and 162–92.

Chapter 3

1. On the Pomssen case and the probable identity of the child, see Udo Benzenhöfer, 'Der Fall "Kind Knauer"', *Deutsches Ärzteblatt*, 95/19, 1998, 954–5, and his 'Genese und Struktur der "NS-Kinder und Jugendlichen-euthanasie"', *Monatschrift Kinderheilkunde*, 10, 2003, 1012–19; Ulf Schmidt, 'Reassessing the Beginning of the "Euthanasia" Programme', *German History*, 17/4, 1999, 543–50; Henry Friedlander, *The Origins of Nazi Genocide: From Euthanasia to the Final Solution*, Chapel Hill 1995, 39. There is now a huge literature on this subject, including pioneering works by Klaus Dörner, 'Nationalsozialismus und Lebensvernichtung', *Vierteljahrshefte für Zeitgeschichte*, 15, 1967, 121–52 and his (ed.) *Der Krieg gegen die psychisch Kranken*, Frankfurt, 1989; Ernst Klee (ed.), *Dokumente zur 'Euthanasie'*, Frankfurt, 1986 and his *'Euthanasie' im NS-Staat: Die 'Vernichtung lebensunwerten Lebens'*, Frankfurt 1983; Götz Aly (ed.), *Aktion T-4 1939–1945: Die 'Euthanasie'-Zentrale in der Tiergartenstrasse 4*, Berlin, 1987; Kurt Nowak, *'Euthanasie' und Sterilisierung im 'Dritten Reich': Die Konfrontation der evangelischen und katholischen Kirche mit dem Gesetz zur Verhütung erbkranken Nachwuchses und der 'Euthanasie'-Aktion* (3rd edn), Göttingen, 1984; Michael Burleigh, *Death and Deliverance: 'Euthanasia' in Germany, 1900–1945*, Cambridge, 1994.
2. The *Kinderfachabteilungen* seem to have been a bureaucratic designation of the child's fate within the asylum, rather than necessarily a separate unit or ward: see Peter Sander, *Verwaltung des Krankenmordes: Der Bezirksverband Nassau im Nationalsozialismus*, Giessen, 2003, 532–3; also Hans Mausbach and Barbara Bromberger, 'Kinder als Opfer der NS-Medizin, unter beson-

derer Berücksichtigung der Kinderfachabteilungen in der Psychiatrie' in Christine Vanja and Martin Vogt (eds), *Euthanasie in Hadamar: Die national-sozialistische Vernichtungspolitik in hessischen Anstalten*, Kassel, 1991, 145–56; Bernhard Richarz, *Heilen, Pflegen, Töten: Zur Alltagsgeschichte einer Heil- und Pflegeanstalt bis zum Ende des Nationalsozialismus*, Göttingen, 1987, 177–89; Andrea Berger and Thomas Oelschläger, '"Ich habe eines natürlichen Todes sterben lassen": Das Krankenhaus im Kalmenhof und die Praxis der nationalsozialistischen Vernichtungsprogramme' in Christian Schrapper and Dieter Sengling (eds), *Die Idee der Bildbarkeit: 100 Jahre sozialpädagogische Praxis in der Heilerziehungsanstalt Kalmenhof*, Weinheim, 1988, 310–31; Dorothea Sick, *'Euthanasie' im Nationalsozialismus am Beispiel des Kalmenhofs in Idstein im Taunus*, Frankfurt, 1983, 57–9; Dorothee Roer and Dieter Henkel (eds), *Psychiatrie im Faschismus: Die Anstalt Hadamar 1933–1945*, Bonn, 1986, 216–18; Udo Benzenhöfer, *'Kinderfachabteilungen' und 'NS-Kindereuthanasie'*, Wetzlar, 2000.

3. Burleigh, *Death and Deliverance*, 99–111.

4. For the units under Kurt Eimann and Herbert Lange, which killed over 10,000 people between December 1939 and the end of March 1940, see Klee, *'Euthanasie' im NS-Staat*, 95ff and 190ff; Aly, *'Final Solution'*, 70–1; Burleigh, *Death and Deliverance*, 111–29; Kuratorium Gedenkstätte Sonnenstein e.V. und Sächsische Landeszentrale für politische Bildung (eds), *Nationalsozialistische Euthanasie-Verbrechen in Sachsen: Beiträge zu ihrer Aufarbeitung*, Dresden, 1993.

5. Aly, *Aktion T-4*, 17; Roer and Henkel, *Psychiatrie im Faschismus*; Landeswohlfahrtsverband Hessen and Bettina Winter (eds), *'Verlegt nach Hadamar': Die Geschichte einer NS-'Euthanasie'-Anstalt*, Kassel, 1994, 68–118; Burleigh, *Death and Deliverance*, 145–9.

6. Ibid., 163–4; 'Da kommt wieder die Mordkiste': cited in Winter, *'Verlegt nach Hadamar'*, 116.

7. Peter Löffler (ed.), *Clemens August Graf von Galen: Akten, Briefe und Predigten 1933–1946*, 2, Mainz, 1988, 878; Burleigh, *Death and Deliverance*, 176–8 and 217.

8. Hugh Trevor-Roper (ed.), *Hitler's Table Talk, 1941–1944*, London, 1953, 555: 4 July 1942; Winter, *'Verlegt nach Hadamar'*, 159; Burleigh, *Death and Deliverance*, 178–80. On policing in general, see Gellately, *The Gestapo and German Society* and his *Backing Hitler*; Johnson, *The Nazi Terror*; Reinhard Mann, *Protest und Kontrolle im Dritten Reich: Nationalsozialistische Herrschaft im Alltag einer rheinischen Grossstadt*, Frankfurt, 1987; Gerhard Paul and Klaus-Michael Mallmann (eds), *Die Gestapo: Mythos und Realität*, Darmstadt, 1995.

9. Burleigh, *Death and Deliverance*, 160.

10. Heinz Faulstich, 'Die Zahl der "Euthanasie"-Opfer' in Andreas Frewer and Clemens Eickhoff (eds), *'Euthanasie' und aktuelle Sterbehilfe-Debatte*, Frankfurt, 2000, 223–7; Burleigh, *Death and Deliverance*, 242: 4,422 of 4,817 transferred to Hadamar between August 1942 and March 1945 died; Sander, *Verwaltung des Krankenmordes*, 607–25; Winter, *'Verlegt nach Hadamar'*, 118–54; Roer and Henkel, *Psychiatrie im Faschismus*, 58–120.

11. Berger and Oelschläger, '"Ich habe eines natürlichen Todes sterben lassen"', 309–22; Alfred Völkel, 'Not just because I was a "bastard"', MS, 1 Aug. 1998, LWV Hessen; LWV Hessen, 5031; Sandner, *Verwaltung des*

Krankenmordes, 542–4; the fullest count, based on individual asylum records, is by Faulstich, but he did not count children separately: Faulstich, 'Die Zahl der "Euthanasie"-Opfer' and his *Hungersterben in der Psychiatrie 1914–1949, mit einer Topographie der NS-Psychiatrie*, Freiburg, 1998.

12. Sick, *'Euthanasie' im Nationalsozialismus*, 73; Gerhard Schmidt, *Selektion in der Heilanstalt 1939–1945*, Frankfurt, 1983, 118–9; Sandner, *Verwaltung des Krankenmordes*, 457, 488–505, 595–6 and 642–3.

13. Interview with Ludwig Heinrich Lohne, b. 1925, in Sick, *'Euthanasie' im Nationalsozialismus*, 82–91.

14. Burleigh, *Death and Deliverance*, 11–53; death in First World War: Heinz Faulstich, *Von der Irrenfürsorge zur 'Euthanasie': Geschichte der badischen Psychiatrie bis 1945*, Freiburg, 1993, 77.

15. Burleigh, *Death and Deliverance*, 183–202, and viii, citing Adolf Dörner (ed.), *Mathematik im Dienste der nationalpolitischen Erziehung mit Anwendungsbeispielen aus Volkswirtschaft, Geländekunde und Naturwissenschaft*, Frankfurt, 1935, 42. Charting public reactions to medical killing is complex and problematic: scholars generally draw heavily on police reports on protests against 'Euthanasia', responses to the film *Ich klage an*, or witness statements to post-war trials of medical personnel, but it does seem to me that the whole trend of the professional lobby, including the Protestant churches, towards punitive treatments during the late 1920s did not command the general endorsement of a population used to comprehensive health care, and led to some pressure on the regime to curtail the numbers of forced sterilisations in the 1930s: Bock, *Zwangssterilisation im Nationalsozialismus*, 278–98; on the Weimar background, see Yong-Sun Hong, *Welfare, Modernity, and the Weimar State, 1919–1933*, Princeton, NJ, 1998; David Crew, *Germans on Welfare: From Weimar to Hitler*, Oxford, 1998; and on public opinion about the social welfare system in the 1930s, Bernd Stöver, *Volksgemeinschaft im Dritten Reich: Die Konsensbereitschaft der Deutschen aus der Sicht sozialistischer Exilberichte*, Düsseldorf, 1993, 151–63.

16. Burleigh, *Death and Deliverance*, 210–19; Boberach, *Meldungen aus dem Reich*, 9, 3175–8: 15 Jan. 1942; Karl Ludwig Rost, *Sterilisation und Euthanasie im Film des 'Dritten Reiches': Nationalsozialistische Propaganda in ihrer Beziehung zu rassenhygienischen Massnahmen des NS-Staates*, Husum, 1987, 208–13; Kurt Nowak, 'Widerstand, Zustimmung, Hinnahme: Das Verhalten der Bevölkerung zur "Euthanasie"' in Norbert Frei (ed.), *Medizin und Gesundheitspolitik in der NS-Zeit*, Munich 1991, 235–51.

17. She had asked to visit a mere four days earlier: LWV Kassel, K12/1864, Dietrich L., b. 10 July 1938, d. Hadamar 9 Mar. 1943, mother to director of Hadamar, 8 and 12 Mar. 1943. As a result, the very few cases where relatives did demand an explanation stand out: e.g., K12/2548, Helmuth K., b. 19 Aug. 1933, d. Hadamar 9 Mar. 1943: Lotte K. (his sister) to director of Hadamar, 16 Mar. and 9 Apr. 1943. On parents' responses, see Burleigh, *Death and Deliverance*, 101–2; Götz Aly, 'Der Mord an behinderten Kindern zwischen 1939 und 1945' in Angelika Ebbinghaus, Heidrun Kaupen-Haas and Karl Heinz Roth (eds), *Heilen und Vernichten im Mustergau Hamburg: Bevölkerungs- und Gesundheitspolitik im Dritten Reich*, Hamburg, 1984, 151–2; Winter, *'Verlegt nach Hadamar'*, 126; an interesting collection of letters was found at Hartheim, though they are difficult to interpret without the relevant case histories: Johannes Neuhauser and Michaela Pfaffenwimmer

(eds), *Hartheim wohin unbekannt: Briefe und Dokumente*, Weitra, 1992.

18. Susanne Scholz and Reinhard Singer, 'Die Kinder in Hadamar' in Roer and Henkel, *Psychiatrie im Faschismus*, 228–9; Renate Otto, 'Die Heilerziehungs- und Pflegeanstalt Scheuern' in Klaus Böhme and Uwe Lohalm (eds), *Wege in den Tod: Hamburgs Anstalt Langenborn und die Euthanasie in der Zeit des Nationalsozialismus*, Hamburg, 1993, 320–33; Sandner, *Verwaltung des Krankenmordes*, 458–9; Uwe Kaminski, *Zwangssterilisation und 'Euthanasie' im Rheinland: Evangelische Erziehungsanstalten sowie Heil- und Pflegean- stalten 1933–1945*, Cologne, 1995, 420–2.

19. Although patients continued to be killed at Hadamar till Mar. 1945, it would seem that Scheuern had emptied at least its children's wing at the beginning of Sept. 1944: see LWV K12/2405, Krankheitsgeschichte, 3 Sept. 1944; LWV K12/2711, Krankheitsgeschichte, 2 Sept. 1944; on Bernotat, see Sander, *Verwaltung des Krankenmordes*, 449–51; 559–63; 645–6.

20. Alfred Völkel survived because the Nuremberg Jugendamt declared that it did not have the right to decide his abode, because this still rested with his 'Aryan' mother, and so requested his return on 20 Sept. 1943; the same was true for one of the other children; the other three were siblings, whose uncle employed a lawyer to have them released, after he learned of the deaths of their three siblings in Hadamar: Winter, *'Verlegt nach Hadamar'*, 136; Scholz and Singer, 'Die Kinder in Hadamar', 229–35; on the whole development, see Sander, *Verwaltung des Krankenmordes*, 654–68; individual files in LWV K12/53, Horst S.; K12/252, Peter W.; K12/1013, Horst St.; K12/1023, Karlheinz Sch.; K12/1050, Willi St.; K12/1071, Edith Sp.; K12/1548, Elias R.; K12/1598, Emmi Sch.; K12/2166, Helmut W.; K12/2918, Ingeborg D.; K12/2957, Georg Br.; K12/3298, Egon H.; K12/3608, Wolfgang Fr.; K12/3615, Klaus Fr.; K12/3750, Leo C.; K12/4769, Ruth B.; K12/5002, Manfred B.; K12/5017, Gerhard K.; K12/5021, Eleonore B.; K12/5028, Erika H.; K12/5030, Sigmund W.; K12/5031, Alfred Völkel; K12/5032, Günther P.; K12/5033, Günther H.; K12/5037, Amanda G.; K12/5038, Klara G.; K12/5039, Alfred G.; K12/5040, Edeltrud G.; K12/5046, Günther M.; K12/5047, Maria L.; K12/5054, Alfred R.; K12/5055, Hermann R.; K12/5056, Johann R.; K12/5057, Irma R.; K12/5058, Anna R.; K12/5059, Friedrich Z.; K12/5060, Jakob H.; K12/5061, Wolfgang H.; K12/5064, Manfred L.; Alfred Völkel, 'Not just because I was a "bastard"' LWV, MS.

21. LWV, K 12/3716, Georg E., b. 13 Jan. 1937, d. Hadamar, 19 Nov. 1943.

22. For the strategies of the poor, see the classic account of Olwen Hufton, *The Poor of Eighteenth-Century France, 1750–1789*, Oxford, 1974; Scholz and Singer, 'Die Kinder in Hadamar', 221–3; LWV, K12/1862, Willi L., b. 19 May 1936, d. Hadamar, 24 Feb. 1943, Krankengeschichte; Kreiswohl- fahrtsamt Diez to Scheuern, 26 Feb. 1941; Anstaltsarzt, Scheuern to Kreiswohlfahrtsamt Diez, 4 Mar. 1941.

23. LWV, K12/1223, Peter Oe., b. 28 Sept. 1928, d. Hadamar, 27 Sept. 1944; Eva Oe. to son, 32.

24. LWV K12/3866, Gertrud D., b. 2 Oct. 1928, d. Hadamar, 24 Feb. 1943: parents, 12 Feb. 1941, thanking her for her card; at this point she had spent eight out of her ten and a half years in the asylum at Scheuern; LWV K12/1848, Alfred K., b. 17 Feb. 1928, d. Hadamar, 11 Mar. 1943, Krankheitsgeschichte, 25 Mar., 29 June and 15 Dec. 1938, and Direktion Hephata to his family, 21 Feb. 1940.

25. LWV K12/1848, Alfred K., Krankengeschichte, 4 Jan. 1941; LWV K12/3865, Krankengeschichte, 14 May 1942; Helena D., b. 10 Dec. 1935, d. Hadamar, 24 Feb. 1943. Cost-cutting and conditions, Sandner, *Verwaltung des Krankenmordes*, 591 and 724; Faulstich, *Hungersterben in der Psychiatrie*, 658.

26. LWV K12/1848, Alfred K., Krankengeschichte, 4 Jan. 1941, and 35–6.

27. LWV K12/1545, Rosemarie R., b. 28 June 1934, d. Hadamar, 3 Mar. 1943, Krankengeschichte, 14 Dec. 1940. Apparently, one of Rosemarie's maternal great-aunts had died in the asylum at Merxhausen: this sufficed for the diagnosis of 'inborn' idiocy; for further letters, see Chefarzt [Adolf Wahlmann], Hadamar, to Soldat Jakob R., 19 Mar. 1943; Soldat Jakob R. to Scheuern, 7 June 1942 and 2 Jan. 1943; Frau R. to Schwester Anna at Scheuern, 22 Dec. 1942.

28. See LWV K12/5002, Edda B., b. 26 Jan. 1940, d. Hadamar, 20 Mar. 1943, Krankheitsgeschichte, 19 Nov. 1942; LWV K12/1862, Willi L., b. 19 May 1936, d. Hadamar 24 Feb. 1943, Krankheitsgeschichte, 5 Mar. 1938.

29. LWV K12/2711, Karl Otto F., b. 19 Jan. 1929, d. Hadamar, 27 Nov. 1944, Krankheitsgeschichte, intelligence test. LWV K12/3866, Gertrud D., Krankheitsgeschichte, 26 Jan. 1936.

30. Scholtz and Singer, 'Die Kinder in Hadamar', 221.

31. LWV K12/4323, Friedrich B., b. 11 June 1930, d. Hadamar, 23 Mar. 1943, Krankheitsgeschichte.

32. See also LWV K12/2405, Helene S., b. 13 Mar. 1928, transferred to Hadamar 3 Sept. 1944, survived; LWV K12/2711, Karl Otto F.

33. LWV K12/3501, Margarethe Elfriede G., b. 28 July 1928, d. Hadamar, 24 Feb. 1943: her year and half in Scheuern is covered by only five entries. Similarly, in the case of Eva H., who also arrived on 22 Nov. 1940 and was transferred to Hadamar in Feb. 1943, her file consists of five brief observations, again testifying to an early judgement in Scheuern that she was not worth trying to help: LWV K12/2747, Eva H., b. 19 Oct. 1936, d. Hadamar, 18 Mar. 1943; LWV K12/5002, Edda B., b. 26 Jan. 1940, d. Hadamar, 20 Mar. 1943, Krankheitsgeschichte, 4 Sept. 1942.

34. LWV K12/4705, Waltraud B., b. 22 Apr. 1937, d. Hadamar, 5 Mar. 1943, Krankengeschichte.

35. LWV K12/4705, Waltraud B. See Scholtz and Singer, 'Die Kinder in Hadamar', 220–1, for the aggregate numbers of the Feb. and Mar. group transfers. The change in typefaces is not always a reliable guide: both are to be found before the 'euthanasia action' got under way.

36. See, for instance, LWV K12/3574, Harald B., b. 16 Oct. 1935, d. Hadamar, 2 Mar. 1943, Krankheitsgeschichte. On staff conditions, see Bronwyn McFarland-Icke, *Nurses in Nazi Germany: Moral Choice in History*, Princeton, NJ, 1999, esp. chapter 8; Hans-Uwe Otto (ed.), *Soziale Arbeit und Faschismus: Volkspflege und Pädagogik im Nationalsozialismus*, Bielefeld, 1986; Sandner, *Verwaltung des Krankenmordes*, 593–605.

37. LWV K12/4705, Waltraud B., b. 22 Apr. 1937, d. Hadamar, 5 Mar. 1943, Krankheitsgeschichte, 5 Sept. 1939, 16 Mar. and 21 June 1940; LWV K12/2544, Karl-Heinz K., b. 11 Dec. 1931, d. Hadamar, 2 Mar. 1943, Krankheitsgeschichte, 10 July 1940; LWV K12/3343, Paul E., b. 4 Sept. 1934, d. Hadamar, 6 Mar. 1943, Krankheitsgeschichte, 17 Aug. 1942.

38. K12/3866, Gertrud D., Krankheitsgeschichte, 27 Feb. and 4 Dec. 1933;

K12/1849, Emma K., b. 3 Mar. 1932, d. Hadamar, 3 Mar. 1943, Krankheitsgeschichte, Oct. 1939 and 17 Jan. 1940; K12/2548, Helmuth K., Krankheitsgeschichte, 7 Sept. 1938 and 21 June 1939.

39. K12/2430, Karl J., b. 30 Jan. 1930, d. Hadamar, 29 Nov. 1943, Krankheitsgeschichte, 15 May 1937 and 12 July 1938; K12/3867, Maria Elise D., b. 30 Apr. 1930, d. Hadamar, 4 Mar. 1943, Krankheitsgeschichte, 'Vorgeschichte', 31 Mar. 1938 and 20 Jan. 1941.

40. LWV K12/2554, Karl-Heinz K., Krankheitsgeschichte, 2 Nov. 1940; 6 Oct. 1937 and 10 Dec. 1938.

41. LWV K12/4860, Willi B., b. 20 Nov. 1937, d. Hadamar, 5 Mar. 1943, Krankheitsgeschichte; LWV K12/1848, Alfred K., Krankengeschichte, 20 Jan. 1937 and 17 May 1940.

42. LWV K12/3574, Harald B., b. 16 Oct. 1935, d. Hadamar, 2 Mar. 1943, Krankengeschichte, 11 Sept. 1940.

43. LWV K12/3866, Gertrud D., Krankheitsgeschichte, 20 Jan. 1941.

44. LWV K12/3866, Gertrud D., Krankheitsgeschichte, 29 Dec. 1937 and 18 Aug. 1938; LWV K12/2711, Karl Otto F., Krankheitsgeschichte, 30 Dec. 1940.

45. LWV K12/2711, Karl Otto F., Krankheitsgeschichte, 17 Aug. 1938:

46. LWV Kassel, K12/1864, Dietrich L: he came to Scheuern on 8 Aug. and his mother wrote on 5 Sept. and 25 Nov. 1940, 8 Apr. and 1 May 1941, 2 Apr. and 15 Sept. 1942.

47. LWV Kassel, K12/1864, Dietrich L., Direktion Scheuern to Frau L., 17 Sept. 1940.

48. Runderlass des Reichsministers des Inneren, 1 July 1940, in Scholtz and Singer 'Die Kinder in Hadamar', 218.

49. Burleigh, *Death and Deliverance*, 21–4 and 98.

Chapter 4

1. Norman Davies, *God's Playground: A History of Poland*, Oxford, 1981, 437; Bethell, *The War Hitler Won*, 27–30 and 98–157; Alan Adelson (ed.), *The Diary of Dawid Sierakowiak: Five Notebooks from the Lódź Ghetto*, Oxford, 1996, 30–2: 30 Aug.–2 Sept. 1939; Wacław Major in Richard C. Lukas, *Did the Children Cry? Hitler's War against Jewish and Polish Children, 1939–1945*, New York, 1994, 11, and Marian Turski (ed.), *Byli wówczas dziećmi*, Warsaw, 1975, 156–7.

2. Adelson, *The Diary of Dawid Sierakowiak*, 34–6: 6–7 Sept.; for expectations of a Polish 'miracle' among students in Warsaw, see Jan Z. Raschke, *Farewell to God*, Dundee, 1977, 11.

3. Mary Berg, *Warsaw Ghetto: A Diary*, S. L. Shneiderman (ed.), New York, 1945, 11–14: 10 Oct. 1939. I have followed the convention of this book and used Berg's original name, Miriam Wattenberg, throughout. She and her American-born mother were among a group of Jews whom the Germans exchanged in 1944. Sections of her diary were translated into Yiddish and appeared in New York in 1944 and the whole diary was published in English before the end of the war in 1945, thus establishing it as the first ghetto diary to be published in the West. In addition to the diary's translation from Polish, it went through two processes of editing, one by herself on her voyage to the USA in 1944 and a second by S. L. Shneiderman, and so it is probably best read as part diary, part memoir: see 'Preface', Berg, *Warsaw Ghetto*, 9–10 and Susan Lee Pentlin, 'Mary Berg (1924–)' in S. Lillian Kremer (ed.),

Holocaust Literature: An Encyclopedia of Writers and their Work, 1, New York, 2003, 138–40; on mounds of corpses on the Warsaw–Kutno road, Lukas, *Did the Children Cry?*, 14.

4. Berg, *Warsaw Ghetto*, 15–16.
5. Adelson, *The Diary of Dawid Sierakowiak*, 34–7: 6–12 Sept. 1939.
6. Phillips, *My Secret Diary*, 57 and 60: 11 and 16 Sept. 1939; Weinberg, *A World at Arms*, 64–9.
7. Campaign and casualties, Weinberg, *A World at Arms*, 56–7; Overmans, *Deutsche militärische Verluste*, 304; Davies, *God's Playground*, 435–9; Madajczyk, *Die Okkupationspolitik Nazideutschlands*, 4; 'Welcome to the Red Army', Irena Grudzińska-Gross and Jan Tomasz Gross (eds), *War through Children's Eyes: The Soviet Occupation of Poland and the Deportations, 1939–1941*, Stanford, 1981, 8–9.
8. Henryk N., Grudzińska-Gross and Gross, *War through Children's Eyes*, doc. 77.
9. Phillips, *My Secret Diary*, 63–4: 20 Sept. 1939.
10. Berg, *Warsaw Ghetto*, 11–19: 10 Oct. 1939.
11. Grudzińska-Gross and Gross, *War through Children's Eyes*, 7–8 and see docs 77, 85, 98, and 104, and Jan Tomasz Gross, *Revolution from Abroad: The Soviet Conquest of Poland's Western Ukraine and Western Belorussia*, Princeton, NJ, 1988; also, Christopher Hann, *A Village without Solidarity: Polish Peasants in Years of Crisis*, New Haven, 1985.
12. Grudzińska-Gross and Gross, *War through Children's Eyes*, 11–16.
13. Helmut Walser Smith, *The Butcher's Tale: Murder and Anti-semitism in a German Town*, New York, 2002, 214–15.
14. See Christian Jansen and Arno Weckbecker, *Der 'Volksdeutsche Selbstschutz' in Polen 1939/40*, Munich, 1992, 27, 116–17, 135–8, 154–9 and 212–28. On Sunday 3 Sept. local Germans at Bromberg were set upon and butchered by their Polish neighbours and retreating Polish soldiers. Perhaps 1,000 people were killed in the area, while as many as 4,000–6,000 ethnic Germans were killed in Poland overall, if those who died fighting in the Polish Army or under German bombs are included. Both Goebbels's media machine and the *Wehrmacht* exaggerated the numbers tenfold, claiming 58,000 ethnic Germans had been killed. While the fighting was still going on, General Brauchitsch himself urged his armies to remember Bromberg and show no mercy to Polish forces. In the German media, especially the weekly cinema news, the *Wochenschau*, Poles were portrayed as a nation of dangerous and criminally degenerate 'sub-humans' who needed to be punished: see Włodzimierz Jastrzębski, *Der Bromberger Blutsonntag: Legende und Wirklichkeit*, Poznań, 1990; Peter Longerich, *Politik der Vernichtung: Eine Gesamtdarstellung der nationalsozialistischen Judenverfolgung*, Munich, 1998, 244; Helmut Krausnick and Hans-Heinrich Wilhelm, *Die Truppe des Weltanschauungskrieges: Die Einsatzgruppen der Sicherheitspolizei und des SD 1938–1942*, Stuttgart, 1981, 56–7; Boy Scouts killed, see Polish Ministry of Information, *The German New Order in Poland*, London, 1942, 26.
15. Bolcek, the local forester paced out the 205 yards of trench and estimated that at least 700 people had been shot there. His notes guided a Polish commission of investigation to the graves of 740 people, when the trenches were dug up after the war: Jansen and Weckbecker, *Der 'Volksdeutsche Selbstschutz'*, 129–32.

16. Numbers killed by the *Einsatzgruppen*, Wolfgang Benz (ed.), *Dimension des Völkermords: Die Zahl der jüdischen Opfer des Nationalsozialismus*, Munich, 1991; techniques of killing, tourism and protests, Jansen and Weckbecker, *Der 'Volksdeutsche Selbstschutz'*, 117–19; Ulrich Herbert, *National Socialist Extermination Policies: Contemporary German Perspectives and Controversies*, New York/Oxford, 2000, 32–7; Klaus-Jürgen Müller, *Das Heer und Hitler: Armee und nationalsozialistisches Regime 1933–1940*, Stuttgart, 1988, 437–50; on reactions to Goebbels propaganda and news of killings in Germany, see Lubien in Wierling, '"Leise versinkt unser Kinderland"', 70; and Boberach, *Meldungen aus dem Reich*, 4, 1073–4: 29 Apr. 1940, and 13, 5144–5: 19 Apr. 1943.

17. I follow the argument of Peter Longerich and Michael Wildt here that the Nazi regime crossed the line separating terror from mass murder at the start of the war: Michael Wildt, *Generation des Unbedingten: Das Führungskorps des Reichssicherheitshauptamtes*, Hamburg, 2002, 480–5; Hitler outlined his expectations in his talk to the military commanders, 22 Aug. 1939, in *Akten zur deutschen Auswärtigen Politik 1918–1945*, Serie D, 7, Baden-Baden and Göttingen, 1956, no. 193.

18. Phillips, *My Secret Diary*, 47–57: 1–11 Sept. 1939; Wanda Przybylska, *Journal de Wanda*, Zofia Bobowicz (ed. and trans.), Paris, 1981, 86–7: 30 June 1944.

19. Phillips, *My Secret Diary*, 94–8: 19 and 22 Dec. 1939, and 13 Mar. 1940.

20. For these games, see Ilona Flatsztejn-Gruda, *Byłam wtedy dzieckiem*, Lublin, 2004, 37–8; Polish Ministry of Information, *The German New Order in Poland*, 27; Tomasz Szarota, *Warschau unter dem Hakenkreuz: Leben und Alltag im besetzten Warschau, 1.10.1939 bis 31.7.1944*, Paderborn, 1985, 100, citing Stanisław Srokowski's diary for 20–21 June 1940.

21. Adelson, *The Diary of Dawid Sierakowiak*, 37–8: 12 Sept. 1939; Berg, *Warsaw Ghetto*, 19–23: 15 Oct.–1 Dec. 1939; in general, see Yisrael Gutman and Shmuel Krakowski, *Unequal Victims: Poles and Jews during World War II*, New York, 1986, 32–5.

22. Adelson, *The Dairy of Dawid Sierakowiak*, 54: 22 Oct. 1939.

23. Ibid., 55–8: 28–31 Oct. 1939.

24. Ibid., 51–3: 9–12 and 16 Oct. 1939.

25. Ibid., 60–3: 8–15 Nov. 1939.

26. Ibid., 63–70: 16 Nov.–13 Dec. 1939.

27. Ibid., 64, 66, 68 and 73–4: 19 Nov. and 1, 7 and 27 Dec. 1939.

28. Aly, *'Final Solution'*, 45–7; Alan Adelson and Robert Lapides, *Łódź Ghetto: Inside a Community under Siege*, New York, 1989, 30–41. We do not know exactly when the Sierakowiaks were forced to move because Dawid's diary for the whole of 1940 was lost.

29. For children's accounts of the deportations from eastern Poland, see Grudzińska-Gross and Gross, *War through Children's Eyes*, xxii–xxiii and docs 5, 9, 23, 25, 31, 46, 54, 84, 104 and 110, and p. 243 n. 13.

30. Aly, *'Final Solution'*, 63–6 and 70–6; Bernhard Stasiewski, 'Die Kirchenpolitik der Nationalsozialisten im Warthegau 1939–45', *Vierteljahrshefte für Zeitgeschichte*, 7/1, 1959, 46–74.

31. Aly, *'Final Solution'*, 77 and 61.

32. See Elizabeth Harvey, *Women and the Nazi East: Agents and Witnesses of Germanization*, New Haven and London, 2003, 154–6.

33. Melita Maschmann, *Account Rendered: A Dossier on My Former Self*, London/New York, 1965, 64–6 and 121 for the following account; on Posen, see Heinrich Schwendemann and Wolfgang Dietsche, *Hitlers Schloss: Die 'Führerresidenz' in Posen*, Berlin, 2003.

34. On Weimar, see Kurt Sontheimer, *Antidemokratisches Denken in der Weimarer Republik*, Munich, 1992; George Mosse, *The Crisis of German Ideology: Ideological Origins of the Third Reich*, London, 1966; Woodruff Smith, *The Ideological Origins of Nazi Imperialism*, New York, 1986; also Birthe Kundrus (ed.), *Phantasiereiche: Zur Kulturgeschichte des Deutschen Kolonialismus*, Frankfurt, 2003; Lora Wildenthal, 'Race, Gender and Citizenship in the German Colonial Empire' in Frederick Cooper and Ann Stoler (eds), *Tensions of Empire: Colonial Cultures in a Bourgeois World*, Berkeley, 1997, 263–83.

35. Hans-Christian Harten, *De-Kulturation und Germanisierung: Die national-sozialistische Rassen- und Erziehungspolitik in Polen 1939–1945*, Frankfurt, 1996, 222–6; Harvey, *Women and the Nazi East*, 165 and 197; see also Alexander Hohenstein, *Wartheländisches Tagebuch aus den Jahren 1941/42*, Stuttgart, 1961, 43–4, 58–61 and 247–8 for similar views; for the national lists, see Isabel Heinemann, *'Rasse, Siedlung, deutsches Blut': Das Rasse- und Siedlungshauptamt der SS und die rassenpolitische Neuordnung Europas*, Göttingen, 2003; on legal discrimination, see Majer, *'Non-Germans' under the Third Reich*; Doris Bergen, 'The Nazi Concept of "Volksdeutsche" and the Exacerbation of Anti-Semitism in Eastern Europe, 1939–45', *Journal of Contemporary History*, 29/4, 1994, 569–82.

36. Gizella cited in Lukas, *Did the Children Cry?*, 18–19.

37. Roman Hrabar, Zofia Tokarz and Jacek Wilczur, *Kinder im Krieg – Krieg gegen Kinder: Die Geschichte der polnischen Kinder 1939–1945*, Hamburg 1981, 83.

38. Madajczyk, *Die Okkupationspolitik Nazideutschlands*, table 15: a further 367,592 Poles were evicted – mainly from rural areas in central Poland near the new Soviet border with the General Government, to make way for military training grounds and SS camps.

39. Madajczyk, *Die Okkupationspolitik Nazideutschlands*, 407–8, citing Tadeusz Norwid, *Kraj bez Quislinga*, Rome, 1945, 30–2. See also Oskar Rosenfeld in Adelson and Lapides, *Lódź Ghetto*, 27; Hrabar, Tokarz and Wilczur, *Kinder im Krieg*, 82–3; Dorothy Macardle, *Children of Europe: A Study of the Children of Liberated Countries: Their War-time Experiences, Their Reactions, and Their Needs, with a Note on Germany*, London, 1949, 68; Dieter Pohl, *Von der 'Judenpolitik' zum Judenmord: Der Distrikt Lublin des Generalgouvernements 1939–1944*, Frankfurt, 1993, 52; on Hitler's reaction to General Blaskowitz's protests, Gerhard Engel, *Heeresadjutant bei Hitler 1938–1943*, Stuttgart, 1974, 68: 18 Nov. 1939, also in Martin Broszat, *Nationalsozialistische Polenpolitik 1939–1945*, Stuttgart, 1961, 41.

40. Aly, *'Final Solution'*, 43; Frank in Lucjan Dobroszycki, *Reptile Journalism: The Official Polish-Language Press under the Nazis, 1939–1945*, New Haven and London, 1994, 134; Madajczyk, *Die Okkupationspolitik Nazideutschlands*, 245–9.

41. Madajczyk, *Die Okkupationspolitik Nazideutschlands*, 261–2; Hohenstein, *Wartheländisches Tagebuch*, 293: 10 July 1942; Harten, *De-Kulturation und Germanisierung*, 192–6.

42. Madajczyk, *Die Okkupationspolitik Nazideutschlands*, 343–53; on the Grey Ranks, see Aleksander Kamiński, *Kamieniena szaniec*, Warsaw, 2001; Phillips, *My Secret Diary*, 151–2; one of the first accounts of the underground state was Jan Karski, *Story of a Secret State*, Boston, 1944.

43. Sosnowski, *The Tragedy of Children under Nazi Rule*, 139–42 and 160–3; Macardle, *Children of Europe*, 69; BDM activist cited in Harvey, *Women and the Nazi East*, 168.

44. Sonia Games, *Escape into Darkness: The True Story of a Young Woman's Extraordinary Survival during World War II*, New York, 1991, 40–1; Harten, *De-Kulturation und Germanisierung*, 197.

45. Jost Hermand, *A Hitler Youth in Poland: The Nazis' Programme for Evacuating Children during World War II*, Evanston, Illinois, 1997, xxix–xxx and 10–11.

46. Ibid., 7–8; other examples in Claus Larass, *Der Zug der Kinder: KLV – Die Evakuierung 5 Millionen deutscher Kinder im 2. Weltkrieg*, Munich, 1983, 211–13.

47. Madajczyk, *Die Okkupationspolitik Nazideutschlands*, 261: after the BBC reported on the '*Grusspflicht*', Goebbels intervened and it was abolished in Pomerania in October 1940 but it continued in the Wartheland for longer and in the Białystok area for the whole period of the occupation. Uncovering for the flag and anthem, Harten, *De-Kulturation und Germanisierung*, 196. Jost Hermand omits any discussion of this issue in his account of life in his KLV home in the eastern Wartheland.

48. Abraham I. Katsh (ed.), *The Warsaw Diary of Chaim A. Kaplan*, New York, 1965, 153–4: 15 May 1940.

49. Szarota, *Warschau unter dem Hakenkreuz*, 293–5, based on the two studies of language during the occupation by Feliks Pluta, *Język polski w okresie drugiej wojny światowej: Studium słowotwórczo-semantyczne*, Opole, 1976, 12–31, and Stanisław Kania, *Polska gwara konspiracyjno-partyzancka czasu okupacji hitlerowskiej 1939–1945*, Zielona Góra, 1976, 74–88.

50. Szarota, *Warschau unter dem Hakenkreuz*, 296–7.

51. Ibid., 145–6, citing Kazimierz Koźniewski, *Zamknięte koło: W podziemnym świecie*, Warsaw, 1967, 71.

52. Szarota, *Warschau unter dem Hakenkreuz*, 120, 147 and 151–2; the demographic imbalance in the population was most marked in the Wartheland, where men were down to 45 per cent of the population: Madajczyk, *Die Okkupationspolitik Nazideutschlands*, 250.

53. According to the Resistance itself, Poles flocked to the cinemas as never before: the Warsaw Film Theatre had 116,000 viewers in Jan. 1940, 235,000 in Jan. 1941 and 501,000 in Jan. 1942; Szarota, *Warschau unter dem Hakenkreuz*, 181–5 and 283.

54. Fabrice Virgili, *Shorn Women: Gender and Punishment in Liberation France*, Oxford, 2002; Veslemøy Kjendsli, *Kinder der Schande*, Berlin, 1988; Ebba Drolshagen, *Nicht ungeschoren davonkommen: Das Schicksal der Frauen in den besetzten Ländern, die Wehrmachtssoldaten liebten*, Hamburg, 1998.

55. Szarota, *Warschau unter dem Hakenkreuz*, 109, citing, *Biuletyn Informacyjny*, 19 June 1941.

56. Kaser and Radice, *The Economic History of Eastern Europe*, 2, 371–81 and 393–7; Madajczyk, *Die Okkupationspolitik Nazideutschlands*, 283; Isaiah Trunk, *Judenrat: The Jewish Councils of Eastern Europe under Nazi*

Occupation, New York, 1972; Gustavo Corni and Horst Gies, *Brot – Butter – Kanonen: Die Ernährungswirtschaft in Deutschland unter der Diktatur Hitler*, Berlin, 1997, 556; Gustavo Corni, *Hitler's Ghettos: Voices from a Beleagured Society, 1939–1944*, London, 2003, 123–39.

57. Szarota, *Warschau unter dem Hakenkreuz*, 118–130.
58. Ibid., 127–8.
59. Ibid., 106, citing Stanisław Srokowski's diary entry, 14–16 Jan. 1941.
60. Katsh, *The Diary of Chaim Kaplan*, 289–90: 4 Jan. 1942; Berg, *Warsaw Diary*, 100: 28 Sept. 1941.
61. Shirli Gilbert's translation of 'Koyft geto-beygelekh' from the Yiddish in Shmerke Kaczerginski and H. Leivick, *Lider fun di getos un lagern*, 1948, New York, 145–6, place of origin unknown, lyricist and composer unknown.
62. Cited in George Eisen, *Children and Play in the Holocaust: Games among the Shadows*, Amherst, Mass., 1988, 77; Sheva Glas-Wiener, *Children of the Ghetto*, Melbourne, 1983, 87–9.
63. Szarota, *Warschau unter dem Hakenkreuz*, 103–5, citing *Nowy Kurier Warszawski* report in the weekend edition, 13–14 Dec. 1941. The director of the Welfare Department in the municipal administration, Jan Starczewski, wrote to the German police administration in Jan. 1942 that of the fathers of these children thirteen were unemployed, nine had been killed during the military campaign, six had been sent to work in Germany, three were unable to work, two fathers had abandoned their families, and two were in the Auschwitz concentration camp.
64. Gunnar S. Paulsson, *Secret City: The Hidden Jews of Warsaw, 1940–1945*, New Haven and London, 2002, 26 and 61–6; Szarota, *Warschau unter dem Hakenkreuz*, 130, citing *Nowy Kurier Warszawski*, 22 Sept. 1941: *Shabbesgoy* literally means the Gentile who does the services Jews are forbidden to do on the Sabbath; smuggling techniques described by H. Passenstein, 'Szmugiel w getcie warszawskim', *Biuletyn ŻIH*, 26, 1958, 42–72; Corni, *Hitler's Ghettos*, 139–46; Janina Pładek in Mary Aitchison, *Caught in the Crossfire: The Story of Janina Pladek*, Fearn, 1995, 38–40.
65. Szarota, *Warschau unter dem Hakenkreuz*, 130; Berg, *Warsaw Ghetto*, 73: 12 June 1941; see also Barbara Engelking-Boni, 'Childhood in the Warsaw Ghetto' in United States Holocaust Memorial Museum, *Children and the Holocaust: Symposium Presentations*, Washington, 2004, 33–42.
66. Paulsson, *Secret City*, 64; Berg, *Warsaw Ghetto*, 73: 12 June 1941.
67. Shirli Gilbert's translation of 'Der kleyner shmugler' from the Yiddish in Kaczerginski and Leivick, *Lider fun di getos un lagern*, 104–5. The text was originally written in Polish by Henryka Łazowert (b. 1909, d. in Treblinka). In the ghetto, she won a prize for her ghetto reporting as well as writing several songs. Henryk Tom, a well-known composer of film music before the war, wrote the music (d. in the Warsaw ghetto of typhus); see also Jadwiga Czachowska and Alicja Szałagan (eds), *Współcześni Polscy Pisarze i Badacze Literatury: Słownik biobibliograficzny*, 5, Warsaw, 1997, 162–3.
68. Jack Klajman, *Out of the Ghetto*, London, 2000, 20–37.
69. Kaplan, *Scroll of Agony*, 269–71 and 332–4: 10 Oct. 1941 and 16 May 1942; Raul Hilberg, Stanisław Staron and Josef Kermisz (eds), *The Warsaw Diary of Adam Czerniakow*, Chicago, 1999, 44; Abraham Lewin, *The Cup of Tears: A Diary of the Warsaw Ghetto*, Oxford, 1988, 127; Lucjan Dobroszycki, *The Chronicle of the Łódź Ghetto 1941–1944*, New Haven

and London, 1984, 43–4, 67: 7 Apr. and 25 July 1941; Adelson, *The Diary of Dawid Sierakowiak*, 115–16: 27 July 1941; Adelson and Lapides, *Łódź Ghetto*, 132; Barbara Engelking-Boni, *Holocaust and Memory: The Experience of the Holocaust and its Consequences: An Investigation Based on Personal Narratives*, London, 2001, 155–77; Yisrael Gutman, *The Jews of Warsaw, 1939–43*, Brighton, 1982, 17 and 69; Corni, *Hitler's Ghettos*, 170–6; on epidemics and health controls, Paul Weindling, *Epidemics and Genocide in Eastern Europe, 1890–1945*, Oxford, 2000.

70. Janina David, *A Square of Sky: The Recollections of a Childhood*, London, 1964, 111–14; Szarota, *Warschau unter dem Hakenkreuz*, 107: even when the Germans authorised Jewish schools to reopen in the Warsaw ghetto in the autumn of 1941, only 5,200 Jewish children out 48,207 of school age had lessons. Walt Disney's *Snow White and the Seven Dwarfs* was the first of his full-length animated feature films, cost $1.5 million to make and set the standard for his later productions: it was released on 21 Dec. 1937.

71. David, *A Square of Sky*, 151–2; Katsh, *The Diary of Chaim Kaplan*, 220: 5 Nov. 1940; Berg, *Warsaw Ghetto*, 61: 20 May 1941.

72. David, *A Square of Sky*, 123 and 129–30.

73. Przybylska, *Journal de Wanda*, 57–8 and 108–34: 21 Jan. 1943 and 1–29 Aug. 1944.

74. Ibid., 18–26, 32, 35, 57–8, 62–5 and 89–90: 7–26 July, 6–7 and 10 Aug. 1942, 21 Jan., 1 and 18 Apr. 1943, 3 May and 2 July 1944.

75. Friedländer, *Nazi Germany and the Jews*, I, 216–19; Stefan, interview 29, in Engelking-Boni, *Holocaust and Memory*, 145; Emmanuel Ringelblum, *Polish–Jewish Relations during the Second World War*, Joseph Kermish and Shmuel Krakowski (eds), New York, 1976, 145–8; on 'statue to the unknown smuggler', see Szarota, *Warschau unter dem Hakenkreuz*, 122.

76. Madajczyk, *Die Okkupationspolitik Nazideutschlands*, 239–43 and 268–70; Heinemann, 'Rasse, Siedlung, deutsches Blut'.

77. Szarota, *Warschau unter dem Hakenkreuz*, 124.

78. Ibid., 241, citing anon., *A Polish Doctor, I Saw Poland Suffer*, 2nd edn, London, 1941, 63 and 67, and the diary of Ludwik Landau, 13 Feb. 1940; Adelson, *The Diary of Dawid Sierakowiak*, 128 n.; Dobroszycki, *The Chronicle of the Łódź Ghetto*, 136–8.

79. Advantages of the other, in Gross, *Polish Society under German Occupation*, 185–6 n. 3, citing 'Informacja: Z placówki rzymsko watykańskiej', PRM 45c/41, General Sikorski Historical Institute, London; Karski cited in Jan Gross, 'A Tangled Web: Confronting Stereotypes concerning Relations between Poles, Germans, Jews, and Communists' in István Deák, Jan Gross and Tony Judt (eds), *The Politics of Retribution in Europe: World War II and its Aftermath*, Princeton, NJ, 2000, 82–3; on this issue see also Gutman and Krakowski, *Unequal Victims*.

80. Shirli Gilbert's translation 'A Yid' from the Yiddish in Kaczerginski and Leivick, *Lider fun di getos un lagern*, 98–9. This song was originally written and performed in Polish, and translated into Yiddish after the war. Text and Music: Paulina Braun (d. in Majdanek, Nov. 1943).

81. Jacob Sloan (ed.), *Notes from the Warsaw Ghetto: The Journal of Emmanuel Ringelblum*, New York and London, 1958, 39: 9 May 1940.

Chapter 5

1. Adelson, *The Diary of Dawid Sierakowiak*, 105: 22 June 1941. David was nearly seventeen.

2. Adelson and Lapides, *Lódź Ghetto*, 487 and 494.

3. Adelson, *The Diary of Dawid Sierakowiak*, 105–6 and 108: 24 and 27 June and 1 July 1941.

4. Ibid., 112–13: 19 and 22 July 1941; and Eisig Silberschlag, *Saul Tschernichowsky: Poet of Revolt*, Ithaca, NY, 1968, 117.

5. Military campaign, Weinberg, *A World at Arms*, 264–81; Catholic bishops in Heinz Boberach (ed.), *Berichte des SD und der Gestapo über Kirchen und Kirchenvolk in Deutschland 1934–1944*, Mainz, 1971, 570–1; also Kershaw, *Hitler*, 2, 427; on broader conservative anti-Communism and support for *Lebensraum*, see Sontheimer, *Antidemokratisches Denken in der Weimarer Republik*; Mosse, *The Crisis of German Ideology*; Woodruff Smith, *The Ideological Origins of Nazi Imperialism*.

6. '"Sehr selten habe ich geweint": Ein Volksschullehrer in Russland' in Hammer and zur Niedern, *Sehr selten habe ich geweint*, 227–8: 23 and 25 June 1941.

7. Ibid., 228–9: 26 June 1941.

8. Ibid., 229–30: 28 June 1941.

9. Ibid., 231: 1 July 1941. Numbers captured, Weinberg, *A World at Arms*, 264–5; David M. Glantz and Jonathan House, *When Titans Clashed: How the Red Army Stopped Hitler*, Edinburgh, 1995, 28–41.

10. Christian Streit, *Keine Kameraden: Die Wehrmacht und die sowjetischen Kriegsgefangenen 1941–1945*, Stuttgart, 1978; Wildt, *Generation des Unbedingten*, 538–61; Longerich, *Politik der Vernichtung*, 293–320 and 405; Christian Gerlach, *Kalkulierte Morde: Die deutsche Wirtschafts- und Vernichtungspolitik in Weissrussland 1941 bis 1944*, Hamburg, 1999, 1060–74.

11. Ortwin Buchbender and Reinhold Sterz (eds), *Das andere Gesicht des Krieges*, Munich, 1982, letter 101, 72–3, cited in Omer Bartov, *Hitler's Army: Soldiers, Nazis and War in the Third Reich*, Oxford/New York, 1991, 153; Security Police, 10 July 1941 in Lacey, *Feminine Frequencies*, 128–9; Nazi propaganda did have some real Soviet atrocities to build upon: Bogdan Musial, *'Konterrevolutionäre Elemente sind zu erschiessen': Die Brutalisierung des deutsch-sowjetischen Krieges im Sommer 1941*, Berlin, 2000.

12. Ludwig Eiber (ed.), '". . . Ein bisschen die Wahrheit": Briefe eines Bremer Kaufmanns von seinem Einsatz beim Polizeibataillon 105 in der Sowjetunion 1941', 1999: *Zeitschrift für Sozialgeschichte des 20. und 21. Jahrhunderts*, 1/1991, 75–6: 3 July and 7 Sept. 1941. Deutsch-Russisches Museum Berlin-Karlshorst, *Mascha + Nina + Katjuscha: Frauen in der Roten Armee, 1941–1945*, Berlin, 2003, 32–3; Boberach, *Meldungen aus dem Reich*, 7, 2564: 24 July 1941.

13. Hammer and zur Niedern, *Sehr selten habe ich geweint*, 255–8: 27–28 Oct. 1941.

14. Ibid., 232–5 and 242–5: 1–2 July and 21–23 Aug. 1941.

15. Ibid., 242 and 265: 20 Aug. and 30 Nov. 1941.

16. Ibid., 267.

17. Eiber, '". . . Ein bisschen die Wahrheit"', 73: 7 Aug. 1941. See also workers' letters to colleagues in Alf Lüdtke, 'The Appeal of Exterminating "Others": German Workers and the Limits of Resistance' in Christian Leitz (ed.), *The Third Reich: The Essential Readings*, Oxford, 1999, 155–77.

18. For all the testimonies about Belaya Tserkov, see Ernst Klee, Willi Dressen and Volker Riess (eds), 'The Good Old Days': The Holocaust as Seen by Its Perpetrators and Bystanders, Old Saybrook, 1991, 138–54.

19. For materials on the massacre at Babi Yar, see ibid., 63–8; Oct. orders in Gerd Überschär and Wolfram Wette (eds), Der deutsche Überfall auf die Sowjetunion: 'Unternehmen Barbarossa' 1941, Paderborn, 1984, 339–40.

20. Following account drawn from Lev Abramovsky, interview with the Metropolitan Police War Crimes Unit, March 1995; I am grateful to Martin Dean for making this testimony available to me, part of which he published in his Collaboration in the Holocaust: Crimes of the Local Police in Belorussia and Ukraine, 1941–44, Basingstoke and London, 2000, 46–50; on Oswald Rufeisen and the break-out from Mir, see also Nechama Tec, In the Lion's Den: The Life of Oswald Rufeisen, New York, 1990, 146–8.

21. For the pogrom in Kovno/Kaunas, see Klee, Dressen and Riess, 'The Good Old Days', 23–45; nonetheless, the Einsatzgruppen were very active in leading the way in the Baltic States: Wildt, Generation des Unbedingten, 578–91; and Longerich, Politik der Vernichtung, 324–37. On the pogroms in eastern Poland, see Jan Tomasz Gross, Neighbors: The Destruction of the Jewish Community in Jedwabne, Poland, Princeton, NJ, 2001, and the Polish official commission's report, Instytut Pamieci Narodowej with Paweł Machcewicz and Krzysztof Persak (eds), Wokół Jedwabnego, Warsaw, 2002; Bogdan Musial has also stressed the extent to which Poles and Ukrainians were taking revenge on the Jews for their supposed involvement in Soviet repression: Musial, 'Konterrevolutionäre Elemente sind zu erschiessen': this interpretation, unfortunately, has also been taken up by those who wish to deny that Poles were responsible for the Jedwabne massacre; for a survey of this debate, see Antony Polonsky and Joanna Michlic (eds), The Neighbors Respond: The Controversy over the Jedwabne Massacre in Poland, Princeton, NJ, 2004. Pogroms also went hand in hand with the reassertion of strong nationalist movements in Central and Eastern Europe, and, compared with its Ukrainian or Polish neighbours, Belorussia had neither a strong nationalist movement, nor did it witness local pogroms: see Gerlach, Kalkulierte Morde, 536–7; Bernhard Chiari, Alltag hinter der Front: Besatzung, Kollaboration und Widerstand in Weissrußland 1941–1944, Düsseldorf, 1998, 245–9. On the occupied Ukraine, see Karel Berkhoff, Harvest of Despair: Life and Death in Ukraine under Nazi Rule, Cambridge, Mass., 2004.

22. Commander of Wehrmacht forces in White Ruthenia, 10 Nov. 1941 in Ernst Klee and Willi Dressen, 'Gott mit uns': Der deutsche Vernichtungskrieg im Osten, Frankfurt, 1989, 110; Chiari, Alltag hinter der Front, 252: 5 Aug. 1941, Ereignismeldung UdSSR, no. 43; Nechama Tec, Defiance: The Bielski Partisans, Oxford, 1993, 92.

23. Tec, Defiance, 41–2; Chiari, Alltag hinter der Front, 255–6; in the Lublin district this developed once more into conflicts between Polish and Ukrainian partisans: see Madajczyk, Die Okkupationspolitik Nazideutschlands, 300.

24. Chiari, Alltag hinter der Front, 200–1 and 256.

25. Ibid., 268–9; Rueben Ainsztein, Jüdischer Widerstand im deutschbesetzten Osteuropa während des Zweiten Weltkrieges, Oldenburg, 1995, 119–21.

26. Chiari, Alltag hinter der Front, 197–8; Tec, In the Lion's Den, 147–8 and her Defiance, 121 and 166–7.

27. Tec, Defiance, 81–9, 119–20, 138–9, 166–7 and 190–2; see Juliane Fürst,

'Heroes, Lovers, Victims – Partisan Girls during the Great Fatherland War', *Minerva: Quarterly Report on Women and the Military*, Fall/Winter 2000, 57–60.

28. Gerlach, *Kalkulierte Morde*, 679–83; Raul Hilberg, *Die Vernichtung der europäischen Juden: Die Gesamtgeschichte des Holocaust*, Berlin, 1982, 378, n. 324; Chiari, *Alltag hinter der Front*, 245 and 257–63; Hohenstein, *Wartheländisches Tagebuch*, 251; Gross, 'A Tangled Web', 88–91; Harvey, *Women and the Nazi East*, 241–4 and 255.

29. Goebbels, 'The Jews are to blame' in Noakes and Pridham, *Nazism*, 3, 515–6; Jürgen Hagemann, *Presselenkung im Dritten Reich*, Bonn, 1970, 146: Hitler may even have told Rosenberg not to speak about extermination in public: Hans-Heinrich Wilhelm, *Rassenpolitik und Kriegführung*, Passau, 1991, 131; Eberhard Jäckel, *Hitler in History*, Hanover, New Hamps., 1984, 55; for the poster, see Kershaw, *Hitler*, 2, plate 45, after 530; 30 Jan. 1939 speech, Hitler, *Reden und Proklamationen, 1932–1945*, 1057–8.

30. Wolfgang Diewerge (ed.) *Feldpostbriefe aus dem Osten: Deutsche Soldaten sehen die Sowjetunion*, Berlin, 1941, 38 and 44; on these and other letters, see Bartov, *Hitler's Army*, 153–69. On growing German knowledge, see Ian Kershaw, 'German Public Opinion during the "Final Solution": Information, Comprehension, Reactions' in Asher Cohen, Joav Gelber and Charlotte Wardi (eds), *Comprehending the Holocaust: Historical and Literary Research*, Frankfurt, 1988, 145–58; and esp. David Bankier, *The Germans and the Final Solution: Public Opinion under Nazism*, Oxford, 1992; for further letters, see Walter Manoschek (ed.), *'Es gibt nur eines für das Judentum: Vernichtung': Das Judenbild in deutschen Soldatenbriefen 1939–1944*, Hamburg, 1995.

31. Stadtarchiv München (ed.), *'Verzogen, unbekannt wohin': Die erste Deportation von Münchener Juden im November 1941*, Zurich, 2000; 'Einstellung der Bevölkerung zur Evakuierung der Juden', SD Aussenstelle Minden, 6 Dec. 1941., M18/11 Bestand: Preussische Regierung Minden/ SD Abschnitt Bielefeld, Nordrhein-Westfälisches Staatsarchiv Detmold, cited in Saul Friedländer, 'Mass Murder and German Society in the Third Reich: Interpretations and Dilemmas', Hayes Robinson Lecture Series no. 5, Royal Holloway, University of London, 2001, 15: very few such local reports seem to have survived the war, and they were consistently excluded from the general weekly reports on public opinion compiled by the Security Police.

32. Liselotte G. in Hammer and zur Niedern, *Sehr selten habe ich geweint*, 278–9: 31 Aug. 1943; Christa J. interview, in Prenzlauer Berg Museum des Kulturamtes Berlin and Annett Gröschner (ed.), *Ich schlug meiner Mutter die brennenden Funken ab: Berliner Schulaufsätze aus dem Jahr 1946*, Berlin, 1996, 356.

33. Lange and Burkard, *'Abends wenn wir essen fehlt uns immer einer'*, 136: Gisela's father, 11 Oct. 1942.

34. Ibid., 209: Ingeborg's father, 19 July 1943, 74–7, and 79–81: 7 and 28 Sept. 1941, and 8 Oct. 1941; Bartov, *Hitler's Army*, 153–63.

35. Lange and Burkard, *'Abends wenn wir essen fehlt uns immer einer'*, 208 and 211–12: 23 May 1943, 5 Dec. 1943 and 26 Jan. 1944.

36. Ibid., 146; Gertrud to father, 12 Sept. 1941.

37. In Sept. 1942, Hitler had apparently also proposed that 400,000 to 500,000 Ukrainian peasant girls should be brought to Germany as domestic servants

in order to 'Germanise' them and boost the national birth rate, but there is no evidence that this idea affected the actual deployment of such girls. See Madajczyk, *Die Okkupationspolitik Nazideutschlands*, 472–3; Mendel, *Zwangsarbeit im Kinderzimmer*, 149 and 156–7.

38. Mendel, *Zwangsarbeit im Kinderzimmer*, 11, 20, 22, 59, 109–10, 144–5, 166, 173–86; Valentina in Susanne Kraatz (ed.), *Verschleppt und Vergessen: Schicksale jugendlicher 'Ostarbeiterinnen' von der Krim im Zweiten Weltkrieg und danach*, Heidelberg, 1995, 143.

39. Mendel, *Zwangsarbeit im Kinderzimmer*, 173–86.

40. Lutz Niethammer, *Ego-Histoire? Und andere Erinnerungs-Versuche*, Vienna and Cologne, 2002, 186–7.

41. Uwe Timm, *Am Beispiel meines Bruders*, Cologne, 2003, 19, 57–8 and 91–2: Karl-Heinz's diary, 21 Mar. 1943, and letters to Uwe, 22 July and to parents, 25 July 1943; Victor Klemperer, *To the Bitter End: The Diaries of Victor Klemperer*, 2, London, 1999, 293: 2 Apr. 1944.

42. Interview with Gertrud L., in Dörr, 'Wer die Zeit nicht miterlebt hat . . .', 2, 219–20.

43. Ibid., 220.

44. DLA, Yvonne H.-R., b. 1931, 'Lebensgeschichte', 7–8; Liselotte G., in Hammer and zur Niedern, *Sehr selten habe ich geweint*, 277–8: 20 Mar. 1943.

45. Lacey, *Feminine Frequencies*, 129–34.

46. Ibid., 134 and 205–6.

47. Chiari, *Alltag hinter der Front*, 257–61; Gerlach, *Kalkulierte Morde*, 46ff, 276–92 and 668–83, and his *Krieg, Ernährung, Völkermord: Forschungen zur deutschen Vernichtungspolitik im Zweiten Weltkrieg*, Hamburg, 1998, 15–16; in the Białystok district of Poland, the German practice was much the same: see Madajczyk, *Die Okkupationspolitik Nazideutschlands*, 300, citing Kazimierz Wyka, *Życie na niby: Szkice z lat 1939–1945*, Warsaw, 1957, 129ff.; and Gross, 'A Tangled Web', 87–92.

48. On living off the land, Bartov, *Hitler's Army*, 130–5; packets home, Eiber, '". . . Ein bisschen die Wahrheit"', 71–3 and 75–6: 20 July 1941 and 7 Sept. 1941; and see also letters of Karl Kretschmer, 27 Sept.–19 Oct. 1942 in Klee, Dressen and Riess, 'The Good Old Days', 163–71.

49. Szarota, *Warschau unter dem Hakenkreuz*, 147–8; David, *A Square of Sky*, 161; Hohenstein, *Wartheländisches Tagebuch*, 212–13: 11 Nov. 1941.

50. Cinema audiences, Steinert, *Hitlers Krieg und die Deutschen*, 211; deaths of prisoners of war, Christian Streit, *Keine Kameraden*; temporary fall in civilian rations, Noakes, *Nazism*, 4, 514–18: but German rations did not drop below 2,000 calories until the spring of 1945.

51. On Poland, Madajczyk, *Die Okkupationspolitik Nazideutschlands*, 255–8, 268–70 and 283–7; on Belorussia, Gerlach, *Kalkulierte Morde*, 276–92; effect of agricultural levies in Eastern Europe, Kaser and Radice, *The Economic History of Eastern Europe*, 2, 371–81 and 393–7; on France, Robert Gildea, *Marianne in Chains: In Search of the German Occupation, 1940–45*, London, 2003, 109–33.

52. Adelson, *The Diary of Dawid Sierakowiak*, 112–43: esp. 19 and 29 July, 8, 24 and 31 Aug., 26 Sept., 6, 9, 12–23 Oct. 1941; Avraham Barkai, 'Between East and West: Jews from Germany in the Łódź Ghetto', *Yad Vashem Studies*, 16, 1984, 275; Sinti and Roma camp, Dobroszycki, *The Chronicle of the*

Łódź Ghetto, 80–103: Nov. and Dec. 1941; Adleson and Lapides, *Łódź Ghetto*, 172–92; Corni, *Hitler's Ghettos*, 179–85.

53. Georg Lilienthal, *Der 'Lebensborn e.V.': Ein Instrument nationalsozialistischer Rassenpolitik*, Frankfurt, 1993, 219–21, citing Himmler's orders to Lorenz and Heydrich of 11 July 1941, and speech of 16 Sept. 1942; Pflaum's report is from 19 July 1942; on the 'tit for tat' link between the deportation of the Volga Germans and the German Jews, see Mark Roseman, *The Villa, the Lake, the Meeting: Wannsee and the Final Solution*, London, 2002, 41.

54. Lilienthal, *Der 'Lebensborn e.V.'*, 209 n. 52 and 215; Czesław Madajczyk (ed.), *Zamojszczyzna – Sonderlaboratorium SS: Zbiór dokumentów polskich i niemieckich z okresu okupacji hitlerowskiej*, 2, Warsaw, 1977, 1, 14, and 2, 9, 95–7 and 189–91; and Madajczyk, *Die Okkupationspolitik Nazideutschlands*, 422–9 and 531.

55. Chiari, *Alltag hinter der Front*, 197–8; Clarissa Henry and Marc Hillel, *Children of the SS*, Hutchinson, 1976, 239–40; Lilienthal, *Der 'Lebensborn e.V.'*, 212–15; Hrabar, Tokarz and Wilczur, *Kinder im Krieg*, 232–3; Roman Hrabar, *Hitlerowski rabunek dzieci polskich: Uprowadzenie i germanizacja dzieci polskich w latach 1939–1945*, Katowice, 1960; Sosnowski, *The Tragedy of Children under Nazi Rule*, annex 15.

56. Sosnowski, *The Tragedy of Children*, annexe 22, 306–7; Lilienthal, *Der 'Lebensborn e.V.'*, 216; 'die gut rassigen Kinder': Himmler to Sollmann, 21 June 1943 in Helmut Heiber (ed.), *Reichsführer! . . . Briefe an und von Himmler*, Stuttgart, 1968, 214; Hrabar, Tokarz and Wilczur, *Kinder im Krieg*, 87; Michael Leapman, *Witnesses to War: Eight True-Life Stories of Nazi Persecution*, London, 2000, 106.

57. Macardle, *Children of Europe*, 235–6 and 238–40.

58. Henryk Tycner, 'Grupa doktora Franciszka Witaszka' in *Przegląd Lekarski*, no. 1, 1967, cited in Madajczyk, *Die Okkupationspolitik Nazideutschlands*, 473 n. 56; see also the interview account in Catrine Clay and Michael Leapman, *Master Race: The Lebensborn Experiment in Nazi Germany*, London 1995, 115–17.

59. Clay and Leapman, *Master Race*, 119–23 for a fascinating interview account. As in many interviews, the interviewee makes mistakes with dates and Michelowski cannot have arrived in Oberweis before it opened in September 1943; nor was the camp run by 'SS guards', although it probably felt like that: Lilienthal, *Der 'Lebensborn e.V.'*, 211 and 57.

60. KA 2073, Ilse-W. P., 'KLV-Tagebuch', 25 Oct. 1941.

61. Ibid., 16 and 22 June 1941.

62. Teenage civilian deaths in the First World War, Jay Winter and Jean-Louis Robert (eds), *Capital Cities at War: Paris, London, Berlin 1914–1919*, Cambridge, 1997, 487–523; also Avner Offer, *The First World War: An Agrarian Interpretation*, Oxford, 1989.

Chapter 6

1. 'Jäger Report' in Klee, Dressen and Riess, *'The Good Old Days'*, 46–58; Christian Gerlach, 'Die Wannsee-Konferenz, das Schicksal der deutschen Juden und Hitlers politische Grundsatzentscheidung, alle Juden Europas zu ermorden', *Werkstattgeschichte*, 18, 1997, 7–44; Longerich, *Politik der Vernichtung*, 419–72; Roseman, *The Villa, the Lake, the Meeting*; Christopher

Browning, 'Nazi Policy: Decisions for the Final Solution' in his *Nazi Policy, Jewish Workers, German Killers*, Cambridge, 2000, 26–57.

2. Goebbels, *Tagebücher*, 2.2: 13 Dec. 1941; Gerlach, 'Die Wannsee-Konferenz', 25; Hitler, *Reden und Proklamationen, 1932–1945*, 1057–8 and 1663; Kershaw, *The 'Hitler Myth'*, 243–4.

3. Frank, cited in Gerlach, *Krieg, Ernährung, Völkermord*, 122; Roseman, *The Villa, the Lake, the Meeting*, 44–8; on the 'Operation Reinhard' death camps, see Yitzhak Arad, *Belzec, Sobibor, Treblinka: The Operation Reinhard Death Camps*, Bloomington, 1987.

4. Roseman, *The Villa, the Lake, the Meeting*, 50, 84 and 112.

5. Adelson, *The Diary of Dawid Sierakowiak*, 131, 135 and 138: 24 and 30 Sept., and 10 Oct. 1941; Dobroszycki, *The Chronicle of the Lódź Ghetto*, 244: 28 Aug. 1942; Corni, *Hitler's Ghettos*, 177–8.

6. Yitzhak Arad, *Ghetto in Flames: The Struggle and Destruction of the Jews in Vilna in the Holocaust*, New York, 1982, 101–19.

7. Translation by Shirli Gilbert of 'Es iz geven a zumer-tog', text by Rikle Glezer, music based on Yiddish theatre song 'Papirosn' (Cigarettes), composed by Herman Yablokoff, Yiddish version in Kaczerginski and Leivick, *Lider fun di getos un lagern*, 7–8.

8. See Shirli Gilbert, 'Music in the Nazi Ghettos and Camps (1939–45)', D. Phil. thesis, Oxford, 2002, chapter 2, for a fascinating account of musical life in the Vilna ghetto; on the shootings at Ponar, see Hermann Kruk, *The Last Days of the Jerusalem of Lithuania: Chronicle from the Vilna Ghetto and the Camps, 1939–1944*, Benjamin Harshav (ed.), New Haven and London, 2002, 88–93: 4 Sept. 1941; Arad, *Ghetto in Flames*, 75–7 and 149–58; Klee, Dressen and Riess, *'The Good Old Days'*, 38–45; Yitskhok Rudashevski, *The Diary of the Vilna Ghetto: June 1941–April 1943*, Tel Aviv, 1973, 43–6.

9. Marc Dvorjetski, 'Adjustment of Detainees to Camp and Ghetto Life and Their Subsequent Readjustment to Normal Society', *Yad Vashem Studies*, 5, 1963, 198; see also Eisen, *Children and Play in the Holocaust*, 76–8; on Bruno Kittel, see Arad, *Ghetto in Flames*, 368.

10. Rudashevski, *The Diary of the Vilna Ghetto*, 113: 28 Dec. 1942; 115–16: 1 Jan. 1943; see also 99: 26 Nov. 1942; 126–7: 27 Jan. 1943, visits the ghetto furniture workshop and finds that the adult workers keep the children in line by threatening them with 'Dear Children, Murer will come and make a fuss'; Arad, *Ghetto in Flames*, 304–5; Eisen, *Children and Play in the Holocaust*, 77: based on testimony of Tzvia Kuretzka.

11. Donald Niewyk (ed.), *Fresh Wounds: Early Narratives of Holocaust Survival*, Chapel Hill, 1998, 176; Adelson, *The Diary of Dawid Sierakowiak*, 142, 161–2 and 258: 19 Oct. 1941, 1–2 May 1942 and 15 Mar 1943; Corni, *Hitler's Ghettos*, 179–82; on ignorance and knowledge within the ghettos during Mar.–Aug. 1942, see Arad, *Belzec, Sobibor, Treblinka*, 241–4.

12. Dobroszycki, *Chronicle of the Lodz Ghetto*, xxiii–xxv, xxxiv–xxxvi, 128 and 133; Hilberg, *Destruction of the European Jews*, 205–214; anon. girl in Zapruder, *Salvaged Pages*, 227–9 and 231–8: 27 Feb.–12 Mar. 1942, 231–8.

13. Adelson, *The Diary of Dawid Sierakowiak*, 212 and 218–20: 1 and 5 Sept. 1942; see also Dobroszycki, *Chronicle of the Lodz Ghetto*, 248–52, and Zelkowicz, 'In these nightmarish days' in Adelson and Lapides, *Lódź Ghetto*, 320–8 and 336–47.

14. Adelson, *The Diary of Dawid Sierakowiak*, 226 and 221: 6 Sept. 1942.

15. Adelson and Lapides, *Lódź Ghetto*, 328–31.

16. Recounted by Ettie's nurse, in Sheva Glas-Wiener, *Children of the Ghetto*, Melbourne, 1983, 86; also cited in Eisen, *Children and Play in the Holocaust*, 76.

17. Berg, *Warsaw Ghetto*, 68–9: 12 June 1941.

18. Janusz Korczak, *Ghetto Diary*, New Haven and London, 1978, 55–6: 29 May 1942.

19. Betty Lifton, *The King of Children: The Life and Death of Janusz Korczak*, New York, 1988, esp. 56–64 and 286–98.

20. Ibid., 295–7 and 308.

21. Ibid., 300–5.

22. Ibid., 301–3; Korczak, *Ghetto Diary*, 65, 76 and 84–5: n.d.

23. Hilberg, Staron and Kermisz, *The Warsaw Diary of Adam Czerniakow*, 352–3: 10 and 14 May 1942.

24. Ibid., 363–4: 7 June 1942; Lifton, *The King of Children*, 311–12.

25. Hilberg, Staron and Kermisz, *The Warsaw Diary of Adam Czerniakow*, 374: 5 and 12 July 1942.

26. Ibid., introduction, 61 and 376–7: 8 July 1942.

27. Katsh, *The Diary of Chaim Kaplan*, 375–6: 16 July 1942; Hilberg, Staron and Kermisz, *The Warsaw Diary of Adam Czerniakow*, 381–3: 16–20 July 1942; Berg, *Warsaw Diary*, 159: 16 July 1942.

28. Hilberg, Staron and Kermisz, *The Warsaw Diary of Adam Czerniakow*, introduction, 63–4.

29. Katsh, *The Diary of Chaim Kaplan*, 360, 369–72 and 379: 25 June, 10–12 and 22 July 1942. On 17 June, Emmanuel Ringelblum had also heard news of the mass gassings and was unsure how to make sense of them: see, Hilberg, Staron and Kermisz, *The Warsaw Diary of Adam Czerniakow*, introduction, 62.

30. Cited in Nora Levin, *The Holocaust: The Destruction of European Jewry, 1933–1945*, New York, 1968, 324–5.

31. For the following account, Lifton, *The King of Children*, 323–4, 338–45 and 348.

32. Ibid., 106–11.

33. David, *A Square of Sky*, 184–6; on work brigades outside the ghetto in this period, Paulsson, *Secret City*, 65–6.

34. Ibid., 79 and further details in his 'Hiding in Warsaw: The Jews on the "Aryan Side" in the Polish Capital, 1940–1945', D. Phil. thesis, Oxford, 1998, 278; Berg, *Warsaw Diary*, 208–10: 17 Dec. 1942.

35. Translated by Shirli Gilbert from the Yiddish, 'Shlof, mayn kind', music and text by M. Shenker, in Kaczerginski and Leivick, *Lider fun di getos un lagern*, 236.

36. Madajczyk, *Die Okkupationspolitik Nazideutschlands*, 254 and 257; Paulsson, *Secret City*, 73–4.

37. Paulsson, *Secret City*, 80–2.

38. Ibid., 53–73.

39. David, *A Square of Sky*, 214–22.

40. Ringelblum, *Polish–Jewish Relations*, 144–5; Paulsson, *Secret City*, 105–11; Nelly S. Toll, *Behind the Secret Window: A Memoir of a Hidden Childhood During World War Two*, New York, 1993, 32–41; see also YVA 0.33 1374 for her MS memoir.

41. Janina David, *A Touch of Earth: A Wartime Childhood*, London, 1966, 8–9; Paulsson, *Secret City*, 49–53.

42. Ringelblum, *Polish–Jewish Relations*, 140–4.

43. Toll, *Behind the Secret Window*, 79–97 and 102.

44. Ibid., 126.

45. See testimonies of Regina Rück, b. 15 July 1935; Maria Kopel, b. 1932; Izak Klajman, b. 10 June 1934; and Dawid Wulf, b. 23 Nov. 1936 in Maria Hochberg-Mariańska and Noe Grüss (eds), *The Children Accuse*, London, 1996, 85, 122, 130 and 171–9; Eisen, *Children and Play in the Holocaust*, 75.

46. Zygmunt Klukowski, diary for 4 Nov. 1942, cited in Gross, 'A Tangled Web', 91 and see 87–92; testimony of Irena Schnitzer, b. 1938; and Fryda Koch, b. 12 Sept. 1932 in Hochberg-Mariańska and Grüss, *The Children Accuse*, 98 and 22; rumours of extermination plans during the Zamość clearances, Madajczyk, *Die Okkupationspolitik Nazideutschlands*, 427, and Dr Wilhelm Hagen to Adolf Hitler, 7 Dec. 1942 in Sosnowski, *The Tragedy of Children*, annexe 29A, 317–20.

47. Przybylska, *Journal de Wanda*, 28–9, 40–1: 1, 17 and 21 Aug. 1942.

48. Izak Klajman, in Hochberg-Mariańska and Grüss, *The Children Accuse*, 127–31; discussed in Gross, 'A Tangled Web', 84; see also testimony of Leon Majblum, b. 14 Dec. 1930; and Fryda Koch, in Hochberg-Mariańska and Grüss, *The Children Accuse*, 26 and 91–2.

49. See the fascinating analysis of this network in Paulsson, *Secret City*, 44–54 and chapter 4; and Bernward Dörner, 'Justiz und Judenmord: Todesurteile gegen Judenhelfer in Polen und der Tschechoslowakei 1942–1944' in Norbert Frei, Sybille Steinbacher and Bernd Wagner (eds), *Ausbeutung, Vernichtung, Öffentlichkeit: Neue Studien zur nationalsozialistischen Lagerpolitik*, Munich, 2000, 249–63.

50. Przybylska, *Journal de Wanda*, 59–62: 24 Feb., 11 and 29 Mar. and 23 June 1943.

51. Joseph Ziemian, *The Cigarette Sellers of Three Crosses Square*, London, 1970, 10–29; Paulsson, *Secret City*, 125–6; see also notes in Władysław Bartoszewski and Zofia Lewin (eds), *Righteous among Nations: How Poles Helped the Jews, 1939–45*, London, 1969, 420–1.

52. Ziemian, *The Cigarette Sellers of Three Crosses Square*, 77 and 80–2.

53. Ibid., 69–70, 149, 63–5, 130–1 and 19–21.

54. Paulsson, *Secret City*, 101–4.

55. Numbers and finance, Paulsson, *Secret City*, 206–10; Bartoszewski and Lewin, *Righteous among Nations*, 420.

56. David, *A Touch of Earth*, 11 and 18–25.

57. Ibid., 24–25 and 15–17; Janina David, *A Square of Sky*, 132.

58. Testimony of Zygmunt Weinreb, b. 26 Nov. 1935, in Hochberg-Mariańska and Grüss, *The Children Accuse*, 114.

59. David, *A Touch of Earth*, 27–104.

60. Paulsson, *Secret City*, 87–8, citing Ringelblum's diary for 14 Dec. 1942; Ringelblum, *Polish–Jewish Relations*, 150–1, a posthumously edited account, puts a different gloss on the failure of this attempted rescue, putting the onus on the Church, whereas the diary entry suggests that it was the Jewish side which rejected the offer. For Jewish children's attraction to the figure of the Virgin Mary, see David, *A Touch of Earth*, 120–2; Saul Friedländer, *When*

Memory Comes, New York, 1979, 120–2; and see Sue Vice, *Children Writing the Holocaust*, London, 2004, 81–100.

Chapter 7

1. Yehuda Bacon, or Juda Bakon, b. 28 July 1929, deported Mährisch-Ostrau to Theresienstadt, 26 Sept. 1942, and deported to Auschwitz-Birkenau, 15 Dec. 1943: see Miroslav Kárný et al. (eds), *Terezínská Pamětní Kniha*, 2, Prague, 1995, 971; YVA 0.3 1202, Yehuda Bacon interviews with Chaim Mass, Jerusalem, 13 Feb. 1959, 13–14 and DöW 13243 with Ben-David Gershon, Jerusalem, 17 Nov. 1964, 29–30; Saul Friedman (ed.), *The Terezin Diary of Gonda Redlich*, Lexington, Kentucky, 1992, 137–8: 19 Dec. 1943; Miroslav Kárný, 'The Genocide of the Czech Jews' in Miroslav Kárný et al., *Terezín Memorial Book: Jewish Victims of Nazi Deportations from Bohemia and Moravia 1941–1945: A Guide to the Czech Original with a Glossary of Czech Terms Used in the Lists*, Prague, 1996, 69–70, and his 'Das Theresienstädter Familienlager in Birkenau', *Judaica Bohemiae*, 15/1, 1979, 3–26.

2. DöW 13243, Bacon, interview with Ben-David Gershon, Jerusalem, 17 Nov. 1964, 17, 24, 68. There is a large literature on Theresienstadt: see Hans Günther Adler, *Theresienstadt, 1941–1945: Das Antlitz einer Zwangsgemeinschaft* (2nd edn), Tübingen, 1960; Miroslav Kárný, Vojtěch Blodig and Margita Kárná (eds), *Theresienstadt in der 'Endlösung der Judenfrage'*, Prague, 1992; Miroslav Kárný and Margita Kárná, 'Kinder in Theresienstadt', *Dachauer Hefte*, 9, 1993, 14–31; on the Theresienstadt artists, see Leo Haas, 'The Affair of the Painters of Terezín' in Massachusetts College of Arts (ed.), *Seeing through 'Paradise': Artists and the Terezín Concentration Camp*, Boston, 1991; Gerald Green, *The Artists of Terezín*, New York, 1978; Památník Terezín (ed.), *Leo Haas*, Terezín, 1969; also Památník Terezín (ed.), *Arts in Terezín, 1941–1945*, Terezín, 1973; Wolf Wagner, *Der Hölle entronnen: Stationen eines Lebens: Eine Biographie des Malers und Graphikers Leo Haas*, Berlin, 1987; Karl Braun, 'Peter Kien oder Ästhetik als Widerstand' in Miroslav Kárný, Raimund Kemper and Margita Kárná (eds), *Theresienstädter Studien und Dokumente*, Prague, 1995, 155–74; on musical life and children, see Wiener Library, K4H, Theresienstadt, Alice Herz-Sommer MS, 'A Memoir'; Victor Ullmann wrote two appreciations of her performances: see Victor Ullmann, *26 Kritiken über musikalische Veranstaltungen in Theresienstadt*, Hamburg, 1993, 61, 84; Joža Karas, *Music in Terezín, 1941–1945*, New York, 1985; JMPTC, 318, for material on cabarets and the children's opera *Brundibar*; JMPTC, 326/67c, for text and music of Carlo and Erika Taube, 'Ein jüdisches Kind'; JMPTC, 326/87b, Erika Taube, 'Theresienstädter Skizzenbuch: Gedanken im Ghetto'; Ilse Weber's poetry has been published as Ilse Weber, *In deinen Mauern wohnt das Leid: Gedichte aus dem KZ Theresienstadt*, Gerlingen, 1991. See JMPTC, 305, for the festival programme of the German home L 414, 4–8 Sept. 1943. See also the published collection of songs and satires in Ulrike Migdal, *Und die Musik spielt dazu: Chansons und Satirien aus dem KZ Theresienstadt*, Munich, 1986.

3. Kárný, 'The Genocide of the Czech Jews', 40–4.

4. Ibid., 49–58; Adler, *Theresienstadt*, 299–300 and 720–2. The average age of death never fell below sixty-three; after Jan. 1942, and for most of the time, it was over seventy: ibid., 527. Aggregate demographic statistics are as

follows: 141,184 people were deported to Theresienstadt; 33,456 died there; 88,202 were deported further (mostly to their deaths in Auschwitz-Birkenau); 1,654 were released prior to liberation; 464 escaped; 276 were arrested (mostly killed in the small fortress); and there were 16,832 survivors on liberation.

5. Kárný, 'The Genocide of the Czech Jews', 54–8; Roseman, *The Villa, the Lake, the Meeting*, appendix, 113; Anita Franková, 'Die Struktur der aus dem Ghetto Theresienstadt zusammengestellten Transporte (1942–1944)', *Judaica Bohemiae*, 25/2, 1989, 63–81.

6. Kárný, 'The Genocide of the Czech Jews', 64–8 and 73–4; Wildt, *Generation des Unbedingten*, 718–24; and for an account based on British and US intelligence which plays up the role of Himmler's masseur, Felix Kersten, see John Waller, *The Devil's Doctor: Felix Kersten and the Secret Plot to Turn Himmler against Hitler*, New York, 2002.

7. Kárný, 'The Genocide of the Czech Jews', 66, 70–1 and 74–5.

8. Heinrich Himmler, *Die Geheimreden 1933 bis 1945*, Bradley Smith and Agnes Peterson (eds), Frankfurt, 1974, 162–83 and 202–5: speeches to *Reich-* and *Gauleiter* at Posen, 6 Oct. 1943 and to the generals at Sonthofen, 5 and 24 May and 21 June 1944; Wildt, *Generation des Unbedingten*, 712–18; Randolph Braham, *The Politics of Genocide: The Holocaust in Hungary*, New York, 1994; Hans Safrian, *Die Eichmann-Männer*, Vienna, 1993; Christian Gerlach and Götz Aly, *Das letzte Kapitel: Der Mord an den ungarischen Juden 1944–1945*, Frankfurt, 2004; on the Slovak rising, see John Erickson, *The Road to Berlin: Stalin's War with Germany*, 2, London, 1983, 290–307; Richard Breitman, 'A Deal with the Nazi Dictatorship? Himmler's Alleged Peace Emissaries in Autumn 1943', *Journal of Contemporary History*, 30, 1995, 411–30; Masur in Leni Yahil, *The Holocaust: The Fate of European Jewry, 1932–1945*, Oxford, 1990, 545.

9. JMPTC, 304, Albert Fischer MS, report on the first year of L417, the Czech boys' home; Marie Rút Křížková, Kurt Jiří Kotouč and Zdeněk Ornest (eds), *We Are Children Just the Same:* Vedem, *the Secret Magazine of the Boys of Terezín*, Philadelphia, 1995, 51–2; Friedman, *The Terezin Diary of Gonda Redlich*, 5 and 7: 9 and 14 Jan. 1942; for Czerniakow's belated attempts to allocate special rations to children, see Hilberg, Staron and Kermisz, *The Warsaw Diary of Adam Czerniakow*, 362 and 267–9: 2, 15 and 22 June 1942, but in practice, children in the orphanages were kept on starvation rations, while the administrators made generous allocations to themselves: Ringelblum, *Polish–Jewish Relations*, 210; in Łódź, Rumkowski did periodically issue ration supplements to children: e.g., Adelson, *The Diary of Dawid Sierakowiak*, 115: 27 July 1942, and Adelson and Lapides, *Łódź Ghetto*, 30–1.

10. See Adler, *Theresienstadt*, 315; as late as 20 March 1945 a new children's home was established by order of the SS to impress Red Cross inspectors that nothing had changed since their previous visit in the summer of 1944: Hans Günther Adler, *Die verheimlichte Wahrheit: Theresienstädter Dokumente*, Tübingen, 1958, 222–4. Willy Groag became the head of this home and the last head of the *Jugendfürsorge* in Theresienstadt: see JMPTC, 343, 88–9, Willy Groag interview with Ben-David Gershon, Kibbutz Maanith, 17 Oct. 1965.

11. Yehuda Bacon, 'Můj život v Terezíně' ('My Life in Terezín'), MS, Jerusalem, 1947, cited in German translation in Alder, *Theresienstadt*, 553. The teachers

even issued certificates and diplomas: Jacob Jacobson and David Cohen, *Terezín: The Daily Life, 1943–45*, London, 1946.

12. Helga Pollak, diary entry for 6 May 1943, in František Ehrmann (ed.), *Terezin*, Prague, 1965, 103. Two autobiographical poems by German boys (both with Jewish fathers) survive on the plight of the *Mischlinge*: JMPTC, 325, anon.; and especially the diaries of Eva Ginzová and Petr Ginz, in Zapruder, *Salvaged Pages*, 160–89. On friendships, see also Ruth Klüger, *Weiter Leben: Eine Jugend*, Göttingen, 1992, 88–90 and 102: she even thought that the close emotional ties she developed in Theresienstadt cured her of the nervous ticks which she put down to her solitary childhood in Vienna. Zdeněk Ohrenstein (Ornest) and Hanus Hachenburg, two of the contributors to *Vedem*, also became very close friends from their time in the Prague orphanage until they were separated by deportation from Theresienstadt: Křížková, Kotouč and Ornest, *We Are Children Just the Same*, 113. On Christian worship in Theresienstadt, see Clara Eisenkraft, *Damals in Theresienstadt: Erlebnisse einer Judenchristin*, Wuppertal, 1977, 48–54; also Stadtarchiv Munich, Familiennachlass 672/2, Karin Vriesländer MS, 'K.-Z. Theresienstadt'.

13. On Eisinger, see Křížková, Kotouč and Ornest, *We Are Children Just the Same*, 40. The Jews of the ghetto were ordered not to doff their hats any longer in preparation for the inspection visit of the International Red Cross in 1944; Helga Pollak interview, in Debórah Dwork, *Children with a Star: Jewish Youth in Nazi Europe*, New Haven, 1991, 128; M. Kryl, 'Das Tagebuch Egon Redlichs' in Kárný, Blodig and Kárná, *Theresienstadt in der 'Endlösung der Judenfrage'*, 152–3. In general, see Nili Keren, 'Ein pädagogisches Poem', in ibid., 157–8; Ruth Bondy, *'Elder of the Jews': Jakob Edelstein of Theresienstadt*, New York, 1989.

14. Bacon, 'Můj život v Terezíně', in Adler, *Theresienstadt*, 552, and YVA 0.3 1202, Bacon interview with Chaim Mass, Jerusalem, 13 Feb. 1959, 14; Křížková, Kotouč and Ornest, *We Are Children Just the Same*, 35 and 160–1; for the diaries of Petr Ginz and his sister Eva as well as a short biographical sketch, see Zapruder, *Salvaged Pages*, 160–89; on conflicts between Germans and Czechs, as well as between Czech- and German-speakers from the 'Protectorate': Ruth Schwertfeger, *Women of Theresienstadt*, New York, 1989, 33–8; the Czech children, even from the more German-orientated communities of Prague and Brno, would have mostly been educated in Czech by the early 1930s: Adler, *Theresienstadt*, 302–3; Hillel J. Kieval, *The Making of Czech Jewry: National Conflict and Jewish Society in Bohemia, 1870–1918*, New York, 1988, 40–6. 'Shkid' was an acronym for Shkola Imeni Dostoyevskovo (Dostoevsky School), a secret kept by the boys and based on the title of one of Eisinger's favourite books, an account of the Petrograd original by two of the boys who had belonged to it.

15. On Friedl Dicker-Brandeis's work, see especially the outstanding exhibition catalogues of Elena Makarova, *From Bauhaus to Terezin: Friedl Dicker-Brandeis and Her Pupils*, Jerusalem, 1990; Stadt Frankfurt, *Vom Bauhaus nach Terezin: Friedl Dicker-Brandeis und die Kinderzeichnungen aus dem Ghetto-Lager Theresienstadt*, Frankfurt, 1991; see also Edith Kramer, 'Erinnerungen an Friedl Dicker-Brandeis', *Mit der Zieharmonika* (special issue, *Zeitschrift der Theodor-Kramer-Gesellschaft*, 3, Sept. 1988), 1–2. Vilem Benda's memoirs are in JMPTC, 343/5; YVA and DöW, Elena Makarova

MS, 1990, 'From Bauhaus to Terezín: Friedl Dicker-Brandeis and her Pupils'; State Jewish Museum in Prague (ed.), *Friedl Dicker-Brandeis, 1898–1944*, Prague, 1988; on the children's art, see Nicholas Stargardt, 'Children's Art of the Holocaust', *Past and Present*, 161, 1998, 192–235.

16. Inge Auerbacher, *I Am a Star: Child of the Holocaust*, New York, 1986, 47.

17. JMPTC, 129.702, Věra Würzelová: b. 10 Dec. 1930; deported to Theresienstadt 13 Aug. 1943; survived; pencil; JMPTC, 129.204, Liliane Franklová: b. 12 Jan. 1931; deported from Brno to Theresienstadt 15 Dec. 1941; deported to Auschwitz 19 Oct. 1944; pencil. The seashore would have had fairy-tale connotations for children growing up in a landlocked country; so, in Ruth Klaubaufová's drawing of a house and garden, the children play just outside the garden fence on the seashore: JMPTC, 129.013.

18. Norbert Troller, *Theresienstadt: Hitler's Gift to the Jews*, Chapel Hill, 1991, 93–5, 119–21, 133; Adler, *Theresienstadt*, 368–77.

19. On the discussion within the Council of Elders over whether to care for the young or the old, see JMPTC, Memories, 343/97, Zeev Scheck, 'Kinder in Theresienstadt: Jugendfürsorge des Ältestenrates', MS; Kárný, 'The Genocide of the Czech Jews', 54–8 and 68.

20. Troller, *Theresienstadt*, 94; Adler, *Theresienstadt*, 299–300. For a collection of women's fantasy recipes, see Cara De Silva (ed.), *In Memory's Kitchen: A Legacy from the Women of Terezín*, Northvale, 1996; also, in general, Elie Cohen, *Human Behaviour in the Concentration Camp*, London, 1988, 131–40.

21. Martha Glass, *'Jeder Tag in Theresin ist ein Geschenk': Die Theresienstädter Tagebücher einer Hamburger Jüdin 1943–1945*, Barbara Müller-Wesemann (ed.), Hamburg, 1996.

22. YVA 0.3 1202, Bacon interview with Chaim Mass, Jerusalem, 13 Feb. 1959, 16. Anna Kovanicová (later Hyndráková), who was fourteen when she was deported to Theresienstadt and entered the Czech girls home, affirms that what made the homes 'the best thing Terezín could have provided for us in the ghetto environment' was that 'we young people lived together without closer contact with the old, sick and wretched': Anita Franková, Anna Hyndráková, Věra Hájková and Františka Faktorová, *The World without Human Dimensions: Four Women's Memories*, Prague, 1991, 157; for children outside the homes, see the anonymous girl's account of staying in her grandmother's room, cited in Adler, *Theresienstadt*, 557–8. Stiassny coined a 'Slogan of the Day: The Young Help the Aged': see Křížková, Kotouč and Ornest, *We Are Children Just the Same*, 137.

23. JMPTC, 129.706, Ilona Weissová; b. 6 Mar. 1932; deported from Prague to Theresienstadt 14 Dec. 1941; deported to Auschwitz 15 May 1944; pencil. *Zmrzlin(a)* is ice cream; *čokoláda* chocolate; *ořisky* nuts; *sardinky* sardines; *med* honey; *bonbony* sweets; *cukr* sugar; *mléko* milk; *Vztup do země blahobytu. Zaplat vtzup 1 Kc* means 'Entry to fantasy land. Entry charge 1 Crown'. On provisioning, see Adler, *Theresienstadt*, 358–63. For a general survey of this motif, see Dieter Richter, *Schlaraffenland: Geschichte einer populären Phantasie*, Frankfurt, 1989, esp. 94–104.

24. Klüger, *Weiter Leben*, 87; Susan Cernyak-Spatz summed it up simply: 'I don't think I ever became so good a cook as I was with my mouth'; cited in Esther Katz and Joan Ringelbaum (eds), *Women Surviving the Holocaust*, New York, 1983, 153.

25. JMPTC, 129.705, Maria Mühlstein(ová): b. 31 Mar. 1932; deported from Prague to Theresienstadt 17 Dec. 1941; deported to Auschwitz 16 Oct. 1944; pencil. Ghetto policemen feature in a number of other drawings: notably, a full-scale watercolour: JMPTC, 129.186, anon.; with a woman who is wearing the yellow star: JMPTC, 125.426, Jiří Beutler; directing non-existent traffic: JMPTC, 121.991, anon.; on a desert island with palm trees and a fantastical animal with the body and head of a cow and camel's hump: JMPTC, 137.669, Gabi Freiová. See also the caricature in *Vedem*, complete with Louis Napoleon moustache and beard and spectacles: Archive, Terezín Memorial, A 1317, *Vedem*, 12 Mar. 1944, 531.

26. For a German example in this style, see Karin Isolde Lehmann, aged twelve, 'Buntes Bild and frisches Leben!', 1945: Hartmut Lehmann, family papers, Göttingen.

27. JMPTC, 129.098, Edita Bikková: b. 9 May 1933; deported to Theresienstadt 24 Oct. 1942; deported to Auschwitz 23 Oct. 1944; pencil and crayon. Although most of the children came from largely secular and assimilated backgrounds, many of their families had continued to celebrate the Jewish festivals; the festival of Passover also gained a special meaning in communities hoping that this time they might survive and escape their bondage, and gave rise to a number of pictures of the Seder: JMPTC, 133.418, Hana Wajlová, and 174.074, Berta Kohnová.

28. JMPTC, 121.899, Jiřina Steinerová: b. 20 Jan. 1930; deported to Theresienstadt 12 Nov. 1942; deported to Auschwitz 4 Oct. 1944; Heim 14 (L 414?); pencil.

29. JMPTC, 129.075, Zuzana Winterová: b. 27 Jan. 1933; deported to Theresienstadt 4 Apr. 1942; deported to Auschwitz 4 Oct. 1944; pencil. JMPTC, Memories 343/95, Willy Groag interview with Ben-David Gershon, Kibbutz Maanith, 17 Oct. 1965.

30. YVA 0.3 1202, Bacon interview with Chaim Mass, Jerusalem, 13 Feb. 1959, 21–2 and 27; Eva Ginzová in Zapruder, *Salvaged Pages*, 175 and 180: 24 June and 28 Sept. 1944; see also Friedman, *The Terezin Diary of Gonda Redlich*, 10 and 14 Nov. 1943, 134–5.

31. After the deportations of Sept. and Oct. 1944, only 819 children were left. This figure had virtually doubled by May 1945, largely due to the arrival of further transports of Slovak Jews, as well as the survivors of evacuation and death marches: Adler, *Theresienstadt, 1941–1945*, 1960, 315; JMPTC, Memoires 343/95, Groag interview with Ben-David Gershon, Kibbutz Maanith, 17 Oct. 1965.

32. Bacon, 30 Oct. 1964 testimony to the Frankfurt trial of the Auschwitz SS, in Inge Deutschkron, . . . *Denn ihrer war die Hölle: Kinder in Gettos und Lagern*, Cologne, 1985, 65, and YVA 0.3 1202, interview with Chaim Mass, Jerusalem, 13 Feb. 1959, 22–4. The transports of Hungarian Jews began in April 1944, three months before the dissolution of the 'family camp': see Ruth Klüger, *Weiter Leben*, 121–2; Filip Müller, *Eyewitness Auschwitz: Three Years in the Gas Chambers*, Susanne Flatauer (ed.), Chicago, 1979, 123–64; Serge Klarsfeld (ed.), *The Auschwitz Album: Lili Jacob's Album*, New York, 1980; Deutschkron, . . . *Denn ihrer war die Hölle*, 105–6, 114, and 131–5; Gerlach and Aly, *Das letzte Kapitel*, 186–239.

33. Yehuda Bacon, video interview in Terezín Foundation, *Terezín Diary*; and

DöW 13243, interview with Ben-David Gershon, Jerusalem, 17 Nov. 1964, 61; Zapruder, *Salvaged Pages*, 166.

34. DöW 13243, Bacon, interview with Ben-David Gershon, Jerusalem, 17 Nov. 1964, 34–7; the 'family camp' was in B2B, with the women's camp (B2C) on one side from 1944, and the quarantine camp (B2A) on the other. At one end ran the camp road, while the infamous ramp was built as an extension to the railway line at the other: see Müller, *Eyewitness Auschwitz*, 175.

35. DöW 13243, Bacon, interview with Ben-David Gershon, Jerusalem, 17 Nov. 1964, 45; JMPTC, 343, 54–8, Willy Groag interview with Ben-David Gershon, 17 Oct. 1965; JMPTC, 343, Elisabeth Kuerti, 'In Memoriam Fredy Hirsch!', MS, 1990.

36. DöW 13243, Bacon interview with Ben-David Gershon, Jerusalem, 17 Nov. 1964, 46; Otto Dov Kulka, evidence given on 30 July 1964 at the Auschwitz trial, reprinted in Deutschkron, . . . *Denn ihrer war die Hölle*, 80; for his later work, see Otto Dov Kulka (ed.), *Judaism and Christianity under the Impact of National Socialism*, Jerusalem, 1987; and (ed.), *Deutsches Judentum unter dem Nationalsozialismus*, Tübingen, 1997; and (ed.), *Die Juden in den geheimen NS-Stimmungsberichten 1933–1945*, Düsseldorf, 2004. For testimony about the child-friendly side of particular SS men, see Deutschkron, . . . *Denn ihrer war die Hölle*, 34, 40–1 and 59, 117; and DöW 13243, Bacon, interview with Ben-David Gershon, Jerusalem, 17 Nov. 1964, 47–8.

37. YVA 0.3 1202, Bacon interview with Chaim Mass, Jerusalem, 13 Feb. 1959, 16; Hanna Hoffmann-Fischel report for Yad Vashem, reprinted in Deutschkron, . . . *Denn ihrer war die Hölle*, 50–1.

38. Ibid., reprinted in Deutschkron, . . . *Denn ihrer war die Hölle*, 54.

39. DöW 13243, Bacon, interview with Ben-David Gershon, Jerusalem, 17 Nov. 1964, 40 and 43; Hoffmann-Fischel in Deutschkron, . . . *Denn ihrer war die Hölle*, 53–4.

40. YVA 0.3 1202, Bacon, interview with Chaim Mass, Jerusalem, 13 Feb. 1959, 17 and DöW 13243, interview with Ben-David Gershon, Jerusalem, 17 Nov. 1964, 49; Hoffmann-Fischel in Deutschkron, . . . *Denn ihrer war die Hölle*, 51.

41. Hoffmann-Fischel in Deutschkron, . . . *Denn ihrer war die Hölle*, 54.

42. Cupik must have been a nickname: he does not appear in Kárný et al., *Terezínská Pamětní Kniha*, 2 vols, Prague, 1995; DöW 13243, Bacon calls Heydebreck 'Heidelberg', interview with Ben-David Gershon, Jerusalem, 17 Nov. 1964, 50; Hoffmann-Fischel, 'Heidebrück', in Deutschkron, . . . *Denn ihrer war die Hölle*, 55.

43. Kulka in Deutschkron, . . . *Denn ihrer war die Hölle*, 57.

44. Müller, *Eyewitness Auschwitz*, 107–11.

45. Ibid., 111–14: I have followed the Czech spelling of her name.

46. Ibid., 117–19.

47. DöW 13243, Bacon, interview with Ben-David Gershon, Jerusalem, 17 Nov. 1964, 51–2.

48. Anna Hyndráková-Kovanicová, 'Letter to my children', *The World without Human Dimensions*, 162.

49. Salmen Gradowski in Miroslav Kárný, 'Eine neue Quelle zur Geschichte der tragischen Nacht vom 8. März 1944', *Judaica Bohemiae*, 25/1, 1989, 53–6; Müller, *Eyewitness Auschwitz*, 120–2.

50. Miroslav Kárný, 'The Vrba and Wetzler Report' in Yisrael Gutman and Michael Berenbaum (eds), *Anatomy of the Auschwitz Death Camp*, Bloomington, Ind., 1994, 553–68.

51. Bankier, *The Germans and the Final Solution*, 113–14; Ursula von Kardorff, *Berliner Aufzeichnungen: Aus den Jahren 1942 bis 1945*, Munich, 1962, 228: 27 Dec. 1944; for Lederer, see Miroslav Kárný, 'Ergebnisse und Aufgaben der Theresienstädter Historiographie' in Kárný, Blodig and Kárná, *Theresienstadt in der 'Endlösung der Judenfrage'*, 34–5. News also spread from the locality – and, although Birkenau was meant to be isolated, the nearby town of Auschwitz was within the Wartheland and designated for German settlement: see Bernd Wagner, 'Gerüchte, Wissen, Verdrängung: Die IG Auschwitz und das Vernichtungslager Birkenau' in Frei, Steinbacher and Wagner, *Ausbeutung, Vernichtung, Öffentlichkeit*, 231–48; and Sybille Steinbacher, *'Musterstadt' Auschwitz: Germanisierungspolitik und Judenmord in Oberschlesien*, Munich, 2000, 178–94.

52. Details of the visit, Kárný, 'The Genocide of the Czech Jews', 74–5.

53. Klüger, *Weiter Leben*, 129–33; Hyndráková-Kovanicová, 'Letter to my children', 163–4; DöW 13243, Bacon, interview with Ben-David Gershon, Jerusalem, 17 Nov. 1964, 55–6.

54. Kulka, in Deutschkron, . . . *Denn ihrer war die Hölle*, 59.

55. DöW 13243, interview with Ben-David Gershon, Jerusalem, 17 Nov. 1964, 57.

56. YVA 0.3 1202, Bacon interviews with Chaim Mass, Jerusalem, 13 Feb. 1959, 34, and DöW 13243, with Ben-David Gershon, Jerusalem, 17 Nov. 1964, 57.

57. YVA 0.3 1202, Bacon interviews with Chaim Mass, Jerusalem, 13 Feb. 1959, 44, and DöW 13243, with Ben-David Gershon, Jerusalem, 17 Nov. 1964, 60.

58. YVA 0.3 1202, Bacon interviews with Chaim Mass, Jerusalem, 13 Feb. 1959, 50–1, and DöW 13243, with Ben-David Gershon, Jerusalem, 17 Nov. 1964, 58.

59. YVA 0.3 1202, Bacon interview with Chaim Mass, Jerusalem, 13 Feb. 1959, 39; see Beno Kaufmann and Zdeněk Taussig, 'Something about the Crematorium', 1943, and Petr Ginz, 'Rambles through Terezín', 1943, in Křížková, Kotouč and Ornest, *We Are Children Just the Same*, 85–7.

60. YVA 0.3 1202, Bacon interviews with Chaim Mass, Jerusalem, 13 Feb. 1959, 21 and 40, and DöW 13243, with Ben-David Gershon, Jerusalem, 17 Nov. 1964, 15.

61. YVA 0.3 1202, Bacon interview with Chaim Mass, Jerusalem, 13 Feb. 1959, 47. The next seven lines are deleted from the transcript.

62. DöW 13243, interview with Ben-David Gershon, Jerusalem, 17 Nov. 1964, 68.

63. YVA 0.3 1202, Bacon interviews with Chaim Mass, Jerusalem, 13 Feb. 1959, 44, and DöW 13243, with Ben-David Gershon, Jerusalem, 17 Nov. 1964, 60; Kárný, 'The Genocide of the Czech Jews', 79.

64. Andrzej Strzelecki, *Endphase des KL Auschwitz: Evakuierung, Liquidierung und Befreiung des Lagers*, Oświęcim-Brzezinka, 1995, 89–92; DöW 13243, Bacon, interview with Ben-David Gershon, Jerusalem, 17 Nov. 1964, 60–3; Müller, *Eyewitness Auschwitz*, 161–5.

Chapter 8

1. KA 4709/2, Klaus S., b. 1926, 'Gomorrah. Bericht über die Luftangriffe auf Hamburg Juli/August 1943', MS, Hamburg, 1993, based on diary and letters to his mother: 25 July 1943. For statistics and background, see Groehler, *Bombenkrieg gegen Deutschland*, 106–21; also Martin Middlebrook, *The Battle of Hamburg: Allied Bomber Forces against a German City in 1943*, London, 1980; Friedrich, *Der Brand*, 192–5.

2. Institut für Geschichte und Biographie, Aussenstelle der Fernuniversität Hagen, Lüdenscheid, Lothar C., diary, 3 June 1943. KA 4709/2, Klaus S., letter to mother, 1 Aug. 1943.

3. KA 4709/2, Klaus S., letters to mother, 28, 30 and 31 July, 1 and 10 Aug. 1943.

4. Ibid., letter to mother, 31 July 1943; Police President of Hamburg, in Noakes, *Nazism*, 4, 554–7.

5. KA 4709/2, Klaus S., letter to mother, 11 Aug. 1943. Sixteen-year-olds were called up to the *Flak* for the first time by a decree issued on 26 Jan. 1943: Jahnke and Buddrus, *Deutsche Jugend 1933–1945*, 359–61; see also the oral history project of Rolf Schörken, *Luftwaffenhelfer und Drittes Reich: Die Entstehung eines politischen Bewusstseins*, Stuttgart, 1984, 101–61; for a study by a former *Flakhelfer*, see Hans-Dietrich Nicolaisen, *Der Einsatz der Luftwaffen- und Marinehelfer im 2. Weltkrieg: Darstellung und Dokumentation*, Büsum, 1981, 168–96; Eggert, *Der Krieg frisst eine Schule*, 104–24; Hans Joachim M., born 1930, cited in Arbeitsgruppe Pädagogisches Museum, *Heil Hitler, Herr Lehrer*, 180; KA 2554, Werner K., '20 Monate Luftwaffenhelfer: Tagebücher 5. Januar 1944–20. August 1945'.

6. Interview, May 1992 with Pavel Vasilievich Pavlenko, in Herbert Diercks (ed.), *Verschleppt nach Deutschland! Jugendliche Häftlinge des KZ Neuengamme aus der Sowjetunion erinnern sich*, Bremen, 2000, 97. Bericht des Polizeipräsidenten, p. 134; see Hans Joachim Schröder, *Die gestohlenen Jahre: Erzählgeschichten und Geschichtserzählung im Interview: Der Zweite Weltkrieg aus der Sicht ehemaliger Mannschaftssoldaten*, Tübingen, 1992, 756–60 and 768–9; Siegfried Gräff, *Tod im Luftangriff: Ergebnisse pathologisch-anatomischer Untersuchungen anlässlich der Angriffe auf Hamburg in den Jahren 1943–45*, Hamburg, 1948, 111 and 116; also Dörr, 'Wer die Zeit nicht miterlebt hat . . .', 2, 276, Roswitha N (1924) for later raids on Stuttgart.

7. Ruth Klein's testimony on looking for her parents after the Heilbronn firestorm of 4 Dec. 1944, in Werkstattgruppe der Frauen für Frieden/Heilbronn (eds), *Heimatfront: Wir überlebten*, Stuttgart, 1985, 214; cited in Dörr, 'Wer die Zeit nicht miterlebt hat . . .', 2, 277–8; and Schröder, *Die gestohlenene Jahre*, 753ff, on soldiers from Hamburg getting lost in their own neighbourhoods.

8. See Groehler, *Bombenkrieg gegen Deutschland*, 119–20; public reactions, Boberach, *Meldungen aus dem Reich*, 14, 5619–21: 16 Aug. 1943; Steinert, *Hitlers Krieg und die Deutschen*, 397–9; supplements and compensation, Noakes, *Nazism*, 4, 558–65; looted Jewish property, Frank Bajohr, *'Aryanisation' in Hamburg: The Economic Exclusion of the Jews and the Confiscation of their Property in Nazi Germany*, Oxford, 2002, 277–82 and 284 n. 34.

9. Harris to Churchill, 3 Nov. 1943, in Charles Webster and Noble Frankland,

The Strategic Air Offensive against Germany, 2, London, 1961, 190; Richard Overy, *Why the Allies Won*, London, 1995, 120–4; Friedrich, *Der Brand*, 92–121; see also critical appraisal of Friedrich in Lothar Kettenacker (ed.), *Ein Volk von Opfern: Die neue Debatte um den Bombenkrieg 1940–45*, Berlin, 2003; on the disastrous Nuremberg raids, see Martin Middlebrook, *The Nuremberg Raid, 30–31 March 1944*, London, 1973.

10. Fear, RA, Burg-Gymnasium Essen, UII/522, anon., b. 1940, 24 Feb. 1956, 1; Burg-Gymnasium Essen, UII/545, 1; Burg-Gymnasium Essen, UII/542, 1; Burg-Gymnasium Essen, UII/548, 1; Berufschule Essen, UI, no number, 1; Luisen-Schule Essen, UI, no number, 1; KA 3187b, Karl-Heinz B., b. 1927, d. 1984, Bismarck-Schule, Schulheft Klasse 4b, Deutsch: 'Flieger über Bochum': 14 May 1942; KA 4145, Ute R., 'Wolke Pink sieben' (MS), 2. Carrying packs, RA, Burg-Gymnasium Essen, anon. (boy), b. 1939, UII/545, 1, and Luisen-Schule Essen, anon. (girl) UI; sleeping in shelters, Luisen-Schule Essen, UI, no number, 2; Luisen-Schule Essen, UI, no number, 1–2; St Nicholas in the bunker, Burg-Gymnasium Essen UII/549, 1; learning to walk in the cellar, Luisen-Schule Essen, UI, no number, 3; being cheered by children's play, see Dörr, 'Wer die Zeit nicht miterlebt hat . . .', 2, 253.

11. RA, Goetheschule Essen, UI/6, 1; Burg-Gymnasium Essen UII/521, 1.

12. Boberach, *Meldungen aus dem Reich*, 17, 6522, 11 May 1944.

13. RA, Burg-Gymnasium Essen, UII/516, anon. 16 years, 14 Feb. 1956, 1.

14. Praying in bunker, RA, Berufschule M2/6, 16 years, 21 Jan. 1956, 1; sounds in Gröschner, *Ich schlug meiner Mutter die brennenden Funken ab*, 35. Even in Berlin, where about a quarter of all German bunkers were built in the programme after the raids on Hamburg, there was capacity for only about 10 per cent of the city's population: Groehler, *Bombenkrieg gegen Deutschland*, 238–54.

15. Liselotte G., in Hammer and zur Niedern, *Sehr selten habe ich geweint*, 288: 29 Dec. 1943. Her confirmation was on *Heldengedenktag*: see entry for 20 Mar. 1943.

16. Ibid., 288: 29 Dec. 1943.

17. Ibid., 283–4: 24 Nov. 1943.

18. Groehler, *Bombenkrieg gegen Deutschland*, 183; see also Martin Middlebrook, *The Berlin Raids: RAF Bomber Command Winter 1943–44*, London, 1988.

19. Alan W. Cooper, *Bombers over Berlin: The RAF Offensive, November 1943–March 1944*, Wellingborough, Northants, 1985 and 1989, 114; Liselotte G., in Hammer and zur Niedern, *Sehr selten habe ich geweint*, 285: 24 Dec. 1943.

20. Liselotte G. in Hammer and zur Niedern, *Sehr selten habe ich geweint*, 285: 24 Dec. 1943.

21. Ibid.: 29 Dec. 1943 and 3 Jan. 1944.

22. Adults' fear and tales to children, see RA, Burg-Gymnasium Essen, UII/552, 16 years, b. 1940, 24 Feb. 1956, 1; Luisen-Schule Essen, UI/7, 1 and 3–4; Burg-Gymnasium Essen UI/522, 17 years, 24 Feb. 1956, 2; Goetheschule Essen, OII/2, 1–5; Burg-Gymnasium Essen, UII/519, 18 years, 24 Feb. 1956, 1; Luisen-Schule Essen, UI/11, 5; Luisen-Schule Essen, UI/6, 18 years, 16 Jan. 1956, 1; Marion to her father, in Lange and Burkard, 'Abends wenn wir essen fehlt uns immer einer', 185: 3 Dec. 1943; dug from rubble, RA, Berufsschule Essen, M2/2, 1–2.

23. RA, Luisen-Schule Essen, UI/7, 9, (Sigrid M., 20 Jan. 1956; b. 1939).

24. For Queen Luise, see RA, Goetheschule Essen, UI/1, 23 Jan. 1956, 3; finding a shoe, see RA, Luisen-Schule Essen, UI/5, 5; RA, Goetheschule Essen UI/3, 6: cannot imagine that all the toys have been destroyed along with the family home.

25. Uwe Timm, *Am Beispiel meines Bruders*, 27 and 37–40: letter from father, 6 Aug., and from Karl-Heinz, 11 Aug. 1943.

26. Harald H., MS, 3: I am grateful to the late W. G. Sebald for sending this to me.

27. RA, Goetheschule Essen, OII, anon. b. 1938, 1; Goetheschule Essen UI/3, 5; RA, Luisen-Schule Essen, UI, no number, Sabine K., 20 Jan. 1956, 2.

28. Kardorff, *Berliner Aufzeichnungen*, 159: 21 June 1944 on Berlin, the swirling clouds of dust and flames as resembling 'purgatory in medieval paintings' and 'all the same having a wild beauty'.

29. Institut für Geschichte und Biographie, Aussenstelle der Fernuniversität Hagen, Lüdenscheid, Lothar C., diary, 30 May 1943; *Flak* fragments, Harald H., MS, 1; 'Stuka' game, RA, Luisen-Schule Essen, UI/ no number, anon. 19 years, 16 Jan. 1956, 2–3.

30. Interview with Pavlenko in Diercks, *Verschleppt nach Deutschland*, 97; RA, Luisen-Schule Essen UI/12, Marie-Luise K., 20 Jan. 1956, 1–2.

31. RA, Berufschule Essen, anon., 16 years, 21 Jan. 1956, M2/6, 1; on air raids and crime, see Wagner, *Volksgemeinschaft ohne Verbrecher*, 316–29.

32. Boberach, *Meldungen aus dem Reich*, 15, 6071–8: 29 Nov. 1943; see also Herbert, *Hitler's Foreign Workers*, 329 and 360–5; Wachsmann, *Hitler's Prisons*, 211 and 221–2; Alexei Antonovich Kutko, interview, Sept. 1993 in Diercks, *Verschleppt nach Deutschland*, 67. See also, Leonid Michailovich Dospechov, Archiv der Gedenkstätte Neuengamme 2.8/1205 Kat. 1.

33. Klimenti Ivanovich Baidak, in Archiv der Gedenkstätte Neuengamme, Ng.2.8./ 1247 Kat. 1. Letter from a French worker in Herbert, *Hitler's Foreign Workers*, 322.

34. Theilen, *Edelweisspiraten*, 26–90; Peukert, *Inside Nazi Germany*, 160–5.

35. Song of the Navajos in Peukert, *Inside Nazi Germany*, 158.

36. See Richard Overy, 'Barbarisch aber sinnvoll' in Kettenacker, *Ein Volk von Opfern?*, 183–7; Groehler, *Bombenkrieg gegen Deutschland*, 190–5; Webster and Frankland, *The Strategic Air Offensive against Germany*, 2, 198–211 and 3, 9–41, for the reluctant subordination of Bomber Command in April 1944 to preparations for the land invasion.

37. Steinert, *Hitlers Krieg und die Deutschen*, 404–24; Wachsmann, *Hitler's Prisons*, 211–12 and 218–26; Overy, *Why the Allies Won*, 90–7 and 129.

38. Groehler, *Bombenkrieg gegen Deutschland*, 238–54.

39. KA 3214 Anna-Matilda M., Klasse 4, 1943–4: Schulhefte 6/7 (Luftschutz).

40. Inge Reininghaus from Hagen, in Sollbach, *Heimat Ade*, 135; see also Steinert, *Hitlers Krieg und die Deutschen*, 425; Boberach, *Meldungen aus dem Reich*, 14, 5643–6: 19 Aug. 1943.

41. Boberach, *Meldungen aus dem Reich*, 14, 5643–6: 19 Aug. 1943.

42. 'Das Bunte Urselbuch: Familienchronik eines Lehrers für seine Tochter' in Hammer and zur Niedern, *Sehr selten habe ich geweint*, 428: 9–10 Feb. 1943: 'Flieger-Anst [sic]!'. Battle for the Ruhr, see Groehler, *Bombenkrieg gegen Deutschland*, 92–105; Klemperer, *To the Bitter End*, 2, 269–70 and 354: 27 and 31 Dec. 1943, and 16 Oct. 1944; Maria P. in Mendel, *Zwangsarbeit im Kinderzimmer*, 67.

43. Liselotte G., in Hammer and zur Niedern, *Sehr selten habe ich geweint*, 288–92: 2–4 Jan. 1944; Boberach, *Meldungen aus dem Reich*, 15, 5885–7: 18 Oct. 1943; Steinert, *Hitlers Krieg und die Deutschen*, 362–72 and 420–4; Noakes, *Nazism*, 4, 467, 498–501 and 567–71.

44. Hitler, *Reden und Proklamationen, 1932–1945*, 2, 1999–2002 and 2050–9: 21 Mar. and 8 Nov. 1943.

45. Steinert, *Hitlers Krieg und die Deutschen*, 421–2; Boberach, *Meldungen aus dem Reich*, 15, 5987–9: 11 Nov. 1943.

46. Liselotte G., in Hammer and zur Niedern, *Sehr selten habe ich geweint*, 282: 8. Nov. 1943. Other references by Hitler to not repeating '1918', see Hitler, *Reden und Proklamtionen*, 2, 1316: speech to Reichstag, 1 Sept. 1939; see also Kershaw, *Hitler*, 1, 104 and 2, 609, 747, 754; clergy unable to counter desire for retaliation even in the Rhineland and Westphalia, Boberach, *Meldungen aus dem Reich*, 15, 5886: 18 Oct. 1943.

47. Both jokes, Boberach, *Meldungen aus dem Reich*, 15, 6187: 27 Dec. 1943.

48. Ibid., 13, 5217: 6 May 1943.

49. See Steinert, *Hitlers Krieg und die Deutschen*, 260–1. Here, BA, R55, 571, 46: Kurt L., 18 May 1944; BA, R55, 571, 145: 4 June 1944, Irma J; BA, R55, 571, 240: K. von N.

50. BA, R55, 571, 123–6: Georg R., 1 June 1944.

51. DLA, Edgar P., b. 15 Sept. 1935, 'Die Russenzeit – ein Zeitzeugnis', MS, 1995, 9–10.

52. See Klemperer, *To the Bitter End*, 289 and 291: 12 and 19 Mar. 1944, and his *The Language of the Third Reich: LTI – Lingua Tertii Imperii: A Philologist's Notebook*, London, 2000, 172–81. On mixed reactions to anti-Semitism until 1939, see Friedländer, *Nazi Germany and the Jews*, 1; on *Kristallnacht* in Franconia, see Wildt, 'Gewalt gegen Juden in Deutschland'.

53. See Bankier, *The Germans and the Final Solution*, 145 and 147, and his 'German Public Awareness of the Final Solution' in David Cesarani (ed.), *The Final Solution: Origins and Implementation*, London, 1994, 215–27, citing Hermann Hirsch in *Stuttgarter NS-Kurier*, 2 Sept. 1943; also Klaus Schickert, 'Kriegsschauplatz Israel' in the Hitler Youth journal *Wille und Macht* for Sept./Oct. 1943; Noakes, *Nazism*, 4, 496–8; Kershaw, *Popular Opinion and Political Dissent*, 369; Frank Trommler, '"Deutschlands Sieg oder Untergang": Perspektiven aus dem Dritten Reich auf die Nachkriegs-entwicklung' in Thomas Koebner, Gert Sautermeister and Sigrid Schneider (eds), *Deutschland nach Hitler*, Opladen, 1987, 214–28. Lothar de la Camp, cited in Renate Hauschild-Thiessen (ed.), *Die Hamburger Katastrophe vom Sommer 1943 in Augenzeugenberichten*, Hamburg, 1993, 230: 28 July 1943; Kardorff, *Berliner Aufzeichnungen*, 40: 3 Mar. 1943.

54. Bankier, 'German Public Awareness of the Final Solution', 216, based on American Intelligence reports from the 12th Army Group.

55. Kock, *'Der Führer sorgt für unsere Kinder . . .'*, 213–25 and 253–5.

56. KA 2808/1, Renate S., b. 1931, 'Ein Schloss voll kleiner Mädchen: Erinnerungen an die Kinderlandverschickung 1943–1945', MS, 2–16.

57. Erwin Ebeling, Inge Reininghaus and report by the rector of a school from Hagen, in Sollbach, *Heimat Ade*, 13, 41, 52 n. 180, 135 and 154–9.

58. Gisela Schwartz (née Vedder) in Sollbach, *Heimat Ade*, 144–5; Boberach, *Meldungen aus dem Reich*, 14, 5643–6: 19 Aug. 1943.

59. Kock, *'Der Führer sorgt für unsere Kinder . . .'*, 218–19, 223–5, 242–4 and

255; Sollbach, *Heimat Ade*, 11–12; Boberach, *Meldungen aus dem Reich*, 15, 5827: 30 Sept. 1943; private arrangements to go to Nauen rather than Zakopane with her school, see Christa G., interview in Gröschner, *Ich schlug meiner Mutter die brennenden Funken ab*, 353–4.

60. Peter Groote and bed-wetting cases in Sollbach, *Heimat Ade*, 36–7 and 51 n. 155; for tales of British children, see Starns and Parsons, 'Against Their Will: The Use and Abuse of British Children during the Second World War' and Parsons, *'I'll Take that One'*.

61. Sollbach, *Heimat Ade*, 25–6 and 29. When the *Gauleiter*'s order was repeated and printed in the press the next day, the grumbling in the streets and shops got louder. See also Boberach, *Meldungen aus dem Reich*, 14, 5643–6 and 15, 6029–31: 19 Aug. and 18 Nov. 1943.

62. Günter Kühnholz, in Sollbach, *Heimat Ade*, 145–7; KA 3221, Friedrich H., 'Reiseheft aus Ungarn 1943', MS, 20 June 1943; KA 2788/1, Karl L., b. 7 Sept. 1936, letters to mother, 13 July and 30 June 1944.

63. Birthe Kundrus, *Kriegerfrauen: Familienpolitik und Geschlechterverhältnisse im Ersten und Zweiten Weltkrieg*, Hamburg, 1995, 261 and 271; Jill Stephenson, '"Emancipation" and Its Problems: War and Society in Württemberg, 1939–45', *European History Quarterly*, 17, 1987, 358–60; also Gerda Szepansky (ed.), *Blitzmädel, Heldenmutter, Kriegerwitwe: Frauenleben im Zweiten Weltkrieg*, Frankfurt, 1986.

64. Noakes, *Nazism*, 4, 502–3; Lacey, *Feminine Frequencies*, 129–30; Liselotte G. in Hammer and zur Niedern, *Sehr selten habe ich geweint*, 293–4: 5 Feb. 1944.

Chapter 9
1. Erickson, *The Road to Berlin*, 198–247 and 326–7; Weinberg, *A World at Arms*, 675–707; 750–1 and 757–65.

2. Overmans, *Deutsche militärische Verluste im zweiten Weltkrieg*, 238–43 and 277–83.

3. July plotters, see Hans Mommsen, 'Gesellschaftsbild und Verfassungspläne des deutschen Widerstandes', in his *Alternative zu Hitler*, Munich, 2000, 53–158; Boberach, *Meldungen aus dem Reich*, 17, 6576–81, 6595–600: 8, 19 and 25 June 1944; but by 28 June the V-1 rockets had already disappointed: 6613–21; 6626–30: 28 and 29 June, and 6 July 1944; Klaus-Dieter Henke, *Die amerikanische Besetzung Deutschlands*, Munich, 1995, 316–17; Steinert, *Hitlers Krieg und die Deutschen*, 455–98, 509–12 and 527–31; see also *Wehrmacht* reports for Berlin in Wolfram Wette, Ricarda Bremer and Detlef Vogel (eds), *Das letzte halbe Jahr: Stimmungsberichte der Wehrmachtpropaganda 1944/45*, Essen, 2001, 127–98: 10 Oct.–31 Dec. 1944.

4. Groehler, *Bombenkrieg gegen Deutschland*, 316–20 and 370–81. All statistics for the numbers of civilians killed are still the subject of political controversy: Groehler bases his on aggregating the numbers reported by the police for different cities; then using test cases to calculate the scale of underreporting at this point in the war and adjusting the overall numbers accordingly. Similar procedures have been used for estimating numbers of military executions and also of civilians who died in, or fleeing from, the eastern provinces: see Overmans, *Deutsche militärische Verluste im zweiten Weltkrieg*, 300–1; Messerschmidt and Wüllner, *Die Wehrmachtjustiz im Dienste des Nationalsozialismus*, 63–89.

5. Verdict, Duisburg Provincial Court, 14 June 1950 in Fritz Bauer, Karl Dietrich

Bracher and H. H. Fuchs (eds), *Justiz und NS-Verbrechen: Sammlung deutscher Strafurteile wegen nationalsozialistischer Tötungsverbrechen 1945–1966*, 6, Amsterdam, 1971, no. 219; also in Herbert, *Hitler's Foreign Workers*, 362 and see 366–9; Theilen, *Edelweisspiraten*, 82–141; Peukert, *Inside Nazi Germany*, 160–5.

6. On the US Air Force's targeting of the transport system, Groehler, *Bombenkrieg gegen Deutschland*, 356–8 and 364–5 and 369–70; extension to dive-bombers, Conrad Crane, *Bombs, Cities, and Civilians: American Airpower Strategy in World War II*, Lawrence, Kansas, 1993, 111; civilian experience, Dörr, 'Wer die Zeit nicht miterlebt hat . . .', 2, 296–8.

7. DLA, Helga F., 'Bericht eines 10-jährigen Kindes zur Zeit des 2. Weltkrieges', MS, 1986, 27; RA, Luisen-Schule Essen, Ul/1, 17 years, 16 Jan. 1956.

8. Wachsmann, *Hitler's Prisons*, 222; Bernward Dörner, *'Heimtücke': Das Gesetz als Waffe: Kontrolle, Abschreckung und Verfolgung in Deutschland 1933–1945*, Paderborn, 1998, 144–5.

9. Military developments, Weinberg, *A World at Arms*, 690–702 and 760–3; foreign boys as SS and anti-aircraft auxiliaries, Gerlach, *Kalkulierte Morde*, 1089–91; David K. Yelton, *Hitler's Volkssturm: The Nazi Militia and the Fall of Germany, 1944–1945*, Lawrence, Kansas, 2002, 120–1.

10. Richard Bessel, *Nazism and War*, London, 2004; Gerhard Hirschfeld and Irina Renz (eds), *Besiegt und Befreit: Stimmen vom Kriegsende 1945*, Gerlingen, 1995; Kershaw, *Hitler*, 2, 713–15; *Volkssturm* decree in Noakes, *Nazism*, 4, 643–4.

11. Yelton, *Hitler's Volkssturm*, 120; Rudolf Semmler, *Goebbels: The Man next to Hitler*, London, 1947, 163–4; 'poetic truth' in Noakes, *Nazism*, 4, 496.

12. For children's games, see chapter 5 above; on 11th Guards Army, see Manfred Zeidler, *Kriegsende im Osten: Die Rote Armee und die Besetzung Deutschlands östlich von Oder und Neisse 1944/45*, Munich, 1996, 150.

13. Stuttgart Security Police, in Noakes, *Nazism*, 4, 652: 6 Nov. 1944.

14. Dörr, 'Wer die Zeit nicht miterlebt hat . . .', 2, 270–6 and 285; Friedrich, *Der Brand*, 335–40; Wette, Bremer and Vogel, *Das letzte halbe Jahr*, 163–4: Berlin, 20–26 Nov. 1944.

15. On the establishment of the *Volkssturm* and Himmler's speech of 18 Oct. 1944, see Noakes, *Nazism*, 4, 643–7; see also Yelton, *Hitler's Volkssturm*; Karl Heinz Jahnke, *Hitlers letztes Aufgebot: Deutsche Jugend im sechsten Kriegsjahr 1944/45*, Essen, 1993.

16. KA 2788/2, Karl L., letters from his brother Kurt to his mother, 22 Oct. 1944; Bergau, *Der Junge von der Bernsteinküste*, 97–107.

17. KA 4448, Monika Schypulla, letters to father, 9 July and 18 Sept. 1944; father to Monika, 29 Sept. 1944 and 10 Jan. 1945.

18. On the military campaign, see Erickson, *The Road to Berlin*, 450, 457–8, 462, 471–2.

19. For mass flight, see esp. Bundesministerium für Vertriebene (ed.), *Die Vertreibung der deutschen Bevölkerung aus den Gebieten östlich der Oder-Neisse*, 1–3, (reprinted) Augsburg, 1993; and for critical appraisals of this project, Matthias Beer, 'Im Spannungsfeld von Politik und Zeitgeschichte: Das Grossforschungsprojekt "Dokumentation der Deutschen aus Ost-Mitteleuropa"', *Vierteljahrshefte für Zeitgeschichte*, 49, 1998, 345–89; Moeller, *War Stories*, 51–87; Breslau as fortress, see Norman Davies and

Roger Moorhouse, *Microcosm: Portrait of a Central European City*, London, 2002, 13–37.

20. Theodor Schieder, 'Einleitende Darstellung' in Bundesministerium für Vertriebene, *Die Vertreibung der deutschen Bevölkerung aus den Gebieten östlich der Oder-Neisse*, 52–3E.

21. Strzelecki, *Endphase des KL Auschwitz*, 155–6 and 308; DöW 13243, Bacon, interview with Ben-David Gershon, 17 Nov. 1964, 63–4; Müller, *Eyewitness Auschwitz*, 166.

22. Strzelecki, *Endphase des KL Auschwitz*, 144–7 and 169–70.

23. Ibid., 188–9, citing Janina Komenda, 1947 testimony, in her *Lager Brzezinka*, Warsaw, 1986, 136.

24. Strzelecki, *Endphase des KL* Auschwitz, 216–18.

25. Ibid., 218; Müller, *Eyewitness Auschwitz*, 167; DöW 13243, Bacon, interview with Ben-David Gershon, 17 Nov. 1964, 64.

26. KA 2084, Gero H., letters to parents, 22 and 26 Jan. 1945.

27. KA 2808/1, Renate S., 'Ein Schloss voll kleiner Mädchen: Erinnerungen an die Kinderlandverschickung 1943–1945', MS; and see KA 3666/3, Gisela G., b. 1933, memoir, 1981.

28. KA 359, Jürgen I., b. 1935, memoir.

29. Gève, *Youth in Chains*, 190–1.

30. Haffner, in Strzelecki, *Endphase des KL Auschwitz*, 141–6; Erickson, *The Road to Berlin*, 238–9 and 471–2; Anna Wiśniewska and Czesław Rajca, *Majdanek: The Concentration Camp of Lublin*, Lublin, 1997, esp. 44–51, 61–5 and 72; Norman Naimark, *The Russians in Germany: A History of the Soviet Zone of Occupation, 1945–1949*, Cambridge, Mass., 1995, 77–8; Alexander Werth, *Russia at War*, New York, 1964, 884–99.

31. East Prussian campaign, see Erickson, *Road to Berlin*, 465–70 and 517–23; Beevor, *Berlin*, 49–51 and 115–22.

32. Swetlana Alexiejewitsch, *Der Krieg hat kein weibliches Gesicht*, Hamburg, 1989, 112; Zeidler, *Kriegsende im Osten*, 150–2; Soviet losses, ibid., 152, and Glantz and House, *When Titans Clashed*, Table B, 299–300.

33. Uspensky, diary, 24 and 27 Jan. 1945, in Zeidler, *Kriegsende im Osten*, 139–40.

34. KA 1920, Charlotte K., b. 1930, memoir MS; the best known of these cases is Marion Gräfin von Dönhoff, *Namen, die keiner mehr nennt: Ostpreussen – Menschen und Geschichte*, Düsseldorf, 1962, though most of her villagers returned home.

35. Erickson, *The Road to Berlin*, 463–70.

36. Hermann Fischer in Wolfgang Benz, *Die Vertreibung der Deutschen aus dem Osten: Ursachen, Ereignisse, Folgen*, Frankfurt, 1985, 106–9: letter 28 Nov. 1946.

37. Zeidler, *Kriegsende im Osten*, 154 and 159.

38. Erickson, *The Road to Berlin*, 463–70; Lore Ehrich in Theodor Schieder (ed.), *The Expulsion of the German Population from the Territories East of the Oder-Neisse-Line*, Bonn, n.d., 135–43.

39. KA 2693/8, Dorothea D., MS, 3–15.

40. For numbers, see Schieder, *The Expulsion of the German Population*, 33; Erickson, *The Road to Berlin*, 470; KA 905, Elisabeth S., diary and memoir, 15 Jan. 1945; Bergau, *Der Junge von der Bernsteinküste*, 108 and 126–7.

41. The main documents are to be found in Shmuel Krakowski, 'Massacre of

Jewish Prisoners on the Samland Peninsula – Documents', *Yad Vashem Studies*, 24, 1994, 349–87; see also Daniel Blatman, 'Die Todesmärsche – Entscheidungsträger, Mörder und Opfer' in Ulrich Herbert, Karin Orth and Christoph Dieckmann (eds), *Die nationalsozialistischen Konzentrationslager – Entwicklung und Struktur*, 2, Göttingen, 1998, 1063–92; Bergau, *Der Junge von der Bernsteinküste*, 108–9.

42. Blatman, 'Die Todesmärsche'; Orth, *Das System der nationalsozialistischen Konzentrationslager*, 283; Erickson, *The Road to Berlin*, 469–70; Bergau, *Der Junge von der Bernsteinküste*, 111–15.

43. Krakowski, 'Massacre of Jewish Prisoners on the Samland Peninsula' and Bergau, *Der Junge von der Bernsteinküste*, 'Anhang', 249–75.

44. Maj. Gen. Kazbintsev (head of Political Directorate, 3rd Belorussian Front), 8 Feb. 1945 in Krakowski, 'Massacre of Jewish Prisoners on the Samland Peninsula', 367–8; soldier's letter, and Uspensky, diary, 2 and 7 Feb. 1945 in Zeidler, *Kriegsende im Osten*, 140 and 154.

45. KA 905, Elisabeth S., diary and memoir, 4 Feb. 1945, and Bergau, *Der Junge von der Bernsteinküste*, 115–19.

46. Schieder, 'Einleitende Darstellung' in Bundesministerium für Vertriebene, *Die Vertreibung der deutschen Bevölkerung aus den Gebieten östlich der Oder-Neisse*, 41–51E.

47. Herbert Hagener and Erwin Ebeling in Sollbach, *Heimat Ade*, 13–14 and 158–9.

48. Schieder, 'Einleitende Darstellung'; Bergau, *Der Junge von der Bernsteinküste*, 119–21.

49. Boberach, *Meldungen aus dem Reich*, 17, 6732–40: 28 Mar. and final and incomplete report for the end of Mar. 1945.

50. Wolfgang Werner, *'Bleib übrig': Deutsche Arbeiter in der nationalsozialistischen Kriegswirtschaft*, Düsseldorf, 1983, 341.

51. Kardorff, *Berliner Aufzeichnungen*, 242: 3 Feb. 1945; Groehler, *Bombenkrieg gegen Deutschland*, 397–8; civilian morale, Wette, Bremer and Vogel, *Das letzte halbe Jahr*, 21–27 Feb. 1945: 271–93.

52. On Kolberg, Welch, *Propaganda and the German Cinema*, 221–37.

53. KA 3186, Ruth Reimann.

54. Liselotte G. in Hammer and zur Niedern, *Sehr selten habe ich geweint*, 289–90: 2 Jan. 1944.

55. KA 3186, Ruth Reimann. On this generation's willingness to go on believing in victory, see also Rosenthal, *Die Hitlerjugend-Generation*, 88–93 and 320–6.

Chapter 10

1. Marianne Peyinghaus, letter to her parents, 25 Mar. 1943, in her (ed.), *Stille Jahre in Gertlauken: Erinnerungen an Ostpreussen*, Berlin, 1988, 92; on *Hitlerjunge Quex*, see Welch, *Propaganda and the German Cinema*, 59–74; slogan from the *Deutscher Ehrenhain für die Helden von 1914/18*, Leipzig, 1931, 7–8; Klaus Latzel, *Vom Sterben im Krieg: Wandlungen in der Einstellung zum Soldatentod vom Siebenjährigen Krieg bis zum II. Weltkrieg*, Warendorf, 1988, 68–92.

2. See Jahnke, *Hitlers letztes Aufgebot*; Jahnke and Buddrus, *Deutsche Jugend 1933–1945*, 386, 392–3 and 400–1; Schörken, *Luftwaffenhelfer und Drittes Reich*, 101; and for a whole class of volunteers in Genthin near Magdeburg, see KA 26, Detlev S., MS, 14.

3. On the student volunteers of 1914, see George Mosse, *Fallen Soldiers: Reshaping the Memory of the World Wars*, New York and Oxford, 1990, 53–80.

4. KA 1997, Werner K., '20 Monate Luftwaffenhelfer: Tagebücher 5. Januar 1944–20. August 1945', 144–5 and 150: 21 and 30 Jan. 1945; similar transition in KA 920, Walter S., 'Mein Tagebuch', 15 Sept.–3 Nov. 1944; Stehkämpfer in Johannes Steinhoff, Peter Pechel and Dennis Showalter, *Voices from the Third Reich: An Oral History*, London, 1991, 362; Arno Klönne, *Gegen den Strom: Bericht über den Jugendwiderstand im Dritten Reich*, Frankfurt, 1958, 143–4; Beevor, *Berlin*, 181.

5. Yelton, *Hitler's Volkssturm*, 105–18.

6. *Niederdeutsche Beobachter*, 8 Feb. 1945, in Jahnke and Buddrus, *Deutsche Jugend 1933–1945*, 404; Yelton, *Hitler's Volkssturm*, 119–31.

7. KA 4025, Heinz M., b. 1928, 'Die Pestbeule: Autobiographische Erinnerungen der Kriegs- und Vorkriegszeit', MS, 195–205.

8. KA 89, Rudi Brill, 'Fronthelfer der HJ', private printing, Bexback, n.d., 3–5 Mar. 1945.

9. Kershaw, *Hitler*, 2, 737–47, 756–8 and 777–85; for an interesting interpretation stressing the element of intentional destruction and self-destruction, see Bernd Wegner, 'Hitler, der Zweite Weltkrieg und die Choreographie des Untergangs', *Geschichte und Gesellschaft*, 26/3, 2000, 493–518.

10. Hitler and the *Gauleiter*, Kershaw, *Hitler*, 2, 779–80; Goebbels to his staff at the Propaganda Ministry, 17 Apr. 1945 in Welch, *Propaganda and the German Cinema*, 234.

11. Kershaw, *Hitler*, 2, 781; Boberach, *Meldungen aus dem Reich*, 17, 6733–4. Letter to Goebbels in BA, R55/578, 210: 25 Oct. 1944, Hans H., Direktor der Staatl. Ingenieurschule in Kaiserslautern und Parteigenosse; BA R55/577, 232–5: 27 Jan. 1945, A. M.

12. Henke, *Die amerikanische Besetzung Deutschlands*, 399–400; Weinberg, *A World at Arms*, 810–14; Lothar Gruchmann, *Der Zweite Weltkrieg: Kriegführung und Politik*, Munich, 1995, 436–43; Winter et al., *Verlegt nach Hadamar*, 166; Ludwig Heinrich Lohne, interview in Sick, *'Euthanasie' im Nationalsozialismus*, 88–9; death rates in asylums, Faulstich, *Hungersterben in der Psychiatrie*, 583–4, 661–717.

13. Ayass, *Das Arbeitshaus Breitenau*, 328–34; Richter, *Breitenau*, 206–15; case files, e.g. LWV 2/7775, Waltraud B., LWV 2/8356, Sonja H., and LWV 2/8194, Anna G.

14. KA 3359, Hella K., Hanover, 'Zwischen Mistbeetfenster und Bombentrichter', MS, 27; Gellately, *Backing Hitler*, 239; Bauer and Bracher, *Justiz und NS-Verbrechen*, 9, 118–28; for a graphic account, see Gerhard Schreiber, *Die italienischen Militärinternierten im deutschen Machtbereich 1943–1945: Verraten – verachtet – vergessen*, Munich, 1990, 563–72; Oberhausen case, in Bauer and Bracher, *Justiz und NS-Verbrechen*, 7, 415–23, and also in Herbert, *Hitler's Foreign Workers*, 363.

15. Gellately, *Backing Hitler*, 230; Kershaw, *Hitler*, 2, 778; Steinert, *Hitlers Krieg und die Deutschen*, 541 and 558–60.

16. See Henke, *Die amerikanische Besetzung Deutschlands*, 844–6; Noakes, *Nazism*, 4, 650–7; Bessel, *Nazism and War*; Hirschfeld and Renz, *Besiegt und befreit*; for an analysis of overall numbers of capital punishment under civil jurisdiction, see Wachsmann, *Hitler's Prisons*, 314–18 and 402–3; for

military executions, see Messerschmidt and Wüllner, *Die Wehrmachtjustiz im Dienste des Nationalsozialismus*, 63–89, who estimate that some 33,000 soldiers were executed during the war; Welch, '"Harsh but just"? German Military Justice in the Second World War'; casualties, Overmans, *Deutsche militärische Verluste im Zweiten Weltkrieg*, 238–43.

17. Mothers fetching boys home, KA 3359, Hella K., 'Zwischen Mistbeetfenster und Bombentrichter', 29; in action, Yelton, *Hitler's Volkssturm*, 137–48; Henke, *Die amerikanische Besetzung Deutschlands*, 954–8.

18. KA 3359, Hella K., 'Zwischen Mistbeetfenster und Bombentrichter', 31–5; KA 89, Rudi Brill, 'Fronthelfer der HJ', 20 Mar. 1945.

19. KA 53, Jürgen H., b. July 1929, 29 Mar.–19 May 1945; KA 4025, Heinz M., 'Die Pestbeule', 206–13.

20. KA 3214, Anna-Matilda M., Schulhefte, 16 Mar. 1945, 'Vorfrühling' and letter to Walter Kempowski, 26 Mar. 1992; KA 4709/1, Agnes S., diary, 'Lüneburger Heide 1945', 18 Mar.–16 Apr. 1945.

21. Stalin to Roosevelt, 7 Apr. 1945, in Erickson, *Road to Berlin*, 540–1.

22. Morale in Berlin, in Wette, Bremer and Vogel, *Das letzte halbe Jahr*, 277–9 and 317: 22 Feb. and 19 Mar. 1945; Steinert, *Hitlers Krieg und die Deutschen*, 552, citing the Propaganda Ministry report for 21 Feb. 1945; Spandau garrison and executions, Messerschmidt and Wüllner, *Die Wehrmachtjustiz im Dienste des Nationalsozialismus*, 86.

23. Liselotte G. in Hammer and zur Niedern, *Sehr selten habe ich geweint*, 309: 12 Apr. 1945. For her earlier knowledge about the murder of the Jews, see ibid., 278–9: 31 Aug. 1943 and chapter 5 above.

24. Ibid., 307–9: 12 Apr. 1945; for a masterful account of the battle for Berlin, see Beevor, *Berlin*, here 177–80; also Erich Kuby, *The Russians and Berlin, 1945*, London, 1968.

25. Liselotte G. in Hammer and zur Niedern, *Sehr selten habe ich geweint*, 310: 17 Apr. 1945.

26. Ibid., 20 Apr. 1945; Kuby, *The Russians and Berlin*, 96–7; Kershaw, *Hitler*, 2, 798.

27. Helga M., interviews with author, Göttingen, May 1998 and Aug. 2004.

28. 'Das bunte Urselbuch' in Hammer and zur Niedern, *Sehr selten habe ich geweint*, 436–7: 11 and 4 Apr. 1945.

29. Ibid., 437: 16 Apr. 1945; Karl Damm, b. 10 Feb. 1927, in Steinhoff, Pechel and Showalter, *Voices from the Third Reich*, 352–4.

30. 'Das bunte Urselbuch' in Hammer and zur Niedern, *Sehr selten habe ich geweint*, 438 and 440-1: 1 July 1945 and letter of 10 Sept. 1945.

31. Yelton, *Hitler's Volkssturm*, 126–7; Beevor, *Berlin*, 287–8; *Völkischer Beobachter*, 20 Apr. 1945; Gröschner, *Ich schlug meiner Mutter die brennenden Funken ab*, 83 and 226: Günther S., Stargarder Str. 47, 6. Klasse, 1946.

32. Rudolf Vilter, b. Jan. 1929, in Steinhoff, Pechel and Showalter, *Voices from the Third Reich*, 355; Gröschner, *Ich schlug meiner Mutter die brennenden Funken ab*, 122–3: Erwin P., Gleimstr., 61; 116–17: Ursula K., Gleimstr., 7. Klasse.

33. Gröschner, *Ich schlug meiner Mutter die brennenden Funken ab*, 185–6: Helga R., Klasse 7, and Renate R., Klasse 5, Hochmeister Str. 29.

34. Ibid., 185–6: Helga R., Klasse 7: 21 Apr. 1945. Ibid., 229: Helga M., Prenzlauer Allee 32.

35. *The Magic Flute*, see *Völkischer Beobachter*, 21 Apr. 1945; KA 3697, Hertha von Gebhardt, b. 1896, diary: 23 Apr. 1945.

36. KA 3697, Gebhardt diary: 24 Apr. 1945; Lothar Loewe, b. 1929, in Steinhoff, Pechel and Showalter, *Voices from the Third Reich*, 347–8.

37. Gröschner, *Ich schlug meiner Mutter die brennenden Funken ab*, 114: Siegried B. (6. Klasse) from Körsorer Str.; 157: Hans Joachim S., Schivelbeinerstr. 7, 7. Klasse; Beevor, *Berlin*, 283–4.

38. KA 3697, Gebhardt, diary: 24 Apr. 1945.

39. Gröschner, *Ich schlug meiner Mutter die brennenden Funken ab*, 143–5: Ingeborg D., Krügerstr., Mädchenmittelschule II, 5. Klasse: 144. See 146, for a similar tale on the same day from Ingrid H., Kuglerstr. 77, 22. Oberschule; Soviet rationing policy, see Kuby, *The Russians and Berlin*, 291–6.

40. KA 3697, Gebhardt, diary: 26 Apr. 45.

41. Interview in Gröschner, *Ich schlug meiner Mutter die brennenden Funken ab*, 347–53:

42. *Niederdeutsche Beobachter*, 27 Apr. 1945, in Jahnke and Buddrus, *Deutsche Jugend 1933–1945*, 410; Tony Le Tissier, *The Battle of Berlin 1945*, London, 1988, 161; Erickson, *The Road to Berlin*, 604.

43. Gerhard Boldt, *Die letzten Tage der Reichskanzlei*, Hamburg, 1947, 156 and 188–9; see also Le Tissier, *The Battle of Berlin 1945*, 198; Arthur Axmann, *'Das kann doch nicht das Ende sein': Hitlers letzter Reichsjugendführer erinnert sich*, Koblenz, 1995, 422–45.

44. Beevor, *Berlin*, 356, 365 and 377–8; Rudolf Vilter in Steinhoff, Pechel and Showalter, *Voices from the Third Reich*, 355–6.

45. Gröschner, *Ich schlug meiner Mutter die brennenden Funken ab*, 157–8: Hans Joachim S., Schivelbeinerstr. 7, 7. Klasse; 208: Jutta P., Allensteiner Str. 12, 3. Klasse.

46. Ibid., 147–9: Christa B., Dänenstr. 1, Mädchenmittelschule II, 4. Klasse.

47. Ibid., 242: R., 6. Klasse Volksschule; 244: Wolfgang S., 6. Klasse; 245–6: Liselotte J., 13 years; 244–5: Walter B., 8. Klasse.

48. Loewe in Steinhoff, Pechel and Showalter, *Voices from the Third Reich*, 348–51; Le Tissier, *The Battle of Berlin*, 214–15; Beevor, *Berlin*, 384–5; for casualties, see Glantz and House, *When Titans Clashed*, 269–71; and Overmans, *Deutsche militärische Verluste im Zweiten Weltkrieg*, 234.

49. DöW 13243, Bacon, interview with Ben-David Gershon, 17 Nov. 1964, 65; Müller, *Eyewitness Auschwitz*, 169–71.

Chapter 11

1. DLA, Edgar P., 'Die Russenzeit – ein Zeitzeugnis', 14–16; RA, Luisen-Schule Essen, UI/[4], 3–4.

2. RA, Goetheschule Essen, UI/[2], 2–4.

3. Kuby, *The Russians and Berlin*, 226 and 283; Sander and Johr, *BeFreier und Befreite*, 55–6: another 2,000 killed themselves in the rest of the year; I am grateful to Christian Goeschel for letting me see the first fruits of his doctoral research on 'Suicide at the end of the Third Reich'.

4. DLA, Karl P., b. 22 Dec. 1939, 'Hunger – Krieg und Kinderjahre!', MS, 1992, 19; DLA, Karl K., b. 1931, 'Kindheit und Jugend im Bergknappendorf Grünbach am Sch.', MS, 1995, 50–1: his father was able to talk to the soldier in Czech; interview with Renate N., b. 1931, 8. Klasse, in Gröschner, *Ich schlug meiner Mutter die brennenden Funken ab*, 345–7.

5. Lieselotte G., diary, 30 Apr. 1945, cited in Reinhard Rürup (ed.), *Berlin 1945: Eine Dokumentation*, Berlin, 1995, 134; this entry does appear in the version of her diary in Hammer and zur Niedern, *Sehr selten habe ich geweint*, 312–13; KA 3697, Hertha von Gebhardt, diary: 27 and 28 Apr. 1945; Kardorff, *Berliner Aufzeichnungen*, 312–14: 23 Sept. 1945; Margaret Boveri, *Tage des Überlebens: Berlin 1945*, Munich, 1968, 119: 6 May 1945; Sander and Johr, *BeFreier und Befreite*, 25–7.

6. Naimark, *The Russians in Germany*, 69–140; Andrea Petö, 'Memory and the Narrative of Rape in Budapest and Vienna in 1945' in Bessel and Schumann, *Life after Death*, 129–48; Irene Bandhauer Schöffmann and Ela Hornung, 'Vom "Dritten Reich" zur Zweiten Republik: Frauen im Wien der Nachkriegszeit' in David F. Good, Margarete Grandner and Mary Jo Maynes (eds), *Frauen in Österreich: Beiträge zu ihrer Situation im 19. und 20. Jahrhundert*, Vienna, 1994, 232–3; Sander and Johr, *BeFreier und Befreite*, 48–51, calculate that a minimum of 110,000 women were raped in Berlin, many more than once, but also argue that there was a tendency among their interviewees to exaggerate the scale of rapes; on rumours of other neighbourhoods, see KA 3697, Gebhardt, diary, 29 and 30 Apr. 1945; see also Anneliese H., diary, 28 Apr. 1945 in Kuby, *The Russians and Berlin*, 224 and 278–9; Boveri, *Tage des Überlebens*, 118–19.

7. Gröschner, *Ich schlug meiner Mutter die brennenden Funken ab*, 215–17: Liane H., Bötzowstr. 57; 94–6: Werner W., 8. Klasse, Schivelbeiner Str. 19; 146: Ingrid H., Kuglerstr. 77; 345–7: Renate N., b. 1931, 8. Klasse; 355: interview with Christa J., b. 1931, Göhrener Str. 3.

8. RA, Luisen-Schule Essen, anon., UI/ no no., 3–4; DLA, Hermine D., b. 28 Aug. 1931, Hundsheim, nr Krems, 'Auch deine Oma war ein Kind', MS, n.d., 42.

9. DLA, Hermann G., b. 24 Oct. 1937, 'Reminiszensen', MS, 1997, 7–8.

10. Ibid., 8–9.

11. Boveri, *Tage des Überlebens*, 119: 6 May 1945; anon., *Eine Frau in Berlin: Tagebuchaufzeichnungen*, Geneva and Frankfurt, 1959, 113 and 220.

12. On CDU propaganda, see Ingrid Schmidt-Harzbach, 'Eine Woche im April' in Sander and Johr, *BeFreier und Befreite*, 35; attitudes in Ruhr and Bavaria, Niethammer, 'Privat – Wirtschaft: Erinnerungsfragmente einer anderen Umerziehung', 29–34; Elizabeth Heineman, 'The Hour of the Woman: Memories of Germany's "Crisis Years" and West German National Identity' in Schissler, *The Miracle Years*, 31 and 38–43; on rejection of racist and anti-Semitic strains of American anti-Communism in 1950s West Germany, see Thomas Mergel, 'Der mediale Stil der "Sachlichkeit": Die gebremste Amerikanisierung des Wahlkampfs in der alten Bundesrepublik' in Bernd Weisbrod (ed.), *Die Politik der Öffentlichkeit – die Öffentlichkeit der Politik: Politische Medialisierung in der Geschichte der Bundesrepublik*, Göttingen, 2003, 29–53.

13. Refused compensation, see Elizabeth Heineman, 'The Hour of the Woman', 32; for women's reluctance to talk, see Petö, 'Memory and the Narrative of Rape in Budapest and Vienna in 1945', 133–4 and 138; Irene Bandhauer Schöffmann and Ela Hornung, 'Vom "Dritten Reich" zur Zweiten Republik', 232–3; also Marianna Baumgartner, 'Zwischen Mythos und Realität: Die Nachkriegsvergewaltigungen im sowjetisch besetzten Mostviertel', *Unsere Heimat: Zeitschrift für Landeskunde von Niederösterreich*, 64/2, 1993,

73–108; Sibylle Meyer and Eva Schulze, '"Als wir wieder zusammen waren, ging der Krieg im Kleinen weiter": Frauen, Männer und Familien in Berlin der vierziger Jahre' in Lutz Niethammer and Alexander von Plato (eds), *'Wir kriegen jetzt andere Zeiten': Auf der Suche nach der Erfahrung des Volkes in nachfaschistischen Ländern*, Bonn, 1985, 314.

14. Timm, *Am Beispiel meines Bruders*, 68–9.

15. DLA, Helga G., b. 29 Dec. 1939, 'Meine Kindheit in P', MS, 1994/5, 11; DLA, Helga F., 'Bericht eines 10-jährigen Kindes zur Zeit des 2. Weltkrieges', MS, 1986, 29–30.

16. Burning own books, DLA, Edgar P., 'Die Russenzeit – ein Zeitzeugnis', MS, 1995, 17; flags on May Day, DLA, Karl P., 'Hunger – Krieg und Kinderjahre!', MS, 1992, 25; not wanting to take off insignia, Lothar C., interview, 26 Mar. 1999, Institut für Geschichte und Biographie, Aussenstelle der Fernuniversität Hagen, Lüdenscheid; turning old 88mm cannons into diving boards, DLA, Imo-Eberhard I., b. 24 Apr. 1934, 'Die Flucht nach Tirol', MS, 1995, 37–8; serious accidents from playing with unexploded ammunition, Hermann G., 'Reminiszenzen', MS, 1997, 6; DLA, Gottlieb G., b. 27 Aug. 1933, '1933–????' [*sic*], MS, 1989, 45; KA 89, Rudi Brill, 'Fronthelfer der HJ', Bexback, n.d., 17–18 May 1945.

17. Biess, 'Survivors of Totalitarianism', 59–61; Dagmar Herzog, 'Desperately Seeking Normality: Sex and Marriage in the Wake of the War' in Bessel and Schumann, *Life after Death*, 177–8; Beate Uhse, 1919–2001, started selling a calendar with contraceptive advice in 1948, before establishing a business in 1951: Burt Herman, AP Berlin, 18 July 2001, obituary.

18. Christa J., interview, in Gröschner, *Ich schlug meiner Mutter die brennenden Funken ab*, 353–8.

19. Interviews with Helga M., May 1998 and Aug. 2004.

20. Meyer and Schulze, '"Als wir wieder zusammen waren, ging der Krieg im Kleinen weiter"', 316–19.

21. Ibid.; Thomas Grotum, *Die Halbstarken; Zur Geschichte einer Jugendkultur der 50er Jahre*, Frankfurt, 1994, 54, 64–9; Christoph Klessmann, *Die doppelte Staatsgründung: Deutsche Geschichte 1945–1955*, Göttingen, 1991, 366–9; Klaus-Jörg Ruhl, *Frauen in der Nachkriegszeit 1945–1963*, Munich, 1988; Ulla Roberts, *Starke Mütter – ferne Väter: Töchter reflektieren ihre Kindheit im Nationalsozialismus und in der Nachkriegszeit*, Frankfurt, 1994; Robert Moeller, *Protecting Motherhood: Women and the Family in the Politics of Postwar West Germany*, Berkeley, 1993; Hanna Schissler, '"Normalization" as Project: Some Thoughts on Gender Relations in West Germany during the 1950s' in her *The Miracle Years*, 359–75; Merith Niehuss, *Familie, Frau und Gesellschaft: Studien zur Strukturgeschichte der Familie in Westdeutschland 1945–1960*, Göttingen, 2001.

22. Helga M., interviews with author, May 1998 and Aug. 2004.

23. Victor Gollancz, *In Darkest Germany: The Record of a Visit*, London, 1947, 65–6; on the bombing of Jülich, see Friedrich, *Der Brand*, 143–5.

24. Gollancz, *In Darkest Germany*, 18–19 and 94–8.

25. Macardle, *Children of Europe*, 289; Klessmann, *Die doppelte Staatsgründung*, 47–8; 'Ascension pass' in Heineman, 'The hour of the Woman', 32: 'Himmelfahrtskarte'.

26. Some schools in Berlin reopened in May, even though 2,474 of Berlin's remaining 5,000 teachers were barred as members of the Nazi Party: Kuby,

The Russians and Berlin, 318–21; also Grotum, *Die Halbstarken*, 45–6: school meals were introduced in the British and then the American Zones in 1946 and 1947. See also RA, Berufsschule Essen, M2/3; Gröschner, *Ich schlug meiner Mutter die brennenden Funken ab*, 255–7 and 262–3: Christa J.; Horst S., Greifenhagener Str. 53.

27. RA, Berufsschule Essen UI, Heinz B., 10 June 1956; Berufsschule Essen, anon., M2/3; Goetheschule Essen, anon., b. 1937; Burg-Gymnasium Essen, UII, anon.; Burg-Gymnasium Essen, UI, anon., 21 Feb. 1956.

28. Gries, *Die Rationen-Gesellschaft*, 27.

29. Norman Naimark, *Fires of Hatred: Ethnic Cleansing in Twentieth-Century Europe*, Cambridge, Mass., 2001, 108–38; Andreas Hofmann, *Nachkriegszeit in Schlesien: Gesellschafts- und Bevölkerungspolitik in den polnischen Siedlungsgebieten 1945–1948*, Cologne, 2000; report of a housing inspector in Bielefeld, 27 July 1946, in Klessmann, *Die doppelte Staatsgründung*, 358–9; on conflicts between locals and refugees, see also Rainer Schulze (ed.), *Unruhige Zeiten: Erlebnisberichte aus dem Landkreis Celle 1945–1949*, Munich, 1990; and his (ed.) *Zwischen Heimat und Zuhause: Deutsche Flüchtlinge und Vertriebene in (West-)Deutschland 1945–2000*, Osnabrück, 2001.

30. KA 3915, Johannes W., 'Die Familie B. 1945/46 in Briefen und Dokumenten', MS, Frau B. to Dr Otto B., Kneese, 10 Dec. 1945; Ingrid B. to father, Kneese, 10 Dec. 1945. For other accounts of the expulsions through children's eyes, see Alena Wagnerová, *1945 waren sie Kinder: Flucht und Vertreibung im Leben einer Generation*, Cologne, 1990.

31. Meyer and Schulze, '"Als wir wieder zusammen waren, ging der Krieg im Kleinen weiter"', 315–19; Jürgen Zinnecker, *Jugendkultur 1940–1985*, Opladen, 1987, 67; dividing the bread, DLA, Annelies G., b. 25 May 1931, 'Vater, Mutter und ich', MS, 71; KA 4622, Peter Laudan, 'Gefährdete Spiele', b. 1935, 34.

32. KA 4622, Peter Laudan, 'Gefährdete Spiele', 34–5.

33. Macardle, *Children of Europe*, 287, citing *International Child Welfare Review*, 2, 1948, 3; Klessmann, *Die doppelte Staatsgründung*, 50–1; Sibylle Meyer and Eva Schulze, *Wie wir das alles geschafft haben: Alleinstehende Frauen berichten über ihr Leben nach 1945*, Munich, 1985, 100–1; Jörg Roesler, 'The Black Market in Post-war Berlin and the Methods Used to Counteract It', *German History*, 7/1, 1989, 92–107.

34. Meyer and Schulze, *Wie wir das alles geschafft haben*, 103–8; A. L. Lloyd, 'Germany's Child Smugglers', *Picture Post*, 4 Oct. 1947, cited in Macardle, *Children of Europe*, 287–8.

35. Sosnowski, *The Tragedy of Children under Nazi Rule*, 167–71.

36. In general, see Thérèse Brosse, *War-Handicapped Children: Report on the European Situation*, Paris, 1950, 77–100, and Sosnowski, *The Tragedy of Children under Nazi Rule*, 175–84; for Breitenau cases, see LWV 2/4379, Hella W., b. 28 Jan. 1932, Amtsgericht Rotenburg/Fulda, 9: 1 Aug. 1946; LWV 2/4743, Elfriede D., b. 9 Apr. 1930, 15; LWV 2/4239 and 4251, Gerda H., b. 7 May 1932; numbers in Ayass, *Das Arbeitshaus Breitenau*, 327 and 336.

37. Looking to forced labourers for protection from the Red Army, see Bundesministerium für Vertriebene, *Dokumentation der Vertreibung*, 1, 199–200 and 205–6; and Moeller, *War Stories*, 81; KA 3666/1, Gisela G.,

b. 15 July 1933, diary: 26 Apr., 12, 26 and 27 May and 6–27 June 1945. Muggings were up 800–1,200 per cent in 1946 compared with 1928, the last year of pre-war Weimar stability, a year chosen also to avoid falsified police data from the Nazi period: Wolfgang Jacobmeyer, *Vom Zwangsarbeiter zum heimatlosen Ausländer: Die Displaced Persons in Westdeutschland 1945–1951*, Göttingen, 1985, 46–50 and 204–15; Herbert, *Hitler's Foreign Workers*, 378–80; and his 'Apartheid nebenan', in Lutz Niethammer (ed.), *'Die Jahre weiss man nicht, wo man die heute hinsetzen soll': Faschismuserfahrungen im Ruhrgebiet*, Berlin, 1983, 258–62.

38. Judgement and similar cases in Richard J. Evans, *Rituals of Retribution: Capital Punishment in Germany, 1600–1987*, Oxford, 1996, 750–5; Jacobmeyer, *Vom Zwangsarbeiter zum heimatlosen Ausländer*, 212–14, 217, 211 and 224–31.

39. KA 3088, Nachlass Richard W., essays from a school in Tegel where he taught: e.g., Renate N. and D.H.; Gröschner, *Ich schlug meiner Mutter die brennenden Funken ab*, 255–7: Christa J., b. 1931, Göhrener Str. 3, Mädchenoberschule, 5. Klasse; and 215–17: Liane H., Bötzowstr. 57.

40. Gröschner, *Ich schlug meiner Mutter die brennenden Funken ab*, 20–1; 258–9: Christel B., Winsstr. 16, Mädchenoberschule, 7. Klasse; and 199–201: Hans H., Diesterwegstr. 7.

41. Hansjörg Riechert, *Im Schatten von Auschwitz: Die nationalsozialistische Sterilisationspolitik gegenüber Sinti und Roma*, Münster, 1995, 124–6; Gilad Margalit, *Germany and Its Gypsies: A Post-Auschwitz Ordeal*, Madison, WI, 2002, 83–142.

42. See chapter 2 above and Krausnick, *Auf Wiedersehen im Himmel*, 77–135.

43. Yara-Colette Lemke Muniz de Faria, *Zwischen Fürsorge und Ausgrenzung: Afrodeutsche 'Besatzungskinder' im Nachkriegsdeutschland*, Berlin, 2002; Heide Fehrenbach, 'Of German Mothers and "Negermischlingskinder": Race, Sex, and the Postwar Nation' in Schissler, *The Miracle Years*, 164–86; Maria Höhn, *GIs and Fräuleins: The German–American Encounter in 1950s West Germany*, Chapel Hill, NC, 2002.

44. For this and the Brno expulsions, see Naimark, *Fires of Hatred*, 114–36; Theodor Schieder, 'Introduction' in his *The Expulsion of the German Population*, 69–94; Alena Wagnerová, *1945 waren sie Kinder*; Alois Harasko, 'Die Vertreibung der Sudetendeutschen: Sechs Erlebnisberichte' in Benz, *Die Vertreibung der Deutschen aus dem Osten*, 109–11; Bundesministerium für Vertriebene, *Dokumentation der Vertreibung*, 2, 158, 202, 210 and 330–1; Alfred-Maurice de Zayas, *A Terrible Revenge: The Ethnic Cleansing of the East European Germans, 1944–1950*, New York, 1994, 86; Enno S. in KA 3245, anon., diary, 1 Mar.–9 July 1945: 6 and 17 May 1945.

45. KA 1110/3, Monika T., 'Meiner lieben Mutter, zum Geburstag 1949'; KA 4058, Hans-Jürgen S.; see also KA 1759 for an East Prussian example; Moeller, *War Stories*, chapter 3.

46. Poll in Anna Merritt and Richard Merritt (eds), *Public Opinion in Occupied Germany: The OMGUS Surveys, 1945–1949*, Urbana, 1970, 18–21; Moeller, *War Stories*, chapter 3, esp. 72–81; Beer, 'Im Spannungsfeld von Politik und Zeitgeschichte: Das Grossforschungsprojekt "Dokumentation der Deutschen aus Ost-Mitteleuropa"'.

47. On sociological surveys, see Volker Ackermann, 'Das Schweigen der Flüchtlingskinder: Psychische Folgen von Krieg, Flucht und Vertreibung bei

den Deutschen nach 1945', *Geschichte und Gesellschaft*, 30/3, 2004, 434–64; I am grateful to Svenja Goltermann for sharing the details of Margarete's case, which she offers a different interpretation of in her forthcoming essay, 'The Imagination of Disaster'; the case is from Hauptarchiv der von Bodelschwinghschen Anstalten Bethel, Bestand Kidron, 4124.

48. The researchers themselves represented the whole range from American-inspired opinion research to Nazi academics working with crude social Darwinist ideas: see Ackermann, 'Das Schweigen der Flüchtlingskinder', 447–52.

49. Overmans, *Deutsche militärische Verluste im zweiten Weltkrieg*, 228–39 and, for a recalculation of the official estimates of deaths of civilians in the East in the light of military losses from the same territories, 298–9; Groehler, *Bombenkrieg gegen Deutschland*, 316–20.

50. Statistics in Grotum, *Die Halbstarken*, 47; Wolfgang Hempel in Schulz, Radebold and Reulecke, *Söhne ohne Väter*, 31–2 and 88–9; Alf Lüdtke, 'Histories of Mourning: Flowers and Stones for the War Dead, Confusion for the Living – Vignettes from East and West Germany' in Gerald Sider and Gavin Smith (eds), *Between History and Histories: The Making of Silences and Commemorations*, Toronto, 1977, 149–79.

51. Neil Gregor, '"Is He still Alive, or Long since Dead?": Loss, Absence and Remembrance in Nuremberg, 1945–1956', *German History*, 21/2, 2003, 186–91. See also Albrecht Lehmann, *Gefangenschaft und Heimkehr: Deutsche Kriegsgefangene in der Sowjetunion*, Munich, 1986, 115–17; Moeller, *War Stories*, chapter 4; Annette Kaminsky (ed.), *Heimkehr 1948: Geschichte und Schicksale deutscher Kriegsgefangener*, Munich, 1998.

52. Bergau, *Der Junge von der Bernsteinküste*, 125–82; KA 4025, Heinz M., 'Die Pestbeule: Autobiographische Erinnerungen der Kriegs- und Vorkriegszeit'; KA 1997, Werner K., '20 Monate Luftwaffenhelfer: Tagebücher 5. Januar 1944–20. August 1945', 19 Aug. 1945; only two of the 1,358 essays collected in Prenzlauer Berg schools in 1946 were written by boys who had served in the *Volkssturm*: Gröschner, *Ich schlug meiner Mutter die brennenden Funken ab*, 12 and 17; on the Hitler Youth generation in post-war East and West Germany, see Alexander von Plato, 'The Hitler Youth Generation and Its Role in the Two Post-war German States' in Roseman, *Generations in Conflict*, 210–26; Bude, *Deutsche Karrieren*.

53. Overmans, *Deutsche militärische Verluste*, 300–1, and 231 and 286; 'Kriegsgefangene und Wehrmachtsvermisste aus Hessen: Vorläufige Ergebnisse der amtlichen Registrierung vom 20.–30. Juni 1947', *Staat und Wirtschaft in Hessen: Statistische Mitteilungen*, 2 (1947), no. 4, 110–12; Burkhart Müller-Hillebrand, *Das Heer 1933–1945*, 3, *Der Zweifrontenkrieg*, Darmstadt, 1969, 263; Arthur Lee Smith, *Die 'vermisste Million': Zum Schicksal deutscher Kriegsgefangener nach dem zweiten Weltkrieg*, Munich, 1992, 62–4; Kurt W. Böhme, *Gesucht wird . . . Die dramatische Geschichte des Suchdienstes*, Munich, 1965, 115 and 234–7.

54. Knoch, *Die Tat als Bild*, 314–23; Moeller, *War Stories*, chapter 4 and figs 11–16; Biess, 'Survivors of Totalitarianism', 57–82, and 63 for letter by Frau R.

55. Liselotte G. in Hammer and zur Niedern, *Sehr selten habe ich geweint*, 314–16: 17 May 1945.

56. Ibid., 316: 17 May 1945.

57. For Aachen in Sept.–Dec. 1944, see Bankier, 'German Public Awareness of the Final Solution', 216; Klessmann, *Die doppelte Staatsgründung*, 372–4: doc. 25, 'Bericht des amerikanischen Geheimdienstes über die Einstellung der deutschen Bevölkerung in der US-Zone', 12 Aug. 1945; Moeller, *War Stories*, 25–49 and 78–9; Anna Merritt and Richard Merritt (eds), *Public Opinion in Semisovereign Germany: The HICOG Surveys, 1949–1955*, Urbana, 1980, 9; on the restitution payments to Israel, see Frank Stern, *The Whitewashing of the Yellow Badge: Antisemitism and Philosemitism in Postwar Germany*, Oxford, 1992, 352, 367 and 382; Constantin Goschler (ed.), *Wiedergutmachung: Westdeutschland und die Verfolgten des Nationalsozialismus (1950–1954)*, Munich, 1992, 257–85; on the Law to Equalise Burdens, see Hans Günther Hockerts, 'Integration der Gesellschaft: Gründungskrise und Sozialpolitik in der frühen Bundesrepublik', *Zeitschrift für Sozialreform*, 32, 1986, 25–41; Michael Hughes, *Shouldering the Burdens of Defeat: West Germany and the Reconstruction of Social Justice*, Chapel Hill, NC, 1999.

58. Mommsen, 'Gesellschaftsbild und Verfassungspläne des deutschen Widerstandes'; Richard Overy, *Interrogations: The Nazi Elite in Allied Hands, 1945*, London, 2001.

59. Merritt and Merritt, *Public Opinion in Occupied Germany*, 32–3; Knoch, *Die Tat als Bild*, 356–425; Hans Wagener, 'Soldaten zwischen Gehorsam und Gewissen: Kriegsromane und Kriegstagebücher' in his (ed.) *Gegenwartsliteratur und Drittes Reich: Deutsche Autoren in der Auseinandersetzung mit der Vergangenheit*, Stuttgart, 1977, 241–64.

60. KA 4500/68, Alfred M., notice, Aug. 1949; wearing mourning, see Alfred M., letter to Walter Kempowski, 15 May 1996. See also Sabine Behrenbeck, 'Between Pain and Silence: Remembering the Victims of Violence in Germany after 1949' in Bessel and Schumann, *Life after Death*, 37–64; Elisabeth Domansky and Jutta de Jong, *Der lange Schatten des Krieges: Deutsche Lebens-Geschichten nach 1945*, Münster, 2000; and Domansky, 'A Lost War: World War Two in Post-war German Memory' in Alvin Rosenfeld (ed.), *Thinking about the Holocaust after Half a Century*, Bloomington, 1997, 233–72.

61. Siegfried Bork, *Missbrauch der Sprache: Tendenzen nationalsozialistischer Sprachregelung*, Bern, 1970, 99. Richard Sheppard has pointed out that 'Die Aktion' and 'Der Sturm' re-entered German culture via an unlikely route: the rediscovery of Expressionism: see the catalogue, *Expressionismus: Literatur und Kunst 1910–1923: Eine Ausstellung des deutschen Literaturarchivs im Schiller-Nationalmuseum Marbach a. N.*, Marbach, 1960.

62. Konrad Ehlich, 'Über den Faschismus sprechen – Analyse und Diskurs' in his (ed.) *Sprache im Faschismus*, Frankfurt, 1989, 7–34; Dolf Sternberger, Gerhard Storz and W. E. Süsking, *Aus dem Wörterbuch des Unmenschen*, Hamburg, 1968, 31–6, 45–50, 57–63, 109–13 and 168–72.

63. See use of these essays made in chapters 8–11 above; on the creation of the collection, see Heinz Abels, Heinz-Hermann Krüger and Hartmut Rohrman, '"Jugend im Erziehungsfeld": Schüleraufsätze aus den fünfziger Jahren im Roessler-Archiv', *BIOS*, 1, 1989, 139–50; on unpopularity of rearmament among the young, see Alan McDougall, 'From *Tag X* to the Prague Spring: Crisis Points in the History of the Free German Youth (FDJ), 1952–1968', D. Phil. thesis, University of Oxford, 2001, 21–9; Grotum, *Die Halbstarken*, 47; see also Uta Poiger, *Jazz, Rock and Rebels: Cold War Politics and American Culture in a Divided Germany*, Berkeley, 2000.

64. Reading in Schulz, Radebold and Reulecke, *Söhne ohne Väter*, 50–5; Manfred Gregor, *Die Brücke*, Munich, 1958; Hans Hellmut Kirst, *08/15: In der Kaserne, Im Krieg, Bis zum Ende: Gesamtausgabe der Trilogie*, Munich, 2001; Albrecht Goes, *Unruhige Nacht*, Hamburg, 1951; Holger Klein, *The Second World War in Fiction*, London, 1984; Wagener, 'Soldaten zwischen Gehorsam und Gewissen'; Knoch, *Die Tat als Bild*, 372–85; Jochen Pfeifer, *Der deutsche Kriegsroman 1945–1960: Ein Versuch zur Vermittlung von Literatur und Sozialgeschichte*, Königstein, 1981; Keith Bullivant and C. Jane Rice, 'Reconstruction and Integration: The Culture of West German Stabilization 1945–1968' in Rob Burns (ed.), *German Cultural Studies: An Introduction*, Oxford, 1995, 225–7.

65. Timm, *Am Beispiel meines Bruders*, 11–16, 57–60, 63–4, 70, 75–6, 89–90, 97–9 and 151.

66. Helmut Schelsky, *Die skeptische Generation: Eine Soziologie der deutschen Jugend*, Düsseldorf, 1957; also Franz-Werner Kersting, 'Helmut Schelskys "Skeptische Generation" von 1957', *Vierteljahrshefte für Zeitgeschichte*, 50, 2002, 465–95.

Chapter 12

1. Angelika Königseder, *Flucht nach Berlin: Jüdische Displaced Persons 1945–1948*, Berlin, 1998, 164–5; YIVO archives, Leo W. Schwarz Papers, 481, press release of the Central Komitet fun di bafrajte Jidn in der amerikaner zone, Department of Public Relations, Munich, 26 Sept. 1947; Menuhin was much criticised in the USA and Israel for championing Furtwängler and also gives a more positive account of this encounter in his memoirs: see Yehudi Menuhin, *Unfinished Journey*, London, 2001, 230–6; Sam Shirakawa, *The Devil's Music Master: The Controversial Life and Career of Wilhelm Furtwängler*, Oxford, 1992, 345–55.

2. Angelika Königseder and Juliane Wetzel, *Lebensmut im Wartesaal: Die jüdischen DPs (Displaced Persons) im Nachkriegsdeutschland*, Frankfurt, 1994, 25, 42 and 47–53.

3. On conflicts between Poles and Jews in Bergen-Belsen, see United Nations Archives, UNRRA, PAG 4/4.2: 82 (S-0524-0106): Office of the Historian, Monographs, DP BR 12, History of Child Welfare Sources, 'Section "F" Repatriation and resettlement of unaccompanied children'; Königseder and Wetzel, *Lebensmut im Wartesaal*, 47, the British numbers were for June 1946; YIVO Archives, Leo W. Schwartz Papers, 54, 89 and 92: Leo W. Schwartz, 'Report on AJDC program in the American Zone' 12 Jan. 1947; Susan Pettiss, 'Report on Jewish infiltree children' and 'Children in German homes and institutions whose nationality is not yet finally established'.

4. YIVO Archives, Leo W. Schwartz Papers, 87, 'Displaced Persons, 1945–1946: Office of the Chief Historian European Command', 61–2; Königseder and Wetzel, *Lebensmut im Wartesaal*, 138; Jacobmeyer, *Vom Zwangsarbeiter zum heimatlosen Ausländer*, 193–4.

5. YIVO Archives, Leo W. Schwartz Papers, 520 and 89, American Joint Distribution Committee (AJDC) Berlin, 'Quarterly Report for the period April 1 to June 30 1947' and Susan Pettiss, 'Report on Jewish infiltree children'.

6. I am grateful to Juliane Wetzel for making the following material available to me: YIVO Archives, DP Collection, Germany, folder 2212, Central

Information Office London: Miriam Warburg, 'Conditions of Jewish children in a Bavarian rehabilitation camp'.

7. Ibid.

8. Ibid.; Königseder and Wetzel, *Lebensmut im Wartesaal*, 110, citing Marie Syrkin, *The State of the Jews*, Washington, 1980, 21–2; on Landsberg, see Angelika Eder, *Flüchtige Heimat: Jüdische Displaced Persons in Landsberg am Lech 1945 bis 1950*, Munich, 1998; Miriam Warburg on a mother being reunited with a daughter she threw from a deportation train from Łódź, Warburg, 'Personal Experiences of camp inmates at D.P. Center of Foehrenwald, Bavaria', *Jews in Europe Today*, 2, Feb. 1946.

9. Sosnowski, *The Tragedy of Children under Nazi Rule*, 172.

10. United Nations Archives, UNRRA, PAG 4/1.1.3.5.6.2: 13 (S-0518-798): Bureau of Administration, Administrative Services Division, Records Section, Central Registry, Registry files (1944–9), Mission files, German Mission, Monthy Narrative Report 46/271, Oct. 1946, Eileen Blackey, 'Minutes of Inter-zonal conference on child search and repatriation, October 16, 17 and 18, 1946'; United Nations Archives, UNRRA, PAG 4/4.2: 82 (S-0524-0106): Office of the Historian, Monographs, DP BR 21A, Michael Sorensen, 'Some observations at the conclusion of six months of child search and investigation', 8 Aug. 1946; United Nations Archives, UNRRA, PAG 4/4.2: 84 (S-0524-0108): Office of the Historian, Monographs, DP BR 32, North Rhine-Westphalia, Miss E. Dunkel, 'Memorandum on child search', 13 June 1947, 460 UNRRA HQ and Brigadier T. J. King, UNRRA Regional Director, North Rhine-Westfalia, 'Unofficial Report for Miss H. Pollak'.

11. Drolshagen, *Nicht ungeschoren davonkommen*; Virgili, *Shorn Women*; Kjendsli, *Kinder der Schande*; Polish claims, Hrabar; Sosnowski; Clay and Leapman, *Master Race*, 128, citing a June 1948 article in the newspaper *Życie Warszawy*.

12. Macardle, *Children of Europe*, 233–4.

13. United Nations Archives, PAG 4/1.1.3.5.6.2: 131 (S-0518–798): UNRRA, Bureau of Administration, Administrative Services Division, Records Section, Central Registry, Registry files (1944–9), Mission files, German Mission, Monthly Narrative Report 46/271, Nov. 1946, Eileen Blackey, 'Report of trip to Poland, 19–27 November 1946'.

14. See the case of Alojzy Twardecki, alias Alfred Binderberger, in Clay and Leapman, *Master Race*, 105–14.

15. See Tycner, 'Grupa doktora Franciszka Witaszka', cited in Madajczyk, *Die Okkupationspolitik Nazideutschlands*, 473 n. 56; Clay and Leapman, *Master Race*, 118–19.

16. Clay and Leapman, *Master Race*, 159–76.

17. Sosnowski, *The Tragedy of Children*, annexe 22, 306–7; Lilienthal, *Der 'Lebensborn e.V.'*, 216; Hrabar, Tokarz and Wilczur, *Kinder im Krieg*, 87; Leapman, *Witnesses to War*, 106; Macardle, *Children of Europe*, 235, 238–40 and 296.

18. United Nations Archives, UNRRA, PAG 4/4.2: 84 (UN, S-0524–0108): Office of the Historian, Monographs, DP BR 32, North Rhine-Westphalia, Dunkel, 'Memorandum on child search'; United Nations Archives, PAG 4/1.1.3.5.6.2: 13 (S-0518–798): UNRRA, Bureau of Administration, Administrative Services Division, Records Section, Central Registry, Registry files (1944–9), Mission files, German Mission, Monthly Narrative Report

46/271, Oct. 1946, Blackey, 'Minutes of Inter-zonal conference on child search and repatriation, October 16, 17 and 18, 1946'; Clay and Leapman, *Master Race*, 128–30.

19. Aitchison, *Caught in the Crossfire*, 66–8 and 197–9.

20. David, *A Touch of Earth*, 162–90.

21. Ibid., 192–3 and 206.

22. Ibid.

23. Martin Gilbert, *The Boys: Triumph over Adversity*, London, 1996, 254–86.

24. Anna Freud and Dorothy Burlingham, *Heimatlose Kinder*, Frankfurt, 1982, 191, and her 1951 essay, 'An Experiment in Group Upbringing' in *The Writings of Anna Freud*, 4, 1968, New York, 163–229. For the children's later lives, see Gilbert, *The Boys*, 286, and Sarah Moskovitz, *Love despite Hate: Child Survivors of the Holocaust and Their Adult Lives*, New York, 1983.

25. Anna Freud, 'Child Observation and Prediction of Development: A Memorial Lecture in Honour of Ernst Kris', in *The Writings of Anna Freud*, 5, 133.

26. Warburg, 'Personal Experiences of camp inmates at D.P. Center of Foehrenwald, Bavaria', 2. The major statement of Anna Freud's position is in her *Ego and the Mechanisms of Defence*, London, 1936; for a brief introduction to the Freud–Klein debate, see 'Ego psychology' in R. D. Hinshelwood, *A Dictionary of Kleinian Thought*, London, 1989, 286–95. Anna Freud's theory that a child deprived of parents early on only encounters difficulties later, during latency and adolescence, in forming any secure and stable sense of self has influenced some subsequent writing in this field: see Edith Ludowyk Gyomroi, 'The Analysis of a Young Concentration Camp Victim', *The Psychoanalytic Study of the Child*, 18, 1963, 484–510; Flora Hogman, 'Displaced Jewish Children during World War II: How They Coped', *Journal of Humanistic Psychology*, 23, 1983, 51–67. For discussions among directors of children's homes, see Thérèse Brosse, *Homeless Children: Report of the Proceedings of the Conference of Directors of the Children's Communities, Trogen, Switzerland*, Paris, 1950, 22, 27 and 43–4; John Bowlby's study of 200 British children under twelve, who had war-related problems, concluded that in one-third of cases evacuation rather than bombing was the cause: John Bowlby, *Child Care and the Growth of Love*, London, 1965, 42; for similar views among German specialists working with German refugee children, see Ackermann, 'Das Schweigen der Flüchtlingskinder', 447–57.

27. Thomas Gève, *Es gibt hier keine Kinder: Auschwitz, Gross-Rosen, Buchenwald: Zeichnungen eines kindlichen Historikers*, Volkhard Knigge (ed.), Göttingen, 1997, 10–11; interview with the author, Southampton, Jan. 2003.

28. Gève, interview with the author, Southampton, Jan. 2003.

29. Gève, *Youth in Chains*, 18; and see chapter 1 above.

30. Kalman Landau, reproduced in *Du* magazine, Mar. 1946.

31. Landau, 'Krematorium', *Du* magazine, Mar. 1946; Gève, 'Auschwitzer Mordkammer', no. 35, in Yad Vashem Art Museum: also in Gève, *Es gibt hier keine Kinder*, 91. See 'Rambles in Terezin' in Křížková, Kotouč and Ornest, *We Are Children Just the Same*, 85–6.

32. Thomas Gève, interview with author and lecture, Southampton, Jan. 2003.

33. Yehuda Bacon, 'Portrait of K. Fuhrman', 1945, Beit Lohamei Haghetaot,

Museum no. 704; 'In Memory of the Czech Transport to the Gas Chambers', 1945, charcoal on paper, on loan to the Yad Vashem Art Museum; for his trial testimony in Frankfurt, see Fritz Bauer Institut (ed.), *Auschwitz-Prozess 4 Ks 2/63 Frankfurt am Main*, Ghent, 2004, 651–3; DöW 13243 Bacon interview with Ben-David Gershon, Jerusalem, 17 Nov. 1964, 68. Bacon may have already been developing some of the ideas for this portrait of his father before the 'family camp' was dissolved: he describes drawing a hand clenched like a claw above the smoking crematorium: ibid., 46–7.

34. Kitty Hart, *Return to Auschwitz: The Remarkable Story of a Girl who Survived the Holocaust*, London, 1983, 14; on silence in the 1950s and 1960s, see Kushner, *The Holocaust and the Liberal Imagination*; and Novick, *The Holocaust and Collective Memory*; for some of the testimonies collected by the Central Jewish Historical Commission in Poland – from 1947, the Jewish Historical Institute in Warsaw – see Hochberg-Mariańska and Grüss, *The Children Accuse*; see also, Natalia Aleksiun, 'Polish Historiography of the Holocaust – Between Silence and Public Debate', *German History*, 22/3, 2004, 406–32; Ilana Tahan, *Memorial Volumes to Jewish Communities Destroyed in the Holocaust: A Bibliography of British Library Holdings*, London, 2003; and for a selection, see Jack Kugelmass and Jonathan Boyarin (eds), *From a Ruined Garden: The Memorial Books of Polish Jewry*, New York, 1983.

35. Davies and Moorhouse, *Microcosm*, 417–44; Gregor Thum, *Die fremde Stadt: Breslau 1945*, Berlin, 2003; Bohdan Kordan, 'Making Borders Stick: Population Transfer and Resettlement in the Trans-Curzon Territories, 1944–1949', *International Migration Review*, 31, no. 3 (1997), 704–20.

36. Lagrou, *The Legacy of Nazi Occupation in Western Europe*; Dmitrów, *Niemcy i okupacja hitlerowska w oczach Polaków*; Steinlauf, *Bondage to the Dead*; Sosnowski, *The Tragedy of Children under Nazi Rule*, 165–7.

37. Zdzisłow Grot and Wincenty Ostrowski, *Wspomnienia młodzieży wielkopolskiej z lat okupacji niemieckiej 1939–1945*, Poznań, 1946, cited in Sosnowski, *The Tragedy of Children under Nazi Rule*, 166; Kamiński, *Kamienie na szaniec*; *Przekrój*, 43, 50–8, 1946; Stephan Szuman, 'La guerre et l'occupation dans les dessins des enfants polonais', *Sauvegarde*, 4, 1949, 28–57; *Berliner Zeitung*, 27 Oct. 1945, cited in Wilfrid Ranke et al. (eds), *Kultur, Pajoks und Care-Pakete: Eine Berliner Chronik 1945–49*, Berlin, 1990, 86–7.

38. Brosse, *War-Handicapped Children*, 19–20 and 77–100; Sosnowski, *The Tragedy of Children under Nazi Rule*, 165–7; Helena Radomska-Strzemecka, 'Okupacja w oczach młodzieży' in Józef Wnuk and Helena Radomska-Strzemecka, *Dzieci polskie oskarżają (1939–1945)*, Warsaw, 1961, 195–379.

39. DöW, MS, Nina Weilová, 'Erinnerungen', 13 and 25; see also chapter 7 above.

40. On the memorial discussion, see Peter Reichel, *Politik mit der Erinnerung: Gedächtnisorte im Streit um die nationalsozialistische Vergangenheit*, Munich and Vienna, 1995; and more generally, see Etienne François and Hagen Schulze (eds), *Deutsche Erinnerungsorte*, 1–3, Munich, 2002; James Young, *The Texture of Memory: Holocaust Memorials and Meaning*, New Haven and London, 1993.

41. Dinora Pines, 'Working with Women Survivors of the Holocaust' in her *A Woman's Unconscious Use of Her Body: A Psychoanalytical Perspective*,

London, 1993, 178–204; Primo Levi, *If This Is Man and The Truce*, London, 1987.

42. Anita Franková, b. 13 July 1930, deported to Theresienstadt 3 Aug. 1942, deported to Auschwitz 18 Dec. 1943, interview with the author, Prague, Apr. 1994, and letter to author, 11 Nov. 2004; see Kárný et al., *Terezínská Pamětní Kniha*, 863.

43. Klemperer, *To the Bitter End*, 2, 387–96: 13–24 Feb. 1945; RA, Burg-Gymnasium Essen, UII/522, anon., 2. See RA, Burg-Gymnasium Essen, UI/641, 2, for a similar record of the excitement of watching the bombing of Essen from a village 20 kilometres away. On Dresden, see also Götz Bergander, *Dresden im Luftkrieg: Vorgeschichte – Zerstörung – Folgen*, Cologne, 1977, 148–95 and 290–2; for destruction of home, see Marion to her father, in Lange and Burkard, '*Abends wenn wir essen fehlt uns immer einer*', 185: 3 Dec. 1943; RA, Berufsschule Essen, M2/2, 1–2; Gröschner, *Ich schlug meiner Mutter die brennenden Funken ab*, 147–9: Christa B., Dänenstr. 1, Mädchenmittelschule II, 4; YVA 0.3 1202 Bacon interviews with Chaim Mass, Jerusalem, 13 Feb. 1959, 17 and 44, and DöW 13243 with Ben-David Gershon, Jerusalem, 17 Nov. 1964, 49 and 60.

44. Timm, *Am Beispiel meines Bruders*, 37–8.

45. Niethammer, *Ego-Histoire?*, 184–5 and 188–91.

46. Ibid.; DLA, Karl P., 'Hunger – Krieg und Kinderjahre!', 12.

47. Passerini, 'Work Ideology and Consensus under Italian Fascism'; Reinhard Sieder, 'A Hitler Youth from a Respectable Family' in Daniel Bertaux and Paul Thompson (eds), *International Yearbook of Oral History and Life Stories*, 2, *Between Generations: Family Models, Myths, and Memories*, Oxford, 1993, 99–120; Rosenthal, *Erlebte und erzählte Lebensgeschichte*; Ulrich Herbert, 'Good Times, Bad Times: Memories of the Third Reich' in Richard Bessel (ed.), *Life in the Third Reich*, Oxford, 1987, 97–110; Michelle Mouton and Helena Pohlandt-McCormick, 'Boundary Crossings: Oral History of Nazi Germany and Apartheid South Africa – A Comparative Perspective', *History Workshop Journal*, 48, Autumn 1999, 41–63; Lawrence Langer, *Holocaust Testimonies: The Ruins of Memory*, New Haven, 1991; and more generally on this open-ended question, see esp. Portelli, 'The Death of Luigi Trastulli: Memory and the Event'; and Figlio, 'Oral History and the Unconscious'; Lothar C., interview with Alexander von Plato and the author, 26 Mar. 1999, Institut für Geschichte und Biographie, Aussenstelle der Fernuniversität Hagen, Lüdenscheid.

48. Hans Medick, b. 1939, interviews with the author in Göttingen, Mar. 1998 and Aug. 2001.

49. KA 2035, Wilhelm Körner., b. 1929, letter to Walter Kempowski, 14 Oct. 1987; also letter to the author, 29 Oct. 2004; diary for 23 Mar. 1942–29 May 1947: 16 May 1945.

50. Harald Welzer, Sabine Moller and Karoline Tschuggnall, '*Opa war kein Nazi*': *Nationalsozialismus und Holocaust im Familiengedächtnis*, Frankfurt, 2002; also Westernhagen, *Die Kinder der Täter*; and Bar-On, *Legacy of Silence*.

51. Anneliese H.'s diary, 1 May 1945, in Kuby, *The Russians and Berlin*, 226.

52. Anne Frank, *Das Tagebuch der Anne Frank: 14. Juni 1942–1. August 1944*, Frankfurt, 1955; Alvin Rosenfeld, 'Popularization and Memory: The Case of Anne Frank' in Peter Hayes (ed.), *Lessons and Legacies: The Meaning of the Holocaust in a Changing World*, Evanston, Ill., 1991,

243–78; Anat Feinberg, *Wiedergutmachung im Programm: Jüdisches Schicksal im deutschen Nachkriegsdrama*, Cologne, 1988, 17–18.

53. Heinrich Böll, *Wo warst du, Adam?*, Frankfurt, 1959; Uwe Johnson, *Mutmassungen über Jakob*, Frankfurt, 1959; Günter Grass, *Hundejahre*, Neuwied, 1963; see Elizabeth Boa and J. H. Reid, *Critical Strategies: German Fiction in the Twentieth Century*, London, 1972.

54. For Rudolf W., see chapter 1, and for Walb, see introduction above.

55. Dr Walter Robert Corti (1910–90). The village still exists, caring for the orphans of international conflicts and victims of Aids.

56. Volkhard Knigge, 'With the eyes of a child historian and engineer' in Gève, *Es gibt hier keine Kinder*, 29–34, citing the diary of Lieselott Walz; Ian Serraillier, *The Silver Sword*, London, 1956, 183–7.

57. Dr Marie Meierhofer (1909–98) in Brosse, *Homeless Children*, 26–7, 30–2 and 43–4; Macardle, *Children of Europe*, 253–4.

GLOSSARY OF PLACE NAMES

German–Polish (unless otherwise specified)

Allenstein	Olsztyn	Kalisch	Kalisz
Auschwitz	Oświęcim	Kamin	Kamień Krajeński
Bad Polzin	Połczyn Zdrój	Kattowitz	Katowice
Beuthen	Bytom	Kirchberg	Wiśniowa Góra
Birkenau	Brzezinka	Königsau	Równe/Rivne
Braunsberg	Braniewo		(Ukrainian)
Breslau	Wrocław	Königsberg	Królewiec/
Brest-Litovsk	Brześć Litewski		Kaliningrad
(Russian)			(Russian)
Brieg	Brzeg	Kolberg	Kołobrzeg
Brockau	Brochów [now	Konitz	Chojnice
	Wrocław-Brochów]	Kulmhof	Chełmno
Bromberg	Bydgoszcz	Küstrin	Kostrzyn
Brünn	Bezrzecze [now	Kremsier	Kromeriz (Czech)
	Szczecin-Bezrzecze]	Lemberg	Lwów/Lviv
Cosel	Koźle		(Ukrainian)/Lvov
Danzig	Gdańsk		(Russian)
Dirschau	Tczew	Leobschütz	Glubczyce
Elbing	Elbląg	Liegnitz	Legnica
Freystadt	Kożuchów (Śląsk)	Lodsch/	Łódź
Frisches Haff	Zalew Wiślany	Litzmannstadt	
Gerdauen	Schelesnidoroschni	Loslau	Wodzisław Śląski
	(Russian)	Mährisch-Ostrau	Moravská Ostrava
Gleiwitz	Gliwice		(Czech)
Glogau	Głogów	Marienburg	Malbork
Gotenhafen/Gdingen	Gdynia	Marienwerder	Kwidzyń
Graudenz	Grudziądz	Märkisch Friedland	Mirosławiec
Gumbinnen	Gusew (Russian)	Mohrungen	Morąg
Heiligenbeil	Mamonowo (Russian)	Neisse	Nysa (river)
Hela	Hel	Neutief	Kosa (Russian)
Hindenburg	Zabrze	Neustadt	Prudnik
Hohensalza	Inowrocław	Oder	Odra (river)
Kahlberg	Krynica Morska	Oppeln	Opole

Osterode	Ostróda	Stolp	Słupsk
Palmnicken	Jantarny (Russia)	Stutthof	Sztutowo
Pillau	Pilawa/Baltijsk	Theresienstadt	Terezín (Czech)
	(Russian)	Thorn	Toruń
Posen	Poznań	Tolkemit	Tolkmicko
Preussisch Holland	Pasłęk	Tschenstochau	Częstochowa
Puschkau	Pastuchów	Turck	Turek
Pyritz	Pyrzyce	Vilnius (Lithuanian)	Wilno (Polish)/Vilna
Rastenburg	Kętrzyn		(Yiddish)
Ratibor	Racibórz	Warthe	Warta (river)
Reppen	Rzepin	Wehlau	Welawa/Znamiensk
Rügenwalde	Darłowo		(Russian)
Schweidnitz	Świdnica	Zempelburg	Sępolno Krajeńskie
Schippenbeil	Sępopol	Zichenau	Ciechanów
Schwetz	Świecie	Züllichau	Sulechów
Stettin	Szczecin		

Polish–German (unless otherwise specified)

Bezrzecze	Brünn	Mamonowo	Heiligenbeil
Braniewo	Braunsberg	(Russian)	
Brochów	Brockau	Mirosławiec	Märkisch Friedland
Brzeg	Brieg	Morąg	Mohrungen
Brześć Litewski	Brest-Litovsk	Nysa	Neisse (river)
	(Russian)	Odra	Oder (river)
Brzezinka	Birkenau	Olsztyn	Allenstein
Bydgoszcz	Bromberg	Opole	Oppeln
Bytom	Beuthen	Moravská Ostrava	Mährisch-Ostrau
Chełmno	Kulmhof	(Czech)	
Chojnice	Konitz	Ostróda	Osterode
Ciechanów	Zichenau	Oświęcim	Auschwitz
Częstochowa	Tschenstochau	Pasłęk	Prussian Holland
Darłowo	Rügenwalde	Pastuchów	Puschkau
Elbląg	Elbing	Pilawa	Pillau/Baltijsk
Gdańsk	Danzig		(Russian)
Gdynia	Gotenhafen/	Połczyn Zdrój	Bad Polzin
	Gdingen	Poznań	Posen
Gliwice	Gleiwitz	Pyrzyce	Pyritz
Głogów	Glogau	Racibórz	Ratibor
Grudziądz	Graudenz	Rzepin	Reppen
Gusew (Russian)	Gumbinnen	Równe	Königsau/Rivne
Hel	Hela		(Ukrainian)
Inowrocław	Hohensalza	Sępolno	Zempelburg
Jantarny (Russian)	Palmnicken	Krajeńskie	
Kalisz	Kalisch	Sępopol	Schippenbeil
Kamień Krajeński	Kamin	Sulechów	Züllichau
Katowice	Kattowitz	Szczecin	Stettin
Kętrzyn	Rastenburg	Sztutowo	Stutthof
Kołobrzeg	Kolberg	Świdnica	Schweidnitz
Kosa (Russia)	Neutief	Świecie	Schwetz
Kostrzyn	Küstrin	Tczew	Dirschau
Kożuchów (Śląsk)	Freystadt	Terezín (Czech)	Theresienstadt
Kromeriz (Czech)	Kremsier	Tolkmicko	Tolkemit
Królewiec	Königsberg/	Toruń	Thorn
	Kaliningrad	Turek	Turck
	(Russian)	Welawa	Wehlau/Znamiensk
Krynica Morska	Kahlberg		(Russian)
Kwidzyń	Marienwerder	Wilno	Vilnius (Lithuanian)/
Legnica	Liegnitz		Vilna (Yiddish)
Lwów	Lemberg/Lviv	Wiśniowa Góra	Kirchberg
	(Ukrainian)/Lvov	Wodzisław Śląski	Loslau
	(Russian)	Wrocław	Breslau
Łódź	Lodsch/	Zabrze	Hindenburg
	Litzmannstadt	Zalew Wiślany	Frisches Haff
Malbork	Marienburg		

ARCHIVAL SOURCES

Bundesarchiv, Berlin (BA)
Dokumentation des österreichischen Widerstandes, Vienna (DöW)
Dokumentation lebensgeschichtlicher Aufzeichnungen, Institut für
  Wirtschafts- und Sozialgeschichte, University of Vienna (DLA)
Gedenkstätte Neuengamme
Institut für Geschichte und Biographie, Aussenstelle der Fernuniversität
  Hagen, Lüdenscheid, Germany
Jewish Musuem, Prague, Terezín Collection (JMPTC)
Das Kempowski-Archiv, Haus Kreienhoop, Nartum, Germany (KA)
Landeswohlfahrtsverband Hessen, Kassel (LWV)
Wilhelm Roessler-Archiv, Institut für Geschichte und Biographie,
  Aussenstelle der Fernuniversität Hagen, Lüdenscheid, Germany (RA)
Stadtarchiv Göttingen
Stadtarchiv Munich
United Nations Archives, New York
Wiener Library, London
Yad Vashem Archive, Jerusalem (YVA)
Yad Vashem Art Museum, Jerusalem
YIVO Archives, New York: copies held on microfilm at the Zentrum
  für Antisemitismusforschung, Technische Universität, Berlin
Zentrum für Antisemitismusforschung, Technische Universität, Berlin

SELECT BIBLIOGRAPHY

ABELS, HEINZ, HEINZ-HERMANN KRÜGER and HARTMUT ROHRMAN, '"Jugend im Erziehungsfeld": Schüleraufsätze aus den fünfziger Jahren im Roessler-Archiv', *BIOS*, 1, 1989, 139–50

ABRAMS, LYNN, *The Orphan Country*, Edinburgh, 1998

ACKERMANN, VOLKER, 'Das Schweigen der Flüchtlingskinder: Psychische Folgen von Krieg, Flucht und Vertreibung bei den Deutschen nach 1945', *Geschichte und Gesellschaft*, 30/3, 2004, 434–64

ADELSON, ALAN (ed.), *The Diary of Dawid Sierakowiak: Five Notebooks from the Łódź Ghetto*, Oxford, 1996

ADELSON, ALAN, and ROBERT LAPIDES (eds), *Łódź Ghetto: Inside a Community under Siege*, New York, 1989

ADLER, HANS GÜNTHER, *Die verheimlichte Wahrheit: Theresienstädter Dokumente*, Tübingen, 1958

ADLER, HANS GÜNTHER, *Theresienstadt, 1941–1945: Das Antlitz einer Zwangsgemeinschaft*, Tübingen, 1960

AITCHISON, MARY, *Caught in the Crossfire: The Story of Janina Pladek*, Fearn, 1995

AINSZTEIN, RUEBEN, *Jüdischer Widerstand im deutschbesetzten Osteuropa während des Zweiten Weltkrieges*, Oldenburg, 1995

Akten zur deutschen Auswärtigen Politik 1918–1945, Serie D, 7, Baden-Baden and Göttingen, 1956

ALEKSIUN, NATALIA, 'Polish Historiography of the Holocaust: Between Silence and Public Debate', *German History*, 22/3, 2004, 406–32

ALEXIEJEWITSCH, SWETLANA, *Der Krieg hat kein weibliches Gesicht*, Hamburg, 1989

ALTER, REINHARD, and PETER MONTEATH (eds), *Rewriting the German Past: History and Identity in the New Germany*, Atlantic Highlands, NJ, 1997

ALY, GÖTZ, 'Der Mord an behinderten Kindern zwischen 1939 und 1945', in Angelika Ebbinghaus, Heidrun Kaupen-Haas and Karl Heinz Roth (eds), *Heilen and Vernichten im Mustergau Hamburg: Bevölkerungs- und Gesundheitspolitik im Dritten Reich*, Hamburg, 1984, 147–55

ALY, GÖTZ (ed.), *Aktion T-4 1939–1945: Die 'Euthanasie'-Zentrale in der Tiergartenstrasse 4*, Berlin, 1987

ALY, GÖTZ, *'Final Solution': Nazi Population Policy and the Murder of the European Jews*, London, 1999

ANDREWS, MOLLY, 'Grand National Narratives and the Project of Truth Commissions: A Comparative Analysis', *Media, Culture and Society*, 25, 2003, 45–65

ARAD, YITZHAK, *Ghetto in Flames: The Struggle and Destruction of the Jews in Vilna in the Holocaust*, New York, 1982

ARAD, YITZHAK, *Belzec, Sobibor, Treblinka: The Operation Reinhard Death Camps*, Bloomington, 1987

Arbeitsgruppe Pädagogisches Museum (ed.), *Heil Hitler, Herr Lehrer: Volksschule 1933–1945: Das Beispiel Berlin*, Hamburg, 1983

AUERBACHER, INGE, *I Am a Star: Child of the Holocaust*, New York, 1986

AXMANN, ARTHUR, *'Das kann doch nicht das Ende sein': Hitlers letzter Reichsjugendführer erinnert sich*, Koblenz, 1995

AYASS, WOLFGANG, *Das Arbeitshaus Breitenau: Bettler, Landstreicher, Prostituierte, Zuhälter und Fürsorgeempfänger in der Korrektions- und Landarmenanstalt Breitenau (1874–1949)*, Kassel, 1992

AYASS, WOLFGANG, 'Die Landesarbeitsanstalt und das Landesfürsorge- heim Breitenau', in Gunnar Richter (ed.), *Breitenau: Zur Geschichte eines nationalsozialistischen Konzentrations- und Arbeitserziehungslagers*, Kassel, 1993, 21–49

AYÇOBERRY, PIERRE, *La société allemande sous le IIIe Reich 1933–1945*, Paris, 1998

BAJOHR, STEFAN, *Die Hälfte der Fabrik: Geschichte der Frauenarbeit in Deutschland 1914 bis 1945*, Marburg, 1979

BAJOHR, FRANK, *'Aryanisation' in Hamburg: The Economic Exclusion of the Jews and the Confiscation of Their Property in Nazi Germany*, Oxford, 2002

BANDHAUER SCHÖFFMANN, IRENE, and ELA HORNUNG, 'Vom "Dritten Reich" zur Zweiten Republik: Frauen im Wien der Nachkriegs- zeit', in David F. Good, Margarete Grandner and Mary Jo Maynes (eds), *Frauen in Österreich: Beiträge zu ihrer Situation im 19. und 20. Jahrhundert*, Vienna, 1994, 225–46

BANKIER, DAVID, *The Germans and the Final Solution: Public Opinion under Nazism*, Oxford, 1992

BANKIER, DAVID, 'German Public Awareness of the Final Solution', in David Cesarani (ed.), *The Final Solution: Origins and Implementation*, London, 1994, 215–27

BARBER, JOHN, and MARK HARRISON, *The Soviet Home Front, 1941–1945: A Social and Economic History of the USSR in World War II*, Harlow, 1991

BARKAI, AVRAHAM, 'Between East and West: Jews from Germany in the Lodz Ghetto', *Yad Vashem Studies*, 16, 1984, 271–332

BAR-ON, DAN, *Legacy of Silence: Encounters with Children of the Third Reich*, Cambridge, Mass., 1989

BARTOSZEWSKI, WŁADYSŁAW, and ZOFIA LEWIN (eds), *Righteous among Nations: How Poles Helped the Jews, 1939–45*, London, 1969

BARTOV, OMER, *Hitler's Army: Soldiers, Nazis and War in the Third Reich*, Oxford and New York, 1991

BAUER, FRITZ, KARL DIETRICH BRACHER and H. H. FUCHS (eds), *Justiz und NS-Verbrechen: Sammlung deutscher Strafurteile wegen nationalsozialistischer Tötungsverbrechen 1945–1968*, 1–27, Amsterdam, 1968–2003

BAUMGART, WILFRIED, 'Zur Ansprache Hitlers vor den Führern der Wehrmacht am 22. August 1939: Eine quellenkritische Untersuchung', *Vierteljahrshefte für Zeitgeschichte*, 16, 1968, 143–9

BAUMGARTNER, MARIANNA, 'Zwischen Mythos und Realität: Die Nachkriegsvergewaltigungen im sowjetisch besetzten Mostviertel', *Unsere Heimat: Zeitschrift für Landeskunde von Niederösterreich*, 64/2, 1993, 73–108

BECHTOLD, GRETEL, *Ein deutsches Kindertagebuch in Bildern, 1933–1945*, Freiburg, 1997

BEER, MATTHIAS, 'Im Spannungsfeld von Politik und Zeitgeschichte: Das Grossforschungsprojekt "Dokumentation der Deutschen aus Ost-Mitteleuropa"', *Vierteljahrshefte für Zeitgeschichte*, 49, 1998, 345–89

BEEVOR, ANTONY, *Berlin: The Downfall 1945*, London, 2002

BENZ, WOLFGANG, *Die Vertreibung der Deutschen aus dem Osten: Ursachen, Ereignisse, Folgen*, Frankfurt, 1985

BENZ, WOLFGANG, (ed.), *Dimension des Völkermords: Die Zahl der jüdischen Opfer des Nationalsozialismus*, Munich, 1991

BENZ, WOLFGANG, and UTE BENZ (eds), *Sozialisation und Traumatisierung: Kinder in der Zeit des Nationalsozialismus*, Frankfurt, 1998

BENZ, WOLFGANG, CLAUDIO CURIO and ANDREA HAMMEL (eds), *Die Kindertransporte 1938/39: Rettung und Integration*, Frankfurt, 2003

BENZENHÖFER, UDO, 'Der Fall "Kind Knauer"', *Deutsches Ärtzeblatt*, 95/19, 1998, 954–5

BENZENHÖFER, UDO, '*Kinderfachabteilungen*' *und* '*NS-Kindereuthanasie*', Wetzlar, 2000

BENZENHÖFER, UDO, 'Genese und Struktur der "NS-Kinder und Jugendlicheneuthanasie"', *Monatschrift für Kinderheilkunde*, 10, 2003, 1012–19

BERG, MARY, *Warsaw Ghetto: A Diary*, S. L. Shneiderman (ed.), New York, 1945

BERGANDER, GÖTZ, *Dresden im Luftkrieg: Vorgeschichte – Zerstörung – Folgen*, Cologne, 1977

BERGAU, MARTIN, *Der Junge von der Bernsteinküste: Erlebte Zeitgeschichte 1938–1948*, Heidelberg, 1994

BERGEN, DORIS, 'The Nazi Concept of "Volksdeutsche" and the Exacerbation of Anti-Semitism in Eastern Europe, 1939–45', *Journal of Contemporary History*, 29/4, 1994, 569–82

BERGER, ANDREA, and THOMAS OELSCHLÄGER, '"Ich habe eines natürlichen Todes sterben lassen": Das Krankenhaus im Kalmenhof und die Praxis der nationalsozialistischen Vernichtungsprogramme', in Christian Schrapper and Dieter Sengling (eds), *Die Idee der Bildbarkeit: 100 Jahre sozialpädagogische Praxis in der Heilerziehungsanstalt Kalmenhof*, Weinheim, 1988, 269–336

BERGHAHN, MARION, *German-Jewish Refugees in England: The Ambiguities of Assimilation*, London, 1984

BERKHOFF, KAREL, *Harvest of Despair: Life and Death in Ukraine under Nazi Rule*, Cambridge, Mass., 2004

BESSEL, RICHARD (ed.), *Life in the Third Reich*, Oxford, 1987

BESSEL, RICHARD, *Nazism and War*, London, 2004

BETHELL, NICHOLAS, *The War Hitler Won: The Fall of Poland, September 1939*, New York, 1972

BETTELHEIM, BRUNO, *The Informed Heart: A Study of the Psychological Consequences of Living under Extreme Fear and Terror*, London, 1991

BIESS, FRANK, 'Survivors of Totalitariansim: Returning POWs and the Reconstruction of Masculine Citizenship in West Germany, 1945–1955', in Hanna Schissler (ed.), *The Miracle Years: A Cultural History of West Germany, 1949–1968*, Princeton, NJ, 2001, 57–82

BLATMAN, DANIEL, 'Die Todesmärsche: Entscheidungsträger, Mörder und Opfer', in Ulrich Herbert, Karin Orth and Christoph Dieckmann (eds), *Die nationalsozialistischen Konzentrationslager: Entwicklung und Struktur*, 2, Göttingen, 1998, 1063–92

BLATTER, JANET, and SYBIL MILTON, *Art of the Holocaust*, New York, 1981

BOA, ELIZABETH, and J. H. REID, *Critical Strategies: German Fiction in the Twentieth Century*, London, 1972

BOBERACH, HEINZ (ed.), *Berichte des SD und der Gestapo über Kirchen und Kirchenvolk in Deutschland 1934–1944*, Mainz, 1971

BOBERACH, HEINZ (ed.), *Meldungen aus dem Reich: Die geheimen Lageberichte des Sicherheitsdienstes der SS 1938–1945*, 1–17, Berlin, 1984

BOCK, GISELA, *Zwangssterilisation im Nationalsozialismus: Studien zur Rassenpolitik und Frauenpolitik*, Opladen, 1986

BODE, SABINE, *Die vergessene Generation: Die Kriegskinder brechen ihr Schweigen*, Stuttgart, 2004

BÖHME, KLAUS, and UWE LOHALM (eds), *Wege in den Tod: Hamburgs Anstalt Langenborn und die Euthanasie in der Zeit des National-sozialismus*, Hamburg, 1993

BÖHME, KURT, *Gesucht wird . . . Die dramatische Geschichte des Suchdienstes*, Munich, 1965

BOLDT, GERHARD, *Die letzten Tage der Reichskanzlei*, Hamburg, 1947

BÖLL, HEINRICH, *Haus ohne Hüter*, Cologne, 1954

BÖLL, HEINRICH, *Wo warst du, Adam?*, Frankfurt, 1959

Bomben auf Engeland, Berlin, 1940

BONDY, RUTH, *'Elder of the Jews': Jakob Edelstein of Theresienstadt*, New York, 1989

BORK, SIEGFRIED, *Missbrauch der Sprache: Tendenzen nationalsozialis-tischer Sprachregelung*, Bern, 1970

BORSDORF, ULRICH, and MATHILDE JAMIN (eds), *Überleben im Krieg: Kriegserfahrungen in einer Industrieregion 1939–1945*, Reinbek, 1989

BOTHIEN, HORST-PIERRE, *Die Jovy-Gruppe: Eine historisch-soziolo-gische Lokalstudie über nonkonforme Jugendliche im 'Dritten Reich'*, Münster, 1994

BOVERI, MARGRET, *Tage des Überlebens: Berlin 1945*, Munich, 1968

BOWLBY, JOHN, *Child Care and the Growth of Love*, London, 1965

BRAHAM, RANDOLPH, *The Politics of Genocide: The Holocaust in Hungary*, New York, 1994

BRAUN, KARL, 'Peter Kien oder Ästhetik als Widerstand', in Miroslav Kárný, Raimund Kemper and Margita Kárná (eds), *Theresienstädter Studien und Dokumente*, Prague, 1995, 155–74

BREITMAN, RICHARD, 'A Deal with the Nazi Dictatorship? Himmler's Alleged Peace Emissaries in Autumn 1943', *Journal of Contemporary History*, 30, 1995, 411–30

BROSSE, THÉRÈSE, *War-Handicapped Children: Report on the European Situation*, Paris, 1950

BROSSE, THÉRÈSE, *Homeless Children: Report of the Proceedings of the*

Conference of Directors of the Children's Communities, Trogen, Switzerland, Paris, 1950

BROSZAT, MARTIN, *Nationalsozialistische Polenpolitik 1939–1945*, Stuttgart, 1961

BROWNING, CHRISTOPHER, *Ordinary Men: Reserve Police Battalion 101 and the Final Solution in Poland*, New York, 1993

BROWNING, CHRISTOPHER, *Nazi Policy, Jewish Workers, German Killers*, Cambridge, 2000

BROWNING, CHRISTOPHER, *The Origins of the Final Solution: The Evolution of Nazi Jewish Policy, September 1939–March 1942*, London, 2004

BUCHBENDER, ORTWIN, and REINHOLD STERZ (eds), *Das andere Gesicht des Krieges: Deutsche Feldpostbriefe 1939–1945*, Munich, 1982

BUDE, HEINZ, *Deutsche Karrieren: Lebenskonstruktionen sozialer Aufsteiger aus der Flakhelfer-Generation*, Frankfurt, 1987

BULLIVANT, KEITH, and C. JANE RICE, 'Reconstruction and Integration: The Culture of West German Stabilization, 1945 to 1968', in Rob Burns (ed.), *German Cultural Studies: An Introduction*, Oxford, 1995, 209–55

BUNDESMINISTERIUM FÜR VERTRIEBENE (ed.), *Die Vertreibung der deutschen Bevölkerung aus den Gebieten östlich der Oder–Neisse*, 1–3, (reprinted) Augsburg, 1993

BURCHARDT, LOTHAR, 'The Impact of the War Economy on the Civilian Population of Germany during the First and Second World Wars', in Wilhelm Deist, *The German Military in the Age of Total War*, Leamington Spa, 1985, 40–70

BURLEIGH, MICHAEL, *Death and Deliverance: 'Euthanasia' in Germany, 1900–1945*, Cambridge, 1994

BURLEIGH, MICHAEL, *The Third Reich: A New History*, London, 2000

BURLEIGH, MICHAEL, *Germany Turns Eastwards: A Study of Ostforschung in the Third Reich*, London, 2002

BURRIN, PHILIPPE, *Hitler and the Jews: The Genesis of the Holocaust*, London, 1994

CALDER, ANGUS, *The People's War*, London, 1969

CARTER, ERICA, *Dietrich's Ghosts: The Sublime and the Beautiful in Third Reich Film*, London, 2004

CERETTI, ADOLFO, *Come pensa il Tribunale per i minorenni: una ricerca sul giudicato penale a Milano dal 1934 al 1990*, Milan, 1996

CHIARI, BERNHARD, *Alltag hinter der Front: Besatzung, Kollaboration und Widerstand in Weissrussland 1941–1944*, Düsseldorf, 1998

CLAY, CATRINE, and MICHAEL LEAPMAN, *Master Race: The Lebensborn Experiment in Nazi Germany*, London, 1995

COHEN, BOAZ, 'Holocaust Heroics: Ghetto Fighters and Partisans in

Israeli Society and Historiography', *Journal of Political and Military Sociology*, 31/2, 2003, 197–213

COHEN, ELIE, *Human Behaviour in the Concentration Camp*, London, 1988

COLDREY, BARRY, *Child Migration under the Auspices of Dr Barnardo's Homes, the Fairbridge Society and the Lady Northcote Trust*, Thornbury, 1999

COOPER, ALAN, *Bombers over Berlin: The RAF Offensive, November 1943–March 1944*, Wellingborough, Northants, 1985 and 1989

CORNI, GUSTAVO, and HORST GIES, *Brot – Butter – Kanonen: Die Ernährungswirtschaft in Deutschland unter der Diktatur Hitlers*, Berlin, 1997

CORNI, GUSTAVO, *Hitler's Ghettos: Voices from a Beleagured Society, 1939–1944*, London, 2003

CRANE, CONRAD, *Bombs, Cities, and Civilians: American Airpower Strategy in World War II*, Lawrence, Kansas, 1993

CREW, DAVID, *Germans on Welfare: From Weimar to Hitler*, Oxford, 1998

CZACHOWSKA, JADWIGA, and ALICJA SZAŁAGAN (eds), *Współcześni Polscy Pisarze i Badacze Literatury: Słownik biobibliograficzny*, 5, Warsaw, 1997

DAVID, JANINA, *A Square of Sky: The Recollections of a Childhood*, London, 1964

DAVID, JANINA, *A Touch of Earth: A Wartime Childhood*, London, 1966

DAVIES, NORMAN, *God's Playground: A History of Poland*, Oxford, 1981

DAVIES, NORMAN, and ROGER MOORHOUSE, *Microcosm: Portrait of a Central European City*, London, 2002

DEAN, MARTIN, *Collaboration in the Holocaust: Crimes of the Local Police in Belorussia and Ukraine, 1941–44*, Basingstoke and London, 2000

DE LORENT, HANS-PETER, 'Hamburger Schulen im Krieg', in Reiner Lehberger and Hans-Peter de Lorent (eds), *'Die Fahne hoch': Schulpolitik und Schulalltag in Hamburg unterm Hakenkreuz*, Hamburg, 1986, 351–69

DE SILVA, CARA (ed.), *In Memory's Kitchen: A Legacy from the Women of Terezín*, Northvale, 1996

DEUTSCH–RUSSISCHES MUSEUM BERLIN-KARLSHORST, *Mascha + Nina + Katjuscha: Frauen in der Roten Armee, 1941–1945*, Berlin, 2003

Deutscher Ehrenhain für die Helden von 1914/18, Leipzig, 1931

DEUTSCHKRON, INGE, *Ich trug den gelben Stern*, Cologne, 1979

DEUTSCHKRON, INGE, . . . *Denn ihrer war die Hölle: Kinder in Gettos und Lagern*, Cologne, 1985

Deutschland-Berichte der Sozialdemokratischen Partei Deutschlands (Sopade) 1934–1940, Frankfurt, 1980

DE ZAYAS, ALFRED-MAURICE, *A Terrible Revenge: The Ethnic Cleansing of the East European Germans, 1944–1950*, New York, 1994

DICKINSON, EDWARD, *The Politics of German Child Welfare from the Empire to the Federal Republic*, Cambridge, Mass., 1996

DIERCKS, HERBERT (ed.), *Verschleppt nach Deutschland! Jugendliche Häftlinge des KZ Neuengamme aus der Sowjetunion erinnern sich*, Bremen, 2000

DIEWERGE, WOLFGANG (ed.), *Feldpostbriefe aus dem Osten: Deutsche Soldaten sehen die Sowjetunion*, Berlin, 1941

DMITRÓW, EDMUND, *Niemcy i okupacja hitlerowska w oczach Polaków: poglady i opinie z lat 1945–1948*, Warsaw, 1987

DOBROSZYCKI, LUCJAN, *The Chronicle of the Łódź Ghetto, 1941–1944*, New Haven and London, 1984

DOBROSZYCKI, LUCJAN, *Reptile Journalism: The Official Polish-Language Press under the Nazis, 1939–1945*, New Haven and London, 1994

DOMANSKY, ELISABETH, 'A Lost War: World War Two in Post-war German Memory', in Alvin Rosenfeld (ed.), *Thinking about the Holocaust after Half a Century*, Bloomington, 1997, 233–72

DOMANSKY, ELISABETH, and JUTTA DE JONG, *Der lange Schatten des Krieges: Deutsche Lebens-Geschichten nach 1945*, Münster, 2000

DÖNHOFF, MARION GRÄFIN VON, *Namen, die keiner mehr nennt: Ostpreussen – Menschen und Geschichte*, Düsseldorf, 1962

DÖRNER, ADOLF (ed.), *Mathematik im Dienste der nationalpolitischen Erziehung mit Anwendungsbeispielen aus Volkswirtschaft, Gelände-kunde und Naturwissenschaft*, Frankfurt, 1935

DÖRNER, BERNWARD, *'Heimtücke': Das Gesetz als Waffe: Kontrolle, Abschreckung und Verfolgung in Deutschland 1933–1945*, Paderborn, 1998

DÖRNER, BERNWARD, 'Justiz und Judenmord: Todesurteile gegen Judenhelfer in Polen und der Tschechoslowakei 1942–1944', in Norbert Frei, Sybille Steinbacher and Bernd Wagner (eds), *Ausbeutung, Vernich-tung, Öffentlichkeit: Neue Studien zur nationalsozialistischen Lager-politik*, Munich, 2000, 249–63

DÖRNER, CHRISTINE, *Erziehung durch Strafe: Die Geschichte des Jugendstrafvollzugs von 1871–1945*, Weinheim, 1991

DÖRNER, KLAUS 'Nationalsozialismus und Lebensvernichtung', *Viertel-jahrshefte für Zeitgeschichte*, 15, 1967, 121–52

DÖRNER, KLAUS (ed.), *Der Krieg gegen die psychisch Kranken*, Frankfurt, 1989

DÖRR, MARGARETE, '*Wer die Zeit nicht miterlebt hat . . .*': *Frauenerfahrungen im Zweiten Weltkrieg und in den Jahren danach*, 1–3, Frankfurt, 1998

DÖTZER, OLIVER, *Aus Menschen werden Briefe: Die Korrespondenz einer jüdischen Familie zwischen Verfolgung und Emigration 1933–1947*, Cologne, 2002

DÖTZER, OLIVER, '"Diese Kriegsspiele, die es dann bei der Hitlerjugend gab, die waren zum Teil denn doch sehr grausam": Männlichkeit und Gewalterfahrung in Kindheiten bürgerlicher Jungen im Nationalsozialismus', in Rolf Schwarz, Uwe Fentsahm and Kay Dohnke (eds), *Kritische Annäherung an den Nationalsozialismus in Norddeutschland: Festschrift für Gerhard Hoch zum 80. Geburtstag*, Kiel, 2003, 8–25

DROBISCH, KLAUS, and GÜNTHER WIELAND, *System der NS-Konzentrationslager 1933–1939*, Berlin, 1993

DROLSHAGEN, EBBA, *Nicht ungeschoren davonkommen: Das Schicksal der Frauen in den besetzten Ländern, die Wehrmachtssoldaten liebten*, Hamburg, 1998

DUNAE, PATRICK, 'Gender, Generations and Social Class: The Fairbridge Society and British Child Migration to Canada, 1930–1960', in Jon Lawrence and Pat Starkey (eds), *Child Welfare and Social Action: International Perspectives*, Liverpool, 2001, 82–100

DVORJETSKI, MARC, 'Adjustment of Detainees to Camp and Ghetto Life and their Subsequent Readjustment to Normal Society', *Yad Vashem Studies*, 5, 1963, 193–220

DWORK, DEBÓRAH, *Children with a Star: Jewish Youth in Nazi Europe*, New Haven, 1991

EDER, ANGELIKA, *Flüchtige Heimat: Jüdische Displaced Persons in Landsberg am Lech 1945 bis 1950*, Munich, 1998

EGGERT, HEINZ-ULRICH (ed.), *Der Krieg frisst eine Schule: Die Geschichte der Oberschule für Jungen am Wasserturm in Münster, 1938–1945*, Münster, 1990

EHLICH, KONRAD (ed.), *Sprache im Faschismus*, Frankfurt, 1989

EHRMANN, FRANTISEK (ed.), *Terezín*, Prague, 1965

EIBER, LUDWIG (ed.), '". . . Ein bisschen die Wahrheit": Briefe eines Bremer Kaufmanns von seinem Einsatz beim Polizeibataillon 105 in der Sowjetunion 1941', *1999: Zeitschrift für Sozialgeschichte des 20. und 21. Jahrhunderts*, 1, 1991, 58–83

EISEN, GEORGE, *Children and Play in the Holocaust: Games among the Shadows*, Amherst, Mass., 1988

EISENBERG, AZRIEL, *The Lost Generation: Children in the Holocaust*, New York, 1982

EISENKRAFT, CLARA, *Damals in Theresienstadt: Erlebnisse einer Judenchristin*, Wuppertal, 1977

ENGEL, GERHARD, *Heeresadjutant bei Hitler 1938–1943*, Stuttgart, 1974

ENGELKING-BONI, BARBARA, *Holocaust and Memory: The Experience of the Holocaust and its Consequences: An Investigation Based on Personal Narratives*, London, 2001

ENGELKING-BONI, BARBARA, 'Childhood in the Warsaw Ghetto', in United States Holocaust Memorial Museum, *Children and the Holocaust: Symposium Presentations*, Washington, DC, 2004, 33–42

ERICKSON, JOHN, *The Road to Berlin: Stalin's War with Germany*, 2, London, 1983

EVANS, RICHARD J., *In Hitler's Shadow*, London, 1989

EVANS, RICHARD J., *Rituals of Retribution: Capital Punishment in Germany, 1600–1987*, Oxford, 1996

EVANS, RICHARD J., *The Coming of the Third Reich*, London, 2003

Expressionismus: Literatur und Kunst 1910–1923: Eine Ausstellung des deutschen Literaturarchivs im Schiller-Nationalmuseum Marbach a. N., Marbach, 1960

FAULSTICH, HEINZ, *Von der Irrenfürsorge zur 'Euthanasie': Geschichte der badischen Psychiatrie bis 1945*, Freiburg, 1993

FAULSTICH, HEINZ, *Hungersterben in der Psychiatrie 1914–1949, mit einer Topographie der NS-Psychiatrie*, Freiburg, 1998

FAULSTICH, HEINZ, 'Die Zahl der "Euthanasie"-Opfer', in Andreas Frewer and Clemens Eickhoff (eds), *'Euthanasie' und aktuelle Sterbehilfe-Debatte*, Frankfurt, 2000, 223–7

FECHNER, FRITZ, *Panzer am Feind: Kampferlebnisse eines Regiments im Westen*, Gütersloh, 1941

FEHRENBACH, HEIDE, 'Of German Mothers and "Negermischlings-kinder": Race, Sex, and the Postwar Nation', in Hanna Schissler (ed.), *The Miracle Years: A Cultural History of West Germany, 1949–1968*, Princeton, NJ, 2001, 164–86

FEINBERG, ANAT, *Wiedergutmachung im Programm: Jüdisches Schicksal im deutschen Nachkriegsdrama*, Cologne, 1988

FIGLIO, KARL, 'Oral History and the Unconscious', *History Workshop Journal*, 26, 1988, 120–32

FISHMAN, SARAH, *The Battle for Children: World War II Youth Crime, and Juvenile Justice in Twentieth-Century France*, Cambridge, Mass., 2002

FITZHERBERT, KATRIN, *True to Both My Selves: A Family Memoir of Germany and England in Two World Wars*, London, 1997

FLATSZTEJN-GRUDA, ILONA, *Bylam wtedy dzieckiem*, Lublin, 2004

FRANÇOIS, ETIENNE, and HAGEN SCHULZE (eds), *Deutsche Erinnerungsorte*, 1–3, Munich, 2002

FRANK, ANNE, *Das Tagebuch der Anne Frank*, Frankfurt, 1955

FRANKOVÁ, ANITA, 'Die Struktur der aus dem Ghetto Theresienstadt zusammengestellten Transporte (1942–1944)', *Judaica Bohemiae*, 25/2, 1989, 63–81

FRANKOVÁ, ANITA, ANNA HYNDRÁKOVÁ, VĚRA HÁJKOVÁ and FRANTIŠKA FAKTOROVÁ, *The World without Human Dimensions: Four Women's Memories*, Prague, 1991

FREI, NORBERT (ed.), *Medizin und Gesundheitspolitik in der NS-Zeit*, Munich, 1991

FREI, NORBERT, *National Socialist Rule in Germany: The Führer State 1933–1945*, Oxford, 1993

FREI, NORBERT, *Vergangenheitspolitik: Die Anfänge der Bundesrepublik und die NS-Vergangenheit*, Munich, 1996

FREI, NORBERT, SYBILLE STEINBACHER and BERND WAGNER (eds), *Ausbeutung, Vernichtung, Öffentlichkeit: Neue Studien zur nationalsozialistischen Lagerpolitik*, Munich, 2000

FREUD, ANNA, *Ego and the Mechanisms of Defence*, London, 1936

FREUD, ANNA, *The Writings of Anna Freud*, 1–8, New York, 1967–81

FRIEDLANDER, HENRY, *The Origins of Nazi Genocide: From Euthanasia to the Final Solution*, Chapel Hill, NC, 1995

FRIEDLÄNDER, SAUL, *When Memory Comes*, New York, 1979

FRIEDLÄNDER, SAUL, *Nazi Germany and the Jews*, 1, *The Years of Persecution, 1933–39*, London, 1997

FRIEDMAN, SAUL (ed.), *The Terezin Diary of Gonda Redlich*, Lexington, Kentucky, 1992

FRIEDRICH, JÖRG, *Der Brand: Deutschland im Bombenkrieg 1940–1945*, Munich, 2002

FRIEDRICH, JÖRG, *Brandstätten: Der Anblick des Bombenkriegs*, Berlin, 2003

FRITZ BAUER INSTITUT (ed.), *Auschwitz-Prozess 4 Ks 2/63 Frankfurt am Main*, Cologne, 2004

FRITZSCHE, PETER, 'Volkstümliche Erinnerung und deutsche Identität nach dem Zweiten Weltkrieg', in Konrad Jarausch and Martin Sabrow (eds), *Verletztes Gedächtnis: Erinnerungskultur und Zeitgeschichte im Konflikt*, Frankfurt, 2002, 75–97

FÜRST, JULIANE, 'Heroes, Lovers, Victims: Partisan Girls during the Great Fatherland War', *Minerva: Quarterly Report on Women and the Military*, Fall/Winter 2000, 38–75

GAMES, SONIA, *Escape into Darkness: The True Story of a Young*

Woman's Extraordinary Survival during World War II, New York, 1991

GEINITZ, CHRISTIAN, *Kriegsfurcht und Kampfbereitschaft: Das Augusterlebnis in Freiburg: Eine Studie zum Kriegsbeginn 1914*, Essen, 1998

GELLATELY, ROBERT, *The Gestapo and German Society: Enforcing Racial Policy, 1933–1945*, Oxford, 1990

GELLATELY, ROBERT, *Backing Hitler: Consent and Coercion in Nazi Germany*, Oxford, 2001

GERLACH, CHRISTIAN, *Krieg, Ernährung, Völkermord: Forschungen zur deutschen Vernichtungspolitik im Zweiten Weltkrieg*, Hamburg, 1998

GERLACH, CHRISTIAN, *Kalkulierte Morde: Die deutsche Wirtschafts- und Vernichtungspolitik in Weissrussland 1941 bis 1944*, Hamburg, 1999

GERLACH, CHRISTIAN, and GÖTZ ALY, *Das letzte Kapitel: Der Mord an den ungarischen Juden 1944–1945*, Frankfurt, 2004

GERWARTH, ROBERT, 'Bismarck in Weimar: Germany's First Democracy and the Civil War of Memories (1918–1933)', D. Phil thesis, Oxford, 2003

GÈVE, THOMAS, *Youth in Chains*, Jerusalem, 1981

GÈVE, THOMAS, *Es gibt hier keine Kinder: Auschwitz, Gross-Rosen, Buchenwald: Zeichnungen eines kindlichen Historikers*, Volkhard Knigge (ed.), Göttingen, 1997

GIESECKE, HERMANN, *Vom Wandervogel bis zur Hitlerjugend: Jugendarbeit zwischen Politik und Pädagogik*, Munich, 1981

GILBERT, SHIRLI, 'Music in the Nazi Ghettos and Camps (1939–45)', D. Phil thesis, Oxford, 2002

GILDEA, ROBERT, *Marianne in Chains: In Search of the German Occupation, 1940–45*, London, 2003

GLANTZ, DAVID, and JONATHAN HOUSE, *When Titans Clashed: How the Red Army Stopped Hitler*, Edinburgh, 1995

GLAS-WIENER, SHEVA, *Children of the Ghetto*, Melbourne, 1983

GLASS, MARTHA, *'Jeder Tag in Theresin ist ein Geschenk': Die Theresienstädter Tagebücher einer Hamburger Jüdin 1943–1945*, Barbara Müller-Wesemann (ed.), Hamburg, 1996

GOEBBELS, JOSEPH, *Die Tagebücher*, Elke Fröhlich (ed.), Munich, 1993–6

GOES, ALBRECHT, *Unruhige Nacht*, Hamburg, 1951

GOLDHAGEN, DANIEL, *Hitler's Willing Exectutioners: Ordinary Germans and the Holocaust*, London, 1996

GOLLANCZ, VICTOR, *In Darkest Germany: The Record of a Visit*, London, 1947

GOLTERMANN, SVENJA, 'The Imagination of Disaster: Death and Survival in Post-war Germany', in Paul Betts, Alon Confino and Dirk Schumann (eds), *Death in Modern Germany*, Cambridge and New York, 2005 (forthcoming)

GÖPFERT, REBEKKA, *Der jüdische Kindertransport von Deutschland nach England, 1938/39: Geschichte und Erinnerung*, Frankfurt, 1999

GOSCHLER, CONSTANTIN (ed.), *Wiedergutmachung: Westdeutschland und die Verfolgten des Nationalsozialismus (1950–1954)*, Munich, 1992

GRÄFF, SIEGFRIED, *Tod im Luftangriff: Ergebnisse pathologisch-anatomischer Untersuchungen anlässlich der Angriffe auf Hamburg in den Jahren 1943–45*, Hamburg, 1948

GRASS, GÜNTER, *Hundejahre*, Neuwied, 1963

GRASS, GÜNTER, *Im Krebsgang*, Göttingen, 2002

GREEN, GERALD, *The Artists of Terezín*, New York, 1978

GREGOR, MANFRED, *Die Brücke*, Munich, 1958

GREGOR, NEIL, 'A *Schicksalsgemeinschaft*? Allied Bombing, Civilian Morale, and Social Dissolution in Nuremberg, 1942–1945', *Historical Journal*, 43/4, 2000, 1051–70

GREGOR, NEIL, '"Is He still Alive, or Long since Dead?": Loss, Absence and Remembrance in Nuremberg, 1945–1956', *German History*, 21/2, 2003, 183–203

GRIES, RAINER, *Die Rationen-Gesellschaft: Versorgungskampf und Vergleichsmentalität: Leipzig, München und Köln nach dem Kriege*, Münster, 1991

GROEHLER, OLAF, *Bombenkrieg gegen Deutschland*, Berlin, 1990

GROSS, JAN TOMASZ, *Polish Society under German Occupation: The Generalgouvernement, 1939–1944*, Princeton, NJ, 1979

GROSS, JAN TOMASZ, *Revolution from Abroad: The Soviet Conquest of Poland's Western Ukraine and Western Belorussia*, Princeton, NJ, 1988

GROSS, JAN TOMASZ, 'A Tangled Web: Confronting Stereotypes Concerning Relations between Poles, Germans, Jews, and Communists', in István Deák, Jan Gross and Tony Judt (eds), *The Politics of Retribution in Europe: World War II and its Aftermath*, Princeton, NJ, 2000, 74–129

GROSS, JAN TOMASZ, *Neighbors: The Destruction of the Jewish Community in Jedwabne, Poland*, Princeton, NJ, 2001

GROSSMAN, ATINA, 'Trauma, Memory, and Motherhood: Germans and Jewish Displaced Persons in Post-Nazi Germany, 1945–1949', *Archiv für Sozialgeschichte*, 38, 1998, 215–39

GROSSMAN, MENDEL, *My Secret Camera: Life in the Lodz Ghetto*, Frank Smith (ed.), London, 2000

GROT, ZDZISLAW, and WINCENTY OSTROWSKI, *Wspomnienia*

młodzieży wielkopolskiej z lat okupacji niemieckiej 1939–1945, Poznań, 1946

GROTUM, THOMAS, *Die Halbstarken: Zur Geschichte einer Jugend-kultur der 50er Jahre*, Frankfurt, 1994

GRUCHMANN, LOTHAR (ed.), *Autobiographie eines Attentäters: Johann Georg Elser: Aussage zum Sprengstoffanschlag im Bürger-bräukeller München am 8. November 1939*, Stuttgart, 1970

GRUCHMANN, LOTHAR, *Justiz im Dritten Reich: Anpassung und Unterwerfung in der Ära Gürtner*, Munich, 1990

GRUCHMANN, LOTHAR, *Der Zweite Weltkrieg: Kriegführung und Politik*, Munich, 1995

GRUDZIŃSKA-GROSS, IRENA, and JAN TOMASZ GROSS (eds), *War through Children's Eyes: The Soviet Occupation of Poland and the Deportations, 1939–1941*, Stanford, 1981

GRUNBERGER, RICHARD, *A Social History of the Third Reich*, New York, 1974

GUSE, MARTIN, ANDREAS KOHRS and FRIEDHELM VAHSEN, 'Das Jugendschutzlager Moringen – Ein Jugendkonzentrationslager', in Hans-Uwe Ott and Heinz Sünker (eds), *Soziale Arbeit und Faschismus*, Frankfurt, 1989, 228–49

GUSE, MARTIN, *'Wir hatten noch gar nicht angefangen zu leben': Eine Ausstellung zu den Jugend-Konzentrationslagern Moringen und Ucker-mark* (3rd edn), Moringen, 1997

GUTMAN, YISRAEL, *The Jews of Warsaw, 1939–43: Ghetto, Underground, Revolt*, Brighton, 1982

GUTMAN, YISRAEL, and SHMUEL KRAKOWSKI, *Unequal Victims: Poles and Jews during World War II*, New York, 1986

GUTMAN, YISRAEL, and MICHAEL BERENBAUM (eds), *Anatomy of the Auschwitz Death Camp*, Bloomington, Ind., 1994

HAAS, LEO, 'The Affair of the Painters of Terezín', in Massachusetts College of Arts (ed.), *Seeing through 'Paradise': Artists and the Terezín Concentration Camp*, Boston, 1991

HAEBICH, ANNA, 'Between Knowing and Not Knowing: Public Knowledge of the Stolen Generations', *Aboriginal History*, 25, 2001, 70–90

HAGEMANN, JÜRGEN, *Presselenkung im Dritten Reich*, Bonn, 1970

HAMMER, INGRID, and SUSANNE ZUR NIEDERN (eds), *Sehr selten habe ich geweint: Briefe und Tagebücher aus dem Zweiten Weltkrieg von Menschen aus Berlin*, Zurich, 1992

HÄMMERLE, CHRISTA, '"Zur Liebesarbeit sind wir hier, Soldatenstrümpfe stricken wir . . ." Zu Formen weiblicher Kriegsfürsorge im ersten Weltkrieg', Ph.D. thesis, University of Vienna, 1996

HÄMMERLE, CHRISTA, '"Habt Dank, Ihr Wiener Mägdelein . . ."

Soldaten und weibliche Liebesgaben im Ersten Weltkrieg', *L'Homme*, 8/1, 1997, 132–54

HANN, CHRISTOPHER, *A Village without Solidarity: Polish Peasants in Years of Crisis*, New Haven, 1985

HANSEN, ECKHARD, *Wohlfahrtspolitik im NS-Staat: Motivationen, Konflikte und Machtstrukturen im 'Sozialismus der Tat' des Dritten Reiches*, Augsburg, 1991

HART, KITTY, *Return to Auschwitz: The Remarkable Story of a Girl Who Survived the Holocaust*, London, 1983

HARTEN, HANS-CHRISTIAN, *De-Kulturation und Germanisierung: Die nationalsozialistische Rassen- und Erziehungspolitik in Polen 1939–1945*, Frankfurt, 1996

HARVEY, ELIZABETH, *Youth and the Welfare State in Weimar Germany*, Oxford, 1993

HARVEY, ELIZABETH, *Women and the Nazi East: Agents and Witnesses of Germanization*, New Haven and London, 2003

HASENCLEVER, CHRISTA, *Jugendhilfe und Jugendgesetzgebung seit 1900*, Göttingen, 1978

HASKINS, VICTORIA, and MARGARET JACOBS, 'Stolen Generations and Vanishing Indians: The Removal of Indigenous Children as a Weapon of War in the United States and Australia, 1870–1940', in James Alan Marten (ed.), *Children and War: A Historical Anthology*, New York and London, 2002, 227–41

HAUPERT, BERNHARD, *Franz-Josef Schäfer: Jugend zwischen Kreuz und Hakenkreuz: Biographische Rekonstruktion als Alltagsgeschichte des Faschismus*, Frankfurt, 1991

HAUSCHILD-THIESSEN, RENATE (ed.), *Die Hamburger Katastrophe vom Sommer 1943 in Augenzeugenberichten*, Hamburg, 1993

HEIBER, HELMUT (ed.), *Reichsführer! . . . Briefe an und von Himmler*, Stuttgart, 1968

HEIMANNSBERG, BARBARA, and CHRISTOPH SCHMIDT (eds), *Das kollektive Schweigen: Nazivergangenheit und gebrochene Identität in der Psychotherapie*, Heidelberg, 1988

HEINEMAN, ELIZABETH, 'The Hour of the Woman: Memories of Germany's "Crisis Years" and West German National Identity', in Hanna Schissler (ed.), *The Miracle Years: A Cultural History of West Germany, 1949–1968*, Princeton, NJ, 2001, 21–56

HEINEMANN, ISABEL, *'Rasse, Siedlung, deutsches Blut': Das Rasse- und Siedlungshauptamt der SS und die rassenpolitische Neuordnung Europas*, Göttingen, 2003

HENKE, KLAUS-DIETER, *Die amerikanische Besetzung Deutschlands*, Munich, 1995

HENRY, CLARISSA, and MARC HILLEL, *Children of the SS*, Hutchinson, 1976

HEPP, MICHAEL, 'Vorhof zur Hölle: Mädchen im "Jugendschutzlager" Uckermark', in Angelika Ebbinghaus (ed.), *Opfer und Täterinnen: Frauenbiographien des Nationalsozialismus*, Nördlingen, 1987, 191–216

HERBERT, ULRICH, 'Von Auschwitz nach Essen: Die Geschichte des KZ-Aussenlagers Humboldtstrasse', *Dachauer Hefte*, 2/2, 1986, 13–34

HERBERT, ULRICH, 'Good Times, Bad Times: Memories of the Third Reich', in Richard Bessel (ed.), *Life in the Third Reich*, Oxford, 1987, 97–110

HERBERT, ULRICH, *Best: Biographische Studien über Radikalismus, Weltanschauung und Vernunft 1903–1989*, Bonn, 1996

HERBERT, ULRICH, *Hitler's Foreign Workers: Enforced Foreign Labor in Germany under the Third Reich*, Cambridge, 1997

HERBERT, ULRICH, KARIN ORTH and CHRISTOPH DIECKMANN (eds), *Die nationalsozialistischen Konzentrationslager: Entwicklung und Struktur*, 1–2, Göttingen, 1998

HERBERT, ULRICH (ed.), *National Socialist Extermination Policies: Contemporary German Perspectives and Controversies*, New York and Oxford, 2000

HERMAND, JOST, *A Hitler Youth in Poland: The Nazis' Programme for Evacuating Children during World War II*, Evanston, Ill., 1997

HERZOG, DAGMAR, 'Desperately Seeking Normality: Sex and Marriage in the Wake of the War', in Richard Bessel and Dirk Schumann (eds), *Life after Death: Approaches to a Cultural and Social History of Europe during the 1940s and 1950s*, Cambridge, 2003, 161–92

HILBERG, RAUL, *Die Vernichtung der europäischen Juden: Die Gesamtgeschichte des Holocaust*, Berlin, 1982

HILBERG, RAUL, STANISŁAW STARON and JOSEF KERMISZ (eds), *The Warsaw Diary of Adam Czerniakow*, Chicago, 1999

HILL, PAULA, 'Anglo-Jewry and the Refugee Children', Ph.D. thesis, University of London, 2001

HIMMLER, HEINRICH, *Die Geheimreden 1933 bis 1945*, Bradley Smith and Agnes Peterson (eds), Frankfurt, 1974

HINSHELWOOD, ROBERT D., *A Dictionary of Kleinian Thought*, London, 1989

HIRSCHFELD, GERHARD, and IRINA RENZ (eds), *Besiegt und Befreit: Stimmen vom Kriegsende 1945*, Gerlingen, 1995

HITLER, ADOLF, *Reden und Proklamationen, 1932–1945*, 1–2, Max Domarus (ed.), Neustadt an der Aisch, 1962–3

HOCHBERG-MARIAŃSKA, MARIA, and NOE GRÜSS (eds), *The Children Accuse*, London, 1996

HOCKERTS, HANS GÜNTHER, 'Integration der Gesellschaft: Gründungskrise und Sozialpolitik in der frühen Bundesrepublik', *Zeitschrift für Sozialreform*, 32, 1986, 25–41

HOFMANN, ANDREAS, *Nachkriegszeit in Schlesien: Gesellschafts- und Bevölkerungspolitik in den polnischen Siedlungsgebieten 1945–1948*, Cologne, 2000

HOGMAN, FLORA, 'Displaced Jewish Children during World War II: How They Coped', *Journal of Humanistic Psychology*, 23, 1983, 51–67

HOHENSTEIN, ALEXANDER, *Wartheländisches Tagebuch aus den Jahren 1941/42*, Stuttgart, 1961

HÖHN, MARIA, *GIs and Fräuleins: The German–American Encounter in 1950s West Germany*, Chapel Hill, NC, 2002

HONG, YONG-SUN, *Welfare, Modernity, and the Weimar State, 1919–1933*, Princeton, NJ, 1998

HRABAR, ROMAN, *Hitlerowski rabunek dzieci polskich: Uprowadzenie i germanizacja dzieci polskich w latach 1939–1945*, Katowice, 1960

HRABAR, ROMAN, ZOFIA TOKARZ and JACEK WILCZUR, *Kinder im Krieg – Krieg gegen Kinder: Die Geschichte der polnischen Kinder 1939–1945*, Hamburg 1981

HUFTON, OLWEN, *The Poor of Eighteenth-Century France, 1750–1789*, Oxford, 1974

HUGHES, MICHAEL, *Shouldering the Burdens of Defeat: West Germany and the Reconstruction of Social Justice*, Chapel Hill, NC, 1999

HUYSSEN, ANDREAS, 'Trauma and Memory: A New Imaginary of Temporality', in Jill Bennett and Rosanne Kennedy (eds), *World Memory: Personal Trajectories in Global Time*, New York, 2003, 16–29

INSTYTUT PAMIECI NARODOWEJ with PAWEŁ MACHCEWICZ and KRZYSZTOF PERSAK (eds), *Wokół Jedwabnego*, Warsaw, 2002

JÄCKEL, EBERHARD, *Hitler in History*, Hanover, New Hamps., 1984

JACOBMEYER, WOLFGANG, *Vom Zwangsarbeiter zum heimatlosen Ausländer: Die Displaced Persons in Westdeutschland 1945–1951*, Göttingen, 1985

JACOBSON, JACOB, and DAVID COHEN, *Terezín: The Daily Life, 1943–45*, London, 1946

JAHNKE, KARL HEINZ, and MICHAEL BUDDRUS, *Deutsche Jugend 1933–1945: Eine Dokumentation*, Hamburg, 1989

JAHNKE, KARL HEINZ, *Hitlers letztes Aufgebot: Deutsche Jugend im sechsten Kriegsjahr 1944/45*, Essen, 1993

JANSEN, CHRISTIAN, and ARNO WECKBECKER, *Der 'Volksdeutsche Selbstschutz' in Polen 1939/40*, Munich, 1992

JASTRZĘBSKI, WŁODZIMIERZ, *Der Bromberger Blutsonntag: Legende und Wirklichkeit*, Poznań, 1990

JOHNSON, ERIC, *The Nazi Terror: Gestapo, Jews and Ordinary Germans*, London, 1999

JOHNSON, UWE, *Mutmassungen über Jakob*, Frankfurt, 1959

JUSTIN, EVA, *Lebensschicksale artfremd erzogener Zigeunerkinder und ihrer Nachkommen*, Berlin, 1944

KACZERGINSKI, SHMERKE, and H. LEIVICK, *Lider fun di getos un lagern*, New York, 1948

KAMIŃSKI, ALEKSANDER, *Kamienie na szaniec*, Warsaw, 2001

KAMINSKI, UWE, *Zwangssterilisation und 'Euthanasie' im Rheinland: Evangelische Erziehungsanstalten sowie Heil- und Pflegeanstalten 1933–1945*, Cologne, 1995

KAMINSKY, ANNETTE (ed.), *Heimkehr 1948: Geschichte und Schicksale deutscher Kriegsgefangener*, Munich, 1998

KANIA, STANISŁAW, *Polska gwara konspiracyjno-partyzancka czasu okupacji hitlerowskiej 1939–1945*, Zielona Góra, 1976

KAPLAN, MARION, *Between Dignity and Despair: Jewish Life in Nazi Germay*, Oxford, 1998

KARAS, JOŽA, *Music in Terezín, 1941–1945*, New York, 1985

KARDORFF, URSULA VON, *Berliner Aufzeichnungen: Aus den Jahren 1942 bis 1945*, Munich, 1962

KÁRNÝ, MIROSLAV, 'Das Theresienstädter Familienlager in Birkenau', *Judaica Bohemiae*, 15/1, 1979, 3–26

KÁRNÝ, MIROSLAV, 'Eine neue Quelle zur Geschichte der tragischen Nacht vom 8. März 1944', *Judaica Bohemiae*, 25/1, 1989, 53–6

KÁRNÝ, MIROSLAV, VOJTĚCH BLODIG and MARGITA KÁRNÁ (eds), *Theresienstadt in der 'Endlösung der Judenfrage'*, Prague, 1992

KÁRNÝ, MIROSLAV, and MARGITA KÁRNÁ, 'Kinder in Theresienstadt', *Dachauer Hefte*, 9, 1993, 14–31

KÁRNÝ, MIROSLAV, et al. (eds), *Terezínská Pamětní Kniha*, 2, Prague, 1995

KÁRNÝ, MIROSLAV, 'The Genocide of the Czech Jews', in Miroslav Kárný et al. (eds), *Terezín Memorial Book: Jewish Victims of Nazi Deportations from Bohemia and Moravia 1941–1945: A Guide to the Czech Original with a Glossary of Czech Terms Used in the Lists*, Prague, 1996, 27–88

KAROWSKI, HERBERT, 'Film im Flug', *Filmwelt*, 24 November 1940

KARSKI, JAN, *Story of a Secret State*, Boston, 1944

KASER, MICHAEL, and EDWARD RADICE (eds), *The Economic History of Eastern Europe, 1919–1975*, 2, *Interwar Policy, the War and Reconstruction*, Oxford, 1986

KATSH, ABRAHAM (ed.), *The Warsaw Diary of Chaim A. Kaplan*, New York, 1965

KATZ, ESTHER, and JOAN RINGELBAUM (eds), *Women Surviving the Holocaust*, New York, 1983

KELLER, ULRICH (ed.), *The Warsaw Ghetto in Photographs: 206 Views Made in 1941*, New York, 1984

KENRICK, DONALD, and GRATTON PUXON, *The Destiny of Europe's Gypsies*, London, 1972

KERBS, DIETHART, and JÜRGEN REULECKE (eds) *Handbuch der deutschen Reformbewegungen, 1880–1933*, Wuppertal, 1998

KERSHAW, IAN, *Popular Opinion and Political Dissent in the Third Reich: Bavaria, 1933–1945*, Oxford, 1983

KERSHAW, IAN, 'German Public Opinion during the "Final Solution": Information, Comprehension, Reactions', in Asher Cohen, Joav Gelber and Charlotte Wardi (eds), *Comprehending the Holocaust: Historical and Literary Research*, Frankfurt, 1988, 145–58

KERSHAW, IAN, *The 'Hitler Myth': Image and Reality in the Third Reich*, Oxford, 1989

KERSHAW, IAN, *Hitler*, 1, *1889–1936: Hubris*, and 2, *1936–1945: Nemesis*, London, 1998–2000

KERSTING, FRANZ-WERNER, 'Helmut Schelskys "Skeptische Generation" von 1957', *Vierteljahrshefte für Zeitgeschichte*, 50, 2002, 465–95

KETTENACKER, LOTHAR (ed.), *Ein Volk von Opfern: Die neue Debatte um den Bombenkrieg 1940–45*, Berlin, 2003

KIEVAL, HILLEL, *The Making of Czech Jewry: National Conflict and Jewish Society in Bohemia, 1870–1918*, New York, 1988

KIRST, HANS HELLMUT, *08/15: In der Kaserne, Im Krieg, Bis zum Ende. Gesamtausgabe der Trilogie*, Munich, 2001

KJENDSLI, VESLEMØY, *Kinder der Schande*, Berlin, 1988

KLARSFELD, SERGE (ed.), *The Auschwitz Album: Lili Jacob's Album*, New York, 1980

KLEE, ERNST, *'Euthanasie' im NS-Staat: Die 'Vernichtung lebensunwerten Lebens'*, Frankfurt, 1983

KLEE, ERNST (ed.), *Dokumente zur 'Euthanasie'*, Frankfurt, 1986

KLEE, ERNST, and WILLI DRESSEN, *'Gott mit uns': Der deutsche Vernichtungskrieg im Osten*, Frankfurt, 1989

KLEE, ERNST, WILLI DRESSEN and VOLKER RIESS (eds), *'The Good Old Days': The Holocaust as Seen by Its Perpetrators and Bystanders*, New York, 1991

KLEIN, HOLGER, *The Second World War in Fiction*, London, 1984

KLEMPERER, VICTOR, *I Shall Bear Witness* and *To the Bitter End: The Diaries of Victor Klemperer*, 1–2, London, 1999

KLEMPERER, VICTOR, *The Language of the Third Reich: LTI – Lingua Tertii Imperii: A Philologist's Notebook*, London, 2000

KLESSMANN, CHRISTOPH, *Die doppelte Staatsgründung: Deutsche Geschichte 1945–1955*, Göttingen, 1991

KLÖNNE, ARNO, *Gegen den Strom: Bericht über den Jugendwiderstand im Dritten Reich*, Frankfurt, 1958

KLÖNNE, ARNO, *Jugend im Dritten Reich: Die Hitler-Jugend und ihre Gegner*, Cologne, 2003

KLÜGER, RUTH, *Weiter Leben: Eine Jugend*, Göttingen, 1992

KNOCH, HABBO, *Die Tat als Bild: Fotografien des Holocaust in der deutschen Erinnerungskultur*, Hamburg, 2001

KOCK, GERHARD, *'Der Führer sorgt für unsere Kinder . . .': Die Kinderlandverschickung im Zweiten Weltkrieg*, Paderborn, 1997

KOEBNER, THOMAS, GERT SAUTERMEISTER and SIGRID SCHNEIDER (eds), *Deutschland nach Hitler*, Opladen, 1987

KÖNIGSEDER, ANGELIKA, *Flucht nach Berlin: Jüdische Displaced Persons 1945–1948*, Berlin, 1998

KÖNIGSEDER, ANGELIKA, and JULIANE WETZEL, *Lebensmut im Wartesaal: Die jüdischen DPs (Displaced Persons) im Nachkriegsdeutschland*, Frankfurt, 1994

KORDAN, BOHDAN, 'Making Borders Stick: Population Transfer and Resettlement in the Trans-Curzon Territories, 1944–1949', *International Migration Review*, 31/3, 1997, 704–20

KOŹNIEWSKI, KAZIMIERZ, *Zamknięte koło: W podziemnym świece*, Warsaw, 1967

KRAATZ, SUSANNE (ed.), *Verschleppt und Vergessen: Schicksale jugendlicher 'OstarbeiterInnen' von der Krim im Zweiten Weltkrieg und danach*, Heidelberg, 1995

KRAKOWSKI, SHMUEL, 'Massacre of Jewish Prisoners on the Samland Peninsula – Documents', *Yad Vashem Studies*, 24, 1994, 349–387

KRAMER, EDITH, 'Erinnerungen an Friedl Dicker-Brandeis', *Mit der Ziehharmonika* (special issue, *Zeitschrift der Theodor-Kramer-Gesellschaft*, 3, September 1988), 1–2

KRAUSE-VILMAR, DIETFRID, *Das Konzentrationslager Breitenau: Ein staatliches Schutzhaftlager 1933/34*, Marburg, 1997

KRAUSNICK, HELMUT, and HANS-HEINRICH WILHELM, *Die Truppe des Weltanschauungskrieges: Die Einsatzgruppen der Sicherheitspolizei und des SD 1938–1942*, Stuttgart, 1981

KRAUSNICK, MICHAIL, *Auf Wiedersehen im Himmel: Die Geschichte der Angela Reinhardt*, Munich, 2001

'Kriegsgefangene und Wehrmachtsvermisste aus Hessen: Vorläufiges Ergebnis der amtlichen Registrierung vom 20.–30. Juni 1947', *Staat und Wirtschaft in Hessen: Statistische Mitteilungen* (2/4), 1947, 110–12

KŘÍŽKOVÁ, MARIE RÚT, KURT JIŘÍ KOTOUČ and ZDENĚK ORNEST (eds), *We Are Children Just the Same: Vedem, the Secret Magazine of the Boys of Terezín*, Philadelphia, 1995

KROCKOW, CHRISTIAN GRAF VON, *Die Stunde der Frauen: Bericht aus Pommern 1944 bis 1947*, Munich, 1991

KRÜGER, NORBERT, 'Die Bombenangriffe auf das Ruhrgebiet', in Ulrich Borsdorf and Mathilde Jamin (eds), *Überleben im Krieg: Kriegserfahrungen in einer Industrieregion 1939–1945*, Reinbek, 1989, 88–100

KRUK, HERMANN, *The Last Days of the Jerusalem of Lithuania: Chronicle from the Vilna Ghetto and the Camps, 1939–1944*, Benjamin Harshav (ed.), New Haven and London, 2002

KUBY, ERICH, *The Russians and Berlin, 1945*, London, 1968

KUGELMASS, JACK, and JONATHAN BOYARIN (eds), *From a Ruined Garden: The Memorial Books of Polish Jewry*, New York, 1983

KÜHL, STEFAN, *The Nazi Connection: Eugenics, American Racism and German National Socialism*, New York, 1994

KUHLMANN, CAROLA, *Erbkrank oder erziehbar? Jugendhilfe als Vorsorge und Aussonderung in der Fürsorgeerziehung in Westfalen von 1933–1945*, Weinheim, 1989

KULKA, OTTO DOV (ed.), *Judaism and Christianity under the Impact of National Socialism*, Jerusalem, 1987

KULKA, OTTO DOV (ed.), *Deutsches Judentum unter dem Nationalsozialismus*, Tübingen, 1997

KULKA, OTTO DOV (ed.), *Die Juden in den geheimen NS-Stimmungsberichten 1933–1945*, Düsseldorf, 2004

KUNDRUS, BIRTHE *Kriegerfrauen: Familienpolitik und Geschlechterverhältnisse im Ersten und Zweiten Weltkrieg*, Hamburg, 1995

KUNDRUS, BIRTHE (ed.), *Phantasiereiche: Zur Kulturgeschichte des deutschen Kolonialismus*, Frankfurt, 2003

KURATORIUM GEDENKSTÄTTE SONNENSTEIN E.V. und SÄCHSISCHE LANDESZENTRALE FÜR POLITISCHE BILDUNG (eds), *Nationalsozialistische Euthanasie-Verbrechen in Sachsen: Beiträge zu ihrer Aufarbeitung*, Dresden, 1993

KUREK-LESIK, EWA, 'The Conditions of Admittance and the Social Background of Jewish Children Saved by Women's Religious Orders in Poland from 1939–1945', *Polin: A Journal of Polish–Jewish Studies*, 13, 1988, 244–75

KUSHNER, TONY, *The Holocaust and the Liberal Imagination: A Social and Cultural History*, Oxford, 1994

LACEY, KATE, *Feminine Frequencies: Gender, German Radio, and the Public Sphere, 1923–1945*, Ann Arbor, Mich., 1996

LAGROU, PIETER, *The Legacy of Nazi Occupation in Western Europe: Patriotic Memory and National Recovery*, Cambridge, 1999

LAGROU, PIETER, 'The Nationalization of Victimhood: Selective Violence and National Grief in Western Europe, 1940–1960', in Richard

Bessel and Dirk Schumann (eds), *Life after Death: Approaches to a Cultural and Social History of Europe during the 1940s and 1950s*, Cambridge, 2003, 243–58

LANDESWOHLFAHRTSVERBAND HESSEN and BETTINA WINTER (eds), *'Verlegt nach Hadamar': Die Geschichte einer NS-'Euthanasie'-Anstalt*, Kassel, 1994

LANGE, HERTA, and BENEDIKT BURKARD (eds), *'Abends wenn wir essen fehlt uns immer einer': Kinder schreiben an die Väter 1939–1945*, Hamburg, 2000

LANGER, LAWRENCE, *Holocaust Testimonies: The Ruins of Memory*, New Haven, 1991

LARASS, CLAUS, *Der Zug der Kinder: KLV – Die Evakuierung 5 Millionen deutscher Kinder im 2. Weltkrieg*, Munich, 1983

LATZEL, KLAUS, *Vom Sterben im Krieg: Wandlungen in der Einstellung zum Soldatentod vom Siebenjährigen Krieg bis zum 2. Weltkrieg*, Warendorf, 1988

LAUBER, HEINZ, *Judenpogrom 'Reichskristallnacht': November 1938 in Grossdeutschland*, Gerlingen, 1981

LEAPMAN, MICHAEL, *Witnesses to War: Eight True-Life Stories of Nazi Persecution*, London, 2000

LEHBERGER, REINER, and HANS-PETER DE LORENT (eds), *'Die Fahne hoch': Schulpolitik und Schulalltag in Hamburg unterm Hakenkreuz*, Hamburg, 1986

LEHMANN, ALBRECHT, *Gefangenschaft und Heimkehr: Deutsche Kriegsgefangene in der Sowjetunion*, Munich, 1986

LEMKE MUNIZ DE FARIA, YARA-COLETTE, *Zwischen Fürsorge und Ausgrenzung: Afrodeutsche 'Besatzungskinder' im Nachkriegsdeutschland*, Berlin, 2002

LESSING, HELLMUT, and MANFRED LIEBEL, *Wilde Cliquen: Szenen einer anderen Arbeiterjugendbewegung*, Bensheim, 1981

LE TISSIER, TONY, *The Battle of Berlin 1945*, London, 1988

LEVI, PRIMO, *If This Is a Man and The Truce*, London, 1987

LEVIN, NORA, *The Holocaust: The Destruction of European Jewry, 1933–1945*, New York, 1968

LEWIN, ABRAHAM, *The Cup of Tears: A Diary of the Warsaw Ghetto*, Oxford, 1988

LIFTON, BETTY, *The King of Children: The Life and Death of Janusz Korczak*, New York, 1988

LILIENTHAL, GEORG, *Der 'Lebensborn e.V.': Ein Instrument national-sozialistischer Rassenpolitik*, Frankfurt, 1993

LINDE, HERTHA (ed.), *So waren wir: Bildband zur Geschichte des BDM*, Munich, 1997

LÖFFLER, PETER (ed.), *Clemens August Graf von Galen: Akten, Briefe und Predigten 1933–1946*, 1–2, Mainz, 1988

LONGERICH, PETER, *Politik der Vernichtung: Eine Gesamtdarstellung der nationalsozialistischen Judenverfolgung*, Munich, 1998

LORENZ, HILKE, *Kriegskinder: Das Schicksal einer Generation Kinder*, Munich, 2003

LOTFI, GABRIELE, *KZ der Gestapo: Arbeitserziehungslager im Dritten Reich*, Stuttgart, 2000

LUDOWYK GYOMROI, EDITH, 'The Analysis of a Young Concentration Camp Victim', *The Psychoanalytic Study of the Child*, 18, 1963, 484–510.

LÜDTKE, ALF, 'Histories of Mourning: Flowers and Stones for the War Dead, Confusion for the Living – Vignettes from East and West Germany', in Gerald Sider and Gavin Smith (eds), *Between History and Histories: The Making of Silences and Commemorations*, Toronto, 1977, 149–79

LÜDTKE, ALF, *Eigen-Sinn: Fabrikalltag, Arbeitererfahrungen und Politik vom Kaiserreich bis in den Faschismus*, Hamburg, 1993

LÜDTKE, ALF, 'The Appeal of Exterminating "Others": German Workers and the Limits of Resistance', in Christian Leitz (ed.), *The Third Reich: The Essential Readings*, Oxford, 1999, 155–77

LUKAS, RICHARD C., *Did the Children Cry? Hitler's War against Jewish and Polish Children, 1939–1945*, New York, 1994

MACARDLE, DOROTHY, *Children of Europe: A Study of the Children of Liberated Countries: Their War-Time Experiences, Their Reactions and Their Needs, with a Note on Germany*, London, 1949

MADAJCZYK, CZESŁAW (ed.), *Zamojszczyzna – Sonderlaboratorium SS: Zbiór dokumentów polskich i niemieckich z okresu okupacji hitlerowskiej*, 1–2, Warsaw, 1977–9

MADAJCZYK, CZESŁAW, *Die Okkupationspolitik Nazideutschlands in Polen 1939–1945*, Cologne, 1988

MAHOOD, LINDA, *Policing Gender, Class and Family: Britain, 1850–1940*, London, 1995

MAIER, CHARLES, *The Unmasterable Past*, Cambridge, Mass., 1988

MAJER, DIEMUT, *'Non-Germans' under the Third Reich: The Nazi Judicial and Administrative System in Germany and Occupied Eastern Europe, with Special Regard to Occupied Poland, 1939–1945*, Baltimore and London, 2003

MAKAROVA, ELENA, *From Bauhaus to Terezin: Friedl Dicker-Brandeis and Her Pupils*, Jerusalem, 1990

MANN, REINHARD, *Protest und Kontrolle im Dritten Reich: Nationalsozialistische Herrschaft im Alltag einer rheinischen Grossstadt*, Frankfurt, 1987

MANOSCHEK, WALTER (ed.), 'Es gibt nur eines für das Judentum: Vernichtung': Das Judenbild in deutschen Soldatenbriefen 1939–1944, Hamburg, 1995

MARGALIT, GILAD, Germany and Its Gypsies: A Post-Auschwitz Ordeal, Madison, Wis., 2002

MARGALIT, GILAD, 'Der Luftangriff auf Dresden: Seine Bedeutung für die Erinnerungspolitik der DDR und für die Herauskristallisierung einer historischen Kriegserinnerung im Westen', in Susanne Düwell and Matthias Schmidt (eds), Narrative der Shoah: Repräsentationen der Vergangenheit in Historiographie, Kunst und Politik, Paderborn, 2002, 189–208

MARTEN, JAMES (ed.), Children and War: A Historical Anthology, New York and London, 2002

MASCHMANN, MELITA, Account Rendered: A Dossier on My Former Self, London and New York, 1965

MASON, TIMOTHY, Arbeiterklasse und Volksgemeinschaft, Opladen, 1975

MASON, TIMOTHY, Nazism, Fascism and the Working Class, Jane Caplan (ed.), Cambridge, 1995

MAUSBACH, HANS, and BARBARA BROMBERGER, 'Kinder als Opfer der NS-Medizin, unter besonderer Berücksichtigung der Kinderfachabteilungen in der Psychiatrie', in Christina Vanja and Martin Vogt (eds), Euthanasie in Hadamar: Die nationalsozialistische Vernichtungspolitik in hessischen Anstalten, Kassel, 1991, 145–56

McDOUGALL, ALAN, 'From Tag X to the Prague Spring: Crisis Points in the History of the Free German Youth (FDJ), 1952–1968', D. Phil thesis, University of Oxford, 2001

McFARLAND-ICKE, BRONWYN, Nurses in Nazi Germany: Moral Choice in History, Princeton, NJ, 1999

MEISTER, JOHANNES, 'Die "Zigeunerkinder" von der St Josefspflege in Mulfingen', 1999: Zeitschrift für Sozialgeschichte des 20. und 21. Jahrhunderts, 2, 1987, 14–51

MENDEL, ANNEKATREIN, Zwangsarbeit im Kinderzimmer: 'Ostarbeiterinnen' in deutschen Familien von 1939 bis 1945: Gespräche mit Polinnen und Deutschen, Frankfurt, 1994

MENNEL, ROBERT, Thorns and Thistles: Juvenile Delinquents in the United States, 1825–1940, Hanover, New Hamps., 1973

MENUHIN, YEHUDI, Unfinished Journey, London, 2001

MERGEL, THOMAS, 'Der mediale Stil der "Sachlichkeit": Die gebremste Amerikanisierung des Wahlkampfs in der alten Bundesrepublik', in Bernd Weisbrod (ed.), Die Politik der Öffentlichkeit – die Öffentlichkeit der Politik: Politische Medialisierung in der Geschichte der Bundesrepublik, Göttingen, 2003, 29–53

MERRITT, ANNA, and RICHARD MERRITT (eds), *Public Opinion in Occupied Germany: The OMGUS Surveys, 1945–1949*, Urbana, Ill., 1970

MERRITT, ANNA, and RICHARD MERRITT (eds), *Public Opinion in Semisovereign Germany: The HICOG Surveys, 1949–1955*, Urbana, Ill., 1980

MESSERSCHMIDT, MANFRED, and FRITZ WÜLLNER, *Die Wehrmachtjustiz im Dienste des Nationalsozialismus: Zerstörung einer Legende*, Baden-Baden, 1987

MEYER, SIBYLLE, and EVA SCHULZE, *Wie wir das alles geschafft haben: Alleinstehende Frauen berichten über ihr Leben nach 1945*, Munich, 1985

MEYER, SIBYLLE, and EVA SCHULZE, '"Als wir wieder zusammen waren, ging der Krieg im Kleinen weiter": Frauen, Männer und Familien in Berlin der vierziger Jahre', in Lutz Niethammer and Alexander von Plato (eds), *'Wir kriegen jetzt andere Zeiten': Auf der Suche nach der Erfahrung des Volkes in nachfaschistischen Ländern*, Bonn, 1985, 305–26

MIDDLEBROOK, MARTIN, *The Battle of Hamburg: Allied Bomber Forces against a German City in 1943*, London, 1980

MIDDLEBROOK, MARTIN, *The Berlin Raids: RAF Bomber Command, Winter 1943–44*, London, 1988

MIDDLEBROOK, MARTIN, and CHRIS EVERITT (eds), *The Bomber Command War Diaries: An Operational Reference Book, 1939–1945*, London, 1990

MIGDAL, ULRIKE, *Und die Musik spielt dazu: Chansons und Satiren aus dem KZ Theresienstadt*, Munich, 1986

MILTON, SYBIL (ed.), *The Art of Jewish Children: Germany 1936–1941: Innocence and Persecution*, New York, 1989

MITSCHERLICH, ALEXANDER, and MARGARETE MITSCHERLICH, *Die Unfähigkeit zu trauern: Grundlagen kollektiven Verhaltens*, Munich, 1967

MOELLER, ROBERT, *Protecting Motherhood: Women and the Family in the Politics of Postwar West Germany*, Berkeley, 1993

MOELLER, ROBERT, *War Stories: The Search for a Usable Past in the Federal Republic of Germany*, Berkeley, 2001

MOMMSEN, HANS, *From Weimar to Auschwitz: Essays in German History*, Princeton, NJ, 1991

MOMMSEN, HANS, *Alternative zu Hitler*, Munich, 2000

MOSKOVITZ, SARAH, *Love despite Hate: Child Survivors of the Holocaust and Their Adult Lives*, New York, 1983

MOSSE, GEORGE, *The Crisis of German Ideology: Intellectual Origins of the Third Reich*, London, 1966

MOSSE, GEORGE, *Fallen Soldiers: Reshaping the Memory of the World Wars*, New York and Oxford, 1990

MOUTON, MICHELLE, and HELENA POHLANDT-McCORMICK, 'Boundary Crossings: Oral History of Nazi Germany and Apartheid South Africa – A Comparative Perspective', *History Workshop Journal*, 48, Autumn 1999, 41–63

MÜLLER, FILIP, *Eyewitness Auschwitz: Three Years in the Gas Chambers*, Susanne Flatauer (ed.), Chicago, 1979

MÜLLER, KLAUS-JÜRGEN, *Das Heer und Hitler: Armee und national-sozialistisches Regime 1933–1940*, Stuttgart, 1988

MÜLLER-HILLEBRAND, BURKHART, *Das Heer 1933–1945*, 1–3, Darmstadt, 1969

MUSIAL, BOGDAN, *'Konterrevolutionäre Elemente sind zu erschiessen': Die Brutalisierung des deutsch-sowjetischen Krieges im Sommer 1941*, Berlin, 2000

NAIMARK, NORMAN, *The Russians in Germany: A History of the Soviet Zone of Occupation, 1945–1949*, Cambridge, Mass., 1995

NAIMARK, NORMAN, *Fires of Hatred: Ethnic Cleansing in Twentieth-Century Europe*, Cambridge, Mass., 2001

NEUHAUSER, JOHANNES, and MICHAELA PFAFFENWIMMER (eds), *Hartheim, wohin unbekannt: Briefe und Dokumente*, Weitra, 1992

NICOLAISEN, HANS-DIETRICH, *Der Einsatz der Luftwaffen- und Marinehelfer im 2. Weltkrieg: Darstellung und Dokumentation*, Büsum, 1981

NIEHUSS, MERITH, *Familie, Frau und Gesellschaft: Studien zur Strukturgeschichte der Familie in Westdeutschland 1945–1960*, Göttingen, 2001

NIETHAMMER, LUTZ (ed.), *'Die Jahre weiss man nicht, wo man die heute hinsetzen soll': Faschismuserfahrungen im Ruhrgebiet*, Berlin, 1983

NIETHAMMER, LUTZ (ed.), *'Hinterher merkt man, dass es richtig war, dass es schiefgegangen ist': Nachkriegserfahrungen im Ruhrgebiet*, Bonn, 1983

NIETHAMMER, LUTZ, and ALEXANDER VON PLATO (eds), *'Wir kriegen jetzt andere Zeiten': Auf der Suche nach der Erfahrung des Volkes in nachfaschistischen Ländern*, Berlin, 1985

NIETHAMMER, LUTZ, *Ego-Histoire? Und andere Erinnerungs-Versuche*, Vienna and Cologne, 2002

NIEWYK, DONALD (ed.), *Fresh Wounds: Early Narratives of Holocaust Survival*, Chapel Hill, NC, 1998

NOAKES, JEREMY, and GEOFFREY PRIDHAM (eds), *Nazism, 1919–1945: A Documentary Reader*, 1–4, Exeter, 1984–98

NORWID, TADEUSZ, *Kraj bez Quislinga*, Rome, 1945

NOVICK, PETER, *The Holocaust and Collective Memory: The American Experience*, London, 1999

NOWAK, KURT, *'Euthanasie' und Sterilisierung im 'Dritten Reich': Die Konfrontation der evangelischen und katholischen Kirche mit dem Gesetz zur Verhütung erbkranken Nachwuchses und der 'Euthanasie'-Aktion* (3rd edn), Göttingen, 1984

NOWAK, KURT, 'Widerstand, Zustimmung, Hinnahme: Das Verhalten der Bevölkerung zur "Euthanasie"', in Norbert Frei (ed.), *Medizin und Gesundheitspolitik in der NS-Zeit*, Munich 1991, 235–51

OBST, DIETER, *'Reichskristallnacht': Ursachen und Verlauf des antisemitischen Pogroms vom November 1938*, Frankfurt, 1991

OFER, DALIA, and LENORE WEITZMAN (eds), *Women in the Holocaust*, New Haven, 1998

OFFER, AVNER, *The First World War: An Agrarian Interpretation*, Oxford, 1989

ORTH, KARIN, *Das System der nationalsozialistischen Konzentrationslager: Eine politische Organisationsgeschichte*, Hamburg, 1999

ORTMEYER, BENJAMIN (ed.), *Berichte gegen Vergessen und Verdrängen von 100 überlebenden jüdischen Schülerinnen und Schülern über die NS-Zeit in Frankfurt am Main*, Alfter, 1994

ORTMEYER, BENJAMIN, *Schulzeit unterm Hitlerbild: Analysen, Berichte, Dokumente*, Frankfurt, 1996

OTTO, HANS-UWE (ed.), *Soziale Arbeit und Faschismus: Volkspflege und Pädagogik im Nationalsozialismus*, Bielefeld, 1986

OTTO, RENATE, 'Die Heilerziehungs- und Pflegeanstalt Scheuern', in Klaus Böhme and Uwe Lohalm (eds), *Wege in den Tod: Hamburgs Anstalt Langenborn und die Euthanasie in der Zeit des Nationalsozialismus*, Hamburg, 1993, 320–33

OVERMANS, RÜDIGER, *Deutsche militärische Verluste im Zweiten Weltkrieg*, Munich, 1999

OVERY, RICHARD, *Goering: The 'Iron Man'*, London, 1984

OVERY, RICHARD, *Why the Allies Won*, London, 1995

OVERY, RICHARD, *Interrogations: The Nazi Elite in Allied Hands, 1945*, London, 2001

PAMÁTNÍK TEREZÍN (ed.), *Leo Haas*, Terezín, 1969

PAMÁTNÍK TEREZÍN (ed.), *Arts in Terezín, 1941–1945*, Terezín, 1973

PANITZ, EBERHARD, *Die Feuer sinken*, Berlin, 1960

PARSONS, MARTIN, *'I'll Take That One': Dispelling the Myths of Civilian Evacuation, 1939–45*, Peterborough, 1998

PASSERINI, LUISA, 'Work Ideology and Consensus under Italian Fascism', *History Workshop Journal*, 8, 1979, 82–108

PASSERINI, LUISA, *Fascism in Popular Memory: The Cultural Experience of the Turin Working Class*, Cambridge, 1987

PAUL, GERHARD, and KLAUS-MICHAEL MALLMANN (eds), *Die Gestapo: Mythos und Realität*, Darmstadt, 1995

PAULSSON, GUNNAR S., 'Hiding in Warsaw: The Jews on the "Aryan Side" in the Polish Capital, 1940–1945', D. Phil thesis, Oxford, 1998

PAULSSON, GUNNAR S., *Secret City: The Hidden Jews of Warsaw, 1940–1945*, New Haven and London, 2002

PENTLIN, SUSAN LEE, 'Mary Berg (1924–)', in S. Lillian Kremer (ed.), *Holocaust Literature: An Encyclopedia of Writers and Their Work*, 1, New York, 2003, 138–40

PETÖ, ANDREA, 'Memory and the Narrative of Rape in Budapest and Vienna in 1945', in Richard Bessel and Dirk Schumann (eds), *Life after Death: Approaches to a Cultural and Social History of Europe during the 1940s and 1950s*, Cambridge, 2003, 129–48

PEUKERT, DETLEV, 'Arbeitslager und Jugend-KZ: Die Behandlung "Gemeinschaftsfremder" im Dritten Reich', in Detlev Peukert and Jürgen Reulecke (eds), *Die Reihen fast geschlossen: Beiträge zur Geschichte des Alltags unterm Nationalsozialismus*, Wuppertal, 1981, 413–34

PEUKERT, DETLEV, *Volksgenossen und Gemeinschaftsfremde: Anpassung, Ausmerze und Aufbegehren unter dem Nationalsozialismus*, Cologne, 1982

PEUKERT, DETLEV, *Grenzen der Sozialdisziplinierung: Aufstieg und Krise der deutschen Jugendfürsorge von 1878 bis 1932*, Cologne, 1986

PEUKERT, DETLEV, *Inside Nazi Germany: Conformity, Opposition and Racism in Everyday Life*, London, 1987

PEYINGHAUS, MARIANNE (ed.), *Stille Jahre in Gertlauken: Erinnerungen an Ostpreussen*, Berlin, 1988

PFAHLMANN, HANS, *Fremdarbeiter und Kriegsgefangene in der deutschen Kriegswirtschaft 1939–1945*, Darmstadt, 1968

PFEIFER, JOCHEN, *Der deutsche Kriegsroman 1945–1960: Ein Versuch zur Vermittlung von Literatur und Sozialgeschichte*, Königstein, 1981

PHILLIPS, JANINE, *My Secret Diary*, London, 1982

PINE, LISA, *Nazi Family Policy, 1933–1945*, Oxford, 1997

PINES, DINORA, *A Woman's Unconscious Use of Her Body: A Psychoanalytical Perspective*, London, 1993

PINFOLD, DEBBIE, *The Child's View of the Third Reich in German Literature: The Eye among the Blind*, Oxford, 2001

PLATO, ALEXANDER VON, 'The Hitler Youth Generation and Its Role in the Two Post-War German States', in Mark Roseman (ed.),

Generations in Conflict: Youth Revolt and Generation Formation in Germany, 1770–1968, Cambridge, 1995, 210–26

PLATT, KRISTIN, and MIHRAN DABAG (eds), *Generation und Gedächtnis: Erinnerungen und kollektive Identitäten*, Opladen, 1995

PLUTA, FELIKS, *Język polski w okresie drugiej wojny światowej: Studium słowotwórczo-semantyczne*, Opole, 1975

POHL, DIETER, *Von der 'Judenpolitik' zum Judenmord: Der Distrikt Lublin des Generalgouvernements 1939–1944*, Frankfurt, 1993

POIGER, UTA, *Jazz, Rock and Rebels: Cold War Politics and American Culture in a Divided Germany*, Berkeley, 2000

POLISH MINISTRY OF INFORMATION, *The German New Order in Poland*, London, 1942

POLONSKY, ANTONY, and JOANNA MICHLIC (eds), *The Neighbors Respond: The Controversy over the Jedwabne Massacre in Poland*, Princeton, NJ, 2004

PORTELLI, ALESSANDRO, 'The Death of Luigi Trastulli: Memory and the Event', in his *The Death of Luigi Trastulli and other Stories*, Albany, 1991, 1–26

PRENZLAUER BERG MUSEUM DES KULTURAMTES BERLIN and ANNETT GRÖSCHNER (ed.), *Ich schlug meiner Mutter die brennenden Funken ab: Berliner Schulaufsätze aus dem Jahr 1946*, Berlin, 1996

PRICE, ALFRED, *Luftwaffe Data Book*, London, 1997

PRZYBYLSKA, WANDA, *Journal de Wanda*, Zofia Bobowicz (ed. and trans.), Paris, 1981

PRZYBYLSKA, WANDA, *Cząstka mego serca: Pamiętniki z lat wojny*, Warsaw, 1985

PRZYREMBEL, ALEXANDRA, *'Rassenschande': Reinheitsmythos und Vernichtungslegitimation im Nationalsozialismus*, Göttingen, 2003

RADEBOLD, HARTMUT, *Abwesende Väter und Kriegskindheit: Fortbestehende Folgen in Psychoanalysen*, Göttingen, 2004

RADOMSKA-STRZEMECKA, HELENA, 'Okupacja w oczach młodzieży', in Józef Wnuk and Helena Radomska-Strzemecka (eds), *Dzieci polskie oskarżają (1939–1945)*, Warsaw, 1961, 195–379

RANKE, WILFRID, et al. (eds), *Kultur, Pajoks und Care-Pakete: Eine Berliner Chronik 1945–49*, Berlin, 1990

RASCHKE, JAN Z., *Farewell to God*, Dundee, 1977

REED, DONNA, *The Novel and the Nazi Past*, New York and Frankfurt, 1985

REICH-RANICKI, MARCEL, *Deutsche Literatur in West und Ost: Prosa seit 1945*, Munich, 1963

REICH-RANICKI, MARCEL (ed.), *Meine Schulzeit im Dritten Reich: Erinnerungen deutscher Schriftsteller*, Cologne, 1982

REICH-RANICKI, MARCEL, *The Author of Himself: The Life of Marcel Reich-Ranicki*, London, 2002

REICHEL, PETER, *Der schöne Schein des Dritten Reiches: Faszination und Gewalt des Faschismus*, Munich, 1992

REICHEL, PETER, *Politik mit der Erinnerung: Gedächtnisorte im Streit um die nationalsozialistische Vergangenheit*, Munich and Vienna, 1995

REULECKE, JÜRGEN, 'The Battle for the Young: Mobilising Young People in Wilhelmine Germany', in Mark Roseman (ed.), *Generations in Conflict: Youth Revolt and Generation Formation in Germany, 1770–1968*, Cambridge, 1995, 92–104

RICHARZ, BERNHARD, *Heilen, Pflegen, Töten: Zur Alltagsgeschichte einer Heil- und Pflegeanstalt bis zum Ende des Nationalsozialismus*, Göttingen, 1987

RICHTER, DIETER, *Schlaraffenland: Geschichte einer populären Phantasie*, Frankfurt, 1989

RICHTER, GUNNAR (ed.), *Breitenau: Zur Geschichte eines national-sozialistischen Konzentrations- und Arbeitserziehungslagers*, Kassel, 1993

RIECHERT, HANSJÖRG, *Im Schatten von Auschwitz: Die national-sozialistische Sterilisationspolitik gegenüber Sinti und Roma*, Münster, 1995

RINGELBLUM, EMMANUEL, *Polish–Jewish Relations during the Second World War*, Joseph Kermish and Shmuel Krakowski (eds), New York, 1976

ROBERTS, ULLA, *Starke Mütter – ferne Väter: Töchter reflektieren ihre Kindheit im Nationalsozialismus und in der Nachkriegszeit*, Frankfurt, 1994

ROER, DOROTHEE, and DIETER HENKEL (eds), *Psychiatrie im Faschismus: Die Anstalt Hadamar 1933–1945*, Bonn, 1986

ROESLER, JÖRG, 'The Black Market in Post-war Berlin and the Methods Used to Counteract It', *German History*, 7/1, 1989, 92–107

ROSEMAN, MARK (ed.), *Generations in Conflict: Youth Revolt and Generation Formation in Germany, 1770–1968*, Cambridge, 1995

ROSEMAN, MARK, *The Past in Hiding*, London, 2000

ROSEMAN, MARK, *The Villa, the Lake, the Meeting: Wannsee and the Final Solution*, London, 2002

ROSENFELD, ALVIN, 'Popularization and Memory: The Case of Anne Frank', in Peter Hayes (ed.), *Lessons and Legacies: The Meaning of the Holocaust in a Changing World*, Evanston, Ill., 1991

ROSENHAFT, EVE, *Beating the Fascists? The German Communists and Political Violence, 1929–1933*, Cambridge, 1983

ROSENSTRAUCH, HAZEL (ed.), *Aus Nachbarn wurden Juden: Ausgrenzung und Selbstbehauptung 1933–1942*, Berlin, 1988

ROSENTHAL, GABRIELE (ed.), *Die Hitlerjugend-Generation: Biographische Thematisierung als Vergangenheitsbewältigung*, Essen, 1986

ROSENTHAL, GABRIELE, *Erlebte und erzählte Lebensgeschichte: Gestalt und Struktur biographischer Selbstbeschreibungen*, Frankfurt, 1995

ROSS, HENRYK, *Łódź Ghetto Album*, Thomas Weber (ed.), London, 2004

ROST, KARL LUDWIG, *Sterilisation und Euthanasie im Film des 'Dritten Reiches': Nationalsozialistische Propaganda in ihrer Beziehung zu rassenhygienischen Massnahmen des NS-Staates*, Husum, 1987

RUDASHEVSKI, YITSKHOK, *The Diary of the Vilna Ghetto: June 1941–April 1943*, Tel Aviv, 1973

RUHL, KLAUS-JÖRG, *Frauen in der Nachkriegszeit 1945–1963*, Munich, 1988

RÜRUP, REINHARD (ed.), *Berlin 1945: Eine Dokumentation*, Berlin, 1995

SACHSE, CAROLA, *Siemens, der Nationalsozialismus und die moderne Familie: Eine Untersuchung zur sozialen Rationalisierung in Deutschland im 20. Jahrhundert*, Hamburg, 1990

SACHSSE, CHRISTOPH, and FLORIAN TENNSTEDT, *Der Wohlfahrtsstaat im Nationalsozialismus*, Stuttgart, 1992

SAFRIAN, HANS, *Die Eichmann-Männer*, Vienna, 1993

SANDER, ELKE, and BARBARA JOHR (eds), *BeFreier und Befreite: Krieg, Vergewaltigungen, Kinder*, Munich, 1992

SANDER, PETER, *Verwaltung des Krankenmordes: Der Bezirksverband Nassau im Nationalsozialismus*, Giessen, 2003

SCHELLENBERGER, BARBARA, *Katholische Jugend und Drittes Reich*, Mainz, 1975

SCHELSKY, HELMUT, *Die skeptische Generation: Eine Soziologie der deutschen Jugend*, Düsseldorf, 1957

SCHERER, KLAUS, *'Asozial' im Dritten Reich: Die vergessenen Verfolgten*, Münster, 1990

SCHICKERT, KLAUS, 'Kriegsschauplatz Israel', in *Wille und Macht*, September/October, 1943

SCHIEDER, THEODOR (ed.), *The Expulsion of the German Population from the Territories East of the Oder-Neisse-Line*, Bonn, n.d.

SCHISSLER, HANNA (ed.), *The Miracle Years: A Cultural History of West Germany, 1949–1968*, Princeton, NJ, 2001

SCHLUMBOHM, JÜRGEN, *Kinderstuben: Wie Kinder zu Bauern, Bürgern, Aristokraten wurden, 1700–1850*, Munich, 1983

SCHMIDT, ULF, 'Reassessing the Beginning of the "Euthanasia" Programme', *German History*, 17/4, 1999, 543–50

SCHMITZ-KÖSTER, DOROTHEE, 'Deutsche Mutter, bist Du bereit . . .': Alltag im Lebensborn, Berlin, 1997

SCHÖRKEN, ROLF, Luftwaffenhelfer und Drittes Reich: Die Entstehung eines politischen Bewusstseins, Stuttgart, 1984

SCHREIBER, GERHARD, Die italienischen Militärinternierten im deutschen Machtbereich 1943–1945: Verraten – verachtet – vergessen, Munich, 1990

SCHRÖDER, HANS JOACHIM, Die gestohlenen Jahre: Erzählgeschichten und Geschichtserzählung im Interview: Der Zweite Weltkrieg aus der Sicht ehemaliger Mannschaftssoldaten, Tübingen, 1992

SCHULTE, THEO, The German Army and Nazi Policies in Occupied Russia, Providence, RI, 1989

SCHULZ, HERMANN, HARTMUT RADEBOLD and JÜRGEN REULECKE, Söhne ohne Väter: Erfahrungen der Kriegsgeneration, Berlin, 2004

SCHULZE, RAINER (ed.), Unruhige Zeiten: Erlebnisberichte aus dem Landkreis Celle 1945–1949, Munich, 1990

SCHULZE, RAINER (ed.), Zwischen Heimat und Zuhause: Deutsche Flüchtlinge und Vertriebene in (West-)Deutschland 1945–2000, Osnabrück, 2001

SCHWARZE, GISELA, Kinder, die nicht zählten: Ostarbeiterinnen und ihre Kinder im Zweiten Weltkrieg, Essen, 1997

SCHWENDEMANN, HEINRICH, and WOLFGANG DIETSCHE, Hitlers Schloss: Die 'Führerresidenz' in Posen, Berlin, 2003

SCHWERTFEGER, RUTH, Women of Theresienstadt, New York, 1989

SEBALD, W. G., On the Natural History of Destruction, London, 2003

SEMMLER, RUDOLF, Goebbels: The Man Next to Hitler, London, 1947

SERRAILLIER, IAN, The Silver Sword, London, 1956

SHIRAKAWA, SAM, The Devil's Music Master: The Controversial Life and Career of Wilhelm Furtwängler, Oxford, 1992

SHIRER, WILLIAM, Berlin Diary, 1934–1941, London, 1970

SICHROVSKY, PETER, Schuldig geboren: Kinder aus Nazifamilien, Cologne, 1987

SICK, DOROTHEA, 'Euthanasie' im Nationalsozialismus am Beispiel des Kalmenhofs in Idstein im Taunus, Frankfurt, 1983

SIEDER, REINHARD, and HANS SAFRIAN, 'Gassenkinder – Strassenkämpfer: Zur politischen Sozialisation einer Arbeitergeneration in Wien 1900 bis 1938', in Lutz Niethammer (ed.), 'Wir kriegen jetzt andere Zeiten': Auf der Suche nach der Erfahrung des Volkes in nach-faschistischen Ländern, Berlin, 1985, 117–51

SIEDER, REINHARD, 'A Hitler Youth from a Respectable Family', in

Daniel Bertaux and Paul Thompson (eds), *International Yearbook of Oral History and Life Stories*, 2, *Between Generations: Family Models, Myths and Memories*, Oxford, 1993, 99–120

SIEDER, REINHARD (ed.), *Brüchiges Leben: Biographien in sozialen Systemen*, Vienna, 1999

SILBERSCHLAG, EISIG, *Saul Tschernichowsky: Poet of Revolt*, Ithaca, NY, 1968

SLOAN, JACOB (ed.), *Notes from the Warsaw Ghetto: The Journal of Emmanuel Ringelblum*, New York and London, 1958

SMITH, ARTHUR LEE, *Die 'Vermisste Million': Zum Schicksal deutscher Kriegsgefangener nach dem zweiten Weltkrieg*, Munich, 1992

SMITH, WOODRUFF, *The Ideological Origins of Nazi Imperialism*, New York, 1986

SOLLBACH, GERHARD, *Heimat Ade! Kinderlandverschickung in Hagen 1941–1945*, Hagen, 1998

SONTHEIMER, KURT, *Antidemokratisches Denken in der Weimarer Republik*, Munich, 1992

SOSNOWSKI, KYRIL, *The Tragedy of Children under Nazi Rule*, Poznań, 1962

STADT FRANKFURT (ed.), *Vom Bauhaus nach Terezin: Friedl Dicker-Brandeis und die Kinderzeichnungen aus dem Ghetto-Lager Theresienstadt*, Frankfurt, 1991

STADTARCHIV MÜNCHEN (ed.), *'Verzogen, unbekannt wohin': Die erste Deportation von Münchener Juden im November 1941*, Zurich, 2000

STARGARDT, NICHOLAS, *The German Idea of Militarism: Radical and Socialist Critics, 1866–1914*, Cambridge, 1994

STARGARDT, NICHOLAS, 'Children's Art of the Holocaust', *Past and Present*, 161, 1998, 192–235

STARNS, PENNY, and MARTIN PARSONS, 'Against Their Will: The Use and Abuse of British Children during the Second World War', in James Alan Marten (ed.), *Children and War: A Historical Anthology*, New York and London, 2002, 266–78

STASIEWSKI, BERNHARD, 'Die Kirchenpolitik der Nationalsozialisten im Warthegau 1939–45', *Vierteljahrshefte für Zeitgeschichte*, 7/1, 1959, 46–74

STATE JEWISH MUSEUM IN PRAGUE (ed.), *Friedl Dicker-Brandeis, 1898–1944*, Prague, 1988

Statistisches Jahrbuch für das Deutsche Reich, 44, 1924–5, Berlin, 1925

STEINBACH, PETER, and JOHANNES TUCHEL, *'Ich habe den Krieg verhindern wollen': George Elser und das Attentat vom 8. November 1939: Eine Dokumentation*, Berlin, 1997

STEINBACHER, SYBILLE, 'Musterstadt' Auschwitz: Germanisierungs-politik und Judenmord in Oberschlesien, Munich, 2000, 178–94

STEINERT, MARLIS, Hitlers Krieg und die Deutschen: Stimmung und Haltung der deutschen Bevölkerung im Zweiten Weltkrieg, Düsseldorf, 1970

STEINHOFF, JOHANNES, PETER PECHEL and DENNIS SHOWALTER, Voices from the Third Reich: An Oral History, London, 1991

STEINLAUF, MICHAEL, Bondage to the Dead: Poland and the Memory of the Holocaust, Syracuse, NY, 1997

STEPHENSON, JILL, '"Emancipation" and its Problems: War and Society in Württemberg, 1939–45', European History Quarterly, 17, 1987, 345–65

STERN, FRANK, The Whitewashing of the Yellow Badge: Antisemitism and Philosemitism in Postwar Germany, Oxford, 1992

STERNBERGER, DOLF, GERHARD STORZ and W. E. SÜSKING, Aus dem Wörterbuch des Unmenschen, Hamburg, 1968

STÖVER, BERND, Volksgemeinschaft im Dritten Reich: Die Konsens-bereitschaft der Deutschen aus der Sicht sozialistischer Exilberichte, Düsseldorf, 1993

STRAUSS, HERBERT, 'Jewish Emigration from Germany, Part I', Leo Baeck Institute Year Book, 25, London, 1980, 313–61

STREIT, CHRISTIAN, Keine Kameraden: Die Wehrmacht und die sowjetischen Kriegsgefangenen 1941–1945, Stuttgart, 1978

STROBL, GERWIN, The Germanic Isle: Nazi Perceptions of Britain, Cambridge, 2000

STRZELECKI, ANDRZEJ, Endphase des KL Auschwitz: Evakuierung, Liquidierung und Befreiung des Lagers, Oświęcim-Brzezinka, 1995

SYRKIN, MARIE, The State of the Jews, Washington, 1980

SZAROTA, TOMASZ, Warschau unter dem Hakenkreuz: Leben und Alltag im besetzten Warschau 1.10.1939 bis 31.7.1944, Paderborn, 1985

SZEPANSKY, GERDA (ed.), Blitzmädel, Heldenmutter, Kriegerwitwe: Frauenleben im Zweiten Weltkrieg, Frankfurt, 1986

SZUMAN, STEPHAN, 'La guerre et l'occupation dans les dessins des enfants polonais', Sauvegarde, 4, 1949, 28–57

TAHAN, ILANA, Memorial Volumes to Jewish Communities Destroyed in the Holocaust: A Bibliography of British Library Holdings, London, 2003

TEC, NECHAMA, In the Lion's Den: The Life of Oswald Rufeisen, New York, 1990

TEC, NECHAMA, Defiance: The Bielski Partisans, Oxford, 1993

THEILEN, FRITZ, Edelweisspiraten, Cologne, 2003

THUM, GREGOR, Die fremde Stadt: Breslau 1945, Berlin, 2003

TIMM, UWE, *Am Beispiel meines Bruders*, Cologne, 2003

TITMUSS, RICHARD, *Problems of Social Policy*, London, 1950

TOLL, NELLY S., *Behind the Secret Window: A Memoir of a Hidden Childhood during World War Two*, New York, 1993

TREVOR-ROPER, HUGH (ed.), *Hitler's Table Talk, 1941–1944*, London, 1953

TROLLER, NORBERT, *Theresienstadt: Hitler's Gift to the Jews*, Chapel Hill, NC, 1991

TROMMLER, FRANK, '"Deutschlands Sieg oder Untergang": Perspektiven aus dem Dritten Reich auf die Nachkriegsentwicklung', in Thomas Koebner, Gert Sautermeister and Sigrid Schneider (eds), *Deutschland nach Hitler*, Opladen, 1987, 214–28

TRUNK, ISAIAH, *Judenrat: The Jewish Councils of Eastern Europe under Nazi Occupation*, New York, 1972

TUCHEL, JOHANNES, *Konzentrationslager: Organisationsgeschichte und Funktion der 'Inspektion der Konzentrationslager' 1934–1938*, Boppard am Rhein, 1991

TURSKI, MARIAN (ed.), *Byli wówczas dziećmi*, Warsaw, 1975

ÜBERSCHÄR, GERD, and WOLFRAM WETTE (eds), *Der deutsche Überfall auf die Sowjetunion: 'Unternehmen Barbarossa' 1941*, Paderborn, 1984

ULLMANN, VICTOR, *26 Kritiken über musikalische Veranstaltungen in Theresienstadt*, Hamburg, 1993

UNGERER, TOMI, *Die Gedanken sind frei: Meine Kindheit im Elsass*, Zurich, 1999

USBOURNE, CORNELIE, *The Politics of the Body in Weimar Germany*, New York, 1992

UTITZ, EMIL, *Psychologie des Lebens im Konzentrationslager Theresienstadt*, Vienna, 1948

VERHEY, JEFFREY, *The Spirit of 1914: Militarism, Myth, and Mobilization in Germany*, Cambridge, 2000

VICE, SUE, *Children Writing the Holocaust*, London, 2004

VIRGILI, FABRICE, *Shorn Women: Gender and Punishment in Liberation France*, Oxford, 2002

VOGEL, DETLEF, and WOLFRAM WETTE (eds), *Andere Helme – andere Menschen? Heimaterfahrung und Frontalltag im Zweiten Weltkrieg: Ein internationaler Vergleich*, Essen, 1995

WACHSMANN, NIKOLAUS, *Hitler's Prisons: Legal Terror in Nazi Germany*, London, 2004

WAGENER, HANS (ed.), *Gegenwartsliteratur und Drittes Reich: Deutsche Autoren in der Auseinandersetzung mit der Vergangenheit*, Stuttgart, 1977

WAGNER, PATRICK, *Volksgemeinschaft ohne Verbrecher: Konzeption und Praxis der Kriminalpolizei in der Zeit der Weimarer Republik und des Nationalsozialismus*, Hamburg, 1996

WAGNER, WOLF, *Der Hölle entronnen: Stationen eines Lebens: Eine Biographie des Malers und Graphikers Leo Haas*, Berlin, 1987

WAGNER, WOLF, *Wo die Schmetterlinge starben: Kinder in Auschwitz*, Berlin, 1995

WAGNEROVÁ, ALENA, *1945 waren sie Kinder: Flucht und Vertreibung im Leben einer Generation*, Cologne, 1990

WALB, LORE, *Ich, die Alte – ich, die Junge: Konfrontation mit meinen Tagebüchern 1933–1945*, Berlin, 1997

WALLER, JOHN, *The Devil's Doctor: Felix Kersten and the Secret Plot to Turn Himmler against Hitler*, New York, 2002

WALSER SMITH, HELMUT, *The Butcher's Tale: Murder and Anti-Semitism in a German Town*, New York, 2002

WEBER, ILSE, *In deinen Mauern wohnt das Leid: Gedichte aus dem KZ Theresienstadt*, Gerlingen, 1991

WEBSTER, CHARLES, and NOBLE FRANKLAND, *The Strategic Air Offensive against Germany*, 1–4, London, 1961

WEGNER, BERND, 'Hitler, der Zweite Weltkrieg und die Choreographie des Untergangs', *Geschichte und Gesellschaft*, 26/3, 2000, 493–518

WEINBERG, GERHARD, *A World at Arms: A Global History of World War II*, Cambridge, 1994

WEINDLING, PAUL, *Health, Race, and German Politics between National Unification and Nazism, 1870–1945*, Cambridge, 1989

WEINDLING, PAUL, *Epidemics and Genocide in Eastern Europe, 1890–1945*, Oxford, 2000

WEISBROD, BERND (ed.), *Die Politik der Öffentlichkeit – die Öffentlichkeit der Politik: Politische Medialisierung in der Geschichte der Bundesrepublik*, Göttingen, 2003

WEISSOVÁ, HELGA, *Zeichne, was Du siehst: Zeichnungen eines Kindes aus Theresienstadt*, Göttingen, 1998

WELCH, DAVID, *Propaganda and the German Cinema*, Oxford, 1985

WELCH, STEVEN, '"Harsh but Just"? German Military Justice in the Second World War: A Comparative Study of the Court-Martialling of German and US Deserters', *German History*, 17/3, 1999, 369–99

WELZER, HARALD, SABINE MOLLER and KAROLINE TSCHUGG-NALL, *'Opa war kein Nazi': Nationalsozialismus und Holocaust im Familiengedächtnis*, Frankfurt, 2002

WERNER, WOLFGANG, *'Bleib übrig': Deutsche Arbeiter in der national-sozialistischen Kriegswirtschaft*, Düsseldorf, 1983

WERTH, ALEXANDER, *Russia at War*, New York, 1964

WESTENRIEDER, NORBERT, *Deutsche Frauen und Mädchen! Vom Alltagsleben 1933–1945*, Düsseldorf, 1984

WESTERNHAGEN, DÖRTE VON, *Die Kinder der Täter: Das Dritte Reich und die Generation danach*, Munich, 1987

WETTE, WOLFRAM, RICARDA BREMER and DETLEF VOGEL (eds), *Das letzte halbe Jahr: Stimmungsberichte der Wehrmachtpropaganda 1944/45*, Essen, 2001

WIERLING, DOROTHEE, '"Leise versinkt unser Kinderland": Marion Lubien schreibt sich durch den Krieg', in Ulrich Borsdorf and Mathilde Jamin (eds), *Überleben im Krieg: Kriegserfahrungen in einer Industrieregion 1939–1945*, Reinbek, 1989, 67–84

WILDENTHAL, LORA, 'Race, Gender and Citizenship in the German Colonial Empire', in Frederick Cooper and Ann Stoler (eds), *Tensions of Empire: Colonial Cultures in a Bourgeois World*, Berkeley, 1997, 263–83

WILDT, MICHAEL, 'Gewalt gegen Juden in Deutschland 1933 bis 1939', *Werkstattgeschichte*, 18, 1997, 59–80

WILDT, MICHAEL, *Generation des Unbedingten: Das Führungskorps des Reichssicherheitshauptamtes*, Hamburg, 2002

WILHELM, HANS-HEINRICH, *Rassenpolitik und Kriegführung*, Passau, 1991

WINKLER, DÖRTE, 'Frauenarbeit versus Frauenideologie: Probleme der weiblichen Erwerbstätigkeit in Deutschland 1930–1945', *Archiv für Sozialgeschichte* 17, 1977, 99–126

WINTER, JAY, and JEAN-LOUIS ROBERT (eds), *Capital Cities at War: Paris, London, Berlin 1914–1919*, Cambridge, 1997

WIŚNIEWSKA, ANNA, and CZESŁAW RAJCA, *Majdanek: The Concentration Camp of Lublin*, Lublin, 1997

WNUK, JÓZEF, and HELENA RADOMSKA-STRZEMECKA (eds), *Dzieci polskie oskarżają (1939–1945)*, Warsaw, 1961

WYKA, KAZIMIERZ, *Życie na niby: Szkice z lat 1939–1945*, Warsaw, 1957

YAHIL, LENI, *The Holocaust: The Fate of European Jewry, 1932–1945*, Oxford, 1990

YELTON, DAVID K., *Hitler's Volkssturm: The Nazi Militia and the Fall of Germany, 1944–1945*, Lawrence, Kansas, 2002

YODER, JENNIFER, 'Truth about Reconciliation: An Appraisal of the Enquete Commission into the SED Dictatorship in Germany', *German Politics*, 8/3, 1999, 59–80

YOUNG, JAMES, *The Texture of Memory: Holocaust Memorials and Meaning*, New Haven and London, 1993

ZAPRUDER, ALEXANDRA (ed.), *Salvaged Pages: Young Writers' Diaries of the Holocaust*, New Haven and London, 2002

ZEIDLER, MANFRED, *Kriegsende im Osten: Die Rote Armee und die Besetzung Deutschlands östlich von Oder und Neisse 1944/45*, Munich, 1996

ZIEMIAN, JOSEPH, *The Cigarette Sellers of Three Crosses Square*, London, 1970

ZIMMERMANN, MICHAEL, *Rassenutopie und Genozid: Die national-sozialistische 'Lösung der Zigeunerfrage'*, Hamburg, 1996

ZINNECKER, JÜRGEN, *Jugendkultur 1940–1985*, Opladen, 1987

INDEX